D0832640

THE LOEB CLASSICAL LIBRARY

FOUNDED BY JAMES LOEB, LL.D.

THUCYDIDES

I

108

PORTRAIT OF PERIKLES.

BRITISH MUSEUM.

THUCYDIDES

WITH AN ENGLISH TRANSLATION BY

CHARLES FORSTER SMITH

OF THE UNIVERSITY OF WISCONSIN

IN FOUR VOLUMES

I

HISTORY OF THE PELOPONNESIAN WAR

BOOKS I AND II

LONDON

WILLIAM HEINEMANN LTD

CAMBRIDGE, MASSACHUSETTS

HARVARD UNIVERSITY PRESS

MCMLXIX

First printed 1919
Revised and Reprinted 1928
Reprinted 1935, 1951, 1956, 1962, 1969

Printed in Great Britain

CONTENTS

MAPS

INTRODUCTION

THREE ancient biographies[1] of Thucydides have come down to us, but they are of little value. They are derived from ancient commentaries, and the biographical details which they contain, wherever they do not rest upon inference from the text of the history itself, are often confused and contradictory. These are supplemented by scattered statements of several ancient writers—Dionysius of Halicarnassus, who wrote two treatises on Thucydides (*De Thucydidis historia iudicium* and the *Second Letter to Ammaeus*), Plutarch (*Cimon* iv), and Pausanias (I. xxxii.).

The only authentic facts about the life of Thucydides are gathered from casual mention in the History. He was the son of Olorus (IV. civ. 4); commenced the compilation of materials for writing the History at the outset of the Peloponnesian War (I. i. 1); and lived through the whole war, ripe in years and

[1] One of these, compiled in three distinct portions "from the commentaries," passed under the name of Marcellinus, who is probably to be identified with the author of Scholia on Hermogenes *περὶ στάσεων*, who seems to have lived in the fifth century A.D.; another was by an anonymous grammarian; and the third is a short notice in Suidas, *s.v.* Θουκυδίδης.

judgment, following it with close attention, that he might acquire accurate information (v. xxvi. 5). He suffered from the plague of 429 B.C. (II. xlviii. 3), of which he wrote his famous account (II. xlvii–liv). Elected one of the ten generals in 424 B.C., he was sent to the coast of Thrace (where he enjoyed the right of working certain gold mines) to operate against Brasidas. Failing to relieve Amphipolis, he was exiled in 424 B.C., and remained in banishment for twenty years, and thus was able to become acquainted with affairs on both sides (v. xxvi. 5).

For other facts we are dependent largely upon inference; some are reasonably certain, others less so. The name of his father was identical with that of the Thracian prince Olorus, whose daughter Hegesipyle was married to Miltiades, and his tomb, having the inscription Θουκυδίδης Ὀλόρου Ἁλιμούσιος, was in the suburb of Athens known as Κοίλη Μελετίδες, adjoining those of Cimon and Miltiades (Plut. *Cim.* iv). We may therefore assume that Olorus, the father of Thucydides, was a near kinsman of the Thracian prince Olorus. If, as Marcellinus says (§ 2), Thucydides' mother was named Hegesipyle, like Cimon's mother, that would be confirmation of the relationship; but Plutarch makes no mention of this. It seems likely, then, that Thucydides was of near kin to Cimon, younger perhaps by one generation. His father Olorus was probably a full citizen of Athens, as is indicated by the fact that, mentioning

himself as στρατηγός (IV. civ. 4), he writes Θουκυδίδην τὸν Ὀλόρου; for only as an Athenian citizen could his father be mentioned in this official style.

As to the date of Thucydides' birth, the only ancient statement that seems worthy of credence was made by Pamphila, a woman writer who in the time of Nero made a great compilation of the results of learning. Aulus Gellius (*N.A.* xv. 23) quotes from Pamphila that, at the beginning of the Peloponnesian War, Hellanicus was sixty-five years of age, Herodotus fifty-three, Thucydides forty. Pamphila's dates were probably taken from the chronological handbook of Apollodorus (second century B.C.), which was generally accepted among the Greeks and Romans. The term forty years used by Pamphila doubtless meant the ἀκμή or prime of Thucydides, and may have been fixed on the basis of his own assertion that he began to collect material at the opening of the war (I. i. 1) and was then in full maturity of mind (v. xxvi. 5). At any rate his own statement, taken with Pamphila's date, has led to the general assumption that the historian was born somewhere about 472 B.C.

It is indicated by Marcellinus (§ 46), and is probable in itself, that the decree for Thucydides' banishment was adopted on the motion of Cleon, who was then at the height of his power; and it is probable that the charge brought against him was treachery (προδοσία), as stated by Marcellinus (§ 55)

and the anonymous biographer (§ 2), and apparently implied by Aristophanes (*Vesp.* 288). His own words, *ξυνέβη μοι φεύγειν*, admit of this interpretation; and the statement of Pausanias (I. xxiii. 9) that he was later recalled from exile on the motion of Oenobius[1] is best understood on this basis. If he had been banished by a simple decree of the people, the general amnesty that followed the capture of Athens by Lysander would have been sufficient for him as for other exiles; if the sentence was more severe, a special decree would be necessary. But it is possible, of course, that the motion of Oenobius antedated the amnesty of Lysander's peace by a few months.

As to Thucydides' death, there was a persistent tradition that he was assassinated, and the fact that the History breaks off suddenly in the midst of exciting events of the Decelean War seems to support the tradition. Plutarch (*Cim.* iv. 3) says that it was commonly reported that he died a violent death at Scapte Hyle; Pausanias (I. xxiii. 9), that he was murdered on his journey home from exile; Marcellinus (§ 10), that after his return from exile he died and was buried in Athens. But whether he died in

[1] The name, which is a rare one in the fifth century, is found as that of a general commanding in the neighbourhood of Thasos in 410–9 B.C. and we hear somewhat later of one Eucles, son of Oenobius; hence it has been conjectured that the father of Oenobius was Eucles, who was Thucydides' colleague in Thrace in 424 B.C. (LV. civ).

Thrace or in Athens, it seems clear from his own words that he outlived the term of his banishment (v. xxvi. 5, ξυνέβη μοι φεύγειν τὴν ἐμαυτοῦ ἔτη εἴκοσι) and that he returned to Athens, since his description of the wall of Themistocles, whose remains "may still be seen at the Peiraeus" (I. xciii. 5), shows that he was there after the destruction of the walls by Lysander. If he had lived to see the restoration of the walls by Conon in 395 B.C., it seems he would certainly have mentioned it. There is another reason, too, for supposing that he did not live to this year: in III. cxvi. 2 he says that the eruption of Aetna, which occurred in the spring of 425 B.C., was the third on record; hence the one mentioned by Diodorus (XIV. lix. 3) for 396 B.C. could not have been known to him. It seems reasonable, then, to assume that he was not alive in 396 B.C.

There is a pretty and oft-repeated story[1] that Thucydides, as a boy, heard Herodotus recite a portion of his History at Olympia and was moved thereby to tears, whereupon Herodotus said, "Olorus, your son's spirit is aflame with a passion for learning." But Lucian, when telling of the powerful effect of Herodotus' recitation at Olympia,[2] would surely have mentioned this circumstance had he known of it; besides, chronology is in the way, it

[1] Suidas *s.v.* ὀργᾶν and Θουκυδίδης; Photius, *Bibl.* 60; Marcellinus, § 54.
[2] *Herod.* i.

we hold to Pamphila's testimony. But if he did not as a boy hear Herodotus recite at Olympia, he must have known him later as a man at Athens. The period of his youth and early manhood fell in the time when Athens was most prolific in great men. It is clear that he had heard and admired Pericles, and he must have seen Aeschylus and known Sophocles, Euripides, Aristophanes, Anaxagoras, Socrates, Gorgias, Antiphon, Pheidias, Polygnotus, Mnesicles, Ictinus, Callicrates, and Hippocrates. Association with such men and the atmosphere of Athens at such a time best explain the development of his genius; but the limits of his subject, as he conceived it, precluded any mention of any of these except Pericles, so that for any personal influence of theirs upon him we are left to inference. The first seven years of the war, before his banishment, were doubtless spent in large part at Athens, where he must have heard the speeches of Pericles, the discussions about Mytilene and about Pylos, as well as about other matters of which we have accounts in this History. But the twenty years of his exile he probably passed largely on his properties in Thrace,[1] engaged in the task of compiling materials for his work about the war, as indeed we are told that he

[1] It was his family connection with Thrace which led to his acquiring the right of working gold mines in that region (IV. cv. 1), which is all that he himself says, though his biographers state that he was the owner of gold mines at Scapte Hyle.

did by Plutarch (*De Exil.* xiv.) and Marcellinus (§§ 25 and 47).

From Thucydides' opening statement, that he began the composition of his History at the outbreak of the war, expecting it to be a great one and more noteworthy than any that had gone before, we should naturally infer that he continued the compilation and composition throughout the war, and in fact—as it is clearly unfinished—until his death. Again, as it was never completed, so it was never completely revised, and it is natural that one can find traces of the different dates at which the several portions were composed. Evidence of this kind has been brought forward in support of different hypotheses as to the composition of the work. The most famous of these was that put forth by F. W. Ullrich in his *Beiträge zur Erklärung des Thukydides,* Hamburg, 1845, in which it is maintained that Books I–V. xxvi, which contain the history of the Archidamian War (432–421 B.C.), formed a separate treatise composed between the Peace of Nicias and the Sicilian Expedition, and that the phrase "this war" in the earlier books refers to the Ten Years' War only.

In v. xxvi Thucydides does make a fresh start with the words, "The same Thucydides recorded the events in order, reckoning by summers and winters,[1]

[1] His division of the year corresponds to the actual conditions of the carrying on of war in ancient times: summer

until the fall of Athens." But he adds, "The war lasted for twenty-seven years, and anyone who declines to count the interval of truce as war is mistaken;" which sounds very much like the opening of a second volume of a work that falls into natural divisions. It is quite likely, as Ullrich maintains, that the account of the Archidamian War (I.–V. xxvi.) was composed mainly in the interval between 421 and 416 B.C.; but that it received important additions after the fall of Athens seems certain, *e.g.* II. lxv. on the career of Pericles. So much may well be admitted for Ullrich's hypothesis, but it is not necessary to admit more. Even the story of the Sicilian expedition, the finest part of the whole work, need not be considered to have been originally a separate treatise, but only to have received especial care. As for the rest, a paragraph from Classen's introduction to Book V outlines a probable order for the growth of the history which seems reasonable: "Though I am convinced that the whole work was written in the shape in which we have it after the conclusion of the Peloponnesian War, and that Thucydides was called away from life when engaged in the last revision and combination of the portions which he had noted down and sketched in outline from the beginning of the war,

—the larger half, including both spring and autumn—covering the time approximately from March to October, winter from November to February.

yet I do not believe that all parts of the work received an equally thorough review. I think that the masterly introduction, which makes our First Book, was completed with the full knowledge of the disastrous result of the twenty-seven years' war; that then the history of the ten years' war and the Sicilian Expedition, for which it is likely that the results of laborious inquiry were already at hand more or less perfectly worked out, received their final touches; and that after this, before the thread of the narrative was taken up again with the Ionic-Decelean War, the intervening period of the εἰρήνη ὕπουλος was described."

The most interesting testimony as to the recognition of the power of Thucydides in ancient times is Lucian's statement (*adv. Indoct.* 102) that Demosthenes copied out the history eight times. Dio Cassius constantly imitated and borrowed from him, and among others of the later historians who emulated him were Philistus, Arrian, and Procopius. There is internal evidence that Tacitus was influenced by him, and Sallust often imitated him. Quintilian's oft-quoted characterization, *Densus et brevis et semper instans sibi Thucydides*, shows his appreciation. In modern times his greatest panegyrist is Macaulay: "There is no prose composition, not even the *De Corona*, which I place so high as the Seventh Book of Thucydides. It is the *ne plus ultra* of human art"; again, "The retreat from Syracuse—Is it or

is it not the finest thing you ever read in your life?"; and still again, "He is the greatest historian that ever lived." John Stuart Mill said, "The most powerful and affecting piece of narrative perhaps in all literature is the account of the Sicilian catastrophe in his Seventh Book." The Earl of Chatham, on sending his son William Pitt to Cambridge, "left to professional teachers the legitimate routine in the classic authors, but made it his particular desire that Thucydides, the eternal manual of statesmen, should be the first Greek which his son read after coming to college." And the Earl of Chatham's estimate is well supported by Sir G. Cornwall Lewis: "For close, cogent, and appropriate reasoning on political questions, the speeches of Thucydides have never been surpassed; and indeed they may be considered as having reached the highest excellence of which the human mind is capable in that department."

In the ordinary narration of events the style of Thucydides is clear, direct, graphic. In strong contrast with this generally simple and lucid form of statement is his style in describing battles and other critical events, in generalizations, and especially in the speeches; here the statement is often so concise and condensed as to become very difficult. Thucydides was not the first to use speeches as a means of vivid presentation of important crises and the actors in them; for that he had the precedent of Homer and the Attic drama. But he used this

means with such impressive effect and success as to induce frequent imitation in later historical writing in ancient times. He does not pretend to give the exact words of the speakers, but says frankly in the Introduction (I. xxii. 1): "As to the speeches that were made by different men, either when they were about to begin the war or when they were already engaged therein, it has been difficult to recall with strict accuracy the words actually spoken, both for me as regards that which I myself heard, and for those who from various other sources have brought me reports. Therefore the speeches are given in the language in which, as it seemed to me, the several speakers would express, on the subjects under consideration, the sentiments most befitting the occasion, though at the same time I have adhered as closely as possible to the general sense of what was actually said." As a natural result the language of the speeches has a uniform character, both in the structure of the sentences and in particular expressions—in other words it is that of Thucydides himself; but at the same time the character and mode of thought of the assumed speaker are clearly manifest in each speech. In the hands of Thucydides such a means of presenting to us a critical situation is extraordinarily effective; here, as in his most striking narrations, his readers become spectators, as Plutarch expressed it. Or as Classen said, "Without our own choice we find ourselves involved in the conflict of

interests, and are put in the position to form judgment for ourselves from the situation and the feeling of parties. Very seldom does the historian himself add a word of comment."

We are accustomed to admire among Thucydides' great qualities as historian, his impartiality, his trustworthiness, vivid description, sense of contrast, conciseness, epigrammatic sententiousness, reserve, pathos. We come to approve heartily his way of leaving facts clearly stated and skilfully grouped to carry their own judgments. He is never a partisan, and the unsophisticated reader might at times wonder what his nationality was did he not frequently subscribe himself "Thucydides the Athenian." Historians sometimes criticise his attitude, but they all accept his statements of fact. His descriptions of battles read as if he himself had been present. He dramatises history by placing events in such juxtaposition that a world of moral is conveyed without a word of comment; for example, when the funeral oration with its splendid eulogy of Athens is followed by the description of the plague, the disgraceful Melian episode is succeeded by the Sicilian disaster, the holiday-like departure from Athens is set over against the distressful flight from Syracuse. He packs his language so full of meaning that at times a sentence does duty for a paragraph, a word for a sentence. "Of all manifestations of power, restraint impresses men most," and however much we regret

his reserve, since for much that he might have told us we have no other witnesses, we come more and more to regard this as great art. As for pathos, no historian ever excelled such passages as those where the utter defeat of a hitherto invincible navy is portrayed (vii. lxxi), or the misery and dejection of the departing Athenian host is described (vii. lxxv), or where the final catastrophe in the river Assinarus seems to occur before our eyes, preparing us for the final sentence: "Fleet and army perished from the face of the earth, nothing was saved, and of the many who went forth few returned home."

BIBLIOGRAPHY

Of Thucydidean manuscripts the following are, according to Hude, the most important:—

A *Cisalpinus sive Italus*, now in Paris (suppl. Gr. 255), parchment, 11th or 12th century.
B *Vaticanus*, Vatican Library at Rome (126), parchment, 11th century.
C *Laurentianus*, Laurentian Library at Florence (69, 2), parchment, 11th century.
E *Palatinus*, Library at Heidelberg (252), parchment, 11th century.
F *Augustanus*, Library at Munich (430), parchment, 11th century.
G *Monacensis*, Library at Munich (228), paper, 13th century.
M *Britannicus*, British Museum (11727), parchment, 11th century.

No one of these manuscripts is of such age or excellence as to deserve preference before all others; but of the two families which may be distinguished, Laurentianus leads the one, namely, C and G, Vaticanus the other, namely, A B E F. Britannicus holds a sort of middle ground between the two. Hude's preference is for Laurentianus; Classen's, following Bekker, for Vaticanus. From VI. xciv on Vaticanus has a special value as coming perhaps from a different copy.

Complete Editions

Aldus: Editio Princeps, Venice, 1502, folio; scholia 1503.
Stephanus: Paris, 1564, folio; with scholia and Valla's Latin version made in 1452. The second edition (1588) is the source of the Vulgate.
I. Bekker: Oxford, 1821, 4 vols., with scholia and Duker's Latin version. Also Ed. ster. altera, Berlin, 1832 ('46, '68).

BIBLIOGRAPHY

Poppo: Leipzig, 1821–40, 11 vols. (prolegomena, commentary, etc.).
Poppo: Minor edition, Leipzig, 1843–51, 4 vols.; revised 1875–85 by Stahl.
Goeller: Leipzig, 1826 and 1836, 2 vols., annotated.
Arnold: London and Oxford, 1830–39, 3 vols., annotated.
Didot: Paris, 1840, text with Latin version by Haase.
Bloomfield: London, 1842–43, 2 vols., annotated.
Krüger: Berlin, 1846–7 and 1858–61, 2 vols., annotated.
Boehme: Leipzig, 1856 and 1871–75, annotated; new edition revised by Widmann.
Classen: Berlin, 1862–76 and 1875–85, 8 vols., annotated; revised by Steup.
Stahl: Editio ster. Leipzig, 1873–74, 2 vols., introduction, text and adnotatio critica.
Van Herwerden: Utrecht, 1877–82, 5 vols., text with critical notes.
Jones: Oxford, 1898, 2 vols., text.
Hude: Leipzig, 1898–1901, text with critical notes.

RECENT EDITIONS

In the Budé series (Paris, 1953–1967) books 1, 2, 4, and 5 have been contributed by Jacqueline de Romilly who helped also in book 3 by R. Weil and in books 6 and 7 by L. Bodin.
H. S. Jones and J. E. Powell: Oxford; the latest edition is 1951–1953.
O. Luschnat: Leipzig, 1960.

OTHER WORKS ON THUCYDIDES

A. W. Gomme: *A Historical Commentary on Thucydides*, Oxford, Vol. I, 1950, Vol. II and Vol. III, 1956.
A. W. Gomme: *Essays in Greek History and Literature*, Oxford, 1936.
A. W. Gomme: *More Essays* etc., Oxford, 1962.
B. W. Henderson: *The Great War between Athens and Sparta*, London, 1927.
G. F. Abbott: *Thucydides*, London, 1925.

BIBLIOGRAPHY

C. N. Cochrane: *Thucydides and the Science of History*, London, 1929.

E. Barker: *Greek Political Theory, Plato and his Predecessors*, London, 1925.

Jacqueline de Romilly: *Thucydide et l'impérialisme athénien*, Paris, 1951. English translation by P. Thody, Oxford, 1963.

Jacqueline de Romilly: *Histoire et Raison chez T.*, Paris, 1956.

THUCYDIDES

BOOK I

ΘΟΥΚΥΔΙΔΟΥ ΙΣΤΟΡΙΑΙ[1]

Α

I. Θουκυδίδης Ἀθηναῖος ξυνέγραψε τὸν πόλεμον τῶν Πελοποννησίων καὶ Ἀθηναίων ὡς
ἐπολέμησαν πρὸς ἀλλήλους, ἀρξάμενος εὐθὺς
καθισταμένου καὶ ἐλπίσας μέγαν τε ἔσεσθαι καὶ
ἀξιολογώτατον τῶν προγεγενημένων, τεκμαιρό-
μενος ὅτι ἀκμάζοντές τε ᾖσαν ἐς αὐτὸν ἀμφότεροι
παρασκευῇ τῇ πάσῃ καὶ τὸ ἄλλο Ἑλληνικὸν
ὁρῶν ξυνιστάμενον πρὸς ἑκατέρους, τὸ μὲν εὐθύς,
2 τὸ δὲ καὶ διανοούμενον. κίνησις γὰρ αὕτη δὴ
μεγίστη τοῖς Ἕλλησιν ἐγένετο καὶ μέρει τινὶ τῶν
βαρβάρων, ὡς δὲ εἰπεῖν καὶ ἐπὶ πλεῖστον ἀνθρώπων. τὰ γὰρ πρὸ αὐτῶν καὶ τὰ ἔτι παλαίτερα
σαφῶς μὲν εὑρεῖν διὰ χρόνου πλῆθος ἀδύνατον
ἦν, ἐκ δὲ τεκμηρίων ὧν ἐπὶ μακρότατον σκοποῦντί
μοι πιστεῦσαι ξυμβαίνει, οὐ μεγάλα νομίζω
γενέσθαι οὔτε κατὰ τοὺς πολέμους οὔτε ἐς τὰ
ἄλλα.

II. Φαίνεται γὰρ ἡ νῦν Ἑλλὰς καλουμένη οὐ πάλαι βεβαίως οἰκουμένη, ἀλλὰ μεταναστάσεις τε οὖσαι τὰ πρότερα καὶ ῥᾳδίως ἕκαστοι τὴν

[1] The Greek text used for this translation of Thucydides is that of Hude. Variations from his text are indicated in footnotes.

THUCYDIDES

BOOK I

I. Thucydides, an Athenian, wrote the history of the war waged by the Peloponnesians and the Athenians against one another. He began the task at the very outset of the war, in the belief that it would be great and noteworthy above all the wars that had gone before, inferring this from the fact that both powers were then at their best in preparedness for war in every way, and seeing the rest of the Hellenic race taking sides with one state or the other, some at once, others planning to do so. For this was the greatest movement that had ever stirred the Hellenes, extending also to some of the Barbarians, one might say even to a very large part of mankind. Indeed, as to the events of the period just preceding this, and those of a still earlier date, it was impossible to get clear information on account of lapse of time; but from evidence which, on pushing my inquiries to the furthest point, I find that I can trust, I think that they were not really great either as regards the wars then waged or in other particulars.

II. For it is plain that what is now called Hellas was not of old settled with fixed habitations, but that migrations were frequent in former times, each tribe readily leaving its own land whenever they were

ἑαυτῶν ἀπολείποντες, βιαζόμενοι ὑπό τινων αἰεὶ
2 πλειόνων. τῆς γὰρ ἐμπορίας οὐκ οὔσης οὐδ'
ἐπιμιγνύντες ἀδεῶς ἀλλήλοις οὔτε κατὰ γῆν οὔτε
διὰ θαλάσσης, νεμόμενοί τε τὰ ἑαυτῶν ἕκαστοι
ὅσον ἀποζῆν καὶ περιουσίαν χρημάτων οὐκ ἔχοντες
οὐδὲ γῆν φυτεύοντες, ἄδηλον ὂν ὁπότε τις ἐπελ-
θών, καὶ ἀτειχίστων ἅμα ὄντων, ἄλλος ἀφαιρή-
σεται, τῆς τε καθ' ἡμέραν ἀναγκαίου τροφῆς
πανταχοῦ ἂν ἡγούμενοι ἐπικρατεῖν οὐ χαλεπῶς
ἀπανίσταντο, καὶ δι' αὐτὸ οὔτε μεγέθει πόλεων
3 ἴσχυον οὔτε τῇ ἄλλῃ παρασκευῇ. μάλιστα δὲ
τῆς γῆς ἡ ἀρίστη αἰεὶ τὰς μεταβολὰς τῶν οἰκη-
τόρων εἶχεν, ἥ τε νῦν Θεσσαλία καλουμένη καὶ
Βοιωτία Πελοποννήσου τε τὰ πολλὰ πλὴν Ἀρ-
4 καδίας τῆς τε ἄλλης ὅσα ἦν κράτιστα. διὰ γὰρ
ἀρετὴν γῆς αἵ τε δυνάμεις τισὶ μείζους ἐγγιγνό-
μεναι στάσεις ἐνεποίουν ἐξ ὧν ἐφθείροντο, καὶ
5 ἅμα ὑπὸ ἀλλοφύλων μᾶλλον ἐπεβουλεύοντο. τὴν
γοῦν Ἀττικὴν ἐκ τοῦ ἐπὶ πλεῖστον διὰ τὸ λεπτό-
γεων ἀστασίαστον οὖσαν ἄνθρωποι ᾤκουν οἱ
6 αὐτοὶ αἰεί. καὶ παράδειγμα τόδε τοῦ λόγου οὐκ
ἐλάχιστόν ἐστι διὰ τὰς μετοικήσεις[1] τὰ ἄλλα μὴ
ὁμοίως αὐξηθῆναι· ἐκ γὰρ τῆς ἄλλης Ἑλλάδος οἱ
πολέμῳ ἢ στάσει ἐκπίπτοντες παρ' Ἀθηναίους
οἱ δυνατώτατοι ὡς βέβαιον ὂν ἀνεχώρουν, καὶ
πολῖται γιγνόμενοι εὐθὺς ἀπὸ παλαιοῦ μείζω ἔτι

[1] So Ullrich: *μετοικίας ἐς* Mn.

forced to do so by any people that was more numerous. For there was no mercantile traffic and the people did not mingle with one another without fear, either on land or by sea, and they each tilled their own land only enough to obtain a livelihood from it, having no surplus of wealth and not planting orchards, since it was uncertain, especially as they were yet without walls, when some invader might come and despoil them. And so, thinking that they could obtain anywhere the sustenance required for their daily needs, they found it easy to change their abodes, and for this reason were not strong as regards either the size of their cities or their resources in general. And it was always the best of the land that was most subject to these changes of inhabitants—the districts now called Thessaly and Boeotia, most of the Peloponnesus except Arcadia, and the most fertile regions in the rest of Hellas. For the greater power that accrued to some communities on account of the fertility of their land occasioned internal quarrels whereby they were ruined, and at the same time these were more exposed to plots from outside tribes. Attica, at any rate, was free from internal quarrels from the earliest times by reason of the thinness of its soil, and therefore was inhabited by the same people always. And here is an excellent illustration of the truth of my statement that it was owing to these migrations that the other parts of Hellas did not increase in the same way as Attica; for the most influential men of the other parts of Hellas, when they were driven out of their own countries by war or sedition, resorted to Athens as being a firmly settled community, and, becoming citizens, from the very earliest times made the city still greater in the

ἐποίησαν πλήθει ἀνθρώπων τὴν πόλιν, ὥστε καὶ ἐς Ἰωνίαν ὕστερον ὡς οὐχ ἱκανῆς οὔσης τῆς Ἀττικῆς ἀποικίας ἐξέπεμψαν.

III. Δηλοῖ δέ μοι καὶ τόδε τῶν παλαιῶν ἀσθένειαν οὐχ ἥκιστα· πρὸ γὰρ τῶν Τρωικῶν οὐδὲν φαίνεται πρότερον κοινῇ ἐργασαμένη ἡ Ἑλλάς·
2 δοκεῖ δέ μοι, οὐδὲ τοὔνομα τοῦτο ξύμπασά πω εἶχεν, ἀλλὰ τὰ μὲν πρὸ Ἕλληνος τοῦ Δευκαλίωνος καὶ πάνυ οὐδὲ εἶναι ἡ ἐπίκλησις αὕτη, κατὰ ἔθνη δὲ ἄλλα τε καὶ τὸ Πελασγικὸν ἐπὶ πλεῖστον ἀφ᾽ ἑαυτῶν τὴν ἐπωνυμίαν παρέχεσθαι, Ἕλληνος δὲ καὶ τῶν παίδων αὐτοῦ ἐν τῇ Φθιώτιδι ἰσχυσάντων, καὶ ἐπαγομένων αὐτοὺς ἐπ᾽ ὠφελίᾳ ἐς τὰς ἄλλας πόλεις, καθ᾽ ἑκάστους μὲν ἤδη τῇ ὁμιλίᾳ μᾶλλον καλεῖσθαι Ἕλληνας, οὐ μέντοι πολλοῦ γε χρόνου ἐδύνατο καὶ ἅπασιν ἐκνικῆσαι.
3 τεκμηριοῖ δὲ μάλιστα Ὅμηρος. πολλῷ γὰρ ὕστερον ἔτι καὶ τῶν Τρωικῶν γενόμενος οὐδαμοῦ οὕτω[1] τοὺς ξύμπαντας ὠνόμασεν οὐδ᾽ ἄλλους ἢ τοὺς μετὰ Ἀχιλλέως ἐκ τῆς Φθιώτιδος, οἵπερ καὶ πρῶτοι Ἕλληνες ἦσαν, Δαναοὺς δὲ ἐν τοῖς ἔπεσι καὶ Ἀργείους καὶ Ἀχαιοὺς ἀνακαλεῖ. οὐ μὴν οὐδὲ βαρβάρους εἴρηκε διὰ τὸ μηδὲ Ἕλληνάς πω, ὡς ἐμοὶ δοκεῖ, ἀντίπαλον ἐς ἓν ὄνομα
4 ἀποκεκρίσθαι. οἱ δ᾽ οὖν ὡς ἕκαστοι Ἕλληνες κατὰ πόλεις τε ὅσοι ἀλλήλων ξυνίεσαν καὶ ξύμπαντες ὕστερον κληθέντες οὐδὲν πρὸ τῶν Τρωικῶν δι᾽ ἀσθένειαν καὶ ἀμειξίαν ἀλλήλων ἁθρόοι

[1] Added by Reiske.

number of its inhabitants; so that Attica proved too small to hold them, and therefore the Athenians eventually sent out colonies even to Ionia.

III. The weakness of the olden times is further proved to me chiefly by this circumstance, that before the Trojan war, Hellas, as it appears, engaged in no enterprise in common. Indeed, it seems to me that as a whole it did not yet have this name, either, but that before the time of Hellen, son of Deucalion, this title did not even exist, and that the several tribes, the Pelasgian most extensively, gave their own names to the several districts; but when Hellen and his sons became strong in Phthiotis and were called in to the aid of the other cities, the clans thenceforth came more and more, by reason of this intercourse, to be called Hellenes, though it was a long time before the name could prevail among them all. The best evidence of this is given by Homer; for, though his time was much later even than the Trojan war, he nowhere uses this name of all, or indeed of any of them except the followers of Achilles of Phthiotis, who were in fact the first Hellenes, but designates them in his poems as Danaans and Argives and Achaeans. And he has not used the term Barbarians, either, for the reason, as it seems to me, that the Hellenes on their part had not yet been separated off so as to acquire one common name by way of contrast. However this may be, those who then received the name of Hellenes, whether severally and in succession, city by city, according as they understood one another's speech, or in a body at a later time, engaged together in no enterprise before the Trojan war, on account of weakness and lack of intercourse

ἔπραξαν. ἀλλὰ καὶ ταύτην τὴν στρατείαν θαλάσσῃ ἤδη πλείω χρώμενοι ξυνῆλθον.

IV. Μίνως γὰρ παλαίτατος ὧν ἀκοῇ ἴσμεν ναυτικὸν ἐκτήσατο καὶ τῆς νῦν Ἑλληνικῆς θαλάσσης ἐπὶ πλεῖστον ἐκράτησε καὶ τῶν Κυκλάδων νήσων ἦρξέ τε καὶ οἰκιστὴς πρῶτος τῶν πλείστων ἐγένετο, Κᾶρας ἐξελάσας καὶ τοὺς ἑαυτοῦ παῖδας ἡγεμόνας ἐγκαταστήσας· τό τε λῃστικόν, ὡς εἰκός, καθῄρει ἐκ τῆς θαλάσσης ἐφ' ὅσον ἐδύνατο, τοῦ τὰς προσόδους μᾶλλον ἰέναι αὐτῷ.

V. Οἱ γὰρ Ἕλληνες τὸ πάλαι καὶ τῶν βαρβάρων οἵ τε ἐν τῇ ἠπείρῳ παραθαλάσσιοι καὶ ὅσοι νήσους εἶχον, ἐπειδὴ ἤρξαντο μᾶλλον περαιοῦσθαι ναυσὶν ἐπ' ἀλλήλους, ἐτράποντο πρὸς λῃστείαν, ἡγουμένων ἀνδρῶν οὐ τῶν ἀδυνατωτάτων κέρδους τοῦ σφετέρου αὐτῶν ἕνεκα καὶ τοῖς ἀσθενέσι τροφῆς, καὶ προσπίπτοντες πόλεσιν ἀτειχίστοις καὶ κατὰ κώμας οἰκουμέναις ἥρπαζον καὶ τὸν πλεῖστον τοῦ βίου ἐντεῦθεν ἐποιοῦντο, οὐκ ἔχοντός πω αἰσχύνην τούτου τοῦ ἔργου,
2 φέροντος δέ τι καὶ δόξης μᾶλλον· δηλοῦσι δὲ τῶν τε ἠπειρωτῶν τινες ἔτι καὶ νῦν, οἷς κόσμος καλῶς τοῦτο δρᾶν, καὶ οἱ παλαιοὶ τῶν ποιητῶν τὰς πύστεις τῶν καταπλεόντων πανταχοῦ ὁμοίως ἐρωτῶντες εἰ λῃσταί εἰσιν, ὡς οὔτε ὧν πυνθάνονται ἀπαξιούντων τὸ ἔργον, οἷς τε ἐπιμελὲς εἴη

with one another. And they united even for this expedition only when they were now making considerable use of the sea.

IV. Minos is the earliest of all those known to us by tradition who acquired a navy. He made himself master of a very great part of what is now called the Hellenic Sea, and became lord of the Cyclades islands and first colonizer of most of them, driving out the Carians and establishing his own sons in them as governors. Piracy, too, he naturally tried to clear from the sea, as far as he could, desiring that his revenues should come to him more readily.

V. It should be explained that in early times both the Hellenes and the Barbarians who dwell on the mainland near the sea,[1] as well as those on the islands, when once they began more frequently to cross over in ships to one another, turned to piracy, under the lead of their most powerful men, whose motive was their own private gain and the support of their weaker followers, and falling upon cities that were unprovided with walls and consisted of groups of villages, they pillaged them and got most of their living from that source. For this occupation did not as yet involve disgrace, but rather conferred something even of glory. This is shown by the practice, even at the present day, of some of the peoples on the mainland, who still hold it an honour to be successful in this business, as well as by the words of the early poets, who invariably ask the question of all who put in to shore, whether they are pirates,[2] the inference being that neither those whom they ask ever disavow that occupation, nor those ever

[1] *e.g.* Phoenicians, Carians, and probably Epirots.
[2] *cf.* Homer, γ 73; ι 252.

3 εἰδέναι οὐκ ὀνειδιζόντων. ἐλῄζοντο δὲ καὶ κατ'
ἤπειρον ἀλλήλους. καὶ μέχρι τοῦδε πολλὰ τῆς
Ἑλλάδος τῷ παλαιῷ τρόπῳ νέμεται περί τε
Λοκροὺς τοὺς Ὀζόλας καὶ Αἰτωλοὺς καὶ Ἀκαρνᾶνας καὶ τὴν ταύτῃ ἤπειρον· τό τε σιδηροφορεῖ-
σθαι τούτοις τοῖς ἠπειρώταις ἀπὸ τῆς παλαιᾶς
λῃστείας ἐμμεμένηκεν.

VI. Πᾶσα γὰρ ἡ Ἑλλὰς ἐσιδηροφόρει διὰ τὰς
ἀφάρκτους τε οἰκήσεις καὶ οὐκ ἀσφαλεῖς παρ'
ἀλλήλους ἐφόδους, καὶ ξυνήθη τὴν δίαιταν μεθ'
2 ὅπλων ἐποιήσαντο ὥσπερ οἱ βάρβαροι. σημεῖον
δ' ἐστὶ ταῦτα τῆς Ἑλλάδος ἔτι οὕτω νεμόμενα
3 τῶν ποτε καὶ ἐς πάντας ὁμοίων διαιτημάτων. ἐν
τοῖς πρῶτοι δὲ Ἀθηναῖοι τόν τε σίδηρον κατέθεντο καὶ ἀνειμένῃ τῇ διαίτῃ ἐς τὸ τρυφερώτερον
μετέστησαν. καὶ οἱ πρεσβύτεροι αὐτοῖς τῶν εὐδαιμόνων διὰ τὸ ἁβροδίαιτον οὐ πολὺς χρόνος
ἐπειδὴ χιτῶνάς τε λινοῦς ἐπαύσαντο φοροῦντες
καὶ χρυσῶν τεττίγων ἐνέρσει κρωβύλον ἀναδούμενοι τῶν ἐν τῇ κεφαλῇ τριχῶν· ἀφ' οὗ καὶ
Ἰώνων τοὺς πρεσβυτέρους κατὰ τὸ ξυγγενὲς ἐπὶ
4 πολὺ αὕτη ἡ σκευὴ κατέσχεν. μετρίᾳ δ' αὖ
ἐσθῆτι καὶ ἐς τὸν νῦν τρόπον πρῶτοι Λακεδαιμόνιοι ἐχρήσαντο καὶ ἐς τὰ ἄλλα πρὸς τοὺς πολλοὺς οἱ τὰ μείζω κεκτημένοι ἰσοδίαιτοι μάλιστα
5 κατέστησαν. ἐγυμνώθησάν τε πρῶτοι καὶ ἐς τὸ

censure it who are concerned to have the information. On the mainland also men plundered one another; and even to-day in many parts of Hellas life goes on under the old conditions, as in the region of the Ozolian Locrians, Aetolians, Acarnanians, and the mainland thereabout. And these mainlanders' habit of carrying arms is a survival of their old freebooting life.

VI. Indeed, all the Hellenes used to carry arms because the places where they dwelt were unprotected, and intercourse with each other was unsafe; and in their everyday life they regularly went armed just as the Barbarians did. And the fact that these districts of Hellas still retain this custom is an evidence that at one time similar modes of life prevailed everywhere. But the Athenians were among the very first to lay aside their arms and, adopting an easier mode of life, to change to more luxurious ways. And indeed, owing to this fastidiousness, it was only recently that their older men of the wealthier class gave up wearing tunics of linen and fastening up their hair in a knot held by a golden grasshopper as a brooch;[1] and this same dress obtained for a long time among the elderly men of the Ionians also, owing to their kinship with the Athenians. An unpretentious costume after the present fashion was first adopted by the Lacedaemonians, and in general their wealthier men took up a style of living that brought them as far as possible into equality with the masses. And they were the first to bare their bodies and, after stripping openly, to anoint

[1] The mode of wearing the hair in a knot on the top of the head with the insertion of a pin in the form of a cicada seems to have persisted long at Athens, a mark of antiquated manners as characteristic as the queue or pig-tail with us.

φανερὸν ἀποδύντες λίπα μετὰ τοῦ γυμνάζεσθαι
ἠλείψαντο. τὸ δὲ πάλαι καὶ ἐν τῷ Ὀλυμπικῷ
ἀγῶνι διαζώματα ἔχοντες περὶ τὰ αἰδοῖα οἱ ἀθλη-
ταὶ ἠγωνίζοντο, καὶ οὐ πολλὰ ἔτη ἐπειδὴ πέπαυν-
ται· ἔτι δὲ καὶ ἐν τοῖς βαρβάροις ἔστιν οἷς νῦν,
καὶ μάλιστα τοῖς Ἀσιανοῖς, πυγμῆς καὶ πάλης
6 ἆθλα τίθεται, καὶ διεζωμένοι τοῦτο δρῶσιν. πολλὰ
δ' ἂν καὶ ἄλλα τις ἀποδείξειε τὸ παλαιὸν Ἑλληνικὸν ὁμοιότροπα τῷ νῦν βαρβαρικῷ διαιτώ-
μενον.

VII. Τῶν δὲ πόλεων ὅσαι μὲν νεώτατα ᾠκίσθησαν καὶ ἤδη πλωιμωτέρων ὄντων περιουσίας μᾶλλον ἔχουσαι χρημάτων, ἐπ' αὐτοῖς τοῖς αἰγιαλοῖς ἐκτίζοντο καὶ τείχεσι τοὺς ἰσθμοὺς ἀπελάμβανον ἐμπορίας τε ἕνεκα καὶ τῆς πρὸς τοὺς προσοίκους ἕκαστοι ἰσχύος· αἱ δὲ παλαιαὶ διὰ τὴν λῃστείαν ἐπὶ πολὺ ἀντίσχουσαν ἀπὸ θαλάσσης μᾶλλον ᾠκίσθησαν, αἵ τε ἐν ταῖς νήσοις καὶ ἐν ταῖς ἠπείροις (ἔφερον γὰρ ἀλλήλους τε καὶ τῶν ἄλλων ὅσοι ὄντες οὐ θαλάσσιοι κάτω ᾤκουν), καὶ μέχρι τοῦδε ἔτι ἀνῳκισμένοι εἰσίν.

VIII. Καὶ οὐχ ἧσσον λῃσταὶ ἦσαν οἱ νησιῶται, Κᾶρές τε ὄντες καὶ Φοίνικες. οὗτοι γὰρ δὴ τὰς πλείστας τῶν νήσων ᾤκησαν. μαρτύριον δέ· Δήλου γὰρ καθαιρομένης ὑπὸ Ἀθηναίων ἐν τῷδε τῷ πολέμῳ καὶ τῶν θηκῶν ἀναιρεθεισῶν, ὅσαι ἦσαν τῶν τεθνεώτων ἐν τῇ νήσῳ, ὑπὲρ ἥμισυ

themselves with oil when they engaged in athletic exercise; for in early times, even in the Olympic games, the athletes wore girdles about their loins in the contests, and it is not many years since the practice has ceased. Indeed, even now among some of the Barbarians, especially those of Asia, where prizes for wrestling and boxing are offered, the contestants wear loin-cloths. And one could show that the early Hellenes had many other customs similar to those of the Barbarians of the present day.

VII. However, the cities which were founded in more recent times, when navigation had at length become safer, and were consequently beginning to have surplus resources, were built right on the seashore, and the isthmuses[1] were occupied and walled off with a view to commerce and to the protection of the several peoples against their neighbours. But the older cities, both on the islands and on the mainland, were built more at a distance from the sea on account of the piracy that long prevailed—for the pirates were wont to plunder not only one another, but also any others who dwelt on the coast but were not sea-faring folk—and even to the present day they lie inland.

VIII. Still more addicted to piracy were the islanders. These included Carians as well as Phoenicians, for Carians inhabited most of the islands, as may be inferred from the fact that, when Delos was purified by the Athenians in this war[2] and the graves of all who had ever died on the island were removed, over half were discovered to be Carians,

[1] *i.e.* fortified cities were established on peninsulas, connected with the mainland by an isthmus, which was then walled off as Epidamnus (ch. xxvi. 5) and Potidaea (IV. cxx. 3).

[2] In the sixth year of the war, 426 B.C. *cf.* III. civ.

Κᾶρες ἐφάνησαν, γνωσθέντες τῇ τε σκευῇ τῶν ὅπλων ξυντεθαμμένῃ καὶ τῷ τρόπῳ ᾧ νῦν ἔτι θάπτουσιν.

2 Καταστάντος δὲ τοῦ Μίνω ναυτικοῦ πλωιμώτερα ἐγένετο παρ' ἀλλήλους (οἱ γὰρ ἐκ τῶν νήσων κακοῦργοι ἀνέστησαν ὑπ' αὐτοῦ, ὅτεπερ καὶ τὰς
3 πολλὰς αὐτῶν κατῴκιζε), καὶ οἱ παρὰ θάλασσαν ἄνθρωποι μᾶλλον ἤδη τὴν κτῆσιν τῶν χρημάτων ποιούμενοι βεβαιότερον ᾤκουν, καί τινες καὶ τείχη περιεβάλλοντο[1] ὡς πλουσιώτεροι ἑαυτῶν γιγνόμενοι· ἐφιέμενοι γὰρ τῶν κερδῶν οἵ τε ἥσσους ὑπέμενον τῶν κρεισσόνων δουλείαν, οἵ τε δυνατώτεροι περιουσίας ἔχοντες προσεποιοῦντο ὑπη-
4 κόους τὰς ἐλάσσους πόλεις. καὶ ἐν τούτῳ τῷ τρόπῳ μᾶλλον ἤδη ὄντες ὕστερον χρόνῳ ἐπὶ Τροίαν ἐστράτευσαν.

IX. Ἀγαμέμνων τέ μοι δοκεῖ τῶν τότε δυνάμει προύχων καὶ οὐ τοσοῦτον τοῖς Τυνδάρεω ὅρκοις κατειλημμένους τοὺς Ἑλένης μνηστῆρας ἄγων τὸν
2 στόλον ἀγεῖραι. λέγουσι δὲ καὶ οἱ τὰ σαφέστατα Πελοποννησίων μνήμῃ παρὰ τῶν πρότερον δεδεγμένοι Πέλοπά τε πρῶτον πλήθει χρημάτων, ἃ ἦλθεν ἐκ τῆς Ἀσίας ἔχων ἐς ἀνθρώπους ἀπόρους, δύναμιν περιποιησάμενον τὴν ἐπωνυμίαν τῆς χώρας ἔπηλυν ὄντα ὅμως σχεῖν, καὶ ὕστερον τοῖς

[1] Hude reads περιεβάλοντο with C_r.

---

[1] According to the post-Homeric legend, all who paid their court to Helen engaged to defend the man of her

being recognized by the fashion of the armour found buried with them, and by the mode of burial, which is that still in use among them.

But when the navy of Minos had been established, navigation between various peoples became safer—for the evil-doers on the islands were expelled by him, and then he proceeded to colonize most of them—and the dwellers on the sea-coast now began to acquire property more than before and to become more settled in their homes, and some, seeing that they were growing richer than before, began also to put walls around their cities. Their more settled life was due to their desire for gain; actuated by this, the weaker citizens were willing to submit to dependence on the stronger, and the more powerful men, with their enlarged resources, were able to make the lesser cities their subjects. And later on, when they had at length more completely reached this condition of affairs, they made the expedition against Troy.

IX. And it was, as I think, because Agamemnon surpassed in power the princes of his time that he was able to assemble his fleet, and not so much because Helen's suitors, whom he led, were bound by oath to Tyndareus.[1] It is said, furthermore, by those of the Peloponnesians who have received the clearest traditional accounts from men of former times, that it was by means of the great wealth which he brought with him from Asia into the midst of a poor people that Pelops first acquired power, and, consequently, stranger though he was, gave his name to the country, and that yet greater things

choice against all wrong. *cf.* Isoc. x. 40; Paus. III. xx. 9; Apollod. III. x. 9.

ἐκγόνοις ἔτι μείζω ξυνενεχθῆναι, Εὐρυσθέως μὲν
ἐν τῇ Ἀττικῇ ὑπὸ Ἡρακλειδῶν ἀποθανόντος,
Ἀτρέως δὲ μητρὸς ἀδελφοῦ ὄντος αὐτῷ καὶ ἐπιτρέψαντος Εὐρυσθέως, ὅτ' ἐστράτευε, Μυκήνας
τε καὶ τὴν ἀρχὴν κατὰ τὸ οἰκεῖον Ἀτρεῖ (τυγχάνειν δὲ αὐτὸν φεύγοντα τὸν πατέρα διὰ τὸν
Χρυσίππου θάνατον), καὶ ὡς οὐκέτι ἀνεχώρησεν
Εὐρυσθεύς, βουλομένων καὶ τῶν Μυκηναίων φόβῳ
τῶν Ἡρακλειδῶν καὶ ἅμα δυνατὸν δοκοῦντα εἶναι
καὶ τὸ πλῆθος τεθεραπευκότα τῶν Μυκηναίων τε
καὶ ὅσων Εὐρυσθεὺς ἦρχε τὴν βασιλείαν Ἀτρέα
παραλαβεῖν καὶ τῶν Περσειδῶν τοὺς Πελοπίδας
3 μείζους καταστῆναι. ἅ μοι δοκεῖ Ἀγαμέμνων
παραλαβὼν καὶ ναυτικῷ δὲ ἅμα ἐπὶ πλέον τῶν
ἄλλων ἰσχύσας τὴν στρατείαν οὐ χάριτι τὸ πλέον
ἢ φόβῳ ξυναγαγὼν ποιήσασθαι. φαίνεται γὰρ
ναυσί τε πλείσταις αὐτὸς ἀφικόμενος καὶ Ἀρκάσι
προσπαρασχών, ὡς Ὅμηρος τοῦτο δεδήλωκεν, εἴ
4 τῳ ἱκανὸς τεκμηριῶσαι. καὶ ἐν τοῦ σκήπτρου
ἅμα τῇ παραδόσει εἴρηκεν αὐτὸν "πολλῇσι νή-
σοισι καὶ Ἄργεϊ παντὶ ἀνάσσειν"· οὐκ ἂν οὖν
νήσων ἔξω τῶν περιοικίδων (αὗται δὲ οὐκ ἂν
πολλαὶ εἶεν) ἠπειρώτης ὢν ἐκράτει, εἰ μή τι καὶ
5 ναυτικὸν εἶχεν. εἰκάζειν δὲ χρὴ καὶ ταύτῃ τῇ
στρατείᾳ οἷα ἦν τὰ πρὸ αὐτῆς.

---

[1] Chrysippus, his half-brother, son of Pelops and Axioche, was killed by Atreus and Thyestes at the instance of their mother Hippodameia.

fell to the lot of his descendants. For when Eurystheus set out on the expedition that resulted in his death in Attica at the hands of the Heracleidae, Atreus, his mother's brother, who chanced to have been banished by his father for the death of Chrysippus,[1] was intrusted by Eurystheus with Mycenae and the sovereignty because he was a kinsman; and when Eurystheus did not return, Atreus, in accordance with the wish of the Mycenaeans, who feared the Heracleidae, and because he seemed to be a man of power and had won the favour of the multitude, received the sovereignty over the Mycenaeans and all who were under the sway of Eurystheus. And so the house of Pelops became greater than the house of Perseus. And it was, I think, because Agamemnon had inherited all this, and at the same time had become strong in naval power beyond the rest, that he was able to collect his armament, not so much by favour as by fear, and so to make the expedition. For it is clear that he himself brought the greatest number of ships, and that he had others with which to supply the Arcadians,[2] as Homer testifies, if he is sufficient witness for anyone. And he says, in the account of the delivery of the sceptre,[3] that Agamemnon "ruled over many islands and all Argos." Now, if he had not had something of a fleet, he could not, as he lived on the mainland, have been lord of any islands except those on the coast, and these would not be "many." And it is from this expedition that we must judge by conjecture what the situation was before that time.

[2] *cf.* Homer, B 576 and 612.
[2] *cf.* Homer, B 101–109.

X. Καὶ ὅτι μὲν Μυκῆναι μικρὸν ἦν, ἢ εἴ τι τῶν τότε πόλισμα νῦν μὴ ἀξιόχρεων δοκεῖ εἶναι, οὐκ ἀκριβεῖ ἄν τις σημείῳ χρώμενος ἀπιστοίη μὴ γενέσθαι τὸν στόλον τοσοῦτον ὅσον οἵ τε ποιηταὶ
2 εἰρήκασι καὶ ὁ λόγος κατέχει. Λακεδαιμονίων μὲν[1] γὰρ εἰ ἡ πόλις ἐρημωθείη, λειφθείη δὲ τά τε ἱερὰ καὶ τῆς κατασκευῆς τὰ ἐδάφη, πολλὴν ἂν οἶμαι ἀπιστίαν τῆς δυνάμεως προελθόντος πολλοῦ χρόνου τοῖς ἔπειτα πρὸς τὸ κλέος αὐτῶν εἶναι (καίτοι Πελοποννήσου τῶν πέντε τὰς δύο μοίρας νέμονται τῆς τε ξυμπάσης ἡγοῦνται καὶ τῶν ἔξω ξυμμάχων πολλῶν· ὅμως δέ, οὔτε ξυνοικισθείσης τῆς[2] πόλεως οὔτε ἱεροῖς καὶ κατασκευαῖς πολυτελέσι χρησαμένης, κατὰ κώμας δὲ τῷ παλαιῷ τῆς Ἑλλάδος τρόπῳ οἰκισθείσης, φαίνοιτ' ἂν ὑποδεεστέρα), Ἀθηναίων δὲ τὸ αὐτὸ τοῦτο παθόντων διπλασίαν ἂν τὴν δύναμιν εἰκάζεσθαι ἀπὸ τῆς
3 φανερᾶς ὄψεως τῆς πόλεως ἢ ἔστιν. οὔκουν ἀπιστεῖν εἰκὸς οὐδὲ τὰς ὄψεις τῶν πόλεων μᾶλλον σκοπεῖν ἢ τὰς δυνάμεις, νομίζειν δὲ τὴν στρατείαν ἐκείνην μεγίστην μὲν γενέσθαι τῶν πρὸ αὐτῆς, λειπομένην δὲ τῶν νῦν, τῇ Ὁμήρου αὖ ποιήσει εἴ τι χρὴ κἀνταῦθα πιστεύειν, ἣν εἰκὸς ἐπὶ τὸ μεῖζον μὲν ποιητὴν ὄντα κοσμῆσαι, ὅμως δὲ φαίνεται
4 καὶ οὕτως ἐνδεεστέρα. πεποίηκε γὰρ χιλίων καὶ διακοσίων νεῶν τὰς μὲν Βοιωτῶν εἴκοσι καὶ ἑκατὸν ἀνδρῶν, τὰς δὲ Φιλοκτήτου πεντήκοντα,

[1] Added by Hude. [2] Added by Stephanus.

X. And because Mycenae was only a small place, or if any particular town of that time seems now to be insignificant, it would not be right for me to treat this as an exact piece of evidence and refuse to believe that the expedition against Troy was as great as the poets have asserted and as tradition still maintains. For if the city of the Lacedaemonians should be deserted, and nothing should be left of it but its temples and the foundations of its other buildings, posterity would, I think, after a long lapse of time, be very loath to believe that their power was as great as their renown. (And yet they occupy two-fifths of the Peloponnesus and have the hegemony of the whole, as well as of their many allies outside; but still, as Sparta is not compactly built as a city and has not provided itself with costly temples and other edifices, but is inhabited village-fashion in the old Hellenic style, its power would appear less than it is.) Whereas, if Athens should suffer the same fate, its power would, I think, from what appeared of the city's ruins, be conjectured double what it is. The reasonable course, therefore, is not to be incredulous or to regard the appearance of cities rather than their power, but to believe that expedition to have been greater than any that preceded it, though falling below those of the present time, if here again one may put any trust in the poetry of Homer; for though it is natural to suppose that he as a poet adorned and magnified the expedition, still even on his showing it was evidently comparatively small. For in the fleet of twelve hundred vessels he has represented the ships of the Boeotians as having one hundred and twenty men each, and those of

δηλῶν, ὡς ἐμοὶ δοκεῖ, τὰς μεγίστας καὶ ἐλαχί-
στας· ἄλλων γοῦν μεγέθους πέρι ἐν νεῶν κατα-
λογῳ οὐκ ἐμνήσθη. αὐτερέται δὲ ὅτι ἦσαν καὶ
μάχιμοι πάντες, ἐν ταῖς Φιλοκτήτου ναυσὶ δεδή-
λωκεν· τοξότας γὰρ πάντας πεποίηκε τοὺς προσ-
κώπους. περίνεως δὲ οὐκ εἰκὸς πολλοὺς ξυμπλεῖν
ἔξω τῶν βασιλέων καὶ τῶν μάλιστα ἐν τέλει,
ἄλλως τε καὶ μέλλοντας πέλαγος περαιώσεσθαι
μετὰ σκευῶν πολεμικῶν οὐδ' αὖ τὰ πλοῖα κατά-
φαρκτα ἔχοντας, ἀλλὰ τῷ παλαιῷ τρόπῳ ληστι-
5 κώτερον παρεσκευασμένα. πρὸς τὰς μεγίστας δ'
οὖν καὶ ἐλαχίστας ναῦς τὸ μέσον σκοποῦντι οὐ
πολλοὶ φαίνονται ἐλθόντες, ὡς ἀπὸ πάσης τῆς
Ἑλλάδος κοινῇ πεμπόμενοι.

XI. Αἴτιον δ' ἦν οὐχ ἡ ὀλιγανθρωπια τοσοῦτον
ὅσον ἡ ἀχρηματία. τῆς γὰρ τροφῆς ἀπορίᾳ τόν
τε στρατὸν ἐλάσσω ἤγαγον καὶ ὅσον ἤλπιζον
αὐτόθεν πολεμοῦντα βιοτεύσειν, ἐπειδὴ δὲ ἀφικόμενοι μάχῃ ἐκράτησαν (δῆλον δέ· τὸ γὰρ ἔρυμα
τῷ στρατοπέδῳ οὐκ ἂν ἐτειχίσαντο), φαίνονται δ'
οὐδ' ἐνταῦθα πάσῃ τῇ δυνάμει χρησάμενοι, ἀλλὰ
πρὸς γεωργίαν τῆς Χερσονήσου τραπόμενοι καὶ
λῃστείαν τῆς τροφῆς ἀπορίᾳ. ᾗ καὶ μᾶλλον οἱ
Τρῶες αὐτῶν διεσπαρμένων τὰ δέκα ἔτη ἀντεῖχον
βίᾳ, τοῖς αἰεὶ ὑπολειπομένοις ἀντίπαλοι ὄντες.
2 περιουσίαν δὲ εἰ ἦλθον ἔχοντες τροφῆς καὶ ὄντες

Philoctetes as having fifty,[1] indicating, it seems to me, the largest and the smallest ships; at any rate, no mention as to the size of any others is made in the Catalogue of Ships. But that all on board were at once rowers and fighting men he has shown in the case of the ships of Philoctetes; for he represents all the oarsmen as archers. And it is not likely that many supernumeraries sailed with the expedition, apart from the kings and those highest in office, especially as they were to cross the open sea with all the equipment of war, and, furthermore, had boats which were not provided with decks, but were built after the early style, more like pirate-boats. In any event, if one takes the mean between the largest ships and the smallest, it is clear that not a large number of men went on the expedition, considering that they were sent out from all Hellas in common.[2]

XI. The cause was not so much lack of men as lack of money. For it was a want of supplies that caused them to take out a comparatively small force, only so large as could be expected to live on the country while at war. And when they arrived and had prevailed in battle—as evidently they did, for otherwise they could not have built the defence around their camp—even then they seem not to have used their whole force, but to have resorted to farming in the Chersonese and to pillaging, through lack of supplies. Wherefore, since they were scattered, the Trojans found it easier to hold the field against them during those ten years, being a match for those who from time to time were left in camp. But if they had taken with them an abundant

[1] Hom. B 510, 719.

[2] The number would be 102,000, *i.e.* 1,200 ships at 85 men each.

ἀθρόοι ἄνευ λῃστείας καὶ γεωργίας ξυνεχῶς τὸν πόλεμον διέφερον, ῥᾳδίως ἂν μάχῃ κρατοῦντες εἷλον, οἵ γε καὶ οὐχ ἀθρόοι, ἀλλὰ μέρει τῷ αἰεὶ παρόντι ἀντεῖχον, πολιορκίᾳ δ' ἂν προσκαθεζόμενοι ἐν ἐλάσσονί τε χρόνῳ καὶ ἀπονώτερον τὴν Τροίαν εἷλον. ἀλλὰ δι' ἀχρηματίαν τά τε πρὸ τούτων ἀσθενῆ ἦν καὶ αὐτά γε δὴ ταῦτα, ὀνομαστότατα τῶν πρὶν γενόμενα, δηλοῦται τοῖς ἔργοις ὑποδεέστερα ὄντα τῆς φήμης καὶ τοῦ νῦν περὶ αὐτῶν διὰ τοὺς ποιητὰς λόγου κατεσχηκότος.

XII. Ἐπεὶ καὶ μετὰ τὰ Τρωικὰ ἡ Ἑλλὰς ἔτι μετανίστατό τε καὶ κατῳκίζετο, ὥστε μὴ ἡσυχά-
2 σασα αὐξηθῆναι. ἥ τε γὰρ ἀναχώρησις τῶν Ἑλλήνων ἐξ Ἰλίου χρονία γενομένη πολλὰ ἐνεόχμωσε, καὶ στάσεις ἐν ταῖς πόλεσιν ὡς ἐπὶ τὸ πολὺ ἐγίγνοντο, ἀφ' ὧν ἐκπίπτοντες τὰς πόλεις
3 ἔκτιζον. Βοιωτοί τε γὰρ οἱ νῦν ἑξηκοστῷ ἔτει μετὰ Ἰλίου ἅλωσιν ἐξ Ἄρνης ἀναστάντες ὑπὸ Θεσσαλῶν τὴν νῦν μὲν Βοιωτίαν, πρότερον δὲ Καδμηίδα γῆν καλουμένην ᾤκησαν (ἦν δὲ αὐτῶν καὶ ἀποδασμὸς ἐν τῇ γῇ ταύτῃ πρότερον, ἀφ' ὧν καὶ ἐς Ἴλιον ἐστράτευσαν), Δωριῆς τε ὀγδοηκοστῷ
4 ἔτει ξὺν Ἡρακλείδαις Πελοπόννησον ἔσχον. μόλις τε ἐν πολλῷ χρόνῳ ἡσυχάσασα ἡ Ἑλλὰς βεβαίως καὶ οὐκέτι ἀνισταμένη ἀποικίας ἐξέ-

supply of food, and, in a body, without resorting to foraging and agriculture, had carried on the war continuously, they would easily have prevailed in battle and taken the city, since even with their forces not united, but with only such part as was from time to time on the spot, they yet held out; whereas, if they could have sat down and laid siege to Troy, they would have taken it in less time and with less trouble. But because of lack of money not only were the undertakings before the Trojan war insignificant, but even this expedition itself, though far more noteworthy than any before, is shown by the facts to have been inferior to its fame and to the tradition about it that now, through the influence of the poets, obtains.

XII. Indeed, even after the Trojan war Hellas was still subject to migrations and in process of settlement, and hence did not get rest and wax stronger. For not only did the return of the Hellenes from Ilium, occurring as it did after a long time, cause many changes; but factions also began to spring up very generally in the cities, and, in consequence of these, men were driven into exile and founded new cities. The present Boeotians, for example, were driven from Arne by the Thessalians in the sixtieth year after the capture of Ilium and settled in the district now called Boeotia, but formerly Cadmeïs; only a portion of these had been in that land before, and it was some of these who took part in the expedition against Ilium. The Dorians, too, in the eightieth year after the war, together with the Heracleidae occupied the Peloponnesus. And so when painfully and after a long course of time Hellas became permanently tranquil and its population was no longer subject to expulsion from their homes, it

πεμπε, καὶ Ἴωνας μὲν Ἀθηναῖοι καὶ νησιωτῶν τοὺς πολλοὺς ᾤκισαν, Ἰταλίας δὲ καὶ Σικελίας τὸ πλέον Πελοποννήσιοι τῆς τε ἄλλης Ἑλλάδος ἔστιν ἃ χωρία. πάντα δὲ ταῦτα ὕστερον τῶν Τρωικῶν ἐκτίσθη.

XIII. Δυνατωτέρας δὲ γιγνομένης τῆς Ἑλλάδος καὶ τῶν χρημάτων τὴν κτῆσιν ἔτι μᾶλλον ἢ πρότερον ποιουμένης τὰ πολλὰ τυραννίδες ἐν ταῖς πόλεσι καθίσταντο, τῶν προσόδων μειζόνων γιγνομένων (πρότερον δὲ ἦσαν ἐπὶ ῥητοῖς γέρασι πατρικαὶ βασιλεῖαι), ναυτικά τε ἐξηρτύετο ἡ Ἑλλὰς καὶ τῆς θαλάσσης μᾶλλον ἀντείχοντο.
2 πρῶτοι δὲ Κορίνθιοι λέγονται ἐγγύτατα τοῦ νῦν τρόπου μεταχειρίσαι τὰ περὶ τὰς ναῦς καὶ τριήρεις πρῶτον ἐν Κορίνθῳ τῆς Ἑλλάδος ἐνναυπη-
3 γηθῆναι. φαίνεται δὲ καὶ Σαμίοις Ἀμεινοκλῆς Κορίνθιος ναυπηγὸς ναῦς ποιήσας τέσσαρας· ἔτη δ' ἐστὶ μάλιστα τριακόσια ἐς τὴν τελευτὴν τοῦδε τοῦ πολέμου, ὅτε Ἀμεινοκλῆς Σαμίοις ἦλθεν.
4 ναυμαχία τε παλαιτάτη ὧν ἴσμεν γίγνεται Κορινθίων πρὸς Κερκυραίους· ἔτη δὲ μάλιστα καὶ ταύτῃ ἑξήκοντα καὶ διακόσιά ἐστι μέχρι τοῦ
5 αὐτοῦ χρόνου. οἰκοῦντες γὰρ τὴν πόλιν οἱ Κορίνθιοι ἐπὶ τοῦ ἰσθμοῦ αἰεὶ δή ποτε ἐμπόριον εἶχον, τῶν Ἑλλήνων τὸ πάλαι κατὰ γῆν τὰ πλείω ἢ κατὰ θάλασσαν, τῶν τε ἐντὸς Πελοποννήσου καὶ τῶν ἔξω, διὰ τῆς ἐκείνων παρ' ἀλλήλους ἐπιμισγόντων, χρήμασί τε δυνατοὶ ἦσαν, ὡς καὶ

began to send out colonies. The Athenians colonized Ionia and most of the islands; the Peloponnesians, the greater part of Italy and Sicily and some portions of the rest of Hellas. And all these colonies were planted after the Trojan war.

XIII. As Hellas grew more powerful and continued to acquire still more wealth than before, along with the increase of their revenue tyrannies began to be established in most of the cities, whereas before that there had been hereditary kingships based on fixed prerogatives. The Hellenes began to fit out navies, too, and to apply themselves more to the sea. And the Corinthians are said to have been the first of all to adopt what was very nearly the modern plan as regards ships and shipping,[1] and Corinth was the first place in all Hellas, we are told, where triremes were built. And it appears that Ameinocles, a Corinthian shipwright, built four ships for the Samians, also; and it was about three hundred years before the end of the Peloponnesian war that Ameinocles came to the Samians.[2] The earliest sea-fight, too, of which we know, was fought by the Corinthians against the Corcyraeans;[3] and this was two hundred and sixty years before the same date. For as the Corinthians had their city on the Isthmus, from the very earliest times they maintained there a market for the exchange of goods, because the Hellenes within and without the Peloponnesus, in olden times communicating with one another more by land than by sea, had to pass through their territory; and so they were powerful and rich, as has

[1] The reference seems to be to the construction of harbours and docks as well as to the structure of the ships, *e.g.* providing them with decks (ch. x. 4).

[2] 704 B.C. [3] 664 B.C.

τοῖς παλαιοῖς ποιηταῖς δεδήλωται· ἀφνειὸν γὰρ ἐπωνόμασαν τὸ χωρίον. ἐπειδή τε οἱ Ἕλληνες μᾶλλον ἔπλῳζον, τὰς ναῦς κτησάμενοι τὸ λῃστικὸν καθῄρουν, καὶ ἐμπόριον παρέχοντες ἀμφότερα δυνατὴν ἔσχον χρημάτων προσόδῳ τὴν πόλιν.
6 καὶ Ἴωσιν ὕστερον πολὺ γίγνεται ναυτικὸν ἐπὶ Κύρου Περσῶν πρώτου βασιλεύοντος καὶ Καμβύσου τοῦ υἱέος αὐτοῦ, τῆς τε καθ' ἑαυτοὺς θαλάσσης Κύρῳ πολεμοῦντες ἐκράτησάν τινα χρόνον. καὶ Πολυκράτης, Σάμου τυραννῶν ἐπὶ Καμβύσου, ναυτικῷ ἰσχύων ἄλλας τε τῶν νήσων ὑπηκόους ἐποιήσατο καὶ Ῥήνειαν ἑλὼν ἀνέθηκε τῷ Ἀπόλλωνι τῷ Δηλίῳ. Φωκαῆς τε Μασσαλίαν οἰκίζοντες Καρχηδονίους ἐνίκων ναυμαχοῦντες.

XIV. Δυνατώτατα γὰρ ταῦτα τῶν ναυτικῶν ἦν. φαίνεται δὲ καὶ ταῦτα, πολλαῖς γενεαῖς ὕστερα γενόμενα τῶν Τρωικῶν, τριήρεσι μὲν ὀλίγαις χρώμενα, πεντηκοντέροις δ' ἔτι καὶ πλοίοις
2 μακροῖς ἐξηρτυμένα ὥσπερ ἐκεῖνα. ὀλίγον τε πρὸ τῶν Μηδικῶν καὶ τοῦ Δαρείου θανάτου, ὃς μετὰ Καμβύσην Περσῶν ἐβασίλευσε, τριήρεις περί τε Σικελίαν τοῖς τυράννοις ἐς πλῆθος ἐγένοντο καὶ Κερκυραίοις· ταῦτα γὰρ τελευταῖα πρὸ τῆς Ξέρξου στρατείας ναυτικὰ ἀξιόλογα ἐν τῇ Ἑλλάδι
3 κατέστη. Αἰγινῆται γὰρ καὶ Ἀθηναῖοι, καὶ

---

[1] *cf.* Hom. B 570; Pind. *Ol.* xiii. 4.
[2] 559–529 B.C. [3] 532–522 B.C. [4] *cf.* III. civ.
[5] Marseilles, founded 600 B.C.

been shown even by the early poets, who called the place "Wealthy Corinth."[1] And when navigation grew more prevalent among the Hellenes, the Corinthians acquired ships and swept the sea of piracy, and offering a market by sea as well as by land, raised their city to great power by means of their revenues. The Ionians, too, acquired a powerful navy later, in the time of Cyrus,[2] the first king of the Persians, and of Cambyses his son; and waging war with Cyrus they maintained control of the sea about their own coasts for some time. Polycrates, also, who was tyrant of Samos in the time of Cambyses,[3] was strong in sea-power and subdued a number of the islands, Rhenea among them, which he captured and consecrated to the Delian Apollo.[4] Finally the Phocaeans, when they were colonizing Massalia,[5] conquered the Carthaginians in a sea-fight.

XIV. These were the most powerful of the fleets; and even these, we learn, though they were formed many generations later than the Trojan war, were provided with only a few triremes, but were still fitted out with fifty-oared galleys and the ordinary long boats,[6] like the navies of that earlier time. Indeed, it was only a little before the Persian war and the death of Darius,[7] who became king of the Persians after Cambyses, that triremes were acquired in large numbers, namely by the tyrants in various parts of Sicily and by the Corcyraeans; and these were the last navies worthy of note that were established in Hellas before the expedition of Xerxes. As for the Athenians and Aeginetans and any other maritime

[6] πλοῖα, usually contrasted with war-ships (τριήρεις), but here marked as ships of war by the epithet μακρά, though probably differing little except in size from trading-vessels.

[7] 485 B.C.

οἵτινες ἄλλοι, βραχέα ἐκέκτηντο καὶ τούτων τὰ πολλὰ πεντηκοντέρους· ὀψέ τε ἀφ' οὗ Ἀθηναίους Θεμιστοκλῆς ἔπεισεν Αἰγινήταις πολεμοῦντας. καὶ ἅμα τοῦ βαρβάρου προσδοκίμου ὄντος, τὰς ναῦς ποιήσασθαι, αἷσπερ καὶ ἐναυμάχησαν· καὶ αὗται οὔπω εἶχον διὰ πάσης καταστρώματα.

XV. Τὰ μὲν οὖν ναυτικὰ τῶν Ἑλλήνων τοιαῦτα ἦν, τά τε παλαιὰ καὶ τὰ ὕστερον γενόμενα. ἰσχὺν δὲ περιεποιήσαντο ὅμως οὐκ ἐλαχίστην οἱ προσσχόντες αὐτοῖς χρημάτων τε προσόδῳ καὶ ἄλλων ἀρχῇ· ἐπιπλέοντες γὰρ τὰς νήσους κατεστρέφοντο, καὶ μάλιστα ὅσοι μὴ διαρκῆ εἶχον
2 χώραν. κατὰ γῆν δὲ πόλεμος, ὅθεν τις κἂν δύναμις περιεγένετο, οὐδεὶς ξυνέστη· πάντες δὲ ἦσαν, ὅσοι καὶ ἐγένοντο, πρὸς ὁμόρους τοὺς σφετέρους ἑκάστοις, καὶ ἐκδήμους στρατείας πολὺ ἀπὸ τῆς ἑαυτῶν ἐπ' ἄλλων καταστροφῇ οὐκ ἐξῇσαν οἱ Ἕλληνες. οὐ γὰρ ξυνειστήκεσαν πρὸς τὰς μεγίστας πόλεις ὑπήκοοι, οὐδ' αὖ αὐτοὶ ἀπὸ τῆς ἴσης κοινὰς στρατείας ἐποιοῦντο, κατ' ἀλλήλους δὲ μᾶλλον ὡς ἕκαστοι οἱ ἀστυγείτονες ἐπολέμουν.
3 μάλιστα δὲ ἐς τὸν πάλαι ποτὲ γενόμενον πόλεμον Χαλκιδέων καὶ Ἐρετριῶν καὶ τὸ ἄλλο Ἑλληνικὸν ἐς ξυμμαχίαν ἑκατέρων διέστη.

---

[1] Referring to Xerxes' invasion. This Aeginetan war is referred to in ch. xli. 2.

powers, the fleets they had acquired were inconsiderable, consisting mostly of fifty-oared galleys; and it was only quite recently that the Athenians, when they were at war with the Aeginetans and were also expecting the Barbarians,[1] built their fleet, at the instance of Themistocles—the very ships with which they fought at Salamis. And these vessels were still without decks throughout their length.

XV. Such were the navies of the Hellenes, both those of early and those of later times; nevertheless those who gave attention to such matters acquired not a little strength by reason both of revenue of money and of sway over others. For they—and especially the peoples whose own territory was insufficient—made expeditions against the islands and subjugated them. But by land no wars arose from which any considerable accession of power resulted; on the contrary, all that did occur were border wars with their several neighbours, and foreign expeditions far from their own country for the subjugation of others were not undertaken by the Hellenes. For they had not yet been brought into union as subjects of the most powerful states, nor, on the other hand, did they of their own accord make expeditions in common as equal allies; it was rather against one another that the neighbouring peoples severally made war. But it was chiefly in the war that arose a long time ago between the Chalcidians and the Eretrians,[2] that all the rest of Hellas took sides in alliance with the one side or the other.

[2] The war for the Lelantine Plain (*cf.* Hdt. v. xcix.; Strabo, x. i. 11); usually placed in the seventh century, but by Curtius in the eighth (see *Hermes*, x. pp. 220 ff.).

XVI. Ἐπεγένετο δὲ ἄλλοις τε ἄλλοθι κωλύματα μὴ αὐξηθῆναι, καὶ Ἴωσι προχωρησάντων ἐπὶ μέγα τῶν πραγμάτων Κῦρος καὶ ἡ Περσικὴ ἐξουσία Κροῖσον καθελοῦσα καὶ ὅσα ἐντὸς Ἅλυος ποταμοῦ πρὸς θάλασσαν, ἐπεστράτευσε καὶ τὰς ἐν τῇ ἠπείρῳ πόλεις ἐδούλωσε, Δαρεῖός τε ὕστερον τῷ Φοινίκων ναυτικῷ κρατῶν καὶ τὰς νήσους.

XVII. Τύραννοί τε ὅσοι ἦσαν ἐν ταῖς Ἑλληνικαῖς πόλεσι, τὸ ἐφ' ἑαυτῶν μόνον προορώμενοι ἔς τε τὸ σῶμα καὶ ἐς τὸ τὸν ἴδιον οἶκον αὔξειν δι' ἀσφαλείας ὅσον ἐδύναντο μάλιστα τὰς πόλεις ᾤκουν, ἐπράχθη τε οὐδὲν ἀπ' αὐτῶν ἔργον ἀξιόλογον, εἰ μὴ εἴ τι πρὸς περιοίκους τοὺς αὐτῶν ἑκάστοις.[1] οὕτω πανταχόθεν ἡ Ἑλλὰς ἐπὶ πολὺν χρόνον κατείχετο μήτε κοινῇ φανερὸν μηδὲν κατεργάζεσθαι, κατὰ πόλεις τε ἀτολμοτέρα εἶναι.

XVIII. Ἐπειδὴ δὲ οἵ τε Ἀθηναίων τύραννοι καὶ οἱ ἐκ τῆς ἄλλης Ἑλλάδος ἐπὶ πολὺ καὶ πρὶν τυραννευθείσης οἱ πλεῖστοι καὶ τελευταῖοι πλὴν τῶν ἐν Σικελίᾳ ὑπὸ Λακεδαιμονίων κατελύθησαν· ἡ γὰρ Λακεδαίμων μετὰ τὴν κτίσιν τῶν νῦν ἐνοικούντων αὐτὴν[2] Δωριῶν ἐπὶ πλεῖστον ὧν ἴσμεν χρόνον στασιάσασα ὅμως ἐκ παλαιτάτου καὶ ηὐνομήθη καὶ αἰεὶ ἀτυράννευτος ἦν· ἔτη γάρ

[1] After ἑκάστοις the MSS. have οἱ γὰρ ἐν Σικελίᾳ ἐπὶ πλεῖστον ἐχώρησαν δυνάμεως, *for those in Sicily advanced to a very great degree of power*, which Wex deletes, followed by most editors. [2] Hude omits with E.

XVI. But different Hellenic peoples in different localities met with obstacles to their continuous growth; for example, after the Ionians had attained great prosperity, Cyrus and the Persian empire, after subduing Croesus[1] and all the territory between the river Halys and the sea, made war against them and enslaved the cities on the mainland, and later on Darius, strong in the possession of the Phoenician fleet, enslaved the islands also.[2]

XVII. The tyrants, moreover—whenever there were tyrants in the Hellenic cities—since they had regard for their own interests only, both as to the safety of their own persons and as to the aggrandizement of their own families, in the administration of their cities made security, so far as they possibly could, their chief aim, and so no achievement worthy of mention was accomplished by them, except perchance by individuals in conflict with their own neighbours. So on all sides Hellas was for a long time kept from carrying out in common any notable undertaking, and also its several states from being more enterprising.

XVIII. But finally the tyrants, not only of Athens but also of the rest of Hellas (which, for a long time before Athens, had been dominated by tyrants)—at least most of them and the last that ever ruled, if we except those in Sicily—were put down by the Lacedaemonians. For although Lacedaemon, after the settlement there of the Dorians who now inhabit it, was, for the longest period of all the places of which we know, in a state of sedition, still it obtained good laws at an earlier time than any other land, and has always been free from tyrants; for the

[1] 546 B.C. [2] 493 B.C.

ἐστι μάλιστα τετρακόσια καὶ ὀλίγῳ πλείω ἐς τὴν
τελευτὴν τοῦδε τοῦ πολέμου, ἀφ' οὗ Λακεδαιμόνιοι τῇ αὐτῇ πολιτείᾳ χρῶνται· καὶ δι' αὐτὸ
δυνάμενοι καὶ τὰ ἐν ταῖς ἄλλαις πόλεσι καθίστασαν. μετὰ δὲ τὴν τῶν τυράννων κατάλυσιν ἐκ
τῆς Ἑλλάδος οὐ πολλοῖς ἔτεσιν ὕστερον καὶ ἡ ἐν
Μαραθῶνι μάχη Μήδων πρὸς Ἀθηναίους ἐγένετο.
2 δεκάτῳ δὲ ἔτει μετ' αὐτὴν αὖθις ὁ βάρβαρος τῷ
μεγάλῳ στόλῳ ἐπὶ τὴν Ἑλλάδα δουλωσόμενος
ἦλθεν. καὶ μεγάλου κινδύνου ἐπικρεμασθέντος
οἵ τε Λακεδαιμόνιοι τῶν ξυμπολεμησάντων Ἑλλήνων ἡγήσαντο δυνάμει προύχοντες, καὶ οἱ Ἀθηναῖοι ἐπιόντων τῶν Μήδων διανοηθέντες ἐκλιπεῖν
τὴν πόλιν καὶ ἀνασκευασάμενοι ἐς τὰς ναῦς
ἐσβάντες ναυτικοὶ ἐγένοντο. κοινῇ τε ἀπωσά-
μενοι τὸν βάρβαρον ὕστερον οὐ πολλῷ διεκρίθησαν πρός τε Ἀθηναίους καὶ Λακεδαιμονίους οἵ τε
ἀποστάντες βασιλέως Ἕλληνες καὶ οἱ ξυμπολε-
μήσαντες· δυνάμει γὰρ ταῦτα μέγιστα διεφάνη·
3 ἴσχυον γὰρ οἱ μὲν κατὰ γῆν, οἱ δὲ ναυσίν. καὶ
ὀλίγον μὲν χρόνον ξυνέμεινεν ἡ ὁμαιχμία, ἔπειτα
διενεχθέντες οἱ Λακεδαιμόνιοι καὶ οἱ Ἀθηναῖοι
ἐπολέμησαν μετὰ τῶν ξυμμάχων πρὸς ἀλλήλους,
καὶ τῶν ἄλλων Ἑλλήνων εἴ τινές που διασταῖεν,
πρὸς τούτους ἤδη ἐχώρουν. ὥστε ἀπὸ τῶν Μηδικῶν ἐς τόνδε αἰεὶ τὸν πόλεμον τὰ μὲν σπενδόμενοι,

---

[1] The legislation of Lycurgus, thus placed by Thucydides at four hundred years or more before 404 B.C., would be about 804 B.C. (Eratosthenes gives 884).

period during which the Lacedaemonians have been enjoying the same constitution[1] covers about four hundred years or a little more down to the end of the Peloponnesian war. And it is for this reason that they became powerful and regulated the affairs of other states as well. Not many years after the overthrow of the tyrants in Hellas by the Lacedaemonians the battle of Marathon[2] was fought between the Athenians and the Persians; and ten years after that the Barbarian came again with his great host against Hellas to enslave it. In the face of the great danger that threatened, the Lacedaemonians, because they were the most powerful, assumed the leadership of the Hellenes that joined in the war; and the Athenians, when the Persians came on, resolved to abandon their city, and packing up their goods embarked on their ships, and so became sailors. By a common effort the Barbarian was repelled; but not long afterwards the other Hellenes, both those who had revolted from the King and those who had joined the first confederacy against him, parted company and aligned themselves with either the Athenians or the Lacedaemonians; for these states had shown themselves the most powerful, the one strong by land and the other on the sea. The defensive alliance lasted only a little while; then the Lacedaemonians and the Athenians quarrelled and, with their respective allies, made war upon one another, and any of the rest of the Hellenes, if they chanced to be at variance, from now on resorted to one or the other. So that from the Persian invasion continually, to this present war, making peace at one time, at another time

[2] 490 B.C.

τὰ δὲ πολεμοῦντες ἢ ἀλλήλοις ἢ τοῖς ἑαυτῶν ξυμμάχοις ἀφισταμένοις εὖ παρεσκευάσαντο τὰ πολέμια καὶ ἐμπειρότεροι ἐγένοντο μετὰ κινδύνων τὰς μελέτας ποιούμενοι.

XIX. Καὶ οἱ μὲν Λακεδαιμόνιοι οὐχ ὑποτελεῖς ἔχοντες φόρου τοὺς ξυμμάχους ἡγοῦντο, κατ' ὀλιγαρχίαν δὲ σφίσιν αὐτοῖς μόνον ἐπιτηδείως ὅπως πολιτεύσουσι θεραπεύοντες, Ἀθηναῖοι δὲ ναῦς τε τῶν πόλεων τῷ χρόνῳ παραλαβόντες, πλὴν Χίων καὶ Λεσβίων, καὶ χρήματα τοῖς πᾶσι τάξαντες φέρειν. καὶ ἐγένετο αὐτοῖς ἐς τόνδε τὸν πόλεμον ἡ ἰδία παρασκευὴ μείζων ἢ ὡς τὰ κράτιστά ποτε μετὰ ἀκραιφνοῦς τῆς ξυμμαχίας ἤνθησαν.

XX. Τὰ μὲν οὖν παλαιὰ τοιαῦτα ηὗρον, χαλεπὰ ὄντα παντὶ ἑξῆς τεκμηρίῳ πιστεῦσαι. οἱ γὰρ ἄνθρωποι τὰς ἀκοὰς τῶν προγεγενημένων, καὶ ἢν ἐπιχώρια σφίσιν ᾖ, ὁμοίως ἀβασανίστως παρ'
2 ἀλλήλων δέχονται. Ἀθηναίων γοῦν τὸ πλῆθος Ἵππαρχον οἴονται ὑφ' Ἁρμοδίου καὶ Ἀριστογείτονος τύραννον ὄντα ἀποθανεῖν καὶ οὐκ ἴσασιν ὅτι Ἱππίας μὲν πρεσβύτατος ὢν ἦρχε τῶν Πεισιστράτου υἱέων, Ἵππαρχος δὲ καὶ Θεσσαλὸς ἀδελφοὶ ἦσαν αὐτοῦ, ὑποτοπήσαντες δέ τι ἐκείνῃ τῇ ἡμέρᾳ καὶ παραχρῆμα Ἁρμόδιος καὶ Ἀριστογείτων ἐκ τῶν ξυνειδότων σφίσιν Ἱππίᾳ μεμηνῦσθαι,

---

[1] *cf.* VI. lxxxv. 2; VII. lvii. 4.

[2] Lost its independence after the revolt of 427 B.C. *cf.* III. l.

[3] *i.e.* as if they took place in some distant land.

fighting with each other or with their own revolted allies, these two states prepared themselves well in matters of war, and became more experienced, taking their training amid actual dangers.

XIX. The Lacedaemonians maintained their hegemony without keeping their allies tributary to them, but took care that these should have an oligarchical form of government conformably to the sole interest of Sparta; the Athenians, on the other hand, maintained theirs by taking over in course of time the ships of the allied cities, with the exception of Chios[1] and Lesbos,[2] and by imposing on them all a tax of money. And so the individual resources of the Athenians available for this war became greater than those of themselves and their allies when that alliance was still unimpaired and strongest.

XX. Now the state of affairs in early times I have found to have been such as I have described, although it is difficult in such matters to credit any and every piece of testimony. For men accept from one another hearsay reports of former events, neglecting to test them just the same,[3] even though these events belong to the history of their own country. Take the Athenians, for example; most of them think that Hipparchus was tyrant when he was slain by Harmodius and Aristogeiton.[4] They do not know that it was Hippias, as the eldest of the sons of Peisistratus, who was ruler, and that Hipparchus and Thessalus were merely his brothers; further, that Harmodius and Aristogeiton, suspecting, on that very day and at the very moment of executing their plan, that information had been conveyed to Hippias by one of their fellow-conspirators,

[4] 514 B.C. On this digression, *cf.* Hdt. v. lv.; VI. cxxiii.; Arist. 'Αθ. Πολ. 17 f.

τοῦ μὲν ἀπέσχοντο ὡς προειδότος, βουλόμενοι δὲ πρὶν ξυλληφθῆναι δράσαντές τι καὶ κινδυνεῦσαι, τῷ Ἱππάρχῳ περιτυχόντες παρὰ τὸ Λεωκόρειον καλούμενον τὴν Παναθηναϊκὴν πομπὴν διακο-
3 σμοῦντι ἀπέκτειναν. πολλὰ δὲ καὶ ἄλλα ἔτι καὶ νῦν ὄντα καὶ οὐ χρόνῳ ἀμνηστούμενα καὶ οἱ ἄλλοι Ἕλληνες οὐκ ὀρθῶς οἴονται, ὥσπερ τούς τε Λακεδαιμονίων βασιλέας μὴ μιᾷ ψήφῳ προστίθεσθαι ἑκάτερον, ἀλλὰ δυοῖν, καὶ τὸν Πιτανάτην λόχον αὐτοῖς εἶναι, ὃς οὐδ' ἐγένετο πώποτε. οὕτως ἀταλαίπωρος τοῖς πολλοῖς ἡ ζήτησις τῆς ἀληθείας καὶ ἐπὶ τὰ ἑτοῖμα μᾶλλον τρέπονται.

XXI. Ἐκ δὲ τῶν εἰρημένων τεκμηρίων ὅμως τοιαῦτα ἄν τις νομίζων μάλιστα ἃ διῆλθον οὐχ ἁμαρτάνοι, καὶ οὔτε ὡς ποιηταὶ ὑμνήκασι περὶ αὐτῶν ἐπὶ τὸ μεῖζον κοσμοῦντες μᾶλλον πιστεύων, οὔτε ὡς λογογράφοι ξυνέθεσαν ἐπὶ τὸ προσαγωγότερον τῇ ἀκροάσει ἢ ἀληθέστερον, ὄντα ἀνεξέλεγκτα καὶ τὰ πολλὰ ὑπὸ χρόνου αὐτῶν ἀπίστως ἐπὶ τὸ μυθῶδες ἐκνενικηκότα, ηὑρῆσθαι δὲ ἡγησάμενος ἐκ τῶν ἐπιφανεστάτων σημείων ὡς παλαιὰ
2 εἶναι ἀποχρώντως. καὶ ὁ πόλεμος οὗτος, καίπερ

---

[1] In the inner Ceramicus near the temple of Apollo Patrous.

[2] Herodotus is doubtless one of the Hellenes here criticised. *cf.* VI. lvii., referring to the two votes; IX. liii., where he seems to have applied a term belonging to a deme (*cf.* Hdt. III. lv.) to a division of the army.

held off from him as forewarned, but wishing to do something before they were seized and then take their chances, fell in with Hipparchus, who was marshalling the Panathenaic procession near the sanctuary called Leocorium,[1] and killed him. There are many other matters, too, belonging to the present and not forgotten through lapse of time, regarding which the other Hellenes[2] as well hold mistaken opinions, for example, that at Lacedaemon the kings cast not one but two votes each, and that the Lacedaemonians have the "Pitana company" in their army, which never at any time existed. So averse to taking pains are most men in the search for the truth, and so prone are they to turn to what lies ready at hand.

XXI. Still, from the evidence that has been given, any one would not err who should hold the view that the state of affairs in antiquity was pretty nearly such as I have described it, not giving greater credence to the accounts, on the one hand, which the poets have put into song, adorning and amplifying their theme, and, on the other, which the chroniclers have composed with a view rather of pleasing the ear[3] than of telling the truth, since their stories cannot be tested and most of them have from lapse of time won their way into the region of the fabulous so as to be incredible. He should regard the facts as having been made out with sufficient accuracy, on the basis of the clearest indications, considering that they have to do with early times. And so, even though men are always

[3] Public recitation was the ordinary mode of getting the works of the poets and early logographers before the people.

τῶν ἀνθρώπων ἐν ᾧ μὲν ἂν πολεμῶσι τὸν παρόντα αἰεὶ μέγιστον κρινόντων, παυσαμένων δὲ τὰ ἀρχαῖα μᾶλλον θαυμαζόντων, ἀπ' αὐτῶν τῶν ἔργων σκοποῦσι δηλώσει ὅμως μείζων γεγενημένος αὐτῶν.

XXII. Καὶ ὅσα μὲν λόγῳ εἶπον ἕκαστοι ἢ μέλλοντες πολεμήσειν ἢ ἐν αὐτῷ ἤδη ὄντες, χαλεπὸν τὴν ἀκρίβειαν αὐτὴν τῶν λεχθέντων διαμνημονεῦσαι ἦν ἐμοί τε ὧν αὐτὸς ἤκουσα καὶ τοῖς ἄλλοθέν ποθεν ἐμοὶ ἀπαγγέλλουσιν· ὡς δ' ἂν ἐδόκουν μοι ἕκαστοι περὶ τῶν αἰεὶ παρόντων τὰ δέοντα μάλιστ' εἰπεῖν, ἐχομένῳ ὅτι ἐγγύτατα τῆς ξυμπάσης γνώ-
2 μης τῶν ἀληθῶς λεχθέντων, οὕτως εἴρηται· τὰ
δ' ἔργα τῶν πραχθέντων ἐν τῷ πολέμῳ οὐκ ἐκ
τοῦ παρατυχόντος πυνθανόμενος ἠξίωσα γράφειν
οὐδ' ὡς ἐμοὶ ἐδόκει, ἀλλ' οἷς τε αὐτὸς παρῆν καὶ
παρὰ τῶν ἄλλων ὅσον δυνατὸν ἀκριβείᾳ περὶ
3 ἑκάστου ἐπεξελθών. ἐπιπόνως δὲ ηὑρίσκετο, διότι
οἱ παρόντες τοῖς ἔργοις ἑκάστοις οὐ ταὐτὰ περὶ
τῶν αὐτῶν ἔλεγον, ἀλλ' ὡς ἑκατέρων τις εὐνοίας
4 ἢ μνήμης ἔχοι. καὶ ἐς μὲν ἀκρόασιν ἴσως τὸ
μὴ μυθῶδες αὐτῶν ἀτερπέστερον φανεῖται· ὅσοι

inclined, while they are engaged in a war, to judge the present one the greatest, but when it is over to regard ancient events with greater wonder, yet this war will prove, for men who judge from the actual facts, to have been more important than any that went before.

XXII. As to the speeches that were made by different men, either when they were about to begin the war or when they were already engaged therein, it has been difficult to recall with strict accuracy the words actually spoken, both for me as regards that which I myself heard, and for those who from various other sources have brought me reports. Therefore the speeches are given in the language in which, as it seemed to me, the several speakers would express, on the subjects under consideration, the sentiments most befitting the occasion, though at the same time I have adhered as closely as possible to the general sense of what was actually said. But as to the facts of the occurrences of the war, I have thought it my duty to give them, not as ascertained from any chance informant nor as seemed to me probable, but only after investigating with the greatest possible accuracy each detail, in the case both of the events in which I myself participated and of those regarding which I got my information from others. And the endeavour to ascertain these facts was a laborious task, because those who were eye-witnesses of the several events did not give the same reports about the same things, but reports varying according to their championship of one side or the other, or according to their recollection. And it may well be that the absence of the fabulous from my narrative will seem

δὲ βουλήσονται τῶν τε γενομένων τὸ σαφὲς σκοπεῖν καὶ τῶν μελλόντων ποτὲ αὖθις κατὰ τὸ ἀνθρώπινον τοιούτων καὶ παραπλησίων ἔσεσθαι, ὠφέλιμα κρίνειν αὐτὰ ἀρκούντως ἕξει. κτῆμά τε ἐς αἰεὶ μᾶλλον ἢ ἀγώνισμα ἐς τὸ παραχρῆμα ἀκούειν ξύγκειται.

XXIII. Τῶν δὲ πρότερον ἔργων μέγιστον ἐπράχθη τὸ Μηδικόν, καὶ τοῦτο ὅμως δυοῖν ναυμαχίαιν καὶ πεζομαχίαιν ταχεῖαν τὴν κρίσιν ἔσχεν. τούτου δὲ τοῦ πολέμου μῆκός τε μέγα προύβη, παθήματά τε ξυνηνέχθη γενέσθαι ἐν αὐτῷ τῇ
2 Ἑλλάδι οἷα οὐχ ἕτερα ἐν ἴσῳ χρόνῳ. οὔτε γὰρ πόλεις τοσαίδε ληφθεῖσαι ἠρημώθησαν, αἱ μὲν ὑπὸ βαρβάρων, αἱ δ' ὑπὸ σφῶν αὐτῶν ἀντιπολεμούντων (εἰσὶ δ' αἳ καὶ οἰκήτορας μετέβαλον ἁλισκόμεναι), οὔτε φυγαὶ τοσαίδε ἀνθρώπων καὶ φόνος, ὁ μὲν κατ' αὐτὸν τὸν πόλεμον, ὁ δὲ διὰ τὸ
3 στασιάζειν. τά τε πρότερον ἀκοῇ μὲν λεγόμενα, ἔργῳ δὲ σπανιώτερον βεβαιούμενα οὐκ ἄπιστα κατέστη, σεισμῶν τε πέρι, οἳ ἐπὶ πλεῖστον ἅμα μέρος γῆς καὶ ἰσχυρότατοι οἱ αὐτοὶ ἐπέσχον, ἡλίου τε ἐκλείψεις, αἳ πυκνότεραι παρὰ τὰ ἐκ τοῦ πρὶν χρόνου μνημονευόμενα ξυνέβησαν, αὐχμοί τε ἔστι παρ' οἷς μεγάλοι καὶ ἀπ' αὐτῶν καὶ λιμοὶ

---

[1] Artemisium and Salamis.
[2] Thermopylae and Plataea.
[3] As Colophon (III. xxxiv.), Mycalessus (VII. xxix.).

less pleasing to the ear; but whoever shall wish to have a clear view both of the events which have happened and of those which will some day, in all human probability, happen again in the same or a similar way—for these to adjudge my history profitable will be enough for me. And, indeed, it has been composed, not as a prize-essay to be heard for the moment, but as a possession for all time.

XXIII. The greatest achievement of former times was the Persian war, and yet this was quickly decided in two sea-fights[1] and two land-battles.[2] But the Peloponnesian war was protracted to a great length, and in the course of it disasters befell Hellas the like of which had never occurred in any equal space of time. Never had so many cities been taken and left desolate, some by the Barbarians,[3] and others by Hellenes[4] themselves warring against one another; while several, after their capture, underwent a change of inhabitants.[5] Never had so many human beings been exiled, or so much human blood been shed, whether in the course of the war itself or as the result of civil dissensions. And so the stories of former times, handed down by oral tradition, but very rarely confirmed by fact, ceased to be incredible: about earthquakes, for instance, for they prevailed over a very large part of the earth and were likewise of the greatest violence; eclipses of the sun, which occurred at more frequent intervals than we find recorded of all former times; great droughts also in some quarters with resultant famines; and lastly—

[4] *e.g.* Plataea (III. lxviii. 3), Thyrea (IV. lvii.).
[5] *e.g.* Sollium (II. xxx.), Potidaea (II. lxx.), Anactorium (IV. xlix.), Scione (V. xxxii.), Melos (V. cxvi.).

καὶ ἡ οὐχ ἥκιστα βλάψασα καὶ μέρος τι φθείρασα
ἡ λοιμώδης νόσος· ταῦτα γὰρ πάντα μετὰ τοῦδε
4 τοῦ πολέμου ἅμα ξυνεπέθετο. ἤρξαντο δὲ αὐτοῦ
Ἀθηναῖοι καὶ Πελοποννήσιοι λύσαντες τὰς τριακοντούτεις σπονδὰς αἳ αὐτοῖς ἐγένοντο μετὰ Εὐ-
5 βοίας ἅλωσιν. δι' ὅ τι δ' ἔλυσαν, τὰς αἰτίας
προύγραψα πρῶτον καὶ τὰς διαφοράς, τοῦ μή
τινα ζητῆσαί ποτε ἐξ ὅτου τοσοῦτος πόλεμος τοῖς
6 Ἕλλησι κατέστη. τὴν μὲν γὰρ ἀληθεστάτην
πρόφασιν, ἀφανεστάτην δὲ λόγῳ τοὺς Ἀθηναίους ἡγοῦμαι μεγάλους γιγνομένους καὶ φόβον παρέχοντας τοῖς Λακεδαιμονίοις ἀναγκάσαι ἐς τὸ πολεμεῖν· αἱ δ' ἐς τὸ φανερὸν λεγόμεναι αἰτίαι αἵδ' ἦσαν ἑκατέρων, ἀφ' ὧν λύσαντες τὰς σπονδὰς ἐς τὸν πόλεμον κατέστησαν.

XXIV. Ἐπίδαμνός ἐστι πόλις ἐν δεξιᾷ ἐσπλέοντι τὸν Ἰόνιον κόλπον· προσοικοῦσι δ' αὐτὴν
2 Ταυλάντιοι βάρβαροι, Ἰλλυρικὸν ἔθνος. ταύτην
ἀπῴκισαν μὲν Κερκυραῖοι, οἰκιστὴς δ' ἐγένετο Φαλίος Ἐρατοκλείδου, Κορίνθιος γένος, τῶν ἀφ' Ἡρακλέους, κατὰ δὴ τὸν παλαιὸν νόμον ἐκ τῆς μητροπόλεως κατακληθείς. ξυνῴκισαν δὲ καὶ Κορινθίων τινὲς καὶ τοῦ ἄλλου Δωρικοῦ γένους.
3 προελθόντος δὲ τοῦ χρόνου ἐγένετο ἡ τῶν Ἐπι-
δαμνίων δύναμις μεγάλη καὶ πολυάνθρωπος.
4 στασιάσαντες δὲ ἐν ἀλλήλοις ἔτη πολλά, ὡς
λέγεται, ἀπὸ πολέμου τινὸς τῶν προσοίκων βαρβάρων ἐφθάρησαν καὶ τῆς δυνάμεως τῆς πολλῆς
5 ἐστερήθησαν. τὰ δὲ τελευταῖα πρὸ τοῦδε τοῦ
πολέμου ὁ δῆμος αὐτῶν ἐξεδίωξε τοὺς δυνατούς, οἱ δὲ ἐπελθόντες μετὰ τῶν βαρβάρων ἐλῄζοντο

To face page 43.

CORCYRA & NORTH-WESTERN HELLAS

English Miles
0 5 10 20 30 40 50

Attic. Stadia
0 50 100 200 300 400

Wm. Heinemann, Ltd. *Edward Stanford Ltd., London*

the disaster which wrought most harm to Hellas and destroyed a considerable part of the people—the noisome pestilence. For all these disasters fell upon them simultaneously with this war. And the war began when the Athenians and Peloponnesians broke the thirty years' truce,[1] concluded between them after the capture of Euboea. The reasons why they broke it and the grounds of their quarrel I have first set forth, that no one may ever have to inquire for what cause the Hellenes became involved in so great a war. The truest explanation, although it has been the least often advanced, I believe to have been the growth of the Athenians to greatness, which brought fear to the Lacedaemonians and forced them to war. But the reasons publicly alleged on either side which led them to break the truce and involved them in the war were as follows.

XXIV. There is a city called Epidamnus on the right hand as one sails into the Ionian gulf, and its next-door neighbours are a barbarian tribe, the Taulantians, of Illyrian race. The city was colonized by the Corcyraeans, and its founder was Phalius, son of Eratocleides, of Corinthian stock and a descendant of Heracles, who was invited from the mother-city according to the ancient custom; but some Corinthians and other Dorians joined the Corcyraeans in establishing the colony. As time passed the city of the Epidamnians became great and populous; but civil wars ensued, lasting, it is said, for many years, and in consequence of a war with the neighbouring barbarians they were crippled and stripped of most of their power. Finally, just before the Peloponnesian war, the populace expelled the aristocrats, and they, making common cause with the barbarians and

[1] 445 B.C.; *cf.* ch. cxv. 1.

τοὺς ἐν τῇ πόλει κατά τε γῆν καὶ κατὰ θάλασ-
6 σαν. οἱ δὲ ἐν τῇ πόλει ὄντες Ἐπιδάμνιοι ἐπειδὴ ἐπιέζοντο, πέμπουσιν ἐς τὴν Κέρκυραν πρέσβεις ὡς μητρόπολιν οὖσαν, δεόμενοι μὴ σφᾶς περιορᾶν φθειρομένους, ἀλλὰ τούς τε φεύγοντας ξυναλλάξαι σφίσι καὶ τὸν τῶν βαρβάρων πό-
7 λεμον καταλῦσαι. ταῦτα δὲ ἱκέται καθεζόμενοι ἐς τὸ Ἥραιον ἐδέοντο. οἱ δὲ Κερκυραῖοι τὴν ἱκετείαν οὐκ ἐδέξαντο, ἀλλ' ἀπράκτους ἀπέπεμψαν.

XXV. Γνόντες δὲ οἱ Ἐπιδάμνιοι οὐδεμίαν σφίσιν ἀπὸ Κερκύρας τιμωρίαν οὖσαν ἐν ἀπόρῳ εἴχοντο θέσθαι τὸ παρόν, καὶ πέμψαντες ἐς Δελφοὺς τὸν θεὸν ἐπηρώτων εἰ παραδοῖεν Κορινθίοις τὴν πόλιν ὡς οἰκισταῖς καὶ τιμωρίαν τινὰ πειρῷντ' ἀπ' αὐτῶν ποιεῖσθαι. ὁ δ' αὐτοῖς ἀνεῖλε παραδοῦναι καὶ ἡγεμόνας ποιεῖσθαι.
2 ἐλθόντες δὲ οἱ Ἐπιδάμνιοι ἐς τὴν Κόρινθον κατὰ τὸ μαντεῖον παρέδοσαν τὴν ἀποικίαν, τόν τε οἰκιστὴν ἀποδεικνύντες σφῶν ἐκ Κορίνθου ὄντα καὶ τὸ χρηστήριον δηλοῦντες, ἐδέοντό τε μὴ σφᾶς περιορᾶν φθειρομένους, ἀλλ' ἐπαμῦναι.
3 Κορίνθιοι δὲ κατά τε τὸ δίκαιον ὑπεδέξαντο τὴν τιμωρίαν, νομίζοντες οὐχ ἧσσον ἑαυτῶν εἶναι τὴν ἀποικίαν ἢ Κερκυραίων, ἅμα δὲ καὶ μίσει τῶν Κερκυραίων, ὅτι αὐτῶν παρημέλουν ὄντες
4 ἄποικοι, οὔτε γὰρ ἐν πανηγύρεσι ταῖς κοιναῖς διδόντες γέρα τὰ νομιζόμενα οὔτε Κορινθίῳ ἀνδρὶ

---

[1] The κοιναὶ πανηγύρεις are the four great games, here doubtless referring especially to the Isthmian Games held at Corinth. The "privileges" would be places of honour (προεδρίαι), animals for sacrifice presented by the colonies of

attacking Epidamnus, plundered those who were in the city both by land and sea. These, when they were being hard pressed, sent envoys to Corcyra, as being their mother-city, begging them not to look on and see them destroyed, but to reconcile them with the exiles and to put a stop to the war with the barbarians. This petition they made, sitting as suppliants in the temple of Hera. But the Corcyraeans denied their supplication, and sent them back unsuccessful.

XXV. The Epidamnians, recognizing that no aid was to be had from Corcyra, were at a loss how to settle their present difficulty; so they sent to Delphi and asked the god whether they should deliver up their city to the Corinthians as founders and try to procure some aid from them. The god answered that they should deliver it up to them and make them leaders. So the Epidamnians went to Corinth and 435 B.C.
delivered up the city as a Corinthian colony, in accordance with the oracle, showing that their founder was from Corinth and stating the response of the oracle; and they begged the Corinthians not to look on and see them utterly destroyed, but to come to their rescue. The Corinthians undertook the task, partly on the ground of right, because they considered that the colony belonged to them quite as much as to the Corcyraeans, partly also through hatred of the Corcyraeans, for the reason that these, though Corinthian colonists, neglected the mother-city. For neither at their common festival gatherings [1] would they concede the customary privileges to Corinthians, nor would they begin with a representative of

the mother-city, sending of delegates (θεωροί) to Corinthian festivals, etc.

προκαταρχόμενοι τῶν ἱερῶν, ὥσπερ αἱ ἄλλαι ἀποικίαι, περιφρονοῦντες δὲ αὐτοὺς κἀν χρημάτων δυνάμει ὄντες κατ' ἐκεῖνον τὸν χρόνον ὁμοῖα τοῖς Ἑλλήνων πλουσιωτάτοις καὶ τῇ ἐς πόλεμον παρασκευῇ δυνατώτεροι, ναυτικῷ δὲ καὶ πολὺ προύχειν ἔστιν ὅτε ἐπαιρόμενοι καὶ κατὰ τὴν Φαιάκων προενοίκησιν τῆς Κερκύρας κλέος ἐχόντων τὰ περὶ τὰς ναῦς· ᾗ καὶ μᾶλλον ἐξηρτύοντο τὸ ναυτικὸν καὶ ἦσαν οὐκ ἀδύνατοι· τριήρεις γὰρ εἴκοσι καὶ ἑκατὸν ὑπῆρχον αὐτοῖς ὅτε ἤρχοντο πολεμεῖν.

XXVI. Πάντων οὖν τούτων ἐγκλήματα ἔχοντες οἱ Κορίνθιοι ἔπεμπον ἐς τὴν Ἐπίδαμνον ἄσμενοι τὴν ὠφελίαν, οἰκήτορά τε τὸν βουλόμενον ἰέναι κελεύοντες καὶ Ἀμπρακιωτῶν καὶ
2 Λευκαδίων καὶ ἑαυτῶν φρουρούς. ἐπορεύθησαν δὲ πεζῇ ἐς Ἀπολλωνίαν Κορινθίων οὖσαν ἀποικίαν, δέει τῶν Κερκυραίων μὴ κωλύωνται ὑπ'
3 αὐτῶν κατὰ θάλασσαν περαιούμενοι. Κερκυραῖοι δὲ ἐπειδὴ ᾔσθοντο τούς τε οἰκήτορας καὶ φρουροὺς ἥκοντας ἐς τὴν Ἐπίδαμνον τήν τε ἀποικίαν Κορινθίοις δεδομένην, ἐχαλέπαινον· καὶ πλεύσαντες εὐθὺς πέντε καὶ εἴκοσι ναυσὶ καὶ ὕστερον ἑτέρῳ στόλῳ τούς τε φεύγοντας ἐκέλευον κατ' ἐπήρειαν δέχεσθαι αὐτούς (ἦλθον γὰρ ἐς τὴν Κέρκυραν οἱ τῶν Ἐπιδαμνίων φυγάδες τάφους τε ἀποδεικνύντες καὶ ξυγγένειαν, ἣν προϊσχόμενοι ἐδέοντο σφᾶς κατάγειν) τούς τε φρουροὺς οὓς

[1] According to the custom obtaining in Hellenic cities, whereby a stranger could offer sacrifice only through a citizen who acted for him. προκαταρχόμενοι, as the Schol. explains, διδόντες πρότερον (sc. ἢ τοῖς ἄλλοις) τὰς καταρχάς, i.e. giving the hair cut from the victim's forehead to a repre-

Corinth the initial rites at sacrifices,[1] as the rest of the colonies did, but they treated them with contempt. For at that time they were in point of wealth equal to the richest of the Hellenes, and in preparation for war even stronger, while in sea-power they sometimes boasted that they were greatly superior, just because of the former occupation of the island by the Phaeacians,[2] whose glory was in their ships. It was for this reason that they kept on developing their navy, and they were in fact powerful; for they had on hand one hundred and twenty triremes when the war began.

XXVI. So the Corinthians, having all these grounds of complaint, gladly sent the desired aid to Epidamnus, inviting whoever wished to go along as settlers and despatching as a garrison some Ambraciots and Leucadians and a detachment of themselves. They proceeded to Apollonia, a colony of the Corinthians, going by land through fear of the Corcyraeans, lest they might be prevented by them if they should attempt to cross the sea. But when the Corcyraeans perceived that the settlers and the garrison had arrived at Epidamnus, and that their colony had been given up to the Corinthians, they were indignant. So they sailed immediately with twenty-five ships, and later with a second fleet, and insolently bade the Epidamnians dismiss the garrison sent by the Corinthians and the settlers, and also receive back their exiles; for the exiled Epidamnians had gone to Corcyra, and pointing to the sepulchres of common ancestors and

sentative of Corinth, that he might throw it on the fire (Classen).

[2] *cf.* III. lxx., where a sacred precinct of Alcinous in Corcyra is mentioned. The ancient belief that Corcyra was the Homeric Scheria has no support in the *Odyssey*.

Κορίνθιοι ἔπεμψαν καὶ τοὺς οἰκήτορας ἀποπέμ-
4 πειν. οἱ δὲ Ἐπιδάμνιοι οὐδὲν αὐτῶν ὑπήκουσαν,
ἀλλὰ στρατεύουσιν ἐπ' αὐτοὺς οἱ Κερκυραῖοι
τεσσαράκοντα ναυσὶ μετὰ τῶν φυγάδων ὡς
κατάξοντες, καὶ τοὺς Ἰλλυριοὺς προσλαβόντες.
5 προσκαθεζόμενοι δὲ τὴν πόλιν προεῖπον Ἐπιδαμνίων τε τὸν βουλόμενον καὶ τοὺς ξένους ἀπα-
θεῖς ἀπιέναι· εἰ δὲ μή, ὡς πολεμίοις χρήσεσθαι.
ὡς δ' οὐκ ἐπείθοντο, οἱ μὲν Κερκυραῖοι (ἔστι δ'
ἰσθμὸς τὸ χωρίον) ἐπολιόρκουν τὴν πόλιν.

XXVII. Κορίνθιοι δ', ὡς αὐτοῖς ἐκ τῆς Ἐπιδάμνου ἦλθον ἄγγελοι ὅτι πολιορκοῦνται, παρεσκευάζοντο στρατείαν, καὶ ἅμα ἀποικίαν ἐς τὴν
Ἐπίδαμνον ἐκήρυσσον ἐπὶ τῇ ἴσῃ καὶ ὁμοίᾳ τὸν
βουλόμενον ἰέναι· εἰ δέ τις τὸ παραυτίκα μὲν
μὴ ἐθέλει ξυμπλεῖν, μετέχειν δὲ βούλεται τῆς
ἀποικίας, πεντήκοντα δραχμὰς καταθέντα Κοριν-
θίας μένειν. ἦσαν δὲ καὶ οἱ πλέοντες πολλοὶ
2 καὶ οἱ τἀργύριον καταβάλλοντες. ἐδεήθησαν δὲ
καὶ τῶν Μεγαρέων ναυσὶ σφᾶς ξυμπροπέμψαι,
εἰ ἄρα κωλύοιντο ὑπὸ Κερκυραίων πλεῖν· οἱ δὲ
παρεσκευάζοντο αὐτοῖς ὀκτὼ ναυσὶ ξυμπλεῖν,
καὶ Παλῆς Κεφαλλήνων τέσσαρσιν. καὶ Ἐπιδαυρίων ἐδεήθησαν, οἳ παρέσχον πέντε, Ἑρμιονῆς
δὲ μίαν καὶ Τροιζήνιοι δύο, Λευκάδιοι δὲ δέκα καὶ
Ἀμπρακιῶται ὀκτώ. Θηβαίους δὲ χρήματα ᾔτησαν καὶ Φλειασίους, Ἠλείους δὲ ναῦς τε κενὰς

invoking the tie of kinship had begged the Corcyraeans to restore them. As the Epidamnians paid no heed to them the Corcyraeans proceeded against them with forty ships, accompanied by the exiles whom they intended to restore, and taking along the Illyrians also. And sitting down before the city they proclaimed that the foreigners and any Epidamnians who wished might go away in safety; otherwise they would treat them as enemies. But when the Epidamnians would not comply, the Corcyraeans laid siege to the city, which is connected with the shore by an isthmus.

XXVII. But the Corinthians, when messengers came from Epidamnus announcing the siege, prepared an expedition and proclaimed at the same time a colony to Epidamnus, saying that any who wished might go there on a basis of equal rights for all, and that if anyone was not inclined to sail at once, but wished to have part in the colony, he might make a deposit of fifty Corinthian drachmae[1] and remain at home. The number that sailed was large, as also of those who deposited the money. Request was also made of the Megarians to convoy them with ships, in case an attempt should be made by the Corcyraeans to prevent their sailing; and these were preparing to accompany them with eight ships, and the Paleans, from Cephallenia, with four. The Epidaurians, of whom a like request was made, furnished five ships, the Hermionians one, the Troezenians two, the Leucadians ten, and the Ambraciots eight. Upon the Thebans and the Phliasians a demand was made for money, and upon the Eleans

[1] The Corinthian drachma was about equivalent to 6*d.*, but of course had greater purchasing power. The Attic drachma = 9¾*d.*

καὶ χρήματα. αὐτῶν δὲ Κορινθίων νῆες παρεσκευάζοντο τριάκοντα καὶ τρισχίλιοι ὁπλῖται.

XXVIII. Ἐπειδὴ δὲ ἐπύθοντο οἱ Κερκυραῖοι
τὴν παρασκευήν, ἐλθόντες ἐς Κόρινθον μετὰ
Λακεδαιμονίων καὶ Σικυωνίων πρέσβεων, οὓς
παρέλαβον, ἐκέλευον Κορινθίους τοὺς ἐν Ἐπιδάμνῳ φρουρούς τε καὶ οἰκήτορας ἀπάγειν, ὡς οὐ
2 μετὸν αὐτοῖς Ἐπιδάμνου. εἰ δέ τι ἀντιποιοῦνται,
δίκας ἤθελον δοῦναι ἐν Πελοποννήσῳ παρὰ πόλεσιν αἷς ἂν ἀμφότεροι ξυμβῶσιν· ὁποτέρων δ'
ἂν δικασθῇ εἶναι τὴν ἀποικίαν, τούτους κρατεῖν·
ἤθελον δὲ καὶ τῷ ἐν Δελφοῖς μαντείῳ ἐπιτρέψαι.
3 πόλεμον δὲ οὐκ εἴων ποιεῖν· εἰ δὲ μή, καὶ αὐτοὶ
ἀναγκασθήσεσθαι ἔφασαν, ἐκείνων βιαζομένων,
φίλους ποιεῖσθαι οὓς οὐ βούλονται, ἑτέρους τῶν
4 νῦν ὄντων μᾶλλον, ὠφελίας ἕνεκα. οἱ δὲ Κορίνθιοι ἀπεκρίναντο αὐτοῖς, ἢν τάς τε ναῦς καὶ τοὺς
βαρβάρους ἀπὸ Ἐπιδάμνου ἀπαγάγωσι, βουλεύ-
σεσθαι· πρότερον δ' οὐ καλῶς ἔχειν τοὺς μὲν
5 πολιορκεῖσθαι, ἑαυτοὺς δὲ δικάζεσθαι. Κερκυραῖοι δὲ ἀντέλεγον, ἢν καὶ ἐκεῖνοι τοὺς ἐν Ἐπιδάμνῳ ἀπαγάγωσι, ποιήσειν ταῦτα· ἑτοῖμοι δὲ
εἶναι καὶ ὥστε ἀμφοτέρους μένειν κατὰ χώραν
σπονδὰς δὲ[1] ποιήσασθαι ἕως ἂν ἡ δίκη γένηται.

[1] Hude deletes δέ, after Poppo.

---

[1] A threat of an alliance with the Athenians, τῶν νῦν ὄντων referring to the Lacedaemonians and other Peloponnesians, not to the Illyrians (*cf.* ch. xxvi. 7), as Poppo suggested.

for unmanned ships as well as for money. And the Corinthians themselves, for their part, made ready thirty ships and three thousand hoplites.

XXVIII. When the Corcyraeans learned of these preparations they went to Corinth, with Lacedaemonian and Sicyonian envoys whom they took with them, and bade the Corinthians withdraw the garrison and settlers at Epidamnus, on the ground that they had no part in Epidamnus. But if they made any claim to it they were willing, they said, to submit the matter for arbitration to any states in the Peloponnesus that both should agree upon, and to whichever party the colony should be adjudged to belong, these should have it; and they were willing also to submit the matter to the oracle at Delphi. War, however, they warned them not to bring on; but if it must be, they too would be compelled, if the Corinthians forced the issue, to make friends with those for whom they had no wish, others beyond their present ones, in order to secure assistance.[1] The Corinthians answered that if the Corcyraeans would withdraw their ships and the barbarians from Epidamnus they would consider the matter, but that meanwhile it was not proper for them[2] to be discussing arbitration while the Epidamnians were undergoing siege. Whereupon the Corcyraeans replied that they would do this if the Corinthians on their part would withdraw their forces at Epidamnus; but they were also ready to arbitrate on condition that both parties should remain where they were and that they should make a truce until the decision should be given.[3]

[2] *i.e.* the envoys and the Corinthians.

[3] Or, omitting δέ, "that they were also ready to make a truce until the decision should be given, on condition that both parties should remain where they were."

XXIX. Κορίνθιοι δὲ οὐδὲν τούτων ὑπήκουον,
ἀλλ' ἐπειδὴ πλήρεις αὐτοῖς ἦσαν αἱ νῆες καὶ οἱ
ξύμμαχοι παρῆσαν, προπέμψαντες κήρυκα πρότερον πόλεμον προεροῦντα Κερκυραίοις, ἄραντες
ἑβδομήκοντα ναυσὶ καὶ πέντε δισχιλίοις τε ὁπλίταις ἔπλεον ἐπὶ τὴν Ἐπίδαμνον, Κερκυραίοις
2 ἐναντία πολεμήσοντες· ἐστρατήγει δὲ τῶν μὲν
νεῶν Ἀριστεὺς ὁ Πελλίχου καὶ Καλλικράτης ὁ
Καλλίου καὶ Τιμάνωρ ὁ Τιμάνθους, τοῦ δὲ πεζοῦ
Ἀρχέτιμός τε ὁ Εὐρυτίμου καὶ Ἰσαρχίδας ὁ
3 Ἰσάρχου. ἐπειδὴ δ' ἐγένοντο ἐν Ἀκτίῳ τῆς
Ἀνακτορίας γῆς, οὗ τὸ ἱερὸν τοῦ Ἀπόλλωνός
ἐστιν, ἐπὶ τῷ στόματι τοῦ Ἀμπρακικοῦ κόλπου,
οἱ Κερκυραῖοι κήρυκά τε προύπεμψαν αὐτοῖς ἐν
ἀκατίῳ ἀπεροῦντα μὴ πλεῖν ἐπὶ σφᾶς, καὶ τὰς
ναῦς ἅμα ἐπλήρουν, ζεύξαντές τε τὰς παλαιὰς
ὥστε πλωίμους εἶναι καὶ τὰς ἄλλας ἐπισκευά-
4 σαντες. ὡς δὲ ὁ κῆρύξ τε ἀπήγγειλεν οὐδὲν
εἰρηναῖον παρὰ τῶν Κορινθίων καὶ αἱ νῆες αὐτοῖς
ἐπεπλήρωντο οὖσαι ὀγδοήκοντα (τεσσαράκοντα
γὰρ Ἐπίδαμνον ἐπολιόρκουν), ἀνταναγαγόμενοι
5 καὶ παραταξάμενοι ἐναυμάχησαν· καὶ ἐνίκησαν
οἱ Κερκυραῖοι παρὰ πολὺ καὶ ναῦς πέντε καὶ
δέκα διέφθειραν τῶν Κορινθίων. τῇ δὲ αὐτῇ
ἡμέρᾳ αὐτοῖς ξυνέβη καὶ τοὺς τὴν Ἐπίδαμνον
πολιορκοῦντας παραστήσασθαι ὁμολογίᾳ ὥστε
τοὺς μὲν ἐπήλυδας ἀποδόσθαι, Κορινθίους δὲ
δήσαντας ἔχειν ἕως ἂν ἄλλο τι δόξῃ.

XXX. Μετὰ δὲ τὴν ναυμαχίαν οἱ Κερκυραῖοι τροπαῖον στήσαντες ἐπὶ τῇ Λευκίμνῃ τῆς Κερκυραίας ἀκρωτηρίῳ τοὺς μὲν ἄλλους οὓς ἔλαβον

XXIX. The Corinthians, however, would not listen to any of these proposals, but, as soon as their ships were manned and their allies were at hand, they sent a herald in advance to declare war against the Corcyraeans; then, setting off with seventy-five ships and two thousand hoplites, they sailed for Epidamnus to give battle to the Corcyraeans. Their ships were under the command of Aristeus son of Pellichus, Callicrates son of Callias, and Timanor son of Timanthes; the infantry under that of Archetimus son of Eurytimus and Isarchidas son of Isarchus. But when they reached Actium in the territory of Anactorium, where is the sanctuary of Apollo at the mouth of the Ambracian gulf, the Corcyraeans sent out a herald in a small boat to forbid their advance, and at the same time proceeded to man their ships, having previously strengthened the old vessels with cross-beams so as to make them seaworthy, and having put the rest in repair. When their herald brought back no message of peace from the Corinthians and their ships were now fully manned, being eighty in number (for forty were besieging Epidamnus), they sailed out against the enemy and, drawing up in line, engaged in battle; and they won a complete victory and destroyed fifteen ships of the Corinthians. On the same day it happened that their troops which were engaged in the siege of Epidamnus forced it to a capitulation, on condition that the other immigrants[1] should be sold into slavery but the Corinthians kept in bonds until something else should be agreed upon.

434 B.C.

XXX. After the sea-fight the Corcyraeans set up a trophy of their victory at Leucimne, a promontory in the territory of Corcyra, and put to death the

[1] *i.e.* the Ambraciots and Leucadians; *cf.* ch. xxvi. 1.

αἰχμαλώτους ἀπέκτειναν, Κορινθίους δὲ δήσαντες
2 εἶχον. ὕστερον δέ, ἐπειδὴ οἱ Κορίνθιοι καὶ οἱ
ξύμμαχοι ἡσσημένοι ταῖς ναυσὶν ἀνεχώρησαν ἐπ'
οἴκου, τῆς θαλάσσης ἁπάσης ἐκράτουν τῆς κατ'
ἐκεῖνα τὰ χωρία οἱ Κερκυραῖοι, καὶ πλεύσαντες
ἐς Λευκάδα τὴν Κορινθίων ἀποικίαν τῆς γῆς ἔτεμον καὶ Κυλλήνην τὸ Ἠλείων ἐπίνειον ἐνέπρησαν,
3 ὅτι ναῦς καὶ χρήματα παρέσχον Κορινθίοις. τοῦ
τε χρόνου τὸν πλεῖστον μετὰ τὴν ναυμαχίαν
ἐπεκράτουν τῆς θαλάσσης καὶ τοὺς τῶν Κορινθίων ξυμμάχους ἐπιπλέοντες ἔφθειρον, μέχρι οὗ Κορίνθιοι περιόντι τῷ θέρει πέμψαντες ναῦς καὶ στρατιάν, ἐπεὶ σφῶν οἱ ξύμμαχοι ἐπόνουν, ἐστρατοπεδεύοντο ἐπὶ Ἀκτίῳ καὶ περὶ τὸ Χειμέριον τῆς Θεσπρωτίδος, φυλακῆς ἕνεκα τῆς τε Λευκάδος καὶ τῶν ἄλλων πόλεων ὅσαι σφίσι φίλιαι ἦσαν.
4 ἀντεστρατοπεδεύοντο δὲ καὶ οἱ Κερκυραῖοι ἐπὶ
τῇ Λευκίμνῃ ναυσί τε καὶ πεζῷ. ἐπέπλεόν τε οὐδέτεροι ἀλλήλοις, ἀλλὰ τὸ θέρος τοῦτο ἀντικαθεζόμενοι χειμῶνος ἤδη ἀνεχώρησαν ἐπ' οἴκου ἑκάτεροι.

XXXI. Τὸν δὲ ἐνιαυτὸν πάντα τὸν μετὰ τὴν ναυμαχίαν καὶ τὸν ὕστερον οἱ Κορίνθιοι ὀργῇ φέροντες τὸν πρὸς Κερκυραίους πόλεμον ἐναυπηγοῦντο καὶ παρεσκευάζοντο τὰ κράτιστα νεῶν στόλον, ἔκ τε αὐτῆς Πελοποννήσου ἀγείροντες καὶ τῆς ἄλλης Ἑλλάδος ἐρέτας μισθῷ πείθοντες.
2 πυνθανόμενοι δὲ οἱ Κερκυραῖοι τὴν παρασκευὴν
αὐτῶν ἐφοβοῦντο, καί (ἦσαν γὰρ οὐδενὸς Ἑλλή-

prisoners they had taken, with the exception of the Corinthians, whom they kept in fetters. But afterwards, when the Corinthians and their allies had gone back home with their ships after their defeat, the Corcyraeans were masters of the whole sea in that quarter, and sailing to Leucas, the colony of the Corinthians, they ravaged the country and burned Cyllene, the naval arsenal of the Eleans, because they had furnished ships and money to the Corinthians. And so for most of the time after the sea-fight they had control over the sea; and sailing against the allies of the Corinthians they kept harrying them, until the Corinthians, as the summer was drawing to an end,[1] seeing that their allies were suffering, sent ships and an army and encamped at Actium and near the promontory of Cheimerium in Thesprotis, as a protection for Leucas and the other cities that were friendly to themselves. And the Corcyraeans encamped on the opposite coast at Leucimne with both ships and infantry. Neither side sailed against the other, but they faced each other for the rest of this summer; it was not until winter had come that they each went back home.

XXXI. During the whole year after the sea-fight and the next year the Corinthians, being angrily indignant about their war with the Corcyraeans, kept building ships and preparing a naval armament with all their might, and collected oarsmen from both the Peloponnesus and the rest of Hellas by the inducement of pay. The Corcyraeans, on the other hand, were alarmed when they learned of their preparations, and since they were without an ally among

[1] περιόντι (as the MSS. read) = περιιόντι. But Ullrich (*Beitr. z. Kr.* iii. p. 5) explains = ἐν τῷ περιόντι τοῦ θέρους, "in what remained of the summer." So Boehme.

νων ἔνσπονδοι οὐδὲ ἐσεγράψαντο ἑαυτοὺς οὔτε ἐς τὰς Ἀθηναίων σπονδὰς οὔτε ἐς τὰς Λακεδαιμονίων) ἔδοξεν αὐτοῖς ἐλθοῦσιν ὡς τοὺς Ἀθηναίους ξυμμάχους γενέσθαι καὶ ὠφελίαν τινὰ πειρᾶ-
3 σθαι ἀπ' αὐτῶν εὑρίσκεσθαι. οἱ δὲ Κορίνθιοι πυθόμενοι ταῦτα ἦλθον καὶ αὐτοὶ ἐς τὰς Ἀθήνας πρεσβευσόμενοι, ὅπως μὴ σφίσι πρὸς τῷ Κερκυραίων ναυτικῷ καὶ τὸ αὐτῶν προσγενόμενον ἐμπόδιον γένηται θέσθαι τὸν πόλεμον ᾗ βού-
4 λονται. καταστάσης δὲ ἐκκλησίας ἐς ἀντιλογίαν ἦλθον. καὶ οἱ μὲν Κερκυραῖοι ἔλεξαν τοιάδε.

XXXII. "Δίκαιον, ὦ Ἀθηναῖοι, τοὺς μήτε εὐεργεσίας μεγάλης μήτε ξυμμαχίας προυφειλομένης ἥκοντας παρὰ τοὺς πέλας ἐπικουρίας, ὥσπερ καὶ ἡμεῖς νῦν, δεησομένους ἀναδιδάξαι πρῶτον, μάλιστα μὲν ὡς καὶ ξύμφορα δέονται, εἰ δὲ μή, ὅτι γε οὐκ ἐπιζήμια, ἔπειτα δὲ ὡς καὶ τὴν χάριν βέβαιον ἕξουσιν· εἰ δὲ τούτων μηδὲν σαφὲς
2 καταστήσουσι, μὴ ὀργίζεσθαι ἢν ἀτυχῶσιν. Κερκυραῖοι δὲ μετὰ τῆς ξυμμαχίας τῆς αἰτήσεως καὶ ταῦτα πιστεύοντες ἐχυρὰ ὑμῖν παρέξεσθαι ἀπέ-
3 στειλαν ἡμᾶς. τετύχηκε δὲ τὸ αὐτὸ ἐπιτήδευμα πρός τε ὑμᾶς ἐς τὴν χρείαν ἡμῶν ἄλογον καὶ ἐς τὰ ἡμέτερα αὐτῶν ἐν τῷ παρόντι ἀξύμφορον.
4 ξύμμαχοί τε γὰρ οὐδενός πω ἐν τῷ πρὸ τοῦ ἑκούσιοι γενόμενοι νῦν ἄλλων τοῦτο δεησόμενοι ἥκομεν, καὶ ἅμα ἐς τὸν παρόντα πόλεμον Κορινθίων ἐρῆμοι δι' αὐτὸ καθέσταμεν. καὶ περιέστηκεν ἡ δοκοῦσα ἡμῶν πρότερον σωφροσύνη, τὸ

the Hellenes and had not enrolled themselves in the alliance either of the Athenians or of the Lacedaemonians, they decided to go to the Athenians, become their allies, and try to procure some aid from them. But the Corinthians also, hearing of this, themselves sent envoys to Athens to prevent the accession of the Athenian fleet to that of the Corcyraeans, as this would hamper them in settling the war as they wished. And when an assembly 438 B.C.
was held opposing speeches were made, and the Corcyraeans spoke as follows:

XXXII. "It is but fair, citizens of Athens, that those who, without any previous claim on the score of important service rendered or of an existing alliance, come to their neighbours to ask aid, as we do now, should show in the first place, if possible, that what they ask is advantageous, or at least that it is not hurtful, and, in the second place, that their gratitude can be depended on; but in case they establish neither of these things clearly, they should not be angry if unsuccessful. Now the Corcyraeans have sent us to ask for an alliance, and in full confidence that they will be able to give you guarantees on just these points. But it so happens that our policy has been at one and the same time inconsistent, as it must seem to you, with our petition, and is also disadvantageous under present circumstances to ourselves; for although heretofore we have freely chosen to be allies of no one, we have now come to ask others for an alliance, and at the same time, in the face of the present war with the Corinthians, we are, because of this very policy, isolated. And so what was formerly fondly imagined to be wise discretion on our part—to enter into no

μὴ ἐν ἀλλοτρίᾳ ξυμμαχίᾳ τῇ τοῦ πέλας γνώμῃ
ξυγκινδυνεύειν, νῦν ἀβουλία καὶ ἀσθένεια φαι-
5 νομένη. τὴν μὲν οὖν γενομένην ναυμαχίαν αὐτοὶ
κατὰ μόνας ἀπεωσάμεθα Κορινθίους· ἐπειδὴ δὲ
μείζονι παρασκευῇ ἀπὸ Πελοποννήσου καὶ τῆς
ἄλλης Ἑλλάδος ἐφ' ἡμᾶς ὥρμηνται καὶ ἡμεῖς
ἀδύνατοι ὁρῶμεν ὄντες τῇ οἰκείᾳ μόνον δυνάμει
περιγενέσθαι, καὶ ἅμα μέγας ὁ κίνδυνος, εἰ ἐσό-
μεθα ὑπ' αὐτοῖς, ἀνάγκη καὶ ὑμῶν καὶ ἄλλου
παντὸς ἐπικουρίας δεῖσθαι, καὶ ξυγγνώμη, εἰ μὴ
μετὰ κακίας, δόξης δὲ μᾶλλον ἁμαρτίᾳ τῇ πρότερον ἀπραγμοσύνῃ ἐναντία τολμῶμεν.

XXXIII. "Γενήσεται δὲ ὑμῖν πειθομένοις
καλὴ ἡ ξυντυχία κατὰ πολλὰ τῆς ἡμετέρας
χρείας, πρῶτον μὲν ὅτι ἀδικουμένοις καὶ οὐχ
ἑτέρους βλάπτουσι τὴν ἐπικουρίαν ποιήσεσθε,
ἔπειτα περὶ τῶν μεγίστων κινδυνεύοντας δεξάμενοι ὡς ἂν μάλιστα μετ' αἰειμνήστου μαρτυρίου
τὴν χάριν καταθήσεσθε, ναυτικόν τε κεκτήμεθα
2 πλὴν τοῦ παρ' ὑμῖν πλεῖστον. καὶ σκέψασθε
τίς εὐπραξία σπανιωτέρα ἢ τίς τοῖς πολεμίοις
λυπηροτερα, εἰ ἣν ὑμεῖς ἂν πρὸ πολλῶν χρημάτων καὶ χάριτος ἐτιμήσασθε δύναμιν ὑμῖν προσ-
γενέσθαι, αὕτη πάρεστιν αὐτεπάγγελτος, ἄνευ
κινδύνων καὶ δαπάνης διδοῦσα ἑαυτὴν καὶ προσέτι φέρουσα ἐς μὲν τοὺς πολλοὺς ἀρετήν, οἷς δὲ
ἐπαμυνεῖτε χάριν, ὑμῖν δ' αὐτοῖς ἰσχύν· ἃ ἐν τῷ

foreign alliance, with the possibility of having to take our share of the danger of our neighbour's policy—has now, in the event, proved want of wisdom and a source of weakness. It is true that, in the sea-fight we have had, we repulsed the Corinthians single-handed; but now that they have set out to attack us with a greater force, drawn from the Peloponnesus and the rest of Hellas, and we see that we are unable to prevail with our own strength alone, and since, further, our peril will be serious if we come into their power, we are constrained to ask help of you and of everyone else; and it is pardonable if we now, actuated by no baseness, but rather acknowledging an error of judgment, venture upon a course that runs counter to our former policy of avoiding foreign entanglements.

XXXIII. "For yourselves, if you concede what we ask, by a happy concurrence of events Athens can get both honour and advantage in many ways: first, you will be giving your aid to those who are wronged and not to those who injure others; next, by taking into alliance men whose most vital interests are at stake, you will lay up for yourselves a claim for gratitude with a record which will abide in our memories for ever; and, lastly, we have a navy greater than any but your own. Think of it now, what good fortune could be rarer, more vexatious to your foes, than this—that the power which you would have accounted it worth much money and gratitude to acquire should become yours unbidden, offering itself to you without danger or expense, and bringing you, besides, a good name before the world, gratitude from those who are to receive your help, and enhanced strength for yourselves? To few in all

παντὶ χρόνῳ ὀλίγοις δὴ ἅμα πάντα ξυνέβη, καὶ ὀλίγοι ξυμμαχίας δεόμενοι οἷς ἐπικαλοῦνται ἀσφάλειαν καὶ κόσμον οὐχ ἧσσον διδόντες ἢ ληψόμενοι παραγίγνονται.

3 "Τὸν δὲ πόλεμον, δι' ὅνπερ χρήσιμοι ἂν εἶμεν, εἴ τις ὑμῶν μὴ οἴεται ἔσεσθαι, γνώμης ἁμαρτάνει καὶ οὐκ αἰσθάνεται τοὺς Λακεδαιμονίους φόβῳ τῷ ὑμετέρῳ πολεμησείοντας καὶ τοὺς Κορινθίους, δυναμένους παρ' αὐτοῖς καὶ ὑμῖν ἐχθροὺς ὄντας,[1] προκαταλαμβάνοντας ἡμᾶς νῦν ἐς τὴν ὑμετέραν ἐπιχείρησιν, ἵνα μὴ τῷ κοινῷ ἔχθει κατ' αὐτοὺς μετ' ἀλλήλων στῶμεν μηδὲ δυοῖν φθάσαι ἁμάρτωσιν, ἢ κακῶσαι ἡμᾶς ἢ σφᾶς αὐ-
4 τοὺς βεβαιώσασθαι. ἡμέτερον δέ γ' αὖ ἔργον προτερῆσαι, τῶν μὲν διδόντων, ὑμῶν δὲ δεξαμένων τὴν ξυμμαχίαν, καὶ προεπιβουλεύειν αὐτοῖς μᾶλλον ἢ ἀντεπιβουλεύειν.

XXXIV. "Ἢν δὲ λέγωσιν ὡς οὐ δίκαιον τοὺς σφετέρους ἀποίκους ὑμᾶς δέχεσθαι, μαθόντων ὡς πᾶσα ἀποικία εὖ μὲν πάσχουσα τιμᾷ τὴν μητρόπολιν, ἀδικουμένη δὲ ἀλλοτριοῦται· οὐ γὰρ ἐπὶ τῷ δοῦλοι, ἀλλ' ἐπὶ τῷ ὁμοῖοι τοῖς λειπομέ-
2 νοις εἶναι ἐκπέμπονται. ὡς δὲ ἠδίκουν σαφές ἐστιν· προκληθέντες γὰρ περὶ Ἐπιδάμνου ἐς κρίσιν πολέμῳ μᾶλλον ἢ τῷ ἴσῳ ἐβουλήθησαν τὰ
3 ἐγκλήματα μετελθεῖν. καὶ ὑμῖν ἔστω τι τεκμή-

[1] καί, before προκαταλαμβάνοντας in the MSS., deleted by Stahl.

---

[1] This allegation is denied in the speech of the Corinthians, ch. xli. 1.

[2] Or, retaining καί before προκαταλαμβάνοντας, "and fails to perceive that the Lacedaemonians, through fear of you,

history have such opportunities fallen all at the same time, and few are they who, when they beg for an alliance, come offering to those to whom they make their appeal as large a degree of security and honour as they expect to receive.

"Now as to the war which would give us occasion to be of service, if anyone of you thinks it will not occur he errs in judgment, and fails to perceive that the Lacedaemonians, through fear of you, are eager for war, and that the Corinthians, who have great influence with them and are enemies of yours,[1] are making a beginning with us now[2] with a view to a subsequent attack upon you, in order that we may not be led by our common hatred to take our stand together against them, and that they may not fail, before we unite, to attain their two objects—to harm us and to strengthen themselves. It is our business, on the other hand, to get the start of them—we offering and you accepting the alliance—and to forestall their schemes rather than to counteract them.

XXXIV. "But if they say that it is not right for you to receive their colonists, let them know that while every colony honours the mother-city so long as it is well treated, yet that if wronged it becomes alienated; for colonists are not sent out to be slaves to those who are left behind, but to be their equals. And that they were in the wrong is manifest; for when challenged to arbitrate the case of Epidamnus they preferred to prosecute their charges by war rather than by equity. And let their present treat-

are eager for war, and that the Corinthians have great influence with them and are enemies of yours, and are making a beginning with us with a view to a subsequent attack upon you . . ."

ριον ἃ πρὸς ἡμᾶς τοὺς ξυγγενεῖς δρῶσιν, ὥστε ἀπάτῃ τε μὴ παράγεσθαι ὑπ' αὐτῶν δεομένοις τε ἐκ τοῦ εὐθέος μὴ ὑπουργεῖν· ὁ γὰρ ἐλαχίστας τὰς μεταμελείας ἐκ τοῦ χαρίζεσθαι τοῖς ἐναντίοις λαμβάνων ἀσφαλέστατος ἂν διατελοίη.

XXXV. "Λύσετε δὲ οὐδὲ τὰς Λακεδαιμονίων σπονδὰς δεχόμενοι ἡμᾶς μηδετέρων ὄντας ξυμμά-
2 χους. εἴρηται γὰρ ἐν αὐταῖς, τῶν Ἑλληνίδων πόλεων ἥτις μηδαμοῦ ξυμμαχεῖ, ἐξεῖναι παρ'
3 ὁποτέρους ἂν ἀρέσκηται ἐλθεῖν. καὶ δεινὸν εἰ τοῖσδε μὲν ἀπό τε τῶν ἐνσπόνδων ἔσται πληροῦν τὰς ναῦς καὶ προσέτι καὶ ἐκ τῆς ἄλλης Ἑλλάδος καὶ οὐχ ἥκιστα ἀπὸ τῶν ὑμετέρων ὑπηκόων, ἡμᾶς δὲ ἀπὸ τῆς προκειμένης τε ξυμμαχίας εἴρξουσι καὶ ἀπὸ τῆς ἄλλοθέν ποθεν ὠφελίας, εἶτα[1] ἐν ἀδικήματι θήσονται πεισθέντων ὑμῶν ἃ δεόμεθα·
4 πολὺ δὲ ἐν πλείονι αἰτίᾳ ἡμεῖς μὴ πείσαντες ὑμᾶς ἕξομεν· ἡμᾶς μὲν γὰρ κινδυνεύοντας καὶ οὐκ ἐχθροὺς ὄντας ἀπώσεσθε, τῶνδε δὲ οὐχ ὅπως κωλυταὶ ἐχθρῶν ὄντων καὶ ἐπιόντων γενήσεσθε, ἀλλὰ καὶ ἀπὸ τῆς ὑμετέρας ἀρχῆς δύναμιν προσλαβεῖν περιόψεσθε· ἣν οὐ δίκαιον, ἀλλ' ἢ κἀκείνων κωλύειν τοὺς ἐκ τῆς ὑμετέρας μισθοφόρους ἢ καὶ ἡμῖν πέμπειν καθ' ὅ τι ἂν πεισθῆτε ὠφελίαν μάλιστα δὲ ἀπὸ τοῦ προφανοῦς δεξαμένους βοη-
5 θεῖν. πολλὰ δέ, ὥσπερ ἐν ἀρχῇ ὑπείπομεν, τὰ ξυμφέροντα ἀποδείκνυμεν, καὶ μέγιστον ὅτι οἵ τε

[1] With the MSS.; Krüger conjectures εἴ τε, followed by Hude.

ment of us, who are their kinsmen, be a warning to you, that you be not misled by their deceit, or, if they seek aid from you directly, that you may refuse it. For whoever finds fewest occasions to regret doing favours to his opponents will ever remain most secure.

XXXV. "Neither will you be breaking your treaty with the Lacedaemonians by receiving us, who are allies of neither party. For in this treaty it is stipulated that if any of the Hellenic cities is a member of no alliance, it is at liberty to join whichever side it pleases. And it is monstrous if they are to be allowed to recruit their navy, not only from their own allies, but also from the rest of Hellas besides, and particularly from your subjects, but are to debar us from the alliance that should naturally be open to us as well as from aid from any other quarter, and then shall count it a crime if you are persuaded to concede what we ask. Far more shall we hold you at fault if we fail to win your consent; for you will be repulsing us who are in peril and are not your enemies, while as regards these men, who are enemies and aggressors, you will not only not be thwarting them, but will even be allowing them to get fresh forces from your own dominions. To that they have no right; but it is right that you should either prevent them from raising mercenaries in places under your control, or else send aid to us also, on whatever terms you may be induced to make; but it would be best of all for you openly to receive and help us. And many, as we suggested at the outset,[1] are the advantages which we can show you, and the most important of all is this, that the enemies of both of

[1] Ch. xxxiii. 1.

αὐτοὶ πολέμιοι ἡμῖν ἦσαν (ὅπερ σαφεστάτη πίστις) καὶ οὗτοι οὐκ ἀσθενεῖς, ἀλλ' ἱκανοὶ τοὺς μεταστάντας βλάψαι. καὶ ναυτικῆς καὶ οὐκ ἠπειρώτιδος τῆς ξυμμαχίας διδομένης οὐχ ὁμοία ἡ ἀλλοτρίωσις, ἀλλὰ μάλιστα μέν, εἰ δύνασθε, μηδένα ἄλλον ἐᾶν κεκτῆσθαι ναῦς, εἰ δὲ μή, ὅστις ἐχυρώτατος, τοῦτον φίλον ἔχειν.

XXXVI. "*Καὶ ὅτῳ τάδε ξυμφέροντα μὲν δοκεῖ λέγεσθαι, φοβεῖται δὲ μὴ δι' αὐτὰ πειθόμενος τὰς σπονδὰς λύσῃ, γνώτω τὸ μὲν δεδιὸς αὐτοῦ ἰσχὺν ἔχον τοὺς ἐναντίους μᾶλλον φοβῆσον, τὸ δὲ θαρσοῦν μὴ δεξαμένου ἀσθενὲς ὂν πρὸς ἰσχύοντας τοὺς ἐχθροὺς ἀδεέστερον ἐσόμενον, καὶ ἅμα οὐ περὶ τῆς Κερκύρας νῦν τὸ πλέον ἢ καὶ τῶν Ἀθηνῶν βουλευόμενος, καὶ οὐ τὰ κράτιστα αὐταῖς προνοῶν, ὅταν ἐς τὸν μέλλοντα καὶ ὅσον οὐ παρόντα πόλεμον τὸ αὐτίκα περισκοπῶν ἐνδοιάζῃ χωρίον προσλαβεῖν ὃ μετὰ μεγίστων*
2 *καιρῶν οἰκειοῦταί τε καὶ πολεμοῦται. τῆς τε γὰρ Ἰταλίας καὶ Σικελίας καλῶς παράπλου κεῖται, ὥστε μήτε ἐκεῖθεν ναυτικὸν ἐᾶσαι Πελοποννησίοις ἐπελθεῖν τό τε ἐντεῦθεν πρὸς τἀκεῖ παραπέμψαι, καὶ ἐς τἆλλα ξυμφορώτατόν ἐστιν.*

---

[1] So *ἦσαν* seems to mean here, where *εἰσί* was to be expected; *cf.* ch. xxxiii. 3.

[2] *δεῖ* or *ξυμφέρει* seems to be implied.

[3] The thirty-years' truce with Sparta; *cf.* ch. xxiii. 4.

us are, as we see,[1] the same—which is the surest guarantee of fidelity—and these are not weak, but able to injure those who withdraw from them. And furthermore, when the alliance that is offered is with a maritime and not with a continental power, the alienation of such an ally is not a matter of indifference; on the contrary, you should [2] by all means, if possible, permit no one else to possess ships; but if that is impossible, you should have as your friend him who is strongest therein.

XXXVI. "If anyone thinks that this course is indeed expedient, but fears that if he yields to this consideration he will be breaking off the truce,[3] he should understand that his fear, if backed by strength, will make his enemies more afraid;[4] whereas, if he reject our alliance, his confidence[5] will be unsupported by might and will therefore be less formidable against enemies that are strong. He should understand, furthermore, that he is deliberating upon the interests, not so much of Corcyra, as of Athens, and that he is not making the best provision for her when, in the face of the war that is impending and all but present, he hesitates, through cautious consideration of the immediate chances, to attach to himself a country which is not made a friend or a foe except with the most momentous consequences. For Corcyra is favourably situated for a coasting voyage either to Italy or Sicily,[6] so that you could prevent a fleet from coming thence to join the Peloponnesians, or could convoy thither a fleet from here; and in other respects it is a most advantageous

[4] *i.e.* of themselves breaking the truce.

[5] *i.e.* in the security of the truce.

[6] Ancient mariners preferred to hug the coast rather than sail through the open sea.

3 βραχυτάτῳ δ' ἂν κεφαλαίῳ, τοῖς τε ξύμπασι καὶ καθ' ἕκαστον, τῷδ' ἂν μὴ προέσθαι ἡμᾶς μάθοιτε· τρία μὲν ὄντα λόγου ἄξια τοῖς Ἕλλησι ναυτικά, τὸ παρ' ὑμῖν καὶ τὸ ἡμέτερον καὶ τὸ Κορινθίων· τούτων δὲ εἰ περιόψεσθε τὰ δύο ἐς ταὐτὸν ἐλθεῖν καὶ Κορίνθιοι ἡμᾶς προκαταλήψονται, Κερκυραίοις τε καὶ Πελοποννησίοις ἅμα ναυμαχήσετε· δεξάμενοι δὲ ἡμᾶς ἕξετε πρὸς αὐτοὺς πλείοσι ναυσὶ ταῖς ἡμετέραις ἀγωνίζεσθαι."

4 Τοιαῦτα μὲν οἱ Κερκυραῖοι εἶπον· οἱ δὲ Κορίνθιοι μετ' αὐτοὺς τοιάδε.

XXXVII. "'Αναγκαῖον Κερκυραίων τῶνδε οὐ μόνον περὶ τοῦ δέξασθαι σφᾶς τὸν λόγον ποιησαμένων, ἀλλ' ὡς καὶ ἡμεῖς τε ἀδικοῦμεν καὶ αὐτοὶ οὐκ εἰκότως πολεμοῦνται, μνησθέντας πρῶτον καὶ ἡμᾶς περὶ ἀμφοτέρων οὕτω καὶ ἐπὶ τὸν ἄλλον λόγον ἰέναι, ἵνα τὴν ἀφ' ἡμῶν τε ἀξίωσιν ἀσφαλέστερον προειδῆτε καὶ τὴν τῶνδε χρείαν μὴ ἀλογίστως ἀπώσησθε.

2 "Φασὶ δὲ ξυμμαχίαν διὰ τὸ σῶφρον οὐδενός πω δέξασθαι· τὸ δ' ἐπὶ κακουργίᾳ καὶ οὐκ ἀρετῇ ἐπετήδευσαν, ξύμμαχόν τε οὐδένα βουλόμενοι πρὸς τἀδικήματα οὔτε[1] μάρτυρα ἔχειν οὐδὲ παρα-
3 καλοῦντες αἰσχύνεσθαι, καὶ ἡ πόλις αὐτῶν ἅμα αὐτάρκη θέσιν κειμένη παρέχει αὐτοὺς δικαστὰς ὧν βλάπτουσί τινα μᾶλλον ἢ κατὰ ξυνθήκας

[1] For οὐδέ of the MSS., Dobree's conjecture. Hude reads οὐδὲ . . . οὐδέ.

place. And by one briefest concluding word, which embraces both the whole issue and all separate facts, you will be convinced that you should not abandon us: The Hellenes have only three fleets that are worthy of mention, yours, ours, and that of the Corinthians; if, now, the Corinthians shall seize us first and you thus let two of these fleets become united, you will have to fight on the sea against both Corcyraeans and Peloponnesians at once; but if you accept us, you will be able to contend against them with your navy augmented by our own."

Thus spoke the Corcyraeans, and after them the Corinthians as follows:

XXXVII. "Since these Corcyraeans have not confined themselves to the question of their admission into your alliance, but have gone further and urged that we are the wrong-doers and they are unfairly attacked, we too must of necessity touch upon both these points before we proceed to our general argument, in order that you may be more definitely forewarned of the nature of the demand we have to make, and may have good grounds for rejecting their petition.

"They say that 'a wise discretion' has hitherto kept them from accepting an alliance with anyone; but the fact is that they adopted this policy with a view to villainy and not from virtuous motives, and because they wished in their misdeeds not to have any ally as witness, or to be put to shame if they invited his presence. Moreover, the insular and independent position of this state causes them to be arbitrary judges of the injuries they do to others instead of being judges appointed by mutual agree-

γίγνεσθαι, διὰ τὸ ἥκιστα ἐπὶ τοὺς πέλας ἐκπλέοντας μάλιστα τοὺς ἄλλους ἀνάγκῃ καταίροντας
4 δέχεσθαι. καὶ τοῦτο τὸ εὐπρεπὲς ἄσπονδον οὐχ
ἵνα μὴ ξυναδικῶσιν ἑτέροις προβέβληνται, ἀλλ'
ὅπως κατὰ μόνας ἀδικῶσι καὶ ὅπως ἐν ᾧ μὲν ἂν
κρατῶσι βιάζωνται, οὗ δ' ἂν λάθωσι πλέον ἔχω-
σιν, ἢν δέ πού τι προλάβωσιν ἀναισχυντῶσιν·
5 καίτοι εἰ ἦσαν ἄνδρες, ὥσπερ φασίν, ἀγαθοί, ὅσῳ
ἀληπτότεροι ἦσαν τοῖς πέλας, τόσῳ δὲ φανερω-
τέραν ἐξῆν αὐτοῖς τὴν ἀρετὴν διδοῦσι καὶ δεχο-
μένοις τὰ δίκαια δεικνύναι.

XXXVIII. "Ἀλλ' οὔτε πρὸς τοὺς ἄλλους οὔτε
ἐς ἡμᾶς τοιοίδε εἰσίν, ἄποικοι δ' ὄντες ἀφεστᾶσί
τε διὰ παντὸς καὶ νῦν πολεμοῦσι, λέγοντες ὡς
2 οὐκ ἐπὶ τῷ κακῶς πάσχειν ἐκπεμφθεῖεν. ἡμεῖς
δὲ οὐδ' αὐτοί φαμεν ἐπὶ τῷ ὑπὸ τούτων ὑβρίζε-
σθαι κατοικίσαι, ἀλλ' ἐπὶ τῷ ἡγεμόνες τε εἶναι
3 καὶ τὰ εἰκότα θαυμάζεσθαι. αἱ γοῦν ἄλλαι
ἀποικίαι τιμῶσιν ἡμᾶς καὶ μάλιστα ὑπὸ ἀποίκων
4 στεργόμεθα· καὶ δῆλον ὅτι, εἰ τοῖς πλέοσιν ἀρέ-
σκοντές ἐσμεν, τοῖσδ' ἂν μόνοις οὐκ ὀρθῶς ἀπαρέ-
σκοιμεν, οὐδ' ἐπιστρατεύομεν ἐκπρεπῶς μὴ καὶ
5 διαφερόντως τι ἀδικούμενοι. καλὸν δ' ἦν, εἰ καὶ
ἡμαρτάνομεν, τοῖσδε μὲν εἶξαι τῇ ἡμετέρᾳ ὀργῇ,
ἡμῖν δὲ αἰσχρὸν βιάσασθαι τὴν τούτων μετρι-

ment; owing to the fact that they resort very little to the ports of their neighbours, but to a very large extent receive into their ports others who are compelled to put in there. And meanwhile they have used as a cloak their specious policy of avoiding alliances, adopted not in order to avoid joining others in wrong-doing, but that they may do wrong all alone; that wherever they have power they may use violence, and wherever they can escape detection they may overreach someone; and if, perchance, they can steal a march on anyone, that they may brazen it out. And yet, if they were really honest men, as they pretend to be, the less liable they were to attack by their neighbours the more clearly they might have demonstrated their virtuous motives by offering and accepting proposals of arbitration.

XXXVIII. "But neither toward others nor toward us have they shown themselves honest men; on the contrary, although they are colonists of ours, they have constantly stood aloof from us, and now they are at war with us, claiming that they were not sent out to be ill treated. But neither did we colonize them to be insulted by them, but to be their leaders and to receive from them all due reverence. The rest of our colonies, at any rate, honour us, and by our colonists we are beloved more than is any other mother-city. And it is clear that, if we are acceptable to the majority, it cannot be on good grounds that we are unacceptable to these alone; nor are we making war upon them in a way so unusual without being also signally wronged. And even if we were at fault, the honourable course for them would have been to make allowance for our temper, in which case it would have been shameful

6 ότητα· ὕβρει δὲ καὶ ἐξουσίᾳ πλούτου πολλὰ ἐς
ἡμᾶς ἄλλα τε ἡμαρτήκασι καὶ Ἐπίδαμνον ἡμετέραν οὖσαν κακουμένην μὲν οὐ προσεποιοῦντο,
ἐλθόντων δὲ ἡμῶν ἐπὶ τιμωρίᾳ ἑλόντες βίᾳ
ἔχουσιν.

XXXIX. "Καὶ φασὶ δὴ δίκῃ πρότερον ἐθε-
λῆσαι κρίνεσθαι, ἥν γε οὐ τὸν προύχοντα καὶ ἐκ
τοῦ ἀσφαλοῦς προκαλούμενον λέγειν τι δοκεῖν
δεῖ, ἀλλὰ τὸν ἐς ἴσον τά τε ἔργα ὁμοίως καὶ τοὺς
2 λόγους πρὶν διαγωνίζεσθαι καθιστάντα. οὗτοι
δὲ οὐ πρὶν πολιορκεῖν τὸ χωρίον, ἀλλ' ἐπειδὴ ἡγήσαντο ἡμᾶς οὐ περιόψεσθαι, τότε καὶ τὸ εὐπρεπὲς
τῆς δίκης παρέσχοντο· καὶ δεῦρο ἥκουσιν, οὐ
τἀκεῖ μόνον αὐτοὶ ἁμαρτόντες, ἀλλὰ καὶ ὑμᾶς
νῦν ἀξιοῦντες οὐ ξυμμαχεῖν, ἀλλὰ ξυναδικεῖν καὶ
3 διαφόρους ὄντας ἡμῖν δέχεσθαι σφᾶς· οὓς χρῆν,
ὅτε ἀσφαλέστατοι ἦσαν, τότε προσιέναι, καὶ μὴ
ἐν ᾧ ἡμεῖς μὲν ἠδικήμεθα, οὗτοι δὲ κινδυνεύουσι,
μηδ' ἐν ᾧ ὑμεῖς τῆς τε δυνάμεως αὐτῶν τότε οὐ
μεταλαβόντες τῆς ὠφελίας νῦν μεταδώσετε καὶ
τῶν ἁμαρτημάτων ἄπο γενόμενοι τῆς ἀφ' ἡμῶν
αἰτίας τὸ ἴσον ἕξετε, πάλαι δὲ κοινώσαντας τὴν
δύναμιν κοινὰ καὶ τὰ ἀποβαίνοντα ἔχειν.[1]

XL. "Ὡς μὲν οὖν αὐτοί τε μετὰ προσηκόντων
ἐγκλημάτων ἐρχόμεθα καὶ οἵδε βίαιοι καὶ πλεο-

[1] ἐγκλημάτων δὲ μόνων ἀμετόχους οὕτως τῶν μετὰ τὰς πράξεις τούτων μὴ κοινωνεῖν, "As, however, you have had no share in the accusations, you should not share in the consequences." This clause is omitted by all good MSS. except G, and by all recent editors except Bloomfield.

for us to outrage their moderation; but in the insolence and arrogance of wealth they have wronged us in many other ways, and particularly in the case of Epidamnus, our colony, which they made no claim to when it was in distress, but seized by force the moment we came to its relief, and continue to hold.

XXXIX. "They pretend, forsooth, that they were the first to agree to an arbitration of the issue; but surely it is not the proposals of the one who has the advantage, and occupies a safe position when he invites arbitration, that ought to have weight, but rather those of the one who has made his actions tally with his professions before appealing to arms. These men, however, bring forward their specious offer of a court of arbitration, not before laying siege to the place, but only after they had concluded that we would not permit it. And now, not satisfied with the blunders they have committed themselves at Epidamnus, they have come here demanding that you too at this juncture, shall be, not their allies, but their accomplices in crime, and that you shall receive them, now that they are at variance with us. But they ought to have come to you when they were in no peril at all, and not at a time when we are victims of their injustice and they are consequently in danger, nor when you, without having had the benefit of their power before, will now have to give them a share of your aid, and, though you had nothing to do with their blunders, will have to bear an equal part of the blame we shall bestow. For only if you from the first had shared their power ought you to share the consequences also now of their acts.

XL. "Now it has been clearly shown that we have come with proper grounds of complaint against

νέκται εἰσὶ δεδήλωται· ὡς δὲ οὐκ ἂν δικαίως
2 αὐτοὺς δέχοισθε μαθεῖν χρή. εἰ γὰρ εἴρηται ἐν
ταῖς σπονδαῖς, ἐξεῖναι παρ᾽ ὁποτέρους τις βούλεται τῶν ἀγράφων πόλεων ἐλθεῖν, οὐ τοῖς ἐπὶ
βλάβῃ ἑτέρων ἰοῦσιν ἡ ξυνθήκη ἐστίν, ἀλλ᾽
ὅστις μὴ ἄλλου ἑαυτὸν ἀποστερῶν ἀσφαλείας
δεῖται καὶ ὅστις μὴ τοῖς δεξαμένοις, εἰ σωφρο-
νοῦσι, πόλεμον ἀντ᾽ εἰρήνης ποιήσει· ὃ νῦν ὑμεῖς
3 μὴ πειθόμενοι ἡμῖν πάθοιτε ἄν. οὐ γὰρ τοῖσδε
μόνον ἐπίκουροι ἂν γένοισθε, ἀλλὰ καὶ ἡμῖν ἀντὶ
ἐνσπόνδων πολέμιοι. ἀνάγκη γάρ, εἰ ἴτε μετ᾽
4 αὐτῶν, καὶ ἀμύνεσθαι μὴ ἄνευ ὑμῶν τούτους. καίτοι δίκαιοί γ᾽ ἐστὲ μάλιστα μὲν ἐκποδὼν στῆναι
ἀμφοτέροις, εἰ δὲ μή, τοὐναντίον ἐπὶ τούτους μεθ᾽
ἡμῶν ἰέναι (Κορινθίοις μέν γε ἔνσπονδοί ἐστε,
Κερκυραίοις δὲ οὐδὲ δι᾽ ἀνοκωχῆς πώποτε ἐγέ-
νεσθε), καὶ τὸν νόμον μὴ καθιστάναι ὥστε τοὺς
5 ἑτέρων ἀφισταμένους δέχεσθαι. οὐδὲ γὰρ ἡμεῖς
Σαμίων ἀποστάντων ψῆφον προσεθέμεθα ἐναν-
τίαν ὑμῖν, τῶν ἄλλων Πελοποννησίων δίχα ἐψη-
φισμένων εἰ χρὴ αὐτοῖς ἀμύνειν, φανερῶς δὲ
ἀντείπομεν τοὺς προσήκοντας ξυμμάχους αὐτόν
6 τινα κολάζειν. εἰ γὰρ τοὺς κακόν τι δρῶντας
δεχόμενοι τιμωρήσετε, φανεῖται καὶ ἃ τῶν ὑμετέ-

---

[1] *i.e.* "who will permit peace to be maintained by their new friends if they exercise ordinary discretion." No new allies should be received who will render ordinary discretion

them and that they are violent and overreaching; but you have still to learn that you have no right to receive them into your alliance. For even though it is stipulated in the treaty that any unenrolled city may join whichever party it pleases, the provision is not intended for those who apply to one side for admission with a view to the injury of the other, but for any one who, without defrauding another state of his services, asks for protection, and any one who to those who received him will not—if they are prudent—bring war instead of peace.[1] But this is precisely what will be your fate if you do not listen to us. For you will not merely become allies to them, but also enemies to us instead of being at truce with us. For it will be necessary for us, if you go with them, to include you when we proceed to take vengeance upon them. And yet the right course for you would be, preferably, to stand aloof from us both,—or else to go with us against them, remembering that you are under treaty with the Corinthians, but have never had with the Corcyraeans even an arrangement to refrain from hostilities for a time,—and not to establish the precedent of admitting into your alliance those who revolt from the other side. Why, when the Samians[2] revolted from you, and the other Peloponnesians were divided in their votes on the question of aiding them, we on our part did not vote against you; on the contrary, we openly maintained that each one should discipline his own allies without interference. If you receive and assist evil-doers, you will surely find that

unavailing to prevent war, as the Corcyraeans are sure to do.

[2] 440 B.C. *cf.* ch. cxv.

ρων οὐκ ἐλάσσω ἡμῖν πρόσεισι, καὶ τὸν νόμον ἐφ' ὑμῖν αὐτοῖς μᾶλλον ἢ ἐφ' ἡμῖν θήσετε.

XLI. "Δικαιώματα μὲν οὖν τάδε πρὸς ὑμᾶς ἔχομεν, ἱκανὰ κατὰ τοὺς Ἑλλήνων νόμους, παραίνεσιν δὲ καὶ ἀξίωσιν χάριτος τοιάνδε, ἣν οὐκ ἐχθροὶ ὄντες ὥστε βλάπτειν οὐδ' αὖ φίλοι ὥστ' ἐπιχρῆσθαι, ἀντιδοθῆναι ἡμῖν ἐν τῷ παρόντι
2 φαμὲν χρῆναι. νεῶν γὰρ μακρῶν σπανίσαντές ποτε πρὸς τὸν Αἰγινητῶν ὑπὲρ τὰ Μηδικὰ[1] πόλεμον παρὰ Κορινθίων εἴκοσι ναῦς ἐλάβετε· καὶ ἡ εὐεργεσία αὕτη τε καὶ ἡ ἐς Σαμίους, τὸ δι' ἡμᾶς Πελοποννησίους αὐτοῖς μὴ βοηθῆσαι, παρέσχεν ὑμῖν Αἰγινητῶν μὲν ἐπικράτησιν, Σαμίων δὲ κόλασιν, καὶ ἐν καιροῖς τοιούτοις ἐγένετο, οἷς μάλιστα ἄνθρωποι ἐπ' ἐχθροὺς τοὺς σφετέρους ἰόντες τῶν ἁπάντων ἀπερίοπτοί εἰσι παρὰ
3 τὸ νικᾶν· φίλον τε γὰρ ἡγοῦνται τὸν ὑπουργοῦντα, ἢν καὶ πρότερον ἐχθρὸς ᾖ, πολέμιόν τε τὸν ἀντιστάντα, ἢν καὶ τύχῃ φίλος ὤν, ἐπεὶ καὶ τὰ οἰκεῖα χεῖρον τίθενται φιλονικίας ἕνεκα τῆς αὐτίκα.

XLII. "Ὧν ἐνθυμηθέντες καὶ νεώτερός τις παρὰ πρεσβυτέρου αὐτὰ μαθὼν ἀξιούτω τοῖς ὁμοίοις ἡμᾶς ἀμύνεσθαι, καὶ μὴ νομίσῃ δίκαια μὲν τάδε λέγεσθαι, ξύμφορα δέ, εἰ πολεμήσει,
2 ἄλλα εἶναι. τό τε γὰρ ξυμφέρον ἐν ᾧ ἄν τις

[1] ὑπὲρ τὰ Μηδικά Krüger deletes, followed by Hude.

full as many of your allies will come over to us, and the precedent you establish will be against yourselves rather than against us.

XLI. "These, then, are the considerations of right which we urge upon you—and they are adequate according to the institutions of the Hellenes; but we have also to remind you of a favour and to urge a claim based upon it; and since we are not your enemies so as to want to injure you, nor yet your friends so that we could make use of you, we think this favour should be repaid us at the present time. It is this: when once, before the Persian war, you were deficient in battle-ships for the war you were waging with the Aeginetans, you borrowed twenty from the Corinthians. And this service and that we rendered in connection with the Samians—our preventing the Peloponnesians from aiding them—enabled you to prevail over the Aeginetans and to chastise the Samians. Both incidents happened, too, at a critical time, when men, engaged in assailing their enemies, are most indifferent to every consideration except victory, regarding any one who assists them as a friend, even if he was an enemy before, and any one who stands in their way as an enemy, even if he happen to be a friend; for they even mismanage their own interests in the eager rivalry of the moment.

XLII. "Bearing these favours in mind—let every young man here be told of them by one who is older—do you consider it your duty to requite us with the like. And do not think that this course is indeed equitable to urge in a speech, but that another course is advantageous if you come to war. For advantage is most likely to result when one

ἐλάχιστα ἁμαρτάνῃ μάλιστα ἕπεται, καὶ τὸ
μέλλον τοῦ πολέμου ᾧ φοβοῦντες ὑμᾶς Κερκυραῖοι κελεύουσιν ἀδικεῖν ἐν ἀφανεῖ ἔτι κεῖται, καὶ οὐκ ἄξιον ἐπαρθέντας αὐτῷ φανερὰν ἔχθραν ἤδη καὶ οὐ μέλλουσαν πρὸς Κορινθίους κτήσασθαι, τῆς δὲ ὑπαρχούσης πρότερον διὰ Μεγαρέας ὑπο-
3 ψίας σῶφρον ὑφελεῖν μᾶλλον (ἡ γὰρ τελευταία
χάρις καιρὸν ἔχουσα, κἂν ἐλάσσων ᾖ, δύναται
4 μεῖζον ἔγκλημα λῦσαι), μηδ' ὅτι ναυτικοῦ ξυμ-
μαχίαν μεγάλην διδόασι, τούτῳ ἐφέλκεσθαι· τὸ γὰρ μὴ ἀδικεῖν τοὺς ὁμοίους ἐχυρωτέρα δύναμις ἢ τῷ αὐτίκα φανερῷ ἐπαρθέντας διὰ κινδύνων τὸ πλέον ἔχειν.

XLIII. "Ἡμεῖς δὲ περιπεπτωκότες οἷς ἐν τῇ Λακεδαίμονι αὐτοὶ προείπομεν, τοὺς σφετέρους ξυμμάχους αὐτόν τινα κολάζειν, νῦν παρ' ὑμῶν τὸ αὐτὸ ἀξιοῦμεν κομίζεσθαι, καὶ μὴ τῇ ἡμετέρᾳ ψήφῳ ὠφεληθέντας τῇ ὑμετέρᾳ ἡμᾶς βλάψαι.
2 τὸ δὲ ἴσον ἀνταπόδοτε, γνόντες τοῦτον ἐκεῖνον
εἶναι τὸν καιρόν, ἐν ᾧ ὅ τε ὑπουργῶν φίλος μά-
3 λιστα καὶ ὁ ἀντιστὰς ἐχθρός. καὶ Κερκυραίους
γε τούσδε μήτε ξυμμάχους δέχεσθε βίᾳ ἡμῶν
4 μήτε ἀμύνετε αὐτοῖς ἀδικοῦσιν. καὶ τάδε ποι-
οῦντες τὰ προσήκοντά τε δράσετε καὶ τὰ ἄριστα βουλεύσεσθε ὑμῖν αὐτοῖς."

XLIV. Τοιαῦτα δὲ καὶ οἱ Κορίνθιοι εἶπον. Ἀθηναῖοι δὲ ἀκούσαντες ἀμφοτέρων, γενομένης

errs least, and the contingency of the war, with which the Corcyraeans would frighten you into wrong-doing, is still uncertain; and it is not worth while for you to be so carried away by it as to acquire an enmity with the Corinthians that will be from that moment on a manifest fact and no longer a contingency. It would be, rather, the prudent course to remove something of the suspicion which has heretofore existed on account of the Megarians[1]; for the favour which comes last, if conferred at the right moment, even though a small one, can cancel a greater offence. Nor ought you to be tempted by their offer of a great naval alliance; for to refrain from wronging equals is a surer strength than to be carried away by present appearances and seek an advantage by incurring dangers.

XLIII. "But we, since events have brought us under the rule which we ourselves proclaimed at Sparta, that each should discipline his own allies, now claim from you in return the same treatment—that you who were then aided by our vote should not injure us by yours. Pay back like with like, determining that this is the supreme moment when assistance is the truest friendship—opposition the worst hostility. We beg you neither to accept the Corcyraeans as your allies in despite of us, nor to aid them in their wrong-doing. And if you do this, you will not only be taking the fitting course, but will also be consulting your own best interests."

XLIV. Thus spoke the Corinthians. And the Athenians, having heard both sides, held a second

[1] Referring apparently to the exclusion of the Megarians from all harbours within the Athenian dominion and from the market at Athens, ch. lxvii. 4.

καὶ δὶς ἐκκλησίας, τῇ μὲν προτέρᾳ οὐχ ἧσσον τῶν Κορινθίων ἀπεδέξαντο τοὺς λόγους, ἐν δὲ τῇ ὑστεραίᾳ μετέγνωσαν Κερκυραίοις ξυμμαχίαν μὲν μὴ ποιήσασθαι ὥστε τοὺς αὐτοὺς ἐχθροὺς καὶ φίλους νομίζειν (εἰ γὰρ ἐπὶ Κόρινθον ἐκέλευον σφίσιν οἱ Κερκυραῖοι ξυμπλεῖν, ἐλύοντ' ἂν αὐτοῖς αἱ πρὸς Πελοποννησίους σπονδαί), ἐπιμαχίαν δὲ ἐποιήσαντο τῇ ἀλλήλων βοηθεῖν, ἐάν τις ἐπὶ Κέρκυραν ἴῃ ἢ Ἀθήνας ἢ τοὺς τούτων ξυμμάχους.
2 ἐδόκει γὰρ ὁ πρὸς Πελοποννησίους πόλεμος καὶ ὣς ἔσεσθαι αὐτοῖς, καὶ τὴν Κέρκυραν ἐβούλοντο μὴ προέσθαι τοῖς Κορινθίοις ναυτικὸν ἔχουσαν τοσοῦτον, ξυγκρούειν δε ὅτι μάλιστα αὐτοὺς ἀλλήλοις, ἵνα ἀσθενεστέροις οὖσιν, ἤν τι δέῃ, Κορινθίοις τε καὶ τοῖς ἄλλοις τοῖς[1] ναυτικὸν
3 ἔχουσιν ἐς πόλεμον καθιστῶνται. ἅμα δὲ τῆς τε Ἰταλίας καὶ Σικελίας καλῶς ἐφαίνετο αὐτοῖς ἡ νῆσος ἐν παράπλῳ κεῖσθαι.

XLV. Τοιαύτῃ μὲν γνώμῃ οἱ Ἀθηναῖοι τοὺς Κερκυραίους προσεδέξαντο, καὶ τῶν Κορινθίων ἀπελθόντων οὐ πολὺ ὕστερον δέκα ναῦς αὐτοῖς
2 ἀπέστειλαν βοηθούς· ἐστρατήγει δὲ αὐτῶν Λακεδαιμόνιός τε ὁ Κίμωνος καὶ Διότιμος ὁ Στρομ-
3 βίχου καὶ Πρωτέας ὁ Ἐπικλέους. προεῖπον δὲ αὐτοῖς μὴ ναυμαχεῖν Κορινθίοις, ἢν μὴ ἐπὶ Κέρκυραν πλέωσι καὶ μέλλωσιν ἀποβαίνειν ἢ ἐς τῶν ἐκείνων τι χωρίων· οὕτω δὲ κωλύειν κατὰ δύναμιν. προεῖπον δὲ ταῦτα τοῦ μὴ λύειν ἕνεκα τὰς σπονδάς.

[1] Added by Bekker.

session of the Ecclesia; and although at the earlier one they were rather inclined to agree with the words of the Corinthians, on the second day they changed their minds in favour of the Corcyraeans, and decided, not, indeed, to make an offensive and defensive alliance with them, for in that case, if the Corcyraeans then asked them to join in an expedition against Corinth, they would have to break, on their own responsibility, the treaty with the Lacedaemonians—but they made a defensive alliance, namely to aid one another in case anyone should attack Corcyra or Athens or the allies of either. For they believed that in any event the war with the Peloponnesians would have to be faced, and they did not wish to give up Corcyra, which had so large a fleet, to the Corinthians, but hoped to wear them out upon one another as much as possible, in order that the Corinthians as well as other naval powers[1] might be found weaker in case they had to go to war with them. Besides, the island seemed to them admirably situated for a coasting voyage to Italy and Sicily.[2]

XLV. With these motives the Athenians received the Corcyraeans into alliance and sent to their aid, soon after the departure of the Corinthians, ten ships commanded by Lacedaemonius son of Cimon, Diotimus son of Strombichus, and Proteas son of Epicles. Orders were given to these not to engage with the Corinthians, unless they should sail against Corcyra and attempt to land there, or to some place belonging to the Corcyraeans; but in that case they were to thwart them if possible. The object of these orders was to avoid breaking the treaty.

[1] Referring especially to those mentioned ch. xxvii. 2.
[2] *cf.* ch. xxxvi. 2.

XLVI. Αἱ μὲν δὴ νῆες ἀφικνοῦνται ἐς τὴν Κέρκυραν. οἱ δὲ Κορίνθιοι, ἐπειδὴ αὐτοῖς παρεσκεύαστο, ἔπλεον ἐπὶ τὴν Κέρκυραν ναυσὶ πεντήκοντα καὶ ἑκατόν. ἦσαν δὲ Ἠλείων μὲν δέκα, Μεγαρέων δὲ δώδεκα καὶ Λευκαδίων δέκα, Ἀμπρακιωτῶν δὲ ἑπτὰ καὶ εἴκοσι καὶ Ἀνακτορίων
2 μία, αὐτῶν δὲ Κορινθίων ἐνενήκοντα· στρατηγοὶ δὲ τούτων ἦσαν μὲν καὶ κατὰ πόλεις ἑκάστων, Κορινθίων δὲ Ξενοκλείδης ὁ Εὐθυκλέους πέμπτος
3 αὐτός. ἐπειδὴ δὲ προσέμειξαν τῇ κατὰ Κέρκυραν ἠπείρῳ ἀπὸ Λευκάδος πλέοντες, ὁρμίζονται ἐς
4 Χειμέριον τῆς Θεσπρωτίδος γῆς. ἔστι δὲ λιμήν, καὶ πόλις ὑπὲρ αὐτοῦ κεῖται ἀπὸ θαλάσσης ἐν τῇ Ἐλαιάτιδι τῆς Θεσπρωτίδος Ἐφύρη. ἐξίησι δὲ παρ' αὐτὴν Ἀχερουσία λίμνη ἐς θάλασσαν· διὰ δὲ τῆς Θεσπρωτίδος Ἀχέρων ποταμὸς ῥέων ἐσβάλλει ἐς αὐτήν, ἀφ' οὗ καὶ τὴν ἐπωνυμίαν ἔχει, ῥεῖ δὲ καὶ Θύαμις ποταμὸς ὁρίζων τὴν Θεσπρωτίδα καὶ Κεστρίνην, ὧν ἐντὸς ἡ ἄκρα
5 ἀνέχει τὸ Χειμέριον. οἱ μὲν οὖν Κορίνθιοι τῆς ἠπείρου ἐνταῦθα ὁρμίζονταί τε καὶ στρατόπεδον ἐποιήσαντο.

XLVII. Οἱ δὲ Κερκυραῖοι ὡς ᾔσθοντο αὐτοὺς προσπλέοντας, πληρώσαντες δέκα καὶ ἑκατὸν ναῦς, ὧν ἦρχε Μικιάδης καὶ Αἰσιμίδης καὶ Εὐρύβατος, ἐστρατοπεδεύσαντο ἐν μιᾷ τῶν νήσων αἳ καλοῦνται Σύβοτα, καὶ αἱ Ἀττικαὶ δέκα παρῆσαν.
2 ἐπὶ δὲ τῇ Λευκίμμῃ αὐτοῖς τῷ ἀκρωτηρίῳ ὁ πεζὸς ἦν καὶ Ζακυνθίων χίλιοι ὁπλῖται βεβοηθηκότες.
3 ἦσαν δὲ καὶ τοῖς Κορινθίοις ἐν τῇ ἠπείρῳ πολλοὶ τῶν βαρβάρων παραβεβοηθηκότες· οἱ γὰρ ταύτῃ ἠπειρῶται αἰεί ποτε φίλοι αὐτοῖς εἰσιν.

XLVI. These ships arrived at Corcyra, and the Corinthians, when their preparations had been made, sailed against Corcyra with one hundred and fifty ships. Of these ten belonged to the Eleans, twelve to the Megarians, ten to the Leucadians, twenty seven to the Ambraciots, one to the Anactorians, and ninety to the Corinthians themselves. The several cities had each its own general, but Xenocleides son of Euthycles and four others commanded the Corinthians. They sailed from Leucas, and when they drew near the mainland over against Corcyra, anchored at Cheimerium in the territory of Thesprotia. It is a harbour, and above it lies a city away from the sea in the Eleatic district of Thesprotia, Ephyra by name. Near it is the outlet into the sea of the Acherusian lake; and the river Acheron runs through Thesprotia and empties into the lake, to which it gives its name. There is also the river Thyamis, which separates Thesprotia and Cestrine, and between these rivers rises the promontory of Cheimerium. It was at this point of the mainland then that the Corinthians cast anchor and made a camp.

XLVII. The Corcyraeans, when they became aware of their approach, manned a hundred and ten ships under the command of Miciades, Aesimides, and Eurybatus, and encamped on one of the islands which are called Sybota, the ten Attic ships being also present. Their land-forces were at the promontory of Leucimne, and also a thousand hoplites of the Zacynthians who had come to aid the Corcyraeans. The Corinthians, also, had the aid of many barbarians who had assembled on the mainland adjacent; for the dwellers on the mainland in that region have always been friendly to them.

XLVIII. Ἐπειδὴ δὲ παρεσκεύαστο τοῖς Κορινθίοις, λαβόντες τριῶν ἡμερῶν σιτία ἀνήγοντο
2 ὡς ἐπὶ ναυμαχίᾳ ἀπὸ τοῦ Χειμερίου νυκτός, καὶ ἅμα ἕῳ πλέοντες καθορῶσι τὰς τῶν Κερκυραίων
3 ναῦς μετεώρους τε καὶ ἐπὶ σφᾶς πλεούσας. ὡς δὲ κατεῖδον ἀλλήλους, ἀντιπαρετάσσοντο, ἐπὶ μὲν τὸ δεξιὸν κέρας Κερκυραίων αἱ Ἀττικαὶ νῆες, τὸ δὲ ἄλλο αὐτοὶ ἐπεῖχον τρία τέλη ποιήσαντες τῶν νεῶν, ὧν ἦρχε τριῶν στρατηγῶν ἑκάστου εἷς. οὕτω μὲν Κερκυραῖοι ἐτάξαντο.
4 Κορινθίοις δὲ τὸ μὲν δεξιὸν κέρας αἱ Μεγαρίδες νῆες εἶχον καὶ αἱ Ἀμπρακιώτιδες, κατὰ δὲ τὸ μέσον οἱ ἄλλοι ξύμμαχοι ὡς ἕκαστοι, εὐώνυμον δὲ κέρας αὐτοὶ οἱ Κορίνθιοι ταῖς ἄριστα τῶν νεῶν πλεούσαις κατὰ τοὺς Ἀθηναίους καὶ τὸ δεξιὸν τῶν Κερκυραίων εἶχον.

XLIX. Ξυμμείξαντες δέ, ἐπειδὴ τὰ σημεῖα ἑκατέροις ἤρθη, ἐναυμάχουν, πολλοὺς μὲν ὁπλίτας ἔχοντες ἀμφότεροι ἐπὶ τῶν καταστρωμάτων, πολλοὺς δὲ τοξότας τε καὶ ἀκοντιστάς, τῷ παλαιῷ
2 τρόπῳ ἀπειρότερον ἔτι παρεσκευασμένοι. ἦν τε ἡ ναυμαχία καρτερά, τῇ μὲν τέχνῃ οὐχ ὁμοίως,
3 πεζομαχίᾳ δὲ τὸ πλέον προσφερὴς οὖσα. ἐπειδὴ γὰρ προσβάλοιεν ἀλλήλοις, οὐ ῥᾳδίως ἀπελύοντο ὑπό τε τοῦ πλήθους καὶ ὄχλου τῶν νεῶν καὶ μᾶλλόν τι πιστεύοντες τοῖς ἐπὶ τοῦ καταστρώματος ὁπλίταις ἐς τὴν νίκην, οἳ καταστάντες ἐμάχοντο ἡσυχαζουσῶν τῶν νεῶν· διέκπλοι δὲ οὐκ ἦσαν, ἀλλὰ θυμῷ καὶ ῥώμῃ τὸ πλέον ἐναυμάχουν ἢ

XLVIII. When their preparations had been made, the Corinthians, taking provisions for three days, put off by night from Cheimerium with the intention of giving battle, and at daybreak as they sailed along they descried the ships of the Corcyraeans out at sea and sailing to meet them. And as soon as they saw one another, they drew up in opposing battle lines, the Attic ships on the right wing of the Corcyraeans, who themselves held the rest of the line forming three divisions, each under the command of one of the three generals. So the Corcyraeans arrayed themselves; but the right wing of the Corinthian fleet was held by the Megarian ships and the Ambracian, in the centre were the other allies with their several contingents, while the left was held by the Corinthians themselves with their best sailing ships, opposed to the Athenians and the right wing of the Corcyraeans.

XLIX. When the standards were raised on either side they joined battle and fought, both having many hoplites on the decks as well as many archers and javelin-men, for they were still equipped rather rudely in the ancient fashion. And so the sea-fight was hotly contested, not so much by reason of the skill displayed as because it was more like a battle on land. For when they dashed against one another they could not easily get clear, partly by reason of the number and throng of the ships, still more because they trusted for victory to the hoplites on the decks, who stood and fought while the ships remained motionless; and there was no cutting of the line,[1] but they fought with fury and brute strength rather than

[1] διέκπλους was a breaking of the line so as to ram the enemy's ship in the flank or astern.

4 ἐπιστήμῃ. πανταχῇ μὲν οὖν πολὺς θόρυβος
καὶ ταραχώδης ἦν ἡ ναυμαχία· ἐν ᾗ αἱ Ἀττικαὶ
νῆες παραγιγνόμεναι τοῖς Κερκυραίοις, εἴ πῃ
πιέζοιντο, φόβον μὲν παρεῖχον τοῖς ἐναντίοις,
μάχης δὲ οὐκ ἦρχον δεδιότες οἱ στρατηγοὶ τὴν
5 πρόρρησιν τῶν Ἀθηναίων. μάλιστα δὲ τὸ δεξιὸν
κέρας τῶν Κορινθίων ἐπόνει. οἱ γὰρ Κερκυραῖοι
εἴκοσι ναυσὶν αὐτοὺς τρεψάμενοι καὶ καταδιώξαντες σποράδας ἐς τὴν ἤπειρον καὶ μέχρι τοῦ
στρατοπέδου πλεύσαντες αὐτῶν καὶ ἐπεκβάντες
ἐνέπρησάν τε τὰς σκηνὰς ἐρήμους καὶ τὰ χρήματα
6 διήρπασαν. ταύτῃ μὲν οὖν οἱ Κορίνθιοι καὶ οἱ
ξύμμαχοι ἡσσῶντό τε καὶ οἱ Κερκυραῖοι ἐπε-
κράτουν· ᾗ δὲ αὐτοὶ ἦσαν οἱ Κορίνθιοι, ἐπὶ τῷ
εὐωνύμῳ, πολὺ ἐνίκων, τοῖς Κερκυραίοις τῶν
εἴκοσι νεῶν ἀπὸ ἐλάσσονος πλήθους ἐκ τῆς διώ-
7 ξεως οὐ παρουσῶν. οἱ δὲ Ἀθηναῖοι ὁρῶντες τοὺς
Κερκυραίους πιεζομένους μᾶλλον ἤδη ἀπροφα-
σίστως ἐπεκούρουν, τὸ μὲν πρῶτον ἀπεχόμενοι
ὥστε μὴ ἐμβάλλειν τινί· ἐπειδὴ δὲ ἡ τροπὴ
ἐγίγνετο λαμπρῶς καὶ ἐνέκειντο οἱ Κορίνθιοι, τότε
δὴ ἔργου πᾶς εἴχετο ἤδη καὶ διεκέκριτο οὐδὲν
ἔτι, ἀλλὰ ξυνέπεσεν ἐς τοῦτο ἀνάγκης ὥστε
ἐπιχειρῆσαι ἀλλήλοις τοὺς Κορινθίους καὶ Ἀθηναίους.

L. Τῆς δὲ τροπῆς γενομένης οἱ Κορίνθιοι τὰ
σκάφη μὲν οὐχ εἷλκον ἀναδούμενοι τῶν νεῶν ἃς
καταδύσειαν, πρὸς δὲ τοὺς ἀνθρώπους ἐτράποντο
φονεύειν διεκπλέοντες μᾶλλον ἢ ζωγρεῖν, τούς τε
αὐτῶν φίλους, οὐκ ᾐσθημένοι ὅτι ἥσσηντο οἱ ἐπὶ
2 τῷ δεξιῷ κέρᾳ, ἀγνοοῦντες ἔκτεινον. πολλῶν γὰρ

with skill. Accordingly there was everywhere much tumult and confusion in the sea-fight. The Attic ships, if they saw the Corcyraeans pressed at any point, came up and kept the enemy in awe; but their generals would not begin fighting, fearing to disobey the instructions of the Athenians. The right wing of the Corinthians suffered most; for the Corcyraeans with twenty ships routed them and pursued them in disorder to the mainland, and then, sailing right up to their camp and disembarking, burned the deserted tents and plundered their property. In that quarter, then, the Corinthians and their allies were worsted, and the Corcyraeans prevailed; but on the left wing where the Corinthians themselves were, they were decidedly superior, for the Corcyraeans, whose numbers were fewer to begin with, had the twenty ships away in the pursuit. But the moment the Athenians saw that the Corcyraeans were being hard pressed, they began to help them more unreservedly, and though they at first refrained from actually attacking an enemy ship, yet when it was conspicuously clear that they were being put to flight and the Corinthians were close in pursuit, then at length every man put his hand to work, and fine distinctions were no longer made; matters had come to such a pass that Corinthians and Athenians of necessity had to attack one another.

L. After the rout of the Corcyraeans the Corinthians did not take in tow and haul off the hulls of the ships which had been disabled, but turned their attention to the men, cruising up and down and killing them in preference to taking them alive; and they unwittingly slew their own friends, not being aware that their right wing had been worsted. For

νεῶν οὐσῶν ἀμφοτέρων καὶ ἐπὶ πολὺ τῆς θαλάσσης ἐπεχουσῶν, ἐπειδὴ ξυνέμειξαν ἀλλήλοις,
οὐ ῥᾳδίως τὴν διάγνωσιν ἐποιοῦντο ὁποῖοι ἐκράτουν ἢ ἐκρατοῦντο· ναυμαχία γὰρ αὕτη Ἕλλησι
πρὸς Ἕλληνας νεῶν πλήθει μεγίστη δὴ τῶν πρὸ
3 αὐτῆς γεγένηται. ἐπειδὴ δὲ κατεδίωξαν τοὺς
Κερκυραίους οἱ Κορίνθιοι ἐς τὴν γῆν, πρὸς τὰ
ναυάγια καὶ τοὺς νεκροὺς τοὺς σφετέρους ἐτράποντο, καὶ τῶν πλείστων ἐκράτησαν ὥστε
προσκομίσαι πρὸς τὰ Σύβοτα, οὗ αὐτοῖς ὁ κατὰ
γῆν στρατὸς τῶν βαρβάρων προσεβεβοηθήκει·
ἔστι δὲ τὰ Σύβοτα τῆς Θεσπρωτίδος λιμὴν
ἐρῆμος. τοῦτο δὲ ποιήσαντες αὖθις ἁθροισθέντες
4 ἐπέπλεον τοῖς Κερκυραίοις. οἱ δὲ ταῖς πλωίμοις
καὶ ὅσαι ἦσαν λοιπαὶ μετὰ τῶν Ἀττικῶν νεῶν
καὶ αὐτοὶ ἀντεπέπλεον, δείσαντες μὴ ἐς τὴν γῆν
5 σφῶν πειρῶσιν ἀποβαίνειν. ἤδη δὲ ἦν ὀψὲ καὶ
ἐπεπαιάνιστο αὐτοῖς ὡς ἐς ἐπίπλουν, καὶ οἱ
Κορίνθιοι ἐξαπίνης πρύμναν ἐκρούοντο, κατιδόντες
εἴκοσι ναῦς Ἀθηναίων προσπλεούσας, ἃς ὕστερον
τῶν δέκα βοηθοὺς ἐξέπεμψαν οἱ Ἀθηναῖοι, δείσαντες, ὅπερ ἐγένετο, μὴ νικηθῶσιν οἱ Κερκυραῖοι
καὶ αἱ σφέτεραι δέκα νῆες ὀλίγαι ἀμύνειν ὦσιν.
LI. ταύτας οὖν προϊδόντες οἱ Κορίνθιοι καὶ
ὑποτοπήσαντες ἀπ' Ἀθηνῶν εἶναι, οὐχ ὅσας
2 ἑώρων ἀλλὰ πλείους, ὑπανεχώρουν. τοῖς δὲ Κερκυραίοις (ἐπέπλεον γὰρ μᾶλλον ἐκ τοῦ ἀφανοῦς)

---

[1] Thucydides makes allowance for Salamis, for example, where Greeks had fought against Persians.

since the ships of the two fleets were many and covered a great stretch of sea, it was not easy, when they joined in combat, for the Corinthians to determine just who were conquering and who were being conquered; for this sea-fight was in number of ships engaged greater than any that Hellenes had ever before fought against Hellenes.[1] But as soon as the Corinthians had chased the Corcyraeans to the shore, they turned to the wrecks and their own dead,[2] and they were able to recover most of them and to fetch them to Sybota, an unused harbour of Thesprotia, whither the land forces of the barbarians had come to their aid. When they had accomplished this, they got their forces together and sailed once more against the Corcyraeans. And they, with such of their vessels as were seaworthy and all the rest that had not been engaged, together with the Attic ships, on their part also sailed to meet them, fearing that they would attempt to disembark on their territory. It was now late and the paean had been sounded for the onset, when the Corinthians suddenly began to back water; for they sighted twenty Attic ships approaching, which the Athenians had sent out after the ten as a reinforcement, fearing just what happened, namely that the Corcyraeans would be defeated and their own ten ships would be too few to help them. LI. So when the Corinthians sighted these ships before the Corcyraeans did, suspecting that they were from Athens and that there were more of them than they saw, they began to withdraw. For the Corcyraeans, however, the Athenian ships were sailing up more out of view and could not be seen by them,

[2] The bodies of the dead which were on the disabled ships.

οὐχ ἑωρῶντο, καὶ ἐθαύμαζον τοὺς Κορινθίους
πρύμναν κρουομένους, πρίν τινες ἰδόντες εἶπον
ὅτι νῆες ἐκεῖναι ἐπιπλέουσιν. τότε δὴ καὶ αὐτοὶ
ἀνεχώρουν (ξυνεσκόταζε γὰρ ἤδη), καὶ οἱ Κορίνθιοι
3 ἀποτραπόμενοι τὴν διάλυσιν ἐποιήσαντο. οὕτω
μὲν ἡ ἀπαλλαγὴ ἐγένετο ἀλλήλων, καὶ ἡ ναυμαχία
4 ἐτελεύτα ἐς νύκτα. τοῖς δὲ Κερκυραίοις στρατο-
πεδευομένοις ἐπὶ τῇ Λευκίμνῃ αἱ εἴκοσι νῆες αἱ
ἐκ τῶν Ἀθηνῶν αὗται, ὧν ἦρχε Γλαύκων τε ὁ
Λεάγρου καὶ Ἀνδοκίδης ὁ Λεωγόρου, διὰ τῶν
νεκρῶν καὶ ναυαγίων προσκομισθεῖσαι κατέπλεον
ἐς τὸ στρατόπεδον οὐ πολλῷ ὕστερον ἢ ὤφθησαν.
5 οἱ δὲ Κερκυραῖοι (ἦν γὰρ νύξ) ἐφοβήθησαν μὴ
πολέμιαι ὦσιν, ἔπειτα δὲ ἔγνωσαν καὶ ὡρμίσαντο.
LII. Τῇ δὲ ὑστεραίᾳ ἀναγαγόμεναι αἵ τε Ἀττικαὶ τριάκοντα νῆες καὶ τῶν Κερκυραίων ὅσαι
πλώιμοι ἦσαν ἐπέπλευσαν ἐπὶ τὸν ἐν τοῖς Συβότοις λιμένα, ἐν ᾧ οἱ Κορίνθιοι ὥρμουν, βουλό-
2 μενοι εἰδέναι εἰ ναυμαχήσουσιν. οἱ δὲ τὰς μὲν
ναῦς ἄραντες ἀπὸ τῆς γῆς καὶ παραταξάμενοι
μετεώρους ἡσύχαζον, ναυμαχίας οὐ διανοούμενοι
ἄρχειν ἑκόντες, ὁρῶντες προσγεγενημένας τε ναῦς
ἐκ τῶν Ἀθηνῶν ἀκραιφνεῖς καὶ σφίσι πολλὰ τὰ
ἄπορα ξυμβεβηκότα, αἰχμαλώτων τε περὶ φυλακῆς, οὓς ἐν ταῖς ναυσὶν εἶχον, καὶ ἐπισκευὴν οὐκ
3 οὖσαν τῶν νεῶν ἐν χωρίῳ ἐρήμῳ· τοῦ δὲ οἴκαδε
πλοῦ μᾶλλον διεσκόπουν ὅπῃ κομισθήσονται, δεδιότες μὴ οἱ Ἀθηναῖοι νομίσαντες λελύσθαι τὰς
σπονδάς, διότι ἐς χεῖρας ἦλθον, οὐκ ἐῶσι σφᾶς
ἀποπλεῖν.

LIII. Ἔδοξεν οὖν αὐτοῖς ἄνδρας ἐς κελήτιον

and so they wondered that the Corinthians were backing water, until some of them caught sight of the ships and said, "Yonder are ships sailing up." Then they too retreated—for it was already getting dark; whereupon the Corinthians put their ships about and broke off the action. Thus they separated, the sea-fight ending at nightfall. And while the Corcyraeans were encamping at Leucimne, the twenty ships from Athens, under the command of Glaucon son of Leagrus and Andocides son of Leogoras, having made their way through the corpses and the wrecks, sailed down to the camp not long after they were sighted. And the Corcyraeans—for it was night—were afraid they were enemies; but afterwards they recognized them and the ships came to anchor.

LII. On the next day the thirty Attic ships and as many of the Corcyraean as were seaworthy put to sea and advanced against the harbour at Sybota, where the Corinthians lay at anchor, wishing to see whether they would fight. But the Corinthians, although they put out from shore and drew up in line in the open sea, kept quiet: for they had no thought of beginning a fight if they could avoid it, as they saw that fresh ships had arrived from Athens and that they themselves were involved in many perplexities, both as regards guarding the captives whom they had in their ships and the impossibility of refitting their ships in a desert place. What they were more concerned about was the voyage home, how they should get back, for they were afraid that the Athenians would consider that the treaty had been broken, since they had come to blows, and would not let them sail away.

LIII. Accordingly they determined to put some

ἐμβιβάσαντας ἄνευ κηρυκείου προσπέμψαι τοῖς
2 Ἀθηναίοις καὶ πεῖραν ποιήσασθαι. πέμψαντές
τε ἔλεγον τοιάδε· "Ἀδικεῖτε, ὦ ἄνδρες Ἀθηναῖοι,
πολέμου ἄρχοντες καὶ σπονδὰς λύοντες· ἡμῖν γὰρ
πολεμίους τοὺς ἡμετέρους τιμωρουμένοις ἐμποδὼν
ἵστασθε ὅπλα ἀνταιρόμενοι. εἰ δ' ὑμῖν γνώμη
ἐστὶ κωλύειν τε ἡμᾶς ἐπὶ Κέρκυραν ἢ ἄλλοσε εἴ
πῃ βουλόμεθα πλεῖν καὶ τὰς σπονδὰς λύετε,
ἡμᾶς τούσδε πρώτους λαβόντες χρήσασθε ὡς
3 πολεμίοις." οἱ μὲν δὴ τοιαῦτα εἶπον· τῶν δὲ
Κερκυραίων τὸ μὲν στρατόπεδον ὅσον ἐπήκουσεν
ἀνεβόησεν εὐθὺς λαβεῖν τε αὐτοὺς καὶ ἀποκτεῖναι,
4 οἱ δὲ Ἀθηναῖοι τοιάδε ἀπεκρίναντο· "Οὔτε ἄρ-
χομεν πολέμου, ὦ ἄνδρες Πελοποννήσιοι, οὔτε
τὰς σπονδὰς λύομεν, Κερκυραίοις δὲ τοῖσδε ξυμμάχοις οὖσι βοηθοὶ ἤλθομεν. εἰ μὲν οὖν ἄλλοσέ
ποι βούλεσθε πλεῖν, οὐ κωλύομεν· εἰ δὲ ἐπὶ
Κέρκυραν πλευσεῖσθε ἢ ἐς τῶν ἐκείνων τι χωρίων,
οὐ περιοψόμεθα κατὰ τὸ δυνατόν."

LIV. Τοιαῦτα τῶν Ἀθηναίων ἀποκριναμένων
οἱ μὲν Κορίνθιοι τόν τε πλοῦν τὸν ἐπ' οἴκου παρεσκευάζοντο καὶ τροπαῖον ἔστησαν ἐν τοῖς ἐν τῇ
ἠπείρῳ Συβότοις· οἱ δὲ Κερκυραῖοι τά τε ναυάγια
καὶ νεκροὺς ἀνείλοντο τὰ κατὰ σφᾶς, ἐξενεχθέν-
των ὑπό τε τοῦ ῥοῦ καὶ ἀνέμου, ὃς γενόμενος τῆς
νυκτὸς διεσκέδασεν αὐτὰ πανταχῇ, καὶ τροπαῖον
ἀντέστησαν ἐν τοῖς ἐν τῇ νήσῳ Συβότοις ὡς
2 νενικηκότες. γνώμῃ δὲ τοιᾷδε ἑκάτεροι τὴν νίκην
προσεποιήσαντο· Κορίνθιοι μὲν κρατήσαντες τῇ

---

[1] To bear a herald's wand would have been a recognition of a state of war, whereas the Corinthians were anxious not to be regarded as enemies by the Athenians.

men, without a herald's wand,[1] into a boat and send them to the Athenians, to test their intentions. And these men bore the following message: "You do wrong, men of Athens, to begin war and break a treaty; for by taking up arms against us you interfere with us when we are but punishing our enemies. But if it is your intention to hinder us from sailing against Corcyra or anywhere else we may wish, and you thus break the treaty, first take us who are here and treat us as enemies." Thus they spoke; and all the host of the Corcyraeans that was within hearing shouted: "Take them and kill them!" But the Athenians made answer as follows: "We are not beginning war, men of the Peloponnesus, nor are we breaking the treaty, but we have come to aid the Corcyraeans here, who are our allies. If, then, you wish to sail anywhere else, we do not hinder you; but if you ever sail against Corcyra or any place of theirs, we shall not permit it, if we are able to prevent it."

LIV. When the Athenians had given this answer, the Corinthians began preparations for the voyage homeward and set up a trophy at Sybota on the mainland; and the Corcyraeans took up the wrecks and dead bodies[2] that had been carried in their direction by the current and by the wind, which had arisen in the night and scattered them in every direction, and set up, as being the victors, a rival trophy at Sybota on the island. Each side claimed the victory on the following grounds: The Corinthians set up a trophy because they had prevailed in

[2] Taking up the dead bodies without asking permission of the enemy indicated that the field was maintained, and was therefore a claim of victory.

ναυμαχίᾳ μέχρι νυκτός, ὥστε καὶ ναυάγια πλεῖστα καὶ νεκροὺς προσκομίσασθαι, καὶ ἄνδρας ἔχοντες αἰχμαλώτους οὐκ ἐλάσσους χιλίων ναῦς τε καταδύσαντες περὶ ἑβδομήκοντα ἔστησαν τροπαῖον·[1] Κερκυραῖοι δὲ τριάκοντα ναῦς μάλιστα διαφθείραντες, καὶ ἐπειδὴ Ἀθηναῖοι ἦλθον, ἀνελόμενοι τὰ κατὰ σφᾶς αὐτοὺς ναυάγια καὶ νεκρούς, καὶ ὅτι αὐτοῖς τῇ τε προτεραίᾳ πρύμναν κρουόμενοι ὑπεχώρησαν οἱ Κορίνθιοι ἰδόντες τὰς Ἀττικὰς ναῦς, καὶ ἐπειδὴ ἦλθον οἱ Ἀθηναῖοι, οὐκ ἀντεπέπλεον ἐκ τῶν Συβότων, διὰ ταῦτα τροπαῖον ἔστησαν. οὕτω μὲν ἑκάτεροι νικᾶν ἠξίουν.

LV. Οἱ δὲ Κορίνθιοι ἀποπλέοντες ἐπ' οἴκου Ἀνακτόριον, ὅ ἐστιν ἐπὶ τῷ στόματι τοῦ Ἀμπρακικοῦ κόλπου, εἷλον ἀπάτῃ (ἦν δὲ κοινὸν Κερκυραίων καὶ ἐκείνων), καὶ καταστήσαντες ἐν αὐτῷ Κορινθίους οἰκήτορας ἀνεχώρησαν ἐπ' οἴκου· καὶ τῶν Κερκυραίων ὀκτακοσίους μὲν οἳ ἦσαν δοῦλοι ἀπέδοντο, πεντήκοντα δὲ καὶ διακοσίους δήσαντες ἐφύλασσον καὶ ἐν θεραπείᾳ εἶχον πολλῇ, ὅπως αὐτοῖς τὴν Κέρκυραν ἀναχωρήσαντες προσποιήσειαν· ἐτύγχανον δὲ καὶ δυνάμει αὐτῶν οἱ πλείους πρῶτοι ὄντες τῆς
2 πόλεως. ἡ μὲν οὖν Κέρκυρα οὕτω περιγίγνεται τῷ πολέμῳ τῶν Κορινθίων, καὶ αἱ νῆες τῶν Ἀθηναίων ἀνεχώρησαν ἐξ αὐτῆς. αἰτία δὲ αὕτη πρώτη ἐγένετο τοῦ πολέμου τοῖς Κορινθίοις ἐς τοὺς Ἀθηναίους, ὅτι σφίσιν ἐν σπονδαῖς μετὰ Κερκυραίων ἐναυμάχουν.

LVI. Μετὰ ταῦτα δ' εὐθὺς καὶ τάδε ξυνέβη

[1] ἔστησαν τροπαῖον bracketed by Hude, following Krüger.

the sea-fight up to nightfall, and had thus been able to carry off a greater number of wrecks and dead bodies, and because they held as prisoners not less than a thousand men and had disabled about seventy ships; and the Corcyraeans, because they had destroyed about thirty ships, and, after the Athenians came, had taken up the wrecks that came their way and the dead bodies, whereas the Corinthians on the day before had backed water and retreated at sight of the Attic ships, and after the Athenians came would not sail out from Sybota and give battle—for these reasons set up a trophy. So each side claimed the victory.

LV. The Corinthians, as they sailed homeward, took by stratagem Anactorium, which is at the mouth of the Ambracian Gulf, a place held by the Corcyraeans and themselves in common, and establishing there some Corinthian colonists returned home. Of their Corcyraean prisoners they sold eight hundred who were slaves, but two hundred and fifty they kept in custody and treated them with much consideration, their motive being that when they returned to Corcyra they might win it over to their side;[1] and it so happened that most of these were among the most influential men of the city. In this way, then, Corcyra had the advantage in the war with the Corinthians, and the ships of the Athenians withdrew from it. And this was the first ground which the Corinthians had for the war against the Athenians, because they had fought with the Corcyraeans against them in time of truce.

LVI. Immediately after this the following events

[1] *cf.* III. lxx. 1, where the carrying out of this plan of the Corinthians leads to the bloody feud at Corcyra.

γενέσθαι τοῖς Ἀθηναίοις καὶ Πελοποννησίοις
2 διάφορα ἐς τὸ πολεμεῖν. τῶν γὰρ Κορινθίων πρασσόντων ὅπως τιμωρήσονται αὐτούς, ὑποτοπήσαντες τὴν ἔχθραν αὐτῶν οἱ Ἀθηναῖοι Ποτειδεάτας, οἳ οἰκοῦσιν ἐπὶ τῷ ἰσθμῷ τῆς Παλλήνης, Κορινθίων ἀποίκους, ἑαυτῶν δὲ ξυμμάχους φόρου ὑποτελεῖς, ἐκέλευον τὸ ἐς Παλλήνην τεῖχος καθελεῖν καὶ ὁμήρους δοῦναι, τούς τε ἐπιδημιουργοὺς ἐκπέμπειν καὶ τὸ λοιπὸν μὴ δέχεσθαι οὓς κατὰ ἔτος ἕκαστον Κορίνθιοι ἔπεμπον, δείσαντες μὴ ἀποστῶσιν ὑπό τε Περδίκκου πειθόμενοι καὶ Κορινθίων, τούς τε ἄλλους τοὺς ἐπὶ Θρᾴκης ξυναποστήσωσι ξυμμάχους.

LVII. Ταῦτα δὲ περὶ τοὺς Ποτειδεάτας οἱ Ἀθηναῖοι προπαρεσκευάζοντο εὐθὺς μετὰ τὴν ἐν
2 Κερκύρᾳ ναυμαχίαν· οἵ τε γὰρ Κορίνθιοι φανερῶς ἤδη διάφοροι ἦσαν, Περδίκκας τε ὁ Ἀλεξάνδρου, Μακεδόνων βασιλεύς, ἐπεπολέμωτο ξύμμαχος
3 πρότερον καὶ φίλος ὤν. ἐπολεμώθη δέ, ὅτι Φιλίππῳ τῷ ἑαυτοῦ ἀδελφῷ καὶ Δέρδᾳ κοινῇ πρὸς αὐτὸν ἐναντιουμένοις οἱ Ἀθηναῖοι ξυμμαχίαν
4 ἐποιήσαντο. δεδιώς τε ἔπρασσεν ἔς τε τὴν Λακεδαίμονα πέμπων ὅπως πόλεμος γένηται αὐτοῖς πρὸς Πελοποννησίους, καὶ τοὺς Κορινθίους προσεποιεῖτο τῆς Ποτειδαίας ἕνεκα ἀποστάσεως·
5 προσέφερε δὲ λόγους καὶ τοῖς ἐπὶ Θρᾴκης Χαλκιδεῦσι καὶ Βοττιαίοις ξυναποστῆναι, νομίζων, εἰ ξύμμαχα ταῦτα ἔχοι, ὅμορα ὄντα, τὰ χωρία,

---

[1] Son of Alexander, who had been a friend of the Hellenes in the Persian war. Perdiccas, who originally possessed only Lower Macedonia, had deprived his brother Philip of

To face page 95.

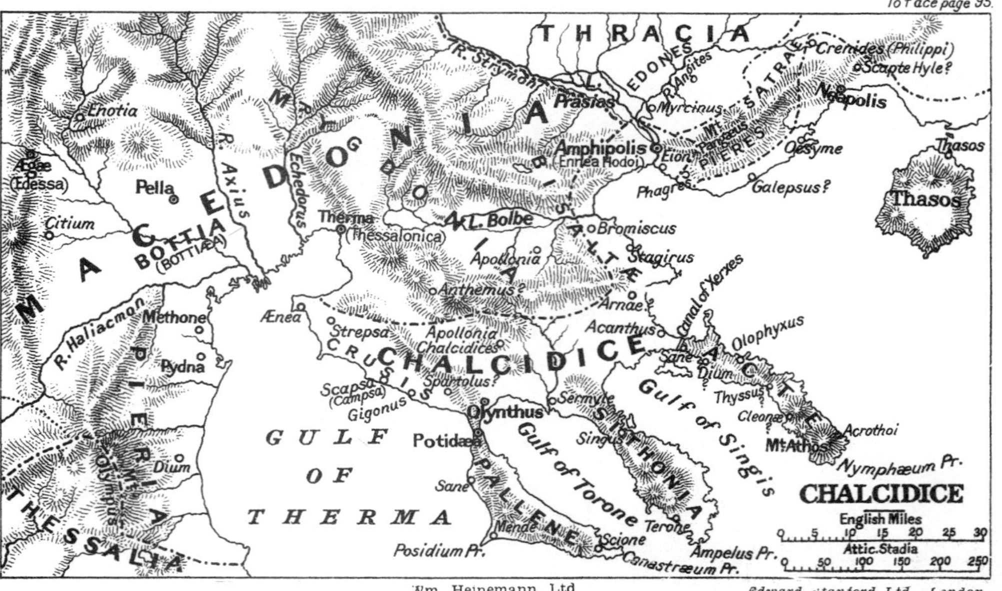

Wm. Heinemann, Ltd

Edward Stanford Ltd. London

also occurred, which caused differences between the Athenians and the Peloponnesians and led to the war. While the Corinthians were devising how they should take vengeance on the Athenians, the latter, suspecting their enmity, required of the Potidaeans (who dwell on the isthmus of Pallene and are colonists of the Corinthians but tributary allies of the Athenians), to pull down their wall on the side of Pallene and give hostages, and, furthermore, to send away and not receive in the future the magistrates whom the Corinthians were accustomed to send every year. For they were afraid that the Potidaeans, persuaded by Perdiccas[1] and the Corinthians, would revolt and cause the rest of the allies in Thrace to revolt with them.

LVII. These precautions the Athenians took with regard to the Potidaeans immediately after the sea-fight at Corcyra; for the Corinthians were now openly at variance with them, and Perdiccas son of Alexander, king of the Macedonians, who had before been an ally and friend, had now become hostile. And he had become hostile because the Athenians had made an alliance with his brother Philip and with Derdas, who were making common cause against himself. Alarmed at this he kept sending envoys to Lacedaemon, trying to bring about a war between Athens and the Peloponnesians. He sought also to win over the Corinthians, with a view to the revolt of Potidaea; and, furthermore, he made overtures to the Chalcidians of Thrace and the Bottiaeans to join in the revolt, thinking that if he had as allies these countries, which bordered on his own, it would be

Upper Macedonia, and now was king of all Macedonia. See, further, II. xcix. ff.

6 ῥᾷον ἂν τὸν πόλεμον μετ' αὐτῶν ποιεῖσθαι. ὧν οἱ Ἀθηναῖοι αἰσθόμενοι καὶ βουλόμενοι προκαταλαμβάνειν τῶν πόλεων τὰς ἀποστάσεις (ἔτυχον γὰρ τριάκοντα ναῦς ἀποστέλλοντες καὶ χιλίους ὁπλίτας ἐπὶ τὴν γῆν αὐτοῦ Ἀρχεστράτου τοῦ Λυκομήδους μετ' ἄλλων τεσσάρων στρατηγοῦντος), ἐπιστέλλουσι τοῖς ἄρχουσι τῶν νεῶν Ποτειδεατῶν τε ὁμήρους λαβεῖν καὶ τὸ τεῖχος καθελεῖν, τῶν τε πλησίον πόλεων φυλακὴν ἔχειν ὅπως μὴ ἀποστήσονται.

LVIII. Ποτειδεᾶται δὲ πέμψαντες μὲν καὶ παρ' Ἀθηναίους πρέσβεις, εἴ πως πείσειαν μὴ σφῶν πέρι νεωτερίζειν μηδέν, ἐλθόντες δὲ καὶ ἐς τὴν Λακεδαίμονα μετὰ Κορινθίων,[1] ὅπως ἑτοιμάσαιντο τιμωρίαν, ἢν δέῃ, ἐπειδὴ ἔκ τε Ἀθηνῶν ἐκ πολλοῦ πράσσοντες οὐδὲν ηὕροντο ἐπιτήδειον, ἀλλ' αἱ νῆες αἱ ἐπὶ Μακεδονίαν καὶ ἐπὶ σφᾶς ὁμοίως ἔπλεον καὶ τὰ τέλη τῶν Λακεδαιμονίων ὑπέσχετο αὐτοῖς, ἢν ἐπὶ Ποτείδαιαν ἴωσιν Ἀθηναῖοι, ἐς τὴν Ἀττικὴν ἐσβαλεῖν, τότε δὴ κατὰ τὸν καιρὸν τοῦτον ἀφίστανται μετὰ Χαλκιδέων καὶ Βοττιαίων κοινῇ ξυνομόσαντες.
2 καὶ Περδίκκας πείθει Χαλκιδέας τὰς ἐπὶ θαλάσσῃ πόλεις ἐκλιπόντας καὶ καταβαλόντας ἀνοικίσασθαι ἐς Ὄλυνθον μίαν τε πόλιν ταύτην ἰσχυρὰν ποιήσασθαι· τοῖς τ' ἐκλιποῦσι τούτοις τῆς ἑαυτοῦ γῆς τῆς Μυγδονίας περὶ τὴν Βόλβην λίμνην ἔδωκε νέμεσθαι, ἕως ἂν ὁ πρὸς Ἀθηναίους πόλε-

[1] ἔπρασσον, before ὅπως in all MSS., deleted by Poppo.

easier, in conjunction with them, to carry on the war. But the Athenians became aware of these designs, and wishing to forestall the revolt of the cities, ordered the commanders of their fleet (since they happened to be sending against the country of Perdiccas thirty ships and a thousand hoplites under the command of Archestratus son of Lycomedes and four others) to take hostages of the Potidaeans and pull down their wall, and also to keep a watch upon the neighbouring towns and prevent them from revolting.

LVIII. The Potidaeans, on the other hand, sent envoys to Athens, to see if they could persuade them not to take any harsh measures with reference to themselves; but envoys of theirs went also to Lacedaemon in the company of the Corinthians, with the object of having assistance ready to hand in case of need. From the Athenians, with whom they carried on protracted negotiation, they obtained no satisfactory result, but on the contrary the ships destined to attack Macedonia proceeded to sail against themselves as well, whereas the magistrates of the Lacedaemonians promised them to invade Attica if the Athenians went against Potidaea; so they seized this opportunity and revolted, entering into a formal alliance with the Chalcidians[1] and Bottiaeans. Perdiccas at the same time persuaded the Chalcidians to abandon and pull down their cities on the sea-coast and settle inland at Olynthus, making there a single strong city; and he gave them, when they abandoned their cities, a part of his own territory of Mygdonia around Lake Bolbe to cultivate as long as they should be at war

[1] *i.e.* the Chalcidians of Thrace.

μος ᾖ. καὶ οἱ μὲν ἀνῳκίζοντό τε καθαιροῦντες
τὰς πόλεις καὶ ἐς πόλεμον παρεσκευάζοντο·
LIX. αἱ δὲ τριάκοντα νῆες τῶν Ἀθηναίων ἀφικνοῦνται ἐς τὰ ἐπὶ Θρᾴκης καὶ καταλαμβάνουσι
2 τήν τε Ποτείδαιαν καὶ τἆλλα ἀφεστηκότα. νομίσαντες δὲ οἱ στρατηγοὶ ἀδύνατα εἶναι πρός τε
Περδίκκαν πολεμεῖν τῇ παρούσῃ δυνάμει καὶ τὰ
ξυναφεστῶτα χωρία, τρέπονται ἐπὶ τὴν Μακεδονίαν, ἐφ' ὅπερ καὶ τὸ πρῶτον ἐξεπέμποντο, καὶ
καταστάντες ἐπολέμουν μετὰ Φιλίππου καὶ τῶν
Δέρδου ἀδελφῶν ἄνωθεν στρατιᾷ ἐσβεβληκότων.

LX. Καὶ ἐν τούτῳ οἱ Κορίνθιοι, τῆς Ποτειδαίας
ἀφεστηκυίας καὶ τῶν Ἀττικῶν νεῶν περὶ Μακεδονίαν οὐσῶν, δεδιότες περὶ τῷ χωρίῳ καὶ οἰκεῖον
τὸν κίνδυνον ἡγούμενοι πέμπουσιν ἑαυτῶν τε
ἐθελοντὰς καὶ τῶν ἄλλων Πελοποννησίων μισθῷ
πείσαντες ἑξακοσίους καὶ χιλίους τοὺς πάντας
2 ὁπλίτας καὶ ψιλοὺς τετρακοσίους. ἐστρατήγει
δὲ αὐτῶν Ἀριστεὺς ὁ Ἀδειμάντου, κατὰ φιλίαν
τε αὐτοῦ οὐχ ἥκιστα οἱ πλεῖστοι ἐκ Κορίνθου
στρατιῶται ἐθελονταὶ ξυνέσποντο· ἦν γὰρ τοῖς
3 Ποτειδεάταις αἰεί ποτε ἐπιτήδειος. καὶ ἀφικνοῦνται τεσσαρακοστῇ ἡμέρᾳ ὕστερον ἐπὶ Θρᾴκης ἢ
Ποτείδαια ἀπέστη.

LXI. Ἦλθε δὲ καὶ τοῖς Ἀθηναίοις εὐθὺς ἡ
ἀγγελία τῶν πόλεων ὅτι ἀφεστᾶσι, καὶ πέμπουσιν, ὡς ᾔσθοντο καὶ τοὺς μετὰ Ἀριστέως
ἐπιπαριόντας, δισχιλίους ἑαυτῶν ὁπλίτας καὶ
τεσσαράκοντα ναῦς πρὸς τὰ ἀφεστῶτα, καὶ Καλ-
λίαν τὸν Καλλιάδου πέμπτον αὐτὸν στρατηγόν·
2 οἳ ἀφικόμενοι ἐς Μακεδονίαν πρῶτον καταλαμβά-

with the Athenians. And so they proceeded to dismantle their cities, move inland, and prepare for war. LIX. But when the thirty ships of the Athenians reached the coast of Thrace, they found Potidaea and the other places already in revolt. Whereupon the generals, thinking it impossible with their present force to wage war with both Perdiccas and the places which had revolted, turned their attention to Macedonia, which was their destination at the start, and when they had got a foothold carried on war in concert with Philip and the brothers of Derdas, who had already invaded Macedonia from the interior with an army.

LX. Thereupon the Corinthians, seeing that Potidaea had revolted and the Attic ships were in the neighbourhood of Macedonia, were alarmed about the place and thinking that the danger came home to them, dispatched volunteers of their own and such other Peloponnesians as they induced by pay, in all sixteen hundred hoplites and four hundred light-armed troops. The general in command was Aristeus son of Adimantus; and it was chiefly because of friendship for him that most of the soldiers from Corinth went along as volunteers; for he had always been on friendly terms with the Potidaeans. And they arrived on the coast of Thrace on the fortieth day after the revolt of Potidaea.

LXI. The news of the revolt of the cities quickly reached the Athenians also; and when they learned that troops under Aristeus were also on the way to support the rebels, they sent against the places in revolt two thousand of their own hoplites and forty ships, under Callias son of Calliades with four other generals. These first came to Macedonia and found

νουσι τοὺς προτέρους χιλίους Θέρμην ἄρτι ᾑρη-
3 κότας καὶ Πύδναν πολιορκοῦντας, προσκαθεζόμενοι δὲ καὶ αὐτοὶ τὴν Πύδναν ἐπολιόρκησαν
μέν, ἔπειτα δὲ ξύμβασιν ποιησάμενοι καὶ ξυμμαχίαν ἀναγκαίαν πρὸς τὸν Περδίκκαν, ὡς αὐτοὺς
κατήπειγεν ἡ Ποτείδαια καὶ ὁ Ἀριστεὺς παρελη-
4 λυθώς, ἀπανίστανται ἐκ τῆς Μακεδονίας, καὶ
ἀφικόμενοι ἐς Βέροιαν κἀκεῖθεν ἐπὶ Στρέψαν[1] καὶ
πειράσαντες πρῶτον τοῦ χωρίου καὶ οὐχ ἑλόντες
ἐπορεύοντο κατὰ γῆν πρὸς τὴν Ποτείδαιαν
τρισχιλίοις μὲν ὁπλίταις ἑαυτῶν, χωρὶς δὲ τῶν
ξυμμάχων πολλοῖς, ἱππεῦσι δὲ ἑξακοσίοις Μακεδόνων τοῖς μετὰ Φιλίππου καὶ Παυσανίου· ἅμα
5 δὲ νῆες παρέπλεον ἑβδομήκοντα. κατ' ὀλίγον δὲ
προϊόντες τριταῖοι ἀφίκοντο ἐς Γίγωνον καὶ
ἐστρατοπεδεύσαντο.

LXII. Ποτειδεᾶται δὲ καὶ οἱ μετὰ Ἀριστέως
Πελοποννήσιοι προσδεχόμενοι τοὺς Ἀθηναίους
ἐστρατοπεδεύοντο πρὸς Ὀλύνθου ἐν τῷ ἰσθμῷ
2 καὶ ἀγορὰν ἔξω τῆς πόλεως ἐπεποίηντο. στρατηγὸν μὲν οὖν τοῦ πεζοῦ παντὸς οἱ ξύμμαχοι
ᾕρηντο Ἀριστέα, τῆς δὲ ἵππου Περδίκκαν· ἀπέστη
γὰρ εὐθὺς πάλιν τῶν Ἀθηναίων καὶ ξυνεμάχει
τοῖς Ποτειδεάταις Ἰόλαον ἀνθ' αὑτοῦ καταστήσας
3 ἄρχοντα. ἦν δὲ ἡ γνώμη τοῦ Ἀριστέως, τὸ μὲν
μεθ' ἑαυτοῦ στρατόπεδον ἔχοντι[2] ἐν τῷ ἰσθμῷ
ἐπιτηρεῖν τοὺς Ἀθηναίους, ἢν ἐπίωσι, Χαλκιδέας
δὲ καὶ τοὺς ἔξω ἰσθμοῦ ξυμμάχους καὶ τὴν παρὰ
Περδίκκου διακοσίαν ἵππον ἐν Ὀλύνθῳ μένειν,

[1] ἐπὶ Στρέψαν, Pluygers' certain emendation for ἐπιστρέψαντες of the MSS.

[2] Madvig deletes, followed by Hude.

that the former thousand had just taken Therme and were besieging Pydna; so they also took part in the siege of Pydna. But afterwards they concluded an agreement and an alliance with Perdiccas, being forced thereto by the situation of Potidaea and the arrival of Aristeus, which compelled them to hasten, and then they withdrew from Macedonia. On their way they came to Beroea and thence to Strepsa,[1] and after an unsuccessful attempt upon this place proceeded overland to Potidaea with three thousand hoplites of their own and with many of their allies besides, and with six hundred Macedonian cavalry, who were under the command of Philip and Pausanias; and at the same time their ships, seventy in number, sailed along the coast. And marching leisurely they arrived on the third day at Gigonus, and went into camp.

LXII. The Potidaeans and the Peloponnesians under Aristeus were awaiting the Athenians, encamped on the Olynthian side of the isthmus; and they had established a market outside of the city. The allies had chosen Aristeus general of all the infantry, and Perdiccas of the cavalry; for Perdiccas had immediately deserted the Athenians again[2] and was now in alliance with the Potidaeans, having appointed Iolaus as his administrator at home. The plan of Aristeus was as follows: he was to hold his own army on the isthmus and watch for the approach of the Athenians, while the Chalcidians and the other allies from outside of the isthmus[3] and the two hundred horse furnished by Perdiccas were to

[1] In Mygdonia, north of Therme.

[2] For his first desertion of the Athenians, see ch. lvii.

[3] *i.e.* the Bottiaeans, who, like the Chalcidians, lived outside the isthmus.

καὶ ὅταν Ἀθηναῖοι ἐπὶ σφᾶς χωρῶσι, κατὰ νώτου
βοηθοῦντας ἐν μέσῳ ποιεῖν αὐτῶν τοὺς πολεμίους.
4 Καλλίας δ' αὖ ὁ τῶν Ἀθηναίων στρατηγὸς καὶ οἱ
ξυνάρχοντες τοὺς μὲν Μακεδόνας ἱππέας καὶ τῶν
ξυμμάχων ὀλίγους ἐπὶ Ὀλύνθου ἀποπέμπουσιν,
ὅπως εἴργωσι τοὺς ἐκεῖθεν ἐπιβοηθεῖν, αὐτοὶ δὲ
ἀναστήσαντες τὸ στρατόπεδον ἐχώρουν ἐπὶ τὴν
5 Ποτείδαιαν. καὶ ἐπειδὴ πρὸς τῷ ἰσθμῷ ἐγένοντο
καὶ εἶδον τοὺς ἐναντίους παρασκευαζομένους ὡς
ἐς μάχην, ἀντικαθίσταντο καὶ αὐτοί, καὶ οὐ πολὺ
6 ὕστερον ξυνέμισγον. καὶ αὐτὸ μὲν τὸ τοῦ Ἀριστέως κέρας καὶ ὅσοι περὶ ἐκεῖνον ἦσαν Κορινθίων
τε καὶ τῶν ἄλλων λογάδες ἔτρεψαν τὸ καθ'
ἑαυτοὺς καὶ ἐπεξῆλθον διώκοντες ἐπὶ πολύ· τὸ
δὲ ἄλλο στρατόπεδον Ποτειδεατῶν καὶ Πελοποννησίων ἡσσᾶτο ὑπὸ τῶν Ἀθηναίων καὶ ἐς τὸ
τεῖχος κατέφυγεν.

LXIII. Ἐπαναχωρῶν δὲ ὁ Ἀριστεὺς ἀπὸ τῆς
διώξεως, ὡς ὁρᾷ τὸ ἄλλο στράτευμα ἡσσημένον,
ἠπόρησε μὲν ὁποτέρωσε διακινδυνεύσῃ χωρήσας,
ἢ ἐπὶ τῆς Ὀλύνθου ἢ ἐς τὴν Ποτείδαιαν· ἔδοξε
δ' οὖν ξυναγαγόντι τοὺς μεθ' ἑαυτοῦ ὡς ἐς
ἐλάχιστον χωρίον δρόμῳ βιάσασθαι ἐς τὴν
Ποτείδαιαν, καὶ παρῆλθε παρὰ τὴν χηλὴν διὰ
τῆς θαλάσσης βαλλόμενός τε καὶ χαλεπῶς, ὀλίγους μέν τινας ἀποβαλών, τοὺς δὲ πλείους σώσας.
2 οἱ δ' ἀπὸ τῆς Ὀλύνθου τοῖς Ποτειδεάταις βοηθοί

remain at Olynthus; then when the Athenians should move against the forces of Aristeus, the others were to come up and attack them in the rear, and thus place the enemy between their two divisions. But Callias, the commander of the Athenians, and his colleagues sent the Macedonian cavalry and a few of the allies toward Olynthus, to shut off aid from that quarter, while they themselves broke camp and advanced against Potidaea. And when they arrived at the isthmus and saw the enemy preparing for battle, they took up their position facing them; and soon the two sides joined battle. And the wing led by Aristeus himself, which included the picked Corinthian and other troops, routed the forces opposed to them and pressed on a long distance in pursuit; but the rest of the army of the Potidaeans and the Peloponnesians was worsted by the Athenians and took refuge within the walls of Potidaea.

LXIII. When Aristeus returned from the pursuit and saw that the rest of the army was defeated, he was at a loss whether he should try to fight his way through towards Olynthus or into Potidaea. He determined, however, to bring his own troops together into as compact a body as possible and to force his way into Potidaea on a run. And he succeeded in getting in by way of the breakwater through the sea, with difficulty, indeed, and harassed by missiles; but though he lost a few men, he saved the greater number of them. Now when the battle began and the standards had been raised,[1] the auxiliaries of

[1] These signals were not for battle, but for the Olynthian auxiliaries to come, and as soon as it became clear, through the speedy success of the Athenians, that their object could not be accomplished, they were lowered.

(ἀπέχει δὲ ἑξήκοντα μάλιστα σταδίους καὶ ἔστι
καταφανές), ὡς ἡ μάχη ἐγίγνετο καὶ τὰ σημεῖα
ἤρθη, βραχὺ μέν τι προῆλθον ὡς βοηθήσοντες,
καὶ οἱ Μακεδόνες ἱππῆς ἀντιπαρετάξαντο ὡς
κωλύσοντες· ἐπειδὴ δὲ διὰ τάχους ἡ νίκη τῶν
Ἀθηναίων ἐγίγνετο καὶ τὰ σημεῖα κατεσπάσθη,
πάλιν ἐπανεχώρουν ἐς τὸ τεῖχος καὶ οἱ Μακεδόνες
παρὰ τοὺς Ἀθηναίους· ἱππῆς δ' οὐδετέροις παρε-
3 γένοντο. μετὰ δὲ τὴν μάχην τροπαῖον ἔστησαν
οἱ Ἀθηναῖοι καὶ τοὺς νεκροὺς ὑποσπόνδους ἀπέδοσαν τοῖς Ποτειδεάταις· ἀπέθανον δὲ Ποτειδεατῶν μὲν καὶ τῶν ξυμμάχων ὀλίγῳ ἐλάσσους
τριακοσίων, Ἀθηναίων δὲ αὐτῶν πεντήκοντα καὶ
ἑκατὸν καὶ Καλλίας ὁ στρατηγός.

LXIV. Τὸ δὲ ἐκ τοῦ ἰσθμοῦ τεῖχος[1] εὐθὺς οἱ
Ἀθηναῖοι ἀποτειχίσαντες ἐφρούρουν· τὸ δ' ἐς τὴν
Παλλήνην ἀτείχιστον ἦν· οὐ γὰρ ἱκανοὶ ἐνόμιζον
εἶναι ἔν τε τῷ ἰσθμῷ φρουρεῖν καὶ ἐς τὴν Παλλήνην διαβάντες τειχίζειν, δεδιότες μὴ σφίσιν οἱ
Ποτειδεᾶται καὶ οἱ ξύμμαχοι γενομένοις δίχα
2 ἐπίθωνται. καὶ πυνθανόμενοι οἱ ἐν τῇ πόλει
Ἀθηναῖοι τὴν Παλλήνην ἀτείχιστον οὖσαν, χρόνῳ
ὕστερον πέμπουσιν ἑξακοσίους καὶ χιλίους
ὁπλίτας ἑαυτῶν καὶ Φορμίωνα τὸν Ἀσωπίου
στρατηγόν· ὃς ἀφικόμενος ἐς τὴν Παλλήνην καὶ ἐξ
Ἀφύτιος ὁρμώμενος προσήγαγε τῇ Ποτειδαίᾳ τὸν

[1] Classen deletes, followed by Hude.

---

[1] On the Athenian side were 600 Macedonian cavalry (ch. lxi. 4), on the Potidaean side 200 Macedonian cavalry under Perdiccas (ch. lxii. 3).

[2] Thucydides omits the loss of the allies of the Athenians.

[3] The wall on the isthmus side of the Potidaeans is the

the Potidaeans in Olynthus—which is only about sixty stadia distant and can be seen from Potidaea—advanced a short distance to give aid, and the Macedonian cavalry drew up in line against them to prevent it. But since the Athenians were soon proving the victors and the standards were pulled down, the auxiliaries retired again within the walls of Olynthus and the Macedonians rejoined the Athenians. And so no cavalry got into action on either side.[1] After the battle the Athenians set up a trophy and gave up their dead under a truce to the Potidaeans. There were slain, of the Potidaeans and their allies a little less than three hundred, and of the Athenians alone[2] about a hundred and fifty, and also their general Callias.

LXIV. The city wall on the isthmus side[3] the Athenians immediately cut off by a transverse wall and set a guard there, but the wall toward Pallene was not shut off.[4] For they thought their numbers were insufficient to maintain a garrison on the isthmus and also to cross over to Pallene and build a wall there too, fearing that, if they divided their forces, the Potidaeans and their allies would attack them. Afterwards, when the Athenians at home learned that Pallene was not blockaded, they sent sixteen hundred of their own hoplites under the command of Phormio son of Asopius; and he, when he arrived at Pallene, making Aphytis his base, brought his army to Potidaea, marching leisurely and ravaging

τεῖχος of ch. lxii. 6; the wall to Pallene is that mentioned in ch. lvi. 2 as τὸ ἐς Παλλήνην τεῖχος.

[4] The investment of Potidaea was effected by walling off first the northern and then also the southern city wall by a blockading wall; on the west and east, where the city extended to the sea, the blockade was made with ships.

στρατόν, κατὰ βραχὺ προϊὼν καὶ κείρων ἅμα τὴν
3 γῆν· ὡς δὲ οὐδεὶς ἐπεξῄει ἐς μάχην, ἀπετείχισε
τὸ ἐκ τῆς Παλλήνης τεῖχος· καὶ οὕτως ἤδη κατὰ
κράτος ἡ Ποτείδαια ἀμφοτέρωθεν ἐπολιορκεῖτο
καὶ ἐκ θαλάσσης ναυσὶν ἅμα ἐφορμούσαις.

LXV. Ἀριστεὺς δὲ ἀποτειχισθείσης αὐτῆς καὶ
ἐλπίδα οὐδεμίαν ἔχων σωτηρίας, ἢν μή τι ἀπὸ
Πελοποννήσου ἢ ἄλλο παρὰ λόγον γίγνηται,
ξυνεβούλευε μὲν πλὴν πεντακοσίων ἄνεμον τη-
ρήσασι τοῖς ἄλλοις ἐκπλεῦσαι, ὅπως ἐπὶ πλέον
ὁ σῖτος ἀντίσχῃ, καὶ αὐτὸς ἤθελε τῶν μενόντων
εἶναι· ὡς δ' οὐκ ἔπειθε, βουλόμενος τὰ ἐπὶ τούτοις
παρασκευάζειν καὶ ὅπως τὰ ἔξωθεν ἕξει ὡς ἄριστα,
ἔκπλουν ποιεῖται λαθὼν τὴν φυλακὴν τῶν Ἀθη-
2 ναίων· καὶ παραμένων ἐν Χαλκιδεῦσι τά τε ἄλλα
ξυνεπολέμει καὶ Σερμυλιῶν λοχήσας πρὸς τῇ
πόλει πολλοὺς διέφθειρεν, ἔς τε τὴν Πελοπόννη-
3 σον ἔπρασσεν ὅπῃ ὠφελία τις γενήσεται. μετὰ
δὲ τῆς Ποτειδαίας τὴν ἀποτείχισιν Φορμίων μὲν
ἔχων τοὺς ἑξακοσιους καὶ χιλίους τὴν Χαλκιδικὴν
καὶ Βοττικὴν ἐδῄου καὶ ἔστιν ἃ καὶ πολίσματα
εἷλεν.

LXVI. Τοῖς δ' Ἀθηναίοις καὶ Πελοποννησίοις αἰτίαι μὲν αὗται προσγεγένηντο[1] ἐς ἀλλήλους, τοῖς μὲν Κορινθίοις[2] ὅτι τὴν Ποτείδαιαν ἑαυτῶν οὖσαν ἀποικίαν καὶ ἄνδρας Κορινθίων τε καὶ

[1] Hude reads προυγεγένηντο, with BCE.
[2] Hude inserts, after Κορινθίοις, the words ἐς τοὺς Ἀθηναίους, following Reiske

the country at the same time. And as no one came out against him to give battle he built a wall to blockade the Pallene wall. And so Potidaea was at length in a state of siege, which was prosecuted vigorously on both sides of it as well as by sea, where a fleet blockaded it.

LXV. As for Aristeus, now that Potidaea was cut off by the blockade and he had no hope of saving it unless help should come from the Peloponnesus or something else should happen beyond his expectation, he advised all the garrison except five hundred men to wait for a wind and sail out of the harbour, that the food might hold out longer, and he himself was ready to be one of those who should remain. But since he could not gain their consent, wishing to do the next best thing and to provide that their affairs outside should be put into the best possible condition, he sailed out, unobserved by the Athenian guard. He then remained among the Chalcidians, whom he assisted generally in carrying on the war, and especially by destroying a large force of Sermylians, whom he ambushed near their city; and meanwhile he kept up negotiations with the Peloponnesians to see if some aid could not be obtained. Phormio, however, after the investment of Potidaea was complete, took his sixteen hundred troops and ravaged Chalcidice and Bottice; and he also captured some towns.

LXVI. As between the Athenians and the Peloponnesians, then, these additional grounds of complaint had arisen on either side, the Corinthians being aggrieved because the Athenians were besieging Potidaea, a colony of theirs with men in it from

Πελοποννησίων ἐν αὐτῇ ὄντας ἐπολιόρκουν, τοῖς δὲ Ἀθηναίοις ἐς τοὺς Πελοποννησίους ὅτι ἑαυτῶν τε πόλιν ξυμμαχίδα καὶ φόρου ὑποτελῆ ἀπέστησαν καὶ ἐλθόντες σφίσιν ἀπὸ τοῦ προφανοῦς ἐμάχοντο μετὰ Ποτειδεατῶν. οὐ μέντοι ὅ γε πόλεμός πω ξυνερρώγει, ἀλλ' ἔτι ἀνοκωχὴ ἦν· ἰδίᾳ γὰρ ταῦτα οἱ Κορίνθιοι ἔπραξαν.

LXVII. Πολιορκουμένης δὲ τῆς Ποτειδαίας οὐχ ἡσύχαζον, ἀνδρῶν τε σφίσιν ἐνόντων καὶ ἅμα περὶ τῷ χωρίῳ δεδιότες. παρεκάλουν τε εὐθὺς ἐς τὴν Λακεδαίμονα τοὺς ξυμμάχους καὶ κατεβόων ἐλθόντες τῶν Ἀθηναίων ὅτι σπονδάς τε λελυκότες εἶεν καὶ ἀδικοῖεν τὴν Πελοπόννησον.
2 Αἰγινῆταί τε φανερῶς μὲν οὐ πρεσβευόμενοι, δεδιότες τοὺς Ἀθηναίους, κρύφα δέ, οὐχ ἥκιστα μετ' αὐτῶν ἐνῆγον τὸν πόλεμον, λέγοντες οὐκ
3 εἶναι αὐτόνομοι κατὰ τὰς σπονδάς. οἱ δὲ Λακεδαιμόνιοι προσπαρακαλέσαντες τῶν ξυμμάχων καὶ[1] εἴ τίς τι ἄλλος ἔφη ἠδικῆσθαι ὑπὸ Ἀθηναίων, ξύλλογον σφῶν αὐτῶν ποιήσαντες τὸν εἰωθότα
4 λέγειν ἐκέλευον. καὶ ἄλλοι τε παριόντες ἐγκλήματα ἐποιοῦντο ὡς ἕκαστοι καὶ Μεγαρῆς, δηλοῦντες μὲν καὶ ἕτερα οὐκ ὀλίγα διάφορα, μάλιστα δὲ λιμένων τε εἴργεσθαι τῶν ἐν τῇ Ἀθηναίων ἀρχῇ καὶ τῆς Ἀττικῆς ἀγορᾶς παρὰ τὰς σπονδάς.
5 παρελθόντες δὲ τελευταῖοι Κορίνθιοι καὶ τοὺς ἄλλους ἐάσαντες πρῶτον παροξῦναι τοὺς Λακεδαιμονίους ἐπεῖπον τοιάδε.

LXVIII. "Τὸ πιστὸν ὑμᾶς, ὦ Λακεδαιμόνιοι, τῆς καθ' ὑμᾶς αὐτοὺς πολιτείας καὶ ὁμιλίας

[1] Hude reads *τε καὶ* with C and some inferior MSS.

Corinth and the Peloponnesus, the Athenians, because the Peloponnesians had brought about the revolt of a city that was an ally and tributary of theirs, and then had come and openly fought with the Potidaeans against themselves. As yet, however, the war had not openly broken out, but there was still a truce for in these things the Corinthians had acted only on their own authority.

LXVII. But when siege was laid to Potidaea they did not take it quietly, not only because Corinthians were in the town, but also because they were in fear about the place; and they immediately summoned the allies to Lacedaemon and, once there, they proceeded to inveigh against the Athenians on the ground that they had broken the treaty and were wronging the Peloponnesus. The Aeginetans also sent delegates—not openly, to be sure, for they feared the Athenians, but secretly—and, acting with the Corinthians, took a leading part in fomenting the war, saying that they were not autonomous as stipulated in the treaty. Then the Lacedaemonians sent out a summons to all the other allies who claimed to have suffered any wrong at the hands of the Athenians, and calling their own customary assembly bade them speak. Others came forward and stated their several complaints, and particularly the Megarians, who presented a great many other grievances, and chiefly this, that they were excluded from the harbours throughout the Athenian dominions and from the Athenian market, contrary to the treaty. Lastly the Corinthians, after they had first allowed the others to exasperate the Lacedaemonians, spoke as follows:—

LXVIII. "That spirit of trust which marks your domestic policy, O Lacedaemonians, and your relations

ἀπιστοτέρους, ἐς τοὺς ἄλλους ἤν τι λέγωμεν, καθίστησιν· καὶ ἀπ' αὐτοῦ σωφροσύνην μὲν ἔχετε, ἀμαθίᾳ δὲ πλέονι πρὸς τὰ ἔξω πράγματα
2 χρῆσθε. πολλάκις γὰρ προαγορευόντων ἡμῶν ἃ ἐμέλλομεν ὑπὸ Ἀθηναίων βλάπτεσθαι, οὐ περὶ ὧν ἐδιδάσκομεν ἑκάστοτε τὴν μάθησιν ἐποιεῖσθε, ἀλλὰ τῶν λεγόντων μᾶλλον ὑπενοεῖτε ὡς ἕνεκα τῶν αὐτοῖς ἰδίᾳ διαφόρων λέγουσιν· καὶ δι' αὐτὸ οὐ πρὶν πάσχειν, ἀλλ' ἐπειδὴ ἐν τῷ ἔργῳ ἐσμέν, τοὺς ξυμμάχους τούσδε παρεκαλέσατε, ἐν οἷς προσήκει ἡμᾶς οὐχ ἥκιστα εἰπεῖν ὅσῳ καὶ μέγιστα ἐγκλήματα ἔχομεν, ὑπὸ μὲν Ἀθηναίων ὑβριζό-
3 μενοι, ὑπὸ δὲ ὑμῶν ἀμελούμενοι. καὶ εἰ μὲν ἀφανεῖς που ὄντες ἠδίκουν τὴν Ἑλλάδα, διδασκαλίας ἂν ὡς οὐκ εἰδόσι προσέδει· νῦν δὲ τί δεῖ μακρηγορεῖν, ὧν τοὺς μὲν δεδουλωμένους ὁρᾶτε, τοῖς δ' ἐπιβουλεύοντας αὐτούς, καὶ οὐχ ἥκιστα τοῖς ἡμετέροις ξυμμάχοις, καὶ ἐκ πολλοῦ προ-
4 παρεσκευασμένους, εἴ ποτε πολεμήσονται; οὐ γὰρ ἂν Κέρκυράν τε ὑπολαβόντες βίᾳ ἡμῶν εἶχον καὶ Ποτείδαιαν ἐπολιόρκουν· ὧν τὸ μὲν ἐπικαιρότατον χωρίον πρὸς τὰ ἐπὶ Θρᾴκης ἀποχρῆσθαι, ἡ δὲ ναυτικὸν ἂν μέγιστον παρέσχε τοῖς Πελοποννησίοις.

LXIX. "Καὶ τῶνδε ὑμεῖς αἴτιοι, τό τε πρῶτον ἐάσαντες αὐτοὺς τὴν πόλιν μετὰ τὰ Μηδικὰ

with one another, renders you more mistrustful if we bring any charge against others, and thus while this quality gives you sobriety, yet because of it you betray a want of understanding in dealing with affairs abroad. For example, although we warned you time and again of the injury the Athenians were intending to do us, you refused to accept the information we kept giving you, but preferred to direct your suspicions against the speakers, feeling that they were actuated by their own private interests. And this is the reason why you did not act before we got into trouble, but it is only when we are in the midst of it that you have summoned these allies, among whom it is especially fitting that we should speak, inasmuch as we have the gravest accusations to bring, insulted as we have long been by the Athenians and neglected by you. And if they were wronging Hellas in some underhand way, you might have needed additional information on the ground of your ignorance; but as the case stands, what need is there of a long harangue, when you see that they have enslaved some of us[1] and are plotting against others, notably against your own allies, and that they have long been making their preparations with a view to the contingency of war? For otherwise they would not have purloined Corcyra, which they still hold in despite of us, and would not be besieging Potidaea—one of these being a most strategic point for operations on the Thracian coast, while the other would have furnished a very large fleet to the Peloponnesians.

LXIX. "And the blame for all this belongs to you, for you permitted them in the first instance to

[1] Referring especially to the Aeginetans, in the other cases to the Megarians and Potidaeans.

κρατῦναι καὶ ὕστερον τὰ μακρὰ στῆσαι τείχη, ἐς τόδε τε αἰεὶ ἀποστεροῦντες οὐ μόνον τοὺς ὑπ' ἐκείνων δεδουλωμένους ἐλευθερίας, ἀλλὰ καὶ τοὺς ὑμετέρους ἤδη ξυμμάχους· οὐ γὰρ ὁ δουλωσάμενος, ἀλλ' ὁ δυνάμενος μὲν παῦσαι, περιορῶν δὲ ἀληθέστερον αὐτὸ δρᾷ, εἴπερ καὶ τὴν ἀξίωσιν τῆς
2 ἀρετῆς ὡς ἐλευθερῶν τὴν Ἑλλάδα φέρεται. μόλις δὲ νῦν γε ξυνήλθομεν καὶ οὐδὲ νῦν ἐπὶ φανεροῖς. χρῆν γὰρ οὐκ εἰ ἀδικούμεθα ἔτι σκοπεῖν, ἀλλὰ καθ' ὅ τι ἀμυνούμεθα· οἱ γὰρ[1] δρῶντες βεβουλευμένοι πρὸς οὐ διεγνωκότας ἤδη καὶ οὐ μέλλοντες
3 ἐπέρχονται. καὶ ἐπιστάμεθα οἵᾳ ὁδῷ οἱ Ἀθηναῖοι καὶ ὅτι κατ' ὀλίγον χωροῦσιν ἐπὶ τοὺς πέλας. καὶ λανθάνειν μὲν οἰόμενοι διὰ τὸ ἀναίσθητον ὑμῶν ἧσσον θαρσοῦσι, γνόντες δὲ
4 εἰδότας περιορᾶν ἰσχυρῶς ἐγκείσονται. ἡσυχάζετε γὰρ μόνοι Ἑλλήνων, ὦ Λακεδαιμόνιοι, οὐ τῇ δυνάμει τινά, ἀλλὰ τῇ μελλήσει ἀμυνόμενοι, καὶ μόνοι οὐκ ἀρχομένην τὴν αὔξησιν τῶν ἐχθρῶν,
5 διπλασιουμένην δὲ καταλύοντες. καίτοι ἐλέγεσθε ἀσφαλεῖς εἶναι, ὧν ἄρα ὁ λόγος τοῦ ἔργου ἐκράτει. τόν τε γὰρ Μῆδον αὐτοὶ ἴσμεν ἐκ περάτων γῆς πρότερον ἐπὶ τὴν Πελοπόννησον ἐλθόντα ἢ τὰ

[1] οἱ γὰρ, so MSS.: Hude reads οἵ γε after Classen.

[1] See ch. xc. ff. [2] See ch. cvii. 1.

[3] Referring to the recent increase of the Athenian navy by the accession of the Corcyraean fleet.

strengthen their city after the Persian war,[1] and afterwards to build their Long Walls,[2] while up to this very hour you are perpetually defrauding of their freedom not only those who have been enslaved by them, but now even your own allies also. For the state which has reduced others to slavery does not in a more real fashion enslave them than the state which has power to prevent it, and yet looks carelessly on, although claiming as its preëminent distinction that it is the liberator of Hellas. And now at last we have with difficulty managed to come together, though even now without a clearly defined purpose. For we ought no longer to be considering whether we are wronged, but how we are to avenge our wrongs. For where men are men of action, it is with resolved plans against those who have come to no decision, it is at once and without waiting, that they advance. We know too by what method the Athenians move against their neighbours—that it is here a little and there a little. And as long as they think that, owing to your want of perception, they are undetected, they are less bold; but once let them learn that you are aware but complaisant, and they will press on with vigour. For indeed, O Lacedaemonians, you alone of the Hellenes pursue a passive policy, defending yourselves against aggression, not by the use of your power, but by your intention to use it; and you alone propose to destroy your enemies' power, not at its inception, but when it is doubling itself.[3] And yet you had the reputation of running no risks; but with you, it would seem, repute goes beyond reality. For example, the Persian, as we ourselves know, came from the ends of the earth as far as the Peloponnesus before your forces went

παρ' ὑμῶν ἀξίως προαπαντῆσαι, καὶ νῦν τοὺς
Ἀθηναίους οὐχ ἑκάς, ὥσπερ ἐκεῖνον, ἀλλ' ἐγγὺς
ὄντας περιορᾶτε, καὶ ἀντὶ τοῦ ἐπελθεῖν αὐτοὶ
ἀμύνεσθαι βούλεσθε μᾶλλον ἐπιόντας καὶ ἐς
τύχας πρὸς πολλῷ δυνατωτέρους ἀγωνιζόμενοι
καταστῆναι, ἐπιστάμενοι καὶ τὸν βάρβαρον αὐτὸν
περὶ αὑτῷ τὰ πλείω σφαλέντα καὶ πρὸς αὐτοὺς
τοὺς Ἀθηναίους πολλὰ ἡμᾶς ἤδη τοῖς ἁμαρτή-
μασιν αὐτῶν μᾶλλον ἢ τῇ ἀφ' ὑμῶν τιμωρίᾳ
περιγεγενημένους· ἐπεὶ αἵ γε ὑμέτεραι ἐλπίδες
ἤδη τινάς που καὶ ἀπαρασκεύους διὰ τὸ πιστεῦ-
6 σαι ἔφθειραν. καὶ μηδεὶς ὑμῶν ἐπ' ἔχθρᾳ τὸ
πλέον ἢ αἰτίᾳ νομίσῃ τάδε λέγεσθαι· αἰτία μὲν
γὰρ φίλων ἀνδρῶν ἐστιν ἁμαρτανόντων, κατη-
γορία δὲ ἐχθρῶν ἀδικησάντων.

LXX. "Καὶ ἅμα, εἴπερ τινὲς καὶ ἄλλοι, νομίζομεν ἄξιοι εἶναι τοῖς πέλας ψόγον ἐπενεγκεῖν,
ἄλλως τε καὶ μεγάλων τῶν διαφερόντων καθεστώτων, περὶ ὧν οὐκ αἰσθάνεσθαι ἡμῖν γε δοκεῖτε οὐδ'
ἐκλογίσασθαι πώποτε πρὸς οἵους ὑμῖν Ἀθηναίους
ὄντας καὶ ὅσον ὑμῶν καὶ ὡς πᾶν διαφέροντας ὁ
2 ἀγὼν ἔσται. οἱ μέν γε νεωτεροποιοὶ καὶ ἐπι-
νοῆσαι ὀξεῖς καὶ ἐπιτελέσαι ἔργῳ ἃ ἂν γνῶσιν,
ὑμεῖς δὲ τὰ ὑπάρχοντά τε σῴζειν καὶ ἐπιγνῶναι
μηδὲν καὶ ἔργῳ οὐδὲ τἀναγκαῖα ἐξικέσθαι.

forth to withstand him in a manner worthy of your power; and now you regard with indifference the Athenians who are not afar off, as the Persian was, but near at hand, and instead of attacking them yourselves, you prefer to ward them off when they attack, and incur hazard by joining in a struggle with opponents who have become far more powerful. Yet you know that the Barbarian failed mostly by his own fault, and that in our struggles with the Athenians themselves we have so far often owed our successes rather to their own errors than to any aid received from you; indeed, it is the hopes they have placed in you that have already ruined more than one state[1] that was unprepared just because of trust in you. And let no one of you think that these things are said more out of hostile feeling than by way of complaint; for complaint is against friends that err, but accusation against enemies that have inflicted an injury.

LXX. "And besides, we have the right, we think, if any men have, to find fault with our neighbours, especially since the interests at stake for us are important. To these interests it seems to us at least that you are insensible, and that you have never even fully considered what sort of men the Athenians are with whom you will have to fight, and how very, how utterly, different they are from you. For they are given to innovation and quick to form plans and to put their decisions into execution, whereas you are disposed merely to keep what you have, to devise nothing new, and, when you do take action, not to carry to completion even what is indispensable.

[1] Alluding perhaps to the Thasians (ch. ci.) and the Euboeans (ch. cxiv.).

3 αὖθις δὲ οἱ μὲν καὶ παρὰ δύναμιν τολμηταὶ καὶ
παρὰ γνώμην κινδυνευταὶ καὶ ἐν τοῖς δεινοῖς
εὐέλπιδες· τὸ δὲ ὑμέτερον τῆς τε δυνάμεως ἐνδεᾶ
πρᾶξαι τῆς τε γνώμης μηδὲ τοῖς βεβαίοις πιστεῦσαι τῶν τε δεινῶν μηδέποτε οἴεσθαι ἀπολυθή-
4 σεσθαι. καὶ μὴν καὶ ἄοκνοι πρὸς ὑμᾶς μελλητὰς
καὶ ἀποδημηταὶ πρὸς ἐνδημοτάτους· οἴονται γὰρ
οἱ μὲν τῇ ἀπουσίᾳ ἄν τι κτᾶσθαι, ὑμεῖς δὲ τῷ
5 ἐξελθεῖν καὶ τὰ ἑτοῖμα ἂν βλάψαι. κρατοῦντές
τε τῶν ἐχθρῶν ἐπὶ πλεῖστον ἐξέρχονται καὶ
6 νικώμενοι ἐπ' ἐλάχιστον ἀναπίπτουσιν. ἔτι δὲ
τοῖς μὲν σώμασιν ἀλλοτριωτάτοις ὑπὲρ τῆς
πόλεως χρῶνται, τῇ δὲ γνώμῃ οἰκειοτάτῃ ἐς τὸ
7 πράσσειν τι ὑπὲρ αὐτῆς· καὶ ἃ μὲν ἂν ἐπινοή-
σαντες μὴ ἐπεξέλθωσιν, οἰκείων στέρεσθαι ἡγοῦνται, ἃ δ' ἂν ἐπελθόντες κτήσωνται, ὀλίγα πρὸς
τὰ μέλλοντα τυχεῖν πράξαντες, ἢν δ' ἄρα του καὶ
πείρᾳ σφαλῶσιν, ἀντελπίσαντες ἄλλα ἐπλήρωσαν
τὴν χρείαν· μόνοι γὰρ ἔχουσί τε ὁμοίως καὶ
ἐλπίζουσιν ἃ ἂν ἐπινοήσωσι διὰ τὸ ταχεῖαν τὴν
8 ἐπιχείρησιν ποιεῖσθαι ὧν ἂν γνῶσιν. καὶ ταῦτα
μετὰ πόνων πάντα καὶ κινδύνων δι' ὅλου τοῦ
αἰῶνος μοχθοῦσι, καὶ ἀπολαύουσιν ἐλάχιστα τῶν
ὑπαρχόντων διὰ τὸ αἰεὶ κτᾶσθαι καὶ μήτε ἑορτὴν
ἄλλο τι ἡγεῖσθαι ἢ τὸ τὰ δέοντα πρᾶξαι ξυμ-
φοράν τε οὐχ ἧσσον ἡσυχίαν ἀπράγμονα ἢ

Again, they are bold beyond their strength, venturesome beyond their better judgment, and sanguine in the face of dangers; while your way is to do less than your strength warrants, to distrust even what your judgment is sure of, and when dangers come to despair of deliverance. Nay more, they are prompt in decision, while you are dilatory; they stir abroad, while you are perfect stay-at-homes; for they expect by absence from home to gain something, while you are afraid that, if you go out after something, you may imperil even what you have. If victorious over their enemies, they pursue their advantage to the utmost; if beaten, they fall back as little as possible. Moreover, they use their bodies in the service of their country as though they were the bodies of quite other men, but their minds as though they were wholly their own, so as to accomplish anything on her behalf. And whenever they have conceived a plan but fail to carry it to fulfilment, they think themselves robbed of a possession of their own; and whenever they go after a thing and obtain it, they consider that they have accomplished but little in comparison with what the future has in store for them; but if it so happens that they try a thing and fail, they form new hopes instead and thus make up the loss. For with them alone is it the same thing to hope for and to attain when once they conceive a plan, for the reason that they swiftly undertake whatever they determine upon. In this way they toil, with hardships and dangers, all their life long; and least of all men they enjoy what they have because they are always seeking more, because they think their only holiday is to do their duty, and because they regard untroubled peace as a far

9 ἀσχολίαν ἐπίπονον· ὥστε εἴ τις αὐτοὺς ξυνελὼν φαίη πεφυκέναι ἐπὶ τῷ μήτε αὐτοὺς ἔχειν ἡσυχίαν μήτε τοὺς ἄλλους ἀνθρώπους ἐᾶν, ὀρθῶς ἂν εἴποι.

LXXI. "Ταύτης μέντοι τοιαύτης ἀντικαθεστηκυίας πόλεως, ὦ Λακεδαιμόνιοι, διαμέλλετε καὶ οἴεσθε τὴν ἡσυχίαν οὐ τούτοις τῶν ἀνθρώπων ἐπὶ πλεῖστον ἀρκεῖν, οἳ ἂν τῇ μὲν παρασκευῇ δίκαια πράσσωσι, τῇ δὲ γνώμῃ, ἢν ἀδικῶνται, δῆλοι ὦσι μὴ ἐπιτρέψοντες, ἀλλ' ἐπὶ τῷ μὴ λυπεῖν τε τοὺς ἄλλους καὶ αὐτοὶ ἀμυνόμενοι μὴ βλάπτεσθαι
2 τὸ ἴσον νέμετε. μόλις δ' ἂν πόλει ὁμοίᾳ παροικοῦντες ἐτυγχάνετε τούτου· νῦν δ', ὅπερ καὶ ἄρτι ἐδηλώσαμεν, ἀρχαιότροπα ὑμῶν τὰ ἐπιτηδεύματα
3 πρὸς αὐτούς ἐστιν. ἀνάγκη δὲ ὥσπερ τέχνης αἰεὶ τὰ ἐπιγιγνόμενα κρατεῖν· καὶ ἡσυχαζούσῃ μὲν πόλει τὰ ἀκίνητα νόμιμα ἄριστα, πρὸς πολλὰ δὲ ἀναγκαζομένοις ἰέναι πολλῆς καὶ τῆς ἐπιτεχνήσεως δεῖ. δι' ὅπερ καὶ τὰ τῶν Ἀθηναίων ἀπὸ τῆς πολυπειρίας ἐπὶ πλέον ὑμῶν κεκαίνωται.

4 "Μέχρι μὲν οὖν τοῦδε ὡρίσθω ὑμῶν ἡ βραδυτής· νῦν δὲ τοῖς τε ἄλλοις καὶ Ποτειδεάταις, ὥσπερ ὑπεδέξασθε, βοηθήσατε κατὰ τάχος ἐσβαλόντες ἐς τὴν Ἀττικήν, ἵνα μὴ ἄνδρας τε φίλους καὶ ξυγγενεῖς τοῖς ἐχθίστοις πρόησθε καὶ ἡμᾶς τοὺς ἄλλους ἀθυμίᾳ πρὸς ἑτέραν τινὰ ξυμμαχίαν

---

[1] *i.e.* you attempt to be fair on the principle that it is wise not to offend others and so run the risk of injury which may

greater calamity than laborious activity. Therefore if a man should sum up and say that they were born neither to have peace themselves nor to let other men have it, he would simply speak the truth.

LXXI. "And yet, although you have such a state ranged against you, O Lacedaemonians, you go on delaying and forget that a peaceful policy suffices long only for those who, while they employ their military strength only for just ends, yet by their spirit show plainly that they will not put up with it if they are treated with injustice; whereas you practise fair dealing on the principle of neither giving offence to others nor exposing yourselves to injury in self-defence.[1] But it would be difficult to carry out such a policy successfully if you had as neighbour a state just like yourselves; whereas now, as we have just shown, your practices are old-fashioned as compared with theirs. But in politics, as in the arts, the new must always prevail over the old. It is true that when a state is at peace the established practices are best left unmodified, but when men are compelled to enter into many undertakings there is need of much improvement in method. It is for this reason that the government of the Athenians, because they have undertaken many things, has undergone greater change than yours.

"Here, then, let your dilatoriness end; at this moment succour both the Potidaeans and the rest of your allies, as you promised to do, by invading Attica without delay, that you may not betray your friends and kinsmen to their bitterest enemies, and drive the rest of us in despair to seek some other

arise in defending yourselves against the attacks you have provoked.

5 τρέψητε. δρῶμεν δ' ἂν ἄδικον οὐδὲν οὔτε πρὸς
θεῶν τῶν ὁρκίων οὔτε πρὸς ἀνθρώπων τῶν αἰσθα-
νομένων· λύουσι γὰρ σπονδὰς οὐχ οἱ δι' ἐρημίαν
ἄλλοις προσιόντες, ἀλλ' οἱ μὴ βοηθοῦντες οἷς ἂν
6 ξυνομόσωσιν. βουλομένων δὲ ὑμῶν προθύμων
εἶναι μενοῦμεν· οὔτε γὰρ ὅσια ἂν ποιοῖμεν μετα-
βαλλόμενοι οὔτε ξυνηθεστέρους ἂν ἄλλους εὕροι-
7 μεν. πρὸς τάδε βουλεύεσθε εὖ καὶ τὴν Πελοπόννησον πειρᾶσθε μὴ ἐλάσσω ἐξηγεῖσθαι ἢ οἱ
πατέρες ὑμῖν παρέδοσαν."

LXXII. Τοιαῦτα μὲν οἱ Κορίνθιοι εἶπον. τῶν
δὲ Ἀθηναίων ἔτυχε γὰρ πρεσβεία πρότερον ἐν
τῇ Λακεδαίμονι περὶ ἄλλων παροῦσα, καὶ ὡς
ᾔσθοντο τῶν λόγων, ἔδοξεν αὐτοῖς παριτητέα ἐς
τοὺς Λακεδαιμονίους εἶναι, τῶν μὲν ἐγκλημάτων
πέρι μηδὲν ἀπολογησομένους, ὧν αἱ πόλεις ἐνε-
κάλουν, δηλῶσαι δὲ περὶ τοῦ παντὸς ὡς οὐ ταχέως
αὐτοῖς βουλευτέον εἴη, ἀλλ' ἐν πλέονι σκεπτέον.
καὶ ἅμα τὴν σφετέραν πόλιν ἐβούλοντο σημῆναι
ὅση εἴη δύναμιν, καὶ ὑπόμνησιν ποιήσασθαι τοῖς
τε πρεσβυτέροις ὧν ᾔδεσαν καὶ τοῖς νεωτέροις
ἐξήγησιν ὧν ἄπειροι ἦσαν, νομίζοντες μᾶλλον ἂν
αὐτοὺς ἐκ τῶν λόγων πρὸς τὸ ἡσυχάζειν τραπέ-
2 σθαι ἢ πρὸς τὸ πολεμεῖν. προσελθόντες οὖν τοῖς
Λακεδαιμονίοις ἔφασαν βούλεσθαι καὶ αὐτοὶ ἐς
τὸ πλῆθος αὐτῶν εἰπεῖν, εἴ τι μὴ ἀποκωλύοι. οἱ
δὲ ἐκέλευόν τε παριέναι, καὶ παρελθόντες οἱ
Ἀθηναῖοι ἔλεγον τοιάδε.

alliance. If we took such a course we should be committing no wrong either in the sight of the gods we have sworn by or of men of understanding; for treaties are broken not by those who when left unsupported join others, but by those who fail to succour allies they have sworn to aid. But if you mean to be zealous allies we will stay; for in that case we should be guilty of impiety if we changed our friends, nor should we find others more congenial. In view of these things, be well advised, and make it your endeavour that the Peloponnesian league shall be no weaker under your leadership than when you inherited it from your fathers."

LXXII. Thus spoke the Corinthians. But there happened to be present at Lacedaemon an embassy of the Athenians that had come on other business, and when they heard the various speeches they deemed it advisable to appear before the Lacedaemonians, not indeed to make any defence on the charges brought by the cities, but to make clear with regard to the whole question at issue that the Lacedaemonians should not decide it hastily but should take more time to consider it. At the same time they wished to show how great was the power of their own city, reminding the older men of what they already knew, and recounting to the younger things of which they were ignorant, in the belief that under the influence of their arguments the Lacedaemonians would be inclined to peace rather than war. Accordingly they approached the Lacedaemonians and said that they also wished, if there was nothing to hinder, to address their assembly. The Lacedaemonians invited them to present themselves, and the Athenians came forward and spoke as follows:

LXXIII. "Ἡ μὲν πρέσβευσις ἡμῶν οὐκ ἐς ἀντιλογίαν τοῖς ὑμετέροις ξυμμάχοις ἐγένετο, ἀλλὰ περὶ ὧν ἡ πόλις ἔπεμψεν· αἰσθανόμενοι δὲ καταβοὴν οὐκ ὀλίγην οὖσαν ἡμῶν παρήλθομεν, οὐ τοῖς ἐγκλήμασι τῶν πόλεων ἀντεροῦντες (οὐ γὰρ παρὰ δικασταῖς ὑμῖν οὔτε ἡμῶν οὔτε τούτων οἱ λόγοι ἂν γίγνοιντο), ἀλλ' ὅπως μὴ ῥᾳδίως περὶ μεγάλων πραγμάτων τοῖς ξυμμάχοις πειθόμενοι χεῖρον βουλεύσησθε, καὶ ἅμα βουλόμενοι περὶ τοῦ παντὸς λόγου τοῦ ἐς ἡμᾶς καθεστῶτος δηλῶσαι ὡς οὔτε ἀπεικότως ἔχομεν ἃ κεκτήμεθα, ἥ τε πόλις ἡμῶν ἀξία λόγου ἐστίν.

2 "Καὶ τὰ μὲν πάνυ παλαιὰ τί δεῖ λέγειν, ὧν ἀκοαὶ μᾶλλον λόγων μάρτυρες ἢ ὄψις τῶν ἀκουσομένων; τὰ δὲ Μηδικὰ καὶ ὅσα αὐτοὶ ξύνιστε, εἰ καὶ δι' ὄχλου μᾶλλον ἔσται αἰεὶ προβαλλομένοις, ἀνάγκη λέγειν. καὶ γὰρ ὅτε ἐδρῶμεν, ἐπ' ὠφελίᾳ ἐκινδυνεύετο, ἧς τοῦ μὲν ἔργου μέρος μετέσχετε, τοῦ δὲ λόγου μὴ παντός, εἴ τι ὠφελεῖ,[1]
3 στερισκώμεθα. ῥηθήσεται δὲ οὐ παραιτήσεως μᾶλλον ἕνεκα ἢ μαρτυρίου καὶ δηλώσεως πρὸς οἵαν ὑμῖν πόλιν μὴ εὖ βουλευομένοις ὁ ἀγὼν καταστήσεται.

4 "Φαμὲν γὰρ Μαραθῶνί τε μόνοι προκινδυνεῦσαι τῷ βαρβάρῳ καὶ ὅτε τὸ ὕστερον ἦλθεν,

[1] ὠφέλει E.

LXXIII. "Our embassy did not come here to enter into a dispute with your allies, but on the business for which our city sent us. Perceiving, however, that no small outcry is being made against us, we have come forward, not to answer the charges of the cities (for it can hardly be that either they or we are addressing you as judges), but in order that you may not, yielding to the persuasion of your allies, lightly make a wrong decision about matters of great importance. And at the same time we wish, as regards the whole outcry that has been raised against us, to show that we are rightfully in possession of what we have acquired, and that our city is not to be despised.

"Now, what need is there to speak about matters quite remote,[1] whose only witnesses are the stories men hear rather than the eyes of those who will hear them told? But concerning the Persian War and all the other events of which you have personal knowledge, we needs must speak, even though it will be rather irksome to mention them, since they are always being paraded. For when we were performing those deeds the risk was taken for a common benefit, and since you got a share of the actual results of that benefit, we should not be wholly deprived of the credit, if there is any benefit in that. And our aim in the recital of the facts will be, not so much to deprecate censure, as to show by evidence with what sort of city you will be involved in war if you are not well advised.

"For we affirm that at Marathon we alone bore the first brunt of the Barbarian's attack, and that

[1] The Schol. remarks τὰ κατὰ Ἀμαζόνας καὶ Θρᾷκας καὶ Ἡρακλείδας, favourite themes in eulogies, panegyric speeches, etc.

οὐχ ἱκανοὶ ὄντες κατὰ γῆν ἀμύνεσθαι, ἐσβάντες ἐς τὰς ναῦς πανδημεὶ ἐν Σαλαμῖνι ξυνναυμαχῆσαι, ὅπερ ἔσχε μὴ κατὰ πόλεις αὐτὸν ἐπιπλέοντα τὴν Πελοπόννησον πορθεῖν, ἀδυνάτων ἂν ὄντων πρὸς ναῦς πολλὰς ἀλλήλοις ἐπιβοηθεῖν. τεκμήριον δὲ μέγιστον αὐτὸς ἐποίησεν· νικηθεὶς γὰρ ταῖς ναυσὶν ὡς οὐκέτι αὐτῷ ὁμοίας οὔσης τῆς δυνάμεως κατὰ τάχος τῷ πλέονι τοῦ στρατοῦ ἀνεχώρησεν.

LXXIV. "Τοιούτου μέντοι τούτου ξυμβάντος καὶ σαφῶς δηλωθέντος ὅτι ἐν ταῖς ναυσὶ τῶν Ἑλλήνων τὰ πράγματα ἐγένετο, τρία τὰ ὠφελιμώτατα ἐς αὐτὸ παρεσχόμεθα, ἀριθμόν τε νεῶν πλεῖστον καὶ ἄνδρα στρατηγὸν ξυνετώτατον καὶ προθυμίαν ἀοκνοτάτην· ναῦς μέν γε ἐς τὰς τετρακοσίας ὀλίγῳ ἐλάσσους τῶν δύο μοιρῶν, Θεμιστοκλέα δὲ ἄρχοντα, ὃς αἰτιώτατος ἐν τῷ στενῷ ναυμαχῆσαι ἐγένετο, ὅπερ σαφέστατα ἔσωσε τὰ πράγματα, καὶ αὐτὸν διὰ τοῦτο ὑμεῖς ἐτιμήσατε μάλιστα δὴ ἄνδρα ξένον τῶν ὡς ὑμᾶς
2 ἐλθόντων· προθυμίαν δὲ καὶ πολὺ τολμηροτάτην ἐδείξαμεν, οἵ γε, ἐπειδὴ ἡμῖν κατὰ γῆν οὐδεὶς ἐβοήθει, τῶν ἄλλων ἤδη μέχρι ἡμῶν δουλευόντων, ἠξιώσαμεν ἐκλιπόντες τὴν πόλιν καὶ τὰ οἰκεῖα διαφθείραντες μηδ᾽ ὣς τὸ τῶν περιλοίπων ξυμμάχων κοινὸν προλιπεῖν μηδὲ σκεδασθέντες ἀχρεῖοι αὐτοῖς γενέσθαι, ἀλλ᾽ ἐσβάντες ἐς τὰς ναῦς κινδυνεῦσαι καὶ μὴ ὀργισθῆναι ὅτι ἡμῖν οὐ

---

¹ Probably a round number for 378 given by Hdt. VIII. xlviii., of which the Athenian contingent (200, *i.e.* 180 + 20 lent to the Chalcidians, Hdt. VIII. i.) could be spoken of as

when he came again, not being able to defend ourselves by land, we embarked in a body on our ships and joined in the sea-fight at Salamis. This prevented his sailing against you city by city and ravaging the Peloponnesus, for you would have been unable to aid one another against a fleet so numerous. And the weightiest testimony to the truth of what we say was afforded by the enemy himself; for when his fleet was defeated, as if aware that his power was no longer a match for that of the Hellenes, he hastily withdrew with the greater part of his army.

LXXIV. "Such, then, was the issue of that battle, and clear proof was given thereby that the salvation of the Hellenes depended upon their ships. To that issue we contributed the three most serviceable elements, namely, the largest number of ships, the shrewdest general, and the most unfaltering zeal. Of the four hundred[1] ships our quota was a little less than two-thirds. The commander was Themistocles, who more than any other was responsible for our fighting the battle in the strait, which most surely was our salvation; and on this account you yourselves honoured him above any stranger who ever visited you.[2] And the zeal we displayed was that of utmost daring, for when there was no one to help us on land, since all the rest up to our very borders were already slaves, we resolved to abandon our city and sacrifice all our possessions; yet not even in that extremity to desert the common cause of the allies who remained, or by dispersing to render ourselves useless to them, but to embark on our ships and fight, and not to be angry because you failed to

πλείους τῶν ἡμισέων or with slight exaggeration as ὀλίγῳ ἐλάσσους τῶν δύο μοιρῶν.

[2] See Hdt. VIII. cxxiv.; Plut. *Them.* xvii. 3.

3 προυτιμωρήσατε. ὥστε φαμὲν οὐχ ἧσσον αὐτοὶ
ὠφελῆσαι ὑμᾶς ἢ τυχεῖν τούτου. ὑμεῖς μὲν γὰρ
ἀπό τε οἰκουμένων τῶν πόλεων καὶ ἐπὶ τῷ τὸ
λοιπὸν νέμεσθαι, ἐπειδὴ ἐδείσατε ὑπὲρ ὑμῶν καὶ
οὐχ ἡμῶν τὸ πλέον, ἐβοηθήσατε (ὅτε γοῦν ἦμεν
ἔτι σῷ, οὐ παρεγένεσθε), ἡμεῖς δὲ ἀπό τε τῆς οὐκ
οὔσης ἔτι ὁρμώμενοι καὶ ὑπὲρ τῆς ἐν βραχείᾳ
ἐλπίδι οὔσης κινδυνεύοντες ξυνεσώσαμεν ὑμᾶς τε
4 τὸ μέρος καὶ ἡμᾶς αὐτούς. εἰ δὲ προσεχωρήσαμεν
πρότερον τῷ Μήδῳ δείσαντες, ὥσπερ καὶ ἄλλοι,
περὶ τῇ χώρᾳ, ἢ μὴ ἐτολμήσαμεν ὕστερον ἐσβῆναι
ἐς τὰς ναῦς ὡς διεφθαρμένοι, οὐδὲν ἂν ἔδει ἔτι
ὑμᾶς[1] μὴ ἔχοντας ναῦς ἱκανὰς ναυμαχεῖν, ἀλλὰ
καθ' ἡσυχίαν ἂν αὐτῷ προυχώρησε τὰ πράγματα
ᾗ ἐβούλετο.

LXXV. "Ἀρ' ἄξιοί ἐσμεν, ὦ Λακεδαιμόνιοι, καὶ προθυμίας ἕνεκα τῆς τότε καὶ γνώμης ξυνέσεως ἀρχῆς γε ἧς ἔχομεν τοῖς Ἕλλησι μὴ οὕτως
2 ἄγαν ἐπιφθόνως διακεῖσθαι; καὶ γὰρ αὐτὴν τήνδε
ἐλάβομεν οὐ βιασάμενοι, ἀλλ' ὑμῶν μὲν οὐκ
ἐθελησάντων παραμεῖναι πρὸς τὰ ὑπόλοιπα τοῦ
βαρβάρου, ἡμῖν δὲ προσελθόντων τῶν ξυμμάχων
3 καὶ αὐτῶν δεηθέντων ἡγεμόνας καταστῆναι. ἐξ
αὐτοῦ δὲ τοῦ ἔργου κατηναγκάσθημεν τὸ πρῶτον

[1] ὑμᾶς: Hude inserts πρὸς before ὑμᾶς.

---

[1] *cf.* the taunt of Adimantus (Hdt. VIII. lvii. 7), περὶ οὐδεμιῆς ἔτι πατρίδος ναυμαχήσεις, "You will fight for a country that is no more," and the famous answer of Themistocles

help us earlier. We therefore maintain that we on our part conferred upon you a benefit at least as great as we received; for whereas the population of the cities from which you brought aid was still undisturbed and you could hope to possess them in the future, and your motive was fear for yourselves rather than for us—at any rate you did not come near so long as we were still unharmed—we on our part, setting forth from a city that was no more,[1] and risking our lives in behalf of one whose future hung upon but a slender hope, bore our part in saving both you and ourselves. But if we had acted as others did, and through fear of losing our territory had gone over to the Persians earlier in the war, or afterwards had lacked the courage to embark on our ships, in the conviction that we were already ruined, it would from that moment have been useless for you, with your inadequate fleet, to fight at sea, but the Persian's plans would have moved on quietly just as he wished.

LXXV. "Considering, then, Lacedaemonians, the zeal and sagacity of judgment which we displayed at that time, do we deserve to be regarded with this excessive jealousy by the Hellenes just on account of the empire we possess? And indeed we did not acquire this empire by force, but only after you had refused to continue to oppose what was left of the barbarian forces, and the allies came to us and of their own accord asked us to assume the leadership. It was under the compulsion of circumstances that

(Hdt. VIII. lxi. 8), *ὡς εἴη καὶ πόλις καὶ γῆ μέζων ἤπερ κείνοισι ἔστ' ἂν διηκόσιαι νέες σφι ἔωσι πεπληρωμέναι*, "We have a city and a country greater than yours as long as we have two hundred ships fully manned."

προαγαγεῖν αὐτὴν ἐς τόδε, μάλιστα μὲν ὑπὸ
δέους, ἔπειτα καὶ τιμῆς, ὕστερον καὶ ὠφελίας,
4 καὶ οὐκ ἀσφαλὲς ἔτι ἐδόκει εἶναι, τοῖς πολλοῖς
ἀπηχθημένους καί τινων καὶ ἤδη ἀποστάντων
κατεστραμμένων, ὑμῶν τε ἡμῖν οὐκέτι ὁμοίως
φίλων, ἀλλ' ὑπόπτων καὶ διαφόρων ὄντων, ἀνέν-
τας κινδυνεύειν (καὶ γὰρ ἂν αἱ ἀποστάσεις πρὸς
5 ὑμᾶς ἐγίγνοντο)· πᾶσι δὲ ἀνεπίφθονον τὰ ξυμφέροντα τῶν μεγίστων περὶ κινδύνων εὖ τίθεσθαι.

LXXVI. "Ὑμεῖς γοῦν, ὦ Λακεδαιμόνιοι, τὰς
ἐν τῇ Πελοποννήσῳ πόλεις ἐπὶ τὸ ὑμῖν ὠφέλιμον
καταστησάμενοι ἐξηγεῖσθε· καὶ εἰ τότε ὑπομείναντες διὰ παντὸς ἀπήχθεσθε ἐν τῇ ἡγεμονίᾳ,
ὥσπερ ἡμεῖς, εὖ ἴσμεν μὴ ἂν ἧσσον ὑμᾶς λυπη-
ροὺς γενομένους τοῖς ξυμμάχοις καὶ ἀναγκασθέν-
τας ἂν ἢ ἄρχειν ἐγκρατῶς ἢ αὐτοὺς κινδυνεύειν.
2 οὕτως οὐδ' ἡμεῖς θαυμαστὸν οὐδὲν πεποιήκαμεν
οὐδ' ἀπὸ τοῦ ἀνθρωπείου τρόπου, εἰ ἀρχήν τε
διδομένην ἐδεξάμεθα καὶ ταύτην μὴ ἀνεῖμεν
ὑπὸ[1] τῶν μεγίστων νικηθέντες, τιμῆς καὶ δέους
καὶ ὠφελίας, οὐδ' αὖ πρῶτοι τοῦ τοιούτου ὑπάρ-
ξαντες, ἀλλ' αἰεὶ καθεστῶτος τὸν ἥσσω ὑπὸ τοῦ
δυνατωτέρου κατείργεσθαι, ἄξιοί τε ἅμα νομίζοντες εἶναι καὶ ὑμῖν δοκοῦντες, μέχρι οὗ τὰ
ξυμφέροντα λογιζόμενοι τῷ δικαίῳ λόγῳ νῦν

[1] Hude inserts τριῶν before τῶν μεγίστων, with van Herwerden and Weil.

we were driven at first to advance our empire to its present state, influenced chiefly by fear, then by honour also, and lastly by self-interest as well; and after we had once incurred the hatred of most of our allies, and several of them had already revolted and been reduced to subjection, and when you were no longer friendly as before but suspicious and at variance with us, it no longer seemed safe to risk relaxing our hold. For all seceders would have gone over to you. And no man is to be blamed for making the most of his advantages when it is a question of the gravest dangers.

LXXVI. "At any rate you, Lacedaemonians, in the exercise of your leadership over the Peloponnesian states regulate their polities[1] according to your own advantage; and if in the Persian war you had held out to the end in the hegemony and had become unpopular in its exercise, as we did, you would certainly have become not less obnoxious to the allies than we are, and would have been compelled either to rule them with a strong hand or yourselves to risk losing the hegemony. Thus there is nothing remarkable or inconsistent with human nature in what we also have done, just because we accepted an empire when it was offered us, and then, yielding to the strongest motives—honour, fear, and self-interest—declined to give it up. Nor, again, are we the first who have entered upon such a course, but it has ever been an established rule that the weaker is kept down by the stronger. And at the same time we thought we were worthy to rule, and used to be so regarded by you also, until you fell to calculating what your interests were and resorted

[1] *i.e.* by setting up oligarchies in them, *cf.* ch. xix.

χρῆσθε, ὃν οὐδείς πω παρατυχὸν ἰσχύι τι κτήσασθαι προθεὶς τοῦ μὴ πλέον ἔχειν ἀπετράπετο.
3 ἐπαινεῖσθαί τε ἄξιοι, οἵτινες χρησάμενοι τῇ
ἀνθρωπείᾳ φύσει ὥστε ἑτέρων ἄρχειν δικαιό-
τεροι ἢ κατὰ τὴν ὑπάρχουσαν δύναμιν γένωνται.
4 ἄλλους γ' ἂν οὖν οἰόμεθα τὰ ἡμέτερα λαβόντας
δεῖξαι ἂν μάλιστα εἴ τι μετριάζομεν, ἡμῖν δὲ καὶ
ἐκ τοῦ ἐπιεικοῦς ἀδοξία τὸ πλέον ἢ ἔπαινος οὐκ
εἰκότως περιέστη.

LXXVII. "Καὶ ἐλασσούμενοι γὰρ ἐν ταῖς
ξυμβολαίαις πρὸς τοὺς ξυμμάχους δίκαις καὶ
παρ' ἡμῖν αὐτοῖς ἐν τοῖς ὁμοίοις νόμοις ποιήσαντες
2 τὰς κρίσεις φιλοδικεῖν δοκοῦμεν. καὶ οὐδεὶς
σκοπεῖ αὐτῶν, τοῖς καὶ ἄλλοθί που ἔχουσιν ἀρχὴν
καὶ ἧσσον ἡμῶν πρὸς τοὺς ὑπηκόους μετρίοις
οὖσι δι' ὅ τι τοῦτο οὐκ ὀνειδίζεται· βιάζεσθαι
γὰρ οἷς ἂν ἐξῇ, δικάζεσθαι οὐδὲν προσδέονται.
3 οἱ δὲ εἰθισμένοι πρὸς ἡμᾶς ἀπὸ τοῦ ἴσου ὁμιλεῖν,
ἤν τι παρὰ τὸ μὴ οἴεσθαι χρῆναι ἢ γνώμῃ ἢ
δυνάμει τῇ διὰ τὴν ἀρχὴν καὶ ὁπωσοῦν ἐλασσω-
θῶσιν, οὐ τοῦ πλέονος μὴ στερισκόμενοι χάριν
ἔχουσιν, ἀλλὰ τοῦ ἐνδεοῦς χαλεπώτερον φέρουσιν
ἢ εἰ ἀπὸ πρώτης ἀποθέμενοι τὸν νόμον φανερῶς

---

[1] These seem to have been disputes in matters of trade tried before federal courts elsewhere than in Athens; whereas *τὰς κρίσεις* refers to compulsory jurisdiction which Athens enforced upon her allies in her own courts.

as you do now, to the plea of justice—which no one, when opportunity offered of securing something by main strength, ever yet put before force and abstained from taking advantage. And they are to be commended who, yielding to the instinct of human nature to rule over others, have been more observant of justice than they might have been, considering their power. At least, if others should seize our power, they would, we think, exhibit the best proof that we show some moderation; but in our case the result of our very reasonableness is, perversely enough, obloquy rather than commendation.

LXXVII. "For although we are at a disadvantage in suits[1] with our allies arising out of commercial agreements, and although in our own courts in Athens, where we have established tribunals, the same laws apply to us as to them, we are thought to insist too much upon our legal rights. And none of our allies observes why it is that those who hold dominion elsewhere, and are less moderate than we are toward their subjects, are not reproached on this account. It is because those who may use might have no need to appeal to right. But if ever our allies, accustomed as they are to associate with us on the basis of equality, come off second best in any matter, however trivial, contrary to their own notion that it ought to be otherwise, whether their discomfiture is due to a legal decision or to the exercise of our imperial power, instead of being grateful that they have not been deprived of what is of greater moment,[2] they are more deeply offended because of their trifling inequality than if we had from the first put aside all legal restraints

[2] Namely, their equality before the law.

ἐπλεονεκτοῦμεν. ἐκείνως δὲ οὐδ' ἂν αὐτοὶ ἀντέλεγον ὡς οὐ χρεὼν τὸν ἥσσω τῷ κρατοῦντι
4 ὑποχωρεῖν. ἀδικούμενοί τε, ὡς ἔοικεν, οἱ ἄνθρωποι μᾶλλον ὀργίζονται ἢ βιαζόμενοι· τὸ μὲν γὰρ
ἀπὸ τοῦ ἴσου δοκεῖ πλεονεκτεῖσθαι, τὸ δ' ἀπὸ
5 τοῦ κρείσσονος καταναγκάζεσθαι. ὑπὸ γοῦν τοῦ
Μήδου δεινότερα τούτων πάσχοντες ἠνείχοντο,
ἡ δὲ ἡμετέρα ἀρχὴ χαλεπὴ δοκεῖ εἶναι, εἰκότως·
6 τὸ παρὸν γὰρ αἰεὶ βαρὺ τοῖς ὑπηκόοις. ὑμεῖς γ'
ἂν οὖν εἰ καθελόντες ἡμᾶς ἄρξαιτε, τάχα ἂν τὴν
εὔνοιαν ἣν διὰ τὸ ἡμέτερον δέος εἰλήφατε μετα-
βάλοιτε, εἴπερ οἷα καὶ τότε πρὸς τὸν Μῆδον δι'
ὀλίγου ἡγησάμενοι ὑπεδείξατε, ὁμοῖα καὶ νῦν
γνώσεσθε. ἄμεικτα γὰρ τά τε καθ' ὑμᾶς αὐτοὺς
νόμιμα τοῖς ἄλλοις ἔχετε καὶ προσέτι εἷς ἕκαστος
ἐξιὼν οὔτε τούτοις χρῆται οὔθ' οἷς ἡ ἄλλη Ἑλλὰς
νομίζει.

LXXVIII. "Βουλεύεσθε οὖν βραδέως ὡς οὐ
περὶ βραχέων, καὶ μὴ ἀλλοτρίαις γνώμαις καὶ
ἐγκλήμασι πεισθέντες οἰκεῖον πόνον πρόσθησθε.
τοῦ δὲ πολέμου τὸν παράλογον ὅσος ἐστί, πρὶν
2 ἐν αὐτῷ γενέσθαι προδιάγνωτε· μηκυνόμενος γὰρ
φιλεῖ ἐς τύχας τὰ πολλὰ περιίστασθαι, ὧν ἴσου
τε ἀπέχομεν καὶ ὁποτέρως ἔσται ἐν ἀδήλῳ κιν-
3 δυνεύεται. ἰόντες τε οἱ ἄνθρωποι ἐς τοὺς πολέμους τῶν ἔργων πρότερον ἔχονται, ἃ χρῆν ὕστερον

and had openly sought our own advantage. In that case even they would not be setting up the claim that the weaker should not have to yield to the stronger. Men, it seems, are more resentful of injustice than of violence; for the former, they feel, is overreaching by an equal, whereas the latter is coercion by a superior. At any rate, they submitted to more grievous wrongs than these at the hands of the Persians, while our rule is hard to bear, as they think; and no wonder, for the present yoke is always heavy to subjects. Certainly you, should you overthrow us and obtain supremacy, would soon lose the good will which you have gained through fear of us—if indeed you mean again to show such temper as you gave a glimpse of at that time when for a little while you had the hegemony against the Persian.[1] For the institutions that prevail among you at home are incompatible with those of other peoples, and, besides, each one of you when he goes abroad uses neither these nor those which the rest of Greece is accustomed to.

LXXVIII. "Be slow, then, in your deliberations, for no slight matters are at stake; and do not, influenced by the opinions and accusations of others, burden yourselves needlessly with trouble of your own. Realise before you get into it how great are the chances of miscalculation in war. For when it is long drawn out, it is wont generally to resolve itself into a mere matter of chance; and over chance both sides equally have no control, and what the outcome will be is unknown and precarious. Most men rush into war and proceed to blows first, although that ought to be the last resort, and then,

[1] *e.g.* the conduct of Pausanias described in ch. cxxx.

δρᾶν, κακοπαθοῦντες δὲ ἤδη τῶν λόγων ἅπτονται.
4 ἡμεῖς δὲ ἐν οὐδεμιᾷ πω τοιαύτῃ ἁμαρτίᾳ ὄντες οὔτ' αὐτοὶ οὔθ' ὑμᾶς ὁρῶντες λέγομεν ὑμῖν, ἕως ἔτι αὐθαίρετος ἀμφοτέροις ἡ εὐβουλία, σπονδὰς μὴ λύειν μηδὲ παραβαίνειν τοὺς ὅρκους, τὰ δὲ
5 διάφορα δίκῃ λύεσθαι κατὰ τὴν ξυνθήκην, ἢ θεοὺς τοὺς ὁρκίους μάρτυρας ποιούμενοι πειρασόμεθα ἀμύνεσθαι πολέμου ἄρχοντας ταύτῃ ᾗ ἂν ὑφηγῆσθε."

LXXIX. Τοιαῦτα δὲ οἱ Ἀθηναῖοι εἶπον. ἐπειδὴ δὲ τῶν τε ξυμμάχων ἤκουσαν οἱ Λακεδαιμόνιοι τὰ ἐγκλήματα τὰ ἐς τοὺς Ἀθηναίους καὶ τῶν Ἀθηναίων ἃ ἔλεξαν, μεταστησάμενοι πάντας ἐβουλεύοντο κατὰ σφᾶς αὐτοὺς περὶ τῶν παρόν-
2 των. καὶ τῶν μὲν πλεόνων ἐπὶ τὸ αὐτὸ αἱ γνῶμαι ἔφερον, ἀδικεῖν τε τοὺς Ἀθηναίους ἤδη καὶ πολεμητέα εἶναι ἐν τάχει· παρελθὼν δὲ Ἀρχίδαμος ὁ βασιλεὺς αὐτῶν, ἀνὴρ καὶ ξυνετὸς δοκῶν εἶναι καὶ σώφρων, ἔλεξε τοιάδε.

LXXX. "Καὶ αὐτὸς πολλῶν ἤδη πολέμων ἔμπειρός εἰμι, ὦ Λακεδαιμόνιοι, καὶ ὑμῶν τοὺς ἐν τῇ αὐτῇ ἡλικίᾳ ὁρῶ, ὥστε μήτε ἀπειρίᾳ ἐπιθυμῆσαί τινα τοῦ ἔργου, ὅπερ ἂν οἱ πολλοὶ πάθοιεν,
2 μήτε ἀγαθὸν καὶ ἀσφαλὲς νομίσαντα. εὕροιτε δ' ἂν τόνδε περὶ οὗ νῦν βουλεύεσθε οὐκ ἂν ἐλάχιστον γενόμενον, εἰ σωφρόνως τις αὐτὸν ἐκλογί-
3 ζοιτο. πρὸς μὲν γὰρ Πελοποννησίους καὶ τοὺς

when they are in distress, at length have recourse to words. But since we ourselves are not as yet involved in any such error and see that you are not, we urge you, while wise counsels are still a matter of free choice to both of us, not to violate the treaty or transgress your oaths, but to let our differences be settled by arbitration according to the agreement. But if you refuse, we shall invoke as witnesses the gods by whom our oaths were sworn, and shall endeavour to make reprisals on those who begin the war, following that path in which you have led the way."

LXXIX. Thus the Athenians spoke. And when the Lacedaemonians had heard the charges brought by the allies against the Athenians, and what the latter said in reply, they caused all others to withdraw and deliberated by themselves on the situation before them. And the opinions of the majority tended to the same conclusion, namely, that the Athenians were already guilty of injustice, and that they must go to war without delay. But Archidamus their king, a man reputed to be both sagacious and prudent, came forward and spoke as follows:

LXXX. "I have both myself, Lacedaemonians, had experience in my day of many wars, and I see men among you who are as old as I am; no one of them, therefore, is eager for war through lack of experience, as would be the case with most men, nor because he thinks it a good or a safe thing. And you would find that this war about which you are now deliberating is likely to prove no trifling matter, if one should reflect upon it soberly. For in a contest with the Peloponnesians or the neighbouring states [1]

[1] By the Peloponnesians Thucydides means the Spartan alliance; the neighbouring states would then be the Peloponnesian states not in the alliance, *e.g.* Argos.

ἀστυγείτονας παρόμοιος ἡμῶν ἡ ἀλκή, καὶ διὰ
ταχέων οἷόν τε ἐφ' ἕκαστα ἐλθεῖν· πρὸς δὲ ἄνδρας
οἳ γῆν τε ἑκὰς ἔχουσι καὶ προσέτι θαλάσσης
ἐμπειρότατοί εἰσι καὶ τοῖς ἄλλοις ἅπασιν ἄριστα
ἐξήρτυνται, πλούτῳ τε ἰδίῳ καὶ δημοσίῳ καὶ
ναυσὶ καὶ ἵπποις καὶ ὅπλοις καὶ ὄχλῳ ὅσος οὐκ
ἐν ἄλλῳ ἑνί γε χωρίῳ Ἑλληνικῷ ἐστιν, ἔτι δὲ καὶ
ξυμμάχους πολλοὺς φόρου ὑποτελεῖς ἔχουσι, πῶς
χρὴ πρὸς τούτους ῥᾳδίως πόλεμον ἄρασθαι καὶ
τίνι πιστεύσαντας ἀπαρασκεύους ἐπειχθῆναι;
4 πότερον ταῖς ναυσίν; ἀλλ' ἥσσους ἐσμέν· εἰ δὲ
μελετήσομεν καὶ ἀντιπαρασκευασόμεθα, χρόνος
ἐνέσται. ἀλλὰ τοῖς χρήμασιν; ἀλλὰ πολλῷ
πλέον ἔτι τούτῳ ἐλλείπομεν καὶ οὔτε ἐν κοινῷ
ἔχομεν οὔτε ἑτοίμως ἐκ τῶν ἰδίων φέρομεν.

LXXXI. "Τάχ' ἄν τις θαρσοίη ὅτι τοῖς ὅπλοις αὐτῶν καὶ τῷ πλήθει ὑπερφέρομεν, ὥστε
2 τὴν γῆν δῃοῦν ἐπιφοιτῶντες. τοῖς δὲ ἄλλη γῆ
ἐστι πολλὴ ἧς ἄρχουσι, καὶ ἐκ θαλάσσης ὧν
3 δέονται ἐπάξονται. εἰ δ' αὖ τοὺς ξυμμάχους
ἀφιστάναι πειρασόμεθα, δεήσει καὶ τούτοις ναυσὶ
4 βοηθεῖν τὸ πλέον οὖσι νησιώταις. τίς οὖν ἔσται
ἡμῶν ὁ πόλεμος; εἰ μὴ γὰρ ἢ ναυσὶ κρατήσομεν
ἢ τὰς προσόδους ἀφαιρήσομεν ἀφ' ὧν τὸ ναυτικὸν
5 τρέφουσι, βλαψόμεθα τὰ πλείω. κἂν τούτῳ
οὐδὲ καταλύεσθαι ἔτι καλόν, ἄλλως τε καὶ εἰ

---

[1] *i.e.* it is military rather than naval; similar, too, in the matter of wealth, equipment, absence of foreign resources, tributary allies, etc.

our power is of the same type with theirs[1] and we can be upon them quickly at every point; but when opposed to men whose territory is far away, who besides are beyond all others experienced in seamanship and are best equipped in all other respects, with wealth both private and public, ships, horses, arms and a larger population than is to be found in any other single district in Hellas, who have, moreover, numerous allies subject to tribute—against such men why should we lightly take up arms? In what do we place our trust that we should attack them unprepared? In our ships? But there we are inferior; and if we train and make ourselves ready to encounter them, that will take time. In our wealth then? But in that respect we are still more deficient, neither having money in the treasury of the state nor finding it easy to raise money from our private resources by taxation.[2]

LXXXI. "Perhaps some of us are emboldened by our superiority in arms and numbers, which enables us freely to invade and lay waste their territory. But there is other territory in plenty over which they hold sway, and they will import by sea whatever they need. And if, on the other hand, we try to induce their allies to revolt, we shall have in addition to protect them with a fleet, since they are chiefly islanders. What then will be the character of the war we shall be waging? Unless we can either win the mastery on the sea or cut off the revenues by which they support their navy, we shall get the worst of it. And, if it comes to that, we can no longer even conclude an honourable peace,

[2] The poverty of the Peloponnesians is referred to by Pericles in ch. cxli. 3. The statement is true especially of the Spartans, but also of all the rest except the Corinthians.

6 δόξομεν ἄρξαι μᾶλλον τῆς διαφορᾶς. μὴ γὰρ δὴ ἐκείνῃ γε τῇ ἐλπίδι ἐπαιρώμεθα ὡς ταχὺ παυσθήσεται ὁ πόλεμος, ἢν τὴν γῆν αὐτῶν τέμωμεν. δέδοικα δὲ μᾶλλον μὴ καὶ τοῖς παισὶν αὐτὸν ὑπολίπωμεν· οὕτως εἰκὸς Ἀθηναίους φρονήματι μήτε τῇ γῇ δουλεῦσαι μήτε ὥσπερ ἀπείρους καταπλαγῆναι τῷ πολέμῳ.

LXXXII. "Οὐ μὴν οὐδὲ ἀναισθήτως αὐτοὺς κελεύω τούς τε ξυμμάχους ἡμῶν ἐᾶν βλάπτειν καὶ ἐπιβουλεύοντας μὴ καταφωρᾶν, ἀλλὰ ὅπλα μὲν μήπω κινεῖν, πέμπειν δὲ καὶ αἰτιᾶσθαι μήτε πόλεμον ἄγαν δηλοῦντας μήθ' ὡς ἐπιτρέψομεν, κἂν τούτῳ καὶ τὰ ἡμέτερ' αὐτῶν ἐξαρτύεσθαι ξυμμάχων τε προσαγωγῇ, καὶ Ἑλλήνων καὶ βαρβάρων, εἴ ποθέν τινα ἢ ναυτικοῦ ἢ χρημάτων δύναμιν προσληψόμεθα (ἀνεπίφθονον δέ, ὅσοι ὥσπερ καὶ ἡμεῖς ὑπ' Ἀθηναίων ἐπιβουλευόμεθα, μὴ Ἕλληνας μόνον, ἀλλὰ καὶ βαρβάρους προσλαβόντας διασωθῆναι), καὶ τὰ αὐτῶν ἅμα ἐκπορι-
2 ζώμεθα. καὶ ἢν μὲν ἐσακούωσί τι πρεσβευομένων ἡμῶν, ταῦτα ἄριστα· ἢν δὲ μή, διελθόντων ἐτῶν δύο καὶ τριῶν ἄμεινον ἤδη, ἢν δοκῇ, πεφραγμένοι
3 ἴμεν ἐπ' αὐτούς. καὶ ἴσως ὁρῶντες ἡμῶν ἤδη τήν τε παρασκευὴν καὶ τοὺς λόγους αὐτῇ ὁμοῖα ὑποσημαίνοντας μᾶλλον ἂν εἴκοιεν, καὶ γῆν ἔτι ἄτμητον ἔχοντες καὶ περὶ παρόντων ἀγαθῶν καὶ οὔπω

especially if it is believed that we rather than they began the quarrel. For we assuredly must not be buoyed up by any such hope as that the war will soon be over if we but ravage their territory. I fear rather that we shall even bequeath it to our children, so improbable it is that the Athenians, high spirited as they are, will either make themselves vassals to their land, or, like novices, become panic-stricken at the war.

LXXXII. "Yet assuredly I do not advise you that you should blindly suffer them to injure our allies and allow their plotting to go undetected, but rather that you should adopt the following course: Do not take up arms yet, but send envoys to them and make complaints, without indicating too clearly whether we shall go to war or put up with their conduct; also in the meantime, let us proceed with our own preparations, in the first place by winning allies to our side, Barbarians as well as Hellenes, in the hope of obtaining from some quarter or other additional resources in ships or money (for those who, like ourselves, are plotted against by the Athenians are not to be blamed if they procure their salvation by gaining the aid, not of Hellenes only, but even of Barbarians); and let us at the same time be developing our resources at home. And if they give any heed to our envoys, there could be nothing better; but if not, then, after the lapse of two or three years, we shall at length be better equipped to go against them, if we decide to do so. Or perhaps when they see our preparations, and that our words correspond thereto, they will be more inclined to yield, for they will both have their land still unravaged and their deliberations will concern goods that are still theirs

4 ἐφθαρμενων βουλευόμενοι. μὴ γὰρ ἄλλο τι
νομίσητε τὴν γῆν αὐτῶν ἢ ὅμηρον ἔχειν καὶ οὐχ
ἧσσον ὅσῳ ἄμεινον ἐξείργασται· ἧς φείδεσθαι
χρὴ ὡς ἐπὶ πλεῖστον, καὶ μὴ ἐς ἀπόνοιαν κατα-
5 στήσαντας αὐτοὺς ἀληπτοτέρους ἔχειν. εἰ γὰρ
ἀπαράσκευοι τοῖς τῶν ξυμμάχων ἐγκλήμασιν
ἐπειχθέντες τεμοῦμεν αὐτήν, ὁρᾶτε ὅπως μὴ
αἴσχιον καὶ ἀπορώτερον τῇ Πελοποννήσῳ πράξο-
6 μεν. ἐγκλήματα μὲν γὰρ καὶ πόλεων καὶ
ἰδιωτῶν οἷόν τε καταλῦσαι· πόλεμον δὲ ξύμπαντας ἀραμένους ἕνεκα τῶν ἰδίων, ὃν οὐχ ὑπάρχει
εἰδέναι καθ' ὅ τι χωρήσει, οὐ ῥᾴδιον εὐπρεπῶς
θέσθαι.

LXXXIII. "Καὶ ἀνανδρία μηδενὶ πολλοὺς μιᾷ
2 πόλει μὴ ταχὺ ἐπελθεῖν δοκείτω εἶναι. εἰσὶ γὰρ
καὶ ἐκείνοις οὐκ ἐλάσσους χρήματα φέροντες
ξύμμαχοι, καὶ ἔστιν ὁ πόλεμος οὐχ ὅπλων τὸ
πλέον, ἀλλὰ δαπάνης, δι' ἣν τὰ ὅπλα ὠφελεῖ,
3 ἄλλως τε καὶ ἠπειρώταις πρὸς θαλασσίους. πο-
ρισώμεθα οὖν πρῶτον αὐτήν, καὶ μὴ τοῖς τῶν
ξυμμάχων λόγοις πρότερον ἐπαιρώμεθα, οἵπερ δὲ
καὶ τῶν ἀποβαινόντων τὸ πλέον ἐπ' ἀμφότερα
τῆς αἰτίας ἕξομεν, οὗτοι καὶ καθ' ἡσυχίαν τι
αὐτῶν προΐδωμεν.

LXXXIV. "Καὶ τὸ βραδὺ καὶ μέλλον, ὃ μέμ-
φονται μάλιστα ἡμῶν, μὴ αἰσχύνεσθε. σπεύ-
δοντές τε γὰρ σχολαίτερον ἂν παύσαισθε διὰ τὸ
ἀπαράσκευοι ἐγχειρεῖν, καὶ ἅμα ἐλευθέραν καὶ

and as yet not ruined. For do not regard their land as anything but a hostage for us to hold, and a better hostage the better it is cultivated. You should therefore spare it as long as possible, instead of making them desperate and thus having a more intractable foe to deal with. For if, without adequate preparation, egged on by the complaints of our allies, we shall ravage their territory, beware lest we adopt a course which might rather[1] result in disgrace and difficulties for the Peloponnesus. For complaints, indeed, whether brought by states, or by individuals, may possibly be adjusted; but when a whole confederacy, for the sake of individual interests, undertakes a war of which no man can foresee the issue, it is not easy to end it with honour.

LXXXIII. "And let no man think it pusillanimous that many states should hesitate to attack a single city. For they also have allies not less numerous than ours who pay tribute; and war is a matter not so much of arms as of money, for it is money alone that makes arms serviceable, especially when an inland opposes a maritime power. Let us therefore provide ourselves with money first, instead of being carried away prematurely by the eloquence of our allies; and, just as it is we who shall bear the greater part of the responsibility for the consequences, whether for good or evil, so let it be our task also calmly to get some forecast of them.

LXXXIV. "And so be not ashamed of the slowness and dilatoriness for which they censure us most; for speed in beginning may mean delay in ending, because you went into the war without preparation, and, moreover, in consequence of our policy we have

[1] *i.e.* than the opposite course.

εὐδοξοτάτην πόλιν διὰ παντὸς νεμόμεθα. καὶ
δύναται μάλιστα σωφροσύνη ἔμφρων τοῦτ᾽ εἶναι·
2 μόνοι γὰρ δι᾽ αὐτὸ εὐπραγίαις τε οὐκ ἐξυβρίζομεν
καὶ ξυμφοραῖς ἧσσον ἑτέρων εἴκομεν, τῶν τε ξὺν
ἐπαίνῳ ἐξοτρυνόντων ἡμᾶς ἐπὶ τὰ δεινὰ παρὰ τὸ
δοκοῦν ἡμῖν οὐκ ἐπαιρόμεθα ἡδονῇ, καὶ ἤν τις
ἄρα ξὺν κατηγορίᾳ παροξύνῃ, οὐδὲν δὴ μᾶλλον
3 ἀχθεσθέντες ἀνεπείσθημεν. πολεμικοί τε καὶ
εὔβουλοι διὰ τὸ εὔκοσμον γιγνόμεθα, τὸ μὲν ὅτι
αἰδὼς σωφροσύνης πλεῖστον μετέχει, αἰσχύνης δὲ
εὐψυχία, εὔβουλοι δὲ ἀμαθέστερον τῶν νόμων
τῆς ὑπεροψίας παιδευόμενοι καὶ ξὺν χαλεπότητι
σωφρονέστερον ἢ ὥστε αὐτῶν ἀνηκουστεῖν, καὶ
μή, τὰ ἀχρεῖα ξυνετοὶ ἄγαν ὄντες, τὰς τῶν πολεμίων παρασκευὰς λόγῳ καλῶς μεμφόμενοι ἀνο-
μοίως ἔργῳ ἐπεξιέναι, νομίζειν δὲ τάς τε διανοίας
τῶν πέλας παραπλησίους εἶναι καὶ τὰς προσπι-
4 πτούσας τύχας οὐ λόγῳ διαιρετάς. αἰεὶ δὲ ὡς πρὸς
εὖ βουλευομένους τοὺς ἐναντίους ἔργῳ παρασκευα-
ζόμεθα· καὶ οὐκ ἐξ ἐκείνων ὡς ἁμαρτησομένων
ἔχειν δεῖ τὰς ἐλπίδας, ἀλλ᾽ ὡς ἡμῶν αὐτῶν ἀσφαλῶς προνοουμένων, πολύ τε διαφέρειν οὐ δεῖ

---

[1] The speaker uses εὔκοσμον, rather than βραδύ employed by the critics of Sparta, to suggest the contrast with impulsiveness or undue haste.

ever inhabited a city at once free and of fairest fame. And, after all, this trait in us may well be in the truest sense intelligent self-control, for by reason of it we alone do not become insolent in prosperity or succumb to adversity as much as others do; and when men try to goad us by praise into dangerous enterprises against our better judgment, we are not carried away by their flattery, or, if any-one goes so far as to attempt to provoke us to action by invective, we are none the more moved to compliance through vexation. Indeed, it is because of our orderly temper[1] that we are brave in war and wise in counsel—brave in war, because self-control is the chief element in self-respect, and respect of self, in turn, is the chief element in courage; and wise in counsel, because we are educated too rudely to despise the laws and with too much severity of discipline to disobey them, and not to be so ultra-clever in useless accomplishments[2] as to disparage our enemy's military preparations in brave words and then fail to go through with the business with corresponding deeds, but rather to consider that the designs of our neighbours are very much like our own and that what may befall from fortune[3] cannot be determined by speeches. But it is our way always to make our preparations by deeds, on the presumption that we go against opponents who are wise in counsel; and we ought never to build our hopes on the chance that they are going to make mistakes, but on the belief that we ourselves are taking safe precautions. And we must not believe that man

[2] With a glance at the Athenians' attention to culture, especially the art of elegant speech.

[3] *cf.* the Corinthians' charge, ch. lxix. 5, that the Spartans trusted to chance.

νομίζειν ἄνθρωπον ἀνθρώπου, κράτιστον δὲ εἶναι ὅστις ἐν τοῖς ἀναγκαιοτάτοις παιδεύεται.

LXXXV. "Ταύτας οὖν ἃς οἱ πατέρες τε ἡμῖν παρέδοσαν μελέτας καὶ αὐτοὶ διὰ παντὸς ὠφελούμενοι ἔχομεν μὴ παρῶμεν, μηδὲ ἐπειχθέντες ἐν βραχεῖ μορίῳ ἡμέρας περὶ πολλῶν σωμάτων καὶ χρημάτων καὶ πόλεων καὶ δόξης βουλεύσωμεν, ἀλλὰ καθ' ἡσυχίαν. ἔξεστι δ' ἡμῖν μᾶλλον ἑτέ-
2 ρων διὰ ἰσχύν. καὶ πρὸς τοὺς Ἀθηναίους πέμπετε μὲν περὶ τῆς Ποτειδαίας, πέμπετε δὲ περὶ ὧν οἱ ξύμμαχοί φασιν ἀδικεῖσθαι, ἄλλως τε καὶ ἑτοίμων ὄντων αὐτῶν δίκας δοῦναι· ἐπὶ δὲ τὸν διδόντα οὐ πρότερον νόμιμον ὡς ἐπ' ἀδικοῦντα ἰέναι. παρασκευάζεσθε δὲ τὸν πόλεμον ἅμα. ταῦτα γὰρ καὶ κράτιστα βουλεύσεσθε καὶ τοῖς ἐναντίοις φοβερώτατα."

3 Καὶ ὁ μὲν Ἀρχίδαμος τοιαῦτα εἶπεν· παρελθὼν δὲ Σθενελᾴδας τελευταῖος, εἷς τῶν ἐφόρων τότε ὤν, ἔλεξεν τοῖς Λακεδαιμονίοις[1] ὧδε.

LXXXVI. "Τοὺς μὲν λόγους τοὺς πολλοὺς τῶν Ἀθηναίων οὐ γιγνώσκω· ἐπαινέσαντες γὰρ πολλὰ ἑαυτοὺς οὐδαμοῦ ἀντεῖπον ὡς οὐκ ἀδικοῦσι τοὺς ἡμετέρους ξυμμάχους καὶ τὴν Πελοπόννησον· καίτοι εἰ πρὸς τοὺς Μήδους ἐγένοντο ἀγαθοὶ τότε, πρὸς δ' ἡμᾶς κακοὶ νῦν, διπλασίας ζημίας ἄξιοί
2 εἰσιν, ὅτι ἀντ' ἀγαθῶν κακοὶ γεγένηνται. ἡμεῖς δὲ ὁμοῖοι καὶ τότε καὶ νῦν ἐσμεν, καὶ τοὺς ξυμμά-

[1] Hude deletes with Krüger.

differs much from man,[1] but that he is best who is trained in the severest discipline.

LXXXV. "These are the practices which our fathers bequeathed to us and we ourselves have maintained from the beginning to our profit; let us not abandon them, nor allow ourselves in a small portion of one day to be hurried into a decision which involves many lives, much money, many cities and a good name; but let us deliberate at our leisure. And this course is permitted to us more than to the supporters of the other view because of our strength. And send envoys to the Athenians to take up the question of Potidaea, and also to take up the matters wherein our allies claim that they are wronged. The chief reason for this is that they are ready[2] to submit to arbitration, and it is not lawful to proceed forthwith against one who offers arbitration as though against a wrong-doer. But all the while prepare yourselves for the war. This decision will be best for yourselves and will inspire most fear in your foes."

Thus spoke Archidamus, and finally Sthenelaidas, one of the ephors at that time, came forward and addressed the Lacedaemonians as follows:

LXXXVI. "The long speeches of the Athenians I cannot understand; for though they indulged in much praise of themselves, they nowhere denied that they are wronging our allies and the Peloponnesus. And yet, if they conducted themselves well against the Persians in former times but are now conducting themselves ill toward us, they deserve two-fold punishment, because they used to be good and have become bad. But we are the same now as we were

[1] *cf.* the Corinthians' praise of Athenian superiority, ch. lxx.
[2] *cf.* ch. lxxviii. 4.

χους, ἢν σωφρονῶμεν, οὐ περιοψόμεθα ἀδικουμένους οὐδὲ μελλήσομεν τιμωρεῖν· οἱ δ' οὐκέτι
3 μέλλουσι κακῶς πάσχειν. ἄλλοις μὲν γὰρ χρήματά ἐστι καὶ νῆες καὶ ἵπποι, ἡμῖν δὲ ξύμμαχοι ἀγαθοί, οὓς οὐ παραδοτέα τοῖς Ἀθηναίοις ἐστίν, οὐδὲ δίκαις καὶ λόγοις διακριτέα μὴ λόγῳ καὶ αὐτοὺς βλαπτομένους, ἀλλὰ τιμωρητέα ἐν τάχει
4 καὶ παντὶ σθένει. καὶ ὡς ἡμᾶς πρέπει βουλεύεσθαι ἀδικουμένους μηδεὶς διδασκέτω, ἀλλὰ τοὺς μέλλοντας ἀδικεῖν μᾶλλον πρέπει πολὺν χρόνον
5 βουλεύεσθαι. ψηφίζεσθε οὖν, ὦ Λακεδαιμόνιοι, ἀξίως τῆς Σπάρτης τὸν πόλεμον καὶ μήτε τοὺς Ἀθηναίους ἐᾶτε μείζους γίγνεσθαι, μήτε τοὺς ξυμμάχους καταπροδιδῶμεν, ἀλλὰ ξὺν τοῖς θεοῖς ἐπίωμεν ἐπὶ τοὺς ἀδικοῦντας."

LXXXVII. Τοιαῦτα λέξας ἐπεψήφιζεν αὐτὸς ἔφορος ὢν ἐς[1] τὴν ἐκκλησίαν τῶν Λακεδαιμονίων.
2 ὁ δέ (κρίνουσι γὰρ βοῇ καὶ οὐ ψήφῳ) οὐκ ἔφη διαγιγνώσκειν τὴν βοὴν ποτέρα μείζων, ἀλλὰ βουλόμενος αὐτοὺς φανερῶς ἀποδεικνυμένους τὴν γνώμην ἐς τὸ πολεμεῖν μᾶλλον ὁρμῆσαι ἔλεξεν· "Ὅτῳ μὲν ὑμῶν, ὦ Λακεδαιμόνιοι, δοκοῦσι λελύσθαι αἱ σπονδαὶ καὶ οἱ Ἀθηναῖοι ἀδικεῖν, ἀναστήτω ἐς ἐκεῖνο τὸ χωρίον," δείξας τι χωρίον αὐτοῖς, "ὅτῳ δὲ μὴ δοκοῦσιν, ἐς τὰ ἐπὶ θάτερα."
3 ἀναστάντες δὲ διέστησαν, καὶ πολλῷ πλείους
4 ἐγένοντο οἷς ἐδόκουν αἱ σπονδαὶ λελύσθαι. προσ-

[1] Hude deletes, after Fr. Müller.

then, and if we are in our right minds, we shall not permit our allies to be wronged or even put off avenging their wrongs, since they cannot longer put off suffering them. Others, indeed, may have money in abundance and ships and horses,[1] but we have brave allies, and they must not be delivered over to the Athenians; nor must we seek redress by means of legal processes and words when it is not in word only that we ourselves are being injured, but we must avenge them speedily and with all our might. And let no man tell us that it befits us to deliberate when a wrong is being done us; nay, it befits rather those who intend to do us a wrong to deliberate a long time. Vote, therefore, Lacedaemonians, for the war as beseems the dignity of Sparta, and do not permit the Athenians to become too great; and let us not prove false to our allies, but let us with the favour of the gods go against the wrong-doer."

LXXXVII. When Sthenelaidas had thus spoken, he himself, since he was an ephor, put the vote to the assembly of the Lacedaemonians. Now in their voting they usually decide by shout and not by ballot, but Sthenelaidas said that he could not distinguish which shout was the louder, and wishing to make the assembly more eager for war by a clear demonstration of their sentiment, he said: "Whoever of you, Lacedaemonians, thinks that the treaty has been broken and the Athenians are doing wrong, let him rise and go to yonder spot (pointing to a certain spot), and whoever thinks otherwise, to the other side." Then they rose and divided, and those who thought the treaty had been broken were found to be in a large majority. Then they called in the

[1] *cf.* ch. lxxx. 3.

καλέσαντές τε τοὺς ξυμμάχους εἶπον ὅτι σφίσι
μὲν δοκοῖεν ἀδικεῖν οἱ Ἀθηναῖοι, βούλεσθαι δὲ
καὶ τοὺς πάντας ξυμμάχους παρακαλέσαντες
ψῆφον ἐπαγαγεῖν, ὅπως κοινῇ βουλευσάμενοι τὸν
5 πόλεμον ποιῶνται, ἢν δοκῇ. καὶ οἱ μὲν ἀπεχώρησαν ἐπ' οἴκου διαπραξάμενοι ταῦτα, καὶ οἱ
Ἀθηναίων πρέσβεις ὕστερον ἐφ' ἅπερ ἦλθον χρη-
ματίσαντες.

6 Ἡ δὲ διαγνώμη αὕτη τῆς ἐκκλησίας τοῦ τὰς
σπονδὰς λελύσθαι[1] ἐγένετο ἐν τετάρτῳ καὶ δεκάτῳ ἔτει τῶν τριακοντουτίδων σπονδῶν προ-
κεχωρηκυιῶν, αἳ ἐγένοντο μετὰ τὰ Εὐβοϊκά.
LXXXVIII. ἐψηφίσαντο δὲ οἱ Λακεδαιμόνιοι
τὰς σπονδὰς λελύσθαι καὶ πολεμητέα εἶναι, οὐ
τοσοῦτον τῶν ξυμμάχων πεισθέντες τοῖς λόγοις
ὅσον φοβούμενοι τοὺς Ἀθηναίους μὴ ἐπὶ μεῖζον
δυνηθῶσιν, ὁρῶντες αὐτοῖς τὰ πολλὰ τῆς Ἑλλάδος ὑποχείρια ἤδη ὄντα.

LXXXIX. Οἱ γὰρ Ἀθηναῖοι τρόπῳ τοιῷδε
2 ἦλθον ἐπὶ τὰ πράγματα ἐν οἷς ηὐξήθησαν. ἐπειδὴ
Μῆδοι ἀνεχώρησαν ἐκ τῆς Εὐρώπης νικηθέντες
καὶ ναυσὶ καὶ πεζῷ ὑπὸ Ἑλλήνων καὶ οἱ καταφυγόντες αὐτῶν ταῖς ναυσὶν ἐς Μυκάλην διεφθάρησαν, Λεωτυχίδης μὲν ὁ βασιλεὺς τῶν Λακεδαιμονίων, ὅσπερ ἡγεῖτο τῶν ἐν Μυκάλῃ Ἑλλήνων,
ἀπεχώρησεν ἐπ' οἴκου ἔχων τοὺς ἀπὸ Πελοποννήσου ξυμμάχους· οἱ δὲ Ἀθηναῖοι καὶ οἱ ἀπὸ

[1] τοῦ τὰς σπονδὰς λελύσθαι, omitted by Hude, following van Herwerden.

allies and told them that, in their opinion, the Athenians were doing wrong, but that they wished to summon the whole body of the allies[1] and put the vote to them, in order that they might all deliberate together and together undertake the war, if it should be so decided. And so the allies who were there went back home, having brought these matters to a settlement, and so did the Athenian envoys later, after they had finished the business on which they had come.

This decision of the assembly, that the treaty had been broken, was made in the fourteenth year[2] from the beginning of the thirty years' truce, which was made after the Euboean war.[3] LXXXVIII. And the vote of the Lacedaemonians that the treaty had been broken and that they must go to war was determined, not so much by the influence of the speeches of their allies, as by fear of the Athenians, lest they become too powerful, seeing that the greater part of Hellas was already subject to them.

LXXXIX. For it was in the following manner that the Athenians found themselves face to face with those circumstances in dealing with which they rose to greatness. When the Persians had retreated from Europe, defeated on both sea and land by the Hellenes,[4] and those of them who with their ships had taken refuge at Mycale had perished there, Leotychides, king of the Lacedaemonians, who was commander of the Hellenes at Mycale, went home with the allies from the Peloponnesus. But the Athenians, together with the allies from Ionia and the

[1] A general convocation of the allies; at this time only part of them had been invited, according to ch. lxvii. See ch. cxix., where the plan is carried out. [2] 445 B.C.
[3] *cf.* ch. cxiv. [4] At Salamis, Plataea, Mycale.

Ἰωνίας καὶ Ἑλλησπόντου ξύμμαχοι, ἤδη ἀφεστηκότες ἀπὸ βασιλέως, ὑπομείναντες Σηστὸν ἐπολιόρκουν Μήδων ἐχόντων, καὶ ἐπιχειμάσαντες εἷλον αὐτὴν ἐκλιπόντων τῶν βαρβάρων, καὶ μετὰ τοῦτο ἀπέπλευσαν ἐξ Ἑλλησπόντου ὡς ἕκαστοι
3 κατὰ πόλεις. Ἀθηναίων δὲ τὸ κοινόν, ἐπειδὴ αὐτοῖς οἱ βάρβαροι ἐκ τῆς χώρας ἀπῆλθον, διεκομίζοντο εὐθὺς ὅθεν ὑπεξέθεντο παῖδας καὶ γυναῖκας καὶ τὴν περιοῦσαν κατασκευήν, καὶ τὴν πόλιν ἀνοικοδομεῖν παρεσκευάζοντο καὶ τὰ τείχη· τοῦ τε γὰρ περιβόλου βραχέα εἱστήκει καὶ οἰκίαι αἱ μὲν πολλαὶ ἐπεπτώκεσαν, ὀλίγαι δὲ περιῆσαν, ἐν αἷς αὐτοὶ ἐσκήνωσαν οἱ δυνατοὶ τῶν Περσῶν.

XC. Λακεδαιμόνιοι δὲ αἰσθόμενοι τὸ μέλλον ἦλθον πρεσβείαν, τὰ μὲν καὶ αὐτοὶ ἥδιον ἂν ὁρῶντες μήτ' ἐκείνους μήτ' ἄλλον μηδένα τεῖχος ἔχοντα, τὸ δὲ πλέον τῶν ξυμμάχων ἐξοτρυνόντων καὶ φοβουμένων τοῦ τε ναυτικοῦ αὐτῶν τὸ πλῆθος, ὃ πρὶν οὐχ ὑπῆρχε, καὶ τὴν ἐς τὸν Μηδικὸν πόλε-
2 μον τόλμαν γενομένην. ἠξίουν τε αὐτοὺς μὴ τειχίζειν, ἀλλὰ καὶ τῶν ἔξω Πελοποννήσου μᾶλλον ὅσοις εἱστήκει ξυγκαθελεῖν μετὰ σφῶν τοὺς περιβόλους, τὸ μὲν βουλόμενον καὶ ὕποπτον τῆς γνώμης οὐ δηλοῦντες ἐς τοὺς Ἀθηναίους, ὡς δὲ τοῦ βαρβάρου, εἰ αὖθις ἐπέλθοι, οὐκ ἂν ἔχοντος

---

[1] The contingents from the islands and the coast of Asia Minor, who, in consequence of the battle at Mycale and the

Hellespont,[1] who were already in revolt from the King, remained at their task and besieged Sestos, which was held by the Persians; and passing the winter there they took it, as it had been deserted by the Barbarians; and after that the contingents of the several cities sailed away from the Hellespont. But the Athenian people, when the Barbarians had departed from their territory, straightway began to fetch back their wives and their children and the remnant of their household goods from where they had placed them for safety,[2] and to rebuild the city and the walls; for of the encircling wall only small portions were left standing, and most of the houses were in ruins, only a few remaining in which the chief men of the Persians had themselves taken quarters.

XC. But the Lacedaemonians, perceiving what was in prospect, came on an embassy, partly because they themselves would have preferred to see neither the Athenians nor anyone else have a wall, but more because their allies urged them on through apprehension, not only of the size of the Athenian navy, which had hitherto not been large, but also of the daring they had shown in the Persian war. So they requested them not to rebuild their walls, but rather to join with them in razing the walls of whatsoever towns outside the Peloponnesus had them standing, giving no indication of their real purpose or of their suspicion with regard to the Athenians, but representing that the Barbarian, if he should attack them again, would not have any stronghold to make his

advance of the victors to Abydos, had been received into the Hellenic alliance.

[2] Salamis, Aegina, and Troezen; *cf.* Hdt. VIII. xli.

ἀπὸ ἐχυροῦ ποθεν, ὥσπερ νῦν ἐκ τῶν Θηβῶν, ὁρμᾶσθαι, τήν τε Πελοπόννησον πᾶσιν ἔφασαν
3 ἀναχώρησίν τε καὶ ἀφορμὴν ἱκανὴν εἶναι. οἱ δ' Ἀθηναῖοι Θεμιστοκλέους γνώμῃ τοὺς μὲν Λακεδαιμονίους ταῦτ' εἰπόντας, ἀποκρινάμενοι ὅτι πέμψουσιν ὡς αὐτοὺς πρέσβεις περὶ ὧν λέγουσιν, εὐθὺς ἀπήλλαξαν· ἑαυτὸν δ' ἐκέλευεν ἀποστέλλειν ὡς τάχιστα ὁ Θεμιστοκλῆς ἐς τὴν Λακεδαίμονα, ἄλλους δὲ πρὸς ἑαυτῷ ἑλομένους πρέσβεις μὴ εὐθὺς ἐκπέμπειν, ἀλλ' ἐπίσχειν μέχρι τοσούτου ἕως ἂν τὸ τεῖχος ἱκανὸν ἄρωσιν ὥστε ἀπομάχεσθαι ἐκ τοῦ ἀναγκαιοτάτου ὕψους· τειχίζειν δὲ πάντας πανδημεὶ τοὺς ἐν τῇ πόλει,[1] καὶ αὐτοὺς καὶ γυναῖκας καὶ παῖδας, φειδομένους μήτε ἰδίου μήτε δημοσίου οἰκοδομήματος ὅθεν τις ὠφελία ἔσται ἐς τὸ ἔργον, ἀλλὰ καθαιροῦντας πάντα.
4 καὶ ὁ μὲν ταῦτα διδάξας καὶ ὑπειπών, τἆλλα ὅτι
5 αὐτὸς τἀκεῖ πράξοι, ᾤχετο. καὶ ἐς τὴν Λακεδαίμονα ἐλθὼν οὐ προσῄει πρὸς τὰς ἀρχάς, ἀλλὰ διῆγε καὶ προυφασίζετο. καὶ ὁπότε τις αὐτὸν ἔροιτο τῶν ἐν τέλει ὄντων ὅ τι οὐκ ἐπέρχεται ἐπὶ τὸ κοινόν, ἔφη τοὺς ξυμπρέσβεις ἀναμένειν, ἀσχολίας δέ τινος οὔσης αὐτοὺς ὑπολειφθῆναι, προσδέχεσθαι μέντοι ἐν τάχει ἥξειν καὶ θαυμάζειν ὡς οὔπω πάρεισιν.

XCI. Οἱ δὲ ἀκούοντες τῷ μὲν Θεμιστοκλεῖ ἐπείθοντο διὰ φιλίαν, τῶν[2] δὲ ἄλλων ἀφικνουμένων καὶ σαφῶς κατηγορούντων ὅτι τειχίζεταί

[1] τοὺς ἐν τῇ πόλει, Krüger brackets, followed by Hude. καὶ αὐτοὺς . . . παῖδας also bracketed by Hude, as not read by Schol.

[2] Hude adopts Shilleto's conjecture αὐτοπτῶν.

base of operations, as lately he had made Thebes; the Peloponnesus, they added, was large enough for all, both as a retreat and as a base of operations. To these proposals of the Lacedaemonians, the Athenians, by the advice of Themistocles, replied that they would send ambassadors to Sparta to discuss these matters, and so got rid of them without delay. Themistocles then proposed that they should send himself as speedily as possible to Lacedaemon; that they should then choose other ambassadors in addition, but, instead of sending them immediately, should wait until they should have raised the wall to such a height as was absolutely necessary for defence; and that the whole population of the city, men, women, and children, should take part in the wall-building, sparing neither private nor public edifice that would in any way help to further the work, but demolishing them all. After he had given these instructions, and an intimation that, for the rest, he would himself look after matters at Sparta, he departed. And when he came to Lacedaemon he did not present himself to the magistrates, but kept putting it off and making excuses; and whenever any one of those in authority asked why he did not come before the people, he said that he was waiting for his colleagues, who had stayed behind on account of some urgent business; he expected them however to come soon, and wondered that they were not already there.

XCI. And the Lacedaemonian magistrates were disposed to be content with this reply by reason of their friendship for Themistocles; but when everybody who came from Athens declared quite positively

τε καὶ ἤδη ὕψος λαμβάνει, οὐκ εἶχον ὅπως χρὴ
2 ἀπιστῆσαι. γνοὺς δὲ ἐκεῖνος κελεύει αὐτοὺς μὴ
λόγοις μᾶλλον παράγεσθαι ἢ πέμψαι σφῶν αὐτῶν ἄνδρας οἵτινες χρηστοὶ καὶ πιστῶς ἀναγγε-
3 λοῦσι σκεψάμενοι. ἀποστέλλουσιν οὖν, καὶ περὶ
αὐτῶν ὁ Θεμιστοκλῆς τοῖς Ἀθηναίοις κρύφα
πέμπει κελεύων[1] ὡς ἥκιστα ἐπιφανῶς κατασχεῖν
καὶ μὴ ἀφεῖναι πρὶν ἂν αὐτοὶ πάλιν κομισθῶσιν
(ἤδη γὰρ καὶ ἧκον αὐτῷ οἱ ξυμπρέσβεις, Ἁβρώ-
νιχός τε ὁ Λυσικλέους καὶ Ἀριστείδης ὁ Λυσι-
μάχου, ἀγγέλλοντες ἔχειν ἱκανῶς τὸ τεῖχος)·
ἐφοβεῖτο γὰρ μὴ οἱ Λακεδαιμόνιοι σφᾶς, ὁπότε
4 σαφῶς ἀκούσειαν, οὐκέτι ἀφῶσιν. οἵ τε οὖν
Ἀθηναῖοι τοὺς πρέσβεις ὥσπερ ἐπεστάλη κατεῖχον, καὶ ὁ Θεμιστοκλῆς ἐπελθὼν τοῖς Λακεδαιμονίοις ἐνταῦθα δὴ φανερῶς εἶπεν ὅτι ἡ μὲν πόλις
σφῶν τετείχισται ἤδη ὥστε ἱκανὴ εἶναι σῴζειν
τοὺς ἐνοικοῦντας, εἰ δέ τι βούλονται Λακεδαιμόνιοι ἢ οἱ ξύμμαχοι πρεσβεύεσθαι παρὰ σφᾶς
ὡς πρὸς διαγιγνώσκοντας τὸ λοιπὸν ἰέναι τά τε
5 σφίσιν αὐτοῖς ξύμφορα καὶ τὰ κοινά. τήν τε γὰρ
πόλιν ὅτε ἐδόκει ἐκλιπεῖν ἄμεινον εἶναι καὶ ἐς τὰς
ναῦς ἐσβῆναι, ἄνευ ἐκείνων ἔφασαν[2] γνόντες τολμῆσαι, καὶ ὅσα αὖ μετ' ἐκείνων βουλεύεσθαι,
6 οὐδενὸς ὕστεροι γνώμῃ φανῆναι. δοκεῖν οὖν σφίσι
καὶ νῦν ἄμεινον εἶναι τὴν ἑαυτῶν πόλιν τεῖχος

[1] Hude omits with Lex. Vindob.
[2] Deleted by Krüger, followed by Hude.

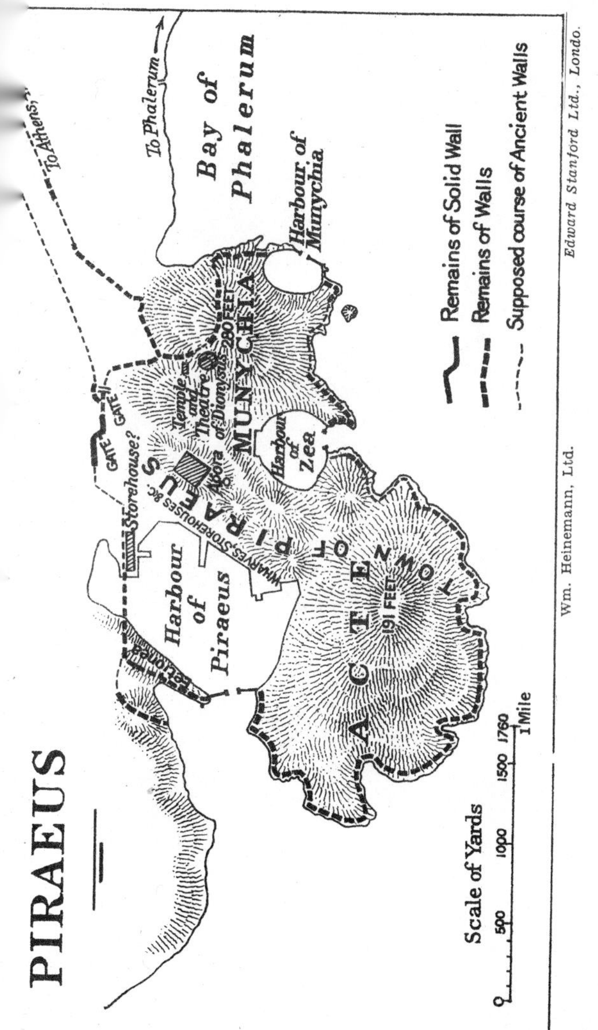

that the wall was going up and was already attaining height, they did not know how to discredit it. Themistocles, however, when he perceived this bade them not to be misled by reports, but rather to send some trustworthy men of their own number who would see for themselves and bring back a faithful report. They did so, and Themistocles sent word secretly to the Athenians to detain the envoys as covertly as possible and not to let them go until they themselves returned—for by this time his colleagues, Habronichus son of Lysicles and Aristides son of Lysimachus, had joined him, with the news that the wall was high enough—the reason for his precaution being that he was afraid the Lacedaemonians, when they heard the truth, would then refuse to let them go. Accordingly the Athenians detained the envoys as they were directed, and Themistocles, appearing before the Lacedaemonians, at length told them frankly that the city was now walled and therefore in a position to protect its inhabitants, and that if the Lacedaemonians or their allies cared to negotiate any matter with them they must hereafter come to them with the understanding that they were dealing with men who were fully aware of what was for their own and the general interest. For when they thought it best to abandon their city and embark on their ships, they had resolved, said the ambassadors, upon this bold step without the advice of the Lacedaemonians, and again in all matters in which the Athenans took counsel with the Lacedaemonians they had shown themselves inferior to none in judgment. Accordingly in the present instance also it seemed to them best that their city should have a wall, and that this course would be of great

ἔχειν, καὶ ἰδίᾳ τοῖς πολίταις καὶ ἐς τοὺς πάντας
7 ξυμμάχους ὠφελιμώτερον ἔσεσθαι· οὐ γὰρ οἷόν τ' εἶναι μὴ ἀπὸ ἀντιπάλου παρασκευῆς ὁμοῖόν τι ἢ ἴσον ἐς τὸ κοινὸν βουλεύεσθαι. ἢ πάντας οὖν ἀτειχίστους ἔφη χρῆναι ξυμμαχεῖν ἢ καὶ τάδε νομίζειν ὀρθῶς ἔχειν.

XCII. Οἱ δὲ Λακεδαιμόνιοι ἀκούσαντες ὀργὴν μὲν φανερὰν οὐκ ἐποιοῦντο τοῖς Ἀθηναίοις (οὐδὲ γὰρ ἐπὶ κωλύμῃ, ἀλλὰ γνώμης παραινέσει δῆθεν τῷ κοινῷ ἐπρεσβεύσαντο, ἅμα δὲ καὶ προσφιλεῖς ὄντες ἐν τῷ τότε διὰ τὴν ἐς τὸν Μῆδον προθυμίαν τὰ μάλιστα αὐτοῖς ἐτύγχανον), τῆς μέντοι βουλήσεως ἁμαρτάνοντες ἀδήλως ἤχθοντο. οἵ τε πρέσβεις ἑκατέρων ἀπῆλθον ἐπ' οἴκου ἀνεπικλήτως.

XCIII. Τούτῳ τῷ τρόπῳ οἱ Ἀθηναῖοι τὴν πό-
2 λιν ἐτείχισαν ἐν ὀλίγῳ χρόνῳ, καὶ δήλη ἡ οἰκοδομία ἔτι καὶ νῦν ἐστιν ὅτι κατὰ σπουδὴν ἐγένετο. οἱ γὰρ θεμέλιοι παντοίων λίθων ὑπόκεινται καὶ οὐ ξυνειργασμένων ἔστιν ᾗ, ἀλλ' ὡς ἕκαστοί[1] ποτε προσέφερον, πολλαί τε στῆλαι ἀπὸ σημάτων καὶ λίθοι εἰργασμένοι ἐγκατελέγησαν. μείζων γὰρ ὁ περίβολος πανταχῇ ἐξήχθη τῆς πό-

[1] Hude reads ἕκαστον with C.

---

[1] The remains of the walls now seen around the Peiraeus are not those of the Themistoclean walls, which were destroyed at the end of the Peloponnesian War, but of the walls built by Conon in 393. A small part of these remains,

To face page 157.

advantage both to themselves in particular, and to the whole body of the allies; for it was impossible for them, he added, to have equal or similar weight in the general councils of the alliance except on the basis of a military strength that was a match for theirs. Therefore, he concluded, the members of the alliance should either dispense with their walls one and all, or regard this act of the Athenians as justified.

XCII. On hearing this, the Lacedaemonians did not openly show any resentment against the Athenians; for they had sent their embassy to Athens, not to stop the work, but to offer, as they professed, a suggestion in the common interest, and besides, they entertained at that time the most friendly feelings for the Athenians on account of their zeal in opposing the Persians; since, however, they had failed in their purpose, they were secretly vexed. So the envoys on either side returned home without making any formal complaint.

XCIII. It was in this manner that the Athenians got their wall built in so short a time, and even to-day the structure shows that it was put together in haste.[1] For the lower courses consist of all sorts of stones, in some cases not even hewn to fit but just as they were when the several workers brought them, and many columns from grave monuments and stones wrought for other purposes were built in. For the circuit-wall of the city was extended in

on the flat ground north of the Peiraeus toward the mainland, answers exactly to Thucydides' description—being of solid stone and over 25 feet thick—but most of the remains are of two outer faces of stone, the intermediate spaces filled in with rubble and earth. On Munychia there is no trace anywhere of a solid wall of the age of Themistocles.

λεως, καὶ διὰ τοῦτο πάντα ὁμοίως κινοῦντες
3 ἠπείγοντο. ἔπεισε δὲ καὶ τοῦ Πειραιῶς τὰ λοιπὰ
ὁ Θεμιστοκλῆς οἰκοδομεῖν (ὑπῆρκτο δ' αὐτοῦ
πρότερον ἐπὶ τῆς ἐκείνου ἀρχῆς ἧς κατ' ἐνιαυτὸν
'Αθηναίοις ἦρξε), νομίζων τό τε χωρίον καλὸν
εἶναι λιμένας ἔχον τρεῖς αὐτοφυεῖς, καὶ αὐτοὺς
ναυτικοὺς γεγενημένους μέγα προφέρειν ἐς τὸ
4 κτήσασθαι δύναμιν (τῆς γὰρ δὴ θαλάσσης πρῶτος ἐτόλμησεν εἰπεῖν ὡς ἀνθεκτέα ἐστί), καὶ τὴν
5 ἀρχὴν εὐθὺς ξυγκατεσκεύαζεν. καὶ ᾠκοδόμησαν
τῇ ἐκείνου γνώμῃ τὸ πάχος τοῦ τείχους ὅπερ νῦν
ἔτι δῆλόν ἐστι περὶ τὸν Πειραιᾶ· δύο γὰρ ἅμαξαι
ἐναντίαι ἀλλήλαις τοὺς λίθους ἐπῆγον, ἐντὸς δὲ
οὔτε χάλιξ οὔτε πηλὸς ἦν, ἀλλὰ ξυνῳκοδομημέ-
νοι μεγάλοι λίθοι καὶ ἐντομῇ ἐγγώνιοι, σιδήρῳ
πρὸς ἀλλήλους τὰ ἔξωθεν καὶ μολύβδῳ δεδεμένοι.
τὸ δὲ ὕψος ἥμισυ μάλιστα ἐτελέσθη οὗ διενοεῖτο.
6 ἐβούλετο γὰρ τῷ μεγέθει καὶ τῷ πάχει ἀφιστάναι
τὰς τῶν πολεμίων ἐπιβουλάς, ἀνθρώπων τε ἐνόμιζεν ὀλίγων καὶ τῶν ἀχρειοτάτων ἀρκέσειν τὴν
φυλακήν, τοὺς δ' ἄλλους ἐς τὰς ναῦς ἐσβήσεσθαι.
7 ταῖς γὰρ ναυσὶ μάλιστα προσέκειτο, ἰδών, ὡς
ἐμοὶ δοκεῖ, τῆς βασιλέως στρατιᾶς τὴν κατὰ
θάλασσαν ἔφοδον εὐπορωτέραν τῆς κατὰ γῆν
οὖσαν· τόν τε Πειραιᾶ ὠφελιμώτερον ἐνόμιζε τῆς
ἄνω πόλεως, καὶ πολλάκις τοῖς 'Αθηναίοις παρῄ-

---

[1] The Peiraeus, here in widest sense, is the peninsula, the heart of which is the steep height of Munychia, from which

every direction, and on this account they laid hands upon everything alike in their haste. Themistocles, moreover, persuaded them also to finish the walls of the Peiraeus, a beginning of which had been made during the year in which he was archon of the Athenians; for he considered that the Peiraeus with its three natural harbours [1] was a fine site to develop and that to have become a nation of seamen would be a great advantage to the Athenians themselves, with a view to their acquisition of power—indeed it was he who first dared declare that they must apply themselves to the sea—and so he immediately took the first steps in this undertaking. [2] And following his advice they built the wall round the Peiraeus of the thickness that may still be observed; for two wagons carrying the stones could meet and pass each other. Inside, moreover, there was neither rubble nor mortar, but stones of large size hewn square were closely laid together, bound to one another on the outside with iron clamps and lead. But the wall was completed to only about half of the height he originally intended, for what he wished was to be able to repel the assaults of the enemy by the very height and thickness of the wall, and he thought that a few men, and these the least effective, would suffice to guard it, while all the rest might man the ships. For Themistocles devoted himself particularly to the navy, because, as it seems to me, he had observed that the approach of the King's forces was easier by sea than by land; and he thought that the Peiraeus would prove more serviceable than the upper city, and often advised the Athenians, if ever they

it stretches into the sea like an indented leaf, forming three natural basins—the Peiraeus, Zea, Munychia.

[2] Others render: immediately began to help them to lay the foundation of their empire.

νει, ἢν ἄρα ποτὲ κατὰ γῆν βιασθῶσι, καταβάντας ἐς αὐτὸν ταῖς ναυσὶ πρὸς ἅπαντας ἀνθίστασθαι.
8 Ἀθηναῖοι μὲν οὖν οὕτως ἐτειχίσθησαν καὶ τἆλλα κατεσκευάζοντο εὐθὺς μετὰ τὴν Μήδων ἀναχώρησιν.

XCIV. Παυσανιας δὲ ὁ Κλεομβροτου ἐκ Λακεδαίμονος στρατηγὸς τῶν Ἑλλήνων ἐξεπέμφθη μετὰ εἴκοσι νεῶν ἀπὸ Πελοποννήσου· ξυνέπλεον δὲ καὶ Ἀθηναῖοι τριάκοντα ναυσὶ καὶ τῶν ἄλλων
2 ξυμμάχων πλῆθος. καὶ ἐστράτευσαν ἐς Κύπρον καὶ αὐτῆς τὰ πολλὰ κατεστρέψαντο, καὶ ὕστερον ἐς Βυζάντιον Μήδων ἐχόντων καὶ ἐξεπολιόρκησαν ἐν τῇδε τῇ ἡγεμονίᾳ.[1]

XCV. Ἤδη δὲ βιαίου ὄντος αὐτοῦ οἵ τε ἄλλοι Ἕλληνες ἤχθοντο καὶ οὐχ ἥκιστα οἱ Ἴωνες καὶ ὅσοι ἀπὸ βασιλέως νεωστὶ ἠλευθέρωντο· φοιτῶντές τε πρὸς τοὺς Ἀθηναίους ἠξίουν αὐτοὺς ἡγεμόνας σφῶν γίγνεσθαι κατὰ τὸ ξυγγενὲς καὶ Παυσανίᾳ μὴ ἐπιτρέπειν, ἤν που
2 βιάζηται. οἱ δὲ Ἀθηναῖοι ἐδέξαντό τε τοὺς λόγους καὶ προσεῖχον τὴν γνώμην ὡς οὐ περιοψόμενοι τἆλλά τε καταστησόμενοι ᾗ φαίνοιτο
3 ἄριστα αὐτοῖς. ἐν τούτῳ δὲ οἱ Λακεδαιμόνιοι μετεπέμποντο Παυσανίαν ἀνακρινοῦντες ὧν πέρι ἐπυνθάνοντο· καὶ γὰρ ἀδικία πολλὴ κατηγορεῖτο αὐτοῦ ὑπὸ τῶν Ἑλλήνων τῶν ἀφικνουμένων, καὶ τυραννίδος μᾶλλον ἐφαίνετο μίμησις ἢ

[1] Hude transfers, with Krüger, ἐν τῇδε τῇ ἡγεμονίᾳ to ch. xcv., deleting δὲ after ἤδη.

were hard pressed on land, to go down to the Peiraeus, and resist all their opponents with their fleet. It was in this way, then, that the Athenians got their walls built, and came to be engaged upon their other fortifications, immediately after the withdrawal of the Persians.

XCIV. Meanwhile Pausanias son of Cleombrotus was sent out from Lacedaemon in command of the Hellenes with twenty ships from Peloponnesus, accompanied by thirty Athenian ships and a multitude of other allies. They made also an expedition against Cyprus, subduing most of it, and afterwards, at the time of Pausanias' leadership, besieged Byzantium, which the Persians then held, and took it.

XCV. But, since he had already become headstrong,[1] the rest of the Hellenes became disaffected, especially the Ionians and all who had been recently emancipated from the King. So they waited upon the Athenians and begged them in the name of their kinship[2] to become their leaders, and to resist Pausanias if he should attempt to coerce them.[3] The Athenians accepted their proposals and gave full attention to the matter with the determination to endure Pausanias' conduct no longer and to settle all other matters as should seem best to themselves. Meanwhile the Lacedaemonians recalled Pausanias in order to interrogate him about reports they were hearing, for much wrongdoing was charged against him by the Hellenes who came to Sparta, and his behaviour seemed an aping of despotic power rather than the conduct of a general.

[1] *cf.* ch. cxxx. 2.
[2] As the mother city; *cf.* ch. ii. (end).
[3] 478 B.C.

4 στρατηγία. ξυνέβη τε αὐτῷ καλεῖσθαί τε ἅμα
καὶ τοὺς ξυμμάχους τῷ ἐκείνου ἔχθει παρ' Ἀθηναίους μετατάξασθαι πλὴν τῶν ἀπὸ Πελοπον-
5 νήσου στρατιωτῶν. ἐλθὼν δὲ ἐς Λακεδαίμονα
τῶν μὲν ἰδίᾳ πρός τινα ἀδικημάτων ηὐθύνθη, τὰ
δὲ μέγιστα ἀπολύεται μὴ ἀδικεῖν· κατηγορεῖτο
δὲ αὐτοῦ οὐχ ἥκιστα μηδισμὸς καὶ ἐδόκει σαφέ-
6 στατον εἶναι. καὶ ἐκεῖνον μὲν οὐκέτι ἐκπέμπου-
σιν ἄρχοντα, Δόρκιν δὲ καὶ ἄλλους τινὰς μετ'
αὐτοῦ στρατιὰν ἔχοντας οὐ πολλήν· οἷς οὐκέτι
7 ἐφίεσαν οἱ ξύμμαχοι τὴν ἡγεμονίαν. οἱ δὲ αἰσθόμενοι ἀπῆλθον, καὶ ἄλλους οὐκέτι ὕστερον
ἐξέπεμψαν οἱ Λακεδαιμόνιοι, φοβούμενοι μὴ
σφίσιν οἱ ἐξιόντες χείρους γίγνωνται, ὅπερ καὶ
ἐν τῷ Παυσανίᾳ ἐνεῖδον, ἀπαλλαξείοντες δὲ καὶ
τοῦ Μηδικοῦ πολέμου καὶ τοὺς Ἀθηναίους νομίζοντες ἱκανοὺς ἐξηγεῖσθαι καὶ σφίσιν ἐν τῷ τότε
παρόντι ἐπιτηδείους.

XCVI. Παραλαβόντες δὲ οἱ Ἀθηναῖοι τὴν
ἡγεμονίαν τούτῳ τῷ τρόπῳ ἑκόντων τῶν ξυμμάχων διὰ τὸ Παυσανίου μῖσος, ἔταξαν ἅς τε ἔδει
παρέχειν τῶν πόλεων χρήματα πρὸς τὸν βάρβαρον καὶ ἃς ναῦς· πρόσχημα γὰρ ἦν ἀμύνεσθαι
2 ὧν ἔπαθον δῃοῦντας τὴν βασιλέως χώραν. καὶ
Ἑλληνοταμίαι τότε πρῶτον Ἀθηναίοις κατέστη
ἀρχή, οἳ ἐδέχοντο τὸν φόρον· οὕτω γὰρ ὠνομάσθη

And it so happened that he was cited before the court at the very time that the allies in vexation at him had gone over to the side of the Athenians, all except the soldiers from the Peloponnesus. And although, on his return to Lacedaemon, Pausanias was held to account for any personal wrongs he had committed against individuals, yet on the principal charges he was acquitted of misconduct; for he was accused most of all of treasonable relations with the Persians, and it seemed to be a very clear case. And they did not again send him out as commander, but Dorcis, together with some others, with an inconsiderable force; but the allies did not entrust these with the chief command. And they, being now aware of the situation, went back home; and the Lacedaemonians sent out no other commanders thereafter, fearing that any who went out might be corrupted, as they saw had happened in the case of Pausanias; they also wanted to be rid of the Persian war, and thought that the Athenians were competent to take the leadership and were friendly to themselves at the time.

XCVI. After the Athenians had succeeded in this way to the leadership over the allies, who freely chose them on account of their hatred of Pausanias, they assessed the amount of their contributions, both for the states which were to furnish money for the war against the Barbarians and for those which were to furnish ships, the avowed object being to avenge themselves for what they had suffered by ravaging the King's territory. And it was then[1] that the Athenians first established the office of Hellenic treasurers, who received the tribute; for so the

[1] 476 B.C.

τῶν χρημάτων ἡ φορά. ἦν δ' ὁ πρῶτος φόρος ταχθεὶς τετρακόσια τάλαντα καὶ ἑξήκοντα, ταμιεῖόν τε Δῆλος ἦν αὐτοῖς καὶ αἱ ξύνοδοι ἐς τὸ ἱερὸν ἐγίγνοντο.

XCVII. Ἡγούμενοι δὲ αὐτονόμων τὸ πρῶτον τῶν ξυμμάχων καὶ ἀπὸ κοινῶν ξυνόδων βουλευόντων τοσάδε ἐπῆλθον πολέμῳ τε καὶ διαχειρίσει πραγμάτων μεταξὺ τοῦδε τοῦ πολέμου καὶ τοῦ Μηδικοῦ, ἃ ἐγένετο πρός τε τὸν βάρβαρον αὐτοῖς καὶ πρὸς τοὺς σφετέρους ξυμμάχους νεωτερίζοντας καὶ Πελοποννησίων τοὺς αἰεὶ προστυγχά-
2 νοντας ἐν ἑκάστῳ. ἔγραψα δὲ αὐτὰ καὶ τὴν ἐκβολὴν τοῦ λόγου ἐποιησάμην διὰ τόδε, ὅτι τοῖς πρὸ ἐμοῦ ἅπασιν ἐκλιπὲς τοῦτο ἦν τὸ χωρίον καὶ ἢ τὰ πρὸ τῶν Μηδικῶν Ἑλληνικὰ ξυνετίθεσαν ἢ αὐτὰ τὰ Μηδικά· τούτων δὲ ὅσπερ καὶ ἥψατο ἐν τῇ Ἀττικῇ ξυγγραφῇ Ἑλλάνικος, βραχέως τε καὶ τοῖς χρόνοις οὐκ ἀκριβῶς ἐπεμνήσθη· ἅμα δὲ καὶ τῆς ἀρχῆς ἀπόδειξιν ἔχει τῆς τῶν Ἀθηναίων ἐν οἵῳ τρόπῳ κατέστη.

XCVIII. Πρῶτον μὲν Ἠιόνα τὴν ἐπὶ Στρυμόνι Μήδων ἐχόντων πολιορκίᾳ εἷλον καὶ ἠνδραπόδισαν Κίμωνος τοῦ Μιλτιάδου στρατηγοῦντος,
2 ἔπειτα Σκῦρον τὴν ἐν τῷ Αἰγαίῳ νῆσον, ἣν ᾤκουν
3 Δόλοπες, ἠνδραπόδισαν[1] καὶ ᾤκισαν αὐτοί. πρὸς δὲ Καρυστίους αὐτοῖς ἄνευ τῶν ἄλλων Εὐβοέων πόλεμος ἐγένετο, καὶ χρόνῳ ξυνέβησαν καθ'

[1] Deleted by Hude, after Cobet.

contribution of money was termed. The amount of the tribute first assessed was four hundred and sixty talents, and the treasury of the allies was Delos, where the meetings were held in the temple.

XCVII. Exercising then what was at first a leadership over allies who were autonomous and took part in the deliberations of common assemblies, the Athenians, in the interval between this war and the Persian, undertook, both in war and in the administration of public affairs, the enterprises now to be related, which were directed against the Barbarian, against their own allies when they attempted revolution, and against such of the Peloponnesians as from time to time came into conflict with them in the course of each attempt. And I have made a digression to write of these matters for the reason that this period has been omitted by all my predecessors, who have confined their narratives either to Hellenic affairs before the Persian War or to the Persian War itself; and Hellanicus, the only one of these who has ever touched upon this period, has in his Attic History treated of it briefly, and with inaccuracy as regards his chronology. And at the same time the narrative of these events serves to explain how the empire of Athens was established.

XCVIII. First, then, under the leadership of Cimon son of Miltiades, they took by siege Eion on the Strymon, which the Persians held, and enslaved its inhabitants[1]; then they enslaved Scyros, the island in the Aegean inhabited by Dolopians, and colonised it themselves. And a war arose between them and the Carystians, the other Euboeans taking no part in it, and after a time terms

[1] 476 B.C.

4 ὁμολογίαν. Ναξίοις δὲ ἀποστᾶσι μετὰ ταῦτα
ἐπολέμησαν καὶ πολιορκίᾳ παρεστήσαντο. πρώτη
τε αὕτη πόλις ξυμμαχὶς παρὰ τὸ καθεστηκὸς
ἐδουλώθη, ἔπειτα δὲ καὶ τῶν ἄλλων ὡς ἑκάστη
ξυνέβη.[1]

XCIX. Αἰτίαι δὲ ἄλλαι τε ἦσαν τῶν ἀποστά-
σεων καὶ μέγισται αἱ τῶν φόρων καὶ νεῶν ἔκδειαι
καὶ λιποστράτιον εἴ τῳ ἐγένετο· οἱ γὰρ Ἀθηναῖοι
ἀκριβῶς ἔπρασσον καὶ λυπηροὶ ἦσαν οὐκ εἰωθό-
σιν οὐδὲ βουλομένοις ταλαιπωρεῖν προσάγοντες
2 τὰς ἀνάγκας. ἦσαν δέ πως καὶ ἄλλως οἱ Ἀθηναῖοι οὐκέτι ὁμοίως ἐν ἡδονῇ ἄρχοντες, καὶ οὔτε
ξυνεστράτευον ἀπὸ τοῦ ἴσου ῥᾴδιόν τε προσά-
γεσθαι ἦν αὐτοῖς τοὺς ἀφισταμένους· ὧν αὐτοὶ
3 αἴτιοι ἐγένοντο οἱ ξύμμαχοι· διὰ γὰρ τὴν ἀπό-
κνησιν ταύτην τῶν στρατειῶν οἱ πλείους αὐτῶν,
ἵνα μὴ ἀπ' οἴκου ὦσι, χρήματα ἐτάξαντο ἀντὶ
τῶν νεῶν τὸ ἱκνούμενον ἀνάλωμα φέρειν, καὶ τοῖς
μὲν Ἀθηναίοις ηὔξετο τὸ ναυτικὸν ἀπὸ τῆς δαπάνης ἣν ἐκεῖνοι ξυμφέροιεν, αὐτοὶ δέ, ὁπότε ἀπο-
σταῖεν, ἀπαράσκευοι καὶ ἄπειροι ἐς τὸν πόλεμον
καθισταντο.

C. Ἐγένετο δὲ μετὰ ταῦτα καὶ ἡ ἐπ' Εὐρυμέ-
δοντι ποταμῷ ἐν Παμφυλίᾳ[2] πεζομαχία καὶ ναυμαχία Ἀθηναίων καὶ τῶν ξυμμάχων πρὸς Μήδους,
καὶ ἐνίκων τῇ αὐτῇ ἡμέρᾳ ἀμφότερα Ἀθηναῖοι

[1] Deleted by Hude as probably not read by Schol.
[2] ἐν Παμφυλίᾳ, omitted by Hude and Stahl, with Codex M.

of capitulation were agreed upon. After this they waged war upon the Naxians,[1] who had revolted, and reduced them by siege. And this was the first allied city to be enslaved in violation of the established rule; but afterwards the others also were enslaved as it happened in each case.

XCIX. Now while there were other causes of revolts, the principal ones were the failures in bringing in the tribute or their quota of ships and, in some cases, refusal of military service; for the Athenians exacted the tribute strictly and gave offence by applying coercive measures to any who were unaccustomed or unwilling to bear the hardships of service. And in some other respects, too, the Athenians were no longer equally agreeable as leaders; they would not take part in expeditions on terms of equality, and they found it easy to reduce those who revolted. For all this the allies themselves were responsible; for most of them, on account of their aversion to military service, in order to avoid being away from home got themselves rated in sums of money instead of ships, which they should pay in as their proportionate contribution, and consequently the fleet of the Athenians was increased by the funds which they contributed, while they themselves, whenever they revolted, entered on the war without preparation and without experience.

C. After this occurred at the river Eurymedon in Pamphylia the land-battle and sea-fight of the Athenians[2] and their allies against the Persians; and the Athenians were victorious in both on the

[1] 466 B.C.

[2] For this glorious victory of Cimon's, whose date (466 B.C.?) is not certain, *cf.* Diod. xi. 60; Plut. *Cim.* xii.

Κίμωνος τοῦ Μιλτιάδου στρατηγοῦντος, καὶ εἷλον
τριήρεις Φοινίκων καὶ διέφθειραν τὰς πάσας ἐς
2 διακοσίας. χρόνῳ δὲ ὕστερον ξυνέβη Θασίους
αὐτῶν ἀποστῆναι διενεχθέντας περὶ τῶν ἐν τῇ
ἀντιπέρας Θρᾴκῃ ἐμπορίων καὶ τοῦ μετάλλου,
ἃ ἐνέμοντο. καὶ ναυσὶ μὲν ἐπὶ Θάσον πλεύσαντες οἱ Ἀθηναῖοι ναυμαχίᾳ ἐκράτησαν καὶ ἐς
3 τὴν γῆν ἀπέβησαν· ἐπὶ δὲ Στρυμόνα πέμψαντες
μυρίους οἰκήτορας αὑτῶν καὶ τῶν ξυμμάχων ὑπὸ
τοὺς αὐτοὺς χρόνους, ὡς οἰκιοῦντες τὰς τότε
καλουμένας Ἐννέα ὁδούς, νῦν δὲ Ἀμφίπολιν, τῶν
μὲν Ἐννέα ὁδῶν αὐτοὶ ἐκράτησαν, ἃς εἶχον Ἠδω-
νοί, προελθόντες δὲ τῆς Θρᾴκης ἐς μεσόγειαν
διεφθάρησαν ἐν Δραβησκῷ τῇ Ἠδωνικῇ ὑπὸ τῶν
Θρᾳκῶν ξυμπάντων οἷς πολέμιον ἦν τὸ χωρίον[1]
κτιζόμενον.

CI. Θάσιοι δὲ νικηθέντες μάχῃ καὶ πολιορκούμενοι Λακεδαιμονίους ἐπεκαλοῦντο καὶ ἐπαμύνειν
2 ἐκέλευον ἐσβαλόντας ἐς τὴν Ἀττικήν. οἱ δὲ
ὑπέσχοντο μὲν κρύφα τῶν Ἀθηναίων καὶ ἔμελλον,
διεκωλύθησαν δὲ ὑπὸ τοῦ γενομένου σεισμοῦ, ἐν ᾧ
καὶ οἱ Εἵλωτες αὐτοῖς καὶ τῶν περιοίκων Θουριᾶ-
ταί τε καὶ Αἰθαιῆς ἐς Ἰθώμην ἀπέστησαν. πλεῖ-

[1] αἱ Ἐννέα ὁδοί, in the MSS. after χωρίον, rejected by Cobet.

---

[1] 465 B.C.

[2] The Thasians had a gold mine at Skapte Hyle on the Thracian coast, from which they drew rich revenues; *cf.* Hdt. VI. xlvi. f.

same day under the command of Cimon son of Miltiades, and they took and destroyed triremes of the Phoenicians to the number of two hundred all told. And some time afterwards it came to pass that the Thasians revolted from them,[1] a quarrel having arisen about the trading posts and the mine[2] on the opposite coast of Thrace, of which the Thasians enjoyed the profits. Thereupon the Athenians sailed with their fleet against Thasos, and, after winning a battle at sea, disembarked on the island. About the same time they sent to the river Strymon ten thousand colonists, consisting of Athenians and their allies, with a view to colonising the place, then called Nine Ways, but now Amphipolis; and though these colonists gained possession of Nine Ways, which was inhabited by Edoni, yet when they advanced into the interior of Thrace they were destroyed at Drabescus in Edonia by the united forces of the Thracians, to whom the settlement of the place was a menace.

CI. As for the Thasians, who had been defeated in battle and were now besieged, they appealed to the Lacedaemonians and urged them to come to their aid by invading Attica. This, unknown to the Athenians, they promised to do, and intended to keep their promise, but were prevented by the earthquake[3] which occurred at the time[4] when both their Helots and the Perioeci of Thuria and Aethaea revolted and went to Ithome.[5] Most of the Helots

[3] Called "the great earthquake" in ch. cxxviii. 1.

[4] 464 B.C.

[5] The Perioeci were the old inhabitants of the country, chiefly of Achaean stock, reduced to a condition of dependence, *i.e.* were not citizens, though not state-slaves as the Helots were.

στοι δὲ τῶν Εἱλώτων ἐγένοντο οἱ τῶν παλαιῶν Μεσσηνίων τότε δουλωθέντων ἀπόγονοι· ᾗ καὶ
3 Μεσσήνιοι ἐκλήθησαν οἱ πάντες. πρὸς μὲν οὖν τοὺς ἐν Ἰθώμῃ πόλεμος καθειστήκει Λακεδαιμονίοις· Θάσιοι δὲ τρίτῳ ἔτει πολιορκούμενοι ὡμολόγησαν Ἀθηναίοις τεῖχός τε καθελόντες καὶ ναῦς παραδόντες, χρήματά τε ὅσα ἔδει ἀποδοῦναι αὐτίκα ταξάμενοι καὶ τὸ λοιπὸν φέρειν, τήν τε ἤπειρον καὶ τὸ μέταλλον ἀφέντες.

CII. Λακεδαιμόνιοι δέ, ὡς αὐτοῖς πρὸς τοὺς ἐν Ἰθώμῃ ἐμηκύνετο ὁ πόλεμος, ἄλλους τε ἐπεκαλέσαντο ξυμμάχους καὶ Ἀθηναίους· οἱ δ' ἦλθον
2 Κίμωνος στρατηγοῦντος πλήθει οὐκ ὀλίγῳ. μάλιστα δ' αὐτοὺς ἐπεκαλέσαντο, ὅτι τειχομαχεῖν ἐδόκουν δυνατοὶ εἶναι, τῆς δὲ πολιορκίας μακρᾶς καθεστηκυίας τούτου ἐνδεᾶ ἐφαίνετο· βίᾳ γὰρ
3 ἂν εἷλον τὸ χωρίον. καὶ διαφορὰ ἐκ ταύτης τῆς στρατείας πρῶτον Λακεδαιμονίοις καὶ Ἀθηναίοις φανερὰ ἐγένετο. οἱ γὰρ Λακεδαιμόνιοι, ἐπειδὴ τὸ χωρίον βίᾳ[1] οὐχ ἡλίσκετο, δείσαντες τῶν Ἀθηναίων τὸ τολμηρὸν καὶ τὴν νεωτεροποιίαν, καὶ ἀλλοφύλους ἅμα ἡγησάμενοι, μή τι, ἢν παραμείνωσιν, ὑπὸ τῶν ἐν Ἰθώμῃ πεισθέντες νεωτερίσωσι, μόνους τῶν ξυμμάχων ἀπέπεμψαν, τὴν μὲν ὑποψίαν οὐ δηλοῦντες, εἰπόντες δὲ ὅτι οὐδὲν
4 προσδέονται αὐτῶν ἔτι. οἱ δ' Ἀθηναῖοι ἔγνωσαν

[1] Krüger deletes, followed by Hude.

were the descendants of the early Messenians who had been enslaved of old,[1] and hence were all called Messenians. The Lacedaemonians, then, were involved in war with the rebels on Ithome; and so the Thasians, who were in the third year of the siege, came to terms with the Athenians, pulling down their walls and delivering over their ships, agreeing to pay forthwith whatever sum of money should be required of them and to render tribute in future, and, finally, giving up both the mainland and the mine.

CII. The Lacedaemonians, on the other hand, when their war with the rebels on Ithome proved a long affair, appealed to their allies in general and especially to the Athenians, who came with a considerable force under the command of Cimon. The principal reason why an appeal was made to them was that they were reputed to be skilful in siege operations, whereas the long continuance of the siege showed their own deficiency in this respect; for otherwise they would have taken the place by assault. And it was in consequence of this expedition that a lack of harmony in the relations of the Lacedaemonians and the Athenians first became manifest. For the Lacedaemonians, when they failed to take the place by storm, fearing the audacity and the fickleness of the Athenians, whom they regarded, besides, as men of another race, thought that, if they remained, they might be persuaded by the rebels on Ithome to change sides; they therefore dismissed them, alone of the allies, without giving any indication of their suspicion, but merely saying that they had no further need of them. The Athenians, however, recognized

[1] Referring to the mythical time of the first Messenian war.

οὐκ ἐπὶ τῷ βελτίονι λόγῳ ἀποπεμπόμενοι, ἀλλά τινος ὑπόπτου γενομένου, καὶ δεινὸν ποιησάμενοι καὶ οὐκ ἀξιώσαντες ὑπὸ Λακεδαιμονίων τοῦτο παθεῖν, εὐθὺς ἐπειδὴ ἀνεχώρησαν, ἀφέντες τὴν γενομένην ἐπὶ τῷ Μήδῳ ξυμμαχίαν πρὸς αὐτοὺς Ἀργείοις τοῖς ἐκείνων πολεμίοις ξύμμαχοι ἐγένοντο, καὶ πρὸς Θεσσαλοὺς ἅμα ἀμφοτέροις οἱ αὐτοὶ ὅρκοι καὶ ξυμμαχία κατέστη.

CIII. Οἱ δ' ἐν Ἰθώμῃ δεκάτῳ ἔτει, ὡς οὐκέτι
ἐδύναντο ἀντέχειν, ξυνέβησαν πρὸς τοὺς Λακεδαιμονίους ἐφ' ᾧ ἐξίασιν ἐκ Πελοποννήσου ὑπόσπονδοι καὶ μηδέποτε ἐπιβήσονται αὐτῆς· ἢν δέ
2 τις ἁλίσκηται, τοῦ λαβόντος εἶναι δοῦλον. ἦν δέ
τι καὶ χρηστήριον τοῖς Λακεδαιμονίοις Πυθικὸν
πρὸ τοῦ, τὸν ἱκέτην τοῦ Διὸς τοῦ Ἰθωμήτα ἀφιέ-
3 ναι. ἐξῆλθον δὲ αὐτοὶ καὶ παῖδες καὶ γυναῖκες, καὶ
αὐτοὺς οἱ Ἀθηναῖοι δεξάμενοι κατὰ ἔχθος ἤδη τὸ
Λακεδαιμονίων ἐς Ναύπακτον κατῴκισαν, ἣν
ἔτυχον ᾑρηκότες νεωστὶ Λοκρῶν τῶν Ὀζολῶν
4 ἐχόντων. προσεχώρησαν δὲ καὶ Μεγαρῆς Ἀθηναίοις ἐς ξυμμαχίαν Λακεδαιμονίων ἀποστάντες,
ὅτι αὐτοὺς Κορίνθιοι περὶ γῆς ὅρων πολέμῳ
κατεῖχον. καὶ ἔσχον Ἀθηναῖοι Μέγαρα καὶ Πηγάς, καὶ τὰ μακρὰ τείχη ᾠκοδόμησαν Μεγαρεῦσι

---

[1] 455 B.C.

that they were not being sent away on the more creditable ground, but because some suspicion had arisen; so because they felt indignant and considered that they had not deserved such treatment at the hands of the Lacedaemonians, the instant they returned home they gave up the alliance which they had made with the Lacedaemonians against the Persians and became allies of their enemies, the Argives. And an alliance at the same time, on the same terms and confirmed by the same oaths, was concluded by both the Athenians and the Argives with the Thessalians.

CIII. In the tenth year[1] the rebels on Ithome found that they could hold out no longer and surrendered to the Lacedaemonians on condition that they should leave the Peloponnesus under a truce and should never set foot in it again; and if any of them should be caught there, he was to be a slave of his captor. Moreover, before this time the Lacedaemonians also received a Pythian oracle, which bade them let go the suppliant of Ithomean Zeus. So the Messenians left the Peloponnesus, themselves and their children and wives; and the Athenians received them, in consequence of the enmity to the Lacedaemonians already existing, and settled them at Naupactus, which they happened to have lately taken from its possessors, the Ozolian Locrians. And the Megarians also entered into alliance with the Athenians, revolting from the Lacedaemonians because the Corinthians were pressing them hard in a war about boundaries; and thus the Athenians secured Megara and Pegae,[2] and they built for the Megarians the long walls which run from the city to

[2] Pegae was the Megarian harbour on the Corinthian gulf: Nisaea, a nearer one, on the Saronic gulf.

τὰ ἀπὸ τῆς πόλεως ἐς Νίσαιαν καὶ ἐφρούρουν αὐτοί. καὶ Κορινθίοις μὲν οὐχ ἥκιστα ἀπὸ τοῦδε τὸ σφοδρὸν μῖσος ἤρξατο πρῶτον ἐς Ἀθηναίους γενέσθαι.

CIV. Ἰνάρως δὲ ὁ Ψαμμητίχου, Λίβυς, βασιλεὺς Λιβύων τῶν πρὸς Αἰγύπτῳ, ὁρμώμενος ἐκ Μαρείας τῆς ὑπὲρ Φάρου πόλεως ἀπέστησεν Αἰγύπτου τὰ πλείω ἀπὸ βασιλέως Ἀρταξέρξου, καὶ αὐτὸς ἄρχων γενόμενος Ἀθηναίους ἐπηγά-
2 γετο. οἱ δὲ (ἔτυχον γὰρ ἐς Κύπρον στρατευόμενοι ναυσὶ διακοσίαις αὐτῶν τε καὶ τῶν ξυμμάχων) ἦλθον ἀπολιπόντες τὴν Κύπρον, καὶ ἀναπλεύσαντες ἀπὸ θαλάσσης ἐς τὸν Νεῖλον τοῦ τε ποταμοῦ κρατοῦντες καὶ τῆς Μέμφιδος τῶν δύο μερῶν πρὸς τὸ τρίτον μέρος ὃ καλεῖται Λευκὸν τεῖχος ἐπολέμουν· ἐνῆσαν δὲ αὐτόθι Περσῶν καὶ Μήδων οἱ καταφυγόντες καὶ Αἰγυπτίων οἱ μὴ ξυναποστάντες.

CV. Ἀθηναίοις δὲ ναυσὶν ἀποβᾶσιν ἐς Ἁλιᾶς πρὸς Κορινθίους καὶ Ἐπιδαυρίους μάχη ἐγένετο, καὶ ἐνίκων Κορίνθιοι. καὶ ὕστερον Ἀθηναῖοι ἐναυμάχησαν ἐπὶ Κεκρυφαλείᾳ Πελοποννησίων
2 ναυσί, καὶ ἐνίκων Ἀθηναῖοι. πολέμου δὲ καταστάντος πρὸς Αἰγινήτας Ἀθηναίοις μετὰ ταῦτα ναυμαχία γίγνεται ἐπ' Αἰγίνῃ μεγάλη Ἀθηναίων καὶ Αἰγινητῶν (καὶ οἱ ξύμμαχοι ἑκατέροις παρῆσαν), καὶ ἐνίκων Ἀθηναῖοι, καὶ ναῦς ἑβδομήκοντα λαβόντες αὐτῶν ἐς τὴν γῆν ἀπέβησαν καὶ ἐπολιόρκουν Λεωκράτους τοῦ Στροίβου στρατηγοῦν-

Nisaea and held it with a garrison of their own troops. And it was chiefly because of this act that the vehement hatred of the Corinthians for the Athenians first arose.

CIV. Meanwhile Inaros, son of Psammetichus, a Libyan and king of the Libyans who are adjacent to Egypt, setting out from Mareia, the city just north of Pharos, caused the greater part of Egypt to revolt from King Artaxerxes,[1] and then, when he had made himself ruler, he called in the Athenians. And they left Cyprus,[2] where they happened to be on an expedition with two hundred ships of their own and of their allies, and went to Egypt, and when they had sailed up the Nile from the sea, finding themselves masters of the river and of two-thirds of Memphis, they proceeded to attack the third part, which is called the White Fortress. And in this fortress were some Persians and Medes who had taken refuge there, and such Egyptians as had not joined in the revolt.

CV. The Athenians also made a descent with a fleet upon Halieis, where they had a battle with some Corinthians and Epidaurians, in which the Corinthians won. And afterwards the Athenians fought a sea-fight at Cecryphaleia with a Peloponnesian fleet, in which the Athenians won. After this war broke out between the Athenians and the Aeginetans, and a great sea-fight occurred between the Athenians and the Aeginetans off Aegina, in which the allies of both sides were present. This the Athenians won and having taken seventy Aeginetan ships they descended upon their territory and laid siege to the city, Leocrates son of Stroebus,

[1] 460 B.C. [2] *cf.* ch. xciv. 2.

3 τος. ἔπειτα Πελοποννήσιοι ἀμύνειν βουλόμενοι
Αἰγινήταις ἐς μὲν τὴν Αἴγιναν τριακοσίους
ὁπλίτας, πρότερον Κορινθίων καὶ Ἐπιδαυρίων
ἐπικούρους, διεβίβασαν, τὰ δὲ ἄκρα τῆς Γερανείας
κατέλαβον καὶ ἐς τὴν Μεγαρίδα κατέβησαν
Κορίνθιοι μετὰ τῶν ξυμμάχων, νομίζοντες ἀδυ-
νάτους ἔσεσθαι Ἀθηναίους βοηθεῖν τοῖς Μεγα-
ρεῦσιν ἔν τε Αἰγίνῃ ἀπούσης στρατιᾶς πολλῆς
καὶ ἐν Αἰγύπτῳ· ἢν δὲ καὶ βοηθῶσιν, ἀπ' Αἰγίνης
4 ἀναστήσεσθαι αὐτούς. οἱ δὲ Ἀθηναῖοι τὸ μὲν
πρὸς Αἰγίνῃ στράτευμα οὐκ ἐκίνησαν, τῶν δ' ἐκ
τῆς πόλεως ὑπολοίπων οἵ τε πρεσβύτατοι καὶ οἱ
νεώτατοι ἀφικνοῦνται ἐς τὰ Μέγαρα Μυρωνίδου
5 στρατηγοῦντος. καὶ μάχης γενομένης ἰσορρόπου
πρὸς Κορινθίους διεκρίθησαν ἀπ' ἀλλήλων, καὶ
ἐνόμισαν αὐτοὶ ἑκάτεροι οὐκ ἔλασσον ἔχειν ἐν τῷ
6 ἔργῳ. καὶ οἱ μὲν Ἀθηναῖοι (ἐκράτησαν γὰρ
ὅμως μᾶλλον) ἀπελθόντων τῶν Κορινθίων τροπαῖον ἔστησαν· οἱ δὲ Κορίνθιοι κακιζόμενοι ὑπὸ
τῶν ἐν τῇ πόλει πρεσβυτέρων καὶ παρασκευασά-
μενοι, ἡμέραις ὕστερον δώδεκα μάλιστα ἐλθόντες
ἀνθίστασαν τροπαῖον καὶ αὐτοὶ ὡς νικήσαντες.
καὶ οἱ Ἀθηναῖοι ἐκβοηθήσαντες ἐκ τῶν Μεγάρων
τούς τε τὸ τροπαῖον ἱστάντας διαφθείρουσι καὶ
τοῖς ἄλλοις ξυμβαλόντες ἐκράτησαν. CVI. οἱ
δὲ νικώμενοι ὑπεχώρουν, καί τι αὐτῶν μέρος οὐκ
ὀλίγον προσβιασθὲν καὶ διαμαρτὸν τῆς ὁδοῦ
ἐσέπεσεν ἔς του χωρίον ἰδιώτου, ᾧ ἔτυχεν

being in command. Thereupon the Peloponnesians, wishing to aid the Aeginetans, sent into Aegina three hundred hoplites, who had previously been assisting the Corinthians and Epidaurians. Moreover, the Corinthians occupied the heights of Geraneia, and made a descent upon the territory of Megara in conjunction with their allies, thinking that the Athenians would be unable to aid the Megarians, since many of their troops were away in Aegina and in Egypt, or if they should attempt it that they would have to withdraw from Aegina. The Athenians, however, did not disturb the army besieging Aegina, but with such forces as were left in the city, consisting of the oldest and the youngest[1] men, marched into Megara, the general in command being Myronides. An indecisive battle was fought with the Corinthians, whereupon they separated, each side thinking they had not got the worst of it in the action. And the Athenians, who had in fact got rather the better of it, when the Corinthians withdrew, set up a trophy; but the Corinthians, being reproached by the older men in their city, made their preparations and about twelve days later came back and set up for themselves a rival trophy, as though they had won. Hereupon the Athenians made a sally from Megara, slew those who were setting up the trophy, and joining battle with the rest defeated them. CVI. The vanquished party now retreated, and a not inconsiderable portion of them, being hard pressed, missed their way and rushed into a piece of land belonging to

[1] These performed military service only in extraordinary cases; the former were between fifty and sixty, the latter under twenty years of age.

2 ὄρυγμα μέγα περιεῖργον καὶ οὐκ ἦν ἔξοδος. οἱ δὲ Ἀθηναῖοι γνόντες κατὰ πρόσωπόν τε εἶργον τοῖς ὁπλίταις καὶ περιστήσαντες κύκλῳ τοὺς ψιλοὺς κατέλευσαν πάντας τοὺς ἐσελθόντας, καὶ πάθος μέγα τοῦτο Κορινθίοις ἐγένετο. τὸ δὲ πλῆθος ἀνεχώρησεν αὐτοῖς τῆς στρατιᾶς ἐπ' οἴκου.

CVII. Ἤρξαντο δὲ κατὰ τοὺς χρόνους τούτους καὶ τὰ μακρὰ τείχη Ἀθηναῖοι ἐς θάλασσαν οἰκοδομεῖν, τό τε Φαληρόνδε καὶ τὸ ἐς Πειραιᾶ.
2 καὶ Φωκέων στρατευσάντων ἐς Δωριᾶς τὴν Λακεδαιμονίων μητρόπολιν, Βοιὸν καὶ Κυτίνιον καὶ Ἐρινεόν, καὶ ἑλόντων ἓν τῶν πολισμάτων τούτων οἱ Λακεδαιμόνιοι Νικομήδους τοῦ Κλεομβρότου ὑπὲρ Πλειστοάνακτος τοῦ Παυσανίου βασιλέως, νέου ὄντος ἔτι, ἡγουμένου ἐβοήθησαν τοῖς Δωριεῦσιν ἑαυτῶν τε πεντακοσίοις καὶ χιλίοις ὁπλίταις καὶ τῶν ξυμμάχων μυρίοις, καὶ τοὺς Φωκέας ὁμολογίᾳ ἀναγκάσαντες ἀποδοῦναι τὴν πόλιν
3 ἀπεχώρουν πάλιν. καὶ κατὰ θάλασσαν μὲν αὐτούς, διὰ τοῦ Κρισαίου κόλπου εἰ βούλοιντο περαιοῦσθαι, Ἀθηναῖοι ναυσὶ περιπλεύσαντες ἔμελλον κωλύσειν· διὰ δὲ τῆς Γερανείας οὐκ ἀσφαλὲς αὐτοῖς ἐφαίνετο Ἀθηναίων ἐχόντων Μέγαρα καὶ Πηγὰς πορεύεσθαι·[1] δύσοδός τε γὰρ ἡ Γεράνεια καὶ ἐφρουρεῖτο αἰεὶ ὑπὸ Ἀθηναίων, καὶ τότε ᾐσθάνοντο αὐτοὺς μέλλοντας καὶ ταύτῃ
4 κωλύσειν. ἔδοξε δὲ αὐτοῖς ἐν Βοιωτοῖς περιμείνασι σκέψασθαι ὅτῳ τρόπῳ ἀσφαλέστατα διαπορεύσονται. τὸ δέ τι καὶ ἄνδρες ἐπῆγον αὐτοὺς

[1] πορεύεσθαι deleted by Hude as not read by Schol.

some private person, which was enclosed by a great ditch and had no exit. And when the Athenians perceived this, they shut them in by barring the entrance with hoplites, and stationing light-armed troops all round stoned all who had entered. And this was a great calamity to the Corinthians; the main body of their army, however, returned home.

CVII. About this period[1] the Athenians began to build their long walls to the sea, one to Phalerum, the other to the Peiraeus. And the Phocians made an expedition against the land of the Dorians, the mother-country of the Lacedaemonians, namely the towns of Boeum, Citinium, and Erineum, one of which they captured; whereupon the Lacedaemonians, under the lead of Nicomedes son of Cleombrotus, acting for King Pleistoanax son of Pausanias, who was still a minor, sent to the aid of the Dorians a force of fifteen hundred hoplites of their own and ten thousand of their allies, and after they had forced the Phocians to make terms and restore the city they began their return homeward. Now if they wished to take the sea-route and make their passage by way of the Crisaean Gulf, the Athenians were sure to take their fleet round the Peloponnesus and block their way; and to march over the Geranaean pass appeared to them hazardous, since the Athenians held Megara and Pegae. Besides, the Geranaean pass was not easy to traverse and was at all times guarded by the Athenians, and at this present time, as the Lacedaemonians perceived, they intended to block their way. So they decided to wait in Boeotia and consider how they might most safely cross over to the Peloponnesus. To this course they were partly influenced by some Athenians, who were

[1] 457 B.C.

τῶν Ἀθηναίων κρύφα, ἐλπίσαντες δῆμόν τε κατα-
παύσειν καὶ τὰ μακρὰ τείχη οἰκοδομούμενα.
5 ἐβοήθησαν δὲ ἐπ' αὐτοὺς οἱ Ἀθηναῖοι πανδημεὶ
καὶ Ἀργείων χίλιοι καὶ τῶν ἄλλων ξυμμάχων
ὡς ἕκαστοι· ξύμπαντες δὲ ἐγένοντο τετρακισχί-
6 λιοι καὶ μύριοι. νομίσαντες δὲ ἀπορεῖν ὅπῃ
διέλθωσιν, ἐπεστράτευσαν αὐτοῖς, καί τι καὶ τοῦ
7 δήμου καταλύσεως ὑποψίᾳ. ἦλθον δὲ καὶ Θεσσαλῶν ἱππῆς τοῖς Ἀθηναίοις κατὰ τὸ ξυμμαχι-
κόν, οἳ μετέστησαν ἐν τῷ ἔργῳ παρὰ τοὺς
Λακεδαιμονίους.

CVIII. Γενομένης δὲ τῆς μάχης ἐν Τανάγρᾳ
τῆς Βοιωτίας ἐνίκων Λακεδαιμόνιοι καὶ οἱ ξύμ-
2 μαχοι, καὶ φόνος ἐγένετο ἀμφοτέρων πολύς. καὶ
Λακεδαιμόνιοι μὲν ἐς τὴν Μεγαρίδα ἐλθόντες καὶ
δενδροτομήσαντες πάλιν ἀπῆλθον ἐπ' οἴκου διὰ
Γερανείας καὶ ἰσθμοῦ· Ἀθηναῖοι δὲ δευτέρᾳ καὶ
ἑξηκοστῇ ἡμέρᾳ μετὰ τὴν μάχην ἐστράτευσαν ἐς
3 Βοιωτοὺς Μυρωνίδου στρατηγοῦντος, καὶ μάχῃ
ἐν Οἰνοφύτοις Βοιωτοὺς νικήσαντες τῆς τε χώρας
ἐκράτησαν τῆς Βοιωτίας καὶ Φωκίδος καὶ Ταναγ-
γραίων τὸ τεῖχος περιεῖλον καὶ Λοκρῶν τῶν
Ὀπουντίων ἑκατὸν ἄνδρας ὁμήρους τοὺς πλου-
σιωτάτους ἔλαβον, τά τε τείχη ἑαυτῶν τὰ μακρὰ
4 ἀπετέλεσαν. ὡμολόγησαν δὲ καὶ οἱ Αἰγινῆται
μετὰ ταῦτα τοῖς Ἀθηναίοις, τείχη τε περιελόντες
καὶ ναῦς παραδόντες φόρον τε ταξάμενοι ἐς τὸν
5 ἔπειτα χρόνον. καὶ Πελοπόννησον περιέπλευσαν
Ἀθηναῖοι Τολμίδου τοῦ Τολμαίου στρατηγοῦντος,

secretly inviting them into their country, in the hope of putting an end to the democracy and to the building of the long walls. But the Athenians went out against the Lacedaemonians with their whole force and with one thousand Argives and contingents of the several allies, the whole body amounting to fourteen thousand men. And they undertook the expedition against them because they believed that they were at a loss how to get through, and partly too on a suspicion of a plot to overthrow the democracy. The forces of the Athenians were strengthened by some Thessalian cavalry, who came in accordance with the terms of the alliance, but they deserted to the Lacedaemonians in the course of the action.

CVIII. The battle took place[1] at Tanagra in Boeotia, and in it the Lacedaemonians and their allies were victorious, and there was much slaughter on both sides. The Lacedaemonians then entered the Megarian territory, cut down the trees, and went back home by way of Geraneia and the Isthmus. But on the sixty-second day after the battle, the Athenians, having made an expedition into Boeotia under Myronides, defeated the Boeotians at Oenophyta, got control of Boeotia and Phocis, pulled down the walls of Tanagra, and took one hundred of the wealthiest men of the Opuntian Locrians as hostages. Meanwhile they completed their own long walls. After this the Aeginetans also capitulated to the Athenians, pulling down their walls, delivering up their ships, and agreeing to pay tribute in future.[2] And the Athenians, under the command of Tolmides son of Tolmaeus, sailed round the Peloponnesus,

[1] 456 B.C. [2] 455 B.C.

καὶ τὸ νεώριον τῶν Λακεδαιμονίων ἐνέπρησαν καὶ Χαλκίδα Κορινθίων εἷλον καὶ Σικυωνίους ἐν ἀποβάσει τῆς γῆς μάχῃ ἐκράτησαν.

CIX. Οἱ δ' ἐν τῇ Αἰγύπτῳ Ἀθηναῖοι καὶ οἱ ξύμμαχοι ἐπέμενον, καὶ αὐτοῖς πολλαὶ ἰδέαι
2 πολέμων κατέστησαν. τὸ μὲν γὰρ πρῶτον ἐκράτουν τῆς Αἰγύπτου οἱ Ἀθηναῖοι, καὶ βασιλεὺς πέμπει ἐς Λακεδαίμονα Μεγάβαζον ἄνδρα Πέρσην χρήματα ἔχοντα, ὅπως ἐς τὴν Ἀττικὴν ἐσβαλεῖν πεισθέντων τῶν Πελοποννησίων ἀπ'
3 Αἰγύπτου ἀπαγάγοι Ἀθηναίους. ὡς δὲ αὐτῷ οὐ προυχώρει καὶ τὰ χρήματα ἄλλως ἀνηλοῦτο, ὁ μὲν Μεγάβαζος καὶ τὰ λοιπὰ τῶν χρημάτων πάλιν ἐς τὴν Ἀσίαν ἀνεκομίσθη, Μεγάβυζον δὲ τὸν Ζωπύρου πέμπει ἄνδρα Πέρσην μετὰ στρα-
4 τιᾶς πολλῆς· ὃς ἀφικόμενος κατὰ γῆν τούς τε Αἰγυπτίους καὶ τοὺς ξυμμάχους μάχῃ ἐκράτησε καὶ ἐκ τῆς Μέμφιδος ἐξήλασε τοὺς Ἕλληνας καὶ τέλος ἐς Προσωπίτιδα τὴν νῆσον κατέκλῃσεν· καὶ ἐπολιόρκει ἐν αὐτῇ ἐνιαυτὸν καὶ ἓξ μῆνας, μέχρι οὗ ξηράνας τὴν διώρυχα καὶ παρατρέψας ἄλλῃ τὸ ὕδωρ τάς τε ναῦς ἐπὶ τοῦ ξηροῦ ἐποίησε καὶ τῆς νήσου τὰ πολλὰ ἠπείρου, καὶ διαβὰς εἷλε τὴν νῆσον πεζῇ.

CX. Οὕτω μὲν τὰ τῶν Ἑλλήνων πράγματα ἐφθάρη ἓξ ἔτη πολεμήσαντα· καὶ ὀλίγοι ἀπὸ πολλῶν πορευόμενοι διὰ τῆς Λιβύης ἐς Κυρήνην
2 ἐσώθησαν, οἱ δὲ πλεῖστοι ἀπώλοντο. Αἴγυπτος δὲ πάλιν ὑπὸ βασιλέα ἐγένετο πλὴν Ἀμυρταίου

burned the dock-yard[1] of the Lacedaemonians, took Chalcis, a city of the Corinthians, and making a descent upon the territory of the Sicyonians defeated them in battle.

CIX. Meanwhile the Athenians and their allies stayed on in Egypt and the war took on many forms. At first the Athenians had the mastery in Egypt, and the King sent to Lacedaemon Megabazus a Persian with a supply of money, in order that the Lacedaemonians might be induced to invade Attica and the Athenians thus be drawn away from Egypt. But when he found that matters did not advance and the money was being spent in vain, Megabazus betook himself back to Asia with the money that was left, and Megabyzus son of Zopyrus,[2] a Persian, was despatched with a large army.[3] He marched thither by land, and defeated the Egyptians and their allies in battle, drove the Hellenes out of Memphis, and finally shut them up in the island of Prosopitis, where he besieged them for a year and six months, then finally, by diverting the water into another course, drained the canal and left the ships high and dry, converting the greater part of the island into mainland; then he crossed over dry-shod and took the island.

CX. Thus this undertaking of the Hellenes came to naught after a war of six years;[4] and but few out of many, making their way through Libya into Cyrene, escaped with their lives; the most of them perished. And all Egypt again came under the King's dominion, except Amyrtaeus, the king of the

[1] Gytheum, on the Laconian gulf.

[2] Hero of the capture of Babylon, Hdt. III. clx.

[3] Diodorus gives him with Artabazus 300,000 men (xi. 75) and 300 ships (xi. 77).

[4] 454 B.C.

τοῦ ἐν τοῖς ἕλεσι βασιλέως· τοῦτον δὲ διὰ μέγεθός τε τοῦ ἕλους οὐκ ἐδύναντο ἑλεῖν καὶ ἅμα
3 μαχιμώτατοί εἰσι τῶν Αἰγυπτίων οἱ ἕλειοι. Ἰνάρως δὲ ὁ Λιβύων βασιλεύς, ὃς τὰ πάντα ἔπραξε περὶ τῆς Αἰγύπτου, προδοσίᾳ ληφθεὶς ἀνεσταυ-
4 ρώθη. ἐκ δὲ τῶν Ἀθηνῶν καὶ τῆς ἄλλης ξυμμαχίδος πεντήκοντα τριήρεις διάδοχοι πλέουσαι ἐς Αἴγυπτον ἔσχον κατὰ τὸ Μενδήσιον κέρας, οὐκ εἰδότες τῶν γεγονότων οὐδέν· καὶ αὐτοῖς ἔκ τε γῆς ἐπιπεσόντες πεζοὶ καὶ ἐκ θαλάσσης Φοινίκων ναυτικὸν διέφθειραν τὰς πολλὰς τῶν νεῶν,
5 αἱ δ' ἐλάσσους διέφυγον πάλιν. τὰ μὲν κατὰ τὴν μεγάλην στρατείαν Ἀθηναίων καὶ τῶν ξυμμάχων ἐς Αἴγυπτον οὕτως ἐτελεύτησεν.

CXI. Ἐκ δὲ Θεσσαλίας Ὀρέστης ὁ Ἐχεκρατίδου υἱὸς τοῦ Θεσσαλῶν βασιλέως φεύγων ἔπεισεν Ἀθηναίους ἑαυτὸν κατάγειν· καὶ παραλαβόντες Βοιωτοὺς καὶ Φωκέας ὄντας ξυμμάχους οἱ Ἀθηναῖοι ἐστράτευσαν τῆς Θεσσαλίας ἐπὶ Φάρσαλον. καὶ τῆς μὲν γῆς ἐκράτουν ὅσα μὴ προϊόντες πολὺ ἐκ τῶν ὅπλων (οἱ γὰρ ἱππῆς τῶν Θεσσαλῶν εἶργον), τὴν δὲ πόλιν οὐχ εἷλον, οὐδ' ἄλλο προυχώρει αὐτοῖς οὐδὲν ὧν ἕνεκα ἐστράτευσαν, ἀλλ' ἀπεχώρησαν πάλιν Ὀρέστην ἔχοντες ἄπρακτοι.

2 Μετὰ δὲ ταῦτα οὐ πολλῷ ὕστερον χίλιοι Ἀθηναίων ἐπὶ τὰς ναῦς τὰς ἐν Πηγαῖς ἐπιβάντες (εἶχον δ' αὐτοὶ τὰς Πηγάς) παρέπλευσαν ἐς Σικυῶνα Περικλέους τοῦ Ξανθίππου στρατηγοῦντος, καὶ ἀποβάντες Σικυωνίων τοὺς προσμεί-

marshes[1]; for the Persians were unable to capture him, both on account of the extent of the marsh and because the marsh people are the best fighters among the Egyptians. Inaros, however, the king of the Libyans, who had been the originator of the whole movement in Egypt, was taken by treachery and impaled. And when fifty triremes, which sailed to Egypt from Athens and the rest of the confederacy to relieve the fleet there, put in at the Mendesian mouth of the Nile, quite unaware of what had happened, the infantry fell upon them from the shore and a Phoenician fleet from the sea and destroyed most of the ships, a small number only escaping. So ended the great expedition against Egypt of the Athenians and their allies.

CXI. And now Orestes son of Echecratidas, king of the Thessalians, who was exiled from Thessaly, persuaded the Athenians to restore him. And they, taking along some Boeotians and Phocians who were allies, made an expedition against Pharsalus in Thessaly. And though they made themselves masters of the land, so far as this was possible without going far from their camp—for the Thessalian cavalry hemmed them in—they failed to capture the city and indeed none of the other objects of their expedition was attained, so they went back home again unsuccessful, having Orestes with them.

Not long after this[2] one thousand Athenians, embarking on the ships at Pegae, which was now in their possession,[3] sailed along the coast to Sicyon under the command of Pericles son of Xanthippus, and disembarking defeated in battle the Sicyonians

[1] *cf.* Hdt. II. cxl.; III. xv.
[2] 454 B.C. [3] *cf.* ch. ciii. 4.

3 ξαντας μαχῃ ἐκράτησαν. καὶ εὐθὺς παραλαβόντες Ἀχαιοὺς καὶ διαπλεύσαντες πέραν, τῆς Ἀκαρνανίας ἐς Οἰνιάδας ἐστράτευσαν καὶ ἐπολιόρκουν, οὐ μέντοι εἷλόν γε, ἀλλ' ἀπεχώρησαν ἐπ' οἴκου.

CXII. Ὕστερον δὲ διαλιπόντων ἐτῶν τριῶν σπονδαὶ γίγνονται Πελοποννησίοις καὶ Ἀθηναίοις
2 πεντέτεις. καὶ Ἑλληνικοῦ μὲν πολέμου ἔσχον οἱ Ἀθηναῖοι, ἐς δὲ Κύπρον ἐστρατεύοντο ναυσὶ διακοσίαις αὐτῶν τε καὶ τῶν ξυμμάχων Κίμωνος
3 στρατηγοῦντος. καὶ ἑξήκοντα μὲν νῆες ἐς Αἴγυπτον ἀπ' αὐτῶν ἔπλευσαν Ἀμυρταίου μεταπέμποντος τοῦ ἐν τοῖς ἕλεσι βασιλέως, αἱ δὲ
4 ἄλλαι Κίτιον ἐπολιόρκουν. Κίμωνος δὲ ἀποθανόντος καὶ λιμοῦ γενομένου ἀπεχώρησαν ἀπὸ Κιτίου· καὶ πλεύσαντες ὑπὲρ Σαλαμῖνος τῆς ἐν Κύπρῳ Φοίνιξι καὶ Κυπρίοις καὶ Κίλιξιν ἐναυμάχησαν καὶ ἐπεζομάχησαν ἅμα, καὶ νικήσαντες ἀμφότερα ἀπεχώρησαν ἐπ' οἴκου καὶ αἱ ἐξ Αἰ-
5 γύπτου νῆες πάλιν ἀνελθοῦσαι μετ' αὐτῶν. Λακεδαιμόνιοι δὲ μετὰ ταῦτα τὸν ἱερὸν καλούμενον πόλεμον ἐστράτευσαν, καὶ κρατήσαντες τοῦ ἐν Δελφοῖς ἱεροῦ παρέδοσαν Δελφοῖς· καὶ αὖθις ὕστερον Ἀθηναῖοι ἀποχωρησάντων αὐτῶν στρατεύσαντες καὶ κρατήσαντες παρέδοσαν Φωκεῦσιν.

CXIII. Καὶ χρόνου ἐγγενομένου μετὰ ταῦτα Ἀθηναῖοι, Βοιωτῶν τῶν φευγόντων ἐχόντων Ὀρχομενὸν καὶ Χαιρώνειαν καὶ ἄλλ' ἄττα χωρία τῆς Βοιωτίας, ἐστράτευσαν ἑαυτῶν μὲν χιλίοις ὁπλίταις, τῶν δὲ ξυμμάχων ὡς ἑκάστοις ἐπὶ τὰ χωρία ταῦτα πολέμια ὄντα, Τολμίδου τοῦ Τολμαίου στρατηγοῦντος. καὶ Χαιρώνειαν ἑλόντες καὶ

who came out against them. Immediately thereafter, taking along some Achaeans and sailing across the gulf, they made an expedition against Oeniadae in Acarnania and laid siege to it; but failing to take it they went back home.

CXII. Three years afterwards[1] a truce was made between the Peloponnesians and Athenians, to last five years. And the Athenians did abstain from warfare against Hellenes, but they made an expedition against Cyprus with two hundred ships of their own and of their allies, under the command of Cimon. Sixty of these ships sailed to Egypt on the summons of Amyrtaeus, the king in the marshes, while the others laid siege to Citium. But Cimon died and a famine arose, and so they withdrew from Citium;[2] and on their way home, when off Salamis in Cyprus, they fought the Phoenicians, Cyprians and Cilicians by sea and on land. Gaining the victory in both battles they went back home, and with them returned the ships that had been in Egypt. After this the Lacedaemonians undertook the so-called sacred war, and getting possession of the temple at Delphi, delivered it to the Delphians; and afterwards, when they had withdrawn, the Athenians made an expedition, got possession of it, and delivered it again to the Phocians.

CXIII. Some time after this[3] the Athenians under the command of Tolmides son of Tolmaeus, with one thousand hoplites of their own and the respective quotas of their allies, made an expedition against Orchomenus and Chaeroneia and some other places in Boeotia, which were in the possession of the Boeotian exiles and therefore hostile. And after taking

[1] 451 B.C. [2] 449 B.C. [3] 447 B.C.

ἀνδραποδίσαντες ἀπεχώρουν φυλακὴν καταστή-
2 σαντες. πορευομένοις δ' αὐτοῖς ἐν Κορωνείᾳ
ἐπιτίθενται οἵ τε ἐκ τῆς Ὀρχομενοῦ φυγάδες
Βοιωτῶν καὶ Λοκροὶ μετ' αὐτῶν καὶ Εὐβοέων
φυγάδες καὶ ὅσοι τῆς αὐτῆς γνώμης ἦσαν· καὶ
μάχῃ κρατήσαντες τοὺς μὲν διέφθειραν τῶν Ἀθη-
3 ναίων, τοὺς δὲ ζῶντας ἔλαβον. καὶ τὴν Βοιωτίαν
ἐξέλιπον Ἀθηναῖοι πᾶσαν, σπονδὰς ποιησάμενοι
4 ἐφ' ᾧ τοὺς ἄνδρας κομιοῦνται. καὶ οἱ φεύγοντες
Βοιωτῶν κατελθόντες καὶ οἱ ἄλλοι πάντες αὐτόνομοι πάλιν ἐγένοντο.

CXIV. Μετὰ δὲ ταῦτα οὐ πολλῷ ὕστερον
Εὔβοια ἀπέστη ἀπὸ Ἀθηναίων. καὶ ἐς αὐτὴν
διαβεβηκότος ἤδη Περικλέους στρατιᾷ Ἀθηναίων
ἠγγέλθη αὐτῷ ὅτι Μέγαρα ἀφέστηκε καὶ Πελοποννήσιοι μέλλουσιν ἐσβάλλειν ἐς τὴν Ἀττικὴν
καὶ οἱ φρουροὶ Ἀθηναίων διεφθαρμένοι εἰσὶν ὑπὸ
Μεγαρέων, πλὴν ὅσοι ἐς Νίσαιαν ἀπέφυγον· ἐπα-
γαγόμενοι δὲ Κορινθίους καὶ Σικυωνίους καὶ Ἐπιδαυρίους ἀπέστησαν οἱ Μεγαρῆς. ὁ δὲ Περικλῆς
πάλιν κατὰ τάχος ἐκόμιζε τὴν στρατιὰν ἐκ τῆς
2 Εὐβοίας. καὶ μετὰ τοῦτο οἱ Πελοποννήσιοι τῆς
Ἀττικῆς ἐς Ἐλευσῖνα καὶ Θριῶζε ἐσβαλόντες
ἐδῄωσαν Πλειστοάνακτος τοῦ Παυσανίου βασιλέως Λακεδαιμονίων ἡγουμένου, καὶ τὸ πλέον
3 οὐκέτι προελθόντες ἀπεχώρησαν ἐπ' οἴκου. καὶ
Ἀθηναῖοι πάλιν ἐς Εὔβοιαν διαβάντες Περικλέους στρατηγοῦντος κατεστρέψαντο πᾶσαν,
καὶ τὴν μὲν ἄλλην ὁμολογίᾳ κατεστήσαντο,
Ἑστιαιᾶς δὲ ἐξοικίσαντες αὐτοὶ τὴν γῆν ἔσχον.

---

445 B.C.

Chaeroneia and selling its inhabitants into slavery, they placed a garrison in it and departed. But while they were on the march they were attacked at Coronea by the Boeotian exiles from Orchomenus, together with some Locrians and Euboean exiles and others who held the same political views, and were defeated, some of the Athenians being slain and others taken alive. Accordingly the Athenians evacuated the whole of Boeotia, making a treaty upon the stipulation that they should receive back their prisoners. And so the Boeotian exiles were restored, and they as well as all the rest of the Boeotians again became autonomous.

CXIV. Not long after this[1] Euboea revolted from Athens; and Pericles had just crossed over to the island with an Athenian army when word was brought to him that Megara had revolted, that the Peloponnesians were about to invade Attica, and that all the Athenian garrison had been destroyed by the Megarians except such as had escaped to Nisaea. The Megarians had effected this revolt by bringing Corinthians, Sicyonians and Epidaurians to their aid. So Pericles in haste brought his army back again from Euboea. After this the Peloponnesians, under the command of Pleistoanax son of Pausanias, king of the Lacedaemonians, advanced into Attica as far as Eleusis and Thria, ravaging the country; but without going further they returned home. Thereupon the Athenians again crossed over into Euboea under the command of Pericles and subdued the whole of it; the rest of the island they settled[2] by agreement, but expelled the Hestiaeans from their homes and themselves occupied their territory.

[2] Setting up democracies, etc. *cf. C.I.A.* iv. 27 a.

CXV. Ἀναχωρήσαντες δὲ ἀπ' Εὐβοίας οὐ πολλῷ ὕστερον σπονδὰς ἐποιήσαντο πρὸς Λακεδαιμονίους καὶ τοὺς ξυμμάχους τριακοντούτεις, ἀποδόντες Νίσαιαν καὶ Πηγὰς καὶ Τροιζῆνα καὶ Ἀχαΐαν· ταῦτα γὰρ εἶχον Ἀθηναῖοι Πελοποννησίων.

2 Ἕκτῳ δὲ ἔτει Σαμίοις καὶ Μιλησίοις πόλεμος ἐγένετο περὶ Πριήνης· καὶ οἱ Μιλήσιοι ἐλασσούμενοι τῷ πολέμῳ παρ' Ἀθηναίους ἐλθόντες κατεβόων τῶν Σαμίων. ξυνεπελάβοντο δὲ καὶ ἐξ αὐτῆς τῆς Σάμου ἄνδρες ἰδιῶται, νεωτερίσαι
3 βουλόμενοι τὴν πολιτείαν.[1] πλεύσαντες οὖν Ἀθηναῖοι ἐς Σάμον ναυσὶ τεσσαράκοντα δημοκρατίαν κατέστησαν καὶ ὁμήρους ἔλαβον τῶν Σαμίων πεντήκοντα μὲν παῖδας, ἴσους δὲ ἄνδρας, καὶ κατέθεντο ἐς Λῆμνον καὶ φρουρὰν ἐγκατα-
4 λιπόντες ἀνεχώρησαν. τῶν δὲ Σαμίων ἦσαν γάρ τινες οἳ οὐχ ὑπέμειναν, ἀλλ' ἔφυγον ἐς τὴν ἤπειρον, ξυνθέμενοι τῶν ἐν τῇ πόλει τοῖς δυνατωτάτοις καὶ Πισσούθνῃ τῷ Ὑστάσπου ξυμμαχίαν, ὃς εἶχε Σάρδεις τότε, ἐπικούρους τε ξυλλέξαντες ἐς ἑπτακοσίους διέβησαν ὑπὸ νύκτα ἐς τὴν Σάμον.
5 καὶ πρῶτον μὲν τῷ δήμῳ ἐπανέστησαν καὶ ἐκράτησαν τῶν πλείστων, ἔπειτα τοὺς ὁμήρους ἐκκλέψαντες ἐκ Λήμνου τοὺς αὑτῶν ἀπέστησαν, καὶ τοὺς φρουροὺς τοὺς Ἀθηναίων καὶ τοὺς ἄρχοντας οἳ ἦσαν παρὰ σφίσιν ἐξέδοσαν Πισσούθνῃ, ἐπί τε Μίλητον εὐθὺς παρεσκευάζοντο στρατεύειν. ξυναπέστησαν δ' αὐτοῖς καὶ Βυζάντιοι.

[1] τὴν πολιτείαν seems not to have been read by the Schol., and so is deleted by van Herwerden and Hude.

CXV. Withdrawing their troops from Euboea not long afterwards they made a truce with the Lacedaemonians and their allies which was to last for thirty years, restoring Nisaea, Pegae, Troezen, and Achaea; for these were the places belonging to the Peloponnesians which the Athenians then held.

Six years later[1] a war arose between the Samians and the Milesians about the possession of Priene, and the Milesians, who were being worsted in the war, went to Athens and cried out against the Samians. They were seconded in their complaint by some private citizens from Samos itself who wished to revolutionize the government. So the Athenians sailed to Samos with forty ships and set up a democracy, taking as hostages of the Samians fifty boys and as many men, whom they deposited in Lemnos; then they withdrew from Samos, leaving a garrison behind. Some of the Samians, however, did not stay, but fled to the mainland, first making an alliance with the most influential men who remained in the city and with Pissuthnes son of Hystaspes, then satrap of Sardis; and collecting mercenary troops to the number of seven hundred they crossed over by night to Samos. First they attacked the popular party and got most of them into their power; then they secretly got their hostages out of Lemnos and revolted from Athens, handing over to Pissuthnes the Athenian officers and garrison that were on the island, and at once set about preparing an expedition against Miletus. And the Byzantines also joined in their revolt.

[1] 440 B.C.

CXVI. Ἀθηναῖοι δὲ ὡς ᾔσθοντο, πλεύσαντες ναυσὶν ἑξήκοντα ἐπὶ Σάμου ταῖς μὲν ἑκκαίδεκα τῶν νεῶν οὐκ ἐχρήσαντο (ἔτυχον γὰρ αἱ μὲν ἐπὶ Καρίας ἐς προσκοπὴν τῶν Φοινισσῶν νεῶν οἰχόμεναι, αἱ δὲ ἐπὶ Χίου καὶ Λέσβου περιαγγέλλουσαι βοηθεῖν), τεσσαράκοντα δὲ ναυσὶ καὶ τέσσαρσι Περικλέους δεκάτου αὐτοῦ στρατηγοῦντος ἐναυμάχησαν πρὸς Τραγίᾳ τῇ νήσῳ Σαμίων ναυσὶν ἑβδομήκοντα, ὧν ἦσαν αἱ εἴκοσι στρατιώτιδες (ἔτυχον δὲ αἱ πᾶσαι ἀπὸ Μιλήτου πλέ-
2 ουσαι), καὶ ἐνίκων Ἀθηναῖοι. ὕστερον δὲ αὐτοῖς ἐβοήθησαν ἐκ τῶν Ἀθηνῶν νῆες τεσσαράκοντα καὶ Χίων καὶ Λεσβίων πέντε καὶ εἴκοσι, καὶ ἀποβάντες καὶ κρατοῦντες τῷ πεζῷ ἐπολιόρκουν τρισὶ τείχεσι τὴν πόλιν καὶ ἐκ θαλάσσης ἅμα.
3 Περικλῆς δὲ λαβὼν ἑξήκοντα ναῦς ἀπὸ τῶν ἐφορμουσῶν ᾤχετο κατὰ τάχος ἐπὶ Καύνου καὶ Καρίας, ἐσαγγελθέντων ὅτι Φοίνισσαι νῆες ἐπ' αὐτοὺς πλέουσιν· ᾤχετο γὰρ καὶ ἐκ τῆς Σάμου πέντε ναυσὶ Στησαγόρας καὶ ἄλλοι ἐπὶ τὰς Φοινίσσας.

CXVII. Ἐν τούτῳ δὲ οἱ Σάμιοι ἐξαπιναίως ἔκπλουν ποιησάμενοι ἀφάρκτῳ τῷ στρατοπέδῳ ἐπιπεσόντες τάς τε προφυλακίδας ναῦς διέφθειραν καὶ ναυμαχοῦντες τὰς ἀνταναγομένας ἐνίκησαν, καὶ τῆς θαλάσσης τῆς καθ' ἑαυτοὺς ἐκράτησαν ἡμέρας περὶ τέσσαρας καὶ δέκα καὶ ἐσεκομίσαντο
2 καὶ ἐξεκομίσαντο ἃ ἐβούλοντο. ἐλθόντος δὲ Περικλέους πάλιν ταῖς ναυσὶ κατεκλῄσθησαν. καὶ ἐκ τῶν Ἀθηνῶν ὕστερον προσεβοήθησαν

CXVI. But when the Athenians heard of this they sailed for Samos with sixty ships. Sixteen of these, however, they did not make use of on this enterprise, for these had already gone, some toward Caria to keep watch upon the Phoenician ships, others towards Chios and Lesbos to summon aid; but with forty-four ships, under the command of Pericles and nine others,[1] they fought a sea-fight at the island of Tragia against seventy ships of the Samians, of which twenty were transport-ships, the whole fleet being on the way back from Miletus; and the Athenians were victorious. Later, having received a reinforcement from Athens of forty ships and from the Chians and Lesbians of twenty-five, they disembarked, and being superior to the Samians with their infantry proceeded to invest the city with three walls, at the same time blockading it by sea as well. But Pericles took sixty ships away from the blockading fleet and departed in haste towards Caunus in Caria, a report having come that a Phoenician fleet was sailing against his forces; for Stesagoras and others had gone from Samos with five vessels to fetch the Phoenician ships.

CXVII. Meanwhile the Samians suddenly made a sally and fell upon the Athenian naval station, which was unprotected by a stockade, destroying the guard-ships and defeating in a sea-fight the ships that put out against them. And for about fourteen days they were masters of the sea off their coast, bringing in and carrying out whatever they wished; but when Pericles came they were again blockaded by sea. And afterwards a reinforcement came from Athens

[1] Sophocles was on the fleet, as one of the ten generals of the year.

τεσσαράκοντα μὲν αἱ μετὰ Θουκυδίδου καὶ Ἅγνωνος καὶ Φορμίωνος νῆες, εἴκοσι δὲ αἱ μετὰ Τληπολέμου καὶ Ἀντικλέους, ἐκ δὲ Χίου καὶ
3 Λέσβου τριάκοντα. καὶ ναυμαχίαν μέν τινα βραχεῖαν ἐποιήσαντο οἱ Σάμιοι, ἀδύνατοι δὲ ὄντες ἀντίσχειν ἐξεπολιορκήθησαν ἐνάτῳ μηνὶ καὶ προσεχώρησαν ὁμολογίᾳ, τεῖχός τε καθελόντες καὶ ὁμήρους δόντες καὶ ναῦς παραδόντες καὶ χρήματα τὰ ἀναλωθέντα ταξάμενοι κατὰ χρόνους ἀποδοῦναι. ξυνέβησαν δὲ καὶ Βυζάντιοι ὥσπερ καὶ πρότερον ὑπήκοοι εἶναι.

CXVIII. Μετὰ ταῦτα δὲ ἤδη γίγνεται οὐ πολλοῖς ἔτεσιν ὕστερον τὰ προειρημένα, τά τε Κερκυραϊκὰ καὶ τὰ Ποτειδεατικὰ καὶ ὅσα πρό-
2 φασις τοῦδε τοῦ πολέμου κατέστη. ταῦτα δὲ ξύμπαντα ὅσα ἔπραξαν οἱ Ἕλληνες πρός τε ἀλλήλους καὶ τὸν βάρβαρον ἐγένετο ἐν ἔτεσι πεντήκοντα μάλιστα μεταξὺ τῆς τε Ξέρξου ἀναχωρήσεως καὶ τῆς ἀρχῆς τοῦδε τοῦ πολέμου· ἐν οἷς οἱ Ἀθηναῖοι τήν τε ἀρχὴν ἐγκρατεστέραν κατεστήσαντο καὶ αὐτοὶ ἐπὶ μέγα ἐχώρησαν δυνάμεως. οἱ δὲ Λακεδαιμόνιοι αἰσθόμενοι οὔτε ἐκώλυον εἰ μὴ ἐπὶ βραχύ, ἡσύχαζόν τε τὸ πλέον τοῦ χρόνου, ὄντες μὲν καὶ πρὸ τοῦ μὴ ταχεῖς ἰέναι ἐς τοὺς πολέμους, ἢν μὴ ἀναγκάζωνται, τὸ δέ τι[1] καὶ πολέμοις οἰκείοις ἐξειργόμενοι, πρὶν δὴ ἡ δύναμις τῶν Ἀθηναίων σαφῶς ᾔρετο καὶ τῆς

[1] τὸ δέ τι, so MSS.: τότε δ' ἔτι is read by Hude, after Reiske (Dion. H. τότε δέ τι).

[1] Possibly the historian, as some have thought; others explain as the son of Melesias and opponent of Pericles; still others as the poet from the deme of Acherdus.

of forty ships under the command of Thucydides,[1] Hagnon and Phormio, twenty under Tlepolemus and Anticles, and thirty from Chios and Lesbos. Now the Samians did indeed put up a sea-fight for a short time, but they were unable to hold out, and in the ninth month [2] were reduced by siege and agreed to a capitulation, pulling down their walls, giving hostages, delivering over their ships, and consenting to pay back by instalments the money spent upon the siege. The Byzantines too came to terms, agreeing to be subjects as before.

CXVIII. It was not many years [3] after this that the events already narrated occurred, namely the Corcyraean affair,[4] the Potidaean,[5] and all the other incidents [6] that furnished an occasion for this war. And all these operations of the Hellenes, against one another and against the Barbarian, took place in the interval of about fifty years between the retreat of Xerxes and the beginning of this war.[7] It was in this period that the Athenians established their rule more firmly and themselves advanced to great power. And the Lacedaemonians, though aware of their growing power, made no attempt to check it, except to a trifling extent, remaining indifferent the greater part of the time, since they had never been quick to go to war except under compulsion, and in this case were in some degree precluded from interference by wars of their own.[8] But at last the power of the Athenians began clearly to exalt itself and they were

[2] 439 B.C.

[3] Hardly four years, since the naval battle between the Corcyraeans and Corinthians seems to have occurred 435 B.C.

[4] Chs. xxiv–lv. [5] Chs. liv–lxvi.

[6] The transactions in the Spartan assembly, chs. lxvii–lxxxviii. [7] 479–432 B.C.

[8] The Helot rebellion, ch. ci. *et seq.*

ξυμμαχίας αὐτῶν ἥπτοντο. τότε δὲ οὐκέτι ἀνασχετὸν ἐποιοῦντο, ἀλλ' ἐπιχειρητέα ἐδόκει εἶναι πάσῃ προθυμίᾳ καὶ καθαιρετέα ἡ ἰσχύς, ἢν δύνωνται, ἀραμένοις δὴ τόνδε τὸν πόλεμον.

3 Αὐτοῖς μὲν οὖν τοῖς Λακεδαιμονίοις διέγνωστο λελύσθαι τε τὰς σπονδὰς καὶ τοὺς Ἀθηναίους ἀδικεῖν, πέμψαντες δὲ ἐς Δελφοὺς ἐπηρώτων τὸν θεὸν εἰ πολεμοῦσιν ἄμεινον ἔσται. ὁ δὲ ἀνεῖλεν αὐτοῖς, ὡς λέγεται, κατὰ κράτος πολεμοῦσι νίκην ἔσεσθαι, καὶ αὐτὸς ἔφη ξυλλήψεσθαι καὶ παρακαλούμενος καὶ ἄκλητος. CXIX. Αὖθις δὲ τοὺς ξυμμάχους παρακαλέσαντες ψῆφον ἐβούλοντο ἐπαγαγεῖν εἰ χρὴ πολεμεῖν. καὶ ἐλθόντων τῶν πρέσβεων ἀπὸ τῆς ξυμμαχίας καὶ ξυνόδου γενομένης οἵ τε ἄλλοι εἶπον ἃ ἐβούλοντο, κατηγοροῦντες οἱ πλείους τῶν Ἀθηναίων καὶ τὸν πόλεμον ἀξιοῦντες γίγνεσθαι, καὶ οἱ Κορίνθιοι δεηθέντες μὲν καὶ κατὰ πόλεις πρότερον ἑκάστων ἰδίᾳ ὥστε ψηφίσασθαι τὸν πόλεμον, δεδιότες περὶ τῇ Ποτειδαίᾳ μὴ προδιαφθαρῇ, παρόντες δὲ καὶ τότε καὶ τελευταῖοι ἐπελθόντες ἔλεγον τοιάδε.

CXX. "Τοὺς μὲν Λακεδαιμονίους, ὦ ἄνδρες ξύμμαχοι, οὐκ ἂν ἔτι αἰτιασαίμεθα ὡς οὐ καὶ αὐτοὶ ἐψηφισμένοι τὸν πόλεμόν εἰσι καὶ ἡμᾶς ἐς τοῦτο νῦν ξυνήγαγον. χρὴ γὰρ τοὺς ἡγεμόνας τὰ ἴδια ἐξ ἴσου νέμοντας τὰ κοινὰ προσκοπεῖν, ὥσπερ καὶ ἐν ἄλλοις ἐκ πάντων προτιμῶνται.

laying hands upon their allies. Then the Lacedaemonians could bear it no longer, but determined that they must attack the Athenian power with all zeal and overthrow it, if they could, by undertaking this war.

The Lacedaemonians themselves, then,[1] had decided that the treaty had been broken and that the Athenians were in the wrong, and sending to Delphi they asked the god if it would be advisable for them to go to war. The god answered them, as it is said, that if they warred with all their might, victory would be theirs, and said that he himself would help them, whether invoked or uninvoked. CXIX. But they wished to summon their allies again and put 432 B.C.
to them the question whether they should go to war. And when the envoys from the allies had come and an assembly was held, the others said what they wished, most of them complaining of the Athenians and demanding that the war should be entered upon, and especially the Corinthians. They had already, before the meeting, privately begged the allies city by city to vote for the war, fearing lest Potidaea would be destroyed before help came, and now, being also present at this meeting, they came forward last of all and spoke as follows:

CXX. "Men of the allies, we can no longer complain of the Lacedaemonians that they have not both themselves voted for the war and also brought us together for this object. And that is right; for it is the duty of leaders, while equitably considering their particular interests, to have special regard for the general weal, just as in other matters they are

[1] Resuming the narrative interrupted at the end of ch. lxxxviii.

2 ἡμῶν δὲ ὅσοι μὲν Ἀθηναίοις ἤδη ξυνηλλάγησαν
οὐχὶ διδαχῆς δέονται ὥστε φυλάξασθαι αὐτούς·
τοὺς δὲ τὴν μεσόγειαν μᾶλλον καὶ μὴ ἐν πόρῳ
κατῳκημένους εἰδέναι χρὴ ὅτι, τοῖς κάτω ἢν μὴ
ἀμύνωσι, χαλεπωτέραν ἕξουσι τὴν κατακομιδὴν
τῶν ὡραίων καὶ πάλιν ἀντίληψιν ὧν ἡ θάλασσα
τῇ ἠπείρῳ δίδωσι, καὶ τῶν νῦν λεγομένων μὴ
κακοὺς κριτὰς ὡς μὴ προσηκόντων εἶναι, προσδέχεσθαι δέ ποτε, εἰ τὰ κάτω πρόοιντο, κἂν μέχρι
σφῶν τὸ δεινὸν προελθεῖν, καὶ περὶ αὑτῶν οὐχ
3 ἧσσον νῦν βουλεύεσθαι. δι' ὅπερ καὶ μὴ ὀκνεῖν
δεῖ αὐτοὺς τὸν πόλεμον ἀντ' εἰρήνης μεταλαμβά-
νειν. ἀνδρῶν γὰρ σωφρόνων μέν ἐστιν, εἰ μὴ
ἀδικοῖντο, ἡσυχάζειν, ἀγαθῶν δὲ ἀδικουμένους ἐκ
μὲν εἰρήνης πολεμεῖν, εὖ δὲ παρασχὸν ἐκ πολέμου πάλιν ξυμβῆναι, καὶ μήτε τῇ κατὰ πόλεμον
εὐτυχίᾳ ἐπαίρεσθαι μήτε τῷ ἡσύχῳ τῆς εἰρήνης
4 ἡδόμενον ἀδικεῖσθαι· ὅ τε γὰρ διὰ τὴν ἡδονὴν
ὀκνῶν τάχιστ' ἂν ἀφαιρεθείη τῆς ῥᾳστώνης τὸ
τερπνὸν δι' ὅπερ ὀκνεῖ, εἰ ἡσυχάζοι,[1] ὅ τε ἐν
πολέμῳ εὐτυχίᾳ πλεονάζων οὐκ ἐντεθύμηται
5 θράσει ἀπίστῳ ἐπαιρόμενος. πολλὰ γὰρ κακῶς
γνωσθέντα ἀβουλοτέρων τῶν ἐναντίων τυχόντα
κατωρθώθη, καὶ ἔτι πλείω καλῶς δοκοῦντα
βουλευθῆναι ἐς τοὐναντίον αἰσχρῶς περιέστη·

[1] εἰ ἡσυχάζοι deleted by Hude, after Lehner.

honoured above all. Now those of us who have had dealings with the Athenians in the past do not need to be taught to be on our guard against them. But those who dwell more in the interior and away from any trade-route should be warned that, if they do not aid those who are on the seaboard, they will find it more difficult to bring the products of the land down to the sea and to get in return what the sea gives to the mainland; and that they should not be careless judges of what is said here, as though it were no concern of theirs, but should expect that, if they abandon the seacoast to its fate, the danger may possibly some day reach them, and that they are deliberating upon their own interests no less than upon ours. They ought not, therefore, to hesitate a moment to adopt war in place of peace. For though it is the part of men of discretion to remain tranquil should they not be wronged, it behooves brave men, when wronged, to go from peace to war, but when a favourable opportunity offers to abandon war and resume peace again, allowing themselves neither to be elated by success in war nor to be so enamoured of the quiet of peace as to submit to wrong. For he who for the sake of his comfort shrinks from war is likely, should he remain tranquil, very speedily to forfeit the delights of ease which caused him to shrink; and he who presumes upon his success in war has failed to reflect how treacherous is the confidence which elates him. For many enterprises which were ill-planned have succeeded because the adversary has proved to be still worse advised, and yet more, which to all appearances were well advised, have turned out the opposite way and brought disgrace. For no one ever carries out a

ἐνθυμεῖται γὰρ οὐδεὶς ὁμοίᾳ[1] τῇ πίστει καὶ ἔργῳ ἐπεξέρχεται, ἀλλὰ μετ' ἀσφαλείας μὲν δοξάζομεν, μετὰ δέους δὲ ἐν τῷ ἔργῳ ἐλλείπομεν.

CXXI. "Ἡμεῖς δὲ νῦν καὶ ἀδικούμενοι τὸν πόλεμον ἐγείρομεν καὶ ἱκανὰ ἔχοντες ἐγκλήματα, καὶ ὅταν ἀμυνώμεθα Ἀθηναίους, καταθησόμεθα
2 αὐτὸν ἐν καιρῷ. κατὰ πολλὰ δὲ ἡμᾶς εἰκὸς ἐπικρατῆσαι, πρῶτον μὲν πλήθει προύχοντας καὶ ἐμπειρίᾳ πολεμικῇ, ἔπειτα ὁμοίως πάντας ἐς τὰ
3 παραγγελλόμενα ἰόντας, ναυτικόν τε, ᾧ ἰσχύουσιν, ἀπὸ τῆς ὑπαρχούσης τε ἑκάστοις οὐσίας ἐξαρτυσόμεθα καὶ ἀπὸ τῶν ἐν Δελφοῖς καὶ Ὀλυμπίᾳ χρημάτων· δάνεισμα γὰρ ποιησάμενοι ὑπολαβεῖν οἷοί τ' ἐσμὲν μισθῷ μείζονι τοὺς ξένους αὐτῶν ναυβάτας. ὠνητὴ γὰρ ἡ Ἀθηναίων δύναμις μᾶλλον ἢ οἰκεία· ἡ δὲ ἡμετέρα ἧσσον ἂν τοῦτο πάθοι, τοῖς σώμασι τὸ πλέον ἰσχύουσα ἢ
4 τοῖς χρήμασιν. μιᾷ τε νίκῃ ναυμαχίας κατὰ τὸ εἰκὸς ἁλίσκονται· εἰ δ' ἀντίσχοιεν, μελετήσομεν καὶ ἡμεῖς ἐν πλέονι χρόνῳ τὰ ναυτικά, καὶ ὅταν τὴν ἐπιστήμην ἐς τὸ ἴσον καταστήσωμεν, τῇ γε εὐψυχίᾳ δήπου περιεσόμεθα· ὃ γὰρ ἡμεῖς ἔχομεν φύσει ἀγαθόν, ἐκείνοις οὐκ ἂν γένοιτο διδαχῇ, ὃ

[1] Reiske's correction for ὅμοια of the MSS.

---

[1] *cf.* II. xiii. 4, where Pericles suggests a similar resource. The Delphic oracle favoured the Peloponnesians, according to ch. cxviii. 3.

plan with the same confidence with which he conceives it; on the contrary we form our fond schemes with a feeling of security, but when it comes to their execution, we are possessed by fear and fall short ot success.

CXXI. "And so now in our own case, it is because we are suffering wrongs and have ample grounds for complaint that we are stirring up this war, and as soon as we have avenged our wrongs upon the Athenians we will bring the war to an end when occasion offers. And for many reasons we are likely to prevail: first, because we are superior in point of numbers and in military experience; secondly, because we all with one accord obey the word of command; and, thirdly, on the sea, where their strength lies, we shall be able to equip a fleet, not only with the means which we severally possess, but also with the funds stored up at Delphi and Olympia.[1] For by contracting a loan we can use the inducement of higher pay to entice away from them their mercenary sailors; for the forces of the Athenians are made up of hirelings rather than of their own citizens, whereas ours, whose strength lies more in the quality of the men than in the pay they get, would be less subject to such defection. And so, if we win a single victory at sea, in all probability they are defeated.[2] If, however, they should still hold out, we on our part shall have more time for practice in seamanship, and as soon as we have brought our skill to a parity with theirs, in courage, assuredly, we shall be superior. For the excellence that nature has given us cannot become theirs through instruction, whereas

[2] Through the mercenary sailors flocking to the Peloponnesian side for higher pay.

δ' ἐκεῖνοι ἐπιστήμῃ προύχουσι, καθαιρετὸν[1] ἡμῖν ἐστι μελέτῃ. χρήματα δὲ ὥστε ἔχειν ἐς αὐτά, οἴσομεν· ἦ δεινὸν ἂν εἴη εἰ οἱ μὲν ἐκείνων ξύμμαχοι ἐπὶ δουλείᾳ τῇ αὐτῶν φέροντες οὐκ ἀπεροῦσιν, ἡμεῖς δ' ἐπὶ τῷ τιμωρούμενοι τοὺς ἐχθροὺς καὶ αὐτοὶ ἅμα σῴζεσθαι οὐκ ἄρα δαπανήσομεν καὶ ἐπὶ τῷ μὴ ὑπ' ἐκείνων αὐτὰ ἀφαιρεθέντες αὐτοῖς τούτοις κακῶς πάσχειν.

CXXII. "Ὑπάρχουσι δὲ καὶ ἄλλαι ὁδοὶ τοῦ πολέμου ἡμῖν, ξυμμάχων τε ἀπόστασις, μάλιστα παραίρεσις οὖσα τῶν προσόδων αἷς ἰσχύουσι, καὶ ἐπιτειχισμὸς τῇ χώρᾳ, ἄλλα τε ὅσα οὐκ ἄν τις νῦν προΐδοι. ἥκιστα γὰρ πόλεμος ἐπὶ ῥητοῖς χωρεῖ, αὐτὸς δὲ ἀφ' αὐτοῦ τὰ πολλὰ τεχνᾶται πρὸς τὸ παρατυγχάνον· ἐν ᾧ ὁ μὲν εὐοργήτως αὐτῷ προσομιλήσας βεβαιότερος, ὁ δ' ὀργισθεὶς περὶ αὐτὸν[2] οὐκ ἐλάσσω πταίει.

2 "Ἐνθυμώμεθα δὲ καὶ ὅτι, εἰ μὲν ἡμῶν ἦσαν ἑκάστοις πρὸς ἀντιπάλους περὶ γῆς ὅρων αἱ διαφοραί, οἰστὸν ἂν ἦν· νῦν δὲ πρὸς ξύμπαντάς τε ἡμᾶς Ἀθηναῖοι ἱκανοὶ καὶ κατὰ πόλιν ἔτι δυνατώτεροι· ὥστε, εἰ μὴ καὶ ἁθρόοι καὶ κατὰ ἔθνη καὶ ἕκαστον ἄστυ μιᾷ γνώμῃ ἀμυνούμεθα αὐτούς, δίχα γε ὄντας ἡμᾶς ἀπόνως χειρώσονται. καὶ τὴν ἧσσαν, εἰ καὶ δεινόν τῳ ἀκοῦσαι, ἴστω οὐκ

[1] καθαιρετόν, which Hude adopts from C and G (*ex corr.*), against καθαιρετέον of the other MSS., is confirmed by the echo in Dio C. xliii. 11, τὸ μὲν γὰρ κτητὸν διὰ βραχέος τοῖς τὸν νοῦν αὐτῷ προσέχουσι καὶ καθαιρετὸν μελέτῃ εἶναι.

[2] Dobree's correction for αὑτὸν of nearly all MSS.

the advantage they have in skill can be acquired by us through practice. And as to the money we need to accomplish all this, we shall provide it by contributions; or strange were it, if their allies should never fail to pay tribute to ensure their own slavery, but we, to secure at once vengeance upon our enemies and safety for ourselves, shall prove unwilling to spend money, aye, and that we may not be robbed of that very wealth and withal have it used to our destruction.

CXXII. "But we have other ways also of waging war—inducing their allies to revolt, which is the best means of depriving them of the revenues in which their strength consists, the planting of forts in their territory, and all the other measures which one cannot now foresee. For war least of all conforms to fixed rules, but itself in most cases has to form its plans to suit the occasion as its own resources allow; when, therefore, a man keeps his temper cool while dealing with war, he is more likely to be safe, while he who loses his temper over it[1] makes more blunders.

"And let us reflect also that, if we individually were involved in a dispute about mere boundary-lines with an enemy who was no more than our equal, that might be borne; but as the case stands, the Athenians are quite a match for us all together, and still more powerful against us city by city. Hence, unless all of us together, every nation and town, with one accord resist them, they will easily overpower us because we shall be divided. And as to defeat—even though this is terrible to hear, let it

[1] Or, reading *αὑτόν* with the MSS., "makes blunders through his own fault as much as anything," *i.e.* "the man who loses his head has only himself to blame for his disasters."

3 ἄλλο τι φέρουσαν ἢ ἄντικρυς δουλείαν· ὃ καὶ λόγῳ ἐνδοιασθῆναι αἰσχρὸν τῇ Πελοποννήσῳ καὶ πόλεις τοσάσδε ὑπὸ μιᾶς κακοπαθεῖν. ἐν ᾧ ἢ δικαίως δοκοῖμεν ἂν πάσχειν ἢ διὰ δειλίαν ἀνέχεσθαι καὶ τῶν πατέρων χείρους φαίνεσθαι, οἳ τὴν Ἑλλάδα ἠλευθέρωσαν· ἡμεῖς δὲ οὐδ' ἡμῖν αὐτοῖς βεβαιοῦμεν αὐτό, τύραννον δὲ ἐῶμεν ἐγκαθεστάναι πόλιν, τοὺς δ' ἐν μιᾷ μονάρχους
4 ἀξιοῦμεν καταλύειν. καὶ οὐκ ἴσμεν ὅπως τάδε τριῶν τῶν μεγίστων ξυμφορῶν ἀπήλλακται, ἀξυνεσίας ἢ μαλακίας ἢ ἀμελείας. οὐ γὰρ δὴ πεφευγότες αὐτὰ ἐπὶ τὴν πλείστους δὴ βλάψασαν καταφρόνησιν κεχωρήκατε, ἣ ἐκ τοῦ πολλοὺς σφάλλειν τὸ ἐναντίον ὄνομα ἀφροσύνη μετωνόμασται.

CXXIII. "Τὰ μὲν οὖν προγεγενημένα τί δεῖ μακρότερον ἢ ἐς ὅσον τοῖς νῦν ξυμφέρει αἰτιᾶσθαι; περὶ δὲ τῶν ἔπειτα μελλόντων τοῖς παροῦσι βοηθοῦντας χρὴ ἐπιταλαιπωρεῖν (πάτριον γὰρ ἡμῖν[1] ἐκ τῶν πόνων τὰς ἀρετὰς κτᾶσθαι), καὶ μὴ μεταβάλλειν τὸ ἔθος, εἰ ἄρα πλούτῳ τε νῦν καὶ ἐξουσίᾳ ὀλίγον προφέρετε (οὐ γὰρ δίκαιον ἃ τῇ ἀπορίᾳ ἐκτήθη τῇ περιουσίᾳ ἀπολέσθαι), ἀλλὰ θαρσοῦντας ἰέναι κατὰ πολλὰ ἐς τὸν πόλεμον, τοῦ τε θεοῦ χρήσαντος καὶ αὐτοῦ ὑποσχομένου

[1] With C, the other MSS. have ὑμῖν.

---

[1] καταφρόνησις is that proud and haughty spirit which precedes and invites a fall. It seems impossible to reproduce in

be well understood that it brings nothing else than downright slavery. That such an outcome should even be spoken of as a possibility, or that so many cities might suffer ill at the hands of one, is a disgrace to the Peloponnesus. In such a case men would say of us, either that we deserved our fate, or that through cowardice we submitted to it, and that we were clearly degenerate sons of our fathers, who liberated Hellas, whereas we, so far from making this liberty secure, should be allowing a city to be established as a tyrant in our midst, though we claim the reputation of deposing the monarchs in single states. We know not how such a course can be acquitted of one of the three gravest errors, stupidity or cowardice, or carelessness. For I cannot suppose that, escaping those errors, you have reached that most fatal spirit of proud disdain [1] which has ruined so many men that it has taken on a new name, that of despicable folly.

CXXIII. "With regard, however, to what is past and done, what need is there to find fault at length, except in so far as that is profitable for what is present? But with a view to what shall be hereafter, we should devote every effort to the task in hand—for to win virtue [2] by toils is our heritage—and make no change of custom because you now have a slight superiority in wealth and power; for it is not right that attributes which have been won through poverty should be lost through prosperity. Nay, you should go into the war with confidence, and for many reasons: the god has spoken through his oracle and promised that he

English the assonance of the words καταφρόνησις ἀφροσύνη. Thucydides was fond of paronomasia; *cf.* ch. xxxiii. 4.

[2] Or, "the rewards of virtue"—honour, renown.

ξυλλήψεσθαι, καὶ τῆς ἄλλης Ἑλλάδος ἁπάσης ξυναγωνιουμένης, τὰ μὲν φόβῳ, τὰ δὲ ὠφελίᾳ.
2 σπονδάς τε οὐ λύσετε πρότεροι, ἅς γε καὶ ὁ θεὸς κελεύων πολεμεῖν νομίζει παραβεβάσθαι, ἠδικημέναις δὲ μᾶλλον βοηθήσετε· λύουσι γὰρ οὐχ οἱ ἀμυνόμενοι, ἀλλ' οἱ πρότεροι ἐπιόντες.

CXXIV. "Ὥστε πανταχόθεν καλῶς ὑπάρχον ὑμῖν πολεμεῖν καὶ ἡμῶν κοινῇ τάδε παραινούντων, εἴπερ βεβαιότατον τὸ ταὐτὰ[1] ξυμφέροντα καὶ πόλεσι καὶ ἰδιώταις εἶναι, μὴ μέλλετε Ποτειδεάταις τε ποιεῖσθαι τιμωρίαν οὖσι Δωριεῦσι καὶ ὑπὸ Ἰώνων πολιορκουμένοις, οὗ πρότερον ἦν τοὐναντίον, καὶ τῶν ἄλλων μετελθεῖν τὴν ἐλευθερίαν, ὡς οὐκέτι ἐνδέχεται περιμένοντας τοὺς μὲν ἤδη βλάπτεσθαι, τοὺς δ', εἰ γνωσθησόμεθα ξυνελθόντες μέν, ἀμύνεσθαι δὲ ἀτολμῶντες,
2 μὴ πολὺ ὕστερον τὸ αὐτὸ πάσχειν· ἀλλὰ νομίσαντες ἐς ἀνάγκην ἀφῖχθαι, ὦ ἄνδρες ξύμμαχοι, καὶ ἅμα τάδε ἄριστα λέγεσθαι, ψηφίσασθε τὸν πόλεμον μὴ φοβηθέντες τὸ αὐτίκα δεινόν, τῆς δ' ἀπ' αὐτοῦ διὰ πλείονος εἰρήνης ἐπιθυμήσαντες· ἐκ πολέμου μὲν γὰρ εἰρήνη μᾶλλον βεβαιοῦται, ἀφ' ἡσυχίας δὲ μὴ πολεμῆσαι οὐχ ὁμοίως ἀκίν-
3 δυνον. καὶ τὴν καθεστηκυῖαν ἐν τῇ Ἑλλάδι πόλιν τύραννον ἡγησάμενοι ἐπὶ πᾶσιν ὁμοίως καθεστάναι, ὥστε τῶν μὲν ἤδη ἄρχειν, τῶν δὲ

[1] So Hude, after Reiske (ταὐτα F, ταυτά γρ.a_2); ταῦτα ABCEGM.

himself will help you; all the rest of Hellas will join you in the struggle, partly through fear and partly through self-interest; and, finally, you will not be the ones to break the treaty, inasmuch as the god, in bidding you go to war, considers it to have been transgressed already, but you will be going to the defence of a treaty that has been violated. For it is not those who fight in self-defence that break a treaty, but those who attack others unprovoked.

CXXIV. "So then, since from every quarter a favourable opportunity offers itself to you to go to war, and since we recommend this course in the common interest—if it be true that identity of interest[1] is the surest policy for states and individuals to follow—make haste to succour the Potidaeans, who are Dorians and besieged by Ionians—the reverse of what used to be—and to recover the liberty of the rest; since it will no longer do for us to wait, when some are already being injured, and others, if it shall become known that we have had a meeting and dare not defend ourselves, will soon suffer the same fate. On the contrary, men of the allies, recognize that we are now facing the inevitable, and at the same time that this proposal is for the best; and vote for the war, not fearing the immediate danger, but coveting the more enduring peace which will result from the war. For peace is more firmly established when it follows war, but to refuse to go to war from a desire for tranquillity is by no means so free from danger. And so, in the conviction that the state which has set itself up as a tyrant in Hellas is a menace to all alike, ruling over some already and

[1] Or, reading ταῦτα, "if it be most certain that *this course* (*i.e.* declaration of war) is advantageous for states as well as individuals."

διανοεῖσθαι, παραστησώμεθα ἐπελθόντες, καὶ αὐτοί τε ἀκινδύνως τὸ λοιπὸν οἰκῶμεν καὶ τοὺς νῦν δεδουλωμένους Ἕλληνας ἐλευθερώσωμεν."

CXXV. Τοιαῦτα μὲν οἱ Κορίνθιοι εἶπον. οἱ δὲ Λακεδαιμόνιοι ἐπειδὴ ἀφ' ἁπάντων ἤκουσαν γνώμην, ψῆφον ἐπήγαγον τοῖς ξυμμάχοις ἅπασιν ὅσοι παρῆσαν ἑξῆς καὶ μείζονι καὶ ἐλάσσονι πό-
2 λει· καὶ τὸ πλῆθος ἐψηφίσαντο πολεμεῖν. δεδογμένον δὲ αὐτοῖς εὐθὺς μὲν ἀδύνατα ἦν ἐπιχειρεῖν ἀπαρασκεύοις οὖσιν, ἐκπορίζεσθαι δὲ ἐδόκει ἑκάστοις ἃ πρόσφορα ἦν καὶ μὴ εἶναι μέλλησιν. ὅμως δὲ καθισταμένοις ὧν ἔδει ἐνιαυτὸς μὲν οὐ διετρίβη, ἔλασσον δέ, πρὶν ἐσβαλεῖν ἐς τὴν Ἀττικὴν καὶ τὸν πόλεμον ἄρασθαι φανερῶς.

CXXVI. Ἐν τούτῳ δὲ ἐπρεσβεύοντο τῷ χρόνῳ πρὸς τοὺς Ἀθηναίους ἐγκλήματα ποιούμενοι, ὅπως σφίσιν ὅτι μεγίστη πρόφασις εἴη τοῦ πολε-
2 μεῖν, ἢν μή τι ἐσακούωσιν. καὶ πρῶτον μὲν πρέσβεις πέμψαντες οἱ Λακεδαιμόνιοι ἐκέλευον
3 τοὺς Ἀθηναίους τὸ ἄγος ἐλαύνειν τῆς θεοῦ. τὸ δὲ ἄγος ἦν τοιόνδε. Κύλων ἦν Ἀθηναῖος ἀνὴρ Ὀλυμπιονίκης τῶν πάλαι εὐγενής τε καὶ δυνατός· ἐγεγαμήκει δὲ θυγατέρα Θεαγένους Μεγαρέως ἀνδρός, ὃς κατ' ἐκεῖνον τὸν χρόνον ἐτυράννει
4 Μεγάρων. χρωμένῳ δὲ τῷ Κύλωνι ἐν Δελφοῖς ἀνεῖλεν ὁ θεὸς ἐν τοῦ Διὸς τῇ μεγίστῃ ἑορτῇ
5 καταλαβεῖν τὴν Ἀθηναίων ἀκρόπολιν. ὁ δὲ παρά τε τοῦ Θεαγένους δύναμιν λαβὼν καὶ τοὺς φίλους ἀναπείσας, ἐπειδὴ ἐπῆλθεν Ὀλύμπια τὰ ἐν Πελοποννήσῳ, κατέλαβε τὴν ἀκρόπολιν ὡς ἐπὶ τυραννίδι, νομίσας ἑορτήν τε τοῦ Διὸς μεγίστην

designing to rule over others, let us attack and reduce it, and henceforth dwell in security ourselves and set free those Hellenes who are already enslaved."

CXXV. Thus spoke the Corinthians. And the Lacedaemonians when they had heard the opinions of all, put the vote in succession to all the allied states which were present, both great and small; and the majority voted for war. But though the decision was made it was impossible for them to take up arms at once, as they were unprepared; it was determined, however, that the several states should make the fitting preparations and that there should be no delay. Nevertheless, in providing themselves with what was needed there was spent, not indeed a full year, but somewhat less, before they invaded Attica and took up the war openly.

CXXVI. During this interval they kept sending embassies to the Athenians and making complaints, that they might have as good a pretext as possible for making war, in case the Athenians should refuse to consider them. And first the Lacedaemonian envoys bade the Athenians drive out the "curse of the goddess." The curse was as follows: There was an Athenian in days of old named Cylon, a victor at Olympia, of noble birth and powerful; and he had married a daughter of Theagenes, a Megarian, who was at that time tyrant of Megara. Now Cylon consulted the oracle at Delphi, and the god in answer told him to seize the Acropolis of Athens "at the greatest festival of Zeus." So he obtained a force from Theagenes and, persuading his friends to help, when the Olympic festival in the Peloponnesus came on he seized the Acropolis with a view to making himself tyrant; for he thought that the

εἶναι καὶ ἑαυτῷ τι προσήκειν Ὀλύμπια νενικη-
6 κότι. εἰ δὲ ἐν τῇ Ἀττικῇ ἢ ἄλλοθί που ἡ μεγίστη
ἑορτὴ εἴρητο, οὔτε ἐκεῖνος ἔτι κατενόησε τό τε
μαντεῖον οὐκ ἐδήλου (ἔστι γὰρ καὶ Ἀθηναίοις
Διάσια, ἃ καλεῖται, Διὸς ἑορτὴ Μειλιχίου μεγίστη, ἔξω τῆς πόλεως, ἐν ᾗ πανδημεὶ θύουσι,
πολλοὶ[1] οὐχ ἱερεῖα ἀλλὰ θύματα ἐπιχώρια),
δοκῶν δὲ ὀρθῶς γιγνώσκειν ἐπεχείρησε τῷ ἔργῳ.
7 οἱ δὲ Ἀθηναῖοι αἰσθόμενοι ἐβοήθησάν τε πανδημεὶ ἐκ τῶν ἀγρῶν ἐπ᾽ αὐτοὺς καὶ προσκαθε-
8 ζόμενοι ἐπολιόρκουν. χρόνου δὲ ἐγγιγνομένου οἱ
Ἀθηναῖοι τρυχόμενοι τῇ προσεδρίᾳ ἀπῆλθον οἱ
πολλοί, ἐπιτρέψαντες τοῖς ἐννέα ἄρχουσι τὴν
φυλακήν τε καὶ τὸ πᾶν αὐτοκράτορσι διαθεῖναι
ᾗ ἂν ἄριστα διαγιγνώσκωσιν· τότε δὲ τὰ πολλὰ
τῶν πολιτικῶν οἱ ἐννέα ἄρχοντες ἔπρασσον.
9 οἱ δὲ μετὰ τοῦ Κύλωνος πολιορκούμενοι φλαύρως
10 εἶχον σίτου τε καὶ ὕδατος ἀπορίᾳ. ὁ μὲν οὖν
Κύλων καὶ ὁ ἀδελφὸς ἐκδιδράσκουσιν· οἱ δ᾽ ἄλλοι
ὡς ἐπιέζοντο καί τινες καὶ ἀπέθνῃσκον ὑπὸ τοῦ
λιμοῦ, καθίζουσιν ἐπὶ τὸν βωμὸν ἱκέται τὸν ἐν τῇ

[1] πολλοὶ: Hude adopts C. F. Hermann's conjecture πολλά, and, after Madvig, inserts ἁγνά before θύματα.

---

[1] On this first attempt to establish a tyranny in Athens, see also Hdt. v. lxxi; Plut. *Solon*, xii. It was not a rising of the people against the nobles, but the attempt of an ambitious man who aspired to royal power, supported only by a few friends and a body of Megarian soldiers. To the mass

Olympic festival was not only the greatest festival of Zeus, but also in a manner was connected with him as having won an Olympic victory.[1] But whether the oracle meant the greatest festival in Attica or somewhere else he did not go on to consider, and the oracle did not make it clear. For, in fact, the Athenians also have a festival in honour of Zeus Meilichius, the Diasia, as it is called, a very great festival celebrated outside the city, whereat all the people offer sacrifices, many making offerings[2] peculiar to the country instead of victims. But Cylon, thinking that he was right in his opinion, made his attempt. And the Athenians, when they were aware of it, came in a body from the fields against them and sitting down before the Acropolis laid siege to it. But as time passed the Athenians grew weary of the siege and most of them went away, committing the task of guarding to the nine Archons, to whom they also gave full power to settle the whole matter as they might determine to be best; for at that time[3] the nine Archons transacted most of the public business. But Cylon and those who were being besieged with him were in hard straits through lack of food and water. So Cylon and his brother escaped; but the rest, when they were in great distress and some of them were even dying of hunger, sat down as suppliants at the

of the people it seemed to portend subjection to Megara, so they flocked in to crush the movement, not, as Cylon hoped, to support it.

[2] A scholiast suggests cakes (πέμματα) made in the forms of animals.

[3] *i.e.* before the legislation of Solon; from that time the power of the Archons decreased, and was restricted chiefly to judicial functions.

11 ἀκροπόλει. ἀναστήσαντες δὲ αὐτοὺς οἱ τῶν Ἀθηναίων ἐπιτετραμμένοι τὴν φυλακήν, ὡς ἑώρων
ἀποθνῄσκοντας ἐν τῷ ἱερῷ, ἐφ᾿ ᾧ μηδὲν κακὸν
ποιήσουσιν, ἀπαγαγόντες ἀπέκτειναν· καθεζομέ-
νους δέ τινας καὶ ἐπὶ τῶν σεμνῶν θεῶν τοῖς
βωμοῖς ἐν τῇ παρόδῳ ἀπεχρήσαντο. καὶ ἀπὸ
τούτου ἐναγεῖς καὶ ἀλιτήριοι τῆς θεοῦ ἐκεῖνοί τε
12 ἐκαλοῦντο καὶ τὸ γένος τὸ ἀπ᾿ ἐκείνων. ἤλασαν
μὲν οὖν καὶ οἱ Ἀθηναῖοι τοὺς ἐναγεῖς τούτους,
ἤλασε δὲ καὶ Κλεομένης ὁ Λακεδαιμόνιος ὕστερον
μετὰ Ἀθηναίων στασιαζόντων, τούς τε ζῶντας
ἐλαύνοντες καὶ τῶν τεθνεώτων τὰ ὀστᾶ ἀνελόντες
ἐξέβαλον· κατῆλθον μέντοι ὕστερον, καὶ τὸ γένος
αὐτῶν ἔτι ἔστιν ἐν τῇ πόλει.

CXXVII. Τοῦτο δὴ τὸ ἄγος οἱ Λακεδαιμόνιοι
ἐκέλευον ἐλαύνειν δῆθεν τοῖς θεοῖς πρῶτον τιμω-
ροῦντες, εἰδότες δὲ Περικλέα τὸν Ξανθίππου
προσεχόμενον αὐτῷ κατὰ τὴν μητέρα καὶ νομίζοντες ἐκπεσόντος αὐτοῦ ῥᾷον ἂν[1] σφίσι προ-
2 χωρεῖν τὰ ἀπὸ τῶν Ἀθηναίων. οὐ μέντοι τοσοῦτον ἤλπιζον παθεῖν ἂν αὐτὸν τοῦτο ὅσον διαβολὴν
οἴσειν αὐτῷ πρὸς τὴν πόλιν, ὡς καὶ διὰ τὴν
3 ἐκείνου ξυμφορὰν τὸ μέρος ἔσται ὁ πόλεμος. ὢν

[1] Added by Stahl.

---

[1] Of Athena Polias.
[2] The sanctuary of the Eumenides, which lay between the Acropolis and the Areopagus.

altar[1] on the Acropolis. And the Athenians who had been charged with guarding them, when they saw them dying in the temple, caused them to arise on promise of doing them no harm, and leading them away put them to death; and some who in passing by took refuge at the altar of the Awful Goddesses[2] they dispatched even there. For this act both they and their descendants[3] were called accursed and sinners against the Goddess. Accordingly the accursed persons were driven out not only by the Athenians but also at a later time by Cleomenes the Lacedaemonian, with the help of a faction of the Athenians, during a civil strife, when they drove out the living and disinterred and cast out the bones of the dead. Afterwards, however, they were restored, and their descendants are still in the city.

CXXVII. It was this "curse" that the Lacedaemonians now bade the Athenians drive out, principally, as they pretended, to avenge the honour of the gods, but in fact because they knew that Pericles son of Xanthippus was implicated in the curse on his mother's side,[4] and thinking that, if he were banished, they would find it easier to get from the Athenians the concessions they hoped for. They did not, however, so much expect that he would suffer banishment, as that they would discredit him with his fellow-citizens, who would feel that to some extent his misfortune[5] would be the cause of the

[3] Chiefly the Alcmaeonidae, whose head was Megacles, Archon at the time of Cylon's attempt.

[4] Pericles was a descendant in the sixth generation from Megacles, his mother Agariste being niece of the Alcmaeonid Cleisthenes (Hdt. VI. cxxxi.).

[5] As belonging to the accursed family.

γὰρ δυνατώτατος τῶν καθ' ἑαυτὸν καὶ ἄγων τὴν πολιτείαν ἠναντιοῦτο πάντα τοῖς Λακεδαιμονίοις, καὶ οὐκ εἴα ὑπείκειν, ἀλλ' ἐς τὸν πόλεμον ὥρμα τοὺς Ἀθηναίους.

CXXVIII. Ἀντεκέλευον δὲ καὶ οἱ Ἀθηναῖοι τοὺς Λακεδαιμονίους τὸ ἀπὸ Ταινάρου ἄγος ἐλαύνειν. οἱ γὰρ Λακεδαιμόνιοι ἀναστήσαντές ποτε ἐκ τοῦ ἱεροῦ τοῦ Ποσειδῶνος ἀπὸ Ταινάρου[1]
τῶν Εἱλώτων ἱκέτας ἀπαγαγόντες διέφθειραν· δι'
ὃ δὴ καὶ σφίσιν αὐτοῖς νομίζουσι τὸν μέγαν
2 σεισμὸν γενέσθαι ἐν Σπάρτῃ. ἐκέλευον δὲ καὶ τὸ
τῆς Χαλκιοίκου ἄγος ἐλαύνειν αὐτούς· ἐγένετο δὲ
3 τοιόνδε. ἐπειδὴ Παυσανίας ὁ Λακεδαιμόνιος τὸ
πρῶτον μεταπεμφθεὶς ὑπὸ Σπαρτιατῶν ἀπὸ τῆς
ἀρχῆς τῆς ἐν Ἑλλησπόντῳ καὶ κριθεὶς ὑπ' αὐτῶν
ἀπελύθη μὴ ἀδικεῖν, δημοσίᾳ μὲν οὐκέτι ἐξεπέμφθη, ἰδίᾳ δὲ αὐτὸς τριήρη λαβὼν Ἑρμιονίδα
ἄνευ Λακεδαιμονίων ἀφικνεῖται ἐς Ἑλλήσποντον,
τῷ μὲν λόγῳ ἐπὶ τὸν Μηδικὸν πόλεμον, τῷ δὲ
ἔργῳ τὰ πρὸς βασιλέα πράγματα πράσσειν,
ὥσπερ καὶ τὸ πρῶτον ἐπεχείρησεν, ἐφιέμενος τῆς
4 Ἑλληνικῆς ἀρχῆς. εὐεργεσίαν δὲ ἀπὸ τοῦδε
πρῶτον ἐς βασιλέα κατέθετο καὶ τοῦ παντὸς
5 πράγματος ἀρχὴν ἐποιήσατο. Βυζάντιον γὰρ

[1] Van Herwerden deletes, followed by Hude.

---

[1] *cf.* ch. ci. 2.

war. For being the most powerful man of his time and the leader of the state, he was opposed to the Lacedaemonians in all things, and would not let the Athenians make concessions, but kept urging them on to the war.

CXXVIII. The Athenians answered with the demand that the Lacedaemonians should drive out the curse of Taenarus. For the Lacedaemonians had on one occasion caused some suppliant Helots to leave their refuge in the temple of Poseidon at Taenarus, then had led them off and put them to death; and the Lacedaemonians believe that it was because of this sacrilege that the great earthquake[1] befell them at Sparta. And the Athenians also bade them drive out the curse of Athena of the Brazen House.[2] And this is the way it was incurred. After Pausanias the Lacedaemonian had been recalled by the Spartans, on the first occasion,[3] from his command on the Hellespont, and on trial had been acquitted of wrong-doing, he was never again sent out in a public capacity, but privately and on his own account he took a trireme of Hermione without authority of the Lacedaemonians and came to the Hellespont, to take part, as he pretended, in the Persian war, but in reality to carry on an intrigue with the Great King—an enterprise to which he had set his hand in the first instance also, his aim being to become master of all Hellas. He had namely first laid up for himself with the King a store of gratitude in the following circumstances, and thus had begun the whole affair. When he was in that quarter before, after

[2] So called from her temple or shrine in the citadel at Sparta. Pausanias says (III. xvii. 2) both temple and statue were of bronze. [3] 477 B.C. *cf.* ch. xcv. 3.

*ἑλὼν τῇ προτέρᾳ παρουσίᾳ μετὰ τὴν ἐκ Κύπρου
ἀναχώρησιν (εἶχον δὲ Μῆδοι αὐτὸ καὶ βασιλέως
προσήκοντές τινες καὶ ξυγγενεῖς, οἳ ἑάλωσαν ἐν
αὐτῷ τότε) τούτους οὓς ἔλαβεν ἀποπέμπει βασιλεῖ κρύφα τῶν ἄλλων ξυμμάχων, τῷ δὲ λόγῳ
6 ἀπέδρασαν αὐτόν. ἔπρασσε δὲ ταῦτα μετὰ Γογ-
γύλου τοῦ Ἐρετριῶς, ᾧπερ ἐπέτρεψε τό τε Βυζάντιον καὶ τοὺς αἰχμαλώτους. ἔπεμψε δὲ καὶ
7 ἐπιστολὴν τὸν Γογγύλον φέροντα αὐτῷ. ἐνε-
γέγραπτο δὲ τάδε ἐν αὐτῇ, ὡς ὕστερον ἀνηυρέθη·*

*"Παυσανίας ὁ ἡγεμὼν τῆς Σπάρτης τούσδε τέ
σοι χαρίζεσθαι βουλόμενος ἀποπέμπει δορὶ ἑλών,
καὶ γνώμην ποιοῦμαι, εἰ καὶ σοὶ δοκεῖ, θυγατέρα
τε τὴν σὴν γῆμαι καί σοι Σπάρτην τε καὶ τὴν
ἄλλην Ἑλλάδα ὑποχείριον ποιῆσαι. δυνατὸς δὲ
δοκῶ εἶναι ταῦτα πρᾶξαι μετὰ σοῦ βουλευόμενος.
εἰ οὖν τί σε τούτων ἀρέσκει, πέμπε ἄνδρα πιστὸν
ἐπὶ θάλασσαν δι' οὗ τὸ λοιπὸν τοὺς λόγους ποιη-
σόμεθα." τοσαῦτα μὲν ἡ γραφὴ ἐδήλου.*

CXXIX. *Ξέρξης δὲ ἥσθη τε τῇ ἐπιστολῇ καὶ
ἀποστέλλει Ἀρτάβαζον τὸν Φαρνάκου ἐπὶ θάλασσαν καὶ κελεύει αὐτὸν τήν τε Δασκυλῖτιν
σατραπείαν παραλαβεῖν Μεγαβάτην ἀπαλλά-
ξαντα, ὃς πρότερον ἦρχε, καὶ παρὰ Παυσανίαν
ἐς Βυζάντιον ἐπιστολὴν ἀντεπετίθει αὐτῷ ὡς
τάχιστα διαπέμψαι καὶ τὴν σφραγῖδα ἀποδεῖξαι,
καὶ ἤν τι αὐτῷ Παυσανίας παραγγέλλῃ περὶ τῶν
ἑαυτοῦ πραγμάτων, πράσσειν ὡς ἄριστα καὶ
2 πιστότατα. ὁ δὲ ἀφικόμενος τά τε ἄλλα ἐποίησεν*

the return of the Hellenic fleet from Cyprus,[1] he had taken Byzantium, then in the possession of the Persians, and certain connections and kinsmen of the King were captured in the place when the city fell. These prisoners he sent back to the King without the knowledge of the allies in general, whom he gave to understand that they had escaped from him. And he was carrying on this intrigue in concert with Gongylus the Eretrian, the very man whom he had placed in charge of Byzantium and the captives. And he also sent a letter by Gongylus to the King, in which the following was written, as was afterwards discovered:

"Pausanias, the Spartan commander, wishing to do you a favour, sends you back these men whom he took with the spear. And I make the proposal, if it seems good to you also, to marry your daughter and to make Sparta and the rest of Hellas subject to you. And I am able, I think, to accomplish these things with the help of your counsel. If any of these things pleases you, send a trusty man to the sea, and through him we shall in future confer." So much the letter disclosed.

CXXIX. Xerxes was pleased with the letter, and sent Artabazus son of Pharnaces to the sea, commanding him to take over the satrapy of Dascylium, superseding Megabates, who was governor before; and he charged him with a letter in reply to Pausanias, bidding him transmit it to him in Byzantium as quickly as possible and to show him the seal, and if Pausanias should give him any direction about the King's affairs, to execute it with all care and fidelity. And he on his arrival did

[1] *cf.* ch. xciv. 2.

ὥσπερ εἴρητο καὶ τὴν ἐπιστολὴν διέπεμψεν. ἀντενεγέγραπτο δὲ τάδε·

3 "Ὧδε λέγει βασιλεὺς Ξέρξης Παυσανίᾳ· καὶ τῶν ἀνδρῶν οὕς μοι πέραν θαλάσσης ἐκ Βυζαντίου ἔσωσας κείσεταί σοι εὐεργεσία ἐν τῷ ἡμετέρῳ οἴκῳ ἐς αἰεὶ ἀνάγραπτος, καὶ τοῖς λόγοις τοῖς ἀπὸ σοῦ ἀρέσκομαι. καί σε μήτε νὺξ μήθ' ἡμέρα ἐπισχέτω ὥστε ἀνεῖναι πράσσειν τι ὧν ἐμοὶ ὑπισχνεῖ, μηδὲ χρυσοῦ καὶ ἀργύρου δαπάνῃ κεκώλυσο μηδὲ στρατιᾶς πλήθει, εἴ ποι δεῖ παραγίγνεσθαι, ἀλλὰ μετ' Ἀρταβάζου ἀνδρὸς ἀγαθοῦ, ὅν σοι ἔπεμψα, πρᾶσσε θαρσῶν καὶ τὰ ἐμὰ καὶ τὰ σὰ ὅπῃ κάλλιστα καὶ ἄριστα ἕξει ἀμφοτέροις."

CXXX. Ταῦτα λαβὼν ὁ Παυσανίας τὰ γράμματα, ὢν καὶ πρότερον ἐν μεγάλῳ ἀξιώματι ὑπὸ τῶν Ἑλλήνων διὰ τὴν Πλαταιᾶσιν ἡγεμονίαν, πολλῷ τότε μᾶλλον ἦρτο καὶ οὐκέτι ἐδύνατο ἐν τῷ καθεστῶτι τρόπῳ βιοτεύειν, ἀλλὰ σκευάς τε Μηδικὰς ἐνδυόμενος ἐκ τοῦ Βυζαντίου ἐξῄει καὶ διὰ τῆς Θρᾴκης πορευόμενον αὐτὸν Μῆδοι καὶ Αἰγύπτιοι ἐδορυφόρουν, τράπεζάν τε Περσικὴν παρετίθετο καὶ κατέχειν τὴν διάνοιαν οὐκ ἐδύνατο, ἀλλ' ἔργοις βραχέσι προυδήλου ἃ τῇ γνώμῃ
2 μειζόνως ἐς ἔπειτα ἔμελλε πράξειν. δυσπρόσοδόν τε αὐτὸν παρεῖχε καὶ τῇ ὀργῇ οὕτω χαλεπῇ ἐχρῆτο ἐς πάντας ὁμοίως ὥστε μηδένα δύνασθαι προσιέναι· δι' ὅπερ καὶ πρὸς τοὺς Ἀθηναίους οὐχ ἥκιστα ἡ ξυμμαχία μετέστη.

CXXXI. Οἱ δὲ Λακεδαιμόνιοι αἰσθόμενοι τό τε πρῶτον δι' αὐτὰ ταῦτα ἀνεκάλεσαν αὐτόν, καὶ

other things as he was told and transmitted the letter. And this reply of the King ran as follows:

"Thus saith King Xerxes to Pausanias: As touching the men whom thou didst save for me out of Byzantium beyond the sea, a store of gratitude is laid up for thee, of record, in our house forever, and with thy words also I am pleased. And let neither night nor day stay thee to make thee remiss in performing aught of what thou dost promise me; and let nothing hinder thee, either expense of gold and silver or number of troops, if there be need of their presence anywhere; but with Artabazus, a good man, whom I have sent to thee, transact with confidence my business and thine as shall be most honourable and best for both of us."

CXXX. When Pausanias received this letter, although even before this he had been held in high consideration by the Hellenes because he had led them at Plataea, he was then far more elated and could no longer bring himself to live in the usual manner of his people, but clad himself in Persian apparel whenever he went forth from Byzantium, and when he travelled through Thrace a body-guard of Medes and Egyptians attended him; he had his table served in Persian style, and indeed could not conceal his real purpose, but by such trifling acts showed plainly what greater designs he purposed in his heart to accomplish thereafter. And so he made himself difficult of access, and indulged in such a violent temper towards everybody that no one could come near him; and this was one of the chief reasons why the allies went over to the Athenians.

CXXXI. Now it was just this conduct that had caused the Lacedaemonians in the first instance to

ἐπειδὴ τῇ Ἑρμιονίδι νηὶ τὸ δεύτερον ἐκπλεύσας οὐ κελευσάντων αὐτῶν τοιαῦτα ἐφαίνετο ποιῶν, καὶ ἐκ τοῦ Βυζαντίου βίᾳ ὑπ' Ἀθηναίων ἐκπολιορκηθεὶς ἐς μὲν τὴν Σπάρτην οὐκ ἐπανεχώρει, ἐς δὲ Κολωνὰς τὰς Τρῳάδας ἱδρυθεὶς πράσσων τε ἐσηγγέλλετο αὐτοῖς ἐς τοὺς βαρβάρους καὶ οὐκ ἐπ' ἀγαθῷ τὴν μονὴν ποιούμενος, οὕτω δὴ οὐκέτι ἐπέσχον, ἀλλὰ πέμψαντες κήρυκα οἱ ἔφοροι καὶ σκυτάλην εἶπον τοῦ κήρυκος μὴ λείπεσθαι, εἰ δὲ μή, πόλεμον αὐτῷ Σπαρτιάτας προαγορεύειν.
2 ὁ δὲ βουλόμενος ὡς ἥκιστα ὕποπτος εἶναι καὶ πιστεύων χρήμασι διαλύσειν τὴν διαβολὴν ἀνεχώρει τὸ δεύτερον ἐς Σπάρτην. καὶ ἐς μὲν τὴν εἱρκτὴν ἐσπίπτει τὸ πρῶτον ὑπὸ τῶν ἐφόρων (ἔξεστι δὲ τοῖς ἐφόροις τὸν βασιλέα δρᾶσαι τοῦτο), ἔπειτα διαπραξάμενος ὕστερον ἐξῆλθε καὶ καθίστησιν ἑαυτὸν ἐς κρίσιν τοῖς βουλομένοις περὶ αὐτῶν ἐλέγχειν.

CXXXII. Καὶ φανερὸν μὲν εἶχον οὐδὲν οἱ Σπαρτιᾶται σημεῖον, οὔτε οἱ ἐχθροὶ οὔτε ἡ πᾶσα πόλις, ὅτῳ ἂν πιστεύσαντες βεβαίως ἐτιμωροῦντο ἄνδρα γένους τε τοῦ βασιλείου ὄντα καὶ ἐν τῷ παρόντι τιμὴν ἔχοντα (Πλείσταρχον γὰρ τὸν Λεωνίδου ὄντα βασιλέα καὶ νέον ἔτι ἀνεψιὸς ὢν
2 ἐπετρόπευεν), ὑποψίας δὲ πολλὰς παρεῖχε τῇ τε

[1] The σκυτάλη was a staff used for writing dispatches. The Lacedaemonians had two round staves of one size, the one kept at Sparta, the other in possession of commanders

recall Pausanias, when they learned of it; and when this second time, on his sailing away in the ship of Hermione without their authority, it was evident that he was acting in the very same manner—when, after being forcibly dislodged from Byzantium by the Athenians, instead of returning to Sparta, he settled at Colonae in the Troad and was reported to the ephors to be intriguing with the Barbarians and tarrying there for no good purpose—then at length they held back no longer, but sent a herald with a skytale-dispatch,[1] in which they told him not to lag behind the herald, or the Spartans would declare war upon him. And he, wishing to avoid suspicion as far as possible, and confident that he could dispose of the charge by the use of money, returned the second time to Sparta. And at first he was thrown into prison by the ephors, who have the power to do this in the case of the king himself; then, having contrived after a time to get out, he offered himself for trial to any who might wish to examine into his case.

CXXXII. There was, indeed, no clear proof in the possession of the Spartans, either his personal enemies or the state at large, on the strength of which they could with entire confidence proceed to punish a man who was of the royal family and held high office for the time being—for as cousin of Pleistarchus son of Leonidas, who was king and still a minor, he was acting as regent for him; but he, by his disregard of propriety, and particularly by

abroad. A strip of paper was rolled slantwise round the staff and the dispatch written lengthwise on it; when unrolled the dispatch was unintelligible, but rolled slantwise round the commander's skytale it could be read.

παρανομίᾳ καὶ ζηλώσει τῶν βαρβάρων μὴ ἴσος βούλεσθαι εἶναι τοῖς παροῦσι, καὶ[1] τά τε ἄλλα αὐτοῦ ἀνεσκόπουν εἴ τί που ἐξεδεδιῄτητο τῶν καθεστώτων νομίμων καὶ ὅτι ἐπὶ τὸν τρίποδά ποτε τὸν ἐν Δελφοῖς, ὃν ἀνέθεσαν οἱ Ἕλληνες ἀπὸ τῶν Μήδων ἀκροθίνιον, ἠξίωσεν ἐπιγράψασθαι αὐτὸς ἰδίᾳ τὸ ἐλεγεῖον τόδε·

Ἑλλήνων ἀρχηγὸς ἐπεὶ στρατὸν ὤλεσε Μήδων,
Παυσανίας Φοίβῳ μνῆμ' ἀνέθηκε τόδε.

3 τὸ μὲν οὖν ἐλεγεῖον οἱ Λακεδαιμόνιοι ἐξεκόλαψαν εὐθὺς τότε ἀπὸ τοῦ τρίποδος τοῦτο καὶ ἐπέγραψαν ὀνομαστὶ τὰς πόλεις ὅσαι ξυγκαθελοῦσαι τὸν βάρβαρον ἔστησαν τὸ ἀνάθημα· τοῦ μέντοι Παυσανίου ἀδίκημα καὶ τότ' ἐδόκει εἶναι, καὶ ἐπεί γε δὴ ἐν τούτῳ καθειστήκει, πολλῷ μᾶλλον παρόμοιον πραχθῆναι ἐφαίνετο τῇ παρούσῃ δια-
4 νοίᾳ. ἐπυνθάνοντο δὲ καὶ ἐς τοὺς Εἵλωτας πράσσειν τι αὐτόν, καὶ ἦν δὲ οὕτως· ἐλευθέρωσίν τε γὰρ ὑπισχνεῖτο αὐτοῖς καὶ πολιτείαν, ἢν ξυνεπαναστῶσι καὶ τὸ πᾶν ξυγκατεργάσωνται.
5 ἀλλ' οὐδ' ὣς οὐδὲ τῶν Εἱλώτων μηνυταῖς τισι πιστεύσαντες ἠξίωσαν νεώτερόν τι ποιεῖν ἐς

[1] Added by Ullrich.

---

[1] A golden tripod set upon a three-headed bronze serpent (Hdt. IX. lxxxi.). The gold tripod was carried off by the Phocians in the Sacred War (Paus. X. xiii. 5), but the bronze pillar, eighteen feet high, of three intertwined snakes, was removed by the Emperor Constantine to Constantinople

his aping of the Barbarians, gave them much ground for suspecting that he did not want to remain an equal in the present order of things at Sparta. And they went back into his past and scrutinized all his other acts, to see if perchance he had in his mode of life departed from established customs, and they recalled especially that he had once presumed, on his own authority, to have inscribed on the tripod at Delphi,[1] which the Hellenes dedicated as first fruits of the spoils they had won from the Persians, the following elegiac couplet:

"When as captain of the Hellenes he had destroyed the Persian host, Pausanias dedicated this memorial to Phoebus."[2]

Now the Lacedaemonians had immediately chiselled off these verses and inscribed on the tripod by name all the cities which had had a part in overthrowing the Barbarians and had together set up this offering. The act of Pausanias, however, was felt at the time to have been a transgression, and now that he had got into this further trouble, it stood out more clearly than ever as having been but a prelude to his present designs. They were informed also that he was intriguing with the Helots; and it was even so, for he was promising them freedom and citizenship if they would join him in a revolt and help him accomplish his whole plan. But not even then, nor relying on certain Helots who had turned informers, did they think it best to take harsh measures against him; they

and placed in the hippodrome, the modern Atmeidan, where it still is. It contains the names of thirty-one Greek states which took part in the Persian War.

[2] The distich was composed by Simonides.

αὐτόν, χρώμενοι τῷ τρόπῳ ᾧπερ εἰώθασιν ἐς σφᾶς αὐτούς, μὴ ταχεῖς εἶναι περὶ ἀνδρὸς Σπαρτιάτου ἄνευ ἀναμφισβητήτων τεκμηρίων βουλεῦσαί τι ἀνήκεστον, πρίν γε δὴ αὐτοῖς, ὡς λέγεται, ὁ μέλλων τὰς τελευταίας βασιλεῖ ἐπιστολὰς πρὸς Ἀρτάβαζον κομιεῖν, ἀνὴρ Ἀργίλιος, παιδικά ποτε ὢν αὐτοῦ καὶ πιστότατος ἐκείνῳ, μηνυτὴς γίγνεται, δείσας κατὰ ἐνθύμησίν τινα ὅτι οὐδείς πω τῶν πρὸ ἑαυτοῦ ἀγγέλων πάλιν ἀφίκετο, καὶ παρασημηνάμενος, ἵνα, ἢν ψευσθῇ τῆς δόξης ἢ καὶ ἐκεῖνός τι μεταγράψαι αἰτήσῃ, μὴ ἐπιγνῷ, λύει τὰς ἐπιστολάς, ἐν αἷς ὑπονοήσας τι τοιοῦτον προσεπεστάλθαι καὶ αὑτὸν ηὗρεν ἐγγεγραμμένον κτείνειν.

CXXXIII. Τότε δὴ οἱ ἔφοροι δείξαντος αὐτοῦ τὰ γράμματα μᾶλλον μὲν ἐπίστευσαν, αὐτήκοοι δὲ βουληθέντες ἔτι γενέσθαι αὐτοῦ Παυσανίου τι λέγοντος, ἀπὸ παρασκευῆς τοῦ ἀνθρώπου ἐπὶ Ταίναρον ἱκέτου οἰχομένου καὶ σκηνωσαμένου διπλῆν διαφράγματι καλύβην, ἐς ἣν τῶν ἐφόρων[1] ἐντός τινας ἔκρυψε, καὶ Παυσανίου ὡς αὐτὸν ἐλθόντος καὶ ἐρωτῶντος τὴν πρόφασιν τῆς ἱκετείας ᾔσθοντο πάντα σαφῶς, αἰτιωμένου τοῦ ἀνθρώπου τά τε περὶ αὐτοῦ γραφέντα καὶ τἆλλ' ἀποφαίνοντος καθ' ἕκαστον, ὡς οὐδὲν πώποτε αὐτὸν ἐν ταῖς πρὸς βασιλέα διακονίαις παραβάλοιτο, προτιμηθείη δὲ ἐν ἴσῳ τοῖς πολλοῖς τῶν

[1] τῶν τε ἐφόρων in the MSS.; Poppo deletes τε.

adhered to their usual method in dealing with men of their own class—not to be hasty, in the case of a Spartan, in adopting an irrevocable decision unless they had indisputable proofs. But at last, as it is said, the man who was to take to Artabazus Pausanias' last letter to the King, a man of Argilus who had once been a favourite of his and had hitherto been most loyal to him, turned informer. For he took fright when he called to mind that no previous messenger had ever come back again; and so, having made a counterfeit seal, in order that his act might not be discovered, in case he should be wrong in his suspicion or in case Pausanias should ask to make some alteration in the letter, he opened the letter and in fact found written therein, as he suspected he should find something of the sort to have been directed, an order for his own death.

CXXXIII. At this point the ephors, when the man showed them the letter, were at last more nearly convinced, but they wished besides to hear with their own ears some word from Pausanias' own lips; so in accordance with a prearranged plan the man went as a suppliant to Taenarus and put up there a hut divided by a partition. In the inner room of the hut he concealed some of the ephors, and when Pausanias visited him and asked the reason of his taking the position of a suppliant, they heard clearly everything that was said: they heard the man accuse Pausanias of having written the order about himself, reveal the other items of the plot in detail, and protest that, though he had never yet compromised Pausanias in his errands to the King, the special honour awarded him was no better than that which the common run of his servants

διακόνων ἀποθανεῖν, κἀκείνου αὐτά τε ταῦτα
ξυνομολογοῦντος καὶ περὶ τοῦ παρόντος οὐκ
ἐῶντος ὀργίζεσθαι, ἀλλὰ πίστιν ἐκ τοῦ ἱεροῦ[1]
διδόντος τῆς ἀναστάσεως καὶ ἀξιοῦντος ὡς τάχιστα πορεύεσθαι καὶ μὴ τὰ πρασσόμενα διακω-
λύειν.

CXXXIV. Ἀκούσαντες δὲ ἀκριβῶς τότε μὲν
ἀπῆλθον οἱ ἔφοροι, βεβαίως δὲ ἤδη εἰδότες ἐν τῇ
πόλει τὴν ξύλληψιν ἐποιοῦντο. λέγεται δ' αὐτὸν
μέλλοντα ξυλληφθήσεσθαι ἐν τῇ ὁδῷ, ἑνὸς μὲν
τῶν ἐφόρων τὸ πρόσωπον προσιόντος ὡς εἶδε,
γνῶναι ἐφ' ᾧ ἐχώρει, ἄλλου δὲ νεύματι ἀφανεῖ
χρησαμένου καὶ δηλώσαντος εὐνοίᾳ, πρὸς τὸ ἱερὸν
τῆς Χαλκιοίκου χωρῆσαι δρόμῳ καὶ προκαταφυ-
γεῖν· ἦν δ' ἐγγὺς τὸ τέμενος. καὶ ἐς οἴκημα οὐ
μέγα ὃ ἦν τοῦ ἱεροῦ ἐσελθών, ἵνα μὴ ὑπαίθριος
2 ταλαιπωροίη, ἡσύχαζεν. οἱ δὲ τὸ παραυτίκα μὲν
ὑστέρησαν τῇ διώξει, μετὰ δὲ τοῦτο τοῦ τε οἰκήματος τὸν ὄροφον ἀφεῖλον καὶ τὰς θύρας ἔνδον
ὄντα τηρήσαντες αὐτὸν καὶ ἀπολαβόντες ἔσω
ἀπῳκοδόμησαν, προσκαθεζόμενοί τε ἐξεπολιόρ-
3 κησαν λιμῷ. καὶ μέλλοντος αὐτοῦ ἀποψύχειν
ὥσπερ εἶχεν ἐν τῷ οἰκήματι, αἰσθόμενοι ἐξά-
γουσιν ἐκ τοῦ ἱεροῦ ἔτι ἔμπνουν ὄντα, καὶ ἐξαχ-
4 θεὶς ἀπέθανε παραχρῆμα. καὶ αὐτὸν ἐμέλλησαν
μὲν ἐς τὸν Καιάδαν, οὗπερ τοὺς κακούργους, ἐσ-

[1] ἐκ τοῦ ἱεροῦ deleted by Hude, after Krüger.

[1] The temple would have been polluted if he had been allowed to die there.

received—to be put to death; and they heard Pausanias acknowledge these same things, urge the man not to be angry with him this time, offer him a guarantee that he might leave the temple in safety, and finally request him to go on his way with all speed and not frustrate the negotiations.

CXXXIV. When the ephors had heard all the details they went back home for the present, but inasmuch as they now had certain knowledge, they were planning to make the arrest in the city. And the story goes that when Pausanias was about to be arrested in the street, he saw the face of one of the ephors as he was approaching and realised for what purpose he was coming, and that another ephor out of friendship warned him by giving a covert nod, whereupon he set off on a run for the temple of Athena of the Brazen House, and reached the refuge first, as the sacred precinct was near by. Entering then into a building of no great size belonging to the temple, that he might not suffer from exposure under the open sky, he kept quiet. For the moment then the ephors were distanced in their pursuit, but afterwards they took the roof off the building and, watching until he was inside and shutting off his retreat, walled up the doors; then they invested the place and starved him to death. And when he was about to expire, imprisoned as he was in the building,[1] they perceived his condition and brought him out of the temple still breathing; but when he was brought out he died immediately. It was their first intention to cast him into the Caeadas,[2] where

[2] A cleft in the mountains not far from the city, probably near the modern Mistra, into which in early times prisoners, in later, corpses of criminals, were thrown; *cf.* Strabo, VIII. v. 7; Paus. IV. xviii. 3.

βάλλειν· ἔπειτα ἔδοξε πλησίον που κατορύξαι. ὁ δὲ θεὸς ὁ ἐν Δελφοῖς τόν τε τάφον ὕστερον ἔχρησε τοῖς Λακεδαιμονίοις μετενεγκεῖν οὗπερ ἀπέθανε (καὶ νῦν κεῖται ἐν τῷ προτεμενίσματι, ὃ γραφῇ στῆλαι δηλοῦσι), καὶ ὡς ἄγος αὐτοῖς ὂν τὸ πεπραγμένον δύο σώματα ἀνθ' ἑνὸς τῇ Χαλκιοίκῳ ἀποδοῦναι. οἱ δὲ ποιησάμενοι χαλκοῦς ἀνδριάντας δύο ὡς ἀντὶ Παυσανίου ἀνέθεσαν.

CXXXV. Οἱ δὲ Ἀθηναῖοι, ὡς καὶ τοῦ θεοῦ ἄγος κρίναντος, ἀντεπέταξαν τοῖς Λακεδαιμονίοις ἐλαύνειν αὐτό.

2 Τοῦ δὲ μηδισμοῦ τοῦ Παυσανίου οἱ Λακεδαιμόνιοι πρέσβεις πέμψαντες παρὰ τοὺς Ἀθηναίους ξυνεπῃτιῶντο καὶ τὸν Θεμιστοκλέα, ὡς ηὕρισκον ἐκ τῶν Παυσανίου ἐλέγχων, ἠξίουν τε τοῖς αὐτοῖς
3 κολάζεσθαι αὐτόν. οἱ δὲ πεισθέντες (ἔτυχε γὰρ ὠστρακισμένος καὶ ἔχων δίαιταν μὲν ἐν Ἄργει, ἐπιφοιτῶν δὲ καὶ ἐς τὴν ἄλλην Πελοπόννησον) πέμπουσι μετὰ τῶν Λακεδαιμονίων ἑτοίμων ὄντων ξυνδιώκειν ἄνδρας οἷς εἴρητο ἄγειν ὅπου ἂν περιτύχωσιν.

CXXXVI. Ὁ δὲ Θεμιστοκλῆς προαισθόμενος φεύγει ἐκ Πελοποννήσου ἐς Κέρκυραν, ὢν αὐτῶν εὐεργέτης. δεδιέναι δὲ φασκόντων Κερκυραίων

---

[1] *cf.* ch. cxxviii. 1.

[2] εὐεργέτης, *benefactor*, a title of honour bestowed upon him, either because he took the part of the Corcyraeans in a dispute with Corinth (Plut. *Them.* xxiv), or because he had

they throw malefactors; but afterwards they decided to bury him somewhere near the city. But the god at Delphi afterwards warned the Lacedaemonians by oracle to transfer him to the place where he died (and he now lies in the entrance to the precinct, as an inscription on some columns testifies), and that they should recompense Athena of the Brazen House with two bodies in place of one, since their act had brought a curse upon them. So they had two bronze statues made and dedicated them to Athena to be a substitute for Pausanias.

CXXXV. Thus it was that the Athenians,[1] in response to the demand of the Lacedaemonians, ordered them to drive out the curse of Taenarus, seeing that the god also declared it to be a curse.

But when Pausanias was thus convicted of treasonable dealings with Persia, the Lacedaemonians sent envoys to the Athenians and accused Themistocles also of complicity in the plot, in accordance with discoveries they had made in connection with their investigation about Pausanias; and they demanded that he be punished in the same way. The Athenians agreed, but as he happened to have been ostracised, and, though living in Argos, frequently visited other parts of the Peloponnesus also, they sent some men, accompanied by the Lacedaemonians (who were quite ready to join in the pursuit), with instructions to arrest him wherever they chanced to find him.

CXXXVI. But Themistocles, forewarned, fled from the Peloponnesus to Corcyra, since he was a benefactor[2] of the Corcyraeans. As they, however, alleged that they were afraid to keep him and thus

excused their absence (Schol.) in the Persian war (Hdt. VII. cxv). Themistocles relied upon the right of asylum, which had doubtless been decreed him as εὐεργέτης.

ἔχειν αὐτὸν ὥστε Λακεδαιμονίοις καὶ Ἀθηναίοις
ἀπεχθέσθαι, διακομίζεται ὑπ' αὐτῶν ἐς τὴν
2 ἤπειρον τὴν καταντικρύ. καὶ διωκόμενος ὑπὸ
τῶν προστεταγμένων κατὰ πύστιν ᾗ χωροίη,
ἀναγκάζεται κατά τι ἄπορον παρὰ Ἄδμητον τὸν
Μολοσσῶν βασιλέα ὄντα αὐτῷ οὐ φίλον κατα-
3 λῦσαι. καὶ ὁ μὲν οὐκ ἔτυχεν ἐπιδημῶν, ὁ δὲ τῆς
γυναικὸς ἱκέτης γενόμενος διδάσκεται ὑπ' αὐτῆς
τὸν παῖδα σφῶν λαβὼν καθέζεσθαι ἐπὶ τὴν
4 ἑστίαν. καὶ ἐλθόντος οὐ πολὺ ὕστερον τοῦ
Ἀδμήτου δηλοῖ τε ὅς ἐστι καὶ οὐκ ἀξιοῖ, εἴ τι
ἄρα αὐτὸς ἀντεῖπεν αὐτῷ Ἀθηναίων δεομένῳ,
φεύγοντα τιμωρεῖσθαι. καὶ γὰρ ἂν ὑπ' ἐκείνου
πολλῷ ἀσθενεστέρου[1] ἐν τῷ παρόντι κακῶς πάσχειν, γενναῖον δὲ εἶναι τοὺς ὁμοίους ἀπὸ τοῦ
ἴσου τιμωρεῖσθαι. καὶ ἅμα αὐτὸς μὲν ἐκείνῳ
χρείας τινὸς καὶ οὐκ ἐς τὸ σῶμα σῴζεσθαι ἐναντιωθῆναι, ἐκεῖνον δ' ἄν, εἰ ἐκδοίη αὐτόν (εἰπὼν
ὑφ' ὧν καὶ ἐφ' ᾧ διώκεται), σωτηρίας ἂν τῆς
ψυχῆς ἀποστερῆσαι.

CXXXVII. Ὁ δὲ ἀκούσας ἀνίστησί τε αὐτὸν
μετὰ τοῦ ἑαυτοῦ υἱέος (ὥσπερ καὶ ἔχων αὐτὸν[2]
ἐκαθέζετο, καὶ μέγιστον ἦν ἱκέτευμα τοῦτο) καὶ
ὕστερον οὐ πολλῷ τοῖς τε Λακεδαιμονίοις καὶ
Ἀθηναίοις ἐλθοῦσι καὶ πολλὰ εἰποῦσιν οὐκ
ἐκδίδωσιν, ἀλλ' ἀποστέλλει βουλόμενον ὡς βασιλέα πορευθῆναι ἐπὶ τὴν ἑτέραν θάλασσαν πεζῇ
2 ἐς Πύδναν τὴν Ἀλεξάνδρου. ἐν ᾗ ὁλκάδος τυχὼν

[1] The reading of nearly all the better MSS.; Hude and many other recent editors adopt the correction of Graevianus ἀσθενέστερος.

[2] Hude deletes, as not read by the Scholiast.

incur the enmity of the Lacedaemonians and Athenians, he was conveyed by them across to the mainland opposite. And being pursued by those who had been appointed to the task, according as they could learn the course he was taking, he was forced in some strait to take lodging with Admetus, king of the Molossians, who was not friendly to him. Admetus happened not to be at home, but Themistocles approached his wife as a suppliant and was instructed by her to take their child and seat himself on the hearth. And when Admetus returned after a short time, Themistocles declared who he was and urged that, if he had ever opposed any request Admetus had made to the Athenians, he ought not to take vengeance on him when a fugitive; for in his present plight he might come to harm at the hands of a far weaker man than Admetus, whereas the noble thing to do was to take vengeance on fair terms upon equals. Besides, he added, he had opposed Admetus merely in the matter of a petition and not of his personal safety; whereas Admetus, if he gave him up to his pursuers (telling who these were and what the charge against him), would deprive him of the salvation of his life.

CXXXVII. Admetus, hearing this, raised him up, together with his own son, even as he still sat holding him, this being the most potent form of supplication. And when, not long afterwards, the Athenians and Lacedaemonians came and made urgent demands for him, Admetus would not give him up, but, since he wished to go to the King, gave him an escort overland to Pydna on the other[1] sea, the capital of Alexander.[2] There he found a

[1] The Aegean. [2] King of Macedonia.

ἀναγομένης ἐπ' Ἰωνίας καὶ ἐπιβὰς καταφέρεται χειμῶνι ἐς τὸ Ἀθηναίων στρατόπεδον ὃ ἐπολιόρκει Νάξον. καὶ (ἦν γὰρ ἀγνὼς τοῖς ἐν τῇ νηί) δείσας φράζει τῷ ναυκλήρῳ ὅστις ἐστὶ καὶ δι' ἃ φεύγει, καὶ εἰ μὴ σώσει αὐτόν, ἔφη ἐρεῖν ὅτι χρήμασι πεισθεὶς αὐτὸν ἄγει· τὴν δὲ ἀσφάλειαν εἶναι μηδένα ἐκβῆναι ἐκ τῆς νεὼς μέχρι πλοῦς γένηται· πειθομένῳ δ' αὐτῷ χάριν ἀπομνήσεσθαι κατ' ἀξίαν. ὁ δὲ ναύκληρος ποιεῖ τε ταῦτα καὶ ἀποσαλεύσας ἡμέραν καὶ νύκτα ὑπὲρ τοῦ στρατο-
3 πέδου ὕστερον ἀφικνεῖται ἐς Ἔφεσον. καὶ ὁ Θεμιστοκλῆς ἐκεῖνόν τε ἐθεράπευσε χρημάτων δόσει (ἦλθε γὰρ αὐτῷ ὕστερον ἔκ τε Ἀθηνῶν παρὰ τῶν φίλων καὶ ἐξ Ἄργους ἃ ὑπεξέκειτο), καὶ μετὰ τῶν κάτω Περσῶν τινος πορευθεὶς ἄνω ἐσπέμπει γράμματα πρὸς βασιλέα Ἀρταξέρξην
4 τὸν Ξέρξου νεωστὶ βασιλεύοντα. ἐδήλου δὲ ἡ γραφὴ ὅτι "Θεμιστοκλῆς ἥκω παρὰ σέ, ὃς κακὰ μὲν πλεῖστα Ἑλλήνων εἴργασμαι τὸν ὑμέτερον οἶκον, ὅσον χρόνον τὸν σὸν πατέρα ἐπιόντα ἐμοὶ ἀνάγκῃ ἠμυνόμην, πολὺ δ' ἔτι πλείω ἀγαθά, ἐπειδὴ ἐν τῷ ἀσφαλεῖ μὲν ἐμοί, ἐκείνῳ δὲ ἐν ἐπικινδύνῳ πάλιν ἡ ἀποκομιδὴ ἐγίγνετο. καί μοι εὐεργεσία ὀφείλεται (γράψας τήν τε ἐκ Σαλαμῖνος προάγγελσιν τῆς ἀναχωρήσεως καὶ τὴν τῶν γεφυρῶν, ἣν ψευδῶς προσεποιήσατο, τότε δι'

merchant vessel putting off for Ionia, and going on board was driven by a storm to the station of the Athenian fleet which was blockading Naxos. Themistocles became afraid and told the captain who he was (for he was unknown to those on board) and why he was in flight, adding that if he did not save him he would tell the Athenians that he had been bribed to give him passage; their only chance for safety, he explained, was that no one be allowed to leave the ship until the voyage could be resumed, and he promised that if he complied with his request he would make a fitting return for the favour. The captain did as he was bidden, and after riding out the gale for a day and a night just outside the Athenian station, duly arrived at Ephesus. And Themistocles rewarded him handsomely with a gift of money (for he soon received from his friends in Athens and from Argos the funds which he had deposited for safekeeping); then proceeding into the interior with one of the Persians who dwelt on the coast, he sent on a letter to King Artaxerxes son of Xerxes, who had lately come to the throne. And the letter ran as follows: "I, Themistocles, am come to you, who of all Hellenes did your house most harm so long as your father assailed me and I was constrained to defend myself, but still greater good by far when, his retreat being in progress, I was in security and he in dire peril. And there is a kindness due to me (here he related the timely warning to retreat given at Salamis, and the failure of the Hellenic fleet to destroy the bridges at that time,[1] which he falsely

[1] For Themistocles' advice given to Xerxes to retreat before it was too late and his claim about the non-destruction of the bridges, *cf.* Hdt. VIII. cviii–cx.

αὐτὸν οὐ διάλυσιν), καὶ νῦν ἔχων σε μεγάλα
ἀγαθὰ δρᾶσαι πάρειμι διωκόμενος ὑπὸ τῶν Ἑλλήνων διὰ τὴν σὴν φιλίαν. βούλομαι δ' ἐνιαυτὸν
ἐπισχὼν αὐτός σοι περὶ ὧν ἥκω δηλῶσαι."

CXXXVIII. Βασιλεὺς δέ, ὡς λέγεται, ἐθαύ-
μασέ τε αὐτοῦ τὴν διάνοιαν καὶ ἐκέλευε ποιεῖν
οὕτω. ὁ δ' ἐν τῷ χρόνῳ ὃν ἐπέσχε τῆς τε Περ-
σίδος γλώσσης ὅσα ἐδύνατο κατενόησε καὶ τῶν
2 ἐπιτηδευμάτων τῆς χώρας· ἀφικόμενος δὲ μετὰ
τὸν ἐνιαυτὸν γίγνεται παρ' αὐτῷ μέγας καὶ ὅσος
οὐδείς πω Ἑλλήνων διά τε τὴν προυπάρχουσαν
ἀξίωσιν καὶ τοῦ Ἑλληνικοῦ ἐλπίδα ἣν ὑπετίθει
αὐτῷ δουλώσειν, μάλιστα δὲ ἀπὸ τοῦ πεῖραν
3 διδοὺς ξυνετὸς φαίνεσθαι. ἦν γὰρ ὁ Θεμιστοκλῆς,
βεβαιότατα δὴ φύσεως ἰσχὺν δηλώσας, καὶ διαφερόντως τι ἐς αὐτὸ μᾶλλον ἑτέρου ἄξιος θαυ-
μάσαι· οἰκείᾳ γὰρ ξυνέσει καὶ οὔτε προμαθὼν ἐς
αὐτὴν οὐδὲν οὔτ' ἐπιμαθών, τῶν τε παραχρῆμα
δι' ἐλαχίστης βουλῆς κράτιστος γνώμων καὶ τῶν
μελλόντων ἐπὶ πλεῖστον τοῦ γενησομένου ἄριστος
εἰκαστής· καὶ ἃ μὲν μετὰ χεῖρας ἔχοι, καὶ
ἐξηγήσασθαι οἷός τε, ὧν δ' ἄπειρος εἴη, κρῖναι
ἱκανῶς οὐκ ἀπήλλακτο, τό τε ἄμεινον ἢ χεῖρον ἐν

---

[1] Or, as some take it, "character." *cf.* Plut. *Them.* xxviii τὸ φρόνημα καὶ τὴν τόλμαν αὐτοῦ, *the boldness of his spirit.*

claimed to have been due to his own efforts), and now I am here, having it in my power to do you great good, being pursued by the Hellenes on account of my friendship to you; and my desire is to wait a year and then in person explain to you that for which I am come."

CXXXVIII. The King, it is said, marvelled at his purpose[1] and bade him do as he desired. And Themistocles, in the interval of his waiting, made himself acquainted, as far as he could, with the Persian language and with the customs of the country; but when the year was ended he came to the King and became more influential with him than any of the Hellenes ever had been before, both because of the reputation he already enjoyed and of the hope which he kept suggesting to him that he would make all Hellas subject to him, but most of all in consequence of the insight he manifested, of which he gave repeated proofs. For indeed Themistocles was a man who had most convincingly demonstrated the strength of his natural sagacity, and was in the very highest degree worthy of admiration in that respect. For by native insight, not reinforced by earlier or later study,[2] he was beyond other men, with the briefest deliberation, both a shrewd judge of the immediate present and wise in forecasting what would happen in the most distant future. Moreover, he had the ability to expound to others the enterprises he had in hand, and on those which he had not yet essayed he could yet without fail pass competent judgment; and he could most clearly foresee the issue for better

[2] *i.e.* without knowledge acquired either before or after the occasion for action had arisen.

τῷ ἀφανεῖ ἔτι προεώρα μάλιστα. καὶ τὸ ξύμπαν
εἰπεῖν φύσεως μὲν δυνάμει, μελέτης δὲ βραχύτητι
κράτιστος δὴ οὗτος αὐτοσχεδιάζειν τὰ δέοντα
ἐγένετο.
4 Νοσήσας δὲ τελευτᾷ τὸν βίον· λέγουσι δέ
τινες καὶ ἑκούσιον φαρμάκῳ ἀποθανεῖν αὐτόν,
ἀδύνατον νομίσαντα εἶναι ἐπιτελέσαι βασιλεῖ ἃ
5 ὑπέσχετο. μνημεῖον μὲν οὖν αὐτοῦ ἐν Μαγνησίᾳ
ἐστὶ τῇ Ἀσιανῇ ἐν τῇ ἀγορᾷ· ταύτης γὰρ ἦρχε
τῆς χώρας, δόντος βασιλέως αὐτῷ Μαγνησίαν
μὲν ἄρτον, ἣ προσέφερε πεντήκοντα τάλαντα τοῦ
ἐνιαυτοῦ, Λάμψακον δὲ οἶνον (ἐδόκει γὰρ πολυ-
οινότατον τῶν τότε εἶναι), Μυοῦντα δὲ ὄψον.
6 τὰ δὲ ὀστᾶ φασι κομισθῆναι αὐτοῦ οἱ προσή-
κοντες οἴκαδε κελεύσαντος ἐκείνου καὶ τεθῆναι
κρύφα Ἀθηναίων ἐν τῇ Ἀττικῇ· οὐ γὰρ ἐξῆν
θάπτειν[1] ὡς ἐπὶ προδοσίᾳ φεύγοντος. τὰ μὲν
κατὰ Παυσανίαν τὸν Λακεδαιμόνιον καὶ Θεμιστοκλέα τὸν Ἀθηναῖον λαμπροτάτους γενομένους
τῶν καθ' ἑαυτοὺς Ἑλλήνων οὕτως ἐτελεύτησεν.

CXXXIX. Λακεδαιμόνιοι δὲ ἐπὶ μὲν τῆς πρώτης πρεσβείας τοιαῦτα ἐπέταξάν τε καὶ ἀντεκελεύσθησαν περὶ τῶν ἐναγῶν τῆς ἐλάσεως· ὕστερον δὲ φοιτῶντες παρὰ Ἀθηναίους Ποτειδαίας τε ἀπανίστασθαι ἐκέλευον καὶ Αἴγιναν αὐτόνομον ἀφιέναι, καὶ μάλιστά γε πάντων καὶ ἐνδηλότατα προύλεγον τὸ περὶ Μεγαρέων ψήφισμα καθελοῦσι

[1] Hude deletes, after Cobet.

or worse that lay in the still dim future. To sum up all in a word, by force of native sagacity and because of the brief preparation he required, he proved himself the ablest of all men instantly to hit upon the right expedient.

He died a natural death, an illness taking him off, though some say that he put an end to his own life by poison[1] when he realised it to be impossible to fulfil his promises to the King. There is a monument to him at Magnesia in Asia, in the market-place; for he was governor of this country, the King having given him, for bread, Magnesia, which brought in a revenue of fifty talents a year, for wine, Lampsacus, reputed to be the best wine country of all places at that time; and Myus for meat. But his bones, his relations say, were fetched home by his own command and buried in Attica unknown to the Athenians; for it was not lawful to bury him there, as he had been banished for treason. Such was the end of Pausanias the Lacedaemonian and of Themistocles the Athenian, the most distinguished of the Hellenes of their time.

CXXXIX. The Lacedaemonians[2] then had on the occasion of their first embassy directed the Athenians, and received a counter demand from them, to take such measures about the expulsion of the accursed. Later, however, they frequently repaired to Athens and bade them withdraw from Potidaea, and give Aegina its independence, and above all they declared in the plainest terms that they could avoid war only by rescinding the decree about the

[1] For the various accounts, see Cic. *Brut.* xi. 43; Plut. *Them.* xxxi.; Diod. xi. 58; Ar. *Eq.* 83.

[2] Taking up the narrative from ch. cxxvi.

μὴ ἂν γίγνεσθαι πόλεμον, ἐν ᾧ εἴρητο αὐτοὺς μὴ χρῆσθαι τοῖς λιμέσι τοῖς ἐν τῇ Ἀθηναίων ἀρχῇ
2 μηδὲ τῇ Ἀττικῇ ἀγορᾷ. οἱ δ' Ἀθηναῖοι οὔτε τἆλλα ὑπήκουον οὔτε τὸ ψήφισμα καθῄρουν ἐπικαλοῦντες ἐπεργασίαν Μεγαρεῦσι τῆς γῆς τῆς ἱερᾶς καὶ τῆς ἀορίστου καὶ ἀνδραπόδων ὑποδοχὴν
3 τῶν ἀφισταμένων. τέλος δὲ ἀφικομένων τῶν τελευταίων πρέσβεων ἐκ Λακεδαίμονος, Ῥαμφίου τε καὶ Μελησίππου καὶ Ἀγησάνδρου, καὶ λεγόντων ἄλλο μὲν οὐδὲν ὧν πρότερον εἰώθεσαν,[1] αὐτὰ δὲ τάδε ὅτι "Λακεδαιμόνιοι βούλονται τὴν εἰρήνην εἶναι, εἴη δ' ἄν, εἰ τοὺς Ἕλληνας αὐτονόμους ἀφεῖτε," ποιήσαντες ἐκκλησίαν οἱ Ἀθηναῖοι γνώμας σφίσιν αὐτοῖς προυτίθεσαν, καὶ ἐδόκει ἅπαξ περὶ ἁπάντων βουλευσαμένους ἀποκρίνασθαι.
4 καὶ παριόντες ἄλλοι τε πολλοὶ ἔλεγον, ἐπ' ἀμφότερα γιγνόμενοι ταῖς γνώμαις καὶ ὡς χρὴ πολεμεῖν καὶ ὡς μὴ ἐμπόδιον εἶναι τὸ ψήφισμα εἰρήνης, ἀλλὰ καθελεῖν, καὶ παρελθὼν Περικλῆς ὁ Ξανθίππου, ἀνὴρ κατ' ἐκεῖνον τὸν χρόνον πρῶτος Ἀθηναίων, λέγειν τε καὶ πράσσειν δυνατώτατος, παρῄνει τοιάδε.

CXL. "Τῆς μὲν γνώμης, ὦ Ἀθηναῖοι, αἰεὶ τῆς αὐτῆς ἔχομαι μὴ εἴκειν Πελοποννησίοις, καίπερ εἰδὼς τοὺς ἀνθρώπους οὐ τῇ αὐτῇ ὀργῇ ἀναπειθομένους τε πολεμεῖν καὶ ἐν τῷ ἔργῳ πράσσοντας, πρὸς δὲ τὰς ξυμφορὰς καὶ τὰς γνώμας τρεπομέ-

[1] εἰώθεσαν deleted by Hude.

---

[1] See ch. lxvii. 4, and the references in Ar. *Acharn.* 520–3 and 533 f. The date of the decree must have been near the outbreak of the war (432).

Megarians,[1] in which they were forbidden to use any of the ports in the Athenian empire or even the Athenian market. But the Athenians would pay no heed to their other demands and declined to rescind the decree, charging the Megarians with encroachment upon the sacred land and the border-land not marked by boundaries,[2] and also with harbouring runaway slaves. But at last a final embassy came from Lacedaemon, consisting of Ramphias, Melesippus, and Agesander, who said nothing of the demands they had hitherto been wont to make, but only this: "The Lacedaemonians desire peace, and there will be peace if you give the Hellenes their independence." Whereupon the Athenians called an assembly and gave their citizens an opportunity to express their opinions; and it was resolved to consider the whole question and then give their answer once for all. And many others came forward and spoke, in support of both sides of the question, some urging that war was necessary, others that the decree should not stand in the way of peace, but should be rescinded; and finally Pericles son of Xanthippus, the foremost man of the Athenians at that time, wielding greatest influence both in speech and in action, came forward and advised them as follows:

CXL. "I hold, men of Athens, to the same judgment as always, that we must not yield to the Peloponnesians, although I know that men are not as a rule moved by the same spirit when they are actually engaged in war as when they are being persuaded to undertake it, but change their judgments in

[2] The reference is, first, to the tillage of land dedicated to the Eleusinian goddesses; second, to land still in dispute between Athens and Megara, and therefore unmarked.

νους. ὁρῶ δὲ καὶ νῦν ὁμοῖα καὶ παραπλήσια ξυμβουλευτέα μοι ὄντα, καὶ τοὺς ἀναπειθομένους ὑμῶν δικαιῶ τοῖς κοινῇ δόξασιν, ἢν ἄρα τι καὶ σφαλλώμεθα, βοηθεῖν, ἢ μηδὲ κατορθοῦντας τῆς ξυνέσεως μεταποιεῖσθαι. ἐνδέχεται γὰρ τὰς ξυμφορὰς τῶν πραγμάτων οὐχ ἧσσον ἀμαθῶς χωρῆσαι ἢ καὶ τὰς διανοίας τοῦ ἀνθρώπου· δι' ὅπερ καὶ τὴν τύχην, ὅσα ἂν παρὰ λόγον ξυμβῇ, εἰώθαμεν αἰτιᾶσθαι.

2 "Λακεδαιμόνιοι δὲ πρότερόν τε δῆλοι ἦσαν ἐπιβουλεύοντες ἡμῖν καὶ νῦν οὐχ ἥκιστα. εἰρημένον γὰρ δίκας μὲν τῶν διαφορῶν ἀλλήλοις διδόναι καὶ δέχεσθαι, ἔχειν δὲ ἑκατέρους ἃ ἔχομεν, οὔτε αὐτοὶ δίκας πω ᾔτησαν οὔτε ἡμῶν διδόντων δέχονται, βούλονται δὲ πολέμῳ μᾶλλον ἢ λόγοις τὰ ἐγκλήματα διαλύεσθαι, καὶ ἐπιτάσσοντες ἤδη
3 καὶ οὐκέτι αἰτιώμενοι πάρεισιν. Ποτειδαίας τε γὰρ ἀπανίστασθαι κελεύουσι καὶ Αἴγιναν αὐτόνομον ἀφιέναι καὶ τὸ Μεγαρέων ψήφισμα καθαιρεῖν· οἱ δὲ τελευταῖοι οἵδε ἥκοντες καὶ τοὺς Ἕλληνας προαγορεύουσιν αὐτονόμους ἀφιέναι.
4 ὑμῶν δὲ μηδεὶς νομίσῃ περὶ βραχέος ἂν πολεμεῖν, εἰ τὸ Μεγαρέων ψήφισμα μὴ καθέλοιμεν, ὅπερ μάλιστα προύχονται εἰ καθαιρεθείη μὴ ἂν γίγνεσθαι τὸν πόλεμον, μηδὲ ἐν ὑμῖν αὐτοῖς αἰτίαν
5 ὑπολίπησθε ὡς διὰ μικρὸν ἐπολεμήσατε. τὸ γὰρ βραχύ τι τοῦτο πᾶσαν ὑμῶν ἔχει τὴν βεβαίωσιν

accordance with events. And now also I see that I must give you the same or nearly the same advice as in the past, and I demand that those of you who are persuaded by what I shall say shall support the common decisions, even if we should in any way fail, or else, in case of success, claim no share in the good judgment shown. For it is just as possible for the course of events to move perversely as for the plans of men; and it is for that very reason that we commonly lay upon fortune the blame for whatever turns out contrary to our calculations.

"As for the Lacedaemonians, it was perfectly clear before that they were plotting against us, and it is now clearer than ever. For whereas it was expressly stipulated that we should submit our differences to arbitration, each side meanwhile keeping what it had, they have never yet asked for arbitration themselves nor do they accept it now when we make the offer. What they want is to redress their grievances by war rather than by discussion, and they are here dictating already and no longer expostulating. For they order us to raise the siege of Potidaea, restore the independence of Aegina, and rescind the Megarian decree; and these men that are just come boldly proclaim that we must give all the Hellenes also their independence. But let no one of you think that we shall be going to war for a trifling matter, if we should refuse to rescind the Megarian decree—the thing they especially insist upon, saying that there will be no war if it is rescinded—and do not let there remain in your minds any self-reproach that it was a small matter for which you went to war. For this trifling thing involves nothing less than the

καὶ πεῖραν τῆς γνώμης, οἷς εἰ ξυγχωρήσετε, καὶ
ἄλλο τι μεῖζον εὐθὺς ἐπιταχθήσεσθε ὡς φόβῳ
καὶ τοῦτο ὑπακούσαντες· ἀπισχυρισάμενοι δὲ
σαφὲς ἂν καταστήσαιτε αὐτοῖς ἀπὸ τοῦ ἴσου
ὑμῖν μᾶλλον προσφέρεσθαι. CXLI. αὐτόθεν δὴ
διανοήθητε ἢ ὑπακούειν πρίν τι βλαβῆναι, ἢ εἰ
πολεμήσομεν, ὥσπερ ἔμοιγε ἄμεινον δοκεῖ εἶναι,
καὶ ἐπὶ μεγάλῃ καὶ ἐπὶ βραχείᾳ ὁμοίως προφάσει
μὴ εἴξοντες μηδὲ ξὺν φόβῳ ἕξοντες ἃ κεκτήμεθα.
τὴν γὰρ αὐτὴν δύναται δούλωσιν ἥ τε μεγίστη
καὶ ἡ ἐλαχίστη δικαίωσις ἀπὸ τῶν ὁμοίων πρὸ
δίκης τοῖς πέλας ἐπιτασσομένη.

2 "Τὰ δὲ τοῦ πολέμου καὶ τῶν ἑκατέροις ὑπαρχόντων ὡς οὐκ ἀσθενέστερα ἕξομεν γνῶτε καθ'
3 ἕκαστον ακούοντες. αὐτουργοί τε γάρ εἰσι Πελοποννήσιοι καὶ οὔτε ἰδίᾳ οὔτ' ἐν κοινῷ χρήματά
ἐστιν, ἔπειτα χρονίων πολέμων καὶ διαποντίων
ἄπειροι διὰ τὸ βραχέως αὐτοὶ ἐπ' ἀλλήλους ὑπὸ
4 πενίας ἐπιφέρειν. καὶ οἱ τοιοῦτοι οὔτε ναῦς πληροῦν οὔτε πεζὰς στρατιὰς πολλάκις ἐκπέμπειν
δύνανται, ἀπὸ τῶν ἰδίων τε ἅμα ἀπόντες καὶ ἀπὸ
τῶν αὐτῶν δαπανῶντες καὶ προσέτι καὶ θαλάσσης
5 εἰργόμενοι· αἱ δὲ περιουσίαι τοὺς πολέμους
μᾶλλον ἢ αἱ βίαιοι ἐσφοραὶ ἀνέχουσιν. σώμασί
τε ἑτοιμότεροι οἱ αὐτουργοὶ τῶν ἀνθρώπων ἢ

---

[1] i.e. by the superior navy of the Athenians.

vindication and proof of your political conviction. If you yield this point to them you will immediately be ordered to yield another and greater one, as having conceded this first point through fear; whereas by a downright refusal you will give them clearly to understand that they must be more disposed to deal with you on terms of equality. CXLI. So make up your minds, here and now, either to take their orders before any damage is done you, or, if we mean to go to war,—as to me at least seems best—do so with the determination not to yield on any pretext, great or small, and not to hold our possessions in fear. For it means enslavement just the same when either the greatest or the least claim is imposed by equals upon their neighbours, not by an appeal to justice but by dictation.

"But as regards the war and the resources of each side, make up your minds, as you hear the particulars from me, that our position will be fully as powerful as theirs. For the Peloponnesians till their lands with their own hands; they have no wealth, either private or public; besides, they have had no experience in protracted or transmarine wars, because, owing to their poverty, they only wage brief campaigns separately against one another. Now people so poor cannot be manning ships or frequently sending out expeditions by land, since they would thus have to be away from their properties and at the same time would be drawing upon their own resources for their expenses, and, besides, are barred from the sea as well.[1] Again, it is accumulated wealth, and not taxes levied under stress, that sustains wars. Men, too, who till their own lands

χρήμασι πολεμεῖν, τὸ μὲν πιστὸν ἔχοντες ἐκ τῶν κινδύνων κἂν περιγενέσθαι, τὸ δὲ οὐ βέβαιον μὴ οὐ προαναλώσειν, ἄλλως τε κἂν παρὰ δόξαν,
6 ὅπερ εἰκός, ὁ πόλεμος αὐτοῖς μηκύνηται. μάχῃ μὲν γὰρ μιᾷ πρὸς ἅπαντας Ἕλληνας δυνατοὶ Πελοποννήσιοι καὶ οἱ ξύμμαχοι ἀντίσχειν, πολεμεῖν δὲ μὴ πρὸς ὁμοίαν ἀντιπαρασκευὴν ἀδύνατοι, ὅταν μήτε βουλευτηρίῳ ἑνὶ χρώμενοι παραχρῆμά τι ὀξέως ἐπιτελῶσι πάντες τε ἰσόψηφοι ὄντες καὶ οὐχ ὁμόφυλοι τὸ ἐφ᾽ ἑαυτὸν ἕκαστος σπεύδῃ,
7 ἐξ ὧν φιλεῖ μηδὲν ἐπιτελὲς γίγνεσθαι. καὶ γὰρ οἱ μὲν ὡς μάλιστα τιμωρήσασθαί τινα βούλονται, οἱ δὲ ὡς ἥκιστα τὰ οἰκεῖα φθεῖραι. χρόνιοί τε ξυνιόντες ἐν βραχεῖ μὲν μορίῳ σκοποῦσί τι τῶν κοινῶν, τῷ δὲ πλέονι τὰ οἰκεῖα πράσσουσι, καὶ ἕκαστος οὐ παρὰ τὴν ἑαυτοῦ ἀμέλειαν οἴεται βλάψειν, μέλειν δέ τινι καὶ ἄλλῳ ὑπὲρ ἑαυτοῦ τι προϊδεῖν, ὥστε τῷ αὐτῷ ὑπὸ ἁπάντων ἰδίᾳ δοξάσματι λανθάνειν τὸ κοινὸν ἁθρόον φθειρόμενον. CXLII. μέγιστον δέ, τῇ τῶν χρημάτων σπάνει κωλύσονται, ὅταν σχολῇ αὐτὰ ποριζόμενοι διαμέλλωσιν· τοῦ δὲ πολέμου οἱ καιροὶ οὐ μενετοί.

2 “Καὶ μὴν οὐδ᾽ ἡ ἐπιτείχισις οὐδὲ τὸ ναυτικὸν

are more ready to risk their lives in war than their property; for they have confident hope of surviving the perils, but no assurance that they will not use up their funds before the war ends, especially if, as may well happen, the war is protracted beyond expectation. Indeed, although in a single battle the Peloponnesians and their allies are strong enough to withstand all the Hellenes, yet they are not strong enough to maintain a war against a military organisation which is so different from theirs, seeing that they have no single general assembly, and therefore cannot promptly put into effect any emergency measure; and as they all have an equal vote and are of different races they each strive to advance their own interests. In such circumstances it usually happens that nothing is accomplished. And indeed it could scarcely be otherwise, for what some of them want is the greatest possible vengeance upon a particular enemy, others the least possible damage to their own property. And when after many delays they do meet, they give but a scant portion of their time to the consideration of any matter of common concern, but the larger portion to their own individual interests. And each one thinks no harm will come from his own negligence, but that it is the business of somebody else to be provident on his behalf; and so, through all separately cherishing the same fancy, universal ruin comes unperceived upon the whole body. CXLII. And what is most important, they will be hampered by scarcity of money, seeing that providing it slowly they are subject to delays; but the opportunities of war wait for no man.

"Moreover, neither the planting of forts in our

3 αὐτῶν ἄξιον φοβηθῆναι. τὴν μὲν γὰρ χαλεπὸν
καὶ ἐν εἰρήνῃ πόλιν ἀντίπαλον κατασκευάσασθαι,
ἦ που δὴ ἐν πολεμίᾳ τε καὶ οὐχ ἧσσον ἐκείνοις
4 ἡμῶν ἀντεπιτετειχισμένων· φρούριον δ' εἰ ποιή-
σονται, τῆς μὲν γῆς βλάπτοιεν ἄν τι μέρος κατα-
δρομαῖς καὶ αὐτομολίαις, οὐ μέντοι ἱκανόν γε
ἔσται ἐπιτειχίζειν τε κωλύειν ἡμᾶς πλεύσαντας
ἐν τῇ ἐκείνων καί, ᾗπερ ἰσχύομεν, ταῖς ναυσὶν
5 ἀμύνεσθαι. πλέον γὰρ ὅμως ἡμεῖς ἔχομεν τοῦ
κατὰ γῆν ἐκ τοῦ ναυτικοῦ ἐμπειρίας ἢ 'κεῖνοι
6 ἐκ τοῦ κατ' ἤπειρον ἐς τὰ ναυτικά. τὸ δὲ τῆς
θαλάσσης ἐπιστήμονας γενέσθαι οὐ ῥᾳδίως αὐτοῖς
7 προσγενήσεται. οὐδὲ γὰρ ὑμεῖς, μελετῶντες αὐτὸ
εὐθὺς ἀπὸ τῶν Μηδικῶν, ἐξείργασθέ πω· πῶς δὴ
ἄνδρες γεωργοὶ καὶ οὐ θαλάσσιοι, καὶ προσέτι
οὐδὲ μελετῆσαι ἐασόμενοι διὰ τὸ ὑφ' ἡμῶν πολλαῖς ναυσὶν αἰεὶ ἐφορμεῖσθαι, ἄξιον ἄν τι δρῷεν;
8 πρὸς μὲν γὰρ ὀλίγας ἐφορμούσας κἂν διακιν-
δυνεύσειαν πλήθει τὴν ἀμαθίαν θρασύνοντες,
πολλαῖς δὲ εἰργόμενοι ἡσυχάσουσι, καὶ ἐν τῷ
μὴ μελετῶντι ἀξυνετώτεροι ἔσονται καὶ δι' αὐτὸ
9 καὶ ὀκνηρότεροι. τὸ δὲ ναυτικὸν τέχνης ἐστίν,
ὥσπερ καὶ ἄλλο τι, καὶ οὐκ ἐνδέχεται, ὅταν τύχῃ,
ἐκ παρέργου μελετᾶσθαι, ἀλλὰ μᾶλλον μηδὲν
ἐκείνῳ πάρεργον ἄλλο γίγνεσθαι.

---

[1] *cf.* ch. cxxii. 1.

territory[1] need cause us to be afraid, nor yet their navy. For as regards the first, it is a difficult matter even in time of peace to construct here a city that will be a match for ours, to say nothing of doing this in a hostile country and at a time when we have fortifications quite as strong to oppose them. But suppose they do establish a fort; although they might injure a part of our territory by making raids and receiving our deserters, yet that will not be sufficient to prevent us from sailing to their land and building forts there, or making reprisals with our fleet, wherein our strength lies. For we have gained more experience of operations on land from our career on the sea than they of naval operations from their career on land. As for their acquiring the art of seamanship, that is an advantage they will not easily secure; for even you, who began practising it immediately after the Persian war, have not yet brought it to perfection. How then could men do anything worth mention who are tillers of the soil and not seamen, especially since they will not even be permitted to practise, because we shall always be lying in wait for them with a large fleet? For if they had to cope with only a small fleet lying in wait, they might perhaps risk an engagement, in their ignorance getting courage from their mere numbers; but if their way is blocked by a large fleet, they will remain inactive, their skill will deteriorate through lack of practice, and that in itself will make them more timid. Seamanship, like any other skill, is a matter of art, and practice in it may not be left to odd times, as a by-work; on the contrary, no other pursuit may be carried on as a by-work to it.

CXLIII. "Εἴ τε καὶ κινήσαντες τῶν Ὀλυμ-
πίασιν ἢ Δελφοῖς χρημάτων μισθῷ μείζονι πει-
ρῷντο ἡμῶν ὑπολαβεῖν τοὺς ξένους τῶν ναυτῶν,
μὴ ὄντων μὲν ἡμῶν ἀντιπάλων ἐσβάντων αὐτῶν
τε καὶ τῶν μετοίκων δεινὸν ἂν ἦν· νῦν δὲ τόδε τε
ὑπάρχει καί, ὅπερ κράτιστον, κυβερνήτας ἔχομεν
πολίτας καὶ τὴν ἄλλην ὑπηρεσίαν πλείους καὶ
2 ἀμείνους ἢ ἅπασα ἡ ἄλλη Ἑλλάς. καὶ ἐπὶ τῷ
κινδύνῳ οὐδεὶς ἂν δέξαιτο τῶν ξένων τήν τε αὑτοῦ
φεύγειν καὶ μετὰ τῆς ἥσσονος ἅμα ἐλπίδος ὀλίγων
ἡμερῶν ἕνεκα μεγάλου μισθοῦ δόσεως ἐκείνοις
ξυναγωνίζεσθαι.
3 "Καὶ τὰ μὲν Πελοποννησίων ἔμοιγε τοιαῦτα
καὶ παραπλήσια δοκεῖ εἶναι, τὰ δὲ ἡμέτερα
τούτων τε ὧνπερ ἐκείνοις ἐμεμψάμην ἀπηλλάχθαι
4 καὶ ἄλλα οὐκ ἀπὸ τοῦ ἴσου μεγάλα ἔχειν. ἤν τε
ἐπὶ τὴν χώραν ἡμῶν πεζῇ ἴωσιν, ἡμεῖς ἐπὶ τὴν
ἐκείνων πλευσούμεθα, καὶ οὐκέτι ἐκ τοῦ ὁμοίου
ἔσται Πελοποννήσου τε μέρος τι τμηθῆναι καὶ
τὴν Ἀττικὴν ἅπασαν· οἱ μὲν γὰρ οὐχ ἕξουσιν
ἄλλην ἀντιλαβεῖν ἀμαχεί, ἡμῖν δ' ἔστι γῆ πολλὴ
καὶ ἐν νήσοις καὶ κατ' ἤπειρον· μέγα γὰρ τὸ τῆς
5 θαλάσσης κράτος. σκέψασθε δέ· εἰ γὰρ ἦμεν
νησιῶται, τίνες ἂν ἀληπτότεροι ἦσαν; καὶ νῦν
χρὴ ὅτι ἐγγύτατα τούτου διανοηθέντας τὴν μὲν
γῆν καὶ οἰκίας ἀφεῖναι, τῆς δὲ θαλάσσης καὶ

---

[1] The mercenaries drawn from the states of the Athenian confederacy; no one of those who had taken part with the Peloponnesians would be allowed to return to his native city.

CXLIII. "Then again, if they should lay hands upon the money at Olympia or Delphi and try to entice away the mercenaries among our sailors by the inducement of higher pay, that indeed might be a dangerous matter if we were not a match for them, assuming that both citizens and our resident aliens have manned our ships. But as a matter of fact we are a match for them, and, what is of the highest importance, we have citizens for pilots, and our crews in general are more numerous and better than those of all the rest of Hellas. And no one of our mercenaries,[1] when it came to facing the risk, would elect to be exiled from his own land and, with a lesser hope of victory at the same time, fight on their side because of the offer of a few days' high pay.

"Such, as it seems to me at least, or approximately such, is the situation as far as the Peloponnesians are concerned; as regards our own, I believe we are free from the defects I have remarked upon in them, and that we have in other respects advantages which more than counterbalance theirs. If they march against our territory, we shall sail against theirs; and the devastation of a part of the Peloponnesus will be quite a different thing from that of the whole of Attica. For they will be unable to get other territory in its place without fighting, while we have an abundance of territory both in the islands and on the mainland. A great thing, in truth, is the control of the sea. Just consider: if we were islanders, who would be more unassailable? So, even now, we must, as near as may be, imagine ourselves such and relinquish our land and houses, but keep watch over the sea and the city;

πόλεως φυλακὴν ἔχειν, καὶ Πελοποννησίοις ὑπὲρ αὐτῶν ὀργισθέντας πολλῷ πλέοσι μὴ διαμάχεσθαι (κρατήσαντές τε γὰρ αὖθις οὐκ ἐλάσσοσι μαχούμεθα καὶ ἢν σφαλῶμεν, τὰ τῶν ξυμμάχων, ὅθεν ἰσχύομεν, προσαπόλλυται· οὐ γὰρ ἡσυχάσουσι μὴ ἱκανῶν ἡμῶν ὄντων ἐπ' αὐτοὺς στρατεύειν), τήν τε ὀλόφυρσιν μὴ οἰκιῶν καὶ γῆς ποιεῖσθαι, ἀλλὰ τῶν σωμάτων· οὐ γὰρ τάδε τοὺς ἄνδρας, ἀλλ' οἱ ἄνδρες ταῦτα κτῶνται. καὶ εἰ ᾤμην πείσειν ὑμᾶς, αὐτοὺς ἂν ἐξελθόντας ἐκέλευον αὐτὰ δῃῶσαι καὶ δεῖξαι Πελοποννησίοις ὅτι τούτων γε ἕνεκα οὐχ ὑπακούσεσθε.

CXLIV. "Πολλὰ δὲ καὶ ἄλλα ἔχω ἐς ἐλπίδα τοῦ περιέσεσθαι, ἢν ἐθέλητε ἀρχήν τε μὴ ἐπικτᾶσθαι ἅμα πολεμοῦντες καὶ κινδύνους αὐθαιρέτους μὴ προστίθεσθαι· μᾶλλον γὰρ πεφόβημαι τὰς οἰκείας ἡμῶν ἁμαρτίας ἢ τὰς τῶν ἐναντίων
2 διανοίας. ἀλλ' ἐκεῖνα μὲν καὶ ἐν ἄλλῳ λόγῳ ἅμα τοῖς ἔργοις δηλωθήσεται· νῦν δὲ τούτοις ἀποκρινάμενοι ἀποπέμψωμεν, Μεγαρέας μὲν ὅτι ἐάσομεν ἀγορᾷ καὶ λιμέσι χρῆσθαι, ἢν καὶ Λακεδαιμόνιοι ξενηλασίας μὴ ποιῶσι μήτε ἡμῶν μήτε τῶν ἡμετέρων ξυμμάχων (οὔτε γὰρ ἐκεῖνο κωλύει ἐν[1] ταῖς σπονδαῖς οὔτε τόδε), τὰς δὲ πόλεις ὅτι αὐτονόμους ἀφήσομεν, εἰ καὶ αὐτονόμους ἔχοντες ἐσπεισάμεθα καὶ ὅταν κἀκεῖνοι ταῖς ἑαυτῶν

[1] ἐν deleted by Hude, after Dion. H.

and we must not give way to resentment against the Peloponnesians on account of our losses and risk a decisive battle with them, far superior in numbers as they are. If we win we shall have to fight them again in undiminished number, and if we fail, our allies, the source of our strength, are lost to us as well; for they will not keep quiet when we are no longer able to proceed in arms against them. And we must not make lament for the loss of houses and land, but for men; for these things do not procure us men, but men these. Indeed, had I thought that I should persuade you, I should have urged you to go forth and lay them waste yourselves, and thus show the Peloponnesians that you will not, for the sake of such things, yield them obedience.

CXLIV. "Many other considerations also lead me to hope that we shall prove superior, if you will consent not to attempt to extend your empire while you are at war and not to burden yourselves needlessly with dangers of your own choosing; for I am more afraid of our own mistakes than of the enemy's plans. But these matters will be explained to you on some later occasion[1] when we are actually at war; at the present time let us send the envoys back with this answer: As to the Megarians, that we will permit them to use our markets and harbours, if the Lacedaemonians on their part will cease passing laws for the expulsion of aliens so far as concerns us or our allies (for nothing in the treaty forbids either our action or theirs); as to the states in our confederacy, that we will give them their independence if they were independent when we made the treaty, and as soon as they on their part

[1] *cf.* II. xiii.

ἀποδῶσι πόλεσι μὴ σφίσιν τοῖς Λακεδαιμονίοις[1] ἐπιτηδείως αὐτονομεῖσθαι, ἀλλ' αὐτοῖς ἑκάστοις ὡς βούλονται· δίκας τε ὅτι ἐθέλομεν δοῦναι κατὰ τὰς ξυνθήκας, πολέμου δὲ οὐκ ἄρξομεν, ἀρχομένους δὲ ἀμυνούμεθα. ταῦτα γὰρ δίκαια καὶ πρέποντα ἅμα τῇδε τῇ πόλει ἀποκρίνασθαι.
3 εἰδέναι δὲ χρὴ ὅτι ἀνάγκη πολεμεῖν (ἢν δὲ ἑκούσιοι μᾶλλον δεχώμεθα, ἧσσον ἐγκεισομένους τοὺς ἐναντίους ἕξομεν), ἔκ τε τῶν μεγίστων κινδύνων ὅτι καὶ πόλει καὶ ἰδιώτῃ μέγισται τιμαὶ περι-
4 γίγνονται. οἱ γοῦν πατέρες ἡμῶν ὑποστάντες Μήδους καὶ οὐκ ἀπὸ τοσῶνδε ὁρμώμενοι, ἀλλὰ καὶ τὰ ὑπάρχοντα ἐκλιπόντες, γνώμῃ τε πλέονι ἢ τύχῃ καὶ τόλμῃ μείζονι ἢ δυνάμει τόν τε βάρβαρον ἀπεώσαντο καὶ ἐς τάδε προήγαγον αὐτά· ὧν οὐ χρὴ λείπεσθαι, ἀλλὰ τούς τε ἐχθροὺς παντὶ τρόπῳ ἀμύνεσθαι καὶ τοῖς ἐπιγιγνομένοις πειρᾶσθαι αὐτὰ μὴ ἐλάσσω παραδοῦναι."

CXLV. Ὁ μὲν Περικλῆς τοιαῦτα εἶπεν. οἱ δὲ Ἀθηναῖοι νομίσαντες ἄριστα σφίσι παραινεῖν αὐτὸν ἐψηφίσαντο ἃ ἐκέλευε, καὶ τοῖς Λακεδαιμονίοις ἀπεκρίναντο τῇ ἐκείνου γνώμῃ, καθ' ἕκαστά τε ὡς ἔφρασε καὶ τὸ ξύμπαν, οὐδὲν κελευόμενοι ποιήσειν, δίκῃ δὲ κατὰ τὰς ξυνθήκας ἑτοῖμοι εἶναι διαλύεσθαι περὶ τῶν ἐγκλημάτων ἐπὶ ἴσῃ καὶ

[1] Deleted by Hude, following Schol.

grant the states in their alliance the right to exercise independence in a manner that conforms, not to the interest of the Lacedaemonians, but to the wishes of the individual states; and as to arbitration, that we are willing to submit to it in accordance with the treaty, and will not begin war, but will defend ourselves against those who do. This answer is just and at the same time consistent with the dignity of the city. But we must realise that war is inevitable, and that the more willing we show ourselves to accept it, the less eager will our enemies be to attack us, and also that it is from the greatest dangers that the greatest honours accrue to a state as well as to an individual. Our fathers, at any rate, withstood the Persians, although they had no such resources as ours, and abandoned even those which they possessed, and by their resolution more than by good fortune and with a courage greater than their strength beat back the Barbarian and advanced our fortunes to their present state. And we must not fall short of their example, but must defend ourselves against our enemies in every way, and must endeavour to hand down our empire undiminished to posterity."

CXLV. Such were the words of Pericles: and the Athenians, thinking that he was advising them for the best, voted as he directed, and answered the Lacedaemonians according to his bidding, both as regards the particulars as he set them forth and on the whole question, to the effect that they would do nothing upon dictation, but were ready in accordance with the treaty to have all complaints adjusted by arbitration on a fair and equal basis. So the

ὁμοίᾳ. καὶ οἱ μὲν ἀπεχώρησαν ἐπ' οἴκου καὶ οὐκέτι ὕστερον ἐπρεσβεύοντο.

CXLVI. Αἰτίαι δὲ αὗται καὶ διαφοραὶ ἐγένοντο ἀμφοτέροις πρὸ τοῦ πολέμου, ἀρξάμεναι εὐθὺς ἀπὸ τῶν ἐν Ἐπιδάμνῳ καὶ Κερκύρᾳ. ἐπεμίγνυντο δὲ ὅμως ἐν αὐταῖς καὶ παρ' ἀλλήλους ἐφοίτων ἀκηρύκτως μέν, ἀνυπόπτως δὲ οὔ· σπονδῶν γὰρ ξύγχυσις τὰ γιγνόμενα ἦν καὶ πρόφασις τοῦ πολεμεῖν.

Lacedaemonian envoys went back home and thereafter came on no further missions.

CXLVI. These were the grounds of complaint and the causes of disagreement on both sides before the war, and they began to appear immediately after the affair of Epidamnus and Corcyra. Nevertheless the two parties continued to have intercourse with one another during these recriminations and visited each other without heralds,[1] though not without suspicion; for the events which were taking place constituted an actual annulment of the treaty and furnished an occasion for war.

[1] *i.e.* without the formalities which are indispensable after war is declared.

BOOK II

B

I. Ἄρχεται δὲ ὁ πόλεμος ἐνθένδε ἤδη Ἀθηναίων καὶ Πελοποννησίων καὶ τῶν ἑκατέροις ξυμμάχων, ἐν ᾧ οὔτε ἐπεμίγνυντο ἔτι ἀκηρυκτὶ παρ' ἀλλήλους καταστάντες τε ξυνεχῶς ἐπολέμουν, καὶ γέγραπται ἑξῆς ὡς ἕκαστα ἐγίγνετο κατὰ θέρος καὶ χειμῶνα.

II. Τέσσαρα καὶ δέκα μὲν ἔτη ἐνέμειναν αἱ τριακοντούτεις σπονδαὶ αἳ ἐγένοντο μετ' Εὐβοίας ἅλωσιν· τῷ δὲ πέμπτῳ καὶ δεκάτῳ ἔτει, ἐπὶ Χρυσίδος ἐν Ἄργει τότε πεντήκοντα δυοῖν δέοντα ἔτη ἱερωμένης καὶ Αἰνησίου ἐφόρου ἐν Σπάρτῃ καὶ Πυθοδώρου ἔτι τέσσαρας μῆνας ἄρχοντος Ἀθηναίοις, μετὰ τὴν ἐν Ποτειδαίᾳ μάχην μηνὶ ἕκτῳ καὶ δεκάτῳ, ἅμα[1] ἦρι ἀρχομένῳ Θηβαίων ἄνδρες ὀλίγῳ πλείους τριακοσίων (ἡγοῦντο δὲ αὐτῶν βοιωταρχοῦντες Πυθάγγελός τε ὁ Φυλείδου καὶ Διέμπορος ὁ Ὀνητορίδου) ἐσῆλθον περὶ πρῶτον ὕπνον ξὺν ὅπλοις ἐς Πλάταιαν τῆς Βοιωτίας

[1] Hude's correction for ἕκτῳ καὶ ἅμα of the MSS. Lipsius suggested ἕκτῳ <καὶ δεκάτῳ> καί.

---

[1] The mode of reckoning customary in the time of Thucydides, and continued long afterwards. In such a scheme the summer included the spring and the winter the autumn:

BOOK II

I. At this point in my narrative begins the account of the actual warfare between the Athenians and the Peloponnesians and their respective allies. While it continued they ceased having communication with one another except through heralds, and when once they were at war they waged it without intermission. The events of the war have been recorded in the order of their occurrence, summer by summer and winter by winter.[1]

II. For fourteen years the thirty years' truce which had been concluded after the capture of Euboea remained unbroken; but in the fifteenth year, when Chrysis was in the forty-eighth year of her priesthood [2] at Argos, and Aenesias was ephor at Sparta, and Pythodorus had still four months to serve as archon at Athens, in the sixteenth month after the battle of Potidaea, at the opening of 431 B.C.
spring, some Thebans, a little more than three hundred in number, under the command of the Boeotarchs Pythangelus son of Phyleidas and Diemporus son of Onetoridas, about the first watch of the night entered under arms into Plataea, a

the summer period was equal to about eight months, the winter to about four.

[2] The commencement of the war is fixed according to the forms of reckoning customary in the three most important Hellenic states.

2 οὖσαν Ἀθηναίων ξυμμαχίδα. ἐπηγάγοντο δὲ καὶ ἀνέῳξαν τὰς πύλας Πλαταιῶν ἄνδρες, Ναυκλείδης τε καὶ οἱ μετ' αὐτοῦ, βουλόμενοι ἰδίας ἕνεκα δυνάμεως ἄνδρας τε τῶν πολιτῶν τοὺς σφίσιν ὑπεναντίους διαφθεῖραι καὶ τὴν πόλιν
3 Θηβαίοις προσποιῆσαι. ἔπραξαν δὲ ταῦτα δι' Εὐρυμάχου τοῦ Λεοντιάδου, ἀνδρὸς Θηβαίων δυνατωτάτου. προϊδόντες γὰρ οἱ Θηβαῖοι ὅτι ἔσοιτο ὁ πόλεμος, ἐβούλοντο τὴν Πλάταιαν αἰεὶ σφίσι διάφορον οὖσαν ἔτι ἐν εἰρήνῃ τε καὶ τοῦ πολέμου μήπω φανεροῦ καθεστῶτος προκαταλαβεῖν. ᾗ καὶ ῥᾷον ἔλαθον ἐσελθόντες, φυλακῆς
4 οὐ προκαθεστηκυίας. θέμενοι δὲ ἐς τὴν ἀγορὰν τὰ ὅπλα τοῖς μὲν ἐπαγαγομένοις οὐκ ἐπείθοντο ὥστε εὐθὺς ἔργου ἔχεσθαι καὶ ἰέναι ἐπὶ τὰς οἰκίας τῶν ἐχθρῶν, γνώμην δ' ἐποιοῦντο κηρύγμασί τε χρήσασθαι ἐπιτηδείοις καὶ ἐς ξύμβασιν μᾶλλον καὶ φιλίαν τὴν πόλιν ἀγαγεῖν (καὶ ἀνεῖπεν ὁ κῆρυξ, εἴ τις βούλεται κατὰ τὰ πάτρια τῶν πάντων Βοιωτῶν ξυμμαχεῖν, τίθεσθαι παρ' αὐτοὺς τὰ ὅπλα), νομίζοντες σφίσι ῥᾳδίως τούτῳ τῷ τρόπῳ προσχωρήσειν τὴν πόλιν.

III. Οἱ δὲ Πλαταιῆς ὡς ᾔσθοντο ἔνδον τε ὄντας τοὺς Θηβαίους καὶ ἐξαπιναίως κατειλημμένην τὴν πόλιν, καταδείσαντες καὶ νομίσαντες πολλῷ πλείους ἐσεληλυθέναι (οὐ γὰρ ἑώρων ἐν τῇ νυκτί) πρὸς ξύμβασιν ἐχώρησαν καὶ τοὺς λόγους δεξά-

town of Boeotia which was in alliance with Athens. They had been invited over by some Plataeans, Naucleides and his partisans, who opened the gates for them, intending, with a view to getting power into their hands, to destroy the citizens who were of the opposite party and make over the city to the Thebans. And they had conducted their intrigue through Eurymachus son of Leontiades, a man of great influence at Thebes. For, as Plataea was always at variance with them, the Thebans, foreseeing that the war[1] was coming, wished to get possession of it while there was still peace and before the war had yet been openly declared. And so they found it easier to make their entry unobserved, because no watch had been set to guard the city. And when they had grounded their arms in the market-place, instead of following the advice of those who had invited them over, namely to set to work at once and enter the houses of their enemies, they determined rather to try conciliatory proclamations and to bring the city to an amicable agreement. The proclamation made by herald was that, if anyone wished to be an ally according to the hereditary usages of the whole body of the Boeotians, he should take his weapons and join them. For they thought that in this way the city would easily be induced to come over to their side.

III. And the Plataeans, when they became aware that the Thebans were inside, and that the city had been taken by surprise, took fright, and, as it was night and they could not see, thinking that a far greater number had come in, they concluded to make terms, and, accepting the proposals

[1] *i.e.* the war between Athens and Sparta.

μενοι ἡσύχαζον, ἄλλως τε καὶ ἐπειδὴ ἐς οὐδένα
2 οὐδὲν ἐνεωτέριζον. πράσσοντες δέ πως ταῦτα
κατενόησαν οὐ πολλοὺς τοὺς Θηβαίους ὄντας καὶ
ἐνόμισαν ἐπιθέμενοι ῥᾳδίως κρατήσειν· τῷ γὰρ
πλήθει τῶν Πλαταιῶν οὐ βουλομένῳ ἦν τῶν
3 Ἀθηναίων ἀφίστασθαι. ἐδόκει οὖν ἐπιχειρητέα
εἶναι καὶ ξυνελέγοντο διορύσσοντες τοὺς κοινοὺς
τοίχους παρ' ἀλλήλους, ὅπως μὴ διὰ τῶν ὁδῶν
φανεροὶ ὦσιν ἰόντες, ἁμάξας τε ἄνευ τῶν ὑπο-
ζυγίων ἐς τὰς ὁδοὺς καθίστασαν, ἵνα ἀντὶ τείχους
ᾖ, καὶ τἆλλα ἐξήρτυον ᾗ ἕκαστον ἐφαίνετο πρὸς
4 τὰ παρόντα ξύμφορον ἔσεσθαι. ἐπεὶ δὲ ὡς ἐκ
τῶν δυνατῶν ἑτοῖμα ἦν, φυλάξαντες ἔτι νύκτα
καὶ αὐτὸ τὸ περίορθρον ἐχώρουν ἐκ τῶν οἰκιῶν
ἐπ' αὐτούς, ὅπως μὴ κατὰ φῶς θαρσαλεωτέροις
οὖσι προσφέροιντο καὶ σφίσιν ἐκ τοῦ ἴσου γίγνωνται, ἀλλ' ἐν νυκτὶ φοβερώτεροι ὄντες ἥσσους
ὦσι τῆς σφετέρας ἐμπειρίας τῆς κατὰ τὴν πόλιν.
προσέβαλόν τε εὐθὺς καὶ ἐς χεῖρας ᾖσαν κατὰ
τάχος.

IV. Οἱ δ' ὡς ἔγνωσαν ἐξηπατημένοι, ξυνεστρέ-
φοντό τε ἐν σφίσιν αὐτοῖς καὶ τὰς προσβολὰς
2 ᾗ προσπίπτοιεν ἀπεωθοῦντο. καὶ δὶς μὲν ἢ τρὶς
ἀπεκρούσαντο, ἔπειτα πολλῷ θορύβῳ αὐτῶν τε
προσβαλόντων καὶ τῶν γυναικῶν καὶ τῶν οἰκετῶν
ἅμα ἀπὸ τῶν οἰκιῶν κραυγῇ τε καὶ ὀλολυγῇ
χρωμένων λίθοις τε καὶ κεράμῳ βαλλόντων, καὶ
ὑετοῦ ἅμα διὰ νυκτὸς πολλοῦ ἐπιγενομένου, ἐφο-

made to them, raised no disturbance, especially as the Thebans did no violence to anyone. But, as it happened, while they were negotiating the terms they perceived that the Thebans were few in number, and thought that by an attack they might easily overpower them; for it was not the wish of the majority of the Plataeans to withdraw from the Athenian alliance. So it was determined to make the attempt, and they began to collect together, reaching each other's houses by digging through the party-walls that they might not be seen going through the streets, and they placed wagons without the draught-animals in the streets to serve as a barricade, and took other measures as each appeared likely to be advantageous in the present emergency. And when all was ready as far as they could make it so, waiting for the time of night just before dawn, they sallied from their houses against the Thebans, not wishing to attack them by day when they might be more courageous and would be on equal terms with them, but at night when they would be more timid and at a disadvantage, in comparison with their own familiarity with the town. And so they fell upon them at once, and speedily came to close quarters.

IV. The Thebans, when they found they had been deceived, drew themselves up in close ranks and sought to repel the assaults of the enemy wherever they fell upon them. And twice or three times they repulsed them; then when the Plataeans charged upon them with a great uproar, and at the same time the women and slaves on the house-tops, uttering screams and yells, kept pelting them with stones and tiles—a heavy rain too had come on

βήθησαν καὶ τραπόμενοι ἔφευγον διὰ τῆς πόλεως,
ἄπειροι μὲν ὄντες οἱ πλείους ἐν σκότῳ καὶ πηλῷ
τῶν διόδων ᾗ χρὴ σωθῆναι (καὶ γὰρ τελευτῶντος
τοῦ μηνὸς τὰ γιγνόμενα ἦν), ἐμπείρους δὲ ἔχοντες
τοὺς διώκοντας τοῦ μὴ ἐκφεύγειν,[1] ὥστε διεφθεί-
3 ροντο πολλοί. τῶν δὲ Πλαταιῶν τις τὰς πύλας
ᾗ ἐσῆλθον καὶ αἵπερ ἦσαν μόναι ἀνεῳγμέναι,
ἔκλῃσε στυρακίῳ ἀκοντίου ἀντὶ βαλάνου χρησά-
μενος ἐς τὸν μοχλόν, ὥστε μηδὲ ταύτῃ ἔξοδον ἔτι
4 εἶναι. διωκόμενοι δὲ κατὰ τὴν πόλιν οἱ μέν τινες
αὐτῶν ἐπὶ τὸ τεῖχος ἀναβάντες ἔρριψαν ἐς τὸ ἔξω
σφᾶς αὐτοὺς καὶ διεφθάρησαν οἱ πλείους, οἱ δὲ
κατὰ πύλας ἐρήμους γυναικὸς δούσης πέλεκυν
λαθόντες[2] διακόψαντες τὸν μοχλὸν ἐξῆλθον
οὐ πολλοί (αἴσθησις γὰρ ταχεῖα ἐπεγένετο),
ἄλλοι δὲ ἄλλῃ τῆς πόλεως σποράδες ἀπώλλυντο.
5 τὸ δὲ πλεῖστον καὶ ὅσον μάλιστα ἦν ξυνεστραμ-
μένον ἐσπίπτουσιν ἐς οἴκημα μέγα, ὃ ἦν τοῦ
τείχους καὶ αἱ[3] θύραι ἀνεῳγμέναι ἔτυχον αὐτοῦ,
οἰόμενοι πύλας τὰς θύρας τοῦ οἰκήματος εἶναι
6 καὶ ἄντικρυς δίοδον ἐς τὸ ἔξω. ὁρῶντες δὲ αὐτοὺς οἱ Πλαταιῆς ἀπειλημμένους ἐβουλεύοντο
εἴτε κατακαύσωσιν ὥσπερ ἔχουσιν, ἐμπρήσαντες
7 τὸ οἴκημα, εἴτε τί ἄλλο χρήσωνται. τέλος δὲ

[1] τοῦ μὴ ἐκφεύγειν Hude deletes, after van Herwerden.
[2] καὶ of MSS. after λαθόντες deleted by van Herwerden.
[3] So Hude with CG; αἱ πλησίον θύραι ABEFm_2. Didot and Haase would transpose thus: τοῦ τείχους πλησίον καὶ αἱ θύραι.

during the night—they became panic-stricken and turned and fled through the city; and since most of them were unfamiliar with the thoroughfares by which they must save themselves amid the darkness and mud—for these things happened at the end of the month[1]—, whereas their pursuers knew full well how to prevent their escape, many of them consequently perished. One of the Plataeans, moreover, had closed the gates by which they had entered—the only gates which had been opened—using the spike of a javelin instead of a pin to fasten the bar, so that there was no longer a way out in that direction either. And being pursued up and down the city, some of them mounted the wall and threw themselves over, most of these perishing; others succeeded in getting out by an unguarded gate without being observed, cutting through the bar with an axe which a woman gave them—but not many, for they were soon discovered; and others got isolated in various parts of the city and were put to death. But the greater number, those who had kept more together than the others, rushed into a large building abutting upon[2] the wall whose doors happened to be open, thinking that the doors of the building were city-gates and that there was a passage right through to the outside. And the Plataeans, seeing that they were cut off, began to deliberate whether they should set fire to the building and burn them up without more ado or what other disposition they should make of them.

[1] When there would be no moon.

[2] Or, as most MSS. read, "a large building . . . whose doors near by happened to be open"; with Didot and Haase, "a large building near the wall whose doors . . ."

οὗτοι τε καὶ ὅσοι ἄλλοι τῶν Θηβαίων περιῆσαν
κατὰ τὴν πόλιν πλανώμενοι, ξυνέβησαν τοῖς
Πλαταιεῦσι παραδοῦναι σφᾶς τε αὐτοὺς καὶ τὰ
ὅπλα χρήσασθαι ὅ τι ἂν βούλωνται.

V. Οἱ μὲν δὴ ἐν τῇ Πλαταίᾳ οὕτως ἐπεπράγε-
σαν. οἱ δ' ἄλλοι Θηβαῖοι οὓς ἔδει ἔτι τῆς νυκτὸς
παραγενέσθαι πανστρατιᾷ, εἴ τι ἄρα μὴ προ-
χωροίη τοῖς ἐσεληλυθόσι, τῆς ἀγγελίας ἅμα καθ'
ὁδὸν αὐτοῖς ῥηθείσης περὶ τῶν γεγενημένων ἐπε-
2 βοήθουν. ἀπέχει δὲ ἡ Πλάταια τῶν Θηβῶν
σταδίους ἑβδομήκοντα, καὶ τὸ ὕδωρ τὸ γενόμενον
τῆς νυκτὸς ἐποίησε βραδύτερον αὐτοὺς ἐλθεῖν·
ὁ γὰρ Ἀσωπὸς ποταμὸς ἐρρύη μέγας καὶ οὐ
3 ῥᾳδίως διαβατὸς ἦν. πορευόμενοί τε ἐν ὑετῷ καὶ
τὸν ποταμὸν μόλις διαβάντες ὕστερον παρε-
γένοντο, ἤδη τῶν ἀνδρῶν τῶν μὲν διεφθαρμένων,
4 τῶν δὲ ζώντων ἐχομένων. ὡς δ' ᾔσθοντο οἱ Θηβαῖοι τὸ γεγενημένον, ἐπεβούλευον τοῖς ἔξω τῆς
πόλεως τῶν Πλαταιῶν (ἦσαν γὰρ καὶ ἄνθρωποι
κατὰ τοὺς ἀγροὺς καὶ κατασκευή, οἷα ἀπροσδοκήτου τοῦ[1] κακοῦ ἐν εἰρήνῃ γενομένου)· ἐβούλοντο γὰρ σφίσιν, εἴ τινα λάβοιεν, ὑπάρχειν
ἀντὶ τῶν ἔνδον, ἢν ἄρα τύχωσί τινες ἐζωγρημένοι.
5 καὶ οἱ μὲν ταῦτα διενοοῦντο· οἱ δὲ Πλαταιῆς ἔτι
διαβουλευομένων αὐτῶν ὑποτοπήσαντες τοιοῦτόν
τι ἔσεσθαι καὶ δείσαντες περὶ τοῖς ἔξω κήρυκα
ἐξέπεμψαν παρὰ τοὺς Θηβαίους, λέγοντες ὅτι
οὔτε τὰ πεποιημένα ὅσια δράσειαν ἐν σπονδαῖς
σφῶν πειράσαντες καταλαβεῖν τὴν πόλιν, τά τε
ἔξω ἔλεγον αὐτοῖς μὴ ἀδικεῖν· εἰ δὲ μή, καὶ αὐτοὶ
ἔφασαν αὐτῶν τοὺς ἄνδρας ἀποκτενεῖν οὓς ἔχουσι

[1] Added by Bredow and Baumeister.

But finally these and the other Thebans who survived and were wandering up and down the city came to an agreement with the Plataeans to surrender themselves and their arms, to be dealt with in any way the Plataeans wished.

V. The Thebans in Plataea had fared thus; but the main body of the Thebans, who were to have come in full force while it was still night, on the chance that things might not go well with those who had entered the city, received while on the way news of what had happened and were now hastening to the rescue. Now Plataea is about seventy stadia distant from Thebes, and the rain that had come on during the night delayed their coming; for the river Asopus was running high and was not easy to cross. And so, marching in the rain and crossing the river with difficulty, they arrived too late, some of their men having already been slain and others taken captive alive. And when the Thebans learned what had happened, they began to plot against the Plataeans who were outside the city—there were, of course, men in the fields and household property, as the trouble had come unexpectedly in time of peace—for they desired to have such men as they could lay hands on as hostages for those within, in case any of them had chanced to be taken captive. Such then were their plans; but the Plataeans, while the Thebans were still deliberating, suspected that something of the sort would be done, and fearing for those outside sent out a herald to the Thebans, saying that they had done an impious thing in trying to seize their city in time of peace, and they bade them do no injury outside the walls; if they did, they on their part would put to death

ζῶντας· ἀναχωρησάντων δὲ πάλιν ἐκ τῆς γῆς
6 ἀποδώσειν αὐτοῖς τοὺς ἄνδρας. Θηβαῖοι μὲν ταῦτα λέγουσι καὶ ἐπομόσαι φασὶν αὐτούς· Πλαταιῆς δ' οὐχ ὁμολογοῦσι τοὺς ἄνδρας εὐθὺς ὑποσχέσθαι ἀποδώσειν, ἀλλὰ λόγων πρῶτον γενομένων ἤν τι ξυμβαίνωσι, καὶ ἐπομόσαι οὔ
7 φασιν. ἐκ δ' οὖν τῆς γῆς ἀνεχώρησαν οἱ Θηβαῖοι οὐδὲν ἀδικήσαντες· οἱ δὲ Πλαταιῆς ἐπειδὴ τὰ ἐκ τῆς χώρας κατὰ τάχος ἐσεκομίσαντο, ἀπέκτειναν τοὺς ἄνδρας εὐθύς. ἦσαν δὲ ὀγδοήκοντα καὶ ἑκατὸν οἱ ληφθέντες, καὶ Εὐρύμαχος αὐτῶν ἦν, πρὸς ὃν ἔπραξαν οἱ προδιδόντες.

VI. Τοῦτο δὲ ποιήσαντες ἔς τε τὰς Ἀθήνας ἄγγελον ἔπεμπον καὶ τοὺς νεκροὺς ὑποσπόνδους ἀπέδοσαν τοῖς Θηβαίοις, τά τε ἐν τῇ πόλει καθίσταντο πρὸς τὰ παρόντα ᾗ ἐδόκει αὐτοῖς.
2 τοῖς δ' Ἀθηναίοις ἠγγέλθη εὐθὺς τὰ περὶ τῶν Πλαταιῶν γεγενημένα, καὶ Βοιωτῶν τε παραχρῆμα ξυνέλαβον ὅσοι ἦσαν ἐν τῇ Ἀττικῇ καὶ ἐς τὴν Πλάταιαν ἔπεμψαν κήρυκα, κελεύοντες εἰπεῖν μηδὲν νεώτερον ποιεῖν περὶ τῶν ἀνδρῶν οὓς ἔχουσι Θηβαίων, πρὶν ἄν τι καὶ αὐτοὶ βουλεύ-
3 σωσι περὶ αὐτῶν· οὐ γὰρ ἠγγέλθη αὐτοῖς ὅτι τεθνηκότες εἶεν. ἅμα γὰρ τῇ ἐσόδῳ γιγνομένῃ τῶν Θηβαίων ὁ πρῶτος ἄγγελος ἐξῄει, ὁ δὲ δεύτερος ἄρτι νενικημένων τε καὶ ξυνειλημμένων, καὶ τῶν ὕστερον οὐδὲν ᾔδεσαν. οὕτω δὴ οὐκ εἰδότες οἱ Ἀθηναῖοι ἐπέστελλον· ὁ δὲ κῆρυξ ἀφικόμενος

the men whom they held captive, but if the Thebans withdrew from their territory they would restore the men to them. Now this is the account which the Thebans give, and they allege that the Plataeans confirmed their promise with an oath; the Plataeans do not admit that they promised to restore the men at once, but only that they would do so in case they should come to an agreement after preliminary negotiations, and they deny that they swore to it. At any rate, the Thebans withdrew from their territory without doing any injury; but the Plataeans, as soon as they had hastily fetched in their property from the country, straightway slew the men. And those who had been taken captive were one hundred and eighty in number, one of them being Eurymachus, with whom the traitors had negotiated.

VI. When they had done this, they sent a messenger to Athens, gave back the dead under a truce to the Thebans, and settled the affairs of the city as seemed best to them in the emergency. The report of what had been done in Plataea was made to the Athenians promptly; and they instantly apprehended all the Thebans who were in Attica and sent a herald to Plataea, bidding him tell them to take no extreme measures regarding the Thebans whom they held captive until they themselves should have taken counsel about them; for the news had not arrived that the men had been put to death. For the first messenger had set out at the time the Thebans were entering the city, the second immediately after their defeat and capture, and the Athenians knew nothing of later events. Consequently the Athenians sent their orders without knowing the facts; and the herald on his

4 ηὗρε τοὺς ἄνδρας διεφθαρμένους. καὶ μετὰ ταῦτα οἱ Ἀθηναῖοι στρατεύσαντες ἐς Πλάταιαν σῖτόν τε ἐσήγαγον καὶ φρουροὺς ἐγκατέλιπον, τῶν τε ἀνθρώπων τοὺς ἀχρειοτάτους ξὺν γυναιξὶ καὶ παισὶν ἐξεκόμισαν.

VII. Γεγενημένου δὲ τοῦ ἐν Πλαταιαῖς ἔργου καὶ λελυμένων λαμπρῶς τῶν σπονδῶν οἱ Ἀθηναῖοι παρεσκευάζοντο ὡς πολεμήσοντες, παρεσκευάζοντο δὲ καὶ Λακεδαιμόνιοι καὶ οἱ ξύμμαχοι, πρεσβείας τε μέλλοντες πέμπειν παρὰ βασιλέα καὶ ἄλλοσε πρὸς τοὺς βαρβάρους, εἴ ποθέν τινα ὠφελίαν ἤλπιζον ἑκάτεροι προσλήψεσθαι, πόλεις τε ξυμμαχίδας ποιούμενοι ὅσαι ἦσαν ἐκτὸς τῆς
2 ἑαυτῶν δυνάμεως. καὶ Λακεδαιμονίοις μὲν πρὸς ταῖς αὐτοῦ ὑπαρχούσαις ἐξ Ἰταλίας καὶ Σικελίας τοῖς τἀκείνων ἑλομένοις ναῦς ἐπετάχθησαν[1] ποιεῖσθαι κατὰ μέγεθος τῶν πόλεων, ὡς ἐς τὸν πάντα ἀριθμὸν πεντακοσίων νεῶν ἐσομένων, καὶ ἀργύριον ῥητὸν ἑτοιμάζειν, τά τε ἄλλα ἡσυχάζοντας καὶ Ἀθηναίους δεχομένους μιᾷ νηὶ ἕως
3 ἂν ταῦτα παρασκευασθῇ. Ἀθηναῖοι δὲ τήν τε ὑπάρχουσαν ξυμμαχίαν ἐξήταζον καὶ ἐς τὰ περὶ Πελοπόννησον μᾶλλον χωρία ἐπρεσβεύοντο, Κέρκυραν καὶ Κεφαλληνίαν καὶ Ἀκαρνᾶνας καὶ Ζάκυνθον, ὁρῶντες, εἰ σφίσι φίλια ταῦτ' εἴη

[1] ἐπετάχθη διακοσίας Hude, with Herbst (ἐπετάχθη σ′).

---

[1] *cf.* ch. lxxviii. 3.

[2] Referring, in the one case, to the unsuccessful embassy of the Lacedaemonians to the King mentioned in ch. lxvii.;

arrival found the men slain. After this the Athenians, marching to Plataea, brought in food and left a garrison,[1] taking away the least efficient of the men along with the women and children.

VII. Now that the affair at Plataea had occurred and the treaty had been glaringly violated, the Athenians began preparing for war, and the Lacedaemonians and their allies also began; both sides were making ready to send embassies to the King and to the barbarians of any other land,[2] where either of them hoped to secure aid, and they were negotiating alliances with such cities as were outside of their own sphere of influence. The Lacedaemonians, on their part, gave orders to those in Italy and Sicily who had chosen their side[3] to build, in proportion to the size of their cities, other ships, in addition to those which were already in Peloponnesian ports, their hope being that their fleet would reach a grand total of five hundred ships, and to provide a stated sum of money; but as to other matters, they were instructed to remain inactive and to refuse their ports to Athenians if they came with more than a single ship, until these preparations had been completed. The Athenians, on the other hand, began to examine their existing list of allies and also sent embassies more particularly to the countries lying about the Peloponnesus—Corcyra, Cephallenia, Acarnania, and Zacynthus—perceiving that if they were sure of the friendship of these

in the other, to the connection of the Athenians with the Odrysian court mentioned in chs. xxix. and lxvii.

[3] Referring to the Dorian colonies in Italy and Sicily (*cf.* III. lxxxvi. 2), which, however, contributed no ships till 412 B.C. (*cf.* VIII. xxvi. 1).

βεβαίως, πέριξ τὴν Πελοπόννησον καταπολεμήσοντες.

VIII. Ὀλίγον τε ἐπενόουν οὐδὲν ἀμφότεροι, ἀλλ' ἔρρωντο ἐς τὸν πόλεμον οὐκ ἀπεικότως· ἀρχόμενοι γὰρ πάντες ὀξύτερον ἀντιλαμβάνονται, τότε δὲ καὶ νεότης πολλὴ μὲν οὖσα ἐν τῇ Πελοποννήσῳ, πολλὴ δ' ἐν ταῖς Ἀθήναις οὐκ ἀκουσίως ὑπὸ ἀπειρίας ἥπτετο τοῦ πολέμου. ἥ τε ἄλλη Ἑλλὰς ἅπασα μετέωρος ἦν ξυνιουσῶν τῶν πρώ-
2 των πόλεων. καὶ πολλὰ μὲν λόγια ἐλέγετο, πολλὰ δὲ χρησμολόγοι ᾖδον ἔν τε τοῖς μέλλουσι
3 πολεμήσειν καὶ ἐν ταῖς ἄλλαις πόλεσιν. ἔτι δὲ Δῆλος ἐκινήθη ὀλίγον πρὸ τούτων, πρότερον οὔπω σεισθεῖσα ἀφ' οὗ Ἕλληνες μέμνηνται. ἐλέγετο δὲ καὶ ἐδόκει ἐπὶ τοῖς μέλλουσι γενήσεσθαι σημῆναι· εἴ τέ τι ἄλλο τοιουτότροπον ξυνέβη γενέσθαι, πάντα ἀνεζητεῖτο.

4 Ἡ δὲ εὔνοια παρὰ πολὺ ἐποίει τῶν ἀνθρώπων μᾶλλον ἐς τοὺς Λακεδαιμονίους, ἄλλως τε καὶ προειπόντων ὅτι τὴν Ἑλλάδα ἐλευθεροῦσιν. ἔρρωτό τε πᾶς καὶ ἰδιώτης καὶ πόλις εἴ τι δύναιτο καὶ λόγῳ καὶ ἔργῳ ξυνεπιλαμβάνειν αὐτοῖς· ἐν τούτῳ τε κεκωλῦσθαι ἐδόκει ἑκάστῳ τὰ πράγ-
5 ματα ᾧ μή τις αὐτὸς παρέσται. οὕτως ἐν[1] ὀργῇ εἶχον οἱ πλείους τοὺς Ἀθηναίους, οἱ μὲν τῆς ἀρχῆς ἀπολυθῆναι βουλόμενοι, οἱ δὲ μὴ ἀρχθῶσι φοβούμενοι.

[1] Added by Stephanus.

places they would be able to encircle the Peloponnesus and subdue it.

VIII. There was nothing paltry in the designs of either side; but both put their whole strength into the war, and not without reason, for men always lay hold with more spirit at the beginning, and at this time, in addition, the young men, who were numerous both in the Peloponnesus and in Athens, were unfamiliar enough with war to welcome it. All the rest of Hellas was in anxious suspense as its foremost cities came into conflict with each other. And many were the prophecies recited and many those which oracle-mongers chanted, both among the peoples who were about to go to war and in the Hellenic cities at large. Moreover, only a short time before this, Delos had been shaken, although it had not before been visited by an earthquake within the memory of the Hellenes.[1] This was said and believed to be ominous of coming events, and indeed every other incident of the sort which chanced to occur was carefully looked into.

The general good-will, however, inclined decidedly to the side of the Lacedaemonians, especially since they proclaimed that they were liberating Hellas. Every person and every state was strongly purposed to assist them in every possible way, whether by word or by deed, and each man thought that wherever he could not himself be present, there the cause had suffered a check. To such an extent were the majority of the Hellenes enraged against the Athenians, some wishing to be delivered from their sway, others fearful of falling under it.

[1] Probably an intentional contradiction of Hdt. VI. xcviii., where it is stated that an earthquake occurred shortly before the battle of Marathon, but none later.

IX. Παρασκευῇ μὲν οὖν καὶ γνώμῃ τοιαύτῃ ὥρμηντο. πόλεις δὲ ἑκάτεροι τάσδε ἔχοντες ξυμ-
2 μάχους ἐς τὸν πόλεμον καθίσταντο. Λακεδαιμονίων μὲν οἵδε ξύμμαχοι· Πελοποννήσιοι μὲν οἱ ἐντὸς ἰσθμοῦ πάντες πλὴν Ἀργείων καὶ Ἀχαιῶν (τούτοις δὲ ἐς ἀμφοτέρους φιλία ἦν· Πελληνῆς δὲ Ἀχαιῶν μόνοι ξυνεπολέμουν τὸ πρῶτον, ἔπειτα δὲ ὕστερον καὶ ἅπαντες), ἔξω δὲ Πελοποννήσου Μεγαρῆς, Βοιωτοί, Λοκροί, Φωκῆς, Ἀμπρακιῶται,
3 Λευκάδιοι, Ἀνακτόριοι. τούτων ναυτικὸν παρείχοντο Κορίνθιοι, Μεγαρῆς, Σικυώνιοι, Πελληνῆς, Ἠλεῖοι, Ἀμπρακιῶται, Λευκάδιοι, ἱππέας δὲ Βοιωτοί, Φωκῆς, Λοκροί, αἱ δ' ἄλλαι πόλεις
4 πεζὸν παρεῖχον.[1] αὕτη μὲν Λακεδαιμονίων ξυμμαχία· Ἀθηναίων δὲ Χῖοι, Λέσβιοι, Πλαταιῆς, Μεσσήνιοι οἱ ἐν Ναυπάκτῳ, Ἀκαρνάνων οἱ πλείους, Κερκυραῖοι, Ζακύνθιοι, καὶ ἄλλαι πόλεις αἱ ὑποτελεῖς οὖσαι ἐν ἔθνεσι τοσοῖσδε, Καρία ἡ ἐπὶ θαλάσσῃ, Δωριῆς Καρσὶ πρόσοικοι, Ἰωνία, Ἑλλήσποντος, τὰ ἐπὶ Θρᾴκης, νῆσοι ὅσαι ἐντὸς Πελοποννήσου καὶ Κρήτης πρὸς ἥλιον
5 ἀνίσχοντα[2] πλὴν Μήλου καὶ Θήρας. τούτων ναυτικὸν παρείχοντο Χῖοι, Λέσβιοι, Κερκυραῖοι,
6 οἱ δ' ἄλλοι πεζὸν καὶ χρήματα. ξυμμαχία μὲν αὕτη ἑκατέρων καὶ παρασκευὴ ἐς τὸν πόλεμον ἦν.

X. Οἱ δὲ Λακεδαιμόνιοι μετὰ τὰ ἐν Πλαταιαῖς εὐθὺς περιήγγελλον κατὰ τὴν Πελοπόννησον καὶ

[1] Herbst deletes, followed by Hude.

[2] Before πλὴν C gives πᾶσαι αἱ Κυκλάδες, the other MSS. πᾶσαι αἱ ἄλλαι Κυκλάδες. Deleted by Dobree.

IX. Such were the preparations and such the feelings with which the Hellenes went into the conflict. And the states which each side had as its allies when it entered the war were as follows. These were the allies of the Lacedaemonians: all the Peloponnesians south of the Isthmus with the exception of the Argives and Achaeans (these latter had friendly relations with both sides, and the Pellenians were the only Achaeans who at first took part in the war with the Lacedaemonians, though eventually all of them did), and outside of the Peloponnesus the Megarians, Boeotians, Locrians, Phocians, Ambraciots, Leucadians, and Anactorians. Of these, the Corinthians, Megarians, Sicyonians, Pellenians, Eleans, Ambraciots, and Leucadians furnished ships, while cavalry was contributed by the Boeotians, Phocians, and Locrians, and infantry by the other states. These were the allies of the Lacedaemonians. Those of the Athenians were: the Chians, Lesbians, Plataeans, the Messenians of Naupactus, most of the Acarnanians, the Corcyraeans, the Zacynthians, and in addition the cities which were tributary in the following countries: the seaboard of Caria, the Dorians adjacent to the Carians, Ionia, the Hellespont, the districts on the coast of Thrace, and the islands which lie between the Peloponnesus and Crete toward the east, with the exception of Melos and Thera. Of these, the Chians, Lesbians, and Corcyraeans furnished ships, the rest infantry and money. Such were the allies of each side and the preparations they made for the war.

X. Immediately after the affair at Plataea the Lacedaemonians sent word around to the various

τὴν ἔξω ξυμμαχίδα στρατιὰν παρασκευάζεσθαι ταῖς πόλεσι τά τε ἐπιτήδεια οἷα εἰκὸς ἐπὶ ἔξοδον ἔκδημον ἔχειν, ὡς ἐσβαλοῦντες ἐς τὴν Ἀττικήν.
2 ἐπειδὴ δὲ ἑκάστοις ἑτοῖμα γίγνοιτο, κατὰ τὸν χρόνον τὸν εἰρημένον ξυνῇσαν τὰ δύο μέρη ἀπὸ
3 πόλεως ἑκάστης ἐς τὸν ἰσθμόν. καὶ ἐπειδὴ πᾶν τὸ στράτευμα ξυνειλεγμένον ἦν, Ἀρχίδαμος ὁ βασιλεὺς τῶν Λακεδαιμονίων, ὅσπερ ἡγεῖτο τῆς ἐξόδου ταύτης, ξυγκαλέσας τοὺς στρατηγοὺς τῶν πόλεων πασῶν καὶ τοὺς μάλιστα ἐν τέλει καὶ ἀξιολογωτάτους παρῄνει τοιάδε.[1]

XI. "Ἄνδρες Πελοποννήσιοι καὶ ξύμμαχοι, καὶ οἱ πατέρες ἡμῶν πολλὰς στρατείας καὶ ἐν αὐτῇ τῇ Πελοποννήσῳ καὶ ἔξω ἐποιήσαντο, καὶ ἡμῶν αὐτῶν οἱ πρεσβύτεροι οὐκ ἄπειροι πολέμων εἰσίν· ὅμως δὲ τῆσδε οὔπω μείζονα παρασκευὴν ἔχοντες ἐξήλθομεν, ἀλλὰ καὶ ἐπὶ πόλιν δυνατωτάτην νῦν ἐρχόμεθα, καὶ αὐτοὶ πλεῖστοι καὶ
2 ἄριστοι στρατεύοντες. δίκαιον οὖν ἡμᾶς μήτε τῶν πατέρων χείρους φαίνεσθαι μήτε ἡμῶν αὐτῶν τῆς δόξης ἐνδεεστέρους. ἡ γὰρ Ἑλλὰς πᾶσα τῇδε τῇ ὁρμῇ ἐπῆρται καὶ προσέχει τὴν γνώμην, εὔνοιαν ἔχουσα διὰ τὸ Ἀθηναίων ἔχθος πρᾶξαι
3 ἡμᾶς ἃ ἐπινοοῦμεν. οὔκουν χρή, εἴ τῳ καὶ δοκοῦμεν πλήθει ἐπιέναι καὶ ἀσφάλεια πολλὴ εἶναι μὴ ἂν ἐλθεῖν τοὺς ἐναντίους ἡμῖν διὰ μάχης, τούτων ἕνεκα ἀμελέστερόν τι παρεσκευασμένους χωρεῖν, ἀλλὰ καὶ πόλεως ἑκάστης ἡγεμόνα καὶ στρατιώτην τὸ καθ' αὑτὸν αἰεὶ προσδέχεσθαι ἐς

[1] Sintenis' correction for παρεῖναι τοιάδ' ἔλεξεν of the MSS.

states in the Peloponnesus and their confederacy outside the Peloponnesus to make ready such troops and supplies as it was appropriate they should have for a foreign expedition, their intention being to invade Attica. When everything was ready in the several states, two-thirds of the contingent of each state assembled at the appointed time at the Isthmus. And when the whole army was assembled, Archidamus, the king of the Lacedaemonians, who was to be the leader of this expedition, called together the generals of all the states as well as the chief officials and the most notable men, and exhorted them as follows:

XI. "Peloponnesians and allies, our fathers made many campaigns both in the Peloponnesus and beyond it, and the elder men also amongst us do not lack experience in warfare, yet never before have we taken the field with a greater armament than this; but though we were never more numerous and puissant, it is also a very powerful state we now go against. It is but right, therefore, that we neither should show ourselves worse men than our fathers nor wanting to our own fame. For all Hellas is stirred by this enterprise of ours, and fixes her gaze upon it, and being friendly to us on account of their hatred of the Athenians hopes that we shall succeed in carrying out our designs. Therefore, even if some of us may think that we are going against them with superior numbers and that in all likelihood the enemy will not risk a pitched battle with us, we must not on that account be a whit less carefully prepared when we advance, but rather must officer and soldier of every state for his own part be always expecting to encounter

4 κίνδυνόν τινα ἥξειν. ἄδηλα γὰρ τὰ τῶν πολέμων,
καὶ ἐξ ὀλίγου τὰ πολλὰ καὶ δι' ὀργῆς αἱ ἐπι-
χειρήσεις γίγνονται· πολλάκις τε τὸ ἔλασσον
πλῆθος δεδιὸς ἄμεινον ἠμύνατο τοὺς πλέονας διὰ
5 τὸ καταφρονοῦντας ἀπαρασκεύους γενέσθαι. χρὴ
δὲ αἰεὶ ἐν τῇ πολεμίᾳ τῇ μὲν γνώμῃ θαρσαλέους
στρατεύειν, τῷ δ' ἔργῳ δεδιότας παρεσκευάσθαι.
οὕτω γὰρ πρός τε τὸ ἐπιέναι τοῖς ἐναντίοις
εὐψυχότατοι ἂν εἶεν, πρός τε τὸ ἐπιχειρεῖσθαι
ἀσφαλέστατοι.
6 "Ἡμεῖς δὲ οὐδ' ἐπὶ ἀδύνατον ἀμύνεσθαι οὕτω[1]
πόλιν ἐρχόμεθα, ἀλλὰ τοῖς πᾶσιν ἄριστα παρε-
σκευασμένην, ὥστε χρὴ καὶ πάνυ ἐλπίζειν διὰ
μάχης ἰέναι αὐτούς, εἰ μὴ καὶ νῦν ὥρμηνται ἐν
ᾧ οὔπω πάρεσμεν, ἀλλ' ὅταν ἐν τῇ γῇ ὁρῶσιν
7 ἡμᾶς δῃοῦντάς τε καὶ τἀκείνων φθείροντας. πᾶσι
γὰρ ἐν τοῖς ὄμμασι καὶ ἐν τῷ παραυτίκα ὁρᾶν
πάσχοντάς τι ἄηθες ὀργὴ προσπίπτει, καὶ οἱ
λογισμῷ ἐλάχιστα χρώμενοι θυμῷ πλεῖστα ἐς
8 ἔργον καθίστανται. Ἀθηναίους δὲ καὶ πλέον τι
τῶν ἄλλων εἰκὸς τοῦτο δρᾶσαι, οἳ ἄρχειν τε τῶν
ἄλλων ἀξιοῦσι καὶ ἐπιόντες τὴν τῶν πέλας δῃοῦν
9 μᾶλλον ἢ τὴν αὑτῶν ὁρᾶν. ὡς οὖν ἐπὶ τοσαύτην
πόλιν στρατεύοντες καὶ μεγίστην δόξαν οἰσόμενοι
τοῖς τε προγόνοις καὶ ὑμῖν αὐτοῖς ἐπ' ἀμφότερα
ἐκ τῶν ἀποβαινόντων, ἕπεσθε ὅπῃ ἄν τις ἡγῆται,
κόσμον καὶ φυλακὴν περὶ παντὸς ποιούμενοι καὶ
τὰ παραγγελλόμενα ὀξέως δεχόμενοι· κάλλιστον

[1] οὕτω deleted by Hude, after Madvig.

some danger. For the events of war cannot be foreseen, and attacks are generally sudden and furious; and oftentimes a smaller force, made cautious by fear, overmatches a larger number that is caught unprepared because it despises the foe. One should, however, when campaigning in an enemy's country always be bold in spirit, but in action cautious and therefore prepared. For thus men will be most valorous in attacking their opponents and most secure against assault.

"And we are going against a city which is not so powerless to defend itself as some may think, but is perfectly prepared in all respects; we have therefore every reason to expect them to risk a battle, if they have not already set out before we are yet there, at any rate when they see us in their territory laying it waste and destroying their property. For with all men, when they suffer an unwonted calamity, it is the sight set then and there before their eyes which makes them angry, and when they are angry they do not pause to think but rush into action. And the Athenians are even more likely than most men to act in this way, since they are more disposed to claim the right to rule over others and to attack and ravage their neighbours' land than to see their own ravaged. Realising, then, how powerful is the city against which you are taking the field, and how great is the fame, for better or for worse, which you are about to win for your ancestors and for yourselves from the outcome, follow wherever your officers lead you, regarding good order and vigilance as all-important, and sharply giving heed to the word of command; for this is the fairest as well as the safest thing—for

γὰρ τόδε καὶ ἀσφαλέστατον πολλοὺς ὄντας ἑνὶ κόσμῳ χρωμένους φαίνεσθαι."

XII. Τοσαῦτα εἰπὼν καὶ διαλύσας τὸν ξύλλογον ὁ Ἀρχίδαμος Μελήσιππον πρῶτον ἀποστέλλει ἐς τὰς Ἀθήνας τὸν Διακρίτου, ἄνδρα Σπαρτιάτην, εἴ τι ἄρα μᾶλλον ἐνδοῖεν οἱ Ἀθηναῖοι ὁρῶν-
2 τες σφᾶς ἤδη ἐν ὁδῷ ὄντας. οἱ δὲ οὐ προσεδέξαντο αὐτὸν ἐς τὴν πόλιν οὐδ' ἐπὶ τὸ κοινόν· ἦν γὰρ Περικλέους γνώμη πρότερον νενικηκυῖα κήρυκα καὶ πρεσβείαν μὴ δέχεσθαι Λακεδαιμονίων ἐξεστρατευμένων. ἀποπέμπουσιν οὖν αὐτὸν πρὶν ἀκοῦσαι καὶ ἐκέλευον ἐκτὸς ὅρων εἶναι αὐθημερόν, τό τε λοιπὸν ἀναχωρήσαντας ἐπὶ τὰ σφέτερα αὐτῶν, ἤν τι βούλωνται, πρεσβεύεσθαι. ξυμπέμπουσί τε τῷ Μελησίππῳ ἀγωγούς, ὅπως
3 μηδενὶ ξυγγένηται. ὁ δ' ἐπειδὴ ἐπὶ τοῖς ὁρίοις ἐγένετο καὶ ἔμελλε διαλύσεσθαι, τοσόνδε εἰπὼν ἐπορεύετο ὅτι "Ἥδε ἡ ἡμέρα τοῖς Ἕλλησι μεγά-
4 λων κακῶν ἄρξει." ὡς δὲ ἀφίκετο ἐς τὸ στρατόπεδον καὶ ἔγνω ὁ Ἀρχίδαμος ὅτι οἱ Ἀθηναῖοι οὐδέν πω ἐνδώσουσιν, οὕτω δὴ ἄρας τῷ στρατῷ
5 προυχώρει ἐς τὴν γῆν αὐτῶν. Βοιωτοὶ δὲ μέρος μὲν τὸ σφέτερον καὶ τοὺς ἱππέας παρείχοντο Πελοποννησίοις ξυστρατεύειν, τοῖς δὲ λειπομένοις ἐς Πλάταιαν ἐλθόντες τὴν γῆν ἐδῄουν.

XIII. Ἔτι δὲ τῶν Πελοποννησίων ξυλλεγομέ-

a great host to show itself subject to a single discipline."

XII. With these words Archidamus dismissed the assembly. He then first sent Melesippus son of Diocritus, a Spartan, to Athens, in the hope that the Athenians, when they saw that the Lacedaemonians were already on the march, might be somewhat more inclined to yield. But they did not allow him to enter the city, much less to appear before the assembly; for a motion of Pericles had already been carried not to admit herald or embassy after the Lacedaemonians had once taken the field. They accordingly dismissed him without hearing him, and ordered him to be beyond their borders that same day; and in future, they added, the Lacedaemonians must first withdraw to their own territory before sending an embassy, if they had any communication to make. They also sent an escort along with Melesippus, in order to prevent his having communication with anyone. And when he arrived at the frontier and was about to leave his escort, he uttered these words before he went his way, "This day will be the beginning of great evils for the Hellenes." When he came to the army, and Archidamus had learned that the Athenians would not as yet make any concession, then at length they broke camp and advanced into Athenian territory. And the Boeotians not only supplied their contingent[1] and the cavalry to serve with the Peloponnesians, but also went to Plataea with their remaining troops and proceeded to ravage the country.

XIII. While the Peloponnesian forces were still

[1] *i.e.* two-thirds of their full appointment; *cf.* ch. x. 2.

νων τε ἐς τὸν ἰσθμὸν καὶ ἐν ὁδῷ ὄντων, πρὶν ἐσβαλεῖν ἐς τὴν Ἀττικήν, Περικλῆς ὁ Ξανθίππου, στρατηγὸς ὢν Ἀθηναίων δέκατος αὐτός, ὡς ἔγνω τὴν ἐσβολὴν ἐσομένην, ὑποτοπήσας, ὅτι Ἀρχίδαμος αὐτῷ ξένος ὢν ἐτύγχανε, μὴ πολλάκις ἢ αὐτὸς ἰδίᾳ βουλόμενος χαρίζεσθαι τοὺς ἀγροὺς αὐτοῦ παραλίπῃ καὶ μὴ δῃώσῃ, ἢ καὶ Λακεδαιμονίων κελευσάντων ἐπὶ διαβολῇ τῇ ἑαυτοῦ γένηται τοῦτο, ὥσπερ καὶ τὰ ἄγη ἐλαύνειν προεῖπον ἕνεκα ἐκείνου, προηγόρευε τοῖς Ἀθηναίοις ἐν τῇ ἐκκλησίᾳ ὅτι Ἀρχίδαμος μέν οἱ ξένος εἴη, οὐ μέντοι ἐπὶ κακῷ γε τῆς πόλεως γένοιτο, τοὺς δὲ ἀγροὺς τοὺς ἑαυτοῦ καὶ οἰκίας ἢν ἄρα μὴ δῃώσωσιν οἱ πολέμιοι ὥσπερ καὶ τὰ τῶν ἄλλων, ἀφίησιν αὐτὰ δημόσια εἶναι, καὶ μηδεμίαν οἱ
2 ὑποψίαν κατὰ ταῦτα γίγνεσθαι. παρῄνει δὲ καὶ περὶ τῶν παρόντων ἅπερ καὶ πρότερον, παρασκευάζεσθαί τε ἐς τὸν πόλεμον καὶ τὰ ἐκ τῶν ἀγρῶν ἐσκομίζεσθαι, ἔς τε μάχην μὴ ἐπεξιέναι, ἀλλὰ τὴν πόλιν ἐσελθόντας φυλάσσειν, καὶ τὸ ναυτικόν, ᾗπερ ἰσχύουσιν, ἐξαρτύεσθαι, τά τε τῶν ξυμμάχων διὰ χειρὸς ἔχειν, λέγων τὴν ἰσχὺν αὐτοῖς ἀπὸ τούτων εἶναι τῶν χρημάτων τῆς προσόδου,[1] τὰ δὲ πολλὰ τοῦ πολέμου γνώμῃ καὶ
3 χρημάτων περιουσίᾳ κρατεῖσθαι. θαρσεῖν τε

[1] τῶν χρημάτων τῆς προσόδου deleted by Hude, after van Herwerden.

collecting at the Isthmus and while they were on the march but had not yet invaded Attica, Pericles son of Xanthippus, who was one of the ten Athenian generals, when he realised that the invasion would be made, conceived a suspicion that perhaps Archidamus, who happened to be a guest-friend of his, might pass by his fields and not lay them waste, doing this either on his own initiative, in the desire to do him a personal favour, or at the bidding of the Lacedaemonians with a view to creating a prejudice against him, just as it was on his account that they had called upon the Athenians to drive out the pollution.[1] So he announced to the Athenians in their assembly that while Archidamus was indeed a guest-friend of his, this relationship had certainly not been entered upon for the detriment of the state; and that in case the enemy might not lay waste his fields and houses like the rest, he now gave them up to be public property, and asked that no suspicion should arise against himself on that account. And he gave them the same advice as before[2] about the present situation: that they should prepare for the war, should bring in their property from the fields, and should not go out to meet the enemy in battle, but should come into the city and there act on the defensive; that they should equip their fleet, in which their strength lay, and keep a firm hand upon their allies, explaining that the Athenian power depended on revenue of money received from the allies, and that, as a general rule, victories in war were won by abundance of money as well as by wise policy. And he bade them be of good courage, as on

[1] *cf.* I. cxxvii. 1.
[2] *cf.* I. cxliii.

ἐκέλευε προσιόντων μὲν ἑξακοσίων ταλάντων ὡς
ἐπὶ τὸ πολὺ φόρου κατ' ἐνιαυτὸν ἀπὸ τῶν ξυμμάχων τῇ πόλει ἄνευ τῆς ἄλλης προσόδου, ὑπαρχόντων δὲ ἐν τῇ ἀκροπόλει ἔτι τότε ἀργυρίου
ἐπισήμου ἑξακισχιλίων ταλάντων (τὰ γὰρ πλεῖστα τριακοσίων ἀποδέοντα μύρια ἐγένετο, ἀφ'
ὧν ἔς τε τὰ προπύλαια τῆς ἀκροπόλεως καὶ τἆλλα οἰκοδομήματα καὶ ἐς Ποτείδαιαν ἀπανηλώθη),
4 χωρὶς δὲ χρυσίου ἀσήμου καὶ ἀργυρίου ἔν τε
ἀναθήμασιν ἰδίοις καὶ δημοσίοις καὶ ὅσα ἱερὰ
σκεύη περί τε τὰς πομπὰς καὶ τοὺς ἀγῶνας καὶ
σκῦλα Μηδικὰ καὶ εἴ τι τοιουτότροπον, οὐκ
5 ἐλάσσονος[1] ἢ πεντακοσίων ταλάντων. ἔτι δὲ
καὶ τὰ ἐκ τῶν ἄλλων ἱερῶν προσετίθει χρήματα
οὐκ ὀλίγα, οἷς χρήσεσθαι αὐτούς, καὶ ἢν πάνυ
ἐξείργωνται πάντων, καὶ αὐτῆς τῆς θεοῦ τοῖς
περικειμένοις χρυσίοις· ἀπέφαινε δ' ἔχον τὸ
ἄγαλμα τεσσαράκοντα τάλαντα σταθμὸν χρυσίου ἀπέφθου καὶ περιαιρετὸν εἶναι ἅπαν. χρη-
σαμένους τε ἐπὶ σωτηρίᾳ ἔφη χρῆναι μὴ ἐλάσσω

[1] ἦν of the MSS., after ἐλάσσονος, deleted by Abresch.

---

[1] About £120,000, or $583,200. The original amount at the institution of the Confederacy of Delos was 460 talents (I. xcvi. 2). The figure here given is an average amount, because the assessment was revised every four years at the Panathenaea.

These figures, and all other equivalents of Greek financial statements, are purely conventional, inasmuch as the purchasing power of money was then very much greater than now.

[2] The ordinary revenue, apart from the tribute, consisted of customs duties, tax on sales, poll tax on resident aliens,

an average six hundred talents[1] of tribute were coming in yearly from the allies to the city, not counting the other sources[2] of revenue, and there were at this time still on hand in the Acropolis six thousand talents[3] of coined silver (the maximum amount had been nine thousand seven hundred talents, from which expenditures had been made for the construction of the Propylaea[4] of the Acropolis and other buildings,[5] as well as for the operations at Potidaea). Besides, there was uncoined gold and silver in public and private dedications, and all the sacred vessels used in the processions and games, and the Persian spoils and other treasures of like nature, worth not less than five hundred talents.[6] And he estimated, besides, the large amount of treasure to be found in the other temples. All this would be available for their use, and, if they should be absolutely cut off from all other resources, they might use even the gold plates with which the statue of the goddess herself was overlaid.[7] The statue, as he pointed out to them, contained forty talents' weight of pure gold, and it was all removable.[8] This treasure they might use for self-preservation, but they must replace as much as they

rents of state property, especially the silver mines, court fees and fines.

[3] About £1,940,000, or $9,428,400.

[4] Completed about 432 B.C.

[5] Such as the Parthenon, the Odeum, and the Telesterion at Eleusis (see Plut. *Per.* xiii.).

[6] About £100,000, or $486,000.

[7] The chryselephantine statue of Athena by Phidias in the Parthenon.

[8] According to Plut. *Per.* xxxi., Phidias, by the advice of Pericles, laid on the gold in such a way that it could all be removed and weighed.

6 ἀντικαταστῆσαι πάλιν. χρήμασι μὲν οὖν οὕτω
ἐθάρσυνεν αὐτούς· ὁπλίτας δὲ τρισχιλίους καὶ
μυρίους εἶναι ἄνευ τῶν ἐν τοῖς φρουρίοις καὶ τῶν
7 παρ' ἔπαλξιν ἑξακισχιλίων καὶ μυρίων. τοσοῦτοι γὰρ ἐφύλασσον τὸ πρῶτον ὁπότε οἱ πολέμιοι
ἐσβάλοιεν, ἀπό τε τῶν πρεσβυτάτων καὶ τῶν
νεωτάτων καὶ μετοίκων ὅσοι ὁπλῖται ἦσαν. τοῦ
τε γὰρ Φαληρικοῦ τείχους στάδιοι ἦσαν πέντε
καὶ τριάκοντα πρὸς τὸν κύκλον τοῦ ἄστεως καὶ
αὐτοῦ τοῦ κύκλου τὸ φυλασσόμενον τρεῖς καὶ
τεσσαράκοντα (ἔστι δὲ αὐτοῦ ὃ καὶ ἀφύλακτον
ἦν, τὸ μεταξὺ τοῦ τε μακροῦ καὶ τοῦ Φαληρικοῦ),
τὰ δὲ μακρὰ τείχη πρὸς τὸν Πειραιᾶ τεσσαράκοντα σταδίων, ὧν τὸ ἔξωθεν ἐτηρεῖτο, καὶ τοῦ
Πειραιῶς ξὺν Μουνιχίᾳ ἑξήκοντα μὲν σταδίων ὁ
ἅπας περίβολος, τὸ δ' ἐν φυλακῇ ὂν ἥμισυ τού-
8 του. ἱππέας δὲ ἀπέφαινε διακοσίους καὶ χιλίους
ξὺν ἱπποτοξόταις, ἑξακοσίους δὲ καὶ χιλίους
τοξότας, καὶ τριήρεις τὰς πλωίμους τριακοσίας.
9 ταῦτα γὰρ ὑπῆρχεν Ἀθηναίοις καὶ οὐκ ἐλάσσω
ἕκαστα τούτων, ὅτε ἡ ἐσβολὴ τὸ πρῶτον ἔμελλε
Πελοποννησίων ἔσεσθαι καὶ ἐς τὸν πόλεμον καθίσταντο. ἔλεγε δὲ καὶ ἄλλα οἷάπερ εἰώθει Περικλῆς ἐς ἀπόδειξιν τοῦ περιέσεσθαι τῷ πολέμῳ.

XIV. Οἱ δὲ Ἀθηναῖοι ἀκούσαντες ἀνεπείθοντό τε καὶ ἐσεκομίζοντο ἐκ τῶν ἀγρῶν παῖδας καὶ γυναῖκας καὶ τὴν ἄλλην κατασκευὴν ᾗ κατ' οἶκον

took. As to their resources in money, then, he thus sought to encourage them; and as to heavy-armed infantry, he told them that there were thirteen thousand, not counting the sixteen thousand men who garrisoned the forts and manned the city walls. For this was the number engaged in garrison duty at first, when the enemy were invading Attica, and they were composed of the oldest and the youngest[1] citizens and of such metics as were heavily armed. For the length of the Phalerian wall was thirty-five stadia to the circuit-wall of the city, and the portion of the circuit-wall itself which was guarded was forty-three stadia (a portion being left unguarded, that between the Long Wall and the Phalerian); and the Long Walls to the Peiraeus were forty stadia in extent, of which only the outside one was guarded; and the whole circuit of the Peiraeus including Munichia was sixty stadia, half of it being under guard. The cavalry, Pericles pointed out, numbered twelve hundred, including mounted archers, the bow-men sixteen hundred, and the triremes that were seaworthy three hundred. For these were the forces, and not less than these in each branch, which the Athenians had on hand when the first invasion of the Peloponnesians was impending and they found themselves involved in the war. And Pericles used still other arguments, as was his wont, to prove that they would be victorious in the war.

XIV. After the Athenians had heard his words they were won to his view, and they began to bring in from the fields their children and wives, and also

[1] The age limits were eighteen to sixty, those from eighteen to twenty (περίπολοι) being called on only for garrison duty within the bounds of Attica. The age of full citizenship was twenty.

ἐχρῶντο, καὶ αὐτῶν τῶν οἰκιῶν καθαιροῦντες τὴν
ξύλωσιν· πρόβατα δὲ καὶ ὑποζύγια ἐς τὴν Εὔβοιαν διεπέμψαντο καὶ τὰς νήσους τὰς ἐπικει-
2 μένας. χαλεπῶς δὲ αὐτοῖς διὰ τὸ αἰεὶ εἰωθέναι
τοὺς πολλοὺς ἐν τοῖς ἀγροῖς διαιτᾶσθαι ἡ ἀνά-
στασις ἐγίγνετο. XV. ξυνεβεβήκει δὲ ἀπὸ τοῦ
πάνυ ἀρχαίου ἑτέρων μᾶλλον Ἀθηναίοις τοῦτο.
ἐπὶ γὰρ Κέκροπος καὶ τῶν πρώτων βασιλέων ἡ
Ἀττικὴ ἐς Θησέα αἰεὶ κατὰ πόλεις ᾠκεῖτο πρυ-
τανεῖά τε ἐχούσας καὶ ἄρχοντας, καὶ ὁπότε μή
τι δείσειαν, οὐ ξυνῇσαν βουλευσόμενοι ὡς τὸν
βασιλέα, ἀλλ' αὐτοὶ ἕκαστοι ἐπολίτευον καὶ
ἐβουλεύοντο· καί τινες καὶ ἐπολέμησάν ποτε αὐτῶν, ὥσπερ καὶ Ἐλευσίνιοι μετ' Εὐμόλπου πρὸς
2 Ἐρεχθέα. ἐπειδὴ δὲ Θησεὺς ἐβασίλευσε, γενόμενος μετὰ τοῦ ξυνετοῦ καὶ δυνατὸς τά τε ἄλλα
διεκόσμησε τὴν χώραν καὶ καταλύσας τῶν ἄλλων πόλεων τά τε βουλευτήρια καὶ τὰς ἀρχὰς ἐς
τὴν νῦν πόλιν οὖσαν, ἓν βουλευτήριον ἀποδείξας
καὶ πρυτανεῖον, ξυνῴκισε πάντας, καὶ νεμομένους
τὰ αὑτῶν ἑκάστους ἅπερ καὶ πρὸ τοῦ ἠνάγκασε
μιᾷ πόλει ταύτῃ χρῆσθαι, ἣ ἁπάντων ἤδη ξυν-
τελούντων ἐς αὐτὴν μεγάλη γενομένη παρεδόθη
ὑπὸ Θησέως τοῖς ἔπειτα· καὶ ξυνοίκια ἐξ ἐκείνου
Ἀθηναῖοι ἔτι καὶ νῦν τῇ θεῷ ἑορτὴν δημοτελῆ
ποιοῦσιν.
3 Τὸ δὲ πρὸ τοῦ ἡ ἀκρόπολις ἡ νῦν οὖσα πόλις

[1] Others render: "since all were now counted as belonging to it."

their household furniture, pulling down even the woodwork of the houses themselves; but sheep and draught-animals they sent over to Euboea and the adjacent islands. And the removal was a hard thing for them to accept, because most of them had always been used to live in the country. XV. And this kind of life had been the characteristic of the Athenians, more than of any other Hellenes, from the very earliest times. For in the time of Cecrops and the earliest kings down to Theseus, Attica had been divided into separate towns, each with its town hall and magistrates, and so long as they had nothing to fear they did not come together to consult with the king, but separately administered their own affairs and took counsel for themselves. Sometimes they even made war upon the king, as, for example, the Eleusinians with Eumolpus did upon Erechtheus. But when Theseus became king and proved himself a powerful as well as a prudent ruler, he not only re-organized the country in other respects, but abolished the councils and magistracies of the minor towns and brought all their inhabitants into union with what is now the city, establishing a single council and town hall, and compelled them, while continuing to occupy each his own lands as before, to use Athens as the sole capital. This became a great city, since all were now paying their taxes to it,[1] and was such when Theseus handed it down to his successors. And from his time even to this day the Athenians have celebrated at the public expense a festival called the Synoecia,[2] in honour of the goddess.

Before this[3] what is now the Acropolis was the

[2] "Feast of the Union," celebrated on the sixteenth of the month Hecatombaeon.

[3] *i.e.* before the Synoecismus, or union of Attica under Theseus.

ἦν, καὶ τὸ ὑπ' αὐτὴν πρὸς νότον μάλιστα τετραμ-
4 μένον. τεκμήριον δέ· τὰ γὰρ ἱερὰ ἐν αὐτῇ τῇ
ἀκροπόλει καὶ ἄλλων θεῶν ἐστι, καὶ τὰ ἔξω
πρὸς τοῦτο τὸ μέρος τῆς πόλεως μᾶλλον ἵδρυται,
τό τε τοῦ Διὸς τοῦ Ὀλυμπίου καὶ τὸ Πύθιον καὶ
τὸ τῆς Γῆς καὶ τὸ τοῦ[1] ἐν Λίμναις Διονύσου, ᾧ
τὰ ἀρχαιότερα Διονύσια τῇ δωδεκάτῃ[2] ποιεῖται
ἐν μηνὶ Ἀνθεστηριῶνι, ὥσπερ καὶ οἱ ἀπ' Ἀθηναίων Ἴωνες ἔτι καὶ νῦν νομίζουσιν. ἵδρυται δὲ
5 καὶ ἄλλα ἱερὰ ταύτῃ ἀρχαῖα. καὶ τῇ κρήνῃ τῇ
νῦν μὲν τῶν τυράννων οὕτως σκευασάντων Ἐν-
νεακρούνῳ καλουμένῃ, τὸ δὲ πάλαι φανερῶν τῶν
πηγῶν οὐσῶν Καλλιρρόῃ ὠνομασμένῃ ἐκεῖνοί τε
ἐγγὺς οὔσῃ τὰ πλείστου ἄξια ἐχρῶντο, καὶ νῦν
ἔτι ἀπὸ τοῦ ἀρχαίου πρό τε γαμικῶν καὶ ἐς ἄλλα
6 τῶν ἱερῶν νομίζεται τῷ ὕδατι χρῆσθαι. καλεῖται
δὲ διὰ τὴν παλαιὰν ταύτῃ κατοίκησιν καὶ ἡ ἀκρόπολις μέχρι τοῦδε ἔτι ὑπ' Ἀθηναίων πόλις.

XVI. Τῇ δ' οὖν ἐπὶ πολὺ κατὰ τὴν χώραν αὐτονόμῳ οἰκήσει[3] οἱ Ἀθηναῖοι, καὶ ἐπειδὴ ξυνῳκίσθησαν, διὰ τὸ ἔθος ἐν τοῖς ἀγροῖς ὅμως οἱ πλείους τῶν τε ἀρχαίων καὶ τῶν ὕστερον

[1] Added by Cobet.
[2] τῇ δωδεκάτῃ deleted by Hude, after Torstrick.
[3] μετεῖχον, in the MSS. before οἱ Ἀθηναῖοι, deleted by Dreissen.

---

[1] It is taken for granted that these temples were ancient foundations.

city, together with the region at the foot of the Acropolis toward the south. And the proof of this is as follows: On the Acropolis itself are the sanctuaries[1] of the other gods as well as of Athena,[2] and the sanctuaries which are outside the Acropolis are situated more in that quarter of the city, namely those of Olympian Zeus, of Pythian Apollo, of Earth, and of Dionysus in Limnae, in whose honour are celebrated the more ancient Dionysia[3] the twelfth of the month Anthesterion, just as the Ionian descendants of the Athenians also are wont even now to celebrate it. In that quarter are also situated still other ancient sanctuaries. And the fountain now called Enneacrunus,[4] from the fashion given it by the tyrants, but which anciently, when the springs were uncovered, was named Callirrhoe, was used by people of those days, because it was close by, for the most important ceremonials; and even now, in accordance with the ancient practice, it is still customary to use its waters in the rites preliminary to marriages and other sacred ceremonies. And, finally, the Acropolis, because the Athenians had there in early times a place of habitation, is still to this day called by them Polis or city.

XVI. Because, then, of their long-continued life of independence in the country districts, most of the Athenians of early times and of their descendants down to the time of this war, from force of habit, even after their political union with the city, continued

[2] A lacuna in the text is generally assumed; Classen would supply καὶ τὰ τῆς Ἀθηνᾶς after θεῶν ἐστι, and I translate this.

[3] The Anthesteria, contrasted with the Lenaea, which was also an ancient festival, but of less antiquity. The city Dionysia was of comparatively recent origin.

[4] Enneacrunus, *Nine Conduits*; Callirrhoe, *Fair Stream*.

μέχρι τοῦδε τοῦ πολέμου πανοικησίᾳ[1] γενόμενοί τε καὶ οἰκήσαντες, οὐ ῥᾳδίως τὰς ἀναστάσεις ἐποιοῦντο, ἄλλως τε καὶ ἄρτι ἀνειληφότες τὰς
2 κατασκευὰς μετὰ τὰ Μηδικά· ἐβαρύνοντο δὲ καὶ χαλεπῶς ἔφερον οἰκίας τε καταλείποντες καὶ ἱερὰ ἃ διὰ παντὸς ἦν αὐτοῖς ἐκ τῆς κατὰ τὸ ἀρχαῖον πολιτείας πάτρια, δίαιτάν τε μέλλοντες μεταβάλλειν καὶ οὐδὲν ἄλλο ἢ πόλιν τὴν αὑτοῦ ἀπολείπων ἕκαστος.

XVII. Ἐπειδὴ δὲ ἀφίκοντο ἐς τὸ ἄστυ, ὀλίγοις μέν τισιν ὑπῆρχον οἰκήσεις καὶ παρὰ φίλων τινὰς ἢ οἰκείων καταφυγή, οἱ δὲ πολλοὶ τά τε ἐρῆμα τῆς πόλεως ᾤκησαν καὶ τὰ ἱερὰ καὶ τὰ ἡρῷα πάντα πλὴν τῆς ἀκροπόλεως καὶ τοῦ Ἐλευσινίου καὶ εἴ τι ἄλλο βεβαίως κληστὸν ἦν· τό τε Πελαργικὸν[2] καλούμενον τὸ ὑπὸ τὴν ἀκρόπολιν, ὃ καὶ ἐπάρατόν τε ἦν μὴ οἰκεῖν καί τι καὶ Πυθικοῦ μαντείου ἀκροτελεύτιον τοιόνδε διεκώλυε, λέγον ὡς "Τὸ Πελαργικὸν ἀργὸν ἄμεινον," ὅμως
2 ὑπὸ τῆς παραχρῆμα ἀνάγκης ἐξῳκήθη. καί μοι δοκεῖ τὸ μαντεῖον τοὐναντίον ξυμβῆναι ἢ προσεδέχοντο, οὐ γὰρ διὰ τὴν παράνομον ἐνοίκησιν αἱ ξυμφοραὶ γενέσθαι τῇ πόλει, ἀλλὰ διὰ τὸν πόλε-

[1] πανοικησίᾳ placed by Hude, following Lipsius, after ῥᾳδίως.

[2] With C and a popular decree found in 1880 (*C.I.A.*, iv. 27 b); the other MSS. Πελασγικόν.

to reside, with their households, in the country where they had been born; and so they did not find it easy to move away, especially since they had only recently finished restoring their establishments after the Persian war. They were dejected and aggrieved at having to leave their homes and the temples which had always been theirs,—relics, inherited from their fathers, of their original form of government—and at the prospect of changing their mode of life, and facing what was nothing less for each of them than forsaking his own town.

XVII. And when they came to the capital, only a few of them were provided with dwellings or places of refuge with friends or relatives, and most of them took up their abode in the vacant places of the city and the sanctuaries and the shrines of heroes, all except the Acropolis and the Eleusinium and any other precinct that could be securely closed. And the Pelargicum,[1] as it was called, at the foot of the Acropolis, although it was under a curse that forbade its use for residence, and this was also prohibited by a verse-end of a Pythian oracle to the following effect:

"The Pelargicum unoccupied is better,"

nevertheless under stress of the emergency was completely filled with buildings. And the oracle, as it seems to me, came true, but in a sense quite the opposite of what was expected; for it was not on account of the unlawful occupation of the place that the city was visited by the calamities, but it was on

[1] A fortification built by the "Pelasgians" on the west side of the Acropolis, the only side accessible to an enemy. It was to the space below and above this fortification that the curse attached.

μον ἡ ἀνάγκη τῆς οἰκήσεως, ὃν οὐκ ὀνομάζον τὸ
μαντεῖον προῄδει μὴ ἐπ' ἀγαθῷ ποτε αὐτὸ κατοι-
3 κισθησόμενον. κατεσκευάσαντο δὲ καὶ ἐν τοῖς
πύργοις τῶν τειχῶν πολλοὶ καὶ ὡς ἕκαστός που
ἐδύνατο· οὐ γὰρ ἐχώρησε ξυνελθόντας αὐτοὺς ἡ
πόλις, ἀλλ' ὕστερον δὴ τά τε μακρὰ τείχη
ᾤκησαν κατανειμάμενοι καὶ τοῦ Πειραιῶς τὰ
4 πολλά. ἅμα δὲ καὶ τῶν πρὸς τὸν πόλεμον
ἥπτοντο, ξυμμάχους τε ἀγείροντες καὶ τῇ Πελο-
5 ποννήσῳ ἑκατὸν νεῶν ἐπίπλουν ἐξαρτύοντες· καὶ
οἱ μὲν ἐν τούτῳ παρασκευῆς ἦσαν.

XVIII. Ὁ δὲ στρατὸς τῶν Πελοποννησίων
προϊὼν ἀφίκετο τῆς Ἀττικῆς ἐς Οἰνόην πρῶτον,
ᾗπερ ἔμελλον ἐσβαλεῖν. καὶ ὡς ἐκαθέζοντο,
προσβολὰς παρεσκευάζοντο τῷ τείχει ποιησό-
2 μενοι μηχαναῖς τε καὶ ἄλλῳ τρόπῳ· ἡ γὰρ Οἰνόη
οὖσα ἐν μεθορίοις τῆς Ἀττικῆς καὶ Βοιωτίας
ἐτετείχιστο καὶ αὐτῷ φρουρίῳ οἱ Ἀθηναῖοι
ἐχρῶντο ὁπότε πόλεμος καταλάβοι. τάς τε οὖν
προσβολὰς ηὐτρεπίζοντο καὶ ἄλλως ἐνδιέτριψαν
3 χρόνον περὶ αὐτήν. αἰτίαν δὲ οὐκ ἐλαχίστην
Ἀρχίδαμος ἔλαβεν ἀπ' αὐτοῦ, δοκῶν καὶ ἐν τῇ
ξυναγωγῇ τοῦ πολέμου μαλακὸς εἶναι καὶ τοῖς
Ἀθηναίοις ἐπιτήδειος, οὐ παραινῶν προθύμως
πολεμεῖν· ἐπειδή τε ξυνελέγετο ὁ στρατός, ἥ τε
ἐν τῷ ἰσθμῷ ἐπιμονὴ γενομένη καὶ κατὰ τὴν

[1] *cf.* I. lxxx.–lxxxv.

account of the war that there was the necessity of its occupation, and the oracle, although it did not mention the war, yet foresaw that the place would never be occupied for any good. Many also established themselves in the towers of the city walls, and whereever each one could find a place; for the city did not have room for them when they were all there together. But afterwards they distributed into lots and occupied the space between the Long Walls and the greater part of the Peiraeus. And while all this was going on, the Athenians applied themselves to the war, bringing together allies and fitting out an expedition of one hundred ships against the Peloponnesus. The Athenians then, were in this stage of their preparations.

XVIII. Meanwhile the army of the Peloponnesians was advancing and the first point it reached in Attica was Oenoe, where they intended to begin the invasion. And while they were establishing their camp there, they prepared to assault the wall with engines and otherwise; for Oenoe, which was on the border between Attica and Boeotia, was a walled town, and was used as a fortress by the Athenians whenever war broke out. So the Lacedaemonians went on with their preparations to assault the place, and in this and other ways wasted time. And it was for his conduct here that Archidamus was most severely censured, though it was thought that in the levying of the war, too, he had been slack and had played into the hands of the Athenians when he did not advise the Peloponnesians to make war with vigour.[1] Again, when the army was being collected, he was criticized for the delay which occurred at the Isthmus, and afterwards for the leisurely way in

ἄλλην πορείαν ἡ σχολαιότης διέβαλεν αὐτόν,
4 μάλιστα δὲ ἡ ἐν τῇ Οἰνόῃ ἐπίσχεσις. οἱ γὰρ
Ἀθηναῖοι ἐσεκομίζοντο ἐν τῷ χρόνῳ τούτῳ, καὶ
ἐδόκουν οἱ Πελοποννήσιοι ἐπελθόντες ἂν διὰ τάχους πάντα ἔτι ἔξω καταλαβεῖν, εἰ μὴ διὰ τὴν
5 ἐκείνου μέλλησιν. ἐν τοιαύτῃ μὲν ὀργῇ ὁ στρατὸς
τὸν Ἀρχίδαμον ἐν τῇ καθέδρᾳ εἶχεν. ὁ δέ, προσ-
δεχόμενος, ὡς λέγεται, τοὺς Ἀθηναίους τῆς γῆς
ἔτι ἀκεραίου οὔσης ἐνδώσειν τι καὶ κατοκνήσειν
περιιδεῖν αὐτὴν τμηθεῖσαν, ἀνεῖχεν.

XIX. Ἐπειδὴ μέντοι προσβαλόντες τῇ Οἰνόῃ
καὶ πᾶσαν ἰδέαν πειράσαντες οὐκ ἐδύναντο ἑλεῖν,
οἵ τε Ἀθηναῖοι οὐδὲν ἐπεκηρυκεύοντο, οὕτω δὴ
ὁρμήσαντες ἀπ' αὐτῆς μετὰ τὰ ἐν Πλαταίᾳ[1]
γενόμενα ἡμέρᾳ ὀγδοηκοστῇ μάλιστα, θέρους καὶ
τοῦ σίτου ἀκμάζοντος, ἐσέβαλον ἐς τὴν Ἀττικήν·
ἡγεῖτο δὲ Ἀρχίδαμος ὁ Ζευξιδάμου, Λακεδαι-
2 μονίων βασιλεύς. καὶ καθεζόμενοι ἔτεμνον πρῶτον μὲν Ἐλευσῖνα καὶ τὸ Θριάσιον πεδίον καὶ
τροπήν τινα τῶν Ἀθηναίων ἱππέων περὶ τοὺς
Ῥείτους καλουμένους ἐποιήσαντο· ἔπειτα πρου-
χώρουν ἐν δεξιᾷ ἔχοντες τὸ Αἰγάλεων ὄρος διὰ
Κρωπιᾶς ἕως ἀφίκοντο ἐς Ἀχαρνάς, χωρίον μέγιστον τῆς Ἀττικῆς τῶν δήμων καλουμένων, καὶ
καθεζόμενοι ἐς αὐτὸν στρατόπεδόν τε ἐποιήσαντο
χρόνον τε πολὺν ἐμμείναντες ἔτεμνον.

XX. Γνώμῃ δὲ τοιᾷδε λέγεται τὸν Ἀρχίδαμον

[1] τῶν ἐσελθόντων Θηβαίων, in the MSS. after Πλαταίᾳ, deleted by Classen.

which the march was made, but most of all for the halt at Oenoe. For in the interval the Athenians continued to bring their property into the city and the Peloponnesians believed that but for his procrastination they could have advanced quickly and found everything still outside. Such was the resentment felt by the army toward Archidamus while they were sitting still. But the reason, it is said, why he kept holding back was that he expected the Athenians would make some concession while their territory was still unravaged and would be loath to see it laid waste.

XIX. When, however, after assaulting Oenoe and trying in every way to take it they were not able to do so, the Athenians meanwhile making no overtures, then at length they set off from there, about eighty days after the events at Plataea, when it was midsummer[1] and the corn was ripe, and invaded Attica, under the command of Archidamus son of Zeuxidamus, king of the Lacedaemonians. Making a halt they proceeded to ravage, first of all, the territory of Eleusis and the Thriasian plain, and they routed the Athenian cavalry near the streams called Rheiti; then they advanced, keeping Mount Aegaleos on their right through Cropia,[2] until they came to Acharnae, the largest of the demes of Attica, as they are called. Halting in the town they made a camp, where they remained for a long time ravaging the country.

XX. And it is said that the motive of Archidamus

[1] The reference is to the Attic summer, which included spring. The date was about the end of May, the average time for cutting grain in Attica.

[2] A deme between Aegaleos and Parnes.

περί τε τὰς Ἀχαρνὰς ὡς ἐς μάχην ταξάμενον μεῖναι καὶ ἐς τὸ πεδίον ἐκείνῃ τῇ ἐσβολῇ οὐ κατα-
2 βῆναι· τοὺς γὰρ Ἀθηναίους ἤλπιζεν, ἀκμάζοντάς τε νεότητι πολλῇ καὶ παρεσκευασμένους ἐς πόλεμον ὡς οὔπω πρότερον, ἴσως ἂν ἐπεξελθεῖν καὶ
3 τὴν γῆν οὐκ ἂν περιιδεῖν τμηθῆναι. ἐπειδὴ οὖν αὐτῷ ἐς Ἐλευσῖνα καὶ τὸ Θριάσιον πεδίον οὐκ ἀπήντησαν, πεῖραν ἐποιεῖτο περὶ τὰς Ἀχαρνὰς
4 καθήμενος εἰ ἐπεξίασιν· ἅμα μὲν γὰρ αὐτῷ ὁ χῶρος ἐπιτήδειος ἐφαίνετο ἐνστρατοπεδεῦσαι, ἅμα δὲ καὶ οἱ Ἀχαρνῆς μέγα μέρος ὄντες τῆς πόλεως (τρισχίλιοι γὰρ ὁπλῖται ἐγένοντο) οὐ περιόψεσθαι ἐδόκουν τὰ σφέτερα διαφθαρέντα, ἀλλ' ὁρμήσειν καὶ τοὺς πάντας ἐς μάχην. εἴ τε καὶ μὴ ἐπεξέλθοιεν ἐκείνῃ τῇ ἐσβολῇ οἱ Ἀθηναῖοι, ἀδεέστερον ἤδη ἐς τὸ ὕστερον τό τε πεδίον τεμεῖν καὶ ἐς αὐτὴν τὴν πόλιν χωρήσεσθαι· τοὺς γὰρ Ἀχαρνέας ἐστερημένους τῶν σφετέρων οὐχ ὁμοίως προθύμους ἔσεσθαι ὑπὲρ τῆς τῶν ἄλλων κινδυ-
5 νεύειν, στάσιν δ' ἐνέσεσθαι τῇ γνώμῃ. τοιαύτῃ μὲν διανοίᾳ ὁ Ἀρχίδαμος περὶ τὰς Ἀχαρνὰς ἦν.

XXI. Ἀθηναῖοι δὲ μέχρι μὲν οὗ περὶ Ἐλευσῖνα καὶ τὸ Θριάσιον πεδίον ὁ στρατὸς ἦν καί τινα ἐλπίδα εἶχον ἐς τὸ ἐγγυτέρω αὐτοὺς μὴ προϊέναι, μεμνημένοι καὶ Πλειστοάνακτα τὸν Παυσανίου Λακεδαιμονίων βασιλέα, ὅτε ἐσβαλὼν τῆς Ἀττικῆς ἐς Ἐλευσῖνα καὶ Θριῶζε στρατῷ Πελοποννησίων πρὸ τοῦδε τοῦ πολέμου τέσσαρσι καὶ δέκα ἔτεσιν ἀνεχώρησε πάλιν ἐς τὸ πλέον οὐκέτι

in waiting about Acharnae with his troops ready for battle, instead of descending into the plain during this invasion, was as follows: He cherished the hope that the Athenians, who were at their very best as regards the multitude of their youth and prepared for war as never before, would perhaps come out against him and not look on and see their land ravaged. So when they did not come to meet him at Eleusis and in the Thriasian plain, he settled down in the neighbourhood of Acharnae, to make a test whether they would come out; for not only did that seem to him a suitable place for his camp, but also the Acharnians were an important part of the state, their hoplites numbering three thousand, and he thought that they would not look on and see their fields ravaged, but would urge the whole people also to fight. And even if the Athenians should not come out against him during this invasion, he would thenceforward proceed with less apprehension to ravage the plain and even advance to the very walls of the city; for the Acharnians, once stripped of their own possessions, would not be as eager to incur danger as before in behalf of the lands of the rest, and so a division would arise in the counsels of the Athenians. It was with this design that Archidamus stayed at Acharnae.

XXI. Now so long as the Peloponnesian army remained in the neighbourhood of Eleusis and the Thriasian plain, the Athenians retained hope that they would not advance nearer; for they remembered that Pleistoanax son of Pausanias, king of the Lacedaemonians, when fourteen years before this war he had invaded Attica with an army of Peloponnesians and proceeded as far as Eleusis and Thria, had advanced

προελθών (δι' ὃ δὴ καὶ ἡ φυγὴ αὐτῷ ἐγένετο ἐκ Σπάρτης δόξαντι χρήμασι πεισθῆναι τὴν ἀναχώ-
2 ρησιν)· ἐπειδὴ δὲ περὶ Ἀχαρνὰς εἶδον τὸν στρατὸν ἑξήκοντα σταδίους τῆς πόλεως ἀπέχοντα, οὐκέτι ἀνασχετὸν ἐποιοῦντο, ἀλλ' αὐτοῖς, ὡς εἰκός, γῆς τεμνομένης ἐν τῷ ἐμφανεῖ, ὃ οὔπω ἑοράκεσαν οἵ γε νεώτεροι, οὐδ' οἱ πρεσβύτεροι πλὴν τὰ Μηδικά, δεινὸν ἐφαίνετο καὶ ἐδόκει τοῖς τε ἄλλοις καὶ μάλιστα τῇ νεότητι ἐπεξιέναι καὶ μὴ περι-
3 ορᾶν. κατὰ ξυστάσεις τε γιγνόμενοι ἐν πολλῇ ἔριδι ἦσαν, οἱ μὲν κελεύοντες ἐπεξιέναι, οἱ δέ τινες οὐκ ἐῶντες. χρησμολόγοι τε ᾖδον χρησμοὺς παντοίους, ὧν ἀκροᾶσθαι ὡς ἕκαστος ὥρμητο.[1] οἵ τε Ἀχαρνῆς οἰόμενοι παρὰ σφίσιν αὐτοῖς οὐκ ἐλαχίστην μοῖραν εἶναι Ἀθηναίων, ὡς αὐτῶν ἡ γῆ ἐτέμνετο, ἐνῆγον τὴν ἔξοδον μάλιστα. παντί τε τρόπῳ ἀνηρέθιστο ἡ πόλις καὶ τὸν Περικλέα ἐν ὀργῇ εἶχον, καὶ ὧν παρῄνεσε πρότερον ἐμέμνηντο οὐδέν, ἀλλ' ἐκάκιζον ὅτι στρατηγὸς ὢν οὐκ ἐπεξάγοι, αἴτιόν τε σφίσιν ἐνόμιζον πάντων ὧν ἔπασχον.

XXII. Περικλῆς δὲ ὁρῶν μὲν αὐτοὺς πρὸς τὸ παρὸν χαλεπαίνοντας καὶ οὐ τὰ ἄριστα φρονοῦντας, πιστεύων δὲ ὀρθῶς γιγνώσκειν περὶ τοῦ μὴ ἐπεξιέναι, ἐκκλησίαν τε οὐκ ἐποίει αὐτῶν οὐδὲ ξύλλογον οὐδένα, τοῦ μὴ ὀργῇ τι μᾶλλον ἢ γνώμῃ ξυνελθόντας ἐξαμαρτεῖν, τήν τε πόλιν ἐφύλασσε

[1] With CEG; ὤργητο ABM.

no farther but had gone back again. (And indeed this was the cause of his banishment from Sparta, since he was thought to have been bribed to retreat.) But when they saw the army in the neighbourhood of Acharnae, only sixty stadia from the city, they thought the situation no longer tolerable; on the contrary, it naturally appeared to them a terrible thing when their land was being ravaged before their eyes, a sight which the younger men had never seen, or even the older men except in the Persian war; and the general opinion, especially on the part of the younger men, was that they ought to go forth and put a stop to it. They gathered in knots and engaged in hot disputes, some urging that they should go out, others opposing this course. Oracle-mongers were chanting oracles of every import, according as each man was disposed to hear them. And the Acharnians, thinking that no insignificant portion of the Athenian people lived at Acharnae, insisted most of all upon going out, as it was their land that was being devastated. Thus in every way the city was in a state of irritation; and they were indignant against Pericles, and remembering none of his earlier warnings they abused him because, though their general, he would not lead them out, and considered him responsible for all their sufferings.

XXII. Pericles, however, seeing them exasperated at the present moment and that their intentions were not for the best, and convinced that his judgment was right about refusing to go out, would not convoke a meeting of the assembly or any gathering whatever, for fear that if they got together there would be an outbreak of passion without judgment that would end in some serious

καὶ δι' ἡσυχίας μάλιστα ὅσον ἐδύνατο εἶχεν.
2 ἱππέας μέντοι ἐξέπεμπεν αἰεὶ τοῦ μὴ προδρόμους ἀπὸ τῆς στρατιᾶς ἐσπίπτοντας ἐς τοὺς ἀγροὺς τοὺς ἐγγὺς τῆς πόλεως κακουργεῖν· καὶ ἱππομαχία τις ἐγένετο βραχεῖα ἐν Φρυγίοις τῶν τε Ἀθηναίων τέλει ἑνὶ τῶν ἱππέων καὶ Θεσσαλοῖς μετ' αὐτῶν πρὸς τοὺς Βοιωτῶν ἱππέας, ἐν ᾗ, οὐκ ἔλασσον ἔσχον οἱ Ἀθηναῖοι καὶ Θεσσαλοί μέχρι οὗ προσβοηθησάντων τοῖς Βοιωτοῖς τῶν ὁπλιτῶν τροπὴ ἐγένετο αὐτῶν· καὶ ἀπέθανον τῶν Θεσσαλῶν καὶ Ἀθηναίων οὐ πολλοί, ἀνείλοντο μέντοι αὐτοὺς αὐθημερὸν ἀσπόνδους. καὶ οἱ Πελοποννήσιοι τροπαῖον τῇ ὑστεραίᾳ ἔστησαν.
3 ἡ δὲ βοήθεια αὕτη τῶν Θεσσαλῶν κατὰ τὸ παλαιὸν ξυμμαχικὸν ἐγένετο τοῖς Ἀθηναίοις, καὶ ἀφίκοντο παρ' αὐτοὺς Λαρισαῖοι, Φαρσάλιοι,[1] Κραννώνιοι, Πυράσιοι, Γυρτώνιοι, Φεραῖοι. ἡγοῦντο δὲ αὐτῶν ἐκ μὲν Λαρίσης Πολυμήδης καὶ Ἀριστόνους, ἀπὸ τῆς στάσεως ἑκάτερος, ἐκ δὲ Φαρσάλου Μένων· ἦσαν δὲ καὶ τῶν ἄλλων κατὰ πόλεις ἄρχοντες.

XXIII. Οἱ δὲ Πελοποννήσιοι, ἐπειδὴ οὐκ ἐπεξῇσαν αὐτοῖς οἱ Ἀθηναῖοι ἐς μάχην, ἄραντες ἐκ τῶν Ἀχαρνῶν ἐδῄουν τῶν δήμων τινὰς ἄλλους τῶν μεταξὺ Πάρνηθος καὶ Βριλησσοῦ ὄρους.
2 ὄντων δὲ αὐτῶν ἐν τῇ γῇ οἱ Ἀθηναῖοι ἀπέστειλαν τὰς ἑκατὸν ναῦς περὶ Πελοπόννησον ἅσπερ παρεσκευάζοντο καὶ χιλίους ὁπλίτας ἐπ' αὐτῶν

[1] Παράσιοι, in MSS. after Φαρσάλιοι, deleted by Heringa.

mistake; moreover he guarded the city, and as far as he could kept it free from disturbances. He did, however, constantly send out detachments of cavalry to prevent flying parties from the main army from raiding the fields near the city and ravaging them; and there was a cavalry skirmish at Phrygia between a company of Athenian horsemen, assisted by some Thessalians, and the Boeotian cavalry, in which the Athenians and Thessalians fully held their own, until their heavy infantry came to the support of the Boeotians, when they were routed. A few of the Thessalians and the Athenians were killed, but their bodies were recovered the same day without a truce; and on the next day the Peloponnesians set up a trophy. This auxiliary force of the Thessalians was sent to the Athenians in accordance with an ancient alliance,[1] and those who came were Larisaeans, Pharsalians, Crannonians, Pyrasians, Gyrtonians, and Pheraeans. And their leaders were, from Larissa, Polymedes and Aristonous, each representing his own faction, and from Pharsalus Menon; and the others had their own commander city by city.

XXIII. The Peloponesians, on the other hand, when the Athenians did not come out to do battle with them broke up their camp at Acharnae and ravaged some of the demes which lie between Mt. Parnes and Mt. Brilessus.[2] But while they were still in their territory the Athenians sent out on an expedition round the Peloponnesus the hundred ships[3] which they had been equipping, and on

[1] *cf.* I. cii. 4.
[2] More generally known as Pentelicus, so called from the deme Pentele on its southern slope.
[3] *cf.* ch. xvii. 4.

καὶ τοξότας τετρακοσίους· ἐστρατήγει δὲ Καρκίνος τε ὁ Ξενοτίμου καὶ Πρωτέας ὁ Ἐπικλέους
3 καὶ Σωκράτης ὁ Ἀντιγένους. καὶ οἱ μὲν ἄραντες τῇ παρασκευῇ ταύτῃ περιέπλεον, οἱ δὲ Πελοποννήσιοι χρόνον ἐμμείναντες ἐν τῇ Ἀττικῇ ὅσου εἶχον τὰ ἐπιτήδεια ἀνεχώρησαν διὰ Βοιωτῶν, οὐχ ᾗπερ ἐσέβαλον· παριόντες δὲ Ὠρωπὸν τὴν γῆν τὴν Γραϊκὴν καλουμένην, ἣν νέμονται Ὠρώπιοι Ἀθηναίων ὑπήκοοι, ἐδῄωσαν. ἀφικόμενοι δὲ ἐς Πελοπόννησον διελύθησαν κατὰ πόλεις ἕκαστοι.

XXIV. Ἀναχωρησάντων δὲ αὐτῶν οἱ Ἀθηναῖοι φυλακὰς κατεστήσαντο κατὰ γῆν καὶ κατὰ θάλασσαν, ὥσπερ δὴ ἔμελλον διὰ παντὸς τοῦ πολέμου φυλάξειν· καὶ χίλια τάλαντα ἀπὸ τῶν ἐν τῇ ἀκροπόλει χρημάτων ἔδοξεν αὐτοῖς ἐξαίρετα ποιησαμένοις χωρὶς θέσθαι καὶ μὴ ἀναλοῦν, ἀλλ' ἀπὸ τῶν ἄλλων πολεμεῖν· ἢν δέ τις εἴπῃ ἢ ἐπιψηφίσῃ κινεῖν τὰ χρήματα ταῦτα ἐς ἄλλο τι, ἢν μὴ οἱ πολέμιοι νηίτῃ στρατῷ ἐπιπλέωσι τῇ πόλει καὶ δέῃ ἀμύνασθαι, θάνατον ζημίαν ἐπέ-
2 θεντο. τριήρεις τε μετ' αὐτῶν ἐξαιρέτους ἐποιήσαντο κατὰ τὸν ἐνιαυτὸν ἑκατὸν τὰς βελτίστας καὶ τριηράρχους αὐταῖς, ὧν μὴ χρῆσθαι μηδεμιᾷ ἐς ἄλλο τι ἢ μετὰ τῶν χρημάτων περὶ τοῦ αὐτοῦ κινδύνου, ἢν δέῃ.

---

1 Named after the ancient town of Γραῖα (Hom. B 498).

them a thousand hoplites and four hundred archers; and the generals in command were Carcinus son of Xenotimus, Proteas son of Epicles, and Socrates son of Antigenes. So they set sail with this force and began their cruise; the Peloponnesians, on the other hand, remained in Attica for as long a time as they were provisioned and then withdrew through Boeotia, taking a different route from that by which they had entered Attica. They passed by Oropus and laid waste the district called Graïce,[1] which the Oropians occupy as subjects of the Athenians.[2] Then on their return to the Peloponnesus they were dismissed to their several cities.

XXIV. After the retreat of the Lacedaemonians, the Athenians set guards to keep watch both by land and sea, their purpose being to maintain a like guard throughout the war. They decided also to set apart one thousand talents[3] of the money stored on the Acropolis as a special reserve fund, and not to spend it, but to use the rest to carry on the war; and if anyone should make or put to vote a proposal to touch this money except in the one case that the enemy should attack the city with a fleet and they should have to defend it, death was to be the penalty. And along with this sum of money they set apart for special service each year one hundred of the very best triremes, appointing trierarchs to command them, and no one of these ships was to be used in any other way than in connection with this particular fund in dealing with the same danger should the emergency arise.

[2] This was written before 412/11, when Oropus was captured by the Boeotians.

[3] About £200,000, or $972,000. This was part of the 6,000 talents stored on the Acropolis (ch. xiii. 3).

XXV. Οἱ δ' ἐν ταῖς ἑκατὸν ναυσὶ περὶ Πελοπόννησον Ἀθηναῖοι καὶ Κερκυραῖοι μετ' αὐτῶν πεντήκοντα ναυσὶ προσβεβοηθηκότες καὶ ἄλλοι τινὲς τῶν ἐκεῖ ξυμμάχων ἄλλα τε ἐκάκουν περιπλέοντες καὶ ἐς Μεθώνην τῆς Λακωνικῆς ἀποβάντες τῷ τείχει προσέβαλον, ὄντι ἀσθενεῖ καὶ
2 ἀνθρώπων οὐκ ἐνόντων. ἔτυχε δὲ περὶ τοὺς χώρους τούτους Βρασίδας ὁ Τέλλιδος, ἀνὴρ Σπαρτιάτης, φρουρὰν ἔχων, καὶ αἰσθόμενος ἐβοήθει τοῖς ἐν τῷ χωρίῳ μετὰ ὁπλιτῶν ἑκατόν. διαδραμὼν δὲ τὸ τῶν Ἀθηναίων στρατόπεδον, ἐσκεδασμένον κατὰ τὴν χώραν καὶ πρὸς τὸ τεῖχος τετραμμένον, ἐσπίπτει ἐς τὴν Μεθώνην καὶ ὀλίγους τινὰς ἐν τῇ ἐσδρομῇ ἀπολέσας τῶν μεθ' αὑτοῦ τήν τε πόλιν περιεποίησε καὶ ἀπὸ τούτου τοῦ τολμήματος πρῶτος τῶν κατὰ τὸν πόλεμον
3 ἐπῃνέθη ἐν Σπάρτῃ. οἱ δὲ Ἀθηναῖοι ἄραντες παρέπλεον, καὶ σχόντες τῆς Ἠλείας ἐς Φειὰν ἐδῄουν τὴν γῆν ἐπὶ δύο ἡμέρας καὶ προσβοηθήσαντας τῶν ἐκ τῆς κοίλης Ἤλιδος τριακοσίους λογάδας καὶ τῶν αὐτόθεν ἐκ τῆς περιοικίδος
4 Ἠλείων μάχῃ ἐκράτησαν. ἀνέμου δὲ κατιόντος μεγάλου χειμαζόμενοι ἐν ἀλιμένῳ χωρίῳ, οἱ μὲν πολλοὶ ἐπέβησαν ἐπὶ τὰς ναῦς καὶ περιέπλεον τὸν Ἰχθῦν καλούμενον τὴν ἄκραν ἐς τὸν ἐν τῇ Φειᾷ λιμένα, οἱ δὲ Μεσσήνιοι ἐν τούτῳ καὶ ἄλλοι τινές, οἱ οὐ δυνάμενοι ἐπιβῆναι, κατὰ γῆν χωρή-
5 σαντες τὴν Φειὰν αἱροῦσιν. καὶ ὕστερον αἵ τε νῆες περιπλεύσασαι ἀναλαμβάνουσιν αὐτοὺς καὶ ἐξανάγονται ἐκλείποντες Φειάν, καὶ τῶν Ἠλείων ἡ πολλὴ ἤδη στρατιὰ προσεβεβοηθήκει. παρα-

XXV. Meanwhile the Athenians who had been despatched in the hundred ships around the Peloponnesus, together with the Corcyraeans, who had reinforced them with fifty ships, and some of their other allies in that quarter, were pillaging various places as they cruised about, and in particular disembarked at Methone in Laconia and assaulted its walls, which were weak and without adequate defenders. But Brasidas, son of Tellis, a Spartan, happened to be in that neighbourhood with a guarding party, and seeing the situation he set out with one hundred hoplites to relieve the garrison. Dashing through the army of the Athenians, which was scattered over the country and was occupied solely with the fortress, he threw his force into Methone, losing a few of his men in the rush, and thus saved the city. This daring exploit, the first of the kind in the war, was acknowledged at Sparta by a vote of thanks. The Athenians then weighed anchor and continued their cruise along the coast, and putting in at Pheia in Elis ravaged the land for two days, defeating in battle a rescue-party of three hundred picked men gathered from the lowlands of Elis and from the immediate neighbourhood of Pheia. But a heavy gale of wind arose, and since they were exposed to the storm in a harbourless region, most of them embarked on their ships and sailed round the promontory called Ichthys into the harbour at Pheia. Meanwhile the Messenians and some others, who could not get on board, marched overland and took Pheia. Afterwards, when the fleet had rounded the promontory, it took up these men, abandoned Pheia, and put out to sea, for meanwhile the main body of the Eleans had come to the rescue. The Athenians now resumed their voyage

πλεύσαντες δὲ οἱ Ἀθηναῖοι ἐπὶ ἄλλα χωρία ἐδῄουν.

XXVI. Ὑπὸ δὲ τὸν αὐτὸν χρόνον τοῦτον Ἀθηναῖοι τριάκοντα ναῦς ἐξέπεμψαν περὶ τὴν Λοκρίδα καὶ [1] Εὐβοίας ἅμα φυλακήν· ἐστρατήγει
2 δὲ αὐτῶν Κλεόπομπος ὁ Κλεινίου. καὶ ἀποβάσεις ποιησάμενος τῆς τε παραθαλασσίου ἔστιν ἃ ἐδῄωσε καὶ Θρόνιον εἷλεν, ὁμήρους τε ἔλαβεν αὐτῶν, καὶ ἐν Ἀλόπῃ τοὺς βοηθήσαντας Λοκρῶν μάχῃ ἐκράτησεν.

XXVII. Ἀνέστησαν δὲ καὶ Αἰγινήτας τῷ αὐτῷ θέρει τούτῳ ἐξ Αἰγίνης Ἀθηναῖοι, αὐτούς τε καὶ παῖδας καὶ γυναῖκας, ἐπικαλέσαντες οὐχ ἥκιστα τοῦ πολέμου σφίσιν αἰτίους εἶναι· καὶ τὴν Αἴγιναν ἀσφαλέστερον ἐφαίνετο τῇ Πελοποννήσῳ ἐπικειμένην αὐτῶν πέμψαντας ἐποίκους ἔχειν. καὶ ἐξέπεμψαν ὕστερον οὐ πολλῷ ἐς αὐτὴν τοὺς
2 οἰκήτορας. ἐκπεσοῦσι δὲ τοῖς Αἰγινήταις οἱ Λακεδαιμόνιοι ἔδοσαν Θυρέαν οἰκεῖν καὶ τὴν γῆν νέμεσθαι, κατά τε τὸ Ἀθηναίων διάφορον καὶ ὅτι σφῶν εὐεργέται ἦσαν ὑπὸ τὸν σεισμὸν καὶ τῶν Εἱλώτων τὴν ἐπανάστασιν. ἡ δὲ Θυρεᾶτις γῆ μεθορία τῆς Ἀργείας καὶ Λακωνικῆς ἐστιν, ἐπὶ θάλασσαν καθήκουσα. καὶ οἱ μὲν αὐτῶν ἐνταῦθα ᾤκησαν, οἱ δὲ ἐσπάρησαν κατὰ τὴν ἄλλην Ἑλλάδα.

XXVIII. Τοῦ δ' αὐτοῦ θέρους νουμηνίᾳ κατὰ σελήνην, ὥσπερ καὶ μόνον δοκεῖ εἶναι γίγνεσθαι

[1] κατ' read by Hude, after Madvig.

along the coast, and visiting other places made depredations.

XXVI. About this same time the Athenians sent out thirty ships to operate around Locris and at the same time to serve as a guard for Euboea. These were under the command of Cleopompus son of Clinias, who made descents upon various places along the seaboard and ravaged them, captured Thronium, some of whose inhabitants he took as hostages, and at Alope defeated in battle the Locrians who came to the defence of the town.

XXVII. In the course of this summer the Athenians also expelled the Aeginetans from Aegina, together with their wives and children, making it their main charge against them that they were responsible for the war in which they were involved; besides Aegina lay close to the Peloponnesus, and it was clearly a safer policy to send colonists of their own to occupy it. And indeed they soon afterwards sent thither the settlers. As for the Aeginetan refugees, the Lacedaemonians gave them Thyrea to dwell in and its territory to cultivate, moved to do this not only by the hostility of the Aeginetans towards the Athenians but also because the Aeginetans had done them a service at the time of the earthquake and the revolt of the Helots.[1] Now the district of Thyrea is the border country between Argolis and Laconia, extending down to the sea. There some of the Aeginetans settled, while some were scattered over the rest of Hellas.

XXVIII. During the same summer at the beginning of a lunar month[2] (the only time, it seems, when

[1] *cf.* I. ci. 2.
[2] August 3rd, 431 B.C.

δυνατόν, ὁ ἥλιος ἐξέλιπε μετὰ μεσημβρίαν καὶ πάλιν ἀνεπληρώθη, γενόμενος μηνοειδὴς καὶ ἀστέρων τινῶν ἐκφανέντων.

XXIX. Καὶ ἐν τῷ αὐτῷ θέρει Νυμφόδωρον τὸν Πύθεω, ἄνδρα Ἀβδηρίτην, οὗ εἶχε τὴν ἀδελφὴν Σιτάλκης, δυνάμενον παρ' αὐτῷ μέγα οἱ Ἀθηναῖοι πρότερον πολέμιον νομίζοντες πρόξενον ἐποιήσαντο καὶ μετεπέμψαντο, βουλόμενοι Σιτάλκην σφίσι τὸν Τήρεω, Θρᾳκῶν βασιλέα, ξύμμαχον
2 γενέσθαι. ὁ δὲ Τήρης οὗτος ὁ τοῦ Σιτάλκου πατὴρ πρῶτος Ὀδρύσαις τὴν μεγάλην βασιλείαν ἐπὶ πλέον τῆς ἄλλης Θρᾴκης ἐποίησεν· πολὺ
3 γὰρ μέρος καὶ αὐτόνομόν ἐστι Θρᾳκῶν. Τηρεῖ δὲ τῷ Πρόκνην τὴν Πανδίονος ἀπ' Ἀθηνῶν σχόντι γυναῖκα προσήκει ὁ Τήρης οὗτος οὐδέν, οὐδὲ τῆς αὐτῆς Θρᾴκης ἐγένοντο, ἀλλ' ὁ μὲν ἐν Δαυλίᾳ τῆς Φωκίδος νῦν καλουμένης γῆς ὁ Τηρεὺς[1] ᾤκει, τότε ὑπὸ Θρᾳκῶν οἰκουμένης, καὶ τὸ ἔργον τὸ περὶ τὸν Ἴτυν αἱ γυναῖκες ἐν τῇ γῇ ταύτῃ ἔπραξαν (πολλοῖς δὲ καὶ τῶν ποιητῶν ἐν ἀηδόνος μνήμῃ Δαυλιὰς ἡ ὄρνις ἐπωνόμασται), εἰκός τε καὶ τὸ κῆδος Πανδίονα ξυνάψασθαι τῆς θυγατρὸς διὰ τοσούτου ἐπ' ὠφελίᾳ τῇ πρὸς ἀλλήλους μᾶλλον ἢ διὰ πολλῶν ἡμερῶν ἐς Ὀδρύσας ὁδοῦ. Τήρης δὲ οὐδὲ τὸ αὐτὸ ὄνομα ἔχων βασιλεὺς[2]

[1] Deleted by Hude, after van Herwerden, as not read by the Scholiast.
[2] τε, in the MSS. after βασιλεὺς, deleted by Classen.

---

[1] *i.e.* their representative to look after Athenian interests in the country of Sitalces and Tereus. The latter had violated

such an occurrence is possible) the sun was eclipsed after midday; it assumed the shape of a crescent and became full again, and during the eclipse some stars became visible.

XXIX. In this summer, too, Nymphodorus son of Pythes, a man of Abdera, whose sister Sitalces had to wife, and possessing great influence with Sitalces, the Athenians made their proxenus[1] with that king, although they had hitherto regarded him as an enemy; and they summoned him to Athens, wishing to gain Sitalces, son of Teres and king of the Thracians, as their ally. Now this Teres, the father of Sitalces, was the first to found the great kingdom of the Odrysians, which extended over the larger part of Thrace; for a considerable portion of the Thracians are independent. This Teres is not in any way connected with Tereus who took from Athens to be his wife Procne the daughter of Pandion, nor indeed did they come from the same Thrace. Tereus dwelt at Daulia in the land now called Phocis, which was then occupied by Thracians, and it was in that land that the women[2] perpetrated their deed upon Itys. In fact many of the poets, when they refer to the nightingale, call it the bird of Daulia. Besides it was natural for Pandion to contract the marriage alliance for his daughter at so short a distance as Daulia with a view to mutual protection, rather than among the Odrysians, who are many days' journey distant. Teres, however, whose name was not the same as the other's, was the first king to attain

Philomela, sister of Procne, and cut out her tongue to prevent her telling of it; but she revealed it by weaving the story into a piece of tapestry.

[2] The women, *i.e.* Procne and Philomela, who murdered Itys, son of Procne.

4 πρῶτος ἐν κράτει Ὀδρυσῶν ἐγένετο. οὗ δὴ ὄντα
τὸν Σιτάλκην οἱ Ἀθηναῖοι ξύμμαχον ἐποιοῦντο,
βουλόμενοι σφίσι τὰ ἐπὶ Θρᾴκης χωρία καὶ
5 Περδίκκαν ξυνεξελεῖν αὐτόν. ἐλθών τε ἐς τὰς
Ἀθήνας ὁ Νυμφόδωρος τήν τε τοῦ Σιτάλκου
ξυμμαχίαν ἐποίησε καὶ Σάδοκον τὸν υἱὸν αὐτοῦ
Ἀθηναῖον, τόν τε ἐπὶ Θρᾴκης πόλεμον ὑπεδέχετο
καταλύσειν· πείσειν γὰρ Σιτάλκην πέμπειν στρατιὰν Θρᾳκίαν Ἀθηναίοις ἱππέων τε καὶ πελ-
6 ταστῶν. ξυνεβίβασε δὲ καὶ τὸν Περδίκκαν τοῖς
Ἀθηναίοις καὶ Θέρμην αὐτῷ ἔπεισεν ἀποδοῦναι·
ξυνεστράτευσέ τε εὐθὺς Περδίκκας ἐπὶ Χαλκιδέας
7 μετὰ Ἀθηναίων καὶ Φορμίωνος. οὕτω μὲν Σιτάλκης τε ὁ Τήρεω, Θρᾳκῶν βασιλεύς, ξύμμαχος
ἐγένετο Ἀθηναίοις καὶ Περδίκκας ὁ Ἀλεξάνδρου,
Μακεδόνων βασιλεύς.

XXX. Οἱ δ' ἐν ταῖς ἑκατὸν ναυσὶν Ἀθηναῖοι
ἔτι ὄντες περὶ Πελοπόννησον Σόλλιόν τε Κορινθίων πόλισμα αἱροῦσι καὶ παραδιδόασι Παλαι-
ρεῦσιν Ἀκαρνάνων μόνοις τὴν γῆν καὶ πόλιν
νέμεσθαι· καὶ Ἀστακόν, ἧς Εὔαρχος ἐτυράννει,
λαβόντες κατὰ κράτος καὶ ἐξελάσαντες αὐτὸν τὸ
2 χωρίον ἐς τὴν ξυμμαχίαν προσεποιήσαντο. ἐπί
τε Κεφαλληνίαν τὴν νῆσον προσπλεύσαντες
προσηγάγοντο ἄνευ μάχης· κεῖται δὲ ἡ Κεφαλ-
ληνία κατὰ Ἀκαρνανίαν καὶ Λευκάδα τετράπολις
3 οὖσα, Παλῆς, Κράνιοι, Σαμαῖοι, Πρωννοι. ὕστερον δ' οὐ πολλῷ ἀνεχώρησαν αἱ νῆες ἐς τὰς
Ἀθήνας.

great power among the Odrysians. And it was his son, Sitalces, whom the Athenians wanted to make their ally, wishing him to help in subduing the places on the coast of Thrace and Perdiccas. So Nymphodorus came to Athens, brought about the alliance with Sitalces, and got Sadocus son of Sitalces made an Athenian citizen; and he promised also to bring the war in Thrace to an end, saying that he would persuade Sitalces to send the Athenians a Thracian force of cavalry and targeteers. Moreover, he brought about a reconciliation between Perdiccas and the Athenians, whom he persuaded to restore Therme[1] to him. Perdiccas immediately joined forces with the Athenians under Phormio[2] and took the field against the Chalcidians. It was in this way that Sitalces son of Teres, king of the Thracians, became an ally of the Athenians, and also Perdiccas son of Alexander, king of the Macedonians.

XXX. Meanwhile the Athenians in the hundred ships, who were still operating on the Peloponnesian coast, took Sollium, a town belonging to the Corinthians, which they then handed over, the territory as well as the city, to the people of Palaerus in Acarnania, for their exclusive occupation. They also stormed Astacus, which Euarchus ruled as tyrant, drove him out, and incorporated the place in their confederacy. Sailing then to the island of Cephallenia, they brought it over to their side without a battle. Now Cephallenia lies over against Acarnania and Leucas and is a union of four communities, the Palians, Cranians, Samaeans, and Pronnians. And not long afterwards the ships withdrew to Athens.

[1] *cf.* I. lxi. 2. [2] *cf.* I. lxiv. 2; lxv. 3.

XXXI. Περὶ δὲ τὸ φθινόπωρον τοῦ θέρους τούτου Ἀθηναῖοι πανδημεί, αὐτοὶ καὶ οἱ μέτοικοι, ἐσέβαλον ἐς τὴν Μεγαρίδα Περικλέους τοῦ Ξανθίππου στρατηγοῦντος. καὶ οἱ περὶ Πελοπόννησον Ἀθηναῖοι ἐν ταῖς ἑκατὸν ναυσίν (ἔτυχον γὰρ ἤδη ἐν Αἰγίνῃ ὄντες ἐπ' οἴκου ἀνακομιζόμενοι) ὡς ᾔσθοντο τοὺς ἐκ τῆς πόλεως πανστρατιᾷ ἐν Μεγάροις ὄντας, ἔπλευσαν παρ'
2 αὐτοὺς καὶ ξυνεμείχθησαν. στρατόπεδόν τε μέγιστον δὴ τοῦτο ἁθρόον Ἀθηναίων ἐγένετο, ἀκμαζούσης ἔτι τῆς πόλεως καὶ οὔπω νενοσηκυίας· μυρίων γὰρ ὁπλιτῶν οὐκ ἐλάσσους ἦσαν αὐτοὶ οἱ Ἀθηναῖοι (χωρὶς δ' αὐτοῖς οἱ ἐν Ποτειδαίᾳ τρισχίλιοι ἦσαν), μέτοικοι δὲ ξυνεσέβαλον οὐκ ἐλάσσους τρισχιλίων ὁπλιτῶν, χωρὶς δὲ ὁ ἄλλος
3 ὅμιλος ψιλῶν οὐκ ὀλίγος. δῃώσαντες δὲ τὰ πολλὰ τῆς γῆς ἀνεχώρησαν. ἐγένοντο δὲ καὶ ἄλλαι ὕστερον ἐν τῷ πολέμῳ κατὰ ἔτος ἕκαστον ἐσβολαὶ Ἀθηναίων ἐς τὴν Μεγαρίδα καὶ ἱππέων καὶ πανστρατιᾷ, μέχρι οὗ Νίσαια ἑάλω ὑπ' Ἀθηναίων.

XXXII. Ἐτειχίσθη δὲ καὶ Ἀταλάντη ὑπὸ Ἀθηναίων φρούριον τοῦ θέρους τούτου τελευτῶντος, ἡ ἐπὶ Λοκροῖς τοῖς Ὀπουντίοις νῆσος, ἐρήμη πρότερον οὖσα, τοῦ μὴ λῃστὰς ἐκπλέοντας ἐξ Ὀποῦντος καὶ τῆς ἄλλης Λοκρίδος κακουργεῖν τὴν Εὔβοιαν. ταῦτα μὲν ἐν τῷ θέρει τούτῳ μετὰ τὴν Πελοποννησίων ἐκ τῆς Ἀττικῆς ἀναχώρησιν ἐγένετο.

XXXIII. Τοῦ δ' ἐπιγιγνομένου χειμῶνος Εὔαρχος ὁ Ἀκαρνάν, βουλόμενος ἐς τὴν Ἀστακὸν

XXXI. Toward the autumn of this year the Athenians with all their military forces, drawn both from the citizens and the resident aliens, invaded Megaris under the command of Pericles son of Xanthippus, who was general.[1] The Athenians of the fleet of one hundred ships operating around Peloponnesus, who happened to be at Aegina on their way home, when they heard that the whole military force of the city was at Megara, sailed over and joined them. This was the largest army of Athenians that had ever been assembled in one body, for the city was still at the height of its strength and not as yet stricken by the plague; the Athenians themselves numbered not less than ten thousand heavy infantry, not including the three thousand at Potidaea,[2] and there were three thousand heavy-armed aliens who took part in the invasion, and, besides, a considerable body of light-armed troops. After they had ravaged most of the Megarian country they retired. Later on in the course of the war still other invasions were made by the Athenians into Megaris every year, both with the cavalry and with the whole army, until Nisaea was captured.[3]

XXXII. Towards the end of this summer the 431 B.C.
Athenians also fortified and garrisoned Atalante, the island which lies off Opuntian Locris and had hitherto been unoccupied. Their object was to prevent pirates sailing from Opus and the other ports of Locris and ravaging Euboea. These were the events which took place during this summer after the withdrawal of the Peloponnesians from Attica.

XXXIII. But in the ensuing winter, Euarchus the Acarnanian, wishing to return to Astacus, persuaded

[1] *i.e.* one of the ten generals elected annually.
[2] *cf.* I. lxi. 4. [3] IV. lxvi.–lxix.

κατελθεῖν, πείθει Κορινθίους τεσσαράκοντα ναυσὶ
καὶ πεντακοσίοις καὶ χιλίοις ὁπλίταις ἑαυτὸν
κατάγειν πλεύσαντας, καὶ αὐτὸς ἐπικούρους τινὰς
προσεμισθώσατο· ἦρχον δὲ τῆς στρατιᾶς Εὐ-
φαμίδας τε ὁ Ἀριστωνύμου καὶ Τιμόξενος ὁ
2 Τιμοκράτους καὶ Εὔμαχος ὁ Χρύσιδος. καὶ
πλεύσαντες κατήγαγον· καὶ τῆς ἄλλης Ἀκαρνανίας τῆς περὶ θάλασσαν ἔστιν ἃ χωρία βουλόμενοι προσποιήσασθαι καὶ πειραθέντες, ὡς οὐκ
3 ἐδύναντο, ἀπέπλεον ἐπ' οἴκου. σχόντες δ' ἐν τῷ
παράπλῳ ἐς Κεφαλληνίαν καὶ ἀπόβασιν ποιησάμενοι ἐς τὴν Κρανίων γῆν, ἀπατηθέντες ὑπ'
αὐτῶν ἐξ ὁμολογίας τινὸς ἄνδρας τε ἀποβάλλουσι
σφῶν αὐτῶν, ἐπιθεμένων ἀπροσδοκήτως τῶν
Κρανίων, καὶ βιαιότερον ἀναγαγόμενοι ἐκομίσθη-
σαν ἐπ' οἴκου.

XXXIV. Ἐν δὲ τῷ αὐτῷ χειμῶνι Ἀθηναῖοι
τῷ πατρίῳ νόμῳ χρώμενοι δημοσίᾳ ταφὰς ἐποιήσαντο τῶν ἐν τῷδε τῷ πολέμῳ πρώτων ἀποθανόν-
2 των τρόπῳ τοιῷδε. τὰ μὲν ὀστᾶ προτίθενται
τῶν ἀπογενομένων πρότριτα σκηνὴν ποιήσαντες,
καὶ ἐπιφέρει τῷ αὑτοῦ ἕκαστος ἤν τι βούληται·
3 ἐπειδὰν δὲ ἡ ἐκφορὰ ᾖ, λάρνακας κυπαρισσίνας
ἄγουσιν ἅμαξαι,[1] φυλῆς ἑκάστης μίαν· ἔνεστι δὲ
τὰ ὀστᾶ ἧς ἕκαστος ἦν φυλῆς. μία δὲ κλίνη
κενὴ φέρεται ἐστρωμένη τῶν ἀφανῶν, οἳ ἂν μὴ
4 εὑρεθῶσιν ἐς ἀναίρεσιν. ξυνεκφέρει δὲ ὁ βουλόμενος καὶ ἀστῶν καὶ ξένων, καὶ γυναῖκες πάρεισιν
αἱ προσήκουσαι ἐπὶ τὸν τάφον ὀλοφυρόμεναι.

[1] Hude inserts δέκα, following Gertz.

the Corinthians to sail with forty ships and fifteen hundred heavy infantry and restore him to power, and for this purpose he himself hired some mercenaries. The commanders of the expedition were Euphamidas son of Aristonymus, Timoxenus son of Timocrates, and Eumachus son of Chrysis. They did in fact sail over and restore him; and wishing to acquire some other places along the seaboard of Acarnania they made the attempt but failed, and thereupon sailed for home. As they skirted the coast they touched at Cephallenia, where they made a descent upon the territory of the Cranians; here deceived by the inhabitants through some sort of agreement they lost a few of their men by an unexpected attack of the Cranians, and finally, after they had got out to sea with considerable difficulty, managed to get back home.

XXXIV. In the course of the same winter the Athenians, following the custom of their fathers, celebrated at the public expense the funeral rites of the first who had fallen in this war. The ceremony is as follows. The bones of the departed lie in state for the space of three days in a tent erected for that purpose, and each one brings to his own dead any offering he desires. On the day of the funeral coffins of cypress wood are borne on wagons, one for each tribe, and the bones of each are in the coffin of his tribe. One empty bier, covered with a pall, is carried in the procession for the missing whose bodies could not be found for burial. Any one who wishes, whether citizen or stranger, may take part in the funeral procession, and the women who are related to the deceased are present at the

5 τιθέασιν οὖν ἐς τὸ δημόσιον σῆμα, ὅ ἐστιν ἐπὶ
τοῦ καλλίστου προαστείου τῆς πόλεως καὶ αἰεὶ
ἐν αὐτῷ θάπτουσι τοὺς ἐκ τῶν πολέμων πλήν γε
τοὺς ἐν Μαραθῶνι· ἐκείνων δὲ διαπρεπῆ τὴν
ἀρετὴν κρίναντες αὐτοῦ καὶ τὸν τάφον ἐποίησαν.
6 ἐπειδὰν δὲ κρύψωσι γῇ, ἀνὴρ ᾑρημένος ὑπὸ τῆς
πόλεως ὃς ἂν γνώμῃ τε δοκῇ μὴ ἀξύνετος εἶναι
καὶ ἀξιώσει προήκῃ, λέγει ἐπ' αὐτοῖς ἔπαινον
7 τὸν πρέποντα· μετὰ δὲ τοῦτο ἀπέρχονται. ὧδε
μὲν θάπτουσιν· καὶ διὰ παντὸς τοῦ πολέμου,
8 ὁπότε ξυμβαίη αὐτοῖς, ἐχρῶντο τῷ νόμῳ. ἐπὶ
δ' οὖν τοῖς πρώτοις τοῖσδε Περικλῆς ὁ Ξανθίππου
ᾑρέθη λέγειν. καὶ ἐπειδὴ καιρὸς ἐλάμβανε,
προελθὼν ἀπὸ τοῦ σήματος ἐπὶ βῆμα ὑψηλὸν
πεποιημένον, ὅπως ἀκούοιτο ὡς ἐπὶ πλεῖστον τοῦ
ὁμίλου, ἔλεγε τοιάδε.

XXXV. "Οἱ μὲν οὖν πολλοὶ τῶν ἐνθάδε ἤδη
εἰρηκότων ἐπαινοῦσι τὸν προσθέντα τῷ νόμῳ τὸν
λόγον τόνδε, ὡς καλὸν ἐπὶ τοῖς ἐκ τῶν πολέμων
θαπτομένοις ἀγορεύεσθαι αὐτόν. ἐμοὶ δὲ ἀρκοῦν
ἂν ἐδόκει εἶναι ἀνδρῶν ἀγαθῶν ἔργῳ γενομένων
ἔργῳ καὶ δηλοῦσθαι τὰς τιμάς, οἷα καὶ νῦν περὶ
τὸν τάφον τόνδε δημοσίᾳ παρασκευασθέντα
ὁρᾶτε, καὶ μὴ ἐν ἑνὶ ἀνδρὶ πολλῶν ἀρετὰς κινδυ-
νεύεσθαι εὖ τε καὶ χεῖρον εἰπόντι πιστευθῆναι.
2 χαλεπὸν γὰρ τὸ μετρίως εἰπεῖν ἐν ᾧ μόλις καὶ ἡ

---

[1] The Outer Cerameicus, just outside the Dipylon gate. This street was to Athens what the Appian Way was to Rome.

burial and make lamentation. The coffins are laid in the public sepulchre, which is situated in the most beautiful suburb[1] of the city; there they always bury those fallen in war, except indeed those who fell at Marathon; for their valour the Athenians judged to be preëminent and they buried them on the spot where they fell. But when the remains have been laid away in the earth, a man chosen by the state, who is regarded as best endowed with wisdom and is foremost in public esteem, delivers over them an appropriate eulogy. After this the people depart. In this manner they bury; and throughout the war, whenever occasion arose, they observed this custom. Now over these, the first victims of the war, Pericles son of Xanthippus was chosen to speak. And when the proper time came, he advanced from the sepulchre and took his stand upon a platform which had been built high in order that his voice might reach as far as possible in the throng, and spoke as follows:

XXXV. "Most of those who have spoken here in the past have commended the law-giver who added this oration to our ceremony, feeling that it is meet and right that it should be spoken at their burial over those who have fallen in war. To me, however, it would have seemed sufficient, when men have proved themselves brave by valiant acts, by act only to make manifest the honours we render them —such honours as to-day you have witnessed in connection with these funeral ceremonies solemnized by the state—and not that the valour of many men should be hazarded on one man to be believed or not according as he spoke well or ill. For it is a hard matter to speak in just measure on an occasion where it is with difficulty that belief in the speaker's

δόκησις τῆς ἀληθείας βεβαιοῦται. ὅ τε γὰρ ξυνειδὼς καὶ εὔνους ἀκροατὴς τάχ᾽ ἄν τι ἐνδεεστέρως πρὸς ἃ βούλεταί τε καὶ ἐπίσταται νομίσειε δηλοῦσθαι, ὅ τε ἄπειρος ἔστιν ἃ καὶ πλεονάζεσθαι, διὰ φθόνον, εἴ τι ὑπὲρ τὴν αὑτοῦ φύσιν ἀκούοι. μέχρι γὰρ τοῦδε ἀνεκτοὶ οἱ ἔπαινοί εἰσι περὶ ἑτέρων λεγόμενοι, ἐς ὅσον ἂν καὶ αὐτὸς ἕκαστος οἴηται ἱκανὸς εἶναι δρᾶσαί τι ὧν ἤκουσεν· τῷ δὲ ὑπερβάλλοντι αὐτῶν φθονοῦντες ἤδη καὶ
3 ἀπιστοῦσιν. ἐπειδὴ δὲ τοῖς πάλαι οὕτως ἐδοκιμάσθη ταῦτα καλῶς ἔχειν, χρὴ καὶ ἐμὲ ἑπόμενον τῷ νόμῳ πειρᾶσθαι ὑμῶν τῆς ἑκάστου βουλήσεώς τε καὶ δόξης τυχεῖν ὡς ἐπὶ πλεῖστον.

XXXVI. "Ἄρξομαι δὲ ἀπὸ τῶν προγόνων πρῶτον· δίκαιον γὰρ αὐτοῖς καὶ πρέπον δὲ ἅμα ἐν τῷ τοιῷδε τὴν τιμὴν ταύτην τῆς μνήμης δίδοσθαι. τὴν γὰρ χώραν οἱ αὐτοὶ αἰεὶ οἰκοῦντες διαδοχῇ τῶν ἐπιγιγνομένων μέχρι τοῦδε ἐλευ-
2 θέραν δι᾽ ἀρετὴν παρέδοσαν. καὶ ἐκεῖνοί τε ἄξιοι ἐπαίνου καὶ ἔτι μᾶλλον οἱ πατέρες ἡμῶν· κτησάμενοι γὰρ πρὸς οἷς ἐδέξαντο ὅσην ἔχομεν ἀρχὴν
3 οὐκ ἀπόνως, ἡμῖν τοῖς νῦν προσκατέλιπον. τὰ δὲ πλείω αὐτῆς αὐτοὶ ἡμεῖς οἵδε οἱ νῦν ἔτι ὄντες μάλιστα ἐν τῇ καθεστηκυίᾳ ἡλικίᾳ ἐπηυξήσαμεν, καὶ τὴν πόλιν τοῖς πᾶσι παρεσκευάσαμεν καὶ ἐς
4 πόλεμον καὶ ἐς εἰρήνην αὐταρκεστάτην. ὧν ἐγὼ

[1] Those enumerated by Pericles in ch. xii.—money, army and navy.

accuracy is established. For the hearer who is cognizant of the facts and partial to the dead will perhaps think that scant justice has been done in comparison with his own wishes and his own knowledge, while he who is not so informed, whenever he hears of an exploit which goes beyond his own capacity, will be led by envy to think there is some exaggeration. And indeed eulogies of other men are tolerable only in so far as each hearer thinks that he too has the ability to perform any of the exploits of which he hears; but whatever goes beyond that at once excites envy and unbelief. However, since our forefathers approved of this practice as right and proper, I also, rendering obedience to the law, must endeavour to the best of my ability to satisfy the wishes and beliefs of each of you.

XXXVI. "I shall speak first of our ancestors, for it is right and at the same time fitting, on an occasion like this, to give them this place of honour in recalling what they did. For this land of ours, in which the same people have never ceased to dwell in an unbroken line of successive generations, they by their valour transmitted to our times a free state. And not only are they worthy of our praise, but our fathers still more; for they, adding to the inheritance which they received, acquired the empire we now possess and bequeathed it, not without toil, to us who are alive to-day. And we ourselves here assembled, who are now for the most part still in the prime of life, have further strengthened the empire in most respects, and have provided our city with all resources,[1] so that it is sufficient for itself both in peace and in war. The military exploits whereby

τὰ μὲν κατὰ πολέμους ἔργα, οἷς ἕκαστα ἐκτήθη, ἢ εἴ τι αὐτοὶ ἢ οἱ πατέρες ἡμῶν βάρβαρον ἢ Ἕλληνα πόλεμον[1] ἐπιόντα προθύμως ἠμυνάμεθα, μακρηγορεῖν ἐν εἰδόσιν οὐ βουλόμενος, ἐάσω· ἀπὸ δὲ οἵας τε ἐπιτηδεύσεως ἤλθομεν ἐπ' αὐτὰ καὶ μεθ' οἵας πολιτείας καὶ τρόπων ἐξ οἵων μεγάλα ἐγένετο, ταῦτα δηλώσας πρῶτον εἶμι καὶ ἐπὶ τὸν τῶνδε ἔπαινον, νομίζων ἐπί τε τῷ παρόντι οὐκ ἂν ἀπρεπῆ λεχθῆναι αὐτὰ καὶ τὸν πάντα ὅμιλον καὶ ἀστῶν καὶ ξένων ξύμφορον εἶναι ἐπακοῦσαι αὐτῶν.

XXXVII. "Χρώμεθα γὰρ πολιτείᾳ οὐ ζηλούσῃ τοὺς τῶν πέλας νόμους, παράδειγμα δὲ μᾶλλον αὐτοὶ ὄντες τισὶν ἢ μιμούμενοι ἑτέρους. καὶ ὄνομα μὲν διὰ τὸ μὴ ἐς ὀλίγους ἀλλ' ἐς πλείονας οἰκεῖν δημοκρατία κέκληται, μέτεστι δὲ κατὰ μὲν τοὺς νόμους πρὸς τὰ ἴδια διάφορα πᾶσι τὸ ἴσον, κατὰ δὲ τὴν ἀξίωσιν, ὡς ἕκαστος ἔν τῳ εὐδοκιμεῖ, οὐκ ἀπὸ μέρους τὸ πλέον ἐς τὰ κοινὰ ἢ ἀπ' ἀρετῆς προτιμᾶται, οὐδ' αὖ κατὰ πενίαν, ἔχων δέ τι ἀγαθὸν δρᾶσαι τὴν πόλιν, ἀξιώματος ἀφανείᾳ
2 κεκώλυται. ἐλευθέρως δὲ τά τε πρὸς τὸ κοινὸν πολιτεύομεν καὶ ἐς τὴν πρὸς ἀλλήλους τῶν καθ' ἡμέραν ἐπιτηδευμάτων ὑποψίαν, οὐ δι' ὀργῆς τὸν πέλας, εἰ καθ' ἡδονήν τι δρᾷ, ἔχοντες, οὐδὲ ἀζη-

[1] πόλεμον, Hude adopts Haase's conjecture πολέμιον.

---

[1] Alluding to the Spartans, whose institutions were said to have been borrowed from Crete; in fact, throughout the whole speech the contrast is with Spartan conditions.

our several possessions were acquired, whether in any case it were we ourselves or our fathers that valiantly repelled the onset of war, Barbarian or Hellenic, I will not recall, for I have no desire to speak at length among those who know. But I shall first set forth by what sort of training we have come to our present position, and with what political institutions and as the result of what manner of life our empire became great, and afterwards proceed to the praise of these men; for I think that on the present occasion such a recital will be not inappropriate and that the whole throng, both of citizens and of strangers, may with advantage listen to it.

XXXVII. "We live under a form of government which does not emulate the institutions of our neighbours[1]; on the contrary, we are ourselves a model which some[2] follow, rather than the imitators of other peoples. It is true that our government is called a democracy, because its administration is in the hands, not of the few, but of the many; yet while as regards the law all men are on an equality for the settlement of their private disputes, as regards the value set on them it is as each man is in any way distinguished that he is preferred to public honours, not because he belongs to a particular class, but because of personal merits; nor, again, on the ground of poverty is a man barred from a public career by obscurity of rank if he but has it in him to do the state a service. And not only in our public life are we liberal, but also as regards our freedom from suspicion of one another in the pursuits of every-day life; for we do not feel resentment at our neighbour

[2] Possible allusion to the embassy sent from Rome in 454 B.C. to examine the laws of Solon (Livy, iii. 31).

μίους μέν, λυπηρὰς δὲ τῇ ὄψει ἀχθηδόνας προστι-
3 θέμενοι. ἀνεπαχθῶς δὲ τὰ ἴδια προσομιλοῦντες τὰ δημόσια διὰ δέος μάλιστα οὐ παρανομοῦμεν, τῶν τε αἰεὶ ἐν ἀρχῇ ὄντων ἀκροάσει καὶ τῶν νόμων, καὶ μάλιστα αὐτῶν ὅσοι τε ἐπ' ὠφελίᾳ τῶν ἀδικουμένων κεῖνται καὶ ὅσοι ἄγραφοι ὄντες αἰσχύνην ὁμολογουμένην φέρουσιν.

XXXVIII. "Καὶ μὴν καὶ τῶν πόνων πλείστας ἀναπαύλας τῇ γνώμῃ ἐπορισάμεθα, ἀγῶσι μέν γε καὶ θυσίαις διετησίοις νομίζοντες, ἰδίαις δὲ κατασκευαῖς εὐπρεπέσιν, ὧν καθ' ἡμέραν ἡ τέρψις
2 τὸ λυπηρὸν ἐκπλήσσει. ἐπεσέρχεται δὲ διὰ μέγεθος τῆς πόλεως ἐκ πάσης γῆς τὰ πάντα, καὶ ξυμβαίνει ἡμῖν μηδὲν οἰκειοτέρᾳ τῇ ἀπολαύσει τὰ αὐτοῦ ἀγαθὰ γιγνόμενα καρποῦσθαι ἢ καὶ τὰ τῶν ἄλλων ἀνθρώπων.

XXXIX. "Διαφέρομεν δὲ κἀν ταῖς τῶν πολεμικῶν μελέταις τῶν ἐναντίων τοῖσδε. τήν τε γὰρ πόλιν κοινὴν παρέχομεν καὶ οὐκ ἔστιν ὅτε ξενηλασίαις ἀπείργομέν τινα ἢ μαθήματος ἢ θεάματος, ὃ μὴ κρυφθὲν ἄν τις τῶν πολεμίων ἰδὼν ὠφεληθείη, πιστεύοντες οὐ ταῖς παρασκευαῖς τὸ

---

[1] Referring especially to the contests at the chief festivals, like the Panathenaea and Dionysia, which by their artistic setting and performance were recreations of mind and spirit quite as much as physical exercises.

[2] Thucydides refers to the spiritual no less than to the physical products which the greatness of Athens attracts to her, to the poetry, music, and art which find there a con-

if he does as he likes, nor yet do we put on sour looks which, though harmless, are painful to behold. But while we thus avoid giving offence in our private intercourse, in our public life we are restrained from lawlessness chiefly through reverent fear, for we render obedience to those in authority and to the laws, and especially to those laws which are ordained for the succour of the oppressed and those which, though unwritten, bring upon the transgressor a disgrace which all men recognize.

XXXVIII. "Moreover, we have provided for the spirit many relaxations from toil: we have games[1] and sacrifices regularly throughout the year and homes fitted out with good taste and elegance; and the delight we each day find in these things drives away sadness. And our city is so great that all the products of all the earth flow in upon us, and ours is the happy lot to gather in the good fruits of our own soil with no more home-felt security of enjoyment than we do those of other lands.[2]

XXXIX. "We are also superior to our opponents in our system of training for warfare, and this in the following respects. In the first place, we throw our city open to all the world and we never by exclusion acts debar any one from learning or seeing anything which an enemy might profit by observing if it were not kept from his sight; for we place our dependence, not so much upon prearranged devices to

genial home as well as to articles of commerce. On these latter compare a passage in the pseudo-Xenophontic *Constitution of Athens* (ii. 7), written somewhat earlier than this portion of Thucydides' history: "Whatever desirable thing is found in Sicily, Italy, Cyprus, Egypt, Lydia, the Pontus, the Peloponnesus, or anywhere else, all these things are brought together at Athens on account of her mastery of the sea."

πλέον καὶ ἀπάταις ἢ τῷ ἀφ' ἡμῶν αὐτῶν ἐς τὰ ἔργα εὐψύχῳ· καὶ ἐν ταῖς παιδείαις οἱ μὲν ἐπιπόνῳ ἀσκήσει εὐθὺς νέοι ὄντες τὸ ἀνδρεῖον μετέρχονται, ἡμεῖς δὲ ἀνειμένως διαιτώμενοι οὐδὲν ἧσσον ἐπὶ τοὺς ἰσοπαλεῖς κινδύνους χωροῦμεν.
2 τεκμήριον δέ· οὔτε γὰρ Λακεδαιμόνιοι καθ' ἑαυτούς, μεθ' ἁπάντων δὲ ἐς τὴν γῆν ἡμῶν στρατεύουσι, τήν τε τῶν πέλας αὐτοὶ ἐπελθόντες οὐ χαλεπῶς ἐν τῇ ἀλλοτρίᾳ τοὺς περὶ τῶν οἰκείων ἀμυνομένους μαχόμενοι τὰ πλείω κρατοῦμεν·
3 ἀθρόᾳ τε τῇ δυνάμει ἡμῶν οὐδείς πω πολέμιος ἐνέτυχε διὰ τὴν τοῦ ναυτικοῦ τε ἅμα ἐπιμέλειαν καὶ τὴν ἐν τῇ γῇ ἐπὶ πολλὰ ἡμῶν αὐτῶν ἐπίπεμψιν· ἤν δέ που μορίῳ τινὶ προσμείξωσι, κρατήσαντές τέ τινας ἡμῶν πάντας αὐχοῦσιν ἀπεῶσθαι καὶ νικηθέντες ὑφ' ἁπάντων ἡσσῆσθαι.
4 καίτοι εἰ ῥᾳθυμίᾳ μᾶλλον ἢ πόνων μελέτῃ καὶ μὴ μετὰ νόμων τὸ πλέον ἢ τρόπων ἀνδρείας ἐθέλομεν κινδυνεύειν, περιγίγνεται ἡμῖν τοῖς τε μέλλουσιν ἀλγεινοῖς μὴ προκάμνειν, καὶ ἐς αὐτὰ ἐλθοῦσι μὴ ἀτολμοτέρους τῶν αἰεὶ μοχθούντων φαίνεσθαι, καὶ ἔν τε τούτοις τὴν πόλιν ἀξίαν εἶναι θαυμάζεσθαι καὶ ἔτι ἐν ἄλλοις.

XL. "Φιλοκαλοῦμέν τε γὰρ μετ' εὐτελείας καὶ φιλοσοφοῦμεν ἄνευ μαλακίας· πλούτῳ τε ἔργου μᾶλλον καιρῷ ἢ λόγου κόμπῳ χρώμεθα, καὶ τὸ

---

[1] Pericles here hints at his policy, outlined in ch. xiii. 2, of always acting on the defensive when the enemy forces are distinctly superior.

deceive, as upon the courage which springs from our own souls when we are called to action. And again, in the matter of education, whereas they from early childhood by a laborious discipline make pursuit of manly courage, we with our unrestricted mode of life are none the less ready to meet any equality of hazard.[1] And here is the proof: When the Lacedaemonians invade our territory they do not come alone but bring all their confederates with them, whereas we, going by ourselves against our neighbours' territory, generally have no difficulty, though fighting on foreign soil against men who are defending their own homes, in overcoming them in battle. And in fact our united forces no enemy has ever yet met, not only because we are constantly attending to the needs of our navy, but also because on land we send our troops on many enterprises; but if they by chance engage with a division of our forces and defeat a few of us, they boast that they have repulsed us all, and if the victory is ours, they claim that they have been beaten by us all. If, then, by taking our ease rather than by laborious training and depending on a courage which springs more from manner of life than compulsion of laws, we are ready to meet dangers, the gain is all ours, in that we do not borrow trouble by anticipating miseries which are not yet at hand, and when we come to the test we show ourselves fully as brave as those who are always toiling; and so our city is worthy of admiration in these respects, as well as in others.

XL. "For we are lovers of beauty yet with no extravagance and lovers of wisdom yet without weakness. Wealth we employ rather as an opportunity for action than as a subject for boasting;

πένεσθαι οὐχ ὁμολογεῖν τινι αἰσχρόν, ἀλλὰ μὴ
2 διαφεύγειν ἔργῳ αἴσχιον. ἔνι τε τοῖς αὐτοῖς
οἰκείων ἅμα καὶ πολιτικῶν ἐπιμέλεια καὶ ἑτέροις[1]
πρὸς ἔργα τετραμμένοις τὰ πολιτικὰ μὴ ἐνδεῶς
γνῶναι· μόνοι γὰρ τόν τε μηδὲν τῶνδε μετέχοντα
οὐκ ἀπράγμονα, ἀλλ' ἀχρεῖον νομίζομεν, καὶ
αὐτοὶ[2] ἤτοι κρίνομέν γε ἢ ἐνθυμούμεθα ὀρθῶς τὰ
πράγματα, οὐ τοὺς λόγους τοῖς ἔργοις βλάβην
ἡγούμενοι, ἀλλὰ μὴ προδιδαχθῆναι μᾶλλον λόγῳ
3 πρότερον ἢ ἐπὶ ἃ δεῖ ἔργῳ ἐλθεῖν. διαφερόντως
γὰρ δὴ καὶ τόδε ἔχομεν ὥστε τολμᾶν τε οἱ αὐτοὶ
μάλιστα καὶ περὶ ὧν ἐπιχειρήσομεν ἐκλογίζεσθαι·
ὃ τοῖς ἄλλοις ἀμαθία μὲν θράσος, λογισμὸς δὲ
ὄκνον φέρει. κράτιστοι δ' ἂν ψυχὴν δικαίως
κριθεῖεν οἱ τά τε δεινὰ καὶ ἡδέα σαφέστατα
γιγνώσκοντες καὶ διὰ ταῦτα μὴ ἀποτρεπόμενοι
4 ἐκ τῶν κινδύνων. καὶ τὰ ἐς ἀρετὴν ἐνηντιώμεθα
τοῖς πολλοῖς· οὐ γὰρ πάσχοντες εὖ, ἀλλὰ δρῶντες
κτώμεθα τοὺς φίλους. βεβαιότερος δὲ ὁ δράσας
τὴν χάριν ὥστε ὀφειλομένην δι' εὐνοίας ᾧ δέδωκε
σῴζειν· ὁ δὲ ἀντοφείλων ἀμβλύτερος, εἰδὼς οὐκ
ἐς χάριν, ἀλλ' ὡς ὀφείλημα τὴν ἀρετὴν ἀποδώ-

[1] ἑτέροις <ἕτερα>, Hude. [2] Hude reads οἱ αὐτοί.

---

[1] As contrasted with the Spartans, whose officials made the most important decisions.

and with us it is not a shame for a man to acknowledge poverty, but the greater shame is for him not to do his best to avoid it. And you will find united in the same persons an interest at once in private and in public affairs, and in others of us who give attention chiefly to business, you will find no lack of insight into political matters. For we alone regard the man who takes no part in public affairs, not as one who minds his own business, but as good for nothing; and we Athenians decide public questions for ourselves[1] or at least endeavour to arrive at a sound understanding of them, in the belief that it is not debate that is a hindrance to action, but rather not to be instructed by debate before the time comes for action. For in truth we have this point also of superiority over other men, to be most daring in action and yet at the same time most given to reflection upon the ventures we mean to undertake; with other men, on the contrary, boldness means ignorance and reflection brings hesitation. And they would rightly be adjudged most courageous who, realizing most clearly the pains no less than the pleasures involved, do not on that account turn away from danger. Again, in nobility of spirit, we stand in sharp contrast to most men; for it is not by receiving kindness, but by conferring it, that we acquire our friends. Now he who confers the favour is a firmer friend, in that he is disposed, by continued goodwill toward the recipient, to keep the feeling of obligation alive in him[2]; but he who owes it is more listless in his friendship, knowing that when he repays the kindness it will count, not as a favour bestowed, but as a debt

[2] This must be the meaning of the ὥστε clause, but something is perhaps wrong with the text.

5 σων. καὶ μόνοι οὐ τοῦ ξυμφέροντος μᾶλλον λογισμῷ ἢ τῆς ἐλευθερίας τῷ πιστῷ ἀδεῶς τινα ὠφελοῦμεν.

XLI. "Ξυνελών τε λέγω τήν τε πᾶσαν πόλιν τῆς Ἑλλάδος παίδευσιν εἶναι καὶ καθ' ἕκαστον δοκεῖν ἄν μοι τὸν αὐτὸν ἄνδρα παρ' ἡμῶν ἐπὶ πλεῖστ' ἂν εἴδη καὶ μετὰ χαρίτων μάλιστ' ἂν
2 εὐτραπέλως τὸ σῶμα αὔταρκες παρέχεσθαι. καὶ ὡς οὐ λόγων ἐν τῷ παρόντι κόμπος τάδε μᾶλλον ἢ ἔργων ἐστὶν ἀλήθεια, αὐτὴ ἡ δύναμις τῆς πόλεως, ἣν ἀπὸ τῶνδε τῶν τρόπων ἐκτησάμεθα,
3 σημαίνει. μόνη γὰρ τῶν νῦν ἀκοῆς κρείσσων ἐς πεῖραν ἔρχεται, καὶ μόνη οὔτε τῷ πολεμίῳ ἐπελθόντι ἀγανάκτησιν ἔχει ὑφ' οἵων κακοπαθεῖ, οὔτε τῷ ὑπηκόῳ κατάμεμψιν ὡς οὐχ ὑπὸ ἀξίων
4 ἄρχεται. μετὰ μεγάλων δὲ σημείων καὶ οὐ δή τοι ἀμάρτυρόν γε τὴν δύναμιν παρασχόμενοι τοῖς τε νῦν καὶ τοῖς ἔπειτα θαυμασθησόμεθα,[1] οὐδὲν προσδεόμενοι οὔτε Ὁμήρου ἐπαινέτου οὔτε ὅστις ἔπεσι μὲν τὸ αὐτίκα τέρψει, τῶν δ' ἔργων τὴν ὑπόνοιαν ἡ ἀλήθεια βλάψει, ἀλλὰ πᾶσαν μὲν θάλασσαν καὶ γῆν ἐσβατὸν τῇ ἡμετέρᾳ τόλμῃ καταναγκάσαντες γενέσθαι, πανταχοῦ δὲ μνημεῖα
5 κακῶν τε κἀγαθῶν ἀίδια ξυγκατοικίσαντες. περὶ τοιαύτης οὖν πόλεως οἵδε τε γενναίως δικαιοῦντες

[1] καὶ, before οὐδὲν in the MSS., deleted by Krüger.

---

[1] The reference is to Athenian colonies and cleruchies, which, according to the bearing of the natives, had been

repaid. And, finally, we alone confer our benefits without fear of consequences, not upon a calculation of the advantage we shall gain, but with confidence in the spirit of liberality which actuates us.

XLI. "In a word, then, I say that our city as a whole is the school of Hellas, and that, as it seems to me, each individual amongst us could in his own person, with the utmost grace and versatility, prove himself self-sufficient in the most varied forms of activity. And that this is no mere boast inspired by the occasion, but actual truth, is attested by the very power of our city, a power which we have acquired in consequence of these qualities. For Athens alone among her contemporaries, when put to the test, is superior to the report of her, and she alone neither affords to the enemy who comes against her cause for irritation at the character of the foe by whom he is defeated, nor to her subject cause for complaint that his masters are unworthy. Many are the proofs which we have given of our power and assuredly it does not lack witnesses, and therefore we shall be the wonder not only of the men of to-day but of after times; we shall need no Homer to sing our praise nor any other poet whose verses may perhaps delight for the moment but whose presentation of the facts will be discredited by the truth. Nay, we have compelled every sea and every land to grant access to our daring, and have everywhere planted[1] everlasting memorials both of evil to foes and of good to friends. Such, then, is the city for which these men nobly fought and died, deeming it their duty not to let her

attended with ill consequences for these (*e.g.* Oreos, and later Aegina) or good (*e.g.* on the Thracian coast).

μὴ ἀφαιρεθῆναι αὐτὴν μαχόμενοι ἐτελεύτησαν, καὶ τῶν λειπομένων πάντα τινὰ εἰκὸς ἐθέλειν ὑπὲρ αὐτῆς κάμνειν.

XLII. "Δι' ὃ δὴ καὶ ἐμήκυνα τὰ περὶ τῆς πόλεως, διδασκαλίαν τε ποιούμενος μὴ περὶ ἴσου ἡμῖν εἶναι τὸν ἀγῶνα καὶ οἷς τῶνδε μηδὲν ὑπάρχει ὁμοίως, καὶ τὴν εὐλογίαν ἅμα ἐφ' οἷς νῦν λέγω
2 φανερὰν σημείοις καθιστάς. καὶ εἴρηται αὐτῆς τὰ μέγιστα· ἃ γὰρ τὴν πόλιν ὕμνησα, αἱ τῶνδε καὶ τῶν τοιῶνδε ἀρεταὶ ἐκόσμησαν, καὶ οὐκ ἂν πολλοῖς τῶν Ἑλλήνων ἰσόρροπος ὥσπερ τῶνδε ὁ λόγος τῶν ἔργων φανείη. δοκεῖ δέ μοι δηλοῦν ἀνδρὸς ἀρετὴν πρώτη τε μηνύουσα καὶ τελευταία
3 βεβαιοῦσα ἡ νῦν τῶνδε καταστροφή. καὶ γὰρ τοῖς τἆλλα χείροσι δίκαιον τὴν ἐς τοὺς πολέμους ὑπὲρ τῆς πατρίδος ἀνδραγαθίαν προτίθεσθαι· ἀγαθῷ γὰρ κακὸν ἀφανίσαντες κοινῶς μᾶλλον
4 ὠφέλησαν ἢ ἐκ τῶν ἰδίων ἔβλαψαν. τῶνδε δὲ οὔτε πλούτου τις τὴν ἔτι ἀπόλαυσιν προτιμήσας ἐμαλακίσθη οὔτε πενίας ἐλπίδι, ὡς κἂν ἔτι διαφυγὼν αὐτὴν[1] πλουτήσειεν, ἀναβολὴν τοῦ δεινοῦ ἐποιήσατο· τὴν δὲ τῶν ἐναντίων τιμωρίαν ποθεινοτέραν αὐτῶν λαβόντες καὶ κινδύνων ἅμα τόνδε κάλλιστον νομίσαντες ἐβουλήθησαν μετ' αὐτοῦ

[1] αὐτήν: Hude brackets.

be taken from them; and it is fitting that every man who is left behind should suffer willingly for her sake.

XLII. "It is for this reason that I have dwelt upon the greatness of our city; for I have desired to show you that we are contending for a higher prize than those who do not enjoy such privileges in like degree, and at the same time to let the praise of these men in whose honour I am now speaking be made manifest by proofs. Indeed, the greatest part of their praise has already been spoken; for when I lauded the city, that was but the praise wherewith the brave deeds of these men and men like them have already adorned her; and there are not many Hellenes whose fame would be found, like theirs, evenly balanced with their deeds. And it seems to me that such a death as these men died gives proof enough of manly courage, whether as first revealing it or as affording its final confirmation. Aye, even in the case of those who in other ways fell short of goodness, it is but right that the valour with which they fought for their country should be set before all else; for they have blotted out evil with good and have bestowed a greater benefit by their service to the state than they have done harm by their private lives. And no one of these men either so set his heart upon the continued enjoyment of wealth as to become a coward, or put off the dreadful day, yielding to the hope which poverty inspires, that if he could but escape it he might yet become rich; but, deeming the punishment of the foe to be more desirable than these things, and at the same time regarding such a hazard as the most glorious of all, they chose, accepting the hazard, to be avenged

τοὺς μὲν τιμωρεῖσθαι, τῶν δὲ ἀφίεσθαι, ἐλπίδι μὲν τὸ ἀφανὲς τοῦ κατορθώσειν ἐπιτρέψαντες, ἔργῳ δὲ περὶ τοῦ ἤδη ὁρωμένου σφίσιν αὐτοῖς ἀξιοῦντες πεποιθέναι· καὶ ἐν αὐτῷ τὸ[1] ἀμύνεσθαι καὶ[2] παθεῖν κάλλιον[3] ἡγησάμενοι ἢ τὸ[4] ἐνδόντες σῴζεσθαι, τὸ μὲν αἰσχρὸν τοῦ λόγου ἔφυγον, τὸ δ' ἔργον τῷ σώματι ὑπέμειναν, καὶ δι' ἐλαχίστου καιροῦ τύχης ἅμα ἀκμῇ τῆς δόξης μᾶλλον ἢ τοῦ δέους ἀπηλλάγησαν.

XLIII. "Καὶ οἵδε μὲν προσηκόντως τῇ πόλει τοιοίδε ἐγένοντο· τοὺς δὲ λοιποὺς χρὴ ἀσφαλεστέραν μὲν εὔχεσθαι, ἀτολμοτέραν δὲ μηδὲν ἀξιοῦν τὴν ἐς τοὺς πολεμίους διάνοιαν ἔχειν, σκοποῦντας μὴ λόγῳ μόνῳ τὴν ὠφελίαν, ἣν ἄν τις πρὸς οὐδὲν χεῖρον αὐτοὺς ὑμᾶς[5] εἰδότας μηκύνοι, λέγων ὅσα ἐν τῷ τοὺς πολεμίους ἀμύνεσθαι ἀγαθὰ ἔνεστιν, ἀλλὰ μᾶλλον τὴν τῆς πόλεως δύναμιν καθ' ἡμέραν ἔργῳ θεωμένους καὶ ἐραστὰς γιγνομένους αὐτῆς, καὶ ὅταν ὑμῖν μεγάλη δόξῃ εἶναι, ἐνθυμουμένους ὅτι τολμῶντες καὶ γιγνώσκοντες τὰ δέοντα καὶ ἐν τοῖς ἔργοις αἰσχυνόμενοι ἄνδρες αὐτὰ ἐκτήσαντο, καὶ ὁπότε καὶ πείρᾳ του σφαλεῖεν, οὐκ οὖν καὶ τὴν πόλιν γε τῆς σφετέρας ἀρετῆς ἀξιοῦντες στερίσκειν, κάλλιστον δὲ ἔρανον

[1] So most MSS. Hude reads τῷ with CG.
[2] καὶ: Hude brackets.
[3] Dobree's correction for μᾶλλον of the MSS. Hude inserts δεῖν and retains μᾶλλον.
[4] Deleted by Hude.
[5] ὑμᾶς: Hude brackets.

upon the enemy and to relinquish these other things, trusting to hope the still obscure possibilities of success, but in action, as to the issue that was before their eyes, confidently relying upon themselves. And then when the moment of combat came, thinking it better to defend themselves and suffer death rather than to yield and save their lives, they fled, indeed, from the shameful word of dishonour, but with life and limb stood stoutly to their task, and in the brief instant ordained by fate, at the crowning moment not of fear but of glory, they passed away.

XLIII. "And so these men then bore themselves after a manner that befits our city; but you who survive, though you may pray that it be with less hazard, should resolve that you will have a spirit to meet the foe which is no whit less courageous; and you must estimate the advantage of such a spirit not alone by a speaker's words, for he could make a long story in telling you—what you yourselves know as well as he—all the advantages that are to be gained by warding off the foe. Nay rather you must daily fix your gaze upon the power of Athens and become lovers of her, and when the vision of her greatness has inspired you, reflect that all this has been acquired by men of courage who knew their duty and in the hour of conflict were moved by a high sense of honour, who, if ever they failed in any enterprise, were resolved that at least their country should not find herself deserted by their valour, but freely sacrificed to her the fairest offering[1] it was in

[1] ἔρανος, a *joint contribution*, the regular term for a contribution made for mutual benefit, *e.g.* to a common meal, to a benevolent society, etc. Demosthenes (*cont. Mid.* 27) represents the state as a sort of benefit society to which every citizen owes a contribution.

2 αὐτῇ προϊέμενοι. κοινῇ γὰρ τὰ σώματα διδόντες
ἰδίᾳ τὸν ἀγήρων ἔπαινον ἐλάμβανον καὶ τὸν
τάφον ἐπισημότατον, οὐκ ἐν ᾧ κεῖνται μᾶλλον,
ἀλλ' ἐν ᾧ ἡ δόξα αὐτῶν παρὰ τῷ ἐντυχόντι αἰεὶ
καὶ λόγου καὶ ἔργου καιρῷ αἰείμνηστος κατα-
3 λείπεται. ἀνδρῶν γὰρ ἐπιφανῶν πᾶσα γῆ τάφος,
καὶ οὐ στηλῶν μόνον ἐν τῇ οἰκείᾳ σημαίνει ἐπι-
γραφή, ἀλλὰ καὶ ἐν τῇ μὴ προσηκούσῃ ἄγραφος
μνήμη παρ' ἑκάστῳ τῆς γνώμης μᾶλλον ἢ τοῦ
4 ἔργου ἐνδιαιτᾶται. οὓς νῦν ὑμεῖς ζηλώσαντες
καὶ τὸ εὔδαιμον τὸ ἐλεύθερον, τὸ δ' ἐλεύθερον τὸ
εὔψυχον κρίναντες, μὴ περιορᾶσθε τοὺς πολεμι-
5 κοὺς κινδύνους. οὐ γὰρ οἱ κακοπραγοῦντες δικαιό-
τερον ἀφειδοῖεν ἂν τοῦ βίου, οἷς ἐλπὶς οὐκ ἔστιν
ἀγαθοῦ, ἀλλ' οἷς ἡ ἐναντία μεταβολὴ ἐν τῷ ζῆν
ἔτι κινδυνεύεται καὶ ἐν οἷς μάλιστα μεγάλα τὰ
6 διαφέροντα, ἤν τι πταίσωσιν. ἀλγεινοτέρα γὰρ
ἀνδρί γε φρόνημα ἔχοντι ἡ μετὰ τοῦ[1] μαλα-
κισθῆναι κάκωσις ἢ ὁ μετὰ ῥώμης καὶ κοινῆς
ἐλπίδος ἅμα γιγνόμενος ἀναίσθητος θάνατος.

XLIV. "Δι' ὅπερ καὶ τοὺς τῶνδε νῦν τοκέας, ὅσοι πάρεστε, οὐκ ὀλοφύρομαι μᾶλλον ἢ παραμυθήσομαι. ἐν πολυτρόποις γὰρ ξυμφοραῖς ἐπίστανται τραφέντες· τὸ δ' εὐτυχές,[2] οἳ ἂν τῆς εὐπρεπεστάτης λάχωσιν, ὥσπερ οἵδε μὲν νῦν, τελευτῆς, ὑμεῖς δὲ λύπης, καὶ οἷς ἐνευδαιμονῆσαί τε ὁ βίος ὁμοίως καὶ ἐντελευτῆσαι ξυνεμετρήθη.

[1] ἐν τῷ, in some MSS. before, in others after, μετὰ τοῦ, deleted by Bredow.

[2] Hude reads τόδε εὐτυχές, following Abresch.

their power to give. For they gave their lives for the common weal, and in so doing won for themselves the praise which grows not old and the most distinguished of all sepulchres—not that in which they lie buried, but that in which their glory survives in everlasting remembrance, celebrated on every occasion which gives rise to word of eulogy or deed of emulation. For the whole world is the sepulchre of famous men, and it is not the epitaph upon monuments set up in their own land that alone commemorates them, but also in lands not their own there abides in each breast an unwritten memorial of them, planted in the heart rather than graven on stone. Do you, therefore, now make these men your examples, and judging freedom to be happiness and courage to be freedom, be not too anxious about the dangers of war. For it is not those that are in evil plight who have the best excuse for being unsparing of their lives, for they have no hope of better days, but rather those who run the risk, if they continue to live, of the opposite reversal of fortune, and those to whom it makes the greatest difference if they suffer a disaster. For to a manly spirit more bitter is humiliation associated with cowardice than death when it comes unperceived in close company with stalwart deeds and public hopes.

XLIV. "Wherefore, I do not commiserate the parents of these men, as many of you as are present here, but will rather try to comfort them. For they know that their lives have been passed amid manifold vicissitudes; and it is to be accounted good fortune when men win, even as these now, a most glorious death—and you a like grief—and when life has been meted out to them to be happy in no less than to

2 χαλεπὸν μὲν οὖν οἶδα πείθειν ὄν, ὧν καὶ πολλάκις ἕξετε ὑπομνήματα ἐν ἄλλων εὐτυχίαις, αἷς ποτε καὶ αὐτοὶ ἠγάλλεσθε· καὶ λύπη οὐχ ὧν ἄν τις μὴ πειρασάμενος ἀγαθῶν στερίσκηται, ἀλλ' οὗ ἂν
3 ἐθὰς γενόμενος ἀφαιρεθῇ. καρτερεῖν δὲ χρὴ καὶ ἄλλων παίδων ἐλπίδι οἷς ἔτι ἡλικία τέκνωσιν ποιεῖσθαι· ἰδίᾳ τε γὰρ τῶν οὐκ ὄντων λήθη οἱ ἐπιγιγνόμενοί τισιν ἔσονται, καὶ τῇ πόλει διχόθεν, ἔκ τε τοῦ μὴ ἐρημοῦσθαι καὶ ἀσφαλείᾳ, ξυνοίσει· οὐ γὰρ οἷόν τε ἴσον τι ἢ δίκαιον βουλεύεσθαι οἳ ἂν μὴ καὶ παῖδας ἐκ τοῦ ὁμοίου παραβαλλόμενοι
4 κινδυνεύωσιν. ὅσοι δ' αὖ παρηβήκατε, τόν τε πλέονα κέρδος ὃν ηὐτυχεῖτε βίον ἡγεῖσθε καὶ τόνδε βραχὺν ἔσεσθαι, καὶ τῇ τῶνδε εὐκλείᾳ κουφίζεσθε. τὸ γὰρ φιλότιμον ἀγήρων μόνον, καὶ οὐκ ἐν τῷ ἀχρείῳ τῆς ἡλικίας τὸ κερδαίνειν, ὥσπερ τινές φασι, μᾶλλον τέρπει, ἀλλὰ τὸ τιμᾶσθαι.

XLV. "Παισὶ δ' αὖ ὅσοι τῶνδε πάρεστε ἢ ἀδελφοῖς ὁρῶ μέγαν τὸν ἀγῶνα (τὸν γὰρ οὐκ ὄντα ἅπας εἴωθεν ἐπαινεῖν), καὶ μόλις ἂν καθ' ὑπερβολὴν ἀρετῆς οὐχ ὁμοῖοι, ἀλλ' ὀλίγῳ χείρους

---

[1] No one could be a member of the Boule or Senate till he was thirty, when he was almost certain to be married; and, according to Deinarchus (§ 71), no man was allowed to speak in the Assembly until he had legitimate male issue (Zimmern).

[2] *e.g* Simonides. *cf.* Plut. *Moral.* 786 b: Σιμωνίδης ἔλεγε πρὸς τοὺς ἐγκαλοῦντας αὐτῷ φιλαργυρίαν, ὅτι τῶν ἄλλων ἀπε-

die in. It will be difficult, I know, to persuade you of the truth of this, when you will constantly be reminded of your loss by seeing others in the enjoyment of blessings in which you too once took delight; and grief, I know, is felt, not for the want of the good things which a man has never known, but for what is taken away from him after he has once become accustomed to it. But those of you who are still of an age to have offspring should bear up in the hope of other children; for not only to many of you individually will the children that are born hereafter be a cause of forgetfulness of those who are gone, but the state also will reap a double advantage—it will not be left desolate and it will be secure. For they cannot possibly offer fair and impartial counsel who, having no children to hazard,[1] do not have an equal part in the risk. But as for you who have passed your prime, count as gain the greater portion of your life during which you were fortunate and remember that the remainder will be short; and be comforted by the fair fame of these your sons. For the love of honour alone is untouched by age, and when one comes to the ineffectual period of life it is not 'gain' as some say,[2] that gives the greater satisfaction, but honour.

XLV. "But for such of you here present as are sons and brothers of these men, I see the greatness of the conflict that awaits you—for the dead are always praised—and even were you to attain to surpassing virtue, hardly would you be judged, I will not say

στερημένος διὰ τὸ γῆρας ἡδονῶν ὑπὸ μιᾶς ἔτι γηροβοσκεῖται, τῆς ἀπὸ τοῦ κερδαίνειν, *Simonides replied to those who charged him with love of money, that, deprived by old age of other pleasures, he is still comforted by one, that of gain.*

κριθεῖτε. φθόνος γὰρ τοῖς ζῶσι πρὸς τὸ ἀντίπαλον,[1] τὸ δὲ μὴ ἐμποδὼν ἀνανταγωνίστῳ εὐνοίᾳ τετίμηται.

2 "Εἰ δέ με δεῖ καὶ γυναικείας τι ἀρετῆς, ὅσαι νῦν ἐν χηρείᾳ ἔσονται, μνησθῆναι, βραχείᾳ παραινέσει ἅπαν σημανῶ. τῆς τε γὰρ ὑπαρχούσης φύσεως μὴ χείροσι γενέσθαι ὑμῖν μεγάλη ἡ δόξα καὶ ἧς ἂν ἐπ' ἐλάχιστον ἀρετῆς πέρι ἢ ψόγου ἐν τοῖς ἄρσεσι κλέος ᾖ.

XLVI. "Εἴρηται καὶ ἐμοὶ λόγῳ κατὰ τὸν νόμον ὅσα εἶχον πρόσφορα, καὶ ἔργῳ οἱ θαπτόμενοι τὰ μὲν ἤδη κεκόσμηνται, τὰ δὲ αὐτῶν τοὺς παῖδας τὸ ἀπὸ τοῦδε δημοσίᾳ ἡ πόλις μέχρι ἥβης θρέψει, ὠφέλιμον στέφανον τοῖσδέ τε καὶ τοῖς λειπομένοις τῶν τοιῶνδε ἀγώνων προτιθεῖσα· ἆθλα γὰρ οἷς κεῖται ἀρετῆς μέγιστα, τοῖς δὲ καὶ
2 ἄνδρες ἄριστοι πολιτεύουσιν. νῦν δὲ ἀπολοφυράμενοι ὃν προσήκει ἑκάστῳ ἄπιτε."

XLVII. Τοιόσδε μὲν ὁ τάφος ἐγένετο ἐν τῷ χειμῶνι τούτῳ· καὶ διελθόντος αὐτοῦ πρῶτον
2 ἔτος τοῦ πολέμου τούτου ἐτελεύτα. τοῦ δὲ θέρους εὐθὺς ἀρχομένου Πελοποννήσιοι καὶ οἱ ξύμμαχοι τὰ δύο μέρη ὥσπερ καὶ τὸ πρῶτον ἐσέβαλον ἐς τὴν Ἀττικήν (ἡγεῖτο δὲ Ἀρχίδαμος ὁ Ζευξιδάμου, Λακεδαιμονίων βασιλεύς), καὶ καθε-
3 ζόμενοι ἐδῄουν τὴν γῆν. καὶ ὄντων αὐτῶν οὐ

[1] πρὸς τὸ ἀντίπαλον, the reading of ABFM[G]; τὸν ἀντίπαλον CE. Hude reads τῶν ἀντιπάλων, after Croiset.

their equals, but even a little inferior. For there is envy of the living on account of rivalry, but that which has been removed from our path is honoured with a good-will that knows no antagonism.

"If I am to speak also of womanly virtues, referring to those of you who will henceforth be in widowhood, I will sum up all in a brief admonition: Great is your glory if you fall not below the standard which nature has set for your sex, and great also is hers of whom there is least talk among men whether in praise or in blame.

XLVI. "I have now spoken, in obedience to the law, such words as I had that were fitting, and those whom we are burying have already in part also received their tribute in our deeds;[1] besides, the state will henceforth maintain their children at the public expense until they grow to manhood, thus offering both to the dead and to their survivors a crown of substantial worth as their prize in such contests. For where the prizes offered for virtue are greatest, there are found the best citizens. And now, when you have made due lament, each for his own dead, depart."

XLVII. Such were the funeral ceremonies that took place during this winter, the close of which brought the first year of this war to an end. At the very beginning of summer the Peloponnesians and their 430 B.C.
allies, with two-thirds of their forces as before,[2] invaded Attica, under the command of Archidamus, son of Zeuxidamus, king of the Lacedaemonians, and establishing themselves proceeded to ravage the country. And before they had been many days in

[1] *i.e.* the honours shown them throughout the rest of the ceremony, described in ch. xxxiv, as contrasted with the words of the eulogist. [2] *cf.* ch. x. 2.

πολλάς πω ἡμέρας ἐν τῇ Ἀττικῇ ἡ νόσος πρῶτον
ἤρξατο γενέσθαι τοῖς Ἀθηναίοις, λεγόμενον μὲν
καὶ πρότερον πολλαχόσε ἐγκατασκῆψαι καὶ περὶ
Λῆμνον καὶ ἐν ἄλλοις χωρίοις, οὐ μέντοι τοσοῦτός
γε λοιμὸς οὐδὲ φθορὰ οὕτως ἀνθρώπων οὐδαμοῦ
4 ἐμνημονεύετο γενέσθαι. οὔτε γὰρ ἰατροὶ ἤρκουν
τὸ πρῶτον θεραπεύοντες ἀγνοίᾳ, ἀλλ' αὐτοὶ μάλιστα ἔθνῃσκον ὅσῳ καὶ μάλιστα προσῄσαν,
οὔτε ἄλλη ἀνθρωπεία τέχνη οὐδεμία· ὅσα τε
πρὸς ἱεροῖς ἱκέτευσαν ἢ μαντείοις καὶ τοῖς τοιούτοις ἐχρήσαντο, πάντα ἀνωφελῆ ἦν, τελευτῶντές
τε αὐτῶν ἀπέστησαν ὑπὸ τοῦ κακοῦ νικώμενοι.

XLVIII. Ἤρξατο δὲ τὸ μὲν πρῶτον, ὡς λέγεται, ἐξ Αἰθιοπίας τῆς ὑπὲρ Αἰγύπτου, ἔπειτα
δὲ καὶ ἐς Αἴγυπτον καὶ Λιβύην κατέβη καὶ ἐς
2 τὴν βασιλέως γῆν τὴν πολλήν. ἐς δὲ τὴν Ἀθηναίων πόλιν ἐξαπιναίως ἐνέπεσε, καὶ τὸ πρῶτον ἐν τῷ Πειραιεῖ ἥψατο τῶν ἀνθρώπων, ὥστε
καὶ ἐλέχθη ὑπ' αὐτῶν ὡς οἱ Πελοποννήσιοι
φάρμακα ἐσβεβλήκοιεν ἐς τὰ φρέατα· κρῆναι
γὰρ οὔπω ἦσαν αὐτόθι. ὕστερον δὲ καὶ ἐς
τὴν ἄνω πόλιν ἀφίκετο καὶ ἔθνῃσκον πολλῷ
3 μᾶλλον ἤδη. λεγέτω μὲν οὖν περὶ αὐτοῦ ὡς
ἕκαστος γιγνώσκει καὶ ἰατρὸς καὶ ἰδιώτης ἀφ'
ὅτου εἰκὸς ἦν[1] γενέσθαι αὐτό, καὶ τὰς αἰτίας
ἅστινας νομίζει τοσαύτης μεταβολῆς ἱκανὰς
εἶναι·[2] ἐγὼ δὲ οἷόν τε ἐγίγνετο λέξω καὶ ἀφ'
ὧν ἄν τις σκοπῶν, εἴ ποτε καὶ αὖθις ἐπιπέσοι,

[1] ἦν: Hude deletes.

[2] δύναμιν ἐς τὸ μεταστῆσαι σχεῖν, in the MSS. after εἶναι, deleted by Gesner; Hude deletes ἱκανὰς εἶναι and ἐς τὸ μεταστῆσαι, with F. Mueller.

Attica the plague[1] began for the first time to show itself among the Athenians. It is said, indeed, to have broken out before in many places, both in Lemnos and elsewhere, though no pestilence of such extent nor any scourge so destructive of human lives is on record anywhere. For neither were physicians able to cope with the disease, since they at first had to treat it without knowing its nature, the mortality among them being greatest because they were most exposed to it, nor did any other human art avail. And the supplications made at sanctuaries, or appeals to oracles and the like, were all futile, and at last men desisted from them, overcome by the calamity.

XLVIII. The disease began, it is said, in Ethiopia beyond Egypt, and then descended into Egypt and Libya and spread over the greater part of the King's territory. Then it suddenly fell upon the city of Athens, and attacked first the inhabitants of the Peiraeus, so that the people there even said that the Peloponnesians had put poison in their cisterns; for there were as yet no public fountains there. But afterwards it reached the upper city also, and from that time the mortality became much greater. Now any one, whether physician or layman, may, each according to his personal opinion, speak about its probable origin and state the causes which, in his view, were sufficient to have produced so great a departure from normal conditions; but I shall describe its actual course, explaining the symptoms, from the study of which a person should be best able,

[1] It is perhaps impossible to identify the plague of Athens with any known disease. Grote describes it as an eruptive typhoid fever. It has perhaps more symptoms in common with typhus than with any other disease.

μάλιστ᾽ ἂν ἔχοι τι προειδὼς μὴ ἀγνοεῖν, ταῦτα δηλώσω αὐτός τε νοσήσας καὶ αὐτὸς ἰδὼν ἄλλους πάσχοντας.

XLIX. Τὸ μὲν γὰρ ἔτος, ὡς ὡμολογεῖτο ἐκ πάντων, μάλιστα δὴ ἐκεῖνο ἄνοσον ἐς τὰς ἄλλας ἀσθενείας ἐτύγχανεν ὄν· εἰ δέ τις καὶ προύκαμνέ
2 τι, ἐς τοῦτο πάντα ἀπεκρίθη. τοὺς δὲ ἄλλους ἀπ᾽ οὐδεμιᾶς προφάσεως, ἀλλ᾽ ἐξαίφνης ὑγιεῖς ὄντας πρῶτον μὲν τῆς κεφαλῆς θέρμαι ἰσχυραὶ καὶ τῶν ὀφθαλμῶν ἐρυθήματα καὶ φλόγωσις ἐλάμβανε, καὶ τὰ ἐντός, ἥ τε φάρυξ καὶ ἡ γλῶσσα, εὐθὺς αἱματώδη ἦν καὶ πνεῦμα ἄτοπον καὶ δυσῶδες
3 ἠφίει· ἔπειτα ἐξ αὐτῶν πταρμὸς καὶ βράγχος ἐπεγίγνετο, καὶ ἐν οὐ πολλῷ χρόνῳ κατέβαινεν ἐς τὰ στήθη ὁ πόνος μετὰ βηχὸς ἰσχυροῦ· καὶ ὁπότε ἐς τὴν καρδίαν στηρίξειεν, ἀνέστρεφέ τε αὐτὴν καὶ ἀποκαθάρσεις χολῆς πᾶσαι ὅσαι ὑπὸ ἰατρῶν
4 ὠνομασμέναι εἰσὶν ἐπῆσαν, καὶ αὐταὶ μετὰ ταλαιπωρίας μεγάλης, λύγξ τε τοῖς πλείοσιν ἐνέπιπτε κενὴ σπασμὸν ἐνδιδοῦσα ἰσχυρόν, τοῖς μὲν μετὰ ταῦτα λωφήσαντα, τοῖς δὲ καὶ πολλῷ ὕστερον.
5 καὶ τῷ μὲν ἔξωθεν ἁπτομένῳ τὸ[1] σῶμα οὔτ᾽ ἄγαν θερμὸν ἦν οὔτε χλωρόν, ἀλλ᾽ ὑπέρυθρον, πελιτνόν, φλυκταίναις μικραῖς καὶ ἕλκεσιν ἐξηνθηκός· τὰ δὲ ἐντὸς οὕτως ἐκαίετο ὥστε μήτε τῶν πάνυ λεπτῶν ἱματίων καὶ σινδόνων τὰς ἐπιβολὰς μηδ᾽ ἄλλο τι ἢ γυμνοὶ ἀνέχεσθαι, ἥδιστά τε ἂν ἐς ὕδωρ ψυχρὸν σφᾶς αὐτοὺς ῥίπτειν (καὶ πολλοὶ τοῦτο τῶν ἠμελημένων ἀνθρώπων καὶ ἔδρασαν ἐς φρέατα) τῇ δίψῃ ἀπαύστῳ ξυνεχόμενοι· καὶ ἐν τῷ ὁμοίῳ καθειστήκει τό τε πλέον καὶ ἔλασσον πο-

[1] Added by Hude.

having knowledge of it beforehand, to recognize it if it should ever break out again. For I had the disease myself and saw others sick of it.

XLIX. That year, as was agreed by all, happened to be unusually free from disease so far as regards the other maladies; but if anyone was already ill of any disease all terminated in this. In other cases from no obvious cause, but suddenly and while in good health, men were seized first with intense heat of the head, and redness and inflammation of the eyes, and the parts inside the mouth, both the throat and the tongue, immediately became blood-red and exhaled an unnatural and fetid breath. In the next stage sneezing and hoarseness came on, and in a short time the disorder descended to the chest, attended by severe coughing. And when it settled in the stomach, that was upset, and vomits of bile of every kind named by physicians ensued, these also attended by great distress; and in most cases ineffectual retching followed producing violent convulsions, which sometimes abated directly, sometimes not until long afterwards. Externally, the body was not so very warm to the touch; it was not pale, but reddish, livid, and breaking out in small blisters and ulcers. But internally it was consumed by such a heat that the patients could not bear to have on them the lightest coverings or linen sheets, but wanted to be quite uncovered and would have liked best to throw themselves into cold water—indeed many of those who were not looked after did throw themselves into cisterns—so tormented were they by thirst which could not be quenched; and it was all the same whether they drank much or little.

6 τόν. καὶ ἡ ἀπορία τοῦ μὴ ἡσυχάζειν καὶ ἡ ἀγρυ-
πνία ἐπέκειτο διὰ παντός. καὶ τὸ σῶμα, ὅσονπερ
χρόνον καὶ ἡ νόσος ἀκμάζοι, οὐκ ἐμαραίνετο, ἀλλ᾽
ἀντεῖχε παρὰ δόξαν τῇ ταλαιπωρίᾳ, ὥστε ἢ διεφθείροντο οἱ πλεῖστοι ἐναταῖοι καὶ ἑβδομαῖοι ὑπὸ
τοῦ ἐντὸς καύματος, ἔτι ἔχοντές τι δυνάμεως, ἢ εἰ
διαφύγοιεν, ἐπικατιόντος τοῦ νοσήματος ἐς τὴν
κοιλίαν καὶ ἑλκώσεώς τε αὐτῇ ἰσχυρᾶς ἐγγιγνο-
μένης καὶ διαρροίας ἅμα ἀκράτου ἐπιπιπτούσης
οἱ πολλοὶ ὕστερον διὰ τὴν ἀσθένειαν διεφθείροντο.
7 διεξῄει γὰρ διὰ παντὸς τοῦ σώματος ἄνωθεν ἀρξά-
μενον τὸ ἐν τῇ κεφαλῇ πρῶτον ἱδρυθὲν κακόν, καὶ
εἴ τις ἐκ τῶν μεγίστων περιγένοιτο, τῶν γε ἀκρω-
8 τηρίων ἀντίληψις αὐτοῦ ἐπεσήμαινεν· κατέσκηπτε
γὰρ καὶ ἐς αἰδοῖα καὶ ἐς ἄκρας χεῖρας καὶ πόδας,
καὶ πολλοὶ στερισκόμενοι τούτων διέφευγον, εἰσὶ
δ᾽ οἳ καὶ τῶν ὀφθαλμῶν. τοὺς δὲ καὶ λήθη ἔλαβε
τὸ παραυτίκα ἀναστάντας πάντων ὁμοίως καὶ
ἠγνόησαν σφᾶς τε αὐτοὺς καὶ τοὺς ἐπιτηδείους.

L. Γενόμενον γὰρ κρεῖσσον λόγου τὸ εἶδος τῆς
νόσου τά τε ἄλλα χαλεπωτέρως ἢ κατὰ τὴν ἀν-
θρωπείαν φύσιν προσέπιπτεν ἑκάστῳ καὶ ἐν τῷδε
ἐδήλωσε μάλιστα ἄλλο τι ὂν ἢ τῶν ξυντρόφων τι·
τὰ γὰρ ὄρνεα καὶ τετράποδα ὅσα ἀνθρώπων ἅπτε-
ται πολλῶν ἀτάφων γενομένων ἢ οὐ προσῄει ἢ
2 γευσάμενα διεφθείρετο. τεκμήριον δέ· τῶν μὲν

They were also beset by restlessness and sleeplessness which never abated. And the body was not wasted while the disease was at its height, but resisted surprisingly the ravages of the disease, so that when the patients died, as most of them did on the seventh or ninth day from the internal heat, they still had some strength left; or, if they passed the crisis, the disease went down into the bowels, producing there a violent ulceration, and at the same time an acute diarrhoea set in, so that in this later stage most of them perished through weakness caused by it. For the malady, starting from the head where it was first seated, passed down until it spread through the whole body, and if one got over the worst, it seized upon the extremities at least and left its marks there; for it attacked the privates and fingers and toes, and many escaped with the loss of these, though some lost their eyes also.[1] In some cases the sufferer was attacked immediately after recovery by loss of memory, which extended to every object alike, so that they failed to recognize either themselves or their friends.

L. Indeed the character of the disease proved such that it baffles description, the violence of the attack being in each case too great for human nature to endure, while in one way in particular it showed plainly that it was different from any of the familiar diseases: the birds, namely, and the fourfooted animals, which usually feed upon human bodies, either would not now come near them, though many lay unburied, or died if they tasted of them. The evidence for this is that birds of this kind became

[1] Evidently as the result of gangrene, due to stoppage of circulation. This after-effect of typhus was of common occurrence in the outbreak in the Balkans in 1915.

τοιούτων ὀρνίθων ἐπίλειψις σαφὴς ἐγένετο, καὶ
οὐχ ἑωρῶντο οὔτε ἄλλως οὔτε περὶ τοιοῦτον οὐδέν·
οἱ δὲ κύνες μᾶλλον αἴσθησιν παρεῖχον τοῦ ἀπο-
βαίνοντος διὰ τὸ ξυνδιαιτᾶσθαι.

LI. Τὸ μὲν οὖν νόσημα, πολλὰ καὶ ἄλλα παρα-
λιπόντι ἀτοπίας, ὡς ἑκάστῳ ἐτύγχανέ τι διαφερόντως ἑτέρῳ πρὸς ἕτερον γιγνόμενον, τοιοῦτον ἦν
ἐπὶ πᾶν τὴν ἰδέαν. καὶ ἄλλο παρελύπει κατ'
ἐκεῖνον τὸν χρόνον οὐδὲν τῶν εἰωθότων· ὃ δὲ καὶ
2 γένοιτο, ἐς τοῦτο ἐτελεύτα. ἔθνῃσκον δὲ οἱ μὲν
ἀμελείᾳ, οἱ δὲ καὶ πάνυ θεραπευόμενοι. ἕν τε
οὐδὲν κατέστη ἴαμα ὡς εἰπεῖν ὅ τι χρῆν προσφέ-
ροντας ὠφελεῖν (τὸ γάρ τῳ ξυνενεγκὸν ἄλλον
3 τοῦτο ἔβλαπτε), σῶμά τε αὔταρκες ὂν οὐδὲν διε-
φάνη πρὸς αὐτὸ ἰσχύος πέρι ἢ ἀσθενείας, ἀλλὰ
πάντα ξυνῄρει καὶ τὰ πάσῃ διαίτῃ θεραπευόμενα.
4 δεινότατον δὲ παντὸς ἦν τοῦ κακοῦ ἥ τε ἀθυμία,
ὁπότε τις αἴσθοιτο κάμνων (πρὸς γὰρ τὸ ἀνέλ-
πιστον εὐθὺς τραπόμενοι τῇ γνώμῃ πολλῷ μᾶλλον προίεντο σφᾶς αὐτοὺς καὶ οὐκ ἀντεῖχον), καὶ
ὅτι ἕτερος ἀφ' ἑτέρου θεραπείᾳ ἀναπιμπλάμενοι
ὥσπερ τὰ πρόβατα ἔθνῃσκον· καὶ τὸν πλεῖστον
5 φθόρον τοῦτο ἐνεποίει. εἴτε γὰρ μὴ 'θέλοιεν δεδιότες ἀλλήλοις προσιέναι, ἀπώλλυντο ἐρῆμοι,
καὶ οἰκίαι πολλαὶ ἐκενώθησαν ἀπορίᾳ τοῦ θερα-
πεύσοντος· εἴτε προσίοιεν, διεφθείροντο, καὶ μά-

noticeably scarce, and they were no longer to be seen either about the bodies or anywhere else; while the dogs gave a still better opportunity to observe what happened, because they live with man.

LI. Such, then, was the general nature of the disease; for I pass over many of the unusual symptoms, since it chanced to affect one man differently as compared with another. And while the plague lasted there were none of the usual complaints, though if any did occur it ended in this. Sometimes death was due to neglect, but sometimes it occurred in spite of careful nursing. And no one remedy was found, I may say, which was sure to bring relief to those applying it—for what helped one man hurt another—and no constitution, as it proved, was of itself sufficient against it, whether as regards physical strength or weakness,[1] but it carried off all without distinction, even those tended with all medical care. And the most dreadful thing about the whole malady was not only the despondency of the victims, when they once became aware that they were sick, for their minds straightway yielded to despair and they gave themselves up for lost instead of resisting, but also the fact that they became infected by nursing one another and died like sheep. And this caused the heaviest mortality; for if, on the one hand, they were restrained by fear from visiting one another, the sick perished uncared for, so that many houses were left empty through lack of anyone to do the nursing; or if, on the other hand, they visited the sick, they perished,

[1] *i.e.* "no constitution was of itself strong enough to resist or weak enough to escape the attacks" (Jowett).

λιστα οἱ ἀρετῆς τι μεταποιούμενοι· αἰσχύνῃ γὰρ ἠφείδουν σφῶν αὐτῶν ἐσιόντες παρὰ τοὺς φίλους, ἐπεὶ καὶ τὰς ὀλοφύρσεις τῶν ἀπογιγνομένων τελευτῶντες καὶ οἱ οἰκεῖοι ἐξέκαμνον ὑπὸ τοῦ πολλοῦ
6 κακοῦ νικώμενοι. ἐπὶ πλέον δ' ὅμως οἱ διαπεφευγότες τόν τε θνῄσκοντα καὶ τὸν πονούμενον ᾠκτίζοντο διὰ τὸ προειδέναι τε καὶ αὐτοὶ ἤδη ἐν τῷ θαρσαλέῳ εἶναι· δὶς γὰρ τὸν αὐτόν, ὥστε καὶ κτείνειν, οὐκ ἐπελάμβανεν. καὶ ἐμακαρίζοντό τε ὑπὸ τῶν ἄλλων καὶ αὐτοὶ τῷ παραχρῆμα περιχαρεῖ καὶ ἐς τὸν ἔπειτα χρόνον ἐλπίδος τι εἶχον κούφης μηδ' ἂν ὑπ' ἄλλου νοσήματός ποτε ἔτι διαφθαρῆναι.

LII. Ἐπίεσε δ' αὐτοὺς μᾶλλον πρὸς τῷ ὑπάρχοντι πόνῳ καὶ ἡ ξυγκομιδὴ ἐκ τῶν ἀγρῶν ἐς τὸ
2 ἄστυ, καὶ οὐχ ἧσσον τοὺς ἐπελθόντας. οἰκιῶν γὰρ οὐχ ὑπαρχουσῶν, ἀλλ' ἐν καλύβαις πνιγηραῖς ὥρᾳ ἔτους διαιτωμένων ὁ φθόρος ἐγίγνετο οὐδενὶ κόσμῳ, ἀλλὰ καὶ νεκροὶ ἐπ' ἀλλήλοις ἀποθνῄσκοντες ἔκειντο καὶ ἐν ταῖς ὁδοῖς ἐκαλινδοῦντο καὶ περὶ τὰς κρήνας ἁπάσας ἡμιθνῆτες τοῦ ὕδατος
3 ἐπιθυμίᾳ. τά τε ἱερὰ ἐν οἷς ἐσκήνηντο νεκρῶν πλέα ἦν, αὐτοῦ ἐναποθνῃσκόντων· ὑπερβιαζομένου γὰρ τοῦ κακοῦ οἱ ἄνθρωποι, οὐκ ἔχοντες ὅ τι γένωνται, ἐς ὀλιγωρίαν ἐτράποντο καὶ ἱερῶν
4 καὶ ὁσίων ὁμοίως. νόμοι τε πάντες ξυνεταράχθησαν οἷς ἐχρῶντο πρότερον περὶ τὰς ταφάς,

especially those who made any pretensions to goodness. For these made it a point of honour to visit their friends without sparing themselves at a time when the very relatives of the dying, overwhelmed by the magnitude of the calamity, were growing weary even of making their lamentations. But still it was more often those who had recovered who had pity for the dying and the sick, because they had learnt what it meant and were themselves by this time confident of immunity; for the disease never attacked the same man a second time, at least not with fatal results. And they were not only congratulated by everybody else, but themselves, in the excess of their joy at the moment, cherished also a fond fancy with regard to the rest of their lives that they would never be carried off by any other disease.

LII. But in addition to the trouble under which they already laboured, the Athenians suffered further hardship owing to the crowding into the city of the people from the country districts; and this affected the new arrivals especially. For since no houses were available for them and they had to live in huts that were stifling in the hot season, they perished in wild disorder. Bodies of dying men lay one upon another, and half-dead people rolled about in the streets and, in their longing for water, near all the fountains. The temples, too, in which they had quartered themselves were full of the corpses of those who had died in them; for the calamity which weighed upon them was so overpowering that men, not knowing what was to become of them, became careless of all law, sacred as well as profane. And the customs which they had hitherto observed regarding burial were all thrown into confusion, and

ἔθαπτον δὲ ὡς ἕκαστος ἐδύνατο. καὶ πολλοὶ ἐς ἀναισχύντους θήκας ἐτράποντο σπάνει τῶν ἐπιτηδείων διὰ τὸ συχνοὺς ἤδη προτεθνάναι σφίσιν· ἐπὶ πυρὰς γὰρ ἀλλοτρίας φθάσαντες τοὺς νήσαντας οἱ μὲν ἐπιθέντες τὸν ἑαυτῶν νεκρὸν ὑφῆπτον, οἱ δὲ καιομένου ἄλλου ἐπιβαλόντες ἄνωθεν ὃν φέροιεν ἀπῇσαν.

LIII. Πρῶτόν τε ἦρξε καὶ ἐς τἆλλα τῇ πόλει ἐπὶ πλέον ἀνομίας τὸ νόσημα. ῥᾷον γὰρ ἐτόλμα τις ἃ πρότερον ἀπεκρύπτετο μὴ καθ' ἡδονὴν ποιεῖν, ἀγχίστροφον τὴν μεταβολὴν ὁρῶντες τῶν τε εὐδαιμόνων καὶ αἰφνιδίως θνῃσκόντων καὶ τῶν οὐδὲν πρότερον κεκτημένων, εὐθὺς δὲ τἀκείνων
2 ἐχόντων. ὥστε ταχείας τὰς ἐπαυρέσεις καὶ πρὸς τὸ τερπνὸν ἠξίουν ποιεῖσθαι, ἐφήμερα τά τε σώ-
3 ματα καὶ τὰ χρήματα ὁμοίως ἡγούμενοι. καὶ τὸ μὲν προταλαιπωρεῖν[1] τῷ δόξαντι καλῷ οὐδεὶς πρόθυμος ἦν, ἄδηλον νομίζων εἰ πρὶν ἐπ' αὐτὸ ἐλθεῖν διαφθαρήσεται, ὅ τι δὲ ἤδη τε ἡδὺ πανταχόθεν τε ἐς αὐτὸ κερδαλέον, τοῦτο καὶ καλὸν καὶ χρήσιμον
4 κατέστη. θεῶν δὲ φόβος ἢ ἀνθρώπων νόμος οὐδεὶς ἀπεῖργε, τὸ μὲν κρίνοντες ἐν ὁμοίῳ καὶ σέβειν καὶ μὴ ἐκ τοῦ πάντας ὁρᾶν ἐν ἴσῳ ἀπολλυμένους, τῶν δὲ ἁμαρτημάτων οὐδεὶς ἐλπίζων μέχρι τοῦ

[1] With CE, the other MSS. προσταλαιπωρεῖν.

---

[1] *i.e.* they concealed the fact that they were acting after their own pleasure (the μὴ being induced by the negative idea in ἀπεκρύπτετο).

they buried their dead each one as he could. And many resorted to shameless modes of burial because so many members of their households had already died that they lacked the proper funeral materials. Resorting to other people's pyres, some, anticipating those who had raised them, would put on their own dead and kindle the fire; others would throw the body they were carrying upon one which was already burning and go away.

LIII. In other respects also the plague first introduced into the city a greater lawlessness. For where men hitherto practised concealment, that they were not acting purely after their pleasure,[1] they now showed a more careless daring. They saw how sudden was the change of fortune in the case both of those who were prosperous and suddenly died, and of those who before had nothing but in a moment were in possession of the property of the others. And so they resolved to get out of life the pleasures which could be had speedily and would satisfy their lusts, regarding their bodies and their wealth alike as transitory. And no one was eager to practise self-denial in prospect of what was esteemed honour,[2] because everyone thought that it was doubtful whether he would live to attain it, but the pleasure of the moment and whatever was in any way conducive to it came to be regarded as at once honourable and expedient. No fear of gods or law of men restrained; for, on the one hand, seeing that all men were perishing alike, they judged that piety and impiety came to the same thing, and, on the other, no one expected that he

[2] Or, reading προσταλαιπωρεῖν, "to take trouble about what was esteemed honour."

δίκην γενέσθαι βιοὺς ἂν τὴν τιμωρίαν ἀντιδοῦναι,
πολὺ δὲ μείζω τὴν ἤδη κατεψηφισμένην σφῶν
ἐπικρεμασθῆναι, ἣν πρὶν ἐμπεσεῖν εἰκὸς εἶναι τοῦ
βίου τι ἀπολαῦσαι.

LIV. Τοιούτῳ μὲν πάθει οἱ Ἀθηναῖοι περιπεσόντες ἐπιέζοντο, ἀνθρώπων τ' ἔνδον θνῃσκόντων
2 καὶ γῆς ἔξω δῃουμένης. ἐν δὲ τῷ κακῷ οἷα εἰκὸς
ἀνεμνήσθησαν καὶ τοῦδε τοῦ ἔπους, φάσκοντες οἱ
πρεσβύτεροι πάλαι ᾄδεσθαι "Ἥξει Δωριακὸς πό-
3 λεμος καὶ λοιμὸς ἅμ' αὐτῷ." ἐγένετο μὲν οὖν ἔρις
τοῖς ἀνθρώποις μὴ λοιμὸν ὠνομάσθαι ἐν τῷ ἔπει
ὑπὸ τῶν παλαιῶν, ἀλλὰ λιμόν, ἐνίκησε δὲ ἐπὶ τοῦ
παρόντος εἰκότως λοιμὸν εἰρῆσθαι· οἱ γὰρ ἄνθρωποι πρὸς ἃ ἔπασχον τὴν μνήμην ἐποιοῦντο. ἢν
δέ γε οἶμαί ποτε ἄλλος πόλεμος καταλάβῃ Δω-
ρικὸς τοῦδε ὕστερος καὶ ξυμβῇ γενέσθαι λιμόν,
4 κατὰ τὸ εἰκὸς οὕτως ᾄσονται. μνήμη δὲ ἐγένετο
καὶ τοῦ Λακεδαιμονίων χρηστηρίου τοῖς εἰδόσιν,
ὅτε ἐπερωτῶσιν αὐτοῖς τὸν θεὸν εἰ χρὴ πολεμεῖν
ἀνεῖλε κατὰ κράτος πολεμοῦσι νίκην ἔσεσθαι, καὶ
5 αὐτὸς ἔφη ξυλλήψεσθαι. περὶ μὲν οὖν τοῦ χρηστηρίου τὰ γιγνόμενα ᾔκαζον ὁμοῖα εἶναι· ἐσβεβληκότων δὲ τῶν Πελοποννησίων ἡ νόσος ἤρξατο
εὐθύς. καὶ ἐς μὲν Πελοπόννησον οὐκ ἐσῆλθεν, ὅ
τι καὶ ἄξιον εἰπεῖν, ἐπενείματο δὲ Ἀθήνας μὲν

---

[1] *cf.* I. cxviii. 3.

would live to be called to account and pay the penalty of his misdeeds. On the contrary, they believed that the penalty already decreed against them, and now hanging over their heads, was a far heavier one, and that before this fell it was only reasonable to get some enjoyment out of life.

LIV. Such then was the calamity that had befallen them by which the Athenians were sore pressed, their people dying within the walls and their land being ravaged without. And in their distress they recalled, as was natural, the following verse which their older men said had long ago been uttered:

"A Dorian war shall come and pestilence with it."

A dispute arose, however, among the people, some contending that the word used in the verse by the ancients was not λοιμός, "pestilence," but λιμός, "famine," and the view prevailed at the time that "pestilence" was the original word; and quite naturally, for men's recollections conformed to their sufferings. But if ever another Dorian war should visit them after the present war and a famine happen to come with it, they would probably, I fancy, recite the verse in that way. Those, too, who were familiar with it, recalled that other oracle given to the Lacedaemonians, when, in answer to their inquiry whether they should go to war, the god responded that if they "warred with all their might victory would be theirs," adding that he himself would assist them.[1] Now so far as the oracle is concerned, they surmised that what was then happening was its fulfilment, for the plague broke out immediately after the Peloponnesians had invaded Attica; and though it did not enter the Peloponnesus to any extent, it devastated Athens most of all, and next

μάλιστα, ἔπειτα δὲ καὶ τῶν ἄλλων χωρίων τὰ πολυανθρωπότατα. ταῦτα μὲν τὰ κατὰ τὴν νόσον γενόμενα.

LV. Οἱ δὲ Πελοποννήσιοι ἐπειδὴ ἔτεμον τὸ πεδίον, παρῆλθον ἐς τὴν Πάραλον γῆν καλουμένην μέχρι Λαυρείου, οὗ τὰ ἀργύρεια μέταλλά ἐστιν Ἀθηναίοις. καὶ πρῶτον μὲν ἔτεμον ταύτην ᾗ πρὸς Πελοπόννησον ὁρᾷ, ἔπειτα δὲ τὴν πρὸς
2 Εὔβοιάν τε καὶ Ἄνδρον τετραμμένην. Περικλῆς δὲ στρατηγὸς ὢν καὶ τότε περὶ μὲν τοῦ μὴ ἐπεξιέναι τοὺς Ἀθηναίους τὴν αὐτὴν γνώμην εἶχεν ὥσπερ καὶ ἐν τῇ προτέρᾳ ἐσβολῇ.

LVI. Ἔτι δ' αὐτῶν ἐν τῷ πεδίῳ ὄντων, πρὶν ἐς τὴν παραλίαν ἐλθεῖν, ἑκατὸν νεῶν ἐπίπλουν τῇ Πελοποννήσῳ παρεσκευάζετο, καὶ ἐπειδὴ
2 ἑτοῖμα ἦν, ἀνήγετο. ἦγε δ' ἐπὶ τῶν νεῶν ὁπλίτας Ἀθηναίων τετρακισχιλίους καὶ ἱππέας τριακοσίους ἐν ναυσὶν ἱππαγωγοῖς πρῶτον τότε ἐκ τῶν παλαιῶν νεῶν ποιηθείσαις· ξυνεστρατεύοντο δὲ
3 καὶ Χῖοι καὶ Λέσβιοι πεντήκοντα ναυσίν. ὅτε δὲ ἀνήγετο ἡ στρατιὰ αὕτη Ἀθηναίων, Πελοποννησίους κατέλιπον τῆς Ἀττικῆς ὄντας ἐν τῇ
4 παραλίᾳ. ἀφικόμενοι δὲ ἐς Ἐπίδαυρον τῆς Πελοποννήσου ἔτεμον τῆς γῆς τὴν πολλήν, καὶ πρὸς τὴν πόλιν προσβαλόντες ἐς ἐλπίδα μὲν ἦλθον
5 τοῦ ἑλεῖν, οὐ μέντοι προυχώρησέ γε. ἀναγαγόμενοι δὲ ἐκ τῆς Ἐπιδαύρου ἔτεμον τήν τε Τροζηνίδα γῆν καὶ Ἁλιάδα καὶ Ἑρμιονίδα· ἔστι δὲ ταῦτα πάντα ἐπιθαλάσσια τῆς Πελοποννήσου.
6 ἄραντες δὲ ἀπ' αὐτῶν ἀφίκοντο ἐς Πρασιάς, τῆς

to Athens the places which had the densest population. So much for the history of the plague.

LV. The Peloponnesians, after ravaging the plain, advanced into the district called Paralus[1] as far as Laurium, where are the silver mines of the Athenians. And first they ravaged that part of this district which looked towards the Peloponnesus, and afterwards the part facing Euboea and Andros. But Pericles, who was general, still held to the same policy as during the earlier invasion, insisting that the Athenians should not take the field against them.

LVI. But before they had left the plain and entered the Paralus, Pericles had begun to equip a fleet of a hundred ships to sail against the Peloponnesus, and when all was ready he put to sea. He took with him on the ships four thousand Athenian hoplites and three hundred cavalry in horse-transports, then employed for the first time, which had been made out of the old galleys. The Chians and Lesbians also took part in the expedition with fifty ships. And when this armament of the Athenians put to sea, the Peloponnesians whom they left in Attica were already in the Paralian district. On reaching Epidaurus in the Peloponnesus the Athenians ravaged most of that land; they also attacked the city, but, though they at first had hopes of taking it, they did not succeed. Then, leaving Epidaurus, they went to sea again, and ravaged the territory of Troezen, Halieis, and Hermione, which are all on the Peloponnesian coast. Sailing next from this region they

[1] The plain referred to was that about Athens, while the Paralian district was the sea-coast, or south-eastern part, terminating in the promontory of Sunium.

Λακωνικῆς πόλισμα ἐπιθαλάσσιον, καὶ τῆς τε γῆς ἔτεμον καὶ αὐτὸ τὸ πόλισμα εἷλον καὶ ἐπόρθησαν. ταῦτα δὲ ποιήσαντες ἐπ' οἴκου ἀνεχώρησαν. τοὺς δὲ Πελοποννησίους οὐκέτι κατέλαβον ἐν τῇ Ἀττικῇ ὄντας, ἀλλ' ἀνακεχωρηκότας.

LVII. Ὅσον δὲ χρόνον οἵ τε Πελοποννήσιοι ἦσαν ἐν τῇ γῇ τῇ Ἀθηναίων καὶ οἱ Ἀθηναῖοι ἐστράτευον ἐπὶ τῶν νεῶν, ἡ νόσος ἔν τε τῇ στρατιᾷ τοὺς Ἀθηναίους ἔφθειρε καὶ ἐν τῇ πόλει, ὥστε καὶ ἐλέχθη τοὺς Πελοποννησίους δείσαντας τὸ νόσημα, ὡς ἐπυνθάνοντο τῶν αὐτομόλων ὅτι ἐν τῇ πόλει εἴη καὶ θάπτοντας ἅμα ᾐσθάνοντο,
2 θᾶσσον ἐκ τῆς γῆς ἐξελθεῖν. τῇ δὲ ἐσβολῇ ταύτῃ πλεῖστόν τε χρόνον ἐνέμειναν καὶ τὴν γῆν πᾶσαν ἔτεμον· ἡμέρας γὰρ τεσσαράκοντα μάλιστα ἐν τῇ γῇ τῇ Ἀττικῇ ἐγένοντο.

LVIII. Τοῦ δ' αὐτοῦ θέρους Ἅγνων ὁ Νικίου καὶ Κλεόπομπος ὁ Κλεινίου, ξυστράτηγοι ὄντες Περικλέους, λαβόντες τὴν στρατιὰν ᾗπερ ἐκεῖνος ἐχρήσατο ἐστράτευσαν εὐθὺς ἐπὶ Χαλκιδέας τοὺς ἐπὶ Θρᾴκης καὶ Ποτείδαιαν ἔτι πολιορκουμένην, ἀφικόμενοι δὲ μηχανάς τε τῇ Ποτειδαίᾳ προσέ-
2 φερον καὶ παντὶ τρόπῳ ἐπειρῶντο ἑλεῖν. προυχώρει δὲ αὐτοῖς οὔτε ἡ αἵρεσις τῆς πόλεως οὔτε τἆλλα τῆς παρασκευῆς ἀξίως· ἐπιγενομένη γὰρ ἡ νόσος ἐνταῦθα δὴ πάνυ ἐπίεσε τοὺς Ἀθηναίους, φθείρουσα τὴν στρατιάν, ὥστε καὶ τοὺς προτέρους στρατιώτας νοσῆσαι τῶν Ἀθηναίων ἀπὸ τῆς ξὺν Ἅγνωνι στρατιᾶς ἐν τῷ πρὸ τοῦ

---

[1] On the expedition against the Peloponnesian coasts, *cf.* ch. lvi.
[2] *cf.* I. lxiv.

came to Prasiae, a town on the coast of Laconia, where they not only ravaged parts of the country, but also captured the town itself and pillaged it. After they had completed these operations they went back home, where they found that the Peloponnesians were no longer in Attica but had retired.

LVII. During this entire period, while the Peloponnesians were in Attica and the fleet of the Athenians was on the expedition, the plague was making havoc among the Athenians, both in their fleet and in the city. The statement was therefore made that the Peloponnesians left Attica in haste because they were afraid of the disease, since they not only heard from deserters that it was in the city, but also could see them burning their dead. In this invasion, however, they remained in Attica longer than at any other time, and also ravaged the entire country; indeed they were in Attica almost forty days.

LVIII. In the same summer Hagnon son of Nicias and Cleopompus son of Clinias, colleagues of Pericles, taking the armament which he had employed,[1] at once set out on an expedition against the Chalcidians in Thrace and against Potidaea, which was still under siege,[2] and on their arrival they brought siege-engines to bear upon Potidaea, and tried in every way to take it. But no success commensurate with the appointments of the expedition attended their efforts, either in their attempt to capture the city or otherwise; for the plague broke out and sorely distressed the Athenians there, playing such havoc in the army that even the Athenian soldiers of the first expedition,[3] who had hitherto been in good health, caught the infection

[3] The 3,000 soldiers of the first expedition; *cf.* ch. xxxi. 2 and I. lxi. 4.

χρόνῳ ὑγιαίνοντας. Φορμίων δὲ καὶ οἱ ἑξακόσιοι
3 καὶ χίλιοι οὐκέτι ἦσαν περὶ Χαλκιδέας. ὁ μὲν
οὖν Ἅγνων ἀνεχώρησε ταῖς ναυσὶν ἐς τὰς Ἀθήνας, ἀπὸ τετρακισχιλίων ὁπλιτῶν χιλίους καὶ πεντήκοντα τῇ νόσῳ ἀπολέσας ἐν τεσσαράκοντα μάλιστα ἡμέραις· οἱ δὲ πρότεροι στρατιῶται κατὰ χώραν μένοντες ἐπολιόρκουν τὴν Ποτείδαιαν.

LIX. Μετὰ δὲ τὴν δευτέραν ἐσβολὴν τῶν Πελοποννησίων οἱ Ἀθηναῖοι, ὡς ἥ τε γῆ αὐτῶν ἐτέτμητο τὸ δεύτερον καὶ ἡ νόσος ἐπέκειτο ἅμα
2 καὶ ὁ πόλεμος, ἠλλοίωντο τὰς γνώμας, καὶ τὸν
μὲν Περικλέα ἐν αἰτίᾳ εἶχον ὡς πείσαντα σφᾶς πολεμεῖν καὶ δι' ἐκεῖνον ταῖς ξυμφοραῖς περιπεπτωκότες, πρὸς δὲ τοὺς Λακεδαιμονίους ὥρμηντο ξυγχωρεῖν· καὶ πρέσβεις τινὰς πέμψαντες ὡς αὐτοὺς ἄπρακτοι ἐγένοντο. πανταχόθεν τε τῇ γνώμῃ ἄποροι καθεστηκότες ἐνέκειντο τῷ
3 Περικλεῖ. ὁ δὲ ὁρῶν αὐτοὺς πρὸς τὰ παρόντα
χαλεπαίνοντας καὶ πάντα ποιοῦντας ἅπερ αὐτὸς ἤλπιζε, ξύλλογον ποιήσας (ἔτι δ' ἐστρατήγει) ἐβούλετο θαρσῦναί τε καὶ ἀπαγαγὼν τὸ ὀργιζόμενον τῆς γνώμης πρὸς τὸ ἠπιώτερον καὶ ἀδεέστερον καταστῆσαι· παρελθὼν δὲ ἔλεξε τοιάδε.

LX. "Καὶ προσδεχομένῳ μοι τὰ τῆς ὀργῆς ὑμῶν ἔς με γεγένηται (αἰσθάνομαι γὰρ τὰς αἰτίας) καὶ ἐκκλησίαν τούτου ἕνεκα ξυνήγαγον, ὅπως ὑπομνήσω καὶ μέμψωμαι εἴ τι μὴ ὀρθῶς ἢ ἐμοὶ

from Hagnon's troops. Phormio, however, and his sixteen hundred men, were no longer in Chalcidice.[1] Accordingly Hagnon took his fleet back to Athens, having lost by the plague in about forty days one thousand and fifty out of a total of four thousand hoplites; but the soldiers of the former expedition remained where they were and continued the siege of Potidaea.

LIX. After the second invasion of the Peloponnesians the Athenians underwent a change of feeling, now that their land had been ravaged a second time while the plague and the war combined lay heavily upon them. They blamed Pericles for having persuaded them to go to war and held him responsible for the misfortunes which had befallen them, and were eager to come to an agreement with the Lacedaemonians. They even sent envoys to them, but accomplished nothing. And now, being altogether at their wits' end, they assailed Pericles. And when he saw that they were exasperated by the present situation and were acting exactly as he had himself expected, he called a meeting of the assembly—for he was still general—wishing to reassure them, and by ridding their minds of resentment to bring them to a milder and less timorous mood. So he came forward and spoke as follows:

LX. "I have been expecting these manifestations of your wrath against me, knowing as I do the causes of your anger, and my purpose in calling an assembly was that I might address to you certain reminders, and remonstrate if in any case you are either angry

[1] *cf.* I. lxiv. 2. Phormio's departure must have occurred before the events described in ch. xxxi. 2, but is nowhere mentioned.

2 χαλεπαίνετε ἢ ταῖς ξυμφοραῖς εἴκετε. ἐγὼ γὰρ
ἡγοῦμαι πόλιν πλείω ξύμπασαν ὀρθουμένην ὠφελεῖν τοὺς ἰδιώτας ἢ καθ' ἕκαστον τῶν πολιτῶν
3 εὐπραγοῦσαν, ἁθρόαν δὲ σφαλλομένην. καλῶς
μὲν γὰρ φερόμενος ἀνὴρ τὸ καθ' ἑαυτὸν διαφθειρο-
μένης τῆς πατρίδος οὐδὲν ἧσσον ξυναπόλλυται,
κακοτυχῶν δὲ ἐν εὐτυχούσῃ πολλῷ μᾶλλον
4 διασῴζεται. ὁπότε οὖν πόλις μὲν τὰς ἰδίας
ξυμφορὰς οἵα τε φέρειν, εἷς δὲ ἕκαστος τὰς ἐκείνης
ἀδύνατος, πῶς οὐ χρὴ πάντας ἀμύνειν αὐτῇ, καὶ
μὴ ὃ νῦν ὑμεῖς δρᾶτε, ταῖς κατ' οἶκον κακο-
πραγίαις ἐκπεπληγμένοι τοῦ κοινοῦ τῆς σωτηρίας
ἀφίεσθε, καὶ ἐμέ τε τὸν παραινέσαντα πολεμεῖν
καὶ ὑμᾶς αὐτοὺς οἳ ξυνέγνωτε δι' αἰτίας ἔχετε.
5 καίτοι ἐμοὶ τοιούτῳ ἀνδρὶ ὀργίζεσθε ὃς οὐδενὸς
ἥσσων οἴομαι εἶναι γνῶναί τε τὰ δέοντα καὶ
ἑρμηνεῦσαι ταῦτα, φιλόπολίς τε καὶ χρημάτων
6 κρείσσων. ὅ τε γὰρ γνοὺς καὶ μὴ σαφῶς διδάξας
ἐν ἴσῳ καὶ εἰ μὴ ἐνεθυμήθη· ὅ τε ἔχων ἀμφότερα,
τῇ δὲ πόλει δύσνους, οὐκ ἂν ὁμοίως τι οἰκείως
φράζοι· προσόντος δὲ καὶ τοῦδε, χρήμασι δὲ
νικωμένου, τὰ ξύμπαντα τούτου ἑνὸς ἂν πωλοῖτο.
7 ὥστ' εἴ μοι καὶ μέσως ἡγούμενοι μᾶλλον ἑτέρων
προσεῖναι αὐτὰ πολεμεῖν ἐπείσθητε, οὐκ ἂν
εἰκότως νῦν τοῦ γε ἀδικεῖν αἰτίαν φεροίμην.

with me or are giving way to your misfortunes without reason. For in my judgment a state confers a greater benefit upon its private citizens when as a whole commonwealth it is successful, than when it prospers as regards the individual but fails as a community. For even though a man flourishes in his own private affairs, yet if his country goes to ruin he perishes with her all the same; but if he is in evil fortune and his country in good fortune, he is far more likely to come through safely. Since, then, the state may bear the misfortunes of her private citizens but the individual cannot bear hers, surely all men ought to defend her, and not to do as you are now doing—proposing to sacrifice the safety of the commonwealth because you are dismayed by the hardships you suffer at home, and are blaming both me who advised you to make war and yourselves who voted with me for it. And yet I, with whom you are angry, am as competent as any man, I think, both to determine upon the right measures and to expound them, and as good a patriot and superior to the influence of money. For he who determines upon a policy, and fails to lay it clearly before others, is in the same case as if he never had a conception of it; and he who has both gifts, but is disloyal to his country, cannot speak with the same unselfish devotion; and if he have loyalty also, but a loyalty that cannot resist money, then for that alone everything will be on sale. If, therefore, when you allowed me to persuade you to go to war, you believed that I possessed these qualities even in a moderate degree more than other men, it is unreasonable that I should now bear the blame, at any rate, of wrongdoing.

LXI. "Καὶ γὰρ οἷς μὲν αἵρεσις γεγένηται τἆλλα εὐτυχοῦσι, πολλὴ ἄνοια πολεμῆσαι· εἰ δ' ἀναγκαῖον ἦν ἢ εἴξαντας εὐθὺς τοῖς πέλας ὑπακοῦσαι ἢ κινδυνεύσαντας περιγενέσθαι, ὁ φυγὼν
2 τὸν κίνδυνον τοῦ ὑποστάντος μεμπτότερος. καὶ ἐγὼ μὲν ὁ αὐτός εἰμι καὶ οὐκ ἐξίσταμαι· ὑμεῖς δὲ μεταβάλλετε, ἐπειδὴ ξυνέβη ὑμῖν πεισθῆναι μὲν ἀκεραίοις, μεταμέλειν δὲ κακουμένοις, καὶ τὸν ἐμὸν λόγον ἐν τῷ ὑμετέρῳ ἀσθενεῖ τῆς γνώμης μὴ ὀρθὸν φαίνεσθαι, διότι τὸ μὲν λυποῦν ἔχει ἤδη τὴν αἴσθησιν ἑκάστῳ, τῆς δὲ ὠφελίας ἄπεστιν ἔτι ἡ δήλωσις ἅπασι, καὶ μεταβολῆς μεγάλης, καὶ ταύτης ἐξ ὀλίγου, ἐμπεσούσης ταπεινὴ ὑμῶν
3 ἡ διάνοια ἐγκαρτερεῖν ἃ ἔγνωτε. δουλοῖ γὰρ φρόνημα τὸ αἰφνίδιον καὶ ἀπροσδόκητον καὶ τὸ πλείστῳ παραλόγῳ ξυμβαῖνον· ὃ ἡμῖν πρὸς τοῖς ἄλλοις οὐχ ἥκιστα καὶ κατὰ τὴν νόσον γεγένηται.
4 ὅμως δὲ πόλιν μεγάλην οἰκοῦντας καὶ ἐν ἤθεσιν ἀντιπάλοις αὐτῇ τεθραμμένους χρεὼν καὶ ξυμφοραῖς ταῖς μεγίσταις ἐθέλειν ὑφίστασθαι καὶ τὴν ἀξίωσιν μὴ ἀφανίζειν (ἐν ἴσῳ γὰρ οἱ ἄνθρωποι δικαιοῦσι τῆς τε ὑπαρχούσης δόξης αἰτιᾶσθαι ὅστις μαλακίᾳ ἐλλείπει καὶ τῆς μὴ προσηκούσης μισεῖν τὸν θρασύτητι ὀρεγόμενον), ἀπαλγήσαντας

---

[1] Described by Pericles in the Funeral Oration, chs. xxxvii–xlii.

LXI. "For though I admit that going to war is always sheer folly for men who are free to choose, and in general are enjoying good fortune, yet if the necessary choice was either to yield and forthwith submit to their neighbours' dictation, or by accepting the hazard of war to preserve their independence, then those who shrink from the hazard are more blameworthy than those who face it. For my part, I stand where I stood before, and do not recede from my position; but it is you who have changed. For it has happened, now that you are suffering, that you repent of the consent you gave me when you were still unscathed, and in your infirmity of purpose my advice now appears to you wrong. The reason is that each one of you is already sensible of his hardships, whereas the proof of the advantages is still lacking to all, and now that a great reverse has come upon you without any warning, you are too dejected in mind to persevere in your former resolutions. For the spirit is cowed by that which is sudden and unexpected and happens contrary to all calculation; and this is precisely the experience you have had, not only in other matters, but especially as regards the plague. Nevertheless, seeing that you are citizens of a great city and have been reared amid customs which correspond to her greatness,[1] you should willingly endure even the greatest calamities and not mar your good fame. For as all men claim the right to detest him who through presumption tries to grasp a reputation to which he has no title, so they equally claim a right to censure him who through faintheartedness fails to live up to the reputation he already enjoys. You should, rather, put away your grief for private ills

δὲ τὰ ἴδια τοῦ κοινοῦ τῆς σωτηρίας ἀντιλαμβάνεσθαι.

LXII. "Τὸν δὲ πόνον τὸν κατὰ τὸν πόλεμον,
μὴ γένηταί τε πολὺς καὶ οὐδὲν μᾶλλον περιγενώ-
μεθα, ἀρκείτω μὲν ὑμῖν καὶ ἐκεῖνα ἐν οἷς ἄλλοτε
πολλάκις γε δὴ ἀπέδειξα οὐκ ὀρθῶς αὐτὸν ὑπο-
πτευόμενον, δηλώσω δὲ καὶ τόδε, ὅ μοι δοκεῖτε
οὔτ' αὐτοὶ πώποτε ἐνθυμηθῆναι ὑπάρχον ὑμῖν
μεγέθους πέρι ἐς τὴν ἀρχὴν οὔτ' ἐγὼ ἐν τοῖς πρὶν
λόγοις· οὐδ' ἂν νῦν ἐχρησάμην κομπωδεστέραν
ἔχοντι τὴν προσποίησιν, εἰ μὴ καταπεπληγμένους
2 ὑμᾶς παρὰ τὸ εἰκὸς ἑώρων. οἴεσθε μὲν γὰρ τῶν
ξυμμάχων μόνων ἄρχειν, ἐγὼ δὲ ἀποφαίνω δύο
μερῶν τῶν ἐς χρῆσιν φανερῶν, γῆς καὶ θαλάσσης,
τοῦ ἑτέρου ὑμᾶς παντὸς κυριωτάτους ὄντας, ἐφ'
ὅσον τε νῦν νέμεσθε καὶ ἢν ἐπὶ πλέον βουληθῆτε·
καὶ οὐκ ἔστιν ὅστις τῇ ὑπαρχούσῃ παρασκευῇ
τοῦ ναυτικοῦ πλέοντας ὑμᾶς οὔτε βασιλεὺς οὔτε
ἄλλο οὐδὲν ἔθνος τῶν ἐν τῷ παρόντι κωλύσει.
3 ὥστε οὐ κατὰ τὴν τῶν οἰκιῶν καὶ τῆς γῆς χρείαν,
ὧν μεγάλων νομίζετε ἐστερῆσθαι, αὕτη ἡ δύναμις
φαίνεται· οὐδ' εἰκὸς χαλεπῶς φέρειν αὐτῶν μᾶλλον ἢ οὐ κηπίον καὶ ἐγκαλλώπισμα πλούτου
πρὸς ταύτην νομίσαντας ὀλιγωρῆσαι καὶ γνῶναι
ἐλευθερίαν μέν, ἢν ἀντιλαμβανόμενοι αὐτῆς δια-
σώσωμεν, ῥᾳδίως ταῦτα ἀναληψομένην, ἄλλων δὲ

---

[1] *cf.* ch. xiii and I. cxl–cxliv.

and devote yourselves to the safety of the commonwealth.

LXII. "As to the hardships involved in this war, and your misgivings lest they prove very great and we succumb after all, let those arguments suffice which I have advanced on many other occasions[1] in order to convince you that your fears are groundless. But there is one point I propose to lay before you on which, I think, you have never yourselves as yet reflected, in spite of the advantage it gives you as regards your empire and its greatness, and which I have never previously dealt with in my speeches, and should not have done so now—for it makes a somewhat boastful claim—had I not seen that you are unreasonably dejected. You think that it is only over your allies that your empire extends, but I declare that of two divisions of the world which lie open to man's use, the land and the sea, you hold the absolute mastery over the whole of one, not only to the extent to which you now exercise it, but also to whatever fuller extent you may choose; and there is no one, either the Great King or any nation of those now on the earth, who will block your path as you sail the seas with such a naval armament as you now possess. This power, therefore, is clearly not to be compared with the mere use of your houses and fields, things which you value highly because you have been dispossessed of them; nor is it reasonable that you should fret about them, but you should make light of them, regarding them in comparison with this power as a mere flower-garden or ornament of a wealthy estate, and should recognize that freedom, if we hold fast to it and preserve it, will easily restore these losses, but let

ὑπακούσασι καὶ τὰ προκεκτημένα[1] φιλεῖν ἐλασσοῦσθαι, τῶν τε πατέρων μὴ χείρους κατ' ἀμφότερα φανῆναι, οἳ μετὰ πόνων καὶ οὐ παρ' ἄλλων
δεξάμενοι κατέσχον τε καὶ προσέτι διασώσαντες
παρέδοσαν ὑμῖν αὐτά (αἴσχιον δὲ ἔχοντας ἀφαιρεθῆναι ἢ κτωμένους ἀτυχῆσαι), ἰέναι δὲ τοῖς
ἐχθροῖς ὁμόσε μὴ φρονήματι μόνον, ἀλλὰ καὶ
4 καταφρονήματι. αὔχημα μὲν γὰρ καὶ ἀπὸ ἀμα-
θίας εὐτυχοῦς καὶ δειλῷ τινι ἐγγίγνεται, καταφρόνησις δὲ ὃς ἂν καὶ γνώμῃ πιστεύῃ τῶν ἐναντίων
5 περιέχειν, ὃ ἡμῖν ὑπάρχει. καὶ τὴν τόλμαν ἀπὸ
τῆς ὁμοίας τύχης ἡ ξύνεσις ἐκ τοῦ ὑπέρφρονος
ἐχυρωτέραν παρέχεται, ἐλπίδι τε ἧσσον πιστεύει,
ἧς ἐν τῷ ἀπόρῳ ἡ ἰσχύς, γνώμῃ δὲ ἀπὸ τῶν ὑπαρχόντων, ἧς βεβαιοτέρα ἡ πρόνοια.

LXIII. "Τῆς τε πόλεως ὑμᾶς εἰκὸς τῷ τιμω-
μένῳ ἀπὸ τοῦ ἄρχειν, ᾧπερ ἅπαντες ἀγάλλεσθε,
βοηθεῖν, καὶ μὴ φεύγειν τοὺς πόνους ἢ μηδὲ τὰς
τιμὰς διώκειν· μηδὲ νομίσαι περὶ ἑνὸς μόνου, δου-
λείας ἀντ' ἐλευθερίας, ἀγωνίζεσθαι, ἀλλὰ καὶ
ἀρχῆς στερήσεως καὶ κινδύνου ὧν ἐν τῇ ἀρχῇ ἀπή-
2 χθεσθε. ἧς οὐδ' ἐκστῆναι ἔτι ὑμῖν ἔστιν, εἴ τις
καὶ τόδε ἐν τῷ παρόντι δεδιὼς ἀπραγμοσύνῃ

[1] So most editors with Gmc$_2$; all other MSS. προσεκτημένα except M προσκεκτημένα.

men once submit to others and even what has been won in the past[1] has a way of being lessened. You must therefore show yourselves not inferior in either of these two respects to your fathers, who by their own labours, and not by inheritance, not only acquired but also preserved this empire and bequeathed it to you (and it is a greater disgrace to let a possession you have be taken away than it is to attempt to gain one and fail); and you must go to meet your enemies not only with confidence in yourselves, but with contempt for them. For even a coward, if his folly is attended with good luck, may boast, but contempt belongs only to the man who is convinced by his reason that he is superior to his opponents, as is the case with us. And, where fortune is impartial, the result of this feeling of contempt is to render courage more effective through intelligence, that puts its trust not so much in hope, which is strongest in perplexity, as in reason supported by the facts, which gives a surer insight into the future.

LXIII. "You may reasonably be expected, moreover, to support the dignity which the state has attained through empire—a dignity in which you all take pride—and not to avoid its burdens, unless you resign its honours also. Nor must you think that you are fighting for the simple issue of slavery or freedom; on the contrary, loss of empire is also involved and danger from the hatred incurred in your sway. From this empire, however, it is too late for you even to withdraw, if any one at the present crisis, through fear and shrinking from action does indeed

[1] Or, reading τὰ προσεκτημένα, "freedom and all that freedom gives" (= πρὸς τῇ ἐλευθερίᾳ κεκτημένα, as Poppo explains).

ἀνδραγαθίζεται· ὡς[1] τυραννίδα γὰρ ἤδη ἔχετε αὐτήν, ἣν λαβεῖν μὲν ἄδικον δοκεῖ εἶναι, ἀφεῖναι
3 δὲ ἐπικίνδυνον. τάχιστ' ἄν τε πόλιν οἱ τοιοῦτοι ἑτέρους τε πείσαντες ἀπολέσειαν καὶ εἴ που ἐπὶ σφῶν αὐτῶν αὐτόνομοι οἰκήσειαν· τὸ γὰρ ἄπραγμον οὐ σῴζεται μὴ μετὰ τοῦ δραστηρίου τεταγμένον, οὐδὲ ἐν ἀρχούσῃ πόλει ξυμφέρει, ἀλλ' ἐν ὑπηκόῳ, ἀσφαλῶς δουλεύειν.

LXIV. "Ὑμεῖς δὲ μήτε ὑπὸ τῶν τοιῶνδε πολιτῶν παράγεσθε μήτε ἐμὲ δι' ὀργῆς ἔχετε, ᾧ καὶ αὐτοὶ ξυνδιέγνωτε πολεμεῖν, εἰ καὶ ἐπελθόντες οἱ ἐναντίοι ἔδρασαν ἅπερ εἰκὸς ἦν μὴ ἐθελησάντων ὑμῶν ὑπακούειν, ἐπιγεγένηταί τε πέρα ὧν προσεδεχόμεθα ἡ νόσος ἥδε, πρᾶγμα μόνον δὴ τῶν πάντων ἐλπίδος κρεῖσσον γεγενημένον. καὶ δι' αὐτὴν οἶδ' ὅτι μέρος τι μᾶλλον ἔτι μισοῦμαι, οὐ δικαίως, εἰ μὴ καὶ ὅταν παρὰ λόγον τι εὖ πράξητε
2 ἐμοὶ ἀναθήσετε. φέρειν δὲ χρὴ τά τε δαιμόνια ἀναγκαίως τά τε ἀπὸ τῶν πολεμίων ἀνδρείως· ταῦτα γὰρ ἐν ἔθει τῇδε τῇ πόλει πρότερόν τε ἦν
3 νῦν τε μὴ ἐν ὑμῖν κωλυθῇ. γνῶτε δὲ ὄνομα μέγιστον αὐτὴν ἔχουσαν ἐν ἅπασιν ἀνθρώποις διὰ τὸ ταῖς ξυμφοραῖς μὴ εἴκειν, πλεῖστα δὲ σώματα καὶ πόνους ἀνηλωκέναι πολέμῳ, καὶ δύναμιν μεγίστην δὴ μέχρι τοῦδε κεκτημένην, ἧς ἐς ἀίδιον τοῖς ἐπι-

[1] Dobree deletes, followed by Hude.

seek thus to play the honest man; for by this time the empire you hold is a tyranny, which it may seem wrong to have assumed, but which certainly it is dangerous to let go. Men like these would soon ruin a state, either here, if they should win others to their views, or if they should settle in some other land and have an independent state all to themselves; for men of peace are not safe unless flanked by men of action; nor is it expedient in an imperial state, but only in a vassal state, to seek safety by submission.

LXIV. "Do not be led astray by such citizens as these, nor persist in your anger with me,—for you yourselves voted for the war the same as I—just because the enemy has come and done exactly what he was certain to do the moment you refused to hearken to his demands, even though, beyond all our expectations, this plague has fallen upon us—the only thing which has happened that has transcended our foresight. I am well aware that your displeasure with me has been aggravated by the plague; but there is no justice in that, unless you mean to give me also the credit whenever any unexpected good fortune falls to your lot. But the right course is to bear with resignation the afflictions sent by heaven and with fortitude the hardships that come from the enemy; for such has been the practice of this city in the past, and let it find no impediment in yourselves. And realize that Athens has a mighty name among all mankind because she has never yielded to misfortunes, but more freely than any other city has lavished lives and labours upon war, and that she possesses to-day a power which is the greatest that ever existed down to our time. The memory of

γιγνομένοις, ἣν καὶ νῦν ὑπενδῶμέν ποτε (πάντα
γὰρ πέφυκε καὶ ἐλασσοῦσθαι), μνήμη καταλελεί-
ψεται, Ἑλλήνων τε ὅτι Ἕλληνες πλείστων δὴ
ἤρξαμεν καὶ πολέμοις μεγίστοις ἀντέσχομεν πρός
τε ξύμπαντας καὶ καθ' ἑκάστους, πόλιν τε τοῖς
4 πᾶσιν εὐπορωτάτην καὶ μεγίστην ᾠκήσαμεν. καίτοι ταῦτα ὁ μὲν ἀπράγμων μέμψαιτ' ἄν, ὁ δὲ δρᾶν
τι καὶ αὐτὸς βουλόμενος ζηλώσει· εἰ δέ τις μὴ
5 κέκτηται, φθονήσει. τὸ δὲ μισεῖσθαι καὶ λυπη-
ροὺς εἶναι ἐν τῷ παρόντι πᾶσι μὲν ὑπῆρξε δὴ
ὅσοι ἕτεροι ἑτέρων ἠξίωσαν ἄρχειν· ὅστις δὲ ἐπὶ
μεγίστοις τὸ ἐπίφθονον λαμβάνει, ὀρθῶς βου-
λεύεται. μῖσος μὲν γὰρ οὐκ ἐπὶ πολὺ ἀντέχει, ἡ
δὲ παραυτίκα τε λαμπρότης καὶ ἐς τὸ ἔπειτα δόξα
6 αἰείμνηστος καταλείπεται. ὑμεῖς δὲ ἔς τε τὸ μέλλον καλὸν προγνόντες ἔς τε τὸ αὐτίκα μὴ αἰσχρὸν
τῷ ἤδη προθύμῳ ἀμφότερα κτήσασθε, καὶ Λακεδαιμονίοις μήτε ἐπικηρυκεύεσθε μήτε ἔνδηλοι ἔστε
τοῖς παροῦσι πόνοις βαρυνόμενοι, ὡς οἵτινες πρὸς
τὰς ξυμφορὰς γνώμῃ μὲν ἥκιστα λυποῦνται, ἔργῳ
δὲ μάλιστα ἀντέχουσιν, οὗτοι καὶ πόλεων καὶ
ἰδιωτῶν κράτιστοί εἰσιν."

LXV. Τοιαῦτα ὁ Περικλῆς λέγων ἐπειρᾶτο
τοὺς Ἀθηναίους τῆς τε ἐς αὐτὸν ὀργῆς παραλύειν
καὶ ἀπὸ τῶν παρόντων δεινῶν ἀπάγειν τὴν γνώ-
2 μην. οἱ δὲ δημοσίᾳ μὲν τοῖς λογοις ἀνεπείθοντο
καὶ οὔτε πρὸς τοὺς Λακεδαιμονίους ἔτι ἔπεμπον
ἔς τε τὸν πόλεμον μᾶλλον ὥρμηντο, ἰδίᾳ δὲ

this greatness, even should we now at last give way a little—for it is the nature of all things to decay as well as to grow—will be left to posterity forever, how that we of all Hellenes held sway over the greatest number of Hellenes, in the greatest wars held out against our foes whether united or single, and inhabited a city that was the richest in all things and the greatest. These things the man who shrinks from action may indeed disparage, but he who, like ourselves, wishes to accomplish something will make them the goal of his endeavour, while every man who does not possess them will be envious. To be hated and obnoxious for the moment has always been the lot of those who have aspired to rule over others; but he who, aiming at the highest ends, accepts the odium, is well advised. For hatred does not last long, but the splendour of the moment and the after-glory are left in everlasting remembrance. Do you, then, providently resolving that yours shall be honour in ages to come and no dishonour in the present, achieve both by prompt and zealous effort. Make no overtures to the Lacedaemonians and do not let them know that you are burdened by your present afflictions; for those who in the face of calamities show least distress of spirit and in action make most vigorous resistance, these are the strongest, whether they be states or individuals."

LXV. By such words Pericles endeavoured to cure the Athenians of their anger toward him, and to divert their minds from their present ills. And as regards public affairs they were won over by his arguments, sending no further envoys to the Lacedaemonians, and were more zealous for the war; but

τοῖς παθήμασιν ἐλυποῦντο, ὁ μὲν δῆμος ὅτι ἀπ'
ἐλασσόνων ὁρμώμενος ἐστέρητο καὶ τούτων, οἱ
δὲ δυνατοὶ καλὰ κτήματα κατὰ τὴν χώραν[1]
οἰκοδομίαις τε καὶ πολυτελέσι κατασκευαῖς ἀπο-
λωλεκότες, τὸ δὲ μέγιστον, πόλεμον ἀντ' εἰρήνης
3 ἔχοντες. οὐ μέντοι πρότερόν γε οἱ ξύμπαντες
ἐπαύσαντο ἐν ὀργῇ ἔχοντες αὐτὸν πρὶν ἐζημίωσαν
4 χρήμασιν. ὕστερον δ' αὖθις οὐ πολλῷ, ὅπερ φιλεῖ ὅμιλος ποιεῖν, στρατηγὸν εἵλοντο καὶ πάντα
τὰ πράγματα ἐπέτρεψαν, ὧν μὲν περὶ τὰ οἰκεῖα
ἕκαστος ἤλγει ἀμβλύτεροι ἤδη ὄντες, ὧν δὲ ἡ
ξύμπασα πόλις προσεδεῖτο πλείστου ἄξιον νομί-
5 ζοντες εἶναι. ὅσον τε γὰρ χρόνον προύστη τῆς
πόλεως ἐν τῇ εἰρήνῃ, μετρίως ἐξηγεῖτο καὶ ἀσφαλῶς διεφύλαξεν αὐτήν, καὶ ἐγένετο ἐπ' ἐκείνου
μεγίστη, ἐπειδή τε ὁ πόλεμος κατέστη, ὁ δὲ φαίνεται καὶ ἐν τούτῳ προγνοὺς τὴν δύναμιν.
6 Ἐπεβίω δὲ δύο ἔτη καὶ ἓξ μῆνας· καὶ ἐπειδὴ
ἀπέθανεν, ἐπὶ πλέον ἔτι ἐγνώσθη ἡ πρόνοια αὐτοῦ
7 ἡ ἐς τὸν πόλεμον. ὁ μὲν γὰρ ἡσυχάζοντάς τε
καὶ τὸ ναυτικὸν θεραπεύοντας καὶ ἀρχὴν μὴ
ἐπικτωμένους ἐν τῷ πολέμῳ μηδὲ τῇ πόλει κινδυνεύοντας ἔφη περιέσεσθαι· οἱ δὲ ταῦτά τε πάντα
ἐς τοὐναντίον ἔπραξαν καὶ ἄλλα ἔξω τοῦ πολέμου
δοκοῦντα εἶναι κατὰ τὰς ἰδίας φιλοτιμίας καὶ
ἴδια κέρδη κακῶς ἔς τε σφᾶς αὐτοὺς καὶ τοὺς

[1] Hude inserts ἐν with Madvig.

---

[1] Eighty talents, according to Diod. XII. xlv.; but according to Plut. *Per.* xxxv. estimates varied from fifteen to fifty

in private they were distressed by their sufferings; for the commons, having less to start with, had been deprived even of this, while the upper classes had lost their beautiful estates in the country, both buildings and costly furniture, and above all they had war instead of peace. Indeed one and all they did not give over their resentment against him until they had imposed a fine[1] upon him. But not long afterwards, as is the way with the multitude, they chose him again as general and entrusted him with the whole conduct of affairs; for they were now becoming individually less keenly sensible of their private griefs, and as to the needs of the state as a whole they esteemed him invaluable. For so long as he presided over the affairs of the state in time of peace he pursued a moderate policy and kept the city in safety, and it was under him that Athens reached the height of her greatness; and, after the war began, here too he appears to have made a far-sighted estimate of her strength.

Pericles lived two years and six months beyond the beginning of the war; and after his death his foresight as to the war was still more fully recognized. For he had told the Athenians that if they would maintain a defensive policy, attend to their navy, and not seek to extend their sway during the war, or do anything to imperil the existence of the state, they would prove superior. But they not only acted contrary to his advice in all these things, but also in matters that apparently had no connection with the war they were led by private ambition and private greed to adopt policies which proved injurious both

talents. The charge was embezzlement, according to Plato, *Gorg.* 576 A.

ξυμμάχους ἐπολίτευσαν, ἃ κατορθούμενα μὲν τοῖς
ἰδιώταις τιμὴ καὶ ὠφελία μᾶλλον ἦν, σφαλέντα
δὲ τῇ πόλει ἐς τὸν πόλεμον βλάβη καθίστατο.
8 αἴτιον δ' ἦν ὅτι ἐκεῖνος μὲν δυνατὸς ὢν τῷ τε
ἀξιώματι καὶ τῇ γνώμῃ χρημάτων τε διαφανῶς
ἀδωρότατος γενόμενος κατεῖχε τὸ πλῆθος ἐλευθέρως, καὶ οὐκ ἤγετο μᾶλλον ὑπ' αὐτοῦ ἢ αὐτὸς
ἦγε, διὰ τὸ μὴ κτώμενος ἐξ οὐ προσηκόντων τὴν
δύναμιν πρὸς ἡδονήν τι λέγειν, ἀλλ' ἔχων ἐπ'
9 ἀξιώσει καὶ πρὸς ὀργήν τι ἀντειπεῖν. ὁπότε γοῦν
αἴσθοιτό τι αὐτοὺς παρὰ καιρὸν ὕβρει θαρσοῦντας, λέγων κατέπλησσεν ἐπὶ τὸ φοβεῖσθαι, καὶ
δεδιότας αὖ ἀλόγως ἀντικαθίστη πάλιν ἐπὶ τὸ
θαρσεῖν. ἐγίγνετό τε λόγῳ μὲν δημοκρατία,
10 ἔργῳ δὲ ὑπὸ τοῦ πρώτου ἀνδρὸς ἀρχή. οἱ δὲ
ὕστερον ἴσοι μᾶλλον αὐτοὶ πρὸς ἀλλήλους ὄντες
καὶ ὀρεγόμενοι τοῦ πρῶτος ἕκαστος γίγνεσθαι
ἐτράποντο καθ' ἡδονὰς τῷ δήμῳ καὶ τὰ πράγματα
11 ἐνδιδόναι. ἐξ ὧν ἄλλα τε πολλά, ὡς ἐν μεγάλῃ
πόλει καὶ ἀρχὴν ἐχούσῃ, ἡμαρτήθη καὶ ὁ ἐς
Σικελίαν πλοῦς, ὃς οὐ τοσοῦτον γνώμης ἁμάρ-
τημα ἦν πρὸς οὓς ἐπῆσαν, ὅσον οἱ ἐκπέμψαντες
οὐ τὰ πρόσφορα τοῖς οἰχομένοις ἐπιγιγνώσκοντες,
ἀλλὰ κατὰ τὰς ἰδίας διαβολὰς περὶ τῆς τοῦ

---

1 The reference is especially to the Sicilian expedition; the pernicious results were seen in the Decelean war.

as to themselves and their allies; for these policies, so long as they were successful, merely brought honour or profit to individual citizens, but when they failed proved detrimental to the state in the conduct of the war.[1] And the reason for this was that Pericles, who owed his influence to his recognized standing and ability, and had proved himself clearly incorruptible in the highest degree, restrained the multitude while respecting their liberties, and led them rather than was led by them, because he did not resort to flattery, seeking power by dishonest means, but was able on the strength of his high reputation to oppose them and even provoke their wrath. At any rate, whenever he saw them unwarrantably confident and arrogant, his words would cow them into fear; and, on the other hand, when he saw them unreasonably afraid, he would restore them to confidence again. And so Athens, though in name a democracy, gradually became in fact a government ruled by its foremost citizen. But the successors of Pericles, being more on an equality with one another and yet striving each to be first, were ready to surrender to the people even the conduct of public affairs to suit their whims. And from this, since it happened in a great and imperial state, there resulted many blunders, especially the Sicilian expedition,[2] which was not so much an error of judgment, when we consider the enemy they went against, as of management; for those who were responsible for it, instead of taking additional measures for the proper support of the first troops which were sent out, gave themselves over to personal intrigues for the sake of

[2] For the history of this expedition, see Books VI and VII.

δήμου προστασίας τά τε ἐν τῷ στρατοπέδῳ ἀμ-
βλύτερα ἐποίουν καὶ τὰ περὶ τὴν πόλιν πρῶτον
12 ἐν ἀλλήλοις ἐταράχθησαν. σφαλέντες δὲ ἐν
Σικελίᾳ ἄλλῃ τε παρασκευῇ καὶ τοῦ ναυτικοῦ τῷ
πλέονι μορίῳ καὶ κατὰ τὴν πόλιν ἤδη ἐν στάσει
ὄντες ὅμως δέκα[1] μὲν ἔτη ἀντεῖχον τοῖς τε πρότερον ὑπάρχουσι πολεμίοις καὶ τοῖς ἀπὸ Σικελίας
μετ' αὐτῶν καὶ τῶν ξυμμάχων ἔτι τοῖς πλέοσιν
ἀφεστηκόσι, Κύρῳ τε ὕστερον βασιλέως παιδὶ
προσγενομένῳ, ὃς παρεῖχε χρήματα Πελοποννησίοις ἐς τὸ ναυτικόν, καὶ οὐ πρότερον ἐνέδοσαν
ἢ αὐτοὶ ἐν[2] σφίσιν αὐτοῖς κατὰ τὰς ἰδίας δια-
13 φορὰς περιπεσόντες ἐσφάλησαν. τοσοῦτον τῷ
Περικλεῖ ἐπερίσσευσε τότε ἀφ' ὧν αὐτὸς προέγνω
καὶ πάνυ ἂν ῥᾳδίως περιγενέσθαι τὴν πόλιν
Πελοποννησίων αὐτῶν τῷ πολέμῳ.

LXVI. Οἱ δὲ Λακεδαιμόνιοι καὶ οἱ ξύμμαχοι
τοῦ αὐτοῦ θέρους ἐστράτευσαν ναυσὶν ἑκατὸν ἐς
Ζάκυνθον τὴν νῆσον, ἣ κεῖται ἀντιπέρας Ἤλιδος·
εἰσὶ δὲ Ἀχαιῶν τῶν ἐκ Πελοποννήσου ἄποικοι
2 καὶ Ἀθηναίοις ξυνεμάχουν. ἐπέπλεον δὲ Λακεδαιμονίων χίλιοι ὁπλῖται καὶ Κνῆμος Σπαρτιάτης
ναύαρχος. ἀποβάντες δὲ ἐς τὴν γῆν ἐδῄωσαν τὰ
πολλά. καὶ ἐπειδὴ οὐ ξυνεχώρουν, ἀπέπλευσαν
ἐπ' οἴκου.

LXVII. Καὶ τοῦ αὐτοῦ θέρους τελευτῶντος
Ἀριστεὺς Κορίνθιος καὶ Λακεδαιμονίων πρέσβεις
Ἀνήριστος καὶ Νικόλαος καὶ Πρατόδαμος καὶ

[1] MSS. read τρία, but Hude follows Haacke in reading δέκα. So also van H., Cl., Stahl, F. Mueller, Croiset, Marchant. ὀκτώ is preferred by Shilleto, Aem. Mueller.

[2] Deleted by van Herwerden, followed by Hude.

gaining the popular leadership and consequently not only conducted the military operations with less rigour, but also brought about, for the first time, civil discord at home. And yet, after they had met with disaster in Sicily, where they lost not only their army but also the greater part of their fleet, and by this time had come to be in a state of sedition at home, they neverthless held out ten years not only against the enemies they had before, but also against the Sicilians, who were now combined with them, and, besides, against most of their allies, who were now in revolt, and later on, against Cyrus son of the King, who joined the Peloponnesians and furnished them with money for their fleet; and they did not finally succumb until they had in their private quarrels fallen upon one another and been brought to ruin. Such abundant grounds had Pericles at that time for his own forecast that Athens might quite easily have triumphed in this war over the Peloponnesians alone.

LXVI. During the same summer the Lacedaemonians and their allies made an expedition with a hundred ships to the island of Zacynthus, which lies over against Elis. The Zacynthians are colonists of the Achaeans in the Peloponnesus and were in alliance with the Athenians. On board the ships were one thousand Lacedaemonian hoplites, and Cnemus a Spartan was admiral. And making a descent upon the land they ravaged most of it; but as the inhabitants would not come to terms they sailed back home.

LXVII. And at the end of the same summer 430 B.C.
Aristeus a Corinthian, three Lacedaemonian envoys, Aneristus, Nicolaus, and Pratodamus, also Timagoras

Τεγεάτης Τιμαγόρας καὶ Ἀργεῖος ἰδίᾳ Πόλλις, πορευόμενοι ἐς τὴν Ἀσίαν ὡς βασιλέα, εἴ πως πείσειαν αὐτὸν χρήματά τε παρασχεῖν καὶ ξυμπολεμεῖν, ἀφικνοῦνται ὡς Σιτάλκην πρῶτον τὸν Τήρεω ἐς Θρᾴκην, βουλόμενοι πεῖσαί τε αὐτόν, εἰ δύναιντο, μεταστάντα τῆς Ἀθηναίων ξυμμαχίας στρατεῦσαι ἐπὶ τὴν Ποτείδαιαν, οὗ ἦν στράτευμα τῶν Ἀθηναίων πολιορκοῦν, καί, ᾗπερ ὥρμηντο, δι' ἐκείνου πορευθῆναι πέραν τοῦ Ἑλλησπόντου ὡς Φαρνάκην τὸν Φαρναβάζου, ὃς αὐτοὺς ἔμελλεν
2 ὡς βασιλέα ἀναπέμψειν. παρατυχόντες δὲ Ἀθηναίων πρέσβεις Λέαρχος Καλλιμάχου καὶ Ἀμεινιάδης Φιλήμονος παρὰ τῷ Σιτάλκῃ πείθουσι τὸν Σάδοκον τὸν γεγενημένον Ἀθηναῖον, Σιτάλκου υἱόν, τοὺς ἄνδρας ἐγχειρίσαι σφίσιν, ὅπως μὴ διαβάντες ὡς βασιλέα τὴν ἐκείνου πόλιν
3 τὸ μέρος βλάψωσιν. ὁ δὲ πεισθεὶς πορευομένους αὐτοὺς διὰ τῆς Θρᾴκης ἐπὶ τὸ πλοῖον ᾧ ἔμελλον τὸν Ἑλλήσποντον περαιώσειν, πρὶν ἐσβαίνειν ξυλλαμβάνει, ἄλλους δὴ ξυμπέμψας μετὰ τοῦ Λεάρχου καὶ Ἀμεινιάδου, καὶ ἐκέλευσεν ἐκείνοις παραδοῦναι· οἱ δὲ λαβόντες ἐκόμισαν ἐς τὰς
4 Ἀθήνας. ἀφικομένων δὲ αὐτῶν δείσαντες οἱ Ἀθηναῖοι τὸν Ἀριστέα μὴ αὖθις σφᾶς ἔτι πλείω κακουργῇ διαφυγών, ὅτι καὶ πρὸ τούτων τὰ τῆς Ποτειδαίας καὶ τῶν ἐπὶ Θρᾴκης πάντα ἐφαίνετο πράξας, ἀκρίτους καὶ βουλομένους ἔστιν ἃ εἰπεῖν αὐθημερὸν ἀπέκτειναν πάντας καὶ ἐς φάραγγα

[1] Because Argos was a neutral state ; *cf.* ch. ix. 2.
[2] Then satrap of Dascylium ; *cf.* I. cxxix. 1.
[3] *cf.* ch. xxix. 5.

of Tegea and Pollis of Argos, the last acting in a private capacity,[1] set out for Asia to the King's court to see if they might persuade him to furnish money and join in the war. On their way they came first to Sitalces son of Teres in Thrace, their desire being to persuade him, if possible, to forsake the Athenian alliance and send a force to relieve Potidaea, where an Athenian army was conducting the siege; and also, in pursuance of their object, with his help to cross the Hellespont to Pharnaces [2] son of Pharnabazus, who was to escort them up the country to the King. But two Athenian envoys, Learchus son of Callimachus and Ameiniades son of Philemon, who chanced to be visiting Sitalces, urged Sadocus son of Sitalces, who had been made an Athenian citizen,[3] to deliver the men into their hands, that they might not cross over to the King and do such injury as might be to his adopted city.[4] To this Sadocus agreed, and sending some troops to accompany Learchus and Ameiniades, seized them as they journeyed through Thrace before they embarked on the boat by which they were to cross the Hellespont. They were then, in accordance with his orders, delivered to the Athenian envoys, who took them and brought them to Athens. When they arrived, the Athenians, in fear that Aristeus might escape and do them still more harm, because he had evidently been the prime mover in all the earlier intrigues at Potidaea and along the coast of Thrace, put them all to death on that very day without a trial, though they wished to say something in their own defence, and threw their bodies into a

[4] Possibly τὴν ἐκείνου πόλιν τὸ μέρος means "a city in a measure his own."

ἐσέβαλον, δικαιοῦντες τοῖς αὐτοῖς ἀμύνεσθαι οἷσπερ καὶ οἱ Λακεδαιμόνιοι ὑπῆρξαν, τοὺς ἐμπόρους οὓς ἔλαβον Ἀθηναίων καὶ τῶν ξυμμάχων ἐν ὁλκάσι περὶ Πελοπόννησον πλέοντας ἀποκτείναντες καὶ ἐς φάραγγας ἐσβαλόντες. πάντας γὰρ δὴ κατ' ἀρχὰς τοῦ πολέμου Λακεδαιμόνιοι ὅσους λάβοιεν ἐν τῇ θαλάσσῃ ὡς πολεμίους διέφθειρον, καὶ τοὺς μετὰ Ἀθηναίων ξυμπολεμοῦντας καὶ τοὺς μηδὲ μεθ' ἑτέρων.

LXVIII. Κατὰ δὲ τοὺς αὐτοὺς χρόνους, τοῦ θέρους τελευτῶντος, καὶ Ἀμπρακιῶται αὐτοί τε καὶ τῶν βαρβάρων πολλοὺς ἀναστήσαντες ἐστράτευσαν ἐπ' Ἄργος τὸ Ἀμφιλοχικὸν καὶ τὴν
2 ἄλλην Ἀμφιλοχίαν. ἔχθρα δὲ πρὸς τοὺς Ἀργείους ἀπὸ τοῦδε αὐτοῖς ἤρξατο πρῶτον γενέσθαι.
3 Ἄργος τὸ Ἀμφιλοχικὸν καὶ Ἀμφιλοχίαν τὴν ἄλλην ἔκτισε μὲν μετὰ τὰ Τρωικὰ οἴκαδε ἀναχωρήσας καὶ οὐκ ἀρεσκόμενος τῇ ἐν Ἄργει καταστάσει Ἀμφίλοχος ὁ Ἀμφιάρεω ἐν τῷ Ἀμπρακικῷ κόλπῳ, ὁμώνυμον τῇ αὐτοῦ πατρίδι Ἄργος
4 ὀνομάσας (καὶ ἦν ἡ πόλις αὕτη μεγίστη τῆς Ἀμφιλοχίας καὶ τοὺς δυνατωτάτους εἶχεν οἰκή-
5 τορας), ὑπὸ ξυμφορῶν δὲ πολλαῖς γενεαῖς ὕστερον πιεζόμενοι Ἀμπρακιώτας ὁμόρους ὄντας τῇ Ἀμφιλοχικῇ ξυνοίκους ἐπηγάγοντο, καὶ ἡλληνίσθησαν τὴν νῦν γλῶσσαν πρῶτον ἀπὸ τῶν Ἀμπρα-

---

[1] Alcmaeon, the elder brother of Amphilochus, had slain their mother Eriphyle (*cf.* ch. cii. 5). The foundation of

pit, thinking it justifiable to employ for their own protection the same measures as had in the first instance been used by the Lacedaemonians when they killed and cast into pits the traders of the Athenians and their allies whom they caught on board merchantmen on the coast of the Peloponnesus. For at the beginning of the war all persons whom the Lacedaemonians captured at sea they destroyed as enemies, whether they were fighting on the side of the Athenians or not even taking part on either side.

LXVIII. About the same time, as the summer was ending, the Ambraciots themselves, with many of the barbarians whom they had summoned to their standard, made an expedition against the Amphilochian Argos and the rest of Amphilochia. And enmity between them and the Argives first began from the following circumstance. Amphilochus son of Amphiaraus, when he returned home after the Trojan war, was dissatisfied with the state of affairs at Argos,[1] and therefore founded Amphilochian Argos on the Ambracian gulf, and occupied the country of Amphilochia, calling the town Argos after the name of his own fatherland. And this city was the largest in Amphilochia and had the wealthiest inhabitants. But many generations later the Amphilochians, under the stress of misfortunes, invited in the Ambraciots, who bordered on Amphilochia, to share the place with them, and these first became Hellenes and adopted their present dialect in consequence of their union with

Amphilochian Argos is ascribed by other authors (Strabo, vii. 326 c; Apollod. III. 7) to Alcmaeon or to his son Amphilochus.

κιωτῶν ξυνοικησάντων· οἱ δὲ ἄλλοι Ἀμφίλοχοι
6 βάρβαροί εἰσιν. ἐκβάλλουσιν οὖν τοὺς Ἀργείους
οἱ Ἀμπρακιῶται χρόνῳ καὶ αὐτοὶ ἴσχουσι τὴν
7 πόλιν. οἱ δ' Ἀμφίλοχοι γενομένου τούτου διδό-
ασιν ἑαυτοὺς Ἀκαρνᾶσι, καὶ προσπαρακαλέσαντες ἀμφότεροι Ἀθηναίους, οἳ αὐτοῖς Φορμίωνά
τε στρατηγὸν ἔπεμψαν καὶ ναῦς τριάκοντα,
ἀφικομένου δὴ τοῦ Φορμίωνος αἱροῦσι κατὰ κράτος Ἄργος καὶ τοὺς Ἀμπρακιώτας ἠνδραπόδισαν,
κοινῇ τε ᾤκισαν αὐτὸ Ἀμφίλοχοι καὶ Ἀκαρνᾶνες.
8 μετὰ δὲ τοῦτο ἡ ξυμμαχία πρῶτον ἐγένετο Ἀθη-
9 ναίοις καὶ Ἀκαρνᾶσιν. οἱ δὲ Ἀμπρακιῶται τὴν
μὲν ἔχθραν ἐς τοὺς Ἀργείους ἀπὸ τοῦ ἀνδρα-
ποδισμοῦ σφῶν αὐτῶν πρῶτον ἐποιήσαντο, ὕστερον δὲ ἐν τῷ πολέμῳ τήνδε τὴν στρατείαν
ποιοῦνται ἑαυτῶν τε καὶ Χαόνων καὶ ἄλλων
τινῶν τῶν πλησιοχώρων βαρβάρων· ἐλθόντες δὲ
πρὸς τὸ Ἄργος τῆς μὲν χώρας ἐκράτουν, τὴν δὲ
πόλιν ὡς οὐκ ἐδύναντο ἑλεῖν προσβαλόντες,
ἀπεχώρησαν ἐπ' οἴκου καὶ διελύθησαν κατὰ ἔθνη.
τοσαῦτα μὲν ἐν τῷ θέρει ἐγένετο.

LXIX. Τοῦ δ' ἐπιγιγνομένου χειμῶνος Ἀθηναῖοι ναῦς ἔστειλαν εἴκοσι μὲν περὶ Πελοπόννησον καὶ Φορμίωνα στρατηγόν, ὃς ὁρμώμενος ἐκ Ναυπάκτου φυλακὴν εἶχε μήτ' ἐκπλεῖν ἐκ Κορίνθου καὶ τοῦ Κρισαίου κόλπου μηδένα μήτ' ἐσπλεῖν, ἑτέρας δὲ ἓξ ἐπὶ Καρίας καὶ Λυκίας καὶ Μελήσανδρον στρατηγόν, ὅπως ταῦτά τε ἀργυρολογῶσι καὶ τὸ λῃστικὸν τῶν Πελοποννησίων μὴ ἐῶσιν αὐτόθεν ὁρμώμενον βλάπτειν τὸν πλοῦν τῶν ὁλκάδων τῶν ἀπὸ Φασήλιδος καὶ Φοινίκης καὶ

the Ambraciots; but the rest of the Amphilochians are still barbarians. Now in course of time the Ambraciots expelled the Argives and themselves seized the city. But the Amphilochians, when this happened, placed themselves under the protection of the Acarnanians, and together they called in the Athenians, who sent to them Phormio as general with thirty ships. On the arrival of Phormio they took Argos by storm and reduced the Ambraciots to slavery, and Amphilochians and Acarnanians settled there together. It was after this that the alliance between the Athenians and the Acarnanians was first established. The Ambraciots first conceived their enmity toward the Argives from this enslavement of their own countrymen; and afterwards in the course of the war they made this expedition, which consisted, besides themselves, of Chaonians and some of the other barbarian tribes of the neighbourhood. And when they came to Argos, although they dominated the country, they were unable to take the city by assault; they therefore went home and the several tribes disbanded. Such were the events of the summer.

LXIX. During the ensuing winter the Athenians sent twenty ships round the Peloponnesus under the command of Phormio, who, making Naupactus his base, kept watch there, so that no one might sail either out of Corinth and the Crisaean Gulf or in; and six other ships were sent to Caria and Lycia, under Melesander as general, to collect arrears of tribute in these places and to prevent the Peloponnesian privateers from establishing a base in these regions and molesting the merchantmen sailing from Phaselis and Phoenicia and the mainland in that

2 τῆς ἐκεῖθεν ἠπείρου. ἀναβὰς δὲ στρατιᾷ Ἀθηναίων τε τῶν ἀπὸ τῶν νεῶν καὶ τῶν ξυμμάχων ἐς τὴν Λυκίαν ὁ Μελήσανδρος ἀποθνῄσκει καὶ τῆς στρατιᾶς μέρος τι διέφθειρε νικηθεὶς μάχῃ.

LXX. Τοῦ δ' αὐτοῦ χειμῶνος οἱ Ποτειδεᾶται ἐπειδὴ οὐκέτι ἐδύναντο πολιορκούμενοι ἀντέχειν, ἀλλ' αἵ τε ἐσβολαὶ ἐς τὴν Ἀττικὴν Πελοποννησίων οὐδὲν μᾶλλον ἀπανίστασαν τοὺς Ἀθηναίους, ὅ τε σῖτος ἐπελελοίπει, καὶ ἄλλα τε πολλὰ ἐπεγεγένητο αὐτόθι ἤδη βρώσεως περὶ ἀναγκαίας καί τινες καὶ ἀλλήλων ἐγέγευντο, οὕτω δὴ λόγους προσφέρουσι περὶ ξυμβάσεως τοῖς στρατηγοῖς τῶν Ἀθηναίων τοῖς ἐπὶ σφίσι τεταγμένοις, Ξενοφῶντί τε τῷ Εὐριπίδου καὶ Ἑστιοδώρῳ τῷ Ἀριστοκλείδου καὶ Φανομάχῳ τῷ Καλλιμάχου.

2 οἱ δὲ προσεδέξαντο, ὁρῶντες μὲν τῆς στρατιᾶς τὴν ταλαιπωρίαν ἐν χωρίῳ χειμερινῷ, ἀνηλωκυίας δὲ ἤδη τῆς πόλεως δισχίλια τάλαντα ἐς τὴν

3 πολιορκίαν. ἐπὶ τοῖσδε οὖν ξυνέβησαν, ἐξελθεῖν αὐτοὺς καὶ παῖδας καὶ γυναῖκας καὶ τοὺς ἐπικούρους ξὺν ἑνὶ ἱματίῳ, γυναῖκας δὲ ξὺν δυοῖν, καὶ

4 ἀργύριόν τι ῥητὸν ἔχοντας ἐφόδιον. καὶ οἱ μὲν ὑπόσπονδοι ἐξῆλθον ἔς τε τὴν Χαλκιδικὴν καὶ ᾗ ἕκαστος ἐδύνατο· Ἀθηναῖοι δὲ τούς τε στρατηγοὺς ἐπῃτιάσαντο ὅτι ἄνευ αὐτῶν ξυνέβησαν (ἐνόμιζον γὰρ ἂν κρατῆσαι τῆς πόλεως ᾗ ἐβούλοντο), καὶ ὕστερον ἐποίκους ἔπεμψαν ἑαυτῶν ἐς

5 τὴν Ποτείδαιαν καὶ κατῴκισαν. ταῦτα μὲν ἐν τῷ

quarter. But Melesander, going inland into Lycia with a force of Athenians from the ships and of allied troops, was defeated in battle and slain, losing a number of his troops.

LXX. During the same winter the Potidaeans found themselves no longer able to endure the siege; and the raids which the Peloponnesians made into Attica did not cause the Athenians to raise the siege any more than before.[1] Their grain had given out, and in addition to many other things which by this time had befallen them in their efforts to get bare subsistence some had even eaten their fellows. In this extremity they made proposals for a capitulation to the Athenian generals who were in charge of the operations against them, namely Xenophon son of Euripides, Hestiodorus son of Aristocleides, and Phanomachus son of Callimachus. And the generals accepted their proposals, seeing the distress which the army was suffering in an exposed place, and taking into consideration that Athens had already spent two thousand talents[2] on the siege. So a capitulation was made on the following terms, that the Potidaeans, with their children and wives and the mercenary troops,[3] were to leave the city with one garment apiece—the women, however, with two—retaining a fixed sum of money for the journey. So they left Potidaea under a truce and went into Chalcidice or wherever each was able to go. The Athenians, however, blamed the generals for granting terms without consulting them—for they thought they could have become masters of the place on their own terms; and afterwards sent settlers of their own into Potidaea and colonized it. These things

[1] *cf.* I. lviii. 1. [2] £400,000, $1,944,000. [3] *cf.* I. lx. 1.

χειμῶνι ἐγένετο, καὶ δεύτερον[1] ἔτος τῷ πολέμῳ ἐτελεύτα τῷδε ὃν Θουκυδίδης ξυνέγραψεν.

LXXI. Τοῦ δ' ἐπιγιγνομένου θέρους οἱ Πελοποννήσιοι καὶ οἱ ξύμμαχοι ἐς μὲν τὴν Ἀττικὴν οὐκ ἐσέβαλον, ἐστράτευσαν δὲ ἐπὶ Πλάταιαν· ἡγεῖτο δὲ Ἀρχίδαμος ὁ Ζευξιδάμου, Λακεδαιμονίων βασιλεύς· καὶ καθίσας τὸν στρατὸν ἔμελλε δῃώσειν τὴν γῆν· οἱ δὲ Πλαταιῆς εὐθὺς πρέσβεις πέμψαντες παρ' αὐτὸν ἔλεγον τοιάδε·

2 "Ἀρχίδαμε καὶ Λακεδαιμόνιοι, οὐ δίκαια ποιεῖτε οὐδ' ἄξια οὔτε ὑμῶν οὔτε πατέρων ὧν ἐστε, ἐς γῆν τὴν Πλαταιῶν στρατεύοντες. Παυσανίας γὰρ ὁ Κλεομβρότου, Λακεδαιμόνιος, ἐλευθερώσας τὴν Ἑλλάδα ἀπὸ τῶν Μήδων μετὰ Ἑλλήνων τῶν ἐθελησάντων ξυνάρασθαι τὸν κίνδυνον τῆς μάχης ἣ παρ' ἡμῖν ἐγένετο, θύσας ἐν τῇ Πλαταιῶν ἀγορᾷ ἱερὰ Διὶ ἐλευθερίῳ καὶ ξυγκαλέσας πάντας τοὺς ξυμμάχους ἀπεδίδου Πλαταιεῦσι γῆν καὶ πόλιν τὴν σφετέραν ἔχοντας αὐτονόμους οἰκεῖν, στρατεῦσαί τε μηδένα ποτὲ ἀδίκως ἐπ' αὐτοὺς μηδ' ἐπὶ δουλείᾳ· εἰ δὲ μή, ἀμύνειν τοὺς παρόντας ξυμμάχους κατὰ δύναμιν.
3 τάδε μὲν ἡμῖν πατέρες οἱ ὑμέτεροι ἔδοσαν ἀρετῆς ἕνεκα καὶ προθυμίας τῆς ἐν ἐκείνοις τοῖς κινδύνοις γενομένης, ὑμεῖς δὲ τἀναντία δρᾶτε· μετὰ γὰρ Θηβαίων τῶν ἡμῖν ἐχθίστων ἐπὶ δουλείᾳ τῇ
4 ἡμετέρᾳ ἥκετε. μάρτυρας δὲ θεοὺς τούς τε ὁρκίους τότε γενομένους ποιούμενοι καὶ τοὺς ὑμετέρους πατρῴους καὶ ἡμετέρους ἐγχωρίους, λέγομεν ὑμῖν γῆν τὴν Πλαταιίδα μὴ ἀδικεῖν μηδὲ

[1] τὸ δεύτερον in the MSS.; τὸ deleted by Poppo.

happened in the winter, and so ended the second year of this war of which Thucydides wrote the history. 430 B.C.

LXXI. In the ensuing summer the Peloponnesians and their allies did not invade Attica, but made an expedition against Plataea. Their leader was Archidamus son of Zeuxidamus, king of the Lacedaemonians, and when he had encamped his army he was about to ravage the land; but the Plataeans straightway sent envoys to him, who spoke as follows:

"Archidamus and Lacedaemonians, you are acting unjustly, and in a manner unworthy either of yourselves or of the fathers from whom you are sprung, when you invade the territory of the Plataeans. For Pausanias son of Cleombrotus, the Lacedaemonian, when he had freed Hellas from the Persians, together with such of the Hellenes as chose to share the danger of the battle[1] that took place in our territory, offered sacrifice in the market-place of the Plataeans to Zeus Eleutherius, and calling together all the allies restored to the Plataeans their land and city to hold and inhabit in independence, and no one was ever to march against them unjustly or for their enslavement; but in that case the allies then present were to defend them with all their might. These privileges your fathers granted to us on account of the valour and zeal we displayed amid those dangers, but you do the very contrary; for with the Thebans, our bitterest enemies, you are come to enslave us. But calling to witness the gods in whose names we then swore and the gods of your fathers and of our country, we say to you, wrong not the land of Plataea nor violate your oaths, but suffer

[1] The battle of Plataea, 479 B.C.

παραβαίνειν τοὺς ὅρκους, ἐὰν δὲ οἰκεῖν αὐτονόμους καθάπερ Παυσανίας ἐδικαίωσεν."

LXXII. Τοσαῦτα εἰπόντων τῶν Πλαταιῶν Ἀρχίδαμος ὑπολαβὼν εἶπεν·

"Δίκαια λέγετε, ὦ ἄνδρες Πλαταιῆς, ἢν ποιῆτε ὁμοῖα τοῖς λόγοις. καθάπερ γὰρ Παυσανίας ὑμῖν παρέδωκεν, αὐτοί τε αὐτονομεῖσθε καὶ τοὺς ἄλλους ξυνελευθεροῦτε ὅσοι μετασχόντες τῶν τότε κινδύνων ὑμῖν τε ξυνώμοσαν καὶ εἰσὶ νῦν ὑπ' Ἀθηναίοις, παρασκευὴ δὲ τοσήδε καὶ πόλεμος γεγένηται αὐτῶν ἕνεκα καὶ τῶν ἄλλων ἐλευθερώσεως. ἧς μάλιστα μὲν μετασχόντες καὶ αὐτοὶ ἐμμείνατε τοῖς ὅρκοις· εἰ δὲ μή, ἅπερ καὶ πρότερον ἤδη προυκαλεσάμεθα, ἡσυχίαν ἄγετε νεμόμενοι τὰ ὑμέτερα αὐτῶν, καὶ ἔστε μηδὲ μεθ' ἑτέρων, δέχεσθε δὲ ἀμφοτέρους φίλους, ἐπὶ πολέμῳ δὲ μηδετέρους. καὶ τάδε ἡμῖν ἀρκέσει."

2 Ὁ μὲν Ἀρχίδαμος τοσαῦτα εἶπεν· οἱ δὲ Πλαταιῶν πρέσβεις ἀκούσαντες ταῦτα ἐσῆλθον ἐς τὴν πόλιν, καὶ τῷ πλήθει τὰ ῥηθέντα κοινώσαντες ἀπεκρίναντο αὐτῷ[1] ὅτι ἀδύνατα σφίσιν εἴη ποιεῖν ἃ προκαλεῖται ἄνευ Ἀθηναίων (παῖδες γὰρ σφῶν καὶ γυναῖκες παρ' ἐκείνοις εἶεν), δεδιέναι δὲ καὶ περὶ τῇ πάσῃ πόλει μὴ 'κείνων ἀποχωρησάντων Ἀθηναῖοι ἐλθόντες σφίσιν οὐκ ἐπιτρέπωσιν, ἢ Θηβαῖοι, ὡς ἔνορκοι ὄντες κατὰ τὸ ἀμφοτέρους δέχεσθαι, αὖθις σφῶν τὴν πόλιν
3 πειράσωσι καταλαβεῖν. ὁ δὲ θαρσύνων αὐτοὺς πρὸς ταῦτα ἔφη·

"Ὑμεῖς δὲ πόλιν μὲν καὶ οἰκίας ἡμῖν παράδοτε

[1] Omitted by Hude, with Lex. Vindob.

us to live independent, according as Pausanias granted that to us as our right."

LXXII. When the Plataeans had so spoken, Archidamus answered and said:

"What you say is just, men of Plataea, if what you do is consistent with your words. For according as Pausanias bestowed that privilege upon you, so do you assert your own independence and help us to set free the others also who, having shared in the dangers of that time, swore the same oaths with you, and are now in subjection to the Athenians; for it is to recover their freedom and that of the rest that these great preparations for war have been made. Therein you should take part, if possible, and yourselves abide by the oaths; otherwise keep quiet, as we have already proposed, continuing to enjoy your own possessions; take part with neither side, receive both sides as friends but for hostile purposes neither. And this will be satisfactory to us."

Thus spoke Archidamus; and the Plataean envoys, on hearing him, went into the city, and after reporting to the people what had been said, answered him, that it was impossible for them to do what he proposed without the consent of the Athenians—for their children and wives were in Athens[1]—adding that they feared for the very existence of the state; for after the departure of the Lacedaemonians the Athenians would come and veto the plan, or else the Thebans, claiming that they were included in the stipulations about receiving both sides, would try again to seize their city. But he, endeavouring to reassure them with regard to these matters, said:

"You need only consign the city and your houses

[1] *cf.* ch. vi. 4.

τοῖς Λακεδαιμονίοις καὶ γῆς ὅρους ἀποδείξατε καὶ δένδρα ἀριθμῷ τὰ ὑμέτερα καὶ ἄλλο εἴ τι δυνατὸν ἐς ἀριθμὸν ἐλθεῖν· αὐτοὶ δὲ μεταχωρήσατε ὅποι βούλεσθε, ἕως ἂν ὁ πόλεμος ᾖ· ἐπειδὰν δὲ παρέλθῃ, ἀποδώσομεν ὑμῖν ἃ ἂν παραλάβωμεν. μέχρι δὲ τοῦδε ἕξομεν παρακαταθήκην, ἐργαζόμενοι καὶ φορὰν φέροντες ἣ ἂν ὑμῖν μέλλῃ ἱκανὴ ἔσεσθαι."

LXXIII. Οἱ δ' ἀκούσαντες ἐσῆλθον αὖθις ἐς τὴν πόλιν, καὶ βουλευσάμενοι μετὰ τοῦ πλήθους ἔλεξαν ὅτι βούλονται ἃ προκαλεῖται Ἀθηναίοις κοινῶσαι πρῶτον καί, ἢν πείθωσιν αὐτούς, ποιεῖν ταῦτα· μέχρι δὲ τούτου σπείσασθαι σφίσιν ἐκέλευον καὶ τὴν γῆν μὴ δῃοῦν. ὁ δὲ ἡμέρας τε ἐσπείσατο ἐν αἷς εἰκὸς ἦν κομισθῆναι καὶ τὴν γῆν
2 οὐκ ἔτεμνεν. ἐλθόντες δὲ οἱ Πλαταιῆς πρέσβεις ὡς τοὺς Ἀθηναίους καὶ βουλευσάμενοι μετ' αὐτῶν πάλιν ἦλθον ἀπαγγέλλοντες τοῖς ἐν τῇ πόλει
3 τοιάδε· "Οὔτ' ἐν τῷ πρὸ τοῦ χρόνῳ, ὦ ἄνδρες Πλαταιῆς, ἀφ' οὗ ξύμμαχοι ἐγενόμεθα, Ἀθηναῖοί φασιν ἐν οὐδενὶ ὑμᾶς προέσθαι ἀδικουμένους οὔτε νῦν περιόψεσθαι, βοηθήσειν δὲ κατὰ δύναμιν. ἐπισκήπτουσί τε ὑμῖν πρὸς τῶν ὅρκων οὓς οἱ πατέρες ὤμοσαν μηδὲν νεωτερίζειν περὶ τὴν ξυμμαχίαν."

LXXIV. Τοιαῦτα τῶν πρέσβεων ἀπαγγειλάντων οἱ Πλαταιῆς ἐβουλεύσαντο Ἀθηναίους μὴ προδιδόναι, ἀλλ' ἀνέχεσθαι καὶ γῆν τεμνομένην, εἰ δεῖ, ὁρῶντας καὶ ἄλλο πάσχοντας ὅ τι ἂν

to us, the Lacedaemonians, pointing out to us the boundaries of your land and telling us the number of your trees and whatever else can be numbered; then as for yourselves migrate to whatever place you please, remaining there while the war lasts; but as soon as the war is over we will give back to you whatever we have received; until then we will hold it all in trust, working the land and paying you whatever rent will satisfy you."

LXXIII. With this answer the Plataean envoys went again into the city, and after they had conferred with the people replied that they wished first to communicate his proposals to the Athenians, and if they could gain their consent would do what he proposed; but meanwhile they requested him to grant them a truce and not to ravage the land. And so he made a truce for the number of days within which their representatives could be expected to go and return, and did not lay waste their land. But the Plataean envoys went to the Athenians and after consulting with them returned with the following message to the people at home: "The Athenians assure you, Plataeans, that as in times past, since you became their allies,[1] they have never on any occasion deserted you when you were being wronged, so now they will not suffer you to be wronged, but will assist you with all their might. They therefore adjure you, by the oaths which your fathers swore, not to break off the alliance."

LXXIV. When the envoys reported this answer, the Plataeans determined not to betray the Athenians, but to endure even to see their lands laid waste, if need be, and to suffer whatever else might happen;

[1] About 520 B.C. *cf.* III. lxviii. 5.

ξυμβαίνῃ· ἐξελθεῖν τε μηδένα ἔτι, ἀλλ' ἀπὸ τοῦ τείχους ἀποκρίνασθαι ὅτι ἀδύνατα σφίσι ποιεῖν
2 ἐστιν ἃ Λακεδαιμόνιοι προκαλοῦνται. ὡς δὲ ἀπεκρίναντο, ἐντεῦθεν δὴ πρῶτον μὲν ἐς ἐπιμαρτυρίαν καὶ θεῶν καὶ ἡρώων τῶν ἐγχωρίων Ἀρχί-
3 δαμος ὁ βασιλεὺς κατέστη λέγων ὧδε· "Θεοὶ ὅσοι γῆν τὴν Πλαταιίδα ἔχετε καὶ ἥρωες, ξυνίστορές ἐστε ὅτι οὔτε τὴν ἀρχὴν ἀδίκως, ἐκλιπόντων δὲ τῶνδε προτέρων τὸ ξυνώμοτον, ἐπὶ γῆν τήνδε ἤλθομεν, ἐν ᾗ οἱ πατέρες ἡμῶν εὐξάμενοι ὑμῖν Μήδων ἐκράτησαν καὶ παρέσχετε αὐτὴν εὐμενῆ ἐναγωνίσασθαι τοῖς Ἕλλησιν, οὔτε νῦν, ἤν τι ποιῶμεν, ἀδικήσομεν· προκαλεσάμενοι γὰρ πολλὰ καὶ εἰκότα οὐ τυγχάνομεν. ξυγγνώμονες δὲ ἔστε τῆς μὲν ἀδικίας κολάζεσθαι τοῖς ὑπάρχουσι προτέροις, τῆς δὲ τιμωρίας τυγχάνειν τοῖς ἐπιφέρουσι νομίμως."

LXXV. Τοσαῦτα ἐπιθειάσας καθίστη ἐς πόλεμον τὸν στρατόν. καὶ πρῶτον μὲν περιεσταύρωσαν αὐτοὺς τοῖς δένδρεσιν ἃ ἔκοψαν, τοῦ μηδένα ἐπεξιέναι, ἔπειτα χῶμα ἔχουν πρὸς τὴν πόλιν, ἐλπίζοντες ταχίστην τὴν[1] αἵρεσιν ἔσεσθαι αὐ-
2 τῶν στρατεύματος τοσούτου ἐργαζομένου. ξύλα μὲν οὖν τέμνοντες ἐκ τοῦ Κιθαιρῶνος παρῳκοδόμουν ἑκατέρωθεν, φορμηδὸν ἀντὶ τοίχων τιθέντες, ὅπως μὴ διαχέοιτο ἐπὶ πολὺ τὸ χῶμα. ἐφόρουν

[1] Added by Classen.

further, that no one should thereafter leave the city, but that the answer should be given from the walls that they found it impossible to do what the Lacedaemonians proposed. And when they had made answer, thereupon king Archidamus first stood forth calling the gods and heroes of the country to witness in the following words: "Ye gods and heroes who protect the land of Plataea, be our witnesses that we did no wrong in the beginning, but only after the Plataeans first abandoned the oath we all swore did we come against this land, where our fathers, invoking you in their prayers, conquered the Persians, and which you made auspicious for the Hellenes to fight in, and that now also, if we take any measures, we shall be guilty of no wrong; for though we have made them many reasonable proposals we have failed. Grant therefore your consent, that those be punished for the wrong who first began it, and that those obtain their revenge who are seeking to exact it lawfully."

LXXV. After this appeal to the gods he began hostilities. In the first place the Lacedaemonians, using the trees which they had cut down, built a stockade round Plataea, that in future no one might leave the place; then they began raising a mound against the town, hoping that with so large an army at work this would be the speediest way of taking it. So they cut timber on Cithaeron and built a structure alongside the mound on either side of it, laying the logs like lattice-work[1] to form a sort of wall, that the mound might not spread too much. Then they

[1] A frame was made like lattice-work or mat-work, the timbers crossing each other at right angles (#).

δὲ ὕλην ἐς αὐτὸ καὶ λίθους καὶ γῆν καὶ εἴ τι ἄλλο
3 ἀνύτειν μέλλοι ἐπιβαλλόμενον. ἡμέρας δὲ ἔχουν
ἑβδομήκοντα καὶ νύκτας ξυνεχῶς, διῃρημένοι
κατ' ἀναπαύλας, ὥστε τοὺς μὲν φέρειν, τοὺς δὲ
ὕπνον τε καὶ σῖτον αἱρεῖσθαι· Λακεδαιμονίων
τε οἱ ξεναγοὶ ἑκάστης πόλεως ξυνεφεστῶτες[1]
4 ἠνάγκαζον ἐς τὸ ἔργον. οἱ δὲ Πλαταιῆς ὁρῶντες
τὸ χῶμα αἰρόμενον, ξύλινον τεῖχος ξυνθέντες καὶ
ἐπιστήσαντες τῷ ἑαυτῶν τείχει ᾗ προσεχοῦτο,
ἐσῳκοδόμουν ἐς αὐτὸ πλίνθους ἐκ τῶν ἐγγὺς οἰ-
5 κιῶν καθαιροῦντες. ξύνδεσμος δ' ἦν αὐτοῖς τὰ
ξύλα, τοῦ μὴ ὑψηλὸν γιγνόμενον ἀσθενὲς εἶναι τὸ
οἰκοδόμημα, καὶ προκαλύμματα εἶχε δέρσεις καὶ
διφθέρας, ὥστε τοὺς ἐργαζομένους καὶ τὰ ξύλα
μήτε πυρφόροις οἰστοῖς βάλλεσθαι ἐν ἀσφαλείᾳ
6 τε εἶναι. ᾔρετο δὲ τὸ ὕψος τοῦ τείχους μέγα, καὶ
τὸ χῶμα οὐ σχολαίτερον ἀντανῄει αὐτῷ. καὶ οἱ
Πλαταιῆς τοιόνδε τι ἐπινοοῦσιν· διελόντες τοῦ
τείχους ᾗ προσέπιπτε τὸ χῶμα ἐσεφόρουν τὴν
γῆν.

LXXVI. Οἱ δὲ Πελοποννήσιοι αἰσθόμενοι ἐν ταρσοῖς καλάμου πηλὸν ἐνίλλοντες ἐσέβαλλον ἐς
τὸ διῃρημένον, ὅπως μὴ διαχεόμενον ὥσπερ ἡ γῆ
2 φοροῖτο. οἱ δὲ ταύτῃ ἀποκλῃόμενοι τοῦτο μὲν
ἐπέσχον, ὑπόνομον δὲ ἐκ τῆς πόλεως ὀρύξαντες
καὶ ξυντεκμηράμενοι ὑπὸ τὸ χῶμα ὑφεῖλκον αὖθις
παρὰ σφᾶς τὸν χοῦν· καὶ ἐλάνθανον ἐπὶ πολὺ

[1] With ABEFM and Suid. Hude reads, with CG, οἱ ξεναγοὶ καὶ ἑκάστης πόλεως <οἱ> ἐφεστῶτες.

brought and threw into the space wood and stones and earth and anything else which when thrown on would serve to build up the mound. And for seventy days and nights continuously they kept on raising the mound, divided into relays, so that while some were carrying others might take sleep and food; and the Lacedaemonian commanders of auxiliaries together with the officers in charge of the contingents from the several cities kept them at their task. But the Plataeans, seeing the mound rising, put together a framework of wood which they set on top of their own wall at the point where the mound was being constructed, and inside this frame they put bricks which they took from the neighbouring houses. The timbers served to hold the bricks together, preventing the structure from becoming weak as it attained height, and they were protected by coverings of skins and hides, so that the workmen and woodwork might be safe and shielded from incendiary arrows. The wall was mounting to a great height, and the opposing mound was rising with equal speed, when the Plataeans thought of a new expedient. They made an opening in that part of the city wall where the mound came into contact with it, and began to draw the earth in.

LXXVI. But the Peloponnesians became aware of this, and threw into the breach clay packed in reed-mats that it might not filter through like the loose earth and be carried away. But the besieged, thwarted in this direction, gave up that plan and dug a mine from the town, and, guessing when they had got beneath the mound, once more began to draw away the earth to their side, this time from underneath; and for a long time they worked

τοὺς ἔξω, ὥστε ἐπιβάλλοντας ἧσσον ἀνύτειν ὑπαγομένου αὐτοῖς κάτωθεν τοῦ χώματος καὶ ἰζάνον-
3 τος αἰεὶ ἐπὶ τὸ κενούμενον. δεδιότες δὲ μὴ οὐδ' οὕτω δύνωνται ὀλίγοι πρὸς πολλοὺς ἀντέχειν, προσεπεξηῦρον τόδε· τὸ μὲν μέγα οἰκοδόμημα ἐπαύσαντο ἐργαζόμενοι τὸ κατὰ τὸ χῶμα, ἔνθεν δὲ καὶ ἔνθεν αὐτοῦ ἀρξάμενοι ἀπὸ τοῦ βραχέος τείχους ἐκ τοῦ ἐντὸς μηνοειδὲς ἐς τὴν πόλιν ἐσῳκοδόμουν, ὅπως, εἰ τὸ μέγα τεῖχος ἁλίσκοιτο, τοῦτ' ἀντέχοι, καὶ δέοι τοὺς ἐναντίους αὖθις πρὸς αὐτὸ χοῦν, καὶ προχωροῦντας ἔσω διπλάσιόν τε πόνον ἔχειν καὶ ἐν ἀμφιβόλῳ μᾶλλον γίγνεσθαι.
4 ἅμα δὲ τῇ χώσει καὶ μηχανὰς προσῆγον οἱ Πελοποννήσιοι τῇ πόλει, μίαν μὲν ἣ τοῦ μεγάλου οἰκοδομήματος κατὰ τὸ χῶμα προσαχθεῖσα ἐπὶ μέγα τε κατέσεισε καὶ τοὺς Πλαταιᾶς ἐφόβησεν, ἄλλας δὲ ἄλλῃ τοῦ τείχους, ἃς βρόχους τε περιβάλλοντες ἀνέκλων οἱ Πλαταιῆς, καὶ δοκοὺς μεγάλας ἀρτήσαντες ἁλύσεσι μακραῖς σιδηραῖς ἀπὸ τῆς τομῆς ἑκατέρωθεν ἀπὸ κεραιῶν δύο ἐπικεκλιμένων καὶ ὑπερτεινουσῶν ὑπὲρ τοῦ τείχους ἀνελκύσαντες ἐγκαρσίας, ὁπότε προσπεσεῖσθαί πῃ μέλλοι ἡ μηχανή, ἀφίεσαν τὴν δοκὸν χαλαραῖς ταῖς ἁλύσεσι καὶ οὐ διὰ χειρὸς ἔχοντες, ἡ δὲ ῥύμῃ ἐμπίπτουσα ἀπεκαύλιζε τὸ προὖχον τῆς ἐμβολῆς.

LXXVII. Μετὰ δὲ τοῦτο οἱ Πελοποννήσιοι, ὡς αἵ τε μηχαναὶ οὐδὲν ὠφέλουν καὶ τῷ χώματι

unnoticed by those outside, so that in spite of what they heaped on these made less progress, because their mound, as it was sapped from below, constantly kept settling down into the hollow space. But fearing that even so they would not be able to hold out, few as they were against a multitude, they devised this further expedient: they stopped working on the high structure opposite the mound, and starting at the low part of the wall on either side of it they began building a crescent-shaped rampart on the inward or city side of it, in order that, if the high wall should be taken, this might offer resistance; the enemy would thus have to raise a second mound to oppose the new rampart, and as they advanced and came inside the crescent they would not only have their labour twice over, but would also be more exposed to attack on both sides. But the Peloponnesians, while going on with their mound, also brought up engines against the city: one was moved forward over the mound, and shook down a great part of the high structure, terrifying the Plataeans, while others were brought to bear at different parts of the wall. But the Plataeans threw nooses over these and pulled them up. They also suspended great beams by long iron chains attached at either end to two poles which rested on the wall and extended over it; then they hauled up the beams at right angles[1] to the battering-ram and when it was about to strike anywhere let go the beam by allowing the chains to run slack and not keeping hold of them; whereupon the beam would fall with a rush and break off the head of the battering-ram.

LXXVII. After this, the Peloponnesians, seeing that their engines were doing no good and that the

[1] *i.e.* parallel to the wall.

τὸ ἀντιτείχισμα ἐγίγνετο, νομίσαντες ἄπορον εἶναι ἀπὸ τῶν παρόντων δεινῶν ἑλεῖν τὴν πόλιν
2 πρὸς τὴν περιτείχισιν παρεσκευάζοντο. πρότερον δὲ πυρὶ ἔδοξεν αὐτοῖς πειρᾶσαι εἰ δύναιντο πνεύματος γενομένου ἐπιφλέξαι τὴν πόλιν οὖσαν οὐ μεγάλην· πᾶσαν γὰρ δὴ ἰδέαν ἐπενόουν, εἴ πως σφίσιν ἄνευ δαπάνης καὶ πολιορκίας προσαχθείη.
3 φοροῦντες δὲ ὕλης φακέλους παρέβαλον ἀπὸ τοῦ χώματος ἐς τὸ μεταξὺ πρῶτον τοῦ τείχους καὶ τῆς προσχώσεως, ταχὺ δὲ πλήρους γενομένου διὰ πολυχειρίαν ἐπιπαρένησαν καὶ τῆς ἄλλης πόλεως ὅσον ἐδύναντο ἀπὸ τοῦ μετεώρου πλεῖστον ἐπισχεῖν, ἐμβαλόντες δὲ πῦρ ξὺν θείῳ καὶ πίσσῃ
4 ἧψαν τὴν ὕλην. καὶ ἐγένετο φλὸξ τοσαύτη ὅσην οὐδείς πω ἔς γε ἐκεῖνον τὸν χρόνον χειροποίητον εἶδεν· ἤδη γὰρ ἐν ὄρεσιν ὕλη τριφθεῖσα ὑπ' ἀνέμων πρὸς αὐτὴν ἀπὸ ταὐτομάτου πῦρ καὶ φλόγα
5 ἀπ' αὐτοῦ ἀνῆκεν. τοῦτο δὲ μέγα τε ἦν καὶ τοὺς Πλαταιᾶς τἆλλα διαφυγόντας ἐλαχίστου ἐδέησε διαφθεῖραι· ἐντὸς γὰρ πολλοῦ χωρίου τῆς πόλεως οὐκ ἦν πελάσαι, πνεῦμά τε εἰ ἐπεγένετο αὐτῇ ἐπίφορον, ὅπερ καὶ ἤλπιζον οἱ ἐναντίοι, οὐκ ἂν
6 διέφυγον. νῦν δὲ καὶ τόδε λέγεται ξυμβῆναι, ὕδωρ πολὺ καὶ βροντὰς γενομένας σβέσαι τὴν φλόγα καὶ οὕτως παυσθῆναι τὸν κίνδυνον.

counter-wall was keeping pace with the mound, and concluding that it was impracticable without more formidable means of attack to take the city, began to make preparations for throwing a wall about it. But before doing that they decided to try fire, in the hope that, if a wind should spring up, they might be able to set the city on fire, as it was not large; indeed, there was no expedient they did not consider, that they might if possible reduce the city without the expense of a siege. Accordingly they brought faggots of brushwood and threw them down from the mound, first into the space between the wall and the mound; and then, since the space was soon filled up by the multitude of workers, they heaped faggots also as far into the city as they could reach from the height, and finally threw fire together with sulphur and pitch upon the wood and set it afire. And a conflagration arose greater than any one had ever seen up to that time, kindled, I mean, by the hand of man; for in times past in the mountains when dry branches have been rubbed against each other a forest has caught fire spontaneously therefrom and produced a conflagration. And this fire was not only a great one, but also very nearly destroyed the Plataeans after they had escaped all earlier perils; for in a large part of the city it was not possible to get near the fire, and if on top of that a breeze had sprung up blowing toward the city, which was precisely what the enemy were hoping for, the Plataeans would not have escaped. But as it was, this also is said to have happened—a heavy thunder-shower came on and quenched the flames, and so the danger was checked.

LXXVIII. Οἱ δὲ Πελοποννήσιοι ἐπειδὴ καὶ τούτου διήμαρτον, μέρος μέν τι καταλιπόντες τοῦ στρατοῦ, τὸ δὲ πλέον ἀφέντες περιετείχιζον τὴν πόλιν κύκλῳ διελόμενοι κατὰ πόλεις τὸ χωρίον· τάφρος δὲ ἐντός τε ἦν καὶ ἔξωθεν ἐξ ἧς ἐπλινθεύ-
2 σαντο. καὶ ἐπειδὴ πᾶν ἐξείργαστο περὶ ἀρκτούρου ἐπιτολάς, καταλιπόντες φυλακὰς τοῦ ἡμίσεος τείχους (τὸ δὲ ἥμισυ Βοιωτοὶ ἐφύλασσον) ἀνεχώρησαν τῷ στρατῷ καὶ διελύθησαν κατὰ πόλεις.
3 Πλαταιῆς δὲ παῖδας μὲν καὶ γυναῖκας καὶ τοὺς πρεσβυτάτους τε καὶ πλῆθος τὸ ἀχρεῖον τῶν ἀνθρώπων πρότερον ἐκκεκομισμένοι ἦσαν ἐς τὰς Ἀθήνας, αὐτοὶ δὲ ἐπολιορκοῦντο ἐγκαταλελειμμένοι τετρακόσιοι, Ἀθηναίων δὲ ὀγδοήκοντα, γυ-
4 ναῖκες δὲ δέκα καὶ ἑκατὸν σιτοποιοί. τοσοῦτοι ἦσαν οἱ ξύμπαντες ὅτε ἐς τὴν πολιορκίαν καθίσταντο, καὶ ἄλλος οὐδεὶς ἦν ἐν τῷ τείχει οὔτε δοῦλος οὔτ' ἐλεύθερος. τοιαύτη μὲν ἡ Πλαταιῶν πολιορκία κατεσκευάσθη.

LXXIX. Τοῦ δ' αὐτοῦ θέρους καὶ ἅμα τῇ τῶν Πλαταιῶν ἐπιστρατείᾳ Ἀθηναῖοι δισχιλίοις ὁπλίταις ἑαυτῶν καὶ ἱππεῦσι διακοσίοις ἐπεστράτευσαν ἐπὶ Χαλκιδέας τοὺς ἐπὶ Θρᾴκης καὶ Βοττιαίους ἀκμάζοντος τοῦ σίτου· ἐστρατήγει δὲ
2 Ξενοφῶν ὁ Εὐριπίδου τρίτος αὐτός. ἐλθόντες δὲ ὑπὸ Σπάρτωλον τὴν Βοττικὴν τὸν σῖτον διέφθειραν. ἐδόκει δὲ καὶ προσχωρήσειν ἡ πόλις ὑπὸ

LXXVIII. When the Peloponnesians had failed in this attempt also, they dismissed the larger part of their army, leaving only a portion of it, and proceeded to throw a wall around the city, apportioning the space to the several cities; and there were ditches both inside and outside the wall, out of which they had taken the clay for the bricks. And when the wall was entirely finished about the time of the rising of Arcturus,[1] they left a guard to watch one half of the wall (the Thebans guarded the other half), and withdrew the main army, the troops dispersing to their several cities. But the Plataeans had previously had their children and wives, as well as the oldest men and the unserviceable part of the population, removed to Athens, and the men left behind to undergo the siege were only four hundred of their own number and eighty Athenians, besides one hundred and ten women to prepare the food. This was the number all told when the siege began, and there was no one else within the walls, slave or freeman. Such were the conditions under which the siege of the Plataeans was established.

LXXIX. During the same summer, when the corn was in full ear,[2] while the expedition against Plataea was in progress, the Athenians with two thousand hoplites of their own and two hundred cavalry marched against the Chalcidians in Thrace and the Bottiaeans, under the command of Xenophon son of Euripides and two others. And coming to Spartolus in Bottice they destroyed the grain. It was believed, moreover, that the city would be delivered over to them by a party inside the town which was

[1] About the middle of September.
[2] In the month of May.

τινων ἔνδοθεν πρασσόντων· προπεμψάντων δὲ ἐς
Ὄλυνθον τῶν οὐ ταὐτὰ βουλομένων ὁπλῖταί τε
ἦλθον καὶ στρατιὰ ἐς φυλακήν· ἧς ἐπεξελθούσης
ἐκ τῆς Σπαρτώλου ἐς μάχην καθίστανται οἱ Ἀθη-
3 ναῖοι ὑπ᾿ αὐτῇ τῇ πόλει. καὶ οἱ μὲν ὁπλῖται τῶν
Χαλκιδέων καὶ ἐπίκουροί τινες μετ᾿ αὐτῶν νικῶν-
ται ὑπὸ τῶν Ἀθηναίων καὶ ἀναχωροῦσιν ἐς τὴν
Σπάρτωλον, οἱ δὲ ἱππῆς τῶν Χαλκιδέων καὶ ψιλοὶ
νικῶσι τοὺς τῶν Ἀθηναίων ἱππέας καὶ ψιλούς.
4 εἶχον δέ τινας οὐ πολλοὺς πελταστὰς ἐκ τῆς
Κρουσίδος γῆς καλουμένης. ἄρτι δὲ τῆς μάχης
γεγενημένης ἐπιβοηθοῦσιν ἄλλοι πελτασταὶ ἐκ
5 τῆς Ὀλύνθου. καὶ οἱ ἐκ τῆς Σπαρτώλου ψιλοὶ
ὡς εἶδον, θαρσήσαντες τοῖς τε προσγιγνομένοις
καὶ ὅτι πρότερον οὐχ ἥσσηντο, ἐπιτίθενται αὖθις
μετὰ τῶν Χαλκιδέων ἱππέων καὶ τῶν προσβοηθησάντων τοῖς Ἀθηναίοις· καὶ ἀναχωροῦσι πρὸς
τὰς δύο τάξεις ἃς κατέλιπον παρὰ τοῖς σκευο-
6 φόροις. καὶ ὁπότε μὲν ἐπίοιεν οἱ Ἀθηναῖοι, ἐνε-
δίδοσαν, ἀναχωροῦσι δὲ ἐνέκειντο καὶ ἐσηκόντιζον.
οἵ τε ἱππῆς τῶν Χαλκιδέων προσιππεύοντες ᾗ
δοκοίη ἐσέβαλλον, καὶ οὐχ ἥκιστα φοβήσαντες
ἔτρεψαν τοὺς Ἀθηναίους καὶ ἐπεδίωξαν ἐπὶ πολύ.
7 καὶ οἱ μὲν Ἀθηναῖοι ἐς τὴν Ποτείδαιαν καταφεύ-
γουσι, καὶ ὕστερον τοὺς νεκροὺς ὑποσπόνδους
κομισάμενοι ἐς τὰς Ἀθήνας ἀναχωροῦσι τῷ περιόντι τοῦ στρατοῦ· ἀπέθανον δὲ αὐτῶν τριάκοντα

negotiating with them; but the opposite faction forestalled this by sending word to Olynthus, and some hoplites and other troops arrived to garrison the place. Now when these made a sally from Spartolus, the Athenians were drawn into a battle with them under the very walls of the city, and although the hoplites of the Chalcidians and some mercenaries with them were defeated by the Athenians and retreated into Spartolus, the cavalry of the Chalcidians and the light-armed troops defeated the Athenian cavalry and light-troops; for the Athenians had a few targeteers from the land called Crousis,[1] and just after the battle was over another force of targeteers came from Olynthus to the help of the garrison. And when the light-armed troops in Spartolus saw them, emboldened by these accessions and because they had not been worsted before, they again, assisted by the Chalcidian cavalry and those who had newly come to their support, attacked the Athenians, who now fell back upon the two companies which they had left with their baggage. And whenever the Athenians advanced, they gave way, but when the Athenians retreated they kept close at their heels, hurling javelins at them. Then the Chalcidian cavalry, riding up, kept charging the Athenians wherever opportunity offered, and throwing them into utter panic routed them and pursued them to a great distance. The Athenians took refuge in Potidaea, and afterwards, having recovered their dead under a truce, returned to Athens with what remained of their army; and they had lost three hundred and thirty

[1] This is evidently a remark in explanation of the presence of light-troops with the Athenians, for there had come from Athens only heavy-armed infantry and cavalry; *cf.* § 1 above.

καὶ τετρακόσιοι καὶ οἱ στρατηγοὶ πάντες. οἱ δὲ Χαλκιδῆς καὶ Βοττιαῖοι τροπαῖόν τε ἔστησαν καὶ τοὺς νεκροὺς τοὺς αὑτῶν ἀνελόμενοι διελύθησαν κατὰ πόλεις.

LXXX. Τοῦ δ' αὐτοῦ θέρους, οὐ πολλῷ ὕστερον τούτων, Ἀμπρακιῶται καὶ Χαόνες, βουλόμενοι Ἀκαρνανίαν τὴν πᾶσαν καταστρέψασθαι καὶ Ἀθηναίων ἀποστῆσαι, πείθουσι Λακεδαιμονίους ναυτικόν τε παρασκευάσαι ἐκ τῆς ξυμμαχίδος καὶ ὁπλίτας χιλίους πέμψαι ἐπ' Ἀκαρνανίαν, λέγοντες ὅτι, ἢν ναυσὶ καὶ πεζῷ ἅμα μετὰ σφῶν ἔλθωσιν, ἀδυνάτων ὄντων ξυμβοηθεῖν τῶν ἀπὸ θαλάσσης Ἀκαρνάνων ῥᾳδίως Ἀκαρνανίαν σχόντες καὶ τῆς Ζακύνθου καὶ Κεφαλληνίας κρατήσουσι, καὶ ὁ περίπλους οὐκέτι ἔσοιτο Ἀθηναίοις ὁμοίως περὶ Πελοπόννησον·
2 ἐλπίδας δ' εἶναι καὶ Ναύπακτον λαβεῖν. οἱ δὲ Λακεδαιμόνιοι πεισθέντες Κνῆμον μὲν ναύαρχον ἔτι ὄντα καὶ τοὺς ὁπλίτας ἐπὶ ναυσὶν ὀλίγαις εὐθὺς πέμπουσι, τῷ δὲ ναυτικῷ περιήγγειλαν παρασκευασαμένῳ ὡς τάχιστα πλεῖν ἐς Λευκάδα.
3 ἦσαν δὲ Κορίνθιοι ξυμπροθυμούμενοι μάλιστα τοῖς Ἀμπρακιώταις ἀποίκοις οὖσιν. καὶ τὸ μὲν ναυτικὸν ἔκ τε Κορίνθου καὶ Σικυῶνος καὶ τῶν ταύτῃ χωρίων ἐν παρασκευῇ ἦν, τὸ δ' ἐκ Λευκάδος καὶ Ἀνακτορίου καὶ Ἀμπρακίας πρότερον
4 ἀφικόμενον ἐν Λευκάδι περιέμενεν. Κνῆμος δὲ καὶ οἱ μετ' αὐτοῦ χίλιοι ὁπλῖται ἐπειδὴ ἐπεραιώθησαν λαθόντες Φορμίωνα, ὃς ἦρχε τῶν εἴκοσι

men and all their generals. The Chalcidians and Bottiaeans set up a trophy, and then, after they had taken up their own dead, dispersed to their several cities.

LXXX. During the same summer, not long after these events, the Ambraciots and Chaonians, wishing to subdue the whole of Acarnania and detach it from Athens, persuaded the Lacedaemonians to fit out a fleet from the countries of the Doric alliance and to send a thousand hoplites against Acarnania, saying that, if they joined forces with them, bringing ships and infantry, it would be an easy matter first to occupy Acarnania since the Acarnanians on[1] the seacoast would be unable to aid those inland, and then to make themselves masters of Zacynthus and Cephallenia also: after that the Athenians would no longer be able to sail round the Peloponnesus in the same way as before; and there was a chance of taking Naupactus also. The Lacedaemonians agreed and at once despatched Cnemus, who was still admiral,[2] and the hoplites on a few ships, and sent round orders to the allied fleet to make their preparations and sail as soon as possible to Leucas. And the Corinthians were especially eager to support the enterprise of the Ambraciots, who were colonists of theirs. The contingent of the fleet to come from Corinth and Sicyon and the places in that quarter was still under preparation, but that from Leucas and Anactorium and Ambracia, arriving first, waited at Leucas. As for Cnemus and the thousand hoplites, as soon as they had succeeded in crossing over without being detected by Phormio, who was in command of the

[1] *i.e.* because of the presence of the Peloponnesian fleet along their coast. [2] *cf.* ch. lxvi. 2.

νεῶν τῶν Ἀττικῶν αἳ περὶ Ναύπακτον ἐφρούρουν, εὐθὺς παρεσκευάζοντο τὴν κατὰ γῆν
5 στρατείαν. καὶ αὐτῷ παρῆσαν Ἑλλήνων μὲν
Ἀμπρακιῶται καὶ Ἀνακτόριοι καὶ Λευκάδιοι
καὶ οὓς αὐτὸς ἔχων ἦλθε χίλιοι Πελοποννησίων,
βάρβαροι δὲ Χαόνες χίλιοι ἀβασίλευτοι, ὧν
ἡγοῦντο ἐπετησίῳ προστατείᾳ ἐκ τοῦ ἀρχικοῦ
γένους Φώτιος καὶ Νικάνωρ. ξυνεστρατεύοντο
δὲ μετὰ Χαόνων καὶ Θεσπρωτοὶ ἀβασίλευτοι.
6 Μολοσσοὺς δὲ ἦγε καὶ Ἀτιντᾶνας Σαβύλινθος
ἐπίτροπος ὢν Θάρυπος τοῦ βασιλέως ἔτι παιδὸς
ὄντος, καὶ Παραυαίους Ὄροιδος βασιλεύων.
Ὀρέσται δὲ χίλιοι, ὧν ἐβασίλευεν Ἀντίοχος,
μετὰ Παραυαίων ξυνεστρατεύοντο Ὀροίδῳ Ἀν-
7 τιόχου ἐπιτρέψαντος. ἔπεμψε δὲ καὶ Περδίκκας
κρύφα τῶν Ἀθηναίων χιλίους Μακεδόνων, οἳ
8 ὕστερον ἦλθον. τούτῳ τῷ στρατῷ ἐπορεύετο
Κνῆμος οὐ περιμείνας τὸ ἀπὸ Κορίνθου ναυτικόν,
καὶ διὰ τῆς Ἀργείας ἰόντες Λιμναίαν, κώμην
ἀτείχιστον, ἐπόρθησαν. ἀφικνοῦνταί τε ἐπὶ
Στράτον, πόλιν μεγίστην τῆς Ἀκαρνανίας, νομίζοντες, εἰ ταύτην πρώτην λάβοιεν, ῥᾳδίως
σφίσι τἆλλα προσχωρήσειν.

LXXXI. Ἀκαρνᾶνες δὲ αἰσθόμενοι κατά τε
γῆν πολλὴν στρατιὰν ἐσβεβληκυῖαν ἔκ τε
θαλάσσης ναυσὶν ἅμα τοὺς πολεμίους παρεσο-
μένους, οὔτε ξυνεβοήθουν ἐφύλασσόν τε τὰ αὑτῶν
ἕκαστοι, παρά τε Φορμίωνα ἔπεμπον κελεύοντες
ἀμύνειν· ὁ δὲ ἀδύνατος ἔφη εἶναι ναυτικοῦ ἐκ
Κορίνθου μέλλοντος ἐκπλεῖν Ναύπακτον ἐρήμην
2 ἀπολιπεῖν. οἱ δὲ Πελοποννήσιοι καὶ οἱ ξύμμα-

twenty Athenian ships that were on guard off Naupactus,[1] they began at once to prepare for the expedition by land. He had with him, of Hellenic troops, some Ambraciots, Anactorians and Leucadians, and the thousand Peloponnesians whom he himself brought; of barbarians, a thousand Chaonians, who, having no king, were led by Photius and Nicanor of the ruling clan who had the annual presidency. With the Chaonian contingent were also some Thesprotians, who likewise have no king. A force of Molossians and Atintanians were led by Sabylinthus, the guardian of king Tharyps, who was still a boy, and of Paravaeans by their king, Oroedus. With the Paravaeans were a thousand Orestians whose king, Antiochus, had entrusted them to Oroedus. And Perdiccas also sent, without the knowledge of the Athenians, a thousand Macedonians, who arrived too late. With this army Cnemus set out, not waiting for the fleet from Corinth; and as they passed through the territory of Argos[2] they sacked Limnaea, an unwalled village. Finally they arrived at Stratus, the largest city of Acarnania, thinking that if they could take this first, the other places would readily come over to them.

LXXXI. Now when the Acarnanians perceived that a large army had invaded them by land and that the enemy would soon be at hand with a fleet by sea as well, they did not attempt combined resistance, but guarding severally their own possessions they sent to Phormio urging him to aid them. But he said that he could not leave Naupactus unprotected, as a hostile fleet was about to sail from Corinth. Meanwhile the Peloponnesians and their

[1] *cf.* ch. lxix. 1. [2] Amphilochian Argos; *cf.* ch. lxviii. 1.

χοι τρία τέλη ποιήσαντες σφῶν αὐτῶν ἐχώρουν πρὸς τὴν τῶν Στρατίων πόλιν, ὅπως ἐγγὺς στρατοπεδευσάμενοι, εἰ μὴ λόγῳ πείθοιεν, ἔργῳ πει-
3 ρῷντο τοῦ τείχους. καὶ τὸ μέσον μὲν ἔχοντες προσῇσαν Χαόνες καὶ οἱ ἄλλοι βάρβαροι, ἐκ δεξιᾶς δ' αὐτῶν Λευκάδιοι καὶ Ἀνακτόριοι καὶ οἱ μετὰ τούτων, ἐν ἀριστερᾷ δὲ Κνῆμος καὶ οἱ Πελοποννήσιοι καὶ Ἀμπρακιῶται· διεῖχον δὲ πολὺ ἀπ' ἀλλήλων καὶ ἔστιν ὅτε οὐδὲ ἑωρῶντο.
4 καὶ οἱ μὲν Ἕλληνες τεταγμένοι τε προσῇσαν καὶ διὰ φυλακῆς ἔχοντες, ἕως ἐστρατοπεδεύσαντο ἐν ἐπιτηδείῳ· οἱ δὲ Χαόνες σφίσι τε αὐτοῖς πιστεύοντες καὶ ἀξιούμενοι ὑπὸ τῶν ἐκείνῃ ἠπειρωτῶν μαχιμώτατοι εἶναι οὔτε ἐπέσχον τοῦ στρατόπεδον καταλαβεῖν, χωρήσαντές τε ῥύμῃ μετὰ τῶν ἄλλων βαρβάρων ἐνόμισαν αὐτοβοεὶ ἂν τὴν πόλιν
5 ἑλεῖν καὶ αὐτῶν τὸ ἔργον γενέσθαι. γνόντες δ' αὐτοὺς οἱ Στράτιοι ἔτι προσιόντας καὶ ἡγησάμενοι, μεμονωμένων εἰ κρατήσειαν, οὐκ ἂν ἔτι σφίσι τοὺς Ἕλληνας ὁμοίως προσελθεῖν, προλοχίζουσι δὴ τὰ περὶ τὴν πόλιν ἐνέδραις, καὶ ἐπειδὴ ἐγγὺς ἦσαν, ἔκ τε τῆς πόλεως ὁμόσε χωρήσαντες
6 καὶ ἐκ τῶν ἐνεδρῶν προσπίπτουσιν. καὶ ἐς φόβον καταστάντων διαφθείρονταί τε πολλοὶ τῶν Χαόνων, καὶ οἱ ἄλλοι βάρβαροι ὡς εἶδον αὐτοὺς ἐνδόντας, οὐκέτι ὑπέμειναν, ἀλλ' ἐς φυγὴν κατέ-
7 στησαν. τῶν δὲ Ἑλληνικῶν στρατοπέδων οὐδέτερον ᾔσθετο τῆς μάχης, διὰ τὸ πολὺ προελθεῖν αὐτοὺς καὶ στρατόπεδον οἰηθῆναι καταληψομέ-

allies, dividing their troops into three divisions, advanced towards the city of the Stratians, their purpose being to encamp near by, and then, if they could not prevail upon them by parleying, to assault the wall. As they advanced, the centre was held by the Chaonians and the other barbarians, while on their right were the Leucadians and Anactorians and those who accompanied them, and on the left Cnemus with his Peloponnesians and the Ambraciots; and the divisions were far apart from each other, sometimes, not even in sight. And the Hellenic troops as they advanced maintained their ranks and were on their guard until they encamped in a suitable place; but the Chaonians, who were not only confident of themselves but were also recognised as very excellent fighting men by the inhabitants of that part of the mainland, did not halt to make camp, but advanced with a rush along with the other barbarians, thinking that they could take the town at the first assault, and thus gain the glory for themselves. But the Stratians noticed that they were still advancing, and thinking that, if they could overcome them while isolated, the Hellenes would no longer be as ready to attack them, set ambushes in the outskirts of the town, and as soon as the barbarians were close at hand, closed in upon them from the city and from the ambushes and fell upon them. Thrown into a panic, many of the Chaonians were slain, and the other barbarians, seeing them give way, no longer held their ground, but took to flight. But neither of the Hellenic divisions was aware of the battle, because their allies had gone far ahead of them, and they thought that they were

8 νους ἐπείγεσθαι. ἐπεὶ δ' ἐνέκειντο φεύγοντες οἱ βάρβαροι, ἀνελάμβανόν τε αὐτοὺς καὶ ξυναγαγόντες τὰ στρατόπεδα ἡσύχαζον αὐτοῦ τὴν ἡμέραν, ἐς χεῖρας μὲν οὐκ ἰόντων σφίσι τῶν Στρατίων διὰ τὸ μήπω τοὺς ἄλλους Ἀκαρνᾶνας ξυμβεβοηθηκέναι, ἄπωθεν δὲ σφενδονώντων καὶ ἐς ἀπορίαν καθιστάντων· οὐ γὰρ ἦν ἄνευ ὅπλων κινηθῆναι. δοκοῦσι δὲ οἱ Ἀκαρνᾶνες κράτιστοι εἶναι τοῦτο ποιεῖν. LXXXII. ἐπειδὴ δὲ νὺξ ἐγένετο, ἀναχωρήσας ὁ Κνῆμος τῇ στρατιᾷ κατὰ τάχος ἐπὶ τὸν Ἄναπον ποταμόν, ὃς ἀπέχει σταδίους ὀγδοήκοντα Στράτου, τούς τε νεκροὺς κομίζεται τῇ ὑστεραίᾳ ὑποσπόνδους καὶ Οἰνιαδῶν ξυμπαραγενομένων κατὰ φιλίαν ἀναχωρεῖ παρ' αὐτοὺς πρὶν τὴν ξυμβοήθειαν ἐλθεῖν. κἀκεῖθεν ἐπ' οἴκου ἀπῆλθον ἕκαστοι. οἱ δὲ Στράτιοι τροπαῖον ἔστησαν τῆς μάχης τῆς πρὸς τοὺς βαρβάρους.

LXXXIII. Τὸ δ' ἐκ τῆς Κορίνθου καὶ τῶν ἄλλων ξυμμάχων τῶν ἐκ τοῦ Κρισαίου κόλπου ναυτικόν, ὃ ἔδει παραγενέσθαι τῷ Κνήμῳ, ὅπως μὴ ξυμβοηθῶσιν οἱ ἀπὸ θαλάσσης ἄνω Ἀκαρνᾶνες, οὐ παραγίγνεται, ἀλλ' ἠναγκάσθησαν περὶ τὰς αὐτὰς ἡμέρας τῇ ἐν Στράτῳ μάχῃ ναυμαχῆσαι πρὸς Φορμίωνα καὶ τὰς εἴκοσι ναῦς τῶν
2 Ἀθηναίων αἳ ἐφρούρουν ἐν Ναυπάκτῳ. ὁ γὰρ Φορμίων παραπλέοντας αὐτοὺς ἔξω τοῦ κόλπου ἐτήρει, βουλόμενος ἐν τῇ εὐρυχωρίᾳ ἐπιθέσθαι.
3 οἱ δὲ Κορίνθιοι καὶ οἱ ξύμμαχοι ἔπλεον μὲν οὐχ ὡς ἐπὶ ναυμαχίᾳ, ἀλλὰ στρατιωτικώτερον παρεσκευασμένοι ἐς τὴν Ἀκαρνανίαν καὶ οὐκ ἂν οἰόμενοι πρὸς ἑπτὰ καὶ τεσσαράκοντα ναῦς τὰς σφετέρας τολμῆσαι τοὺς Ἀθηναίους εἴκοσι ταῖς

pressing on in order to find a camp. But when the barbarians in their flight broke in upon them, they took them in and uniting their two divisions kept quiet there during the day, the Stratians not coming to close quarters with them, because the rest of the Acarnanians had not yet come to their support, but using their slings against them from a distance and distressing them; for it was not possible for them to stir without armour; and indeed the Acarnanians are famous for their excellence in the use of the sling. LXXXII. But when night came on, Cnemus hastily retreated with his army to the river Anapus, which is eighty stadia distant from Stratus, and on the following day took up his dead under a truce; and since the Oeniadae had joined his expedition in token of their friendly feelings, he withdrew to their country before the combined forces of the Acarnanians had arrived, and from there they returned severally to their homes. As for the Stratians, they set up a trophy of their battle with the barbarians.

LXXXIII. Meanwhile the fleet from Corinth and from the other allies on the Crisaean Gulf, which was to have joined Cnemus in order to prevent the Acarnanians on the sea-coast from aiding those in the interior, did not arrive, but was obliged, about the day of the battle at Stratus, to fight with Phormio and the twenty Athenian ships which were on guard at Naupactus. For Phormio was watching them as they sailed along the coast out of the gulf, preferring to attack them in the open water. Now the Corinthians and their allies on their way to Acarnania were not equipped for fighting at sea, but rather for operations on land, and they had no idea that the Athenians with their twenty ships would dare to

ἑαυτῶν ναυμαχίαν ποιήσασθαι· ἐπειδὴ μέντοι
ἀντιπαραπλέοντάς τε ἑώρων αὐτούς, παρὰ γῆν
σφῶν κομιζομένων, καὶ ἐκ Πατρῶν τῆς Ἀχαΐας
πρὸς τὴν ἀντιπέρας ἤπειρον διαβάλλοντες ἐπ'
Ἀκαρνανίας κατεῖδον τοὺς Ἀθηναίους ἀπὸ τῆς
Χαλκίδος καὶ τοῦ Εὐήνου ποταμοῦ προσπλέοντας
σφίσι καὶ οὐκ ἔλαθον νυκτὸς ἀφορμισάμενοι,[1]
οὕτω δὴ ἀναγκάζονται ναυμαχεῖν κατὰ μέσον τὸν
4 πορθμόν. στρατηγοὶ δὲ ἦσαν μὲν καὶ κατὰ
πόλεις ἑκάστων οἳ παρεσκευάζοντο, Κορινθίων
δὲ Μαχάων καὶ Ἰσοκράτης καὶ Ἀγαθαρχίδας.
5 καὶ οἱ μὲν Πελοποννήσιοι ἐτάξαντο κύκλον τῶν
νεῶν ὡς μέγιστον οἷοί τ' ἦσαν μὴ διδόντες διέκ-
πλουν, τὰς πρῴρας μὲν ἔξω, ἔσω δὲ τὰς πρύ-
μνας, καὶ τά τε λεπτὰ πλοῖα ἃ ξυνέπλει ἐντὸς
ποιοῦνται καὶ πέντε ναῦς τὰς ἄριστα πλεούσας,
ὅπως ἐκπλέοιεν διὰ βραχέος παραγιγνόμεναι, εἴ
πῃ προσπίπτοιεν οἱ ἐναντίοι.

LXXXIV. Οἱ δ' Ἀθηναῖοι κατὰ μίαν ναῦν
τεταγμένοι περιέπλεον αὐτοὺς κύκλῳ καὶ ξυνῆ-
γον ἐς ὀλίγον, ἐν χρῷ αἰεὶ παραπλέοντες καὶ
δόκησιν παρέχοντες αὐτίκα ἐμβαλεῖν· προείρητο
δ' αὐτοῖς ὑπὸ Φορμίωνος μὴ ἐπιχειρεῖν πρὶν ἂν
2 αὐτὸς σημήνῃ. ἤλπιζε γὰρ αὐτῶν οὐ μενεῖν τὴν

[1] Bloomfield's correction for ὑφορμισάμενοι of the MSS.

---

[1] Or, retaining ὑφορμισάμενοι, "they had tried to anchor under cover of night, but had been detected."

bring on an engagement with their own forty-seven. When, however, they saw that the Athenians kept sailing along the opposite coast as long as they themselves continued to skirt the southern shore, and when, as they attempted to cross from Patrae in Achaia to the mainland opposite, making for Acarnania, they observed that the Athenians were bearing down upon them from Chalcis and the river Evenus, and finally when, during the night, they had tried to slip their moorings[1] and get away but had been detected, under these circumstances they were forced to fight in the middle of the channel.[2] Their fleet was commanded by generals from the several states which contributed contingents, the Corinthian squadron by Machaon, Isocrates, and Agatharchidas. The Peloponnesians drew up their ships in as large a circle as they could without allowing the enemy an opportunity to break through,[3] prows outward, sterns inward; and inside the circle they placed the light boats which accompanied them, and also five of their swiftest ships, in order that they might have only a short distance to sail out and bring support at any point where the enemy attacked.

LXXXIV. As for the Athenians, drawn up in single column they kept sailing round the Peloponnesian fleet in a circle, hemming it into a narrower and narrower space, always just grazing by and giving the impression that they would charge at any moment. But orders had been given by Phormio not to attack until he should give the signal; for he hoped that the enemy's ships would not keep in line,

[2] *i.e.* in the open water between Patrae and the mouth of the Evenus, as opposed to the regions along the shore of the Gulf, where their fleet might run into a harbour.

[3] See note on I. xlix. 3.

τάξιν, ὥσπερ ἐν γῇ πεζήν, ἀλλὰ ξυμπεσεῖσθαι
πρὸς ἀλλήλας τὰς ναῦς καὶ τὰ πλοῖα ταραχὴν
παρέξειν, εἴ τ' ἐκπνεύσειεν ἐκ τοῦ κόλπου τὸ
πνεῦμα, ὅπερ ἀναμένων τε περιέπλει καὶ εἰώθει
γίγνεσθαι ἐπὶ τὴν ἕω, οὐδένα χρόνον ἡσυχασειν
αὐτούς· καὶ τὴν ἐπιχείρησιν ἐφ' αὑτῷ τε ἐνόμιζεν
εἶναι, ὁπόταν βούληται, τῶν νεῶν ἄμεινον πλεου-
3 σῶν, καὶ τότε καλλίστην γίγνεσθαι. ὡς δὲ τό τε
πνεῦμα κατῄει καὶ αἱ νῆες ἐν ὀλίγῳ ἤδη οὖσαι
ὑπ' ἀμφοτέρων, τοῦ τε ἀνέμου τῶν τε πλοίων,
ἅμα προσκειμένων ἐταράσσοντο, καὶ ναῦς τε νηὶ
προσέπιπτε καὶ τοῖς κοντοῖς διεωθοῦντο, βοῇ τε
χρώμενοι καὶ πρὸς ἀλλήλους ἀντιφυλακῇ τε καὶ
λοιδορίᾳ οὐδὲν κατήκουον οὔτε τῶν παραγγελλο-
μένων οὔτε τῶν κελευστῶν, καὶ τὰς κώπας ἀδύνατοι ὄντες ἐν κλύδωνι ἀναφέρειν ἄνθρωποι ἄπειροι
τοῖς κυβερνήταις ἀπειθεστέρας τὰς ναῦς παρεῖχον, τότε δὴ κατὰ τὸν καιρὸν τοῦτον σημαίνει,
καὶ οἱ Ἀθηναῖοι προσπεσόντες πρῶτον μὲν κατα-
δύουσι τῶν στρατηγίδων νεῶν μίαν, ἔπειτα δὲ καὶ
τὰς ἄλλας ᾗ χωρήσειαν διέφθειρον, καὶ κατέστησαν ἐς ἀλκὴν μὲν μηδένα τρέπεσθαι αὐτῶν ὑπὸ
τῆς ταραχῆς, φεύγειν δὲ ἐς Πάτρας καὶ Δύμην
4 τῆς Ἀχαΐας. οἱ δὲ Ἀθηναῖοι καταδιώξαντες καὶ
ναῦς δώδεκα λαβόντες τούς τε ἄνδρας ἐξ αὐτῶν
τοὺς πλείστους ἀνελόμενοι ἐς Μολύκρειον ἀπέπλεον, καὶ τροπαῖον στήσαντες ἐπὶ τῷ Ῥίῳ καὶ
ναῦν ἀναθέντες τῷ Ποσειδῶνι ἀνεχώρησαν ἐς
5 Ναύπακτον. παρέπλευσαν δὲ καὶ οἱ Πελοπον-

like infantry on land, but would fall foul of one another, and also be thrown into confusion by the small boats, and then if the breeze for which he was waiting while he sailed round, which usually blew from the gulf towards dawn, should spring up, they would not remain steady for any length of time. As for the attack, he thought that was in his power whenever he chose, since his ships were better sailers, and that then was the most favourable moment for it. So when the wind began to come up, and the ships, already hemmed in a narrow space, were being thrown into confusion both by the violence of the wind and the pressure of the small boats, when ship was dashing against ship and the crews were trying to push them apart with poles, all the while keeping up such shouts and warning cries and abuse of one another that they could not hear either the word of command or the coxswains' calls, and, finally, when the inexperienced rowers, unable to get their oars clear of the water in a heavy sea, were rendering the ships less obedient to the helmsmen, then at this critical moment Phormio gave the signal. Thereupon the Athenians fell upon them; first they sank one of the admirals' ships, and then destroyed the rest as well wherever they came upon them, reducing them to such straits that in their confusion no one turned for defence, but all fled to Patrae and Dyme in Achaia. But the Athenians gave chase, and after they had captured twelve ships and had taken on board most of their crews sailed away to Molycreum; then they set up a trophy on Rhium, dedicated a ship to Poseidon, and returned to Naupactus. The Peloponnesians also

νήσιοι εὐθὺς ταῖς περιλοίποις τῶν νεῶν ἐκ τῆς Δύμης καὶ Πατρῶν ἐς Κυλλήνην τὸ Ἠλείων ἐπίνειον· καὶ ἀπὸ Λευκάδος Κνῆμος καὶ αἱ ἐκείνων νῆες, ἃς ἔδει ταύταις ξυμμεῖξαι, ἀφικνοῦνται μετὰ τὴν ἐν Στράτῳ μάχην ἐς τὴν Κυλλήνην.

LXXXV. Πέμπουσι δὲ καὶ οἱ Λακεδαιμόνιοι τῷ Κνήμῳ ξυμβούλους ἐπὶ τὰς ναῦς Τιμοκράτη καὶ Βρασίδαν καὶ Λυκόφρονα, κελεύοντες ἄλλην ναυμαχίαν βέλτιον παρασκευάζεσθαι καὶ μὴ ὑπ'
2 ὀλίγων νεῶν εἴργεσθαι τῆς θαλάσσης. ἐδόκει γὰρ αὐτοῖς ἄλλως τε καὶ πρῶτον ναυμαχίας πειρασαμένοις πολὺς ὁ παράλογος εἶναι καὶ οὐ τοσούτῳ ᾤοντο σφῶν τὸ ναυτικὸν λείπεσθαι, γεγενῆσθαι δέ τινα μαλακίαν, οὐκ ἀντιτιθέντες τὴν Ἀθηναίων ἐκ πολλοῦ ἐμπειρίαν τῆς σφετέρας δι' ὀλίγου
3 μελέτης. ὀργῇ οὖν ἀπέστελλον. οἱ δὲ ἀφικόμενοι μετὰ τοῦ Κνήμου ναῦς τε προσπεριήγγειλαν κατὰ πόλεις καὶ τὰς προϋπαρχούσας ἐξηρτύοντο
4 ὡς ἐπὶ ναυμαχίαν. πέμπει δὲ καὶ ὁ Φορμίων ἐς τὰς Ἀθήνας τήν τε παρασκευὴν αὐτῶν ἀγγελοῦντας καὶ περὶ τῆς ναυμαχίας ἣν ἐνίκησαν φράσοντας καὶ κελεύων αὐτῷ ναῦς ὅτι πλείστας διὰ τάχους ἀποστεῖλαι, ὡς καθ' ἡμέραν ἑκάστην ἐλ-
5 πίδος οὔσης αἰεὶ ναυμαχήσειν. οἱ δὲ ἀποπέμπουσιν εἴκοσι ναῦς αὐτῷ, τῷ δὲ κομίζοντι αὐτὰς προσεπέστειλαν ἐς Κρήτην πρῶτον ἀφικέσθαι. Νικίας γὰρ Κρὴς Γορτύνιος πρόξενος ὢν πείθει

sailed away immediately with the ships that were left, proceeding from Dyme and Patrae along the coast to Cyllene, the shipyard of the Eleans; and Cnemus likewise, coming from Leucas together with the ships from that quarter[1] which were to have joined the Corinthian fleet, came to Cyllene after the battle at Stratus.

LXXXV. The Lacedaemonians now sent to the fleet Timocrates, Brasidas, and Lycophron as advisers to Cnemus, directing them to make better preparation for another sea-fight, and not to be driven off the sea by a few ships. For the issue of the recent battle seemed to them utterly incomprehensible, especially since this was their first attempt at a sea-fight, and they could not believe that their fleet was so greatly inferior, but thought that there had been cowardice somewhere, failing to take into account the long experience of the Athenians as compared with their own brief practice. In a rage, then, they dispatched the advisers. And these on their arrival, acting in conjunction with Cnemus, sent round a call to the allied cities for additional ships, and set about equipping those already at hand, with a view to a sea-fight. And Phormio on his part sent messengers to Athens to give information of the enemy's preparations and to tell about the battle which they had won, urging them also to send to him speedily as many ships as possible, since there was always a prospect that a battle might be fought any day. So they sent him twenty ships, but gave the commander in charge of them special orders to sail first to Crete. For Nicias, a Cretan of Gortys, who was a proxenus[2] of theirs, persuaded

[1] The contingents from Leucas, Anactorium, and Ambracia, ch. lxxx. 2, 3. [2] See ch. xxix. 1, note.

αὐτοὺς ἐπὶ Κυδωνίαν πλεῦσαι, φάσκων προσποιήσειν αὐτὴν οὖσαν πολεμίαν· ἐπῆγε δὲ Πολιχνίταις χαριζόμενος ὁμόροις τῶν Κυδωνιατῶν.
6 καὶ ὁ μὲν λαβὼν τὰς ναῦς ᾤχετο ἐς Κρήτην καὶ μετὰ τῶν Πολιχνιτῶν ἐδῄου τὴν γῆν τῶν Κυδωνιατῶν, καὶ ὑπ᾽ ἀνέμων καὶ ἀπλοίας ἐνδιέτριψεν οὐκ ὀλίγον χρόνον.

LXXXVI. Οἱ δ᾽ ἐν τῇ Κυλλήνῃ Πελοποννήσιοι ἐν τούτῳ, ἐν ᾧ οἱ Ἀθηναῖοι περὶ Κρήτην κατείχοντο, παρεσκευασμένοι ὡς ἐπὶ ναυμαχίαν παρέπλευσαν ἐς Πάνορμον τὸν Ἀχαϊκόν, οὗπερ αὐτοῖς ὁ κατὰ γῆν στρατὸς τῶν Πελοποννησίων προσ-
2 εβεβοηθήκει. παρέπλευσε δὲ καὶ ὁ Φορμίων ἐπὶ τὸ Ῥίον τὸ Μολυκρικὸν καὶ ὡρμίσατο ἔξω αὐτοῦ
3 ναυσὶν εἴκοσι, αἷσπερ καὶ ἐναυμάχησεν. ἦν δὲ τοῦτο μὲν τὸ Ῥίον φίλιον τοῖς Ἀθηναίοις, τὸ δ᾽ ἕτερον Ῥίον ἐστὶν ἀντιπέρας τὸ ἐν τῇ Πελοποννήσῳ· διέχετον δὲ ἀπ᾽ ἀλλήλων σταδίους μάλιστα ἑπτὰ τῆς θαλάσσης, τοῦ δὲ Κρισαίου κόλπου
4 στόμα τοῦτό ἐστιν. ἐπὶ οὖν τῷ Ῥίῳ τῷ Ἀχαϊκῷ οἱ Πελοποννήσιοι ἀπέχοντι οὐ πολὺ τοῦ Πανόρμου, ἐν ᾧ αὐτοῖς ὁ πεζὸς ἦν, ὡρμίσαντο καὶ αὐτοὶ ναυσὶν ἑπτὰ καὶ ἑβδομήκοντα,[1] ἐπειδὴ καὶ τοὺς
5 Ἀθηναίους εἶδον. καὶ ἐπὶ μὲν ἓξ ἢ ἑπτὰ ἡμέρας ἀνθώρμουν ἀλλήλοις μελετῶντές τε καὶ παρασκευαζόμενοι τὴν ναυμαχίαν, γνώμην ἔχοντες οἱ μὲν μὴ ἐκπλεῖν ἔξω τῶν Ῥίων ἐς τὴν εὐρυχωρίαν, φοβούμενοι τὸ πρότερον πάθος, οἱ δὲ μὴ ἐσπλεῖν ἐς τὰ στενά, νομίζοντες πρὸς ἐκείνων εἶναι τὴν ἐν
6 ὀλίγῳ ναυμαχίαν. ἔπειτα ὁ Κνῆμος καὶ ὁ Βρασίδας καὶ οἱ ἄλλοι τῶν Πελοποννησίων στρατηγοί, βουλόμενοι ἐν τάχει τὴν ναυμαχίαν ποιῆσαι πρίν

[1] Hude reads πεντήκοντα, with C.

them to sail against Cydonia, a hostile town, promising to bring it over to the Athenians; but he was really asking them to intervene to gratify the people of Polichne, who are neighbours of the Cydonians. So the officer in charge took the ships, went to Crete, and helped the Polichnitans to ravage the lands of the Cydonians, and by reason of winds and stress of weather wasted not a little time.

LXXXVI. Meantime, while the Athenians were detained in Crete, the Peloponnesians at Cyllene, equipped and ready for a battle, sailed along the coast to Panormus in Achaia, where the land-forces of the Peloponnesians had come to their support. And Phormio also sailed along the coast to the Molycrian Rhium and anchored outside with the twenty ships with which he had fought before. This Rhium was friendly to the Athenians, and opposite is the other Rhium, that in the Peloponnesus; and the distance between them is about seven stadia by sea, constituting the mouth of the Crisaean Gulf. Accordingly the Peloponnesians, when they saw the Athenians come to anchor, likewise anchored with seventy-seven ships at the Achaian Rhium, which is not far from Panormus, where their land-forces were. And for six or seven days they lay at anchor opposite one another, practising and preparing for battle, the one side resolved not to sail outside the two Rhia into the open water, fearing a recurrence of their disaster, the other not to sail into the straits, thinking that fighting in a narrow space was in the enemy's favour. At last Cnemus and Brasidas and the other Peloponnesian commanders, wishing to bring on the engagement

τι καὶ ἀπὸ τῶν Ἀθηναίων ἐπιβοηθῆσαι, ξυνεκάλεσαν τοὺς στρατιώτας πρῶτον, καὶ ὁρῶντες αὐτῶν τοὺς πολλοὺς διὰ τὴν προτέραν ἧσσαν φοβουμένους καὶ οὐ προθύμους ὄντας παρεκελεύσαντο καὶ ἔλεξαν τοιάδε.

LXXXVII. "Ἡ μὲν γενομένη ναυμαχία, ὦ ἄνδρες Πελοποννήσιοι, εἴ τις ἄρα δι' αὐτὴν ὑμῶν φοβεῖται τὴν μέλλουσαν, οὐχὶ δικαίαν ἔχει τέκ-
2 μαρσιν τὸ ἐκφοβῆσαι. τῇ τε γὰρ παρασκευῇ ἐνδεὴς ἐγένετο, ὥσπερ ἴστε, καὶ οὐχὶ ἐς ναυμαχίαν μᾶλλον ἢ ἐπὶ στρατείαν ἐπλέομεν· ξυνέβη δὲ καὶ τὰ ἀπὸ τῆς τύχης οὐκ ὀλίγα ἐναντιωθῆναι, καί πού τι καὶ ἡ ἀπειρία πρῶτον ναυμαχοῦντας
3 ἔσφηλεν. ὥστε οὐ κατὰ τὴν ἡμετέραν κακίαν τὸ ἡσσᾶσθαι προσεγένετο, οὐδὲ δίκαιον τῆς γνώμης τὸ μὴ κατὰ κράτος νικηθέν, ἔχον δέ τινα ἐν αὐτῷ ἀντιλογίαν, τῆς γε ξυμφορᾶς τῷ ἀποβάντι ἀμβλύνεσθαι, νομίσαι δὲ ταῖς μὲν τύχαις ἐνδέχεσθαι σφάλλεσθαι τοὺς ἀνθρώπους, ταῖς δὲ γνώμαις τοὺς αὐτοὺς αἰεὶ ὀρθῶς[1] ἀνδρείους εἶναι, καὶ μὴ ἀπειρίαν τοῦ ἀνδρείου παρόντος προβαλλομένους
4 εἰκότως ἂν ἔν τινι κακοὺς γενέσθαι. ὑμῶν δὲ οὐδ' ἡ ἀπειρία τοσοῦτον λείπεται ὅσον τόλμῃ προύχετε· τῶνδε δὲ ἡ ἐπιστήμη, ἣν μάλιστα φοβεῖσθε, ἀνδρείαν μὲν ἔχουσα καὶ μνήμην ἕξει ἐν τῷ δεινῷ ἐπιτελεῖν ἃ ἔμαθεν, ἄνευ δὲ εὐψυχίας οὐδεμία τέχνη πρὸς τοὺς κινδύνους ἰσχύει. φόβος γὰρ μνήμην ἐκπλήσσει, τέχνη δὲ ἄνευ ἀλκῆς οὐ-

[1] Hude writes ὀρθούς and deletes ἀνδρείους (with Badham).

soon, before reinforcements came from Athens, first called their soldiers together, and seeing that most of them were frightened on account of their previous defeat and not eager for battle, encouraged them and spoke as follows:

LXXXVII. "The recent sea-fight, Peloponnesians, if possibly it has caused any man among you to be afraid of the one before us, affords no just grounds for your alarm. For our preparation was deficient, as you know, and the object of our voyage was not so much to fight at sea as operations on land; and it happened, furthermore, that not a few of the chances of war were against us, and doubtless also our inexperience had something to do with our failure in the first sea-fight. It was not then our cowardice that brought about defeat, nor is it right that the spirit, which force cannot conquer, but which has in it something defiant, should be dulled and blunted by the outcome of mere chance; rather you ought to reflect that although men may suffer reverse in their fortunes, yet in their spirit brave men are rightly considered always brave, and when courage is present no inexperience can properly be urged as an excuse for being cowards under any circumstances. And, after all, your inexperience is more than counterbalanced by your superiority in daring; and though the enemy's skill, which you particularly dread, will indeed, so long as bravery goes with it, have the presence of mind in the moment of danger to put into effect the lessons it has learned, yet without valour no amount of proficiency avails against such dangers. For fear drives presence of mind away, and skill without

5 δὲν ὠφελεῖ. πρὸς μὲν οὖν τὸ ἐμπειρότερον αὐτῶν
τὸ τολμηρότερον ἀντιτάξασθε, πρὸς δὲ τὸ διὰ
τὴν ἧσσαν δεδιέναι τὸ ἀπαράσκευοι τότε τυχεῖν.
6 περιγίγνεται δὲ ἡμῖν πλῆθός τε νεῶν καὶ πρὸς τῇ
γῇ οἰκείᾳ οὔσῃ ὁπλιτῶν παρόντων ναυμαχεῖν· τὰ
δὲ πολλὰ τῶν πλεόνων καὶ ἄμεινον παρεσκευασ-
7 μένων τὸ κράτος ἐστίν. ὥστε οὐδὲ καθ' ἓν εὑρί-
σκομεν εἰκότως ἂν ἡμᾶς σφαλλομένους· καὶ ὅσα
ἡμάρτομεν πρότερον, νῦν αὐτὰ ταῦτα προσγενό-
8 μενα διδασκαλίαν παρέξει. θαρσοῦντες οὖν καὶ
κυβερνῆται καὶ ναῦται τὸ καθ' ἑαυτὸν ἕκαστος
ἕπεσθε, χώραν μὴ προλείποντες ᾗ ἄν τις προσ-
9 ταχθῇ. τῶν δὲ πρότερον ἡγεμόνων οὐ χεῖρον τὴν
ἐπιχείρησιν ἡμεῖς παρασκευάσομεν καὶ οὐκ ἐνδώ-
σομεν πρόφασιν οὐδενὶ κακῷ γενέσθαι· ἢν δέ τις
ἄρα καὶ βουληθῇ, κολασθήσεται τῇ πρεπούσῃ
ζημίᾳ, οἱ δὲ ἀγαθοὶ τιμήσονται τοῖς προσήκουσιν
ἄθλοις τῆς ἀρετῆς."

LXXXVIII. Τοιαῦτα μὲν τοῖς Πελοποννησίοις
οἱ ἄρχοντες παρεκελεύσαντο. ὁ δὲ Φορμίων
δεδιὼς καὶ αὐτὸς τὴν τῶν στρατιωτῶν ὀρρωδίαν
καὶ αἰσθόμενος ὅτι τὸ πλῆθος τῶν νεῶν κατὰ
σφᾶς αὐτοὺς ξυνιστάμενοι ἐφοβοῦντο, ἐβούλετο
ξυγκαλέσας θαρσῦναί τε καὶ παραίνεσιν ἐν τῷ
2 παρόντι ποιήσασθαι. πρότερον μὲν γὰρ αἰεὶ
αὐτοῖς ἔλεγε καὶ προπαρεσκεύαζε τὰς γνώμας ὡς
οὐδὲν αὐτοῖς πλῆθος νεῶν τοσοῦτον, ἢν ἐπιπλέῃ,
ὅ τι οὐχ ὑπομενετέον ἐστί, καὶ οἱ στρατιῶται ἐκ
πολλοῦ ἐν σφίσιν αὐτοῖς τὴν ἀξίωσιν ταύτην

intrepidity is of no avail. Therefore, against their greater experience set your greater daring, and against the fear caused by your defeat set the accident of your being at the moment unprepared. You have the advantage, both in number of ships and in fighting close to the land, which is friendly to us, and you are supported by hoplites; and victory is generally on the side of those who are the more numerous and better prepared. There is accordingly not a single reason that we can find why we should fail; and as to our earlier mistakes, the very fact that they were made will teach us a lesson. Be of good courage, then, and let each man, both helmsman and sailor, follow our lead as best he can, not leaving the post to which he may be assigned. We shall prepare for the attack at least as well as your former commanders, and shall give no one an excuse to act like a coward; but if anyone should be inclined that way, he shall be punished with the penalty he deserves, while the brave shall be honoured with rewards such as befit their valour."

LXXXVIII. With such words the Peloponnesian commanders encouraged their men. But Phormio, being himself also uneasy about the apprehension felt by his troops, and observing that they were gathering in knots amongst themselves in alarm at the superior number of the enemy's ships, wished to call them together in order to hearten them and make an exhortation to suit the present emergency. For in the past he had always told them, by way of bracing their minds, that there was no number of ships, however great, whose attack men such as they could not withstand; and his sailors had long since held among themselves the conviction that they,

εἰλήφεσαν μηδένα ὄχλον Ἀθηναῖοι ὄντες Πελο-
3 πουνησίων νεῶν ὑποχωρεῖν· τότε δὲ πρὸς τὴν
παροῦσαν ὄψιν ὁρῶν αὐτοὺς ἀθυμοῦντας ἐβούλετο ὑπόμνησιν ποιήσασθαι τοῦ θαρσεῖν, καὶ
ξυγκαλέσας τοὺς Ἀθηναίους ἔλεγε τοιάδε.

LXXXIX. "Ὁρῶν ὑμᾶς, ὦ ἄνδρες στρατιῶται,
πεφοβημένους τὸ πλῆθος τῶν ἐναντίων ξυνεκά-
λεσα, οὐκ ἀξιῶν τὰ μὴ δεινὰ ἐν ὀρρωδίᾳ ἔχειν.
2 οὗτοι γὰρ πρῶτον μὲν διὰ τὸ προνενικῆσθαι καὶ
μηδ' αὐτοὶ οἴεσθαι ὁμοῖοι ἡμῖν εἶναι τὸ πλῆθος
τῶν νεῶν καὶ οὐκ ἀπὸ τοῦ ἴσου παρεσκευάσαντο·
ἔπειτα ᾧ μάλιστα πιστεύοντες προσέρχονται, ὡς
προσῆκον σφίσιν ἀνδρείοις εἶναι, οὐ δι' ἄλλο τι
θαρσοῦσιν ἢ διὰ τὴν ἐν τῷ πεζῷ ἐμπειρίαν τὰ
πλείω κατορθοῦντες καὶ οἴονται σφίσι καὶ ἐν τῷ
3 ναυτικῷ ποιήσειν τὸ αὐτό. τὸ δ' ἐκ τοῦ δικαίου
ἡμῖν μᾶλλον νῦν περιέσται, εἴπερ καὶ τούτοις ἐν
ἐκείνῳ, ἐπεὶ εὐψυχίᾳ γε οὐδὲν προφέρουσι, τῷ δὲ
ἑκάτεροί τι εἶναι ἐμπειρότεροι θρασύτεροί ἐσμεν.
4 Λακεδαιμόνιοί τε ἡγούμενοι αὐτῶν διὰ τὴν σφετέραν δόξαν ἄκοντας προσάγουσι τοὺς πολλοὺς
ἐς τὸν κίνδυνον, ἐπεὶ οὐκ ἄν ποτε ἐνεχείρησαν
5 ἡσσηθέντες παρὰ πολὺ αὖθις ναυμαχεῖν. μὴ δὴ
αὐτῶν τὴν τόλμαν δείσητε. πολὺ δὲ ὑμεῖς ἐκείνοις πλείω φόβον παρέχετε καὶ πιστότερον κατά

being Athenians, must never give ground before any number of Peloponnesian ships. But at this time, seeing that they were dispirited by what they saw before their eyes, and wishing to remind them of their old-time confidence, he called them together and spoke as follows:

LXXXIX. "Observing that you have become alarmed, soldiers, at the numbers of the enemy, I have called you together, because I do not want you to be in dread of imaginary dangers. For, in the first place, it is just because these men have been beaten before, and do not even themselves believe that they are a match for us, that they have provided themselves with this large and disproportionate number of ships; then, too, as regards their courage,—the thing on which they chiefly rely when they come against us, as if it were their peculiar province to be brave,—the only reasonable ground they have for confidence is that their experience in fighting on land has generally brought them success, and so they think this will achieve the same result for them at sea as well. But in all reason the advantage to-day will rather be ours, if they on their side have it on land; for in valour assuredly they are nowise superior, but we are both more confident just as in any way we have more experience. Besides, since the Lacedaemonians lead their allies for their own glory, the majority of them have to be dragged into battle against their will, for otherwise they would never, after their decisive defeat, have attempted to fight a second time at sea. Hence you need not fear their daring. On the contrary, you inspire in them a dread far greater and better justified, both because you have already

τε τὸ προνενικηκέναι καὶ ὅτι οὐκ ἂν ἡγοῦνται μὴ
μέλλοντάς τι ἄξιον τοῦ παρὰ πολὺ πράξειν ἀνθί-
6 στασθαι ὑμᾶς. ἀντίπαλοι μὲν γὰρ οἱ[1] πλείους,
ὥσπερ οὗτοι, τῇ δυνάμει τὸ πλέον πίσυνοι ἢ τῇ
γνώμῃ ἐπέρχονται· οἱ δὲ ἐκ πολλῷ ὑποδεεστέρων
καὶ ἅμα οὐκ ἀναγκαζόμενοι, μέγα τι τῆς διανοίας
τὸ βέβαιον ἔχοντες ἀντιτολμῶσιν. ἃ λογιζόμενοι
οὗτοι τῷ οὐκ εἰκότι πλέον πεφόβηνται ἡμᾶς ἢ τῇ
7 κατὰ λόγον παρασκευῇ. πολλὰ δὲ καὶ στρατόπεδα ἤδη ἔπεσεν ὑπ᾽ ἐλασσόνων τῇ ἀπειρίᾳ, ἔστι
δὲ ἃ καὶ τῇ ἀτολμίᾳ· ὧν οὐδετέρου ἡμεῖς νῦν
8 μετέχομεν. τὸν δὲ ἀγῶνα οὐκ ἐν τῷ κόλπῳ ἑκὼν
εἶναι ποιήσομαι οὐδ᾽ ἐσπλεύσομαι ἐς αὐτόν. ὁρῶ
γὰρ ὅτι πρὸς πολλὰς ναῦς ἀνεπιστήμονας ὀλίγαις
ναυσὶν ἐμπείροις καὶ ἄμεινον πλεούσαις ἡ στενο-
χωρία οὐ ξυμφέρει. οὔτε γὰρ ἂν ἐπιπλεύσειέ
τις ὡς χρὴ ἐς ἐμβολὴν μὴ ἔχων τὴν πρόσοψιν
τῶν πολεμίων ἐκ πολλοῦ, οὔτ᾽ ἂν ἀποχωρήσειεν
ἐν δέοντι πιεζόμενος· διέκπλοι τε οὐκ εἰσὶν οὐδ᾽
ἀναστροφαί, ἅπερ νεῶν ἄμεινον πλεουσῶν ἔργα
ἐστίν, ἀλλὰ ἀνάγκη ἂν εἴη τὴν ναυμαχίαν πεζο-
μαχίαν καθίστασθαι, καὶ ἐν τούτῳ αἱ πλείους
9 νῆες κρείσσους γίγνονται. τούτων μὲν οὖν ἐγὼ

[1] Hude adopts Madvig's conjecture ἢ for οἱ.

defeated them and because they think that you would not be facing them at all unless you expected to achieve a result commensurate with the very great odds. For most men, when, like our present opponents, they are equal to their foes, rely more upon their strength when they advance to the attack than upon their resolution; whereas those who dare oppose them with greatly inferior numbers, and at the same time without being compelled to do so, must possess in a high degree the quality of unwavering resolution. Taking all these things into consideration, our enemies have come to fear us more on account of what is amazing in our conduct than they would if our preparations were less out of proportion to their own. Furthermore many an army has before now been overthrown by smaller numbers through its own want of experience, and some too through a deficiency of daring, and at this moment we can be charged with neither. As for the contest, I will not risk it in the gulf if I can help it, nor will I sail into the gulf. For I am aware that a confined space is not an advantage to a fleet of a few ships which are better sailers and have experienced crews, when it is opposed to a large number of ships which are badly managed. For one cannot charge properly upon an enemy ship to ram her side, through not having a clear view of her a long way off, nor can one retire at need when hard pressed; and there is no chance for such manoeuvres as breaking through the line or whirling around to ram, though these are precisely the proper tactics of fast sailing ships, but the sea-fight would have to be turned into a land-battle, and in that case it is the larger fleet that wins. For these

ἔξω τὴν πρόνοιαν κατὰ τὸ δυνατόν· ὑμεῖς δὲ
εὔτακτοι παρὰ ταῖς ναυσὶ μένοντες τά τε παραγγελλόμενα ὀξέως δέχεσθε, ἄλλως τε καὶ δι' ὀλίγου
τῆς ἐφορμήσεως οὔσης, καὶ ἐν τῷ ἔργῳ κόσμον
καὶ σιγὴν περὶ πλείστου ἡγεῖσθε, ὃ ἔς τε τὰ
πολλὰ τῶν πολεμικῶν[1] ξυμφέρει κἂν ναυμαχίᾳ
οὐχ ἥκιστα, ἀμύνεσθέ τε τούσδε ἀξίως τῶν προ-
10 ειργασμένων. ὁ δὲ ἀγὼν μέγας ὑμῖν, ἢ καταλῦσαι Πελοποννησίων τὴν ἐλπίδα τοῦ ναυτικοῦ ἢ
ἐγγυτέρω καταστῆσαι Ἀθηναίοις τὸν φόβον
11 περὶ τῆς θαλάσσης. ἀναμιμνῄσκω δ' αὖ ὑμᾶς
ὅτι νενικήκατε αὐτῶν τοὺς πολλούς· ἡσσημένων
δὲ ἀνδρῶν οὐκ ἐθέλουσιν αἱ γνῶμαι πρὸς τοὺς
αὐτοὺς κινδύνους ὁμοῖαι εἶναι."

XC. Τοιαῦτα δὲ καὶ ὁ Φορμίων παρεκελεύσατο.
οἱ δὲ Πελοποννήσιοι, ἐπειδὴ αὐτοῖς οἱ Ἀθηναῖοι
οὐκ ἐπέπλεον ἐς τὸν κόλπον καὶ τὰ στενά, βουλόμενοι ἄκοντας ἔσω προαγαγεῖν αὐτούς, ἀναγαγόμενοι ἅμα ἕῳ ἔπλεον, ἐπὶ τεσσάρων ταξάμενοι
τὰς ναῦς, παρὰ[2] τὴν ἑαυτῶν γῆν ἔσω ἐπὶ[3] τοῦ
κόλπου δεξιῷ κέρᾳ ἡγουμένῳ, ὥσπερ καὶ ὥρμουν·
2 ἐπὶ δ' αὐτῷ εἴκοσι ἔταξαν τὰς ἄριστα πλεούσας,
ὅπως, εἰ ἄρα νομίσας ἐπὶ τὴν Ναύπακτον αὐτοὺς
πλεῖν ὁ Φορμίων καὶ αὐτὸς ἐπιβοηθῶν ταύτῃ

[1] Hude reads πολεμίων, with C.
[2] With CG; the other MSS. and the Schol. ἐπί.
[3] Hude deletes ἐπί, after Krüger.

---

[1] In the first sea-fight the Peloponnesians had forty-seven ships (ch. lxxxiii. 3) against Phormio's twenty (ch. lxxxiii. 1); in the second battle the Peloponnesians had seventy-seven ships (ch. lxxxvi. 4). Since the Peloponnesians lost twelve ships in the first battle (ch. lxxxiv. 4), the expression "most of them" is not quite exact here.

matters, however, I shall make provision to the best of my ability. As for you, keep good order, stay near your ships, give heed sharply to the word of command, especially since the two fleets are at watch so near one another; and when it comes to action, regard discipline and silence, which are generally advantageous in warfare, but especially so at sea, as all important, and ward off the enemy yonder in a manner worthy of your past exploits. The contest is a momentous one for you—whether you are to shatter the hopes which the Peloponnesians have in their fleet, or to bring closer home to the Athenians their fear about the sea. Once more I remind you that you have beaten most of them [1] already; and when men have once suffered defeat, their spirit is never the same as before if they are called upon to face the same dangers."

XC. Such were the words with which Phormio also encouraged his men. And the Peloponnesians, when the Athenians did not sail into the gulf and the narrows to meet them, wished to draw them in against their will; so they put out to sea at dawn, and, after lining up their ships four deep,[2] sailed along their own shore towards the inner part of the gulf, in the same order as they had lain at anchor,[3] their right wing leading the way.[4] Upon their right wing they had placed their twenty best sailing ships, in order that, if Phormio got the impression that their objective was Naupactus

[2] Or, as some take it, "in a column four abreast."

[3] Only now the four ships which had lain at anchor one behind the other sailed, after the turn to the right, abreast.

[4] Or, retaining ἐπὶ instead of παρὰ, "after lining up their ships four deep against their own shore (*i.e.* with it at their backs), sailed toward the inner part of the gulf . . . ."

παραπλέοι, μὴ διαφύγοιεν πλέοντες τὸν ἐπίπλουν σφῶν οἱ Ἀθηναῖοι ἔξω τοῦ ἑαυτῶν κέρως, ἀλλ'
3 αὗται αἱ νῆες περικλῄσειαν. ὁ δέ, ὅπερ ἐκεῖνοι προσεδέχοντο, φοβηθεὶς περὶ τῷ χωρίῳ ἐρήμῳ ὄντι, ὡς ἑώρα ἀναγομένους αὐτούς, ἄκων καὶ κατὰ σπουδὴν ἐμβιβάσας ἔπλει παρὰ τὴν γῆν· καὶ ὁ
4 πεζὸς ἅμα τῶν Μεσσηνίων παρεβοήθει. ἰδόντες δὲ οἱ Πελοποννήσιοι κατὰ μίαν ἐπὶ κέρως παραπλέοντας καὶ ἤδη ὄντας ἐντὸς τοῦ κόλπου τε καὶ πρὸς τῇ γῇ, ὅπερ ἐβούλοντο μάλιστα, ἀπὸ σημείου ἑνὸς ἄφνω ἐπιστρέψαντες τὰς ναῦς μετωπηδὸν ἔπλεον ὡς εἶχε τάχους ἕκαστος ἐπὶ τοὺς Ἀθηναίους, καὶ ἤλπιζον πάσας τὰς ναῦς ἀπολή-
5 ψεσθαι. τῶν δὲ ἕνδεκα μέν τινες αἵπερ ἡγοῦντο ὑπεκφεύγουσι τὸ κέρας τῶν Πελοποννησίων καὶ τὴν ἐπιστροφὴν ἐς τὴν εὐρυχωρίαν· τὰς δ' ἄλλας ἐπικαταλαβόντες ἐξέωσάν τε πρὸς τὴν γῆν ὑποφευγούσας καὶ διέφθειραν, ἄνδρας τε τῶν Ἀθη-
6 ναίων ἀπέκτειναν ὅσοι μὴ ἐξένευσαν αὐτῶν. καὶ τῶν νεῶν τινας ἀναδούμενοι εἷλκον κενάς (μίαν δὲ αὐτοῖς ἀνδράσιν εἷλον ἤδη), τὰς δέ τινας οἱ Μεσσήνιοι παραβοηθήσαντες καὶ ἐπεσβαίνοντες ξὺν τοῖς ὅπλοις ἐς τὴν θάλασσαν καὶ ἐπιβάντες ἀπὸ τῶν καταστρωμάτων μαχόμενοι ἀφείλοντο ἑλκομένας ἤδη.

XCI. Ταύτῃ μὲν οὖν οἱ Πελοποννήσιοι ἐκράτουν τε καὶ διέφθειραν τὰς Ἀττικὰς ναῦς· αἱ δὲ εἴκοσι νῆες αὐτῶν αἱ ἀπὸ τοῦ δεξιοῦ κέρως ἐδίωκον τὰς ἕνδεκα ναῦς τῶν Ἀθηναίων αἵπερ

and should, following the coast, sail in that direction to its aid, the Athenians might not be able to escape their attack by sailing outside their wing, but might be enveloped by these ships. Now he did just what they expected him to do; when he saw them put to sea, fearing for the safety of the place, which was unprotected, he reluctantly and in haste embarked his crews and sailed along the coast, the Messenian army moving along the shore to support him. And when the Peloponnesians saw that they were skirting the coast in single file and were already inside the gulf and close to shore, which was just what they most desired, at one signal they suddenly veered about, bore down with ships in line as fast as each could upon the Athenians, hoping to cut off all their ships. But eleven of these, which were in the lead, got past the Peloponnesian wing, as it swung round, and escaped into the open water; but the rest were overtaken, driven ashore as they attempted to escape, and disabled, and all the Athenians on them who did not succeed in swimming ashore were slain. Some of the ships they made fast to their own and proceeded to tow away empty—though they had already captured one with its crew—but some others, which were already in tow, were taken from them by the Messenians, who came to the rescue, rushed armed as they were into the sea, boarded the ships, and fought from their decks.

XCI. In this quarter, then, the Peloponnesians were victorious and had disabled the Athenian ships; but the twenty ships covering their right wing were pursuing the eleven Athenian ships which had got

ὑπεξέφυγον τὴν ἐπιστροφὴν ἐς τὴν εὐρυχωρίαν. καὶ φθάνουσιν αὐτοὺς πλὴν μιᾶς νεὼς προκαταφυγοῦσαι πρὸς τὴν Ναύπακτον, καὶ σχοῦσαι ἀντίπρῳροι κατὰ τὸ Ἀπολλώνιον παρεσκευάζοντο ἀμυνούμενοι, ἢν ἐς τὴν γῆν ἐπὶ σφᾶς
2 πλέωσιν. οἱ δὲ παραγενόμενοι ὕστερον ἐπαιάνιζόν τε ἅμα πλέοντες ὡς νενικηκότες, καὶ τὴν μίαν ναῦν τῶν Ἀθηναίων τὴν ὑπόλοιπον ἐδίωκε
3 Λευκαδία ναῦς μία πολὺ πρὸ τῶν ἄλλων. ἔτυχε δὲ ὁλκὰς ὁρμοῦσα μετέωρος, περὶ ἣν ἡ Ἀττικὴ ναῦς φθάσασα καὶ περιπλεύσασα τῇ Λευκαδίᾳ
4 διωκούσῃ ἐμβάλλει μέσῃ καὶ καταδύει. τοῖς μὲν οὖν Πελοποννησίοις γενομένου τούτου ἀπροσδοκήτου τε καὶ παρὰ λόγον φόβος ἐμπίπτει, καὶ ἅμα ἀτάκτως διώκοντες διὰ τὸ κρατεῖν αἱ μέν τινες τῶν νεῶν καθεῖσαι τὰς κώπας ἐπέστησαν τοῦ πλοῦ, ἀξύμφορον δρῶντες πρὸς τὴν ἐξ ὀλίγου ἀντεξόρμησιν, βουλόμενοι τὰς πλείους περιμεῖναι, αἱ δὲ καὶ ἐς βράχεα ἀπειρίᾳ χωρίων ὤκειλαν.

XCII. Τοὺς δ' Ἀθηναίους ἰδόντας ταῦτα γιγνόμενα θάρσος τε ἔλαβε καὶ ἀπὸ ἑνὸς κελεύσματος ἐμβοήσαντες ἐπ' αὐτοὺς ὥρμησαν. οἱ δὲ διὰ τὰ ὑπάρχοντα ἁμαρτήματα καὶ τὴν παροῦσαν ἀταξίαν ὀλίγον μὲν χρόνον ὑπέμειναν, ἔπειτα δὲ ἐτράποντο ἐς τὸν Πάνορμον, ὅθενπερ ἀνηγάγοντο.
2 ἐπιδιώκοντες δὲ οἱ Ἀθηναῖοι τάς τε ἐγγὺς οὔσας μάλιστα ναῦς ἔλαβον ἓξ καὶ τὰς ἑαυτῶν ἀφείλοντο ἃς ἐκεῖνοι πρὸς τῇ γῇ διαφθείραντες τὸ

past them as they swung round and had escaped into the open water. And all the eleven except one reached Naupactus ahead of them, and riding at anchor off the Temple of Apollo, prows outward, made ready to defend themselves if the enemy put in toward the shore to attack them. When the Peloponnesians came up they were singing the paean as they rowed as if they were victorious already, and one Leucadian ship, far ahead of the rest, was chasing the single Athenian ship which lagged behind. But, as it chanced, a merchantman was lying at anchor in deep water and this the Athenian ship succeeded in reaching first and, sailing round it, rammed the pursuing Leucadian vessel amidships and sank her. At this unexpected and amazing feat consternation fell upon the Peloponnesians, who were, moreover, pursuing in disorder because they had the upper hand; on some of their ships the rowers sank their oars into the water and checked the headway of their vessels, intending to await the main body of their fleet – a serious mistake to make in the face of an enemy lying near and ready for the charge— while others, unfamiliar with the waters there, ran aground in the shallows.

XCII. As for the Athenians, when they saw what was happening, they took courage, and at a single word of command gave a shout and dashed at them. But the Peloponnesians had made so many mistakes and were at present in such disorder, that, although they resisted a little while, they soon turned and fled to Panormus, whence they had put to sea. The Athenians gave chase, and not only captured the six ships that were nearest, but also recovered their own ships which the enemy had disabled in the beginning

πρῶτον ἀνεδήσαντο· ἄνδρας τε τοὺς μὲν ἀπέκτει-
3 ναν, τινὰς δὲ καὶ ἐζώγρησαν. ἐπὶ δὲ τῆς Λευκα-
δίας νεώς, ἣ περὶ τὴν ὁλκάδα κατέδυ, Τιμοκράτης
ὁ Λακεδαιμόνιος πλέων, ὡς ἡ ναῦς διεφθείρετο,
ἔσφαξεν ἑαυτόν, καὶ ἐξέπεσεν ἐς τὸν Ναυπακτίων
4 λιμένα. ἀναχωρήσαντες δὲ οἱ Ἀθηναῖοι τροπαῖον
ἔστησαν ὅθεν ἀναγαγόμενοι ἐκράτησαν, καὶ τοὺς
νεκροὺς καὶ τὰ ναυάγια ὅσα πρὸς τῇ ἑαυτῶν ἦν
ἀνείλοντο, καὶ τοῖς ἐναντίοις τὰ ἐκείνων ὑπό-
5 σπονδα ἀπέδοσαν. ἔστησαν δὲ καὶ Πελοποννήσιοι τροπαῖον ὡς νενικηκότες τῆς τροπῆς, ἃς
πρὸς τῇ γῇ διέφθειραν ναῦς· καὶ ἥνπερ ἔλαβον
ναῦν, ἀνέθεσαν ἐπὶ τὸ Ῥίον τὸ Ἀχαϊκὸν παρὰ τὸ
6 τροπαῖον. μετὰ δὲ ταῦτα φοβούμενοι τὴν ἀπὸ
τῶν Ἀθηναίων βοήθειαν ὑπὸ νύκτα ἐσέπλευσαν
ἐς τὸν κόλπον τὸν Κρισαῖον καὶ Κόρινθον ἅπαντες
7 πλὴν Λευκαδίων. καὶ οἱ ἐκ τῆς Κρήτης Ἀθηναῖοι ταῖς εἴκοσι ναυσίν, αἷς ἔδει πρὸ τῆς ναυμαχίας τῷ Φορμίωνι παραγενέσθαι, οὐ πολλῷ
ὕστερον τῆς ἀναχωρήσεως τῶν νεῶν ἀφικνοῦνται
ἐς τὴν Ναύπακτον. καὶ τὸ θέρος ἐτελεύτα.

XCIII. Πρὶν δὲ διαλῦσαι τὸ ἐς Κόρινθόν τε καὶ τὸν Κρισαῖον κόλπον ἀναχωρῆσαν ναυτικόν, ὁ Κνῆμος καὶ ὁ Βρασίδας καὶ οἱ ἄλλοι ἄρχοντες τῶν Πελοποννησίων ἀρχομένου τοῦ χειμῶνος ἐβούλοντο διδαξάντων τῶν Μεγαρέων ἀποπειρᾶσαι τοῦ Πειραιῶς τοῦ λιμένος τῶν Ἀθηναίων· ἦν δὲ ἀφύλακτος καὶ ἄκληστος εἰκότως διὰ τὸ

of the fight near the shore and taken in tow; and of the men they killed some and took others alive. But Timocrates the Lacedaemonian, who was on board the Leucadian ship which was sunk near the merchantmen, slew himself when he saw that his ship was lost, and his body was washed up in the harbour of Naupactus. The Athenians now withdrew and set up a trophy at the place [1] from which they had set out and won the victory; and they took up their dead and such of the wrecked ships as were close to their own shore, giving back to the enemy under a truce those which belonged to them. But the Peloponnesians also set up, in token of victory, a trophy for the defeat of the ships which had been disabled near the shore. And the ships which they had taken they dedicated on the Achaean Rhium by the side of the trophy. And after this, fearing the reinforcements expected from Athens,[2] they sailed under cover of night into the Crisaean Gulf and to Corinth, all except the Leucadians. And not long after their retreat the twenty Athenian ships from Crete,[3] which were to have joined Phormio in time for the battle, arrived at Naupactus. And so the summer ended.

XCIII. However, before dispersing the fleet which had retired to Corinth and the Crisaean Gulf, at the beginning of the winter Cnemus and Brasidas and the other Peloponnesian commanders, instigated by the Megarians, wished to make an attempt upon the Peiraeus, the port of Athens; for it was unguarded and unclosed, and quite naturally, since the Athen-

[1] The point is not certain; either near the Molycrian Rhium (ch. lxxxvi. 2), or off the Apollonium (ch. xci. 1).

[2] *cf.* ch. lxxxvi. 6. [3] *cf.* ch. lxxxv. 5.

2 ἐπικρατεῖν πολὺ τῷ ναυτικῷ. ἐδόκει δὲ λαβόντα τῶν ναυτῶν ἕκαστον τὴν κώπην καὶ τὸ ὑπηρέσιον καὶ τὸν τροπωτῆρα πεζῇ ἰέναι ἐκ Κορίνθου ἐπὶ τὴν πρὸς Ἀθήνας θάλασσαν, καὶ ἀφικομένους κατὰ τάχος ἐς Μέγαρα καθελκύσαντας ἐκ Νισαίας τοῦ νεωρίου αὐτῶν τεσσαράκοντα ναῦς, αἳ ἔτυχον αὐτόθι οὖσαι, πλεῦσαι εὐθὺς ἐπὶ τὸν Πει-
3 ραιᾶ· οὔτε γὰρ ναυτικὸν ἦν προφυλάσσον ἐν αὐτῷ οὐδὲν οὔτε προσδοκία οὐδεμία μὴ ἄν ποτε οἱ πολέμιοι ἐξαπιναίως οὕτως ἐπιπλεύσειαν, ἐπεὶ οὔτ' ἀπὸ τοῦ προφανοῦς τολμῆσαι ἄν, καθ' ἡσυχίαν δ'[1] εἰ διανοοῖντο, μὴ οὐκ ἂν προαισθέσθαι.
4 ὡς δὲ ἔδοξεν αὐτοῖς, καὶ ἐχώρουν εὐθύς· καὶ ἀφικόμενοι νυκτὸς καὶ καθελκύσαντες ἐκ τῆς Νισαίας τὰς ναῦς ἔπλεον ἐπὶ μὲν τὸν Πειραιᾶ οὐκέτι, ὥσπερ διενοοῦντο, καταδείσαντες τὸν κίνδυνον (καί τις καὶ ἄνεμος αὐτοὺς λέγεται κωλῦσαι), ἐπὶ δὲ τῆς Σαλαμῖνος τὸ ἀκρωτήριον τὸ πρὸς Μέγαρα ὁρῶν· καὶ φρούριον[2] ἐπ' αὐτοῦ ἦν καὶ νεῶν τριῶν φυλακὴ τοῦ μὴ ἐσπλεῖν Μεγαρεῦσι μηδὲ ἐκπλεῖν μηδέν. τῷ τε φρουρίῳ προσέβαλον καὶ τὰς τριήρεις ἀφείλκυσαν κενάς, τήν τε ἄλλην Σαλαμῖνα ἀπροσδοκήτοις ἐπιπεσόντες ἐπόρθουν.

XCIV. Ἐς δὲ τὰς Ἀθήνας φρυκτοί τε ᾔροντο πολέμιοι καὶ ἔκπληξις ἐγένετο οὐδεμιᾶς τῶν κατὰ τὸν πόλεμον ἐλάσσων. οἱ μὲν γὰρ ἐν τῷ ἄστει ἐς τὸν Πειραιᾶ ᾤοντο τοὺς πολεμίους ἐσπεπλευκέναι ἤδη, οἱ δ' ἐν τῷ Πειραιεῖ τήν τε Σαλαμῖνα ᾑρῆσθαι καὶ παρὰ σφᾶς ὅσον οὐκ ἐσπλεῖν αὐτούς·

[1] So Hude, adopting Madvig's conjecture δ' (for οὐδ') and punctuating after τολμῆσαι ἄν.

[2] Hude inserts γάρ after φρούριον, with van Herwerden, and includes in parentheses φρούριον . . . μηδέν.

ians were decidedly superior at sea. And it was determined that each sailor, taking his oar and cushion and oar-loop, should go on foot from Corinth to the sea on the Athenian side and hastening to Megara should launch from the docks at Nisaea forty ships of theirs which chanced to be there, and then sail straight for the Peiraeus. For there was no fleet on guard in the harbour, nor was there any expectation that the enemy would ever suddenly attack it in this way, since they would not dare such a thing openly, and if they should plan it secretly they would not fail to be detected in time. But once they had determined upon the scheme they set to work immediately. Reaching Nisaea at night they launched the ships and sailed, not now to the Peiraeus as they had intended, since they were appalled by the risk—and a wind, too, is said to have prevented them—but to the promontory of Salamis that looks towards Megara. There was a fort here and a guard of three ships to prevent anything from entering or leaving the harbour of the Megarians. This fort they assaulted, towed away the triremes without their crews, and ravaged the rest of Salamis, falling on the inhabitants unawares.

XCIV. Meanwhile fire-signals indicating a hostile attack were flashed to Athens, where a panic was caused as great as any in this war.[1] For the inhabitants of the city thought that the enemy had already entered the Peiraeus, and those of the Peiraeus that they had taken Salamis and were all but sailing into their own harbour—as

[1] This must refer to the so-called Decelean War (or last ten years of the Peloponnesian War), for in VIII. xcvi. 1 we read that a panic occurred greater than any before (τοῖς Ἀθηναίοις . . . ἔκπληξις μεγίστη δὴ τῶν πρὶν παρέστη).

ὅπερ ἄν, εἰ ἐβουλήθησαν μὴ κατοκνῆσαι, ῥᾳδίως
2 ἐγένετο· καὶ οὐκ ἂν ἄνεμος ἐκώλυσεν. βοηθήσαντες δὲ ἅμ' ἡμέρᾳ πανδημεὶ οἱ Ἀθηναῖοι ἐς τὸν Πειραιᾶ ναῦς τε καθεῖλκον καὶ ἐσβάντες κατὰ σπουδὴν καὶ πολλῷ θορύβῳ ταῖς μὲν ναυσὶν ἐπὶ τὴν Σαλαμῖνα ἔπλεον, τῷ πεζῷ δὲ φυλακὰς τοῦ
3 Πειραιῶς καθίσταντο. οἱ δὲ Πελοποννήσιοι ὡς ᾐσθάνοντο τὴν βοήθειαν, καταδραμόντες τῆς Σαλαμῖνος τὰ πολλὰ καὶ ἀνθρώπους καὶ λείαν λαβόντες καὶ τὰς τρεῖς ναῦς ἐκ τοῦ Βουδόρου τοῦ φρουρίου κατὰ τάχος ἐπὶ τῆς Νισαίας ἀπέπλεον· ἔστι γὰρ ὅ τι καὶ αἱ νῆες αὐτοὺς διὰ χρόνου καθελκυσθεῖσαι καὶ οὐδὲν στέγουσαι ἐφόβουν. ἀφικόμενοι δὲ ἐς Μέγαρα πάλιν ἐπὶ τῆς Κορίνθου
4 ἀπεχώρησαν πεζῇ· οἱ δ' Ἀθηναῖοι οὐκέτι καταλαβόντες πρὸς τῇ Σαλαμῖνι ἀπέπλευσαν καὶ αὐτοί· καὶ μετὰ τοῦτο φυλακὴν ἤδη τοῦ Πειραιῶς μᾶλλον τὸ λοιπὸν ἐποιοῦντο λιμένων τε κλῄσει καὶ τῇ ἄλλῃ ἐπιμελείᾳ.

XCV. Ὑπὸ δὲ τοὺς αὐτοὺς χρόνους, τοῦ χειμῶνος τούτου ἀρχομένου, Σιτάλκης ὁ Τήρεω Ὀδρύσης, Θρᾳκῶν βασιλεύς, ἐστράτευσεν ἐπὶ Περδίκκαν τὸν Ἀλεξάνδρου, Μακεδονίας βασιλέα, καὶ ἐπὶ Χαλκιδέας τοὺς ἐπὶ Θρᾴκης, δύο ὑποσχέσεις τὴν μὲν βουλόμενος ἀναπρᾶξαι, τὴν
2 δὲ αὐτὸς ἀποδοῦναι. ὅ τε γὰρ Περδίκκας αὐτῷ ὑποσχόμενος, εἰ Ἀθηναίοις τε διαλλάξειεν ἑαυτὸν κατ' ἀρχὰς τῷ πολέμῳ πιεζόμενον καὶ Φίλιππον

indeed might easily have happened if the enemy had resolved that there should be no flinching; and no mere wind would have prevented them. But at dawn the Athenians hastened down to the Peiraeus with all their forces, launched ships, and embarking in haste and with much confusion sailed with the fleet to Salamis, setting their land-forces to guard the Peiraeus. The Peloponnesians had already overrun most of Salamis and had taken prisoners and booty and the three ships at the fort of Budorum, when they saw the relief expedition coming, whereupon they sailed in haste toward Nisaea; to some extent too there was apprehension about their own ships, which had not been drawn down into the sea for a long time and were anything but water-tight. On reaching Megara they withdrew on foot to Corinth, and the Athenians, finding them no longer at Salamis, likewise sailed back. After this they kept stricter guard over the Peiraeus, closing up the harbour[1] as well as taking other precautions.

XCV. About the same time, at the beginning of this winter, Sitalces the Odrysian, a son of Teres, king of the Thracians, made an expedition against Perdiccas son of Alexander, king of Macedonia, and against the Chalcidians of Thrace, wishing to exact fulfilment of one promise and to make good another. For when Perdiccas was being hard pressed at the beginning of the war he had made Sitalces a promise on condition that he should reconcile him to the Athenians and should not bring back his brother Philip, who was

[1] *i.e.* by prolonging the walls at the entrance so as to leave only a narrow passage in the centre, which could be closed by a chain.

τὸν ἀδελφὸν αὐτοῦ πολέμιον ὄντα μὴ καταγάγοι ἐπὶ βασιλείᾳ, ἃ ὑπεδέξατο οὐκ ἐπετέλει· τοῖς τε Ἀθηναίοις αὐτὸς ὡμολογήκει ὅτε τὴν ξυμμαχίαν ἐποιεῖτο τὸν ἐπὶ Θρᾴκης Χαλκιδικὸν πόλεμον
3 καταλύσειν. ἀμφοτέρων οὖν ἕνεκα τὴν ἔφοδον ἐποιεῖτο καὶ τόν τε Φιλίππου υἱὸν Ἀμύνταν ὡς ἐπὶ βασιλείᾳ τῶν Μακεδόνων ἦγε καὶ τῶν Ἀθηναίων πρέσβεις, οἳ ἔτυχον παρόντες τούτων ἕνεκα, καὶ ἡγεμόνα Ἅγνωνα· ἔδει γὰρ καὶ τοὺς Ἀθηναίους ναυσί τε καὶ στρατιᾷ ὡς πλείστῃ ἐπὶ τοὺς Χαλκιδέας παραγενέσθαι.

XCVI. Ἀνίστησιν οὖν ἐκ τῶν Ὀδρυσῶν ὁρμώμενος πρῶτον μὲν τοὺς ἐντὸς τοῦ Αἵμου τε ὄρους καὶ τῆς Ῥοδόπης Θρᾷκας ὅσων ἦρχε μέχρι θαλάσσης ἐς τὸν Εὔξεινόν τε πόντον καὶ τὸν Ἑλλήσποντον,[1] ἔπειτα τοὺς ὑπερβάντι Αἷμον Γέτας καὶ ὅσα ἄλλα μέρη ἐντὸς τοῦ Ἴστρου ποταμοῦ πρὸς θάλασσαν μᾶλλον τὴν τοῦ Εὐξείνου πόντου κατῴκητο· εἰσὶ δ' οἱ Γέται καὶ οἱ ταύτῃ ὅμοροί τε τοῖς Σκύθαις καὶ ὁμόσκευοι, πάντες
2 ἱπποτοξόται. παρεκάλει δὲ καὶ τῶν ὀρεινῶν Θρᾳκῶν πολλοὺς τῶν αὐτονόμων καὶ μαχαιροφόρων, οἳ Δῖοι καλοῦνται, τὴν Ῥοδόπην οἱ πλεῖστοι οἰκοῦντες· καὶ τοὺς μὲν μισθῷ ἔπειθεν, οἱ δ'
3 ἐθελονταὶ ξυνηκολούθουν. ἀνίστη δὲ καὶ Ἀγριᾶ-

[1] ἐς . . . Ἑλλήσποντον deleted by Hude and others as not read by the Schol. (μέχρι θαλάσσης, ἕως τοῦ Εὐξείνου πόντου καὶ τοῦ Ἑλλησπόντου). Classen understands the Schol. to support the text reading.

hostile, to make him king; but Perdiccas would not fulfil his promise. On the other hand, Sitalces had made an agreement with the Athenians,[1] at the time he entered into the alliance with them, to bring to an end their war with the Chalcidians in Thrace. For both these reasons, then, he now began the invasion, and he took with him Philip's son, Amyntas,[2] with a view to making him king of the Macedonians, as well as some Athenian envoys who had come to see him on this business, and Hagnon as commander[3]; for the Athenians were to furnish a fleet and as large an army as possible[4] for the war against the Chalcidians.

XCVI. Sitalces, accordingly, beginning with the Odrysians, summoned to his standard, first the Thracians under his sway between the mountains Haemus[5] and Rhodope[6] and the sea,—as far as the shores of the Euxine and the Hellespont,—then, beyond Haemus, the Getae, and all the other tribes that are settled south of the river Ister[7] in the general direction of the seaboard of the Euxine sea; and the Getae and the people of that region are not only neighbours of the Scythians but are also equipped like them, all of them being mounted archers. And he summoned also many of the mountain Thracians who are independent and wear short swords, who are called Dii, most of them inhabiting Rhodope; and some of these were won to his service by pay, while others came along as volunteers. He called out, further, the

[1] *cf.* ch. xxix. 4.

[2] Philip died meanwhile.

[3] As commander of expected Athenian troops, which however failed to come (ch. ci. 1).

[4] *cf.* ch. ci. 1.

[5] The modern Balkans.

[6] Now Despotodagh.

[7] Danube.

νας καὶ Λαιαίους καὶ ἄλλα ὅσα ἔθνη Παιονικά, ὧν ἦρχε· καὶ ἔσχατοι τῆς ἀρχῆς οὗτοι ἦσαν· μέχρι γὰρ Λαιαίων Παιόνων καὶ τοῦ Στρυμόνος ποταμοῦ, ὃς ἐκ τοῦ Σκόμβρου ὄρους δι' Ἀγριάνων καὶ Λαιαίων ῥεῖ,[1] ὡρίζετο ἡ ἀρχὴ τὰ πρὸς
4 Παίονας αὐτονόμους ἤδη. τὰ δὲ πρὸς Τριβαλλούς, καὶ τούτους αὐτονόμους, Τρῆρες ὥριζον καὶ Τιλαταῖοι· οἰκοῦσι δ' οὗτοι πρὸς βορέαν τοῦ Σκόμβρου ὄρους καὶ παρήκουσι πρὸς ἡλίου δύσιν μέχρι τοῦ Ὀσκίου ποταμοῦ. ῥεῖ δ' οὗτος ἐκ τοῦ ὄρους ὅθενπερ καὶ ὁ Νέστος καὶ ὁ Ἕβρος· ἔστι δὲ ἐρῆμον τὸ ὄρος καὶ μέγα, ἐχόμενον τῆς Ῥοδόπης.

XCVII. Ἐγένετο δὲ ἡ ἀρχὴ ἡ Ὀδρυσῶν μέγεθος ἐπὶ μὲν θάλασσαν καθήκουσα ἀπὸ Ἀβδήρων πόλεως ἐς τὸν Εὔξεινον πόντον μέχρι Ἴστρου ποταμοῦ· αὕτη περίπλους ἐστὶν ἡ γῆ τὰ ξυντομώτατα, ἢν αἰεὶ κατὰ πρύμναν ἵστηται τὸ πνεῦμα, νηὶ στρογγύλῃ τεσσάρων ἡμερῶν καὶ ἴσων νυκτῶν· ὁδῷ δὲ τὰ ξυντομώτατα ἐξ Ἀβδήρων ἐς Ἴστρον ἀνὴρ εὔζωνος ἑνδεκαταῖος τελεῖ.
2 τὰ μὲν πρὸς θάλασσαν τοσαύτη ἦν, ἐς ἤπειρον δὲ ἀπὸ Βυζαντίου ἐς Λαιαίους καὶ ἐπὶ τὸν Στρυμόνα (ταύτῃ γὰρ διὰ πλείστου ἀπὸ θαλάσσης ἄνω ἐγίγνετο) ἡμερῶν ἀνδρὶ εὐζώνῳ τριῶν
3 καὶ δέκα ἀνύσαι. φόρος τε ἐκ πάσης τῆς βαρβάρου καὶ τῶν Ἑλληνίδων πόλεων ὅσωνπερ

[1] οὐ, in the MSS. before ὡρίζετο, deleted by Arnold.

---

[1] Paeonian tribes that dwelt in the mountain regions bordering on Macedonia, watered by the Upper Strymon and the Axius; most of them were afterwards subject to Macedonia.

Agrianians and Laeaeans, and all the other Paeonian tribes which were under his sway.[1] These peoples were at the outer limits of his empire; for the bounds of his empire extended, on the side towards the Paeonians, who are independent, as far as the Laeaean Paeonians and the river Strymon,[2] which flows from mount Scombrus through the country of the Agrianians and the Laeaeans. On the side toward the Triballi, who also are independent, the boundary is formed by the Treres and Tilataeans; and these dwell to the north of Mount Scombrus and extend toward the west as far as the river Oscius.[3] This river has its source in the same mountains as the Nestus[4] and the Hebrus[5]—a mountain range of great extent and uninhabited that is adjacent to Rhodope.

XCVII. Now the empire of the Odrysians[6] in respect to its size extended along the sea-coast from the city of Abdera to the Euxine Sea as far as the river Ister. This stretch of coast constitutes a voyage for a merchant-vessel, if the shortest course is taken and the wind keeps steady astern, of four days and as many nights; but the journey by land from Abdera to the Ister can be accomplished by an active man, taking the shortest route, in eleven days. Such was its extent on its seaboard; but inland the distance from Byzantium to the Laeaeans and the river Strymon—for this was its inland point farthest distant from the sea—it is possible for an active man to cover in thirteen days. As for the tribute which came in from the barbarian territory and from all the Hellenic cities over which the

[2] Now Struma. [3] Now Isker.
[4] Now Masta. [5] Now Maritza.
[6] Coinciding in the main with modern Bulgaria.

ἦρξαν ἐπὶ Σεύθου, ὃς ὕστερον Σιτάλκου βασι-
λεύσας πλεῖστον δὴ ἐποίησε, τετρακοσίων ταλάντων ἀργυρίου μάλιστα δύναμις, ἃ χρυσὸς
καὶ ἄργυρος ᾔει· καὶ δῶρα οὐκ ἐλάσσω τούτων
χρυσοῦ τε καὶ ἀργύρου προσεφέρετο, χωρὶς δὲ
ὅσα ὑφαντά τε καὶ λεῖα καὶ ἡ ἄλλη κατασκευή,
καὶ οὐ μόνον αὐτῷ, ἀλλὰ καὶ τοῖς παραδυνα-
4 στεύουσί τε καὶ γενναίοις Ὀδρυσῶν. κατεστήσαντο γὰρ τοὐναντίον τῆς Περσῶν βασιλείας
τὸν νόμον ὄντα μὲν καὶ τοῖς ἄλλοις Θρᾳξὶ
λαμβάνειν μᾶλλον ἢ διδόναι (καὶ αἴσχιον ἦν
αἰτηθέντα μὴ δοῦναι ἢ αἰτήσαντα μὴ τυχεῖν),
ὅμως δὲ κατὰ τὸ δύνασθαι ἐπὶ πλέον αὐτῷ ἐχρή-
σαντο· οὐ γὰρ ἦν πρᾶξαι οὐδὲν μὴ διδόντα δῶρα.
5 ὥστε ἐπὶ μέγα ἡ βασιλεία ἦλθεν ἰσχύος. τῶν
γὰρ ἐν τῇ Εὐρώπῃ ὅσαι μεταξὺ τοῦ Ἰονίου
κόλπου καὶ τοῦ Εὐξείνου πόντου μεγίστη ἐγένετο
χρημάτων προσόδῳ καὶ τῇ ἄλλῃ εὐδαιμονίᾳ,
ἰσχύι δὲ μάχης καὶ στρατοῦ πλήθει πολὺ δευτέρα
6 μετὰ τὴν Σκυθῶν. ταύτῃ δὲ ἀδύνατα ἐξισοῦσθαι
οὐχ ὅτι τὰ ἐν τῇ Εὐρώπῃ, ἀλλ' οὐδ' ἐν τῇ Ἀσίᾳ
ἔθνος ἓν πρὸς ἓν οὐκ ἔστιν ὅ τι δυνατὸν Σκύθαις
ὁμογνωμονοῦσι πᾶσιν ἀντιστῆναι. οὐ μὴν οὐδ'

---

[1] Nephew and successor of Sitalces ; *cf.* ch. ci. 5, 6 ; IV. ci. 5.

[2] £81,000, $388,800.

[3] Among the Persians the monarch gave rather than received presents : *cf.* Xen. *Cyrop.* VIII. ii. 7, διαμένει ἔτι καὶ νῦν τοῖς βασιλεῦσιν ἡ πολυδωρία.

Odrysians acquired sway in the time of Seuthes[1]—who, succeeding Sitalces on the throne, brought the revenues to their maximum—its value was about four hundred talents[2] in coin, and was paid in gold and silver; and gifts equal in value to the tribute, not only of gold and silver, but besides these all manner of stuffs, both embroidered and plain, and other articles for household use, were brought as offerings to the king, and not for him only, but also for the subordinate princes and nobles of the Odrysians. For these kings had established a custom which was just the opposite of that prevailing in the kingdom of the Persians,[3] namely, to take rather than to give; indeed it was more disgraceful for a man not to give when asked than to ask and be refused. This custom was observed among the other Thracians also; but the Odrysian kings, as they were more powerful, followed it more extensively; indeed it was not possible to accomplish anything without giving gifts. Consequently the kingdom attained to a great degree of power. For of all the kingdoms in Europe between the Ionian Gulf and the Euxine Sea it was the greatest in revenue of money and in general prosperity; but as regards the strength and size of its army, it was distinctly inferior to the Scythian kingdom.[4] With that not only are the nations of Europe unable to compete, but even in Asia, nation against nation, there is none which can make a stand against the Scythians if they all act in concert. However, with

[4] Contradicting Hdt. v. iii.: Θρηΐκων δὲ ἔθνος μέγιστόν ἐστι μετά γε Ἰνδοὺς πάντων ἀνθρώπων· εἰ δὲ ὑπ' ἑνὸς ἄρχοιτο ἢ φρονέοι κατὰ τὠυτό, ἄμαχον τ' ἂν εἴη καὶ πολλῷ κράτιστον πάντων ἐθνέων κατὰ γνώμην τὴν ἐμήν.

ἐς τὴν ἄλλην εὐβουλίαν καὶ ξύνεσιν περὶ τῶν παρόντων ἐς τὸν βίον ἄλλοις ὁμοιοῦνται.

XCVIII. Σιτάλκης μὲν οὖν χώρας τοσαύτης βασιλεύων παρεσκευάζετο τὸν στρατόν. καὶ ἐπειδὴ αὐτῷ ἑτοῖμα ἦν, ἄρας ἐπορεύετο ἐπὶ τὴν Μακεδονίαν πρῶτον μὲν διὰ τῆς αὐτοῦ ἀρχῆς, ἔπειτα διὰ Κερκίνης ἐρήμου ὄρους, ὅ ἐστι μεθόριον Σιντῶν καὶ Παιόνων. ἐπορεύετο δὲ δι' αὐτοῦ τῇ ὁδῷ ἣν πρότερον αὐτὸς ἐποιήσατο τεμὼν τὴν ὕλην, ὅτε ἐπὶ Παίονας ἐστράτευσεν.
2 τὸ δὲ ὄρος ἐξ 'Οδρυσῶν διιόντες ἐν δεξιᾷ μὲν εἶχον Παίονας, ἐν ἀριστερᾷ δὲ Σιντοὺς καὶ Μαιδούς. διελθόντες δὲ αὐτὸ ἀφίκοντο ἐς Δό-
3 βηρον τὴν Παιονικήν. πορευομένῳ δὲ αὐτῷ ἀπεγίγνετο μὲν οὐδὲν τοῦ στρατοῦ εἰ μή τι νόσῳ, προσεγίγνετο δέ. πολλοὶ γὰρ τῶν αὐτονόμων Θρᾳκῶν ἀπαράκλητοι ἐφ' ἁρπαγὴν ἠκολούθουν, ὥστε τὸ πᾶν πλῆθος λέγεται οὐκ ἔλασσον πέντε
4 καὶ δέκα μυριάδων γενέσθαι· καὶ τούτου τὸ μὲν πλέον πεζὸν ἦν, τριτημόριον δὲ μάλιστα ἱππικόν. τοῦ δ' ἱππικοῦ τὸ πλεῖστον αὐτοὶ 'Οδρύσαι παρείχοντο καὶ μετ' αὐτοὺς Γέται. τοῦ δὲ πεζοῦ οἱ μαχαιροφόροι μαχιμώτατοι μὲν ἦσαν οἱ ἐκ τῆς 'Ροδόπης αὐτόνομοι καταβάντες, ὁ δὲ ἄλλος ὅμιλος ξύμμεικτος πλήθει φοβερώτατος ἠκολούθει.

XCIX. Ξυνηθροίζοντο οὖν ἐν τῇ Δοβήρῳ καὶ παρεσκευάζοντο ὅπως κατὰ κορυφὴν ἐσβαλοῦσιν ἐς τὴν κάτω Μακεδονίαν, ἧς ὁ Περδίκκας ἦρχεν.

reference to wise counsel and intelligence about the things that belong to the enrichment of life the Scythians are not to be compared with other nations.

XCVIII. Such then was the extent of the country over which Sitalces ruled at the time when he was preparing his army. But when everything was ready, he set out for Macedonia, proceeding first through his own territory, then through the desolate range of Cercine, which lies between the Sinti and Paeonians. And he passed over this mountain by the road which he himself had constructed before, when he made an expedition against the Paeonians, cutting a path through the forest. As his army crossed the mountain, leaving the country of the Odrysians, they had the Paeonians on the right and on the left the Sinti and Maedi; and when they came out on the other side they arrived at Doberus in Paeonia. On the march his army suffered no loss, except from sickness, but rather was augmented; for many of the independent Thracians joined the expedition unsummoned, in the hope of plunder, so that the whole number is said to have been not less than a hundred and fifty thousand, the greater part being infantry, about one-third cavalry. Of the cavalry the Odrysians themselves furnished the largest contingent, and next to them the Getae; while of the infantry the sword-wearers, independent tribes that came down from Mount Rhodope, were the best fighters, the rest ot the army that followed, a miscellaneous horde, being formidable chiefly on account of its numbers.

XCIX. So Sitalces' army was being mustered at Doberus and preparing to pass over the mountain crest and descend upon lower Macedonia, of which

2 τῶν γὰρ Μακεδόνων εἰσὶ καὶ Λυγκησταὶ καὶ
Ἐλιμιῶται καὶ ἄλλα ἔθνη ἐπάνωθεν, ἃ ξύμμαχα
μέν ἐστι τούτοις καὶ ὑπήκοα, βασιλείας δ' ἔχει
3 καθ' αὑτά. τὴν δὲ παρὰ θάλασσαν νῦν Μακεδονίαν Ἀλέξανδρος ὁ Περδίκκου πατὴρ καὶ οἱ
πρόγονοι αὐτοῦ Τημενίδαι τὸ ἀρχαῖον ὄντες ἐξ
Ἄργους πρῶτοι ἐκτήσαντο καὶ ἐβασίλευσαν
ἀναστήσαντες μάχῃ ἐκ μὲν Πιερίας Πίερας, οἳ
ὕστερον ὑπὸ τὸ Πάγγαιον πέραν Στρυμόνος
ᾤκησαν Φάγρητα καὶ ἄλλα χωρία (καὶ ἔτι καὶ
νῦν Πιερικὸς κόλπος καλεῖται ἡ ὑπὸ τῷ Παγγαίῳ
πρὸς θάλασσαν γῆ), ἐκ δὲ τῆς Βοττίας καλουμένης Βοττιαίους, οἳ νῦν ὅμοροι Χαλκιδέων οἰκοῦ-
4 σιν· τῆς δὲ Παιονίας παρὰ τὸν Ἄξιον ποταμὸν
στενήν τινα καθήκουσαν ἄνωθεν μέχρι Πέλλης
καὶ θαλάσσης ἐκτήσαντο, καὶ πέραν Ἀξίου μέχρι
Στρυμόνος τὴν Μυγδονίαν καλουμένην Ἠδῶνας
5 ἐξελάσαντες νέμονται. ἀνέστησαν δὲ καὶ ἐκ τῆς
νῦν Ἐορδίας καλουμένης Ἐορδούς, ὧν οἱ μὲν
πολλοὶ ἐφθάρησαν, βραχὺ δέ τι αὐτῶν περὶ
Φύσκαν κατῴκηται, καὶ ἐξ Ἀλμωπίας Ἄλμωπας.
6 ἐκράτησαν δὲ καὶ τῶν ἄλλων ἐθνῶν οἱ Μακεδόνες
οὗτοι ἃ καὶ νῦν ἔτι ἔχουσι, τόν τε Ἀνθεμοῦντα
καὶ Γρηστωνίαν καὶ Βισαλτίαν καὶ Μακεδόνων
αὐτῶν πολλήν. τὸ δὲ ξύμπαν Μακεδονία καλεῖται καὶ Περδίκκας Ἀλεξάνδρου βασιλεὺς αὐτῶν
ἦν ὅτε Σιτάλκης ἐπῄει.

Perdiccas was ruler. For the Macedonian race includes also the Lyncestians, Elimiotes, and other tribes of the upper country, which, though in alliance with the nearer Macedonians and subject to them, have kings of their own; but the country by the sea which is now called Macedonia, was first acquired and made their kingdom by Alexander, the father of Perdiccas, and his forefathers, who were originally Temenidae from Argos. They defeated and expelled from Pieria the Pierians, who afterwards took up their abode in Phagres and other places at the foot of Mount Pangaeus beyond the Strymon (and even to this day the district at the foot of Mount Pangaeus toward the sea is called the Pierian Valley), and also, from the country called Bottia, the Bottiaeans, who now dwell on the borders of the Chalcidians; they acquired, further, a narrow strip of Paeonia extending along the river Axius[1] from the interior to Pella and the sea; and beyond the Axius they possess the district as far as the Strymon which is called Mygdonia, having driven out the Edonians. Moreover, they expelled from the district now called Eordia the Eordians, most of whom were destroyed, but a small portion is settled in the neighbourhood of Physca; and also from Almopia the Almopians. These Macedonians also made themselves masters of certain places, which they still hold, belonging to the other tribes, namely, of Anthemus, Grestonia, Bisaltia, as well as of a large part of Macedonia proper. But the whole is now called Macedonia, and Perdiccas son of Alexander was king when Sitalces made his invasion.

[1] Now Vardar.

C. Καὶ οἱ μὲν Μακεδόνες οὗτοι ἐπιόντος πολλοῦ στρατοῦ ἀδύνατοι ὄντες ἀμύνεσθαι ἔς τε τὰ καρτερὰ καὶ τὰ τείχη ὅσα ἦν ἐν τῇ χώρᾳ ἐσεκο-
2 μίσθησαν· ἦν δὲ οὐ πολλά, ἀλλὰ ὕστερον Ἀρχέλαος ὁ Περδίκκου υἱὸς βασιλεὺς γενόμενος τὰ νῦν ὄντα ἐν τῇ χώρᾳ ᾠκοδόμησε καὶ ὁδοὺς εὐθείας ἔτεμε καὶ τἆλλα διεκόσμησε τὰ[1] κατὰ τὸν πόλεμον ἵπποις καὶ ὅπλοις καὶ τῇ ἄλλῃ παρασκευῇ κρείσσονι ἢ ξύμπαντες οἱ ἄλλοι βασιλῆς
3 ὀκτὼ οἱ πρὸ αὐτοῦ γενόμενοι. ὁ δὲ στρατὸς τῶν Θρᾳκῶν ἐκ τῆς Δοβήρου ἐσέβαλε πρῶτον μὲν ἐς τὴν Φιλίππου πρότερον οὖσαν ἀρχήν, καὶ εἷλεν Εἰδομενὴν μὲν κατὰ κράτος, Γορτυνίαν δὲ καὶ Ἀταλάντην καὶ ἄλλα ἄττα χωρία ὁμολογίᾳ διὰ τὴν Ἀμύντου φιλίαν προσχωροῦντα, τοῦ Φιλίππου υἱέος, παρόντος· Εὐρωπὸν δὲ ἐπολιόρκησαν
4 μέν, ἑλεῖν δὲ οὐκ ἐδύναντο. ἔπειτα δὲ καὶ ἐς τὴν ἄλλην Μακεδονίαν προυχώρει τὴν ἐν ἀριστερᾷ Πέλλης καὶ Κύρρου. ἔσω δὲ τούτων ἐς τὴν Βοττιαίαν καὶ Πιερίαν οὐκ ἀφίκοντο, ἀλλὰ τήν τε Μυγδονίαν καὶ Γρηστωνίαν καὶ Ἀνθεμοῦντα
5 ἐδῄουν. οἱ δὲ Μακεδόνες πεζῷ μὲν οὐδὲ διενοοῦντο ἀμύνεσθαι, ἵππους δὲ προσμεταπεμψάμενοι ἀπὸ τῶν ἄνω ξυμμάχων, ὅπῃ δοκοίη, ὀλίγοι πρὸς πολλοὺς ἐσέβαλλον ἐς τὸ στράτευμα τῶν Θρᾳ-
6 κῶν. καὶ ᾗ μὲν προσπέσοιεν, οὐδεὶς ὑπέμενεν ἄνδρας ἱππέας τε ἀγαθοὺς καὶ τεθωρακισμένους, ὑπὸ δὲ πλήθους περικλῃόμενοι αὐτοὺς πολλα-

[1] τέ, in the MSS. after τὰ, deleted by Haacke.

C. The Macedonians of this region, unable to defend themselves against so great an invading army, betook themselves to the strong places and fortresses that were in the country. These were not many; but subsequently Archelaus son of Perdiccas, when he became king,[1] built those that are now in the country, and cut straight roads, and in general organized his country for war by providing cavalry, arms and other equipment beyond anything achieved by all the eight kings who preceded him. But the Thracian army, advancing from Doberus, invaded first the province which before had belonged to Philip, and took Idomene by storm; but Gortynia, Atalanta, and some other places capitulated voluntarily out of friendship for Amyntas son of Philip, who accompanied Sitalces; moreover they laid siege to Europus, but were unable to take it. Next they advanced into the other part of Macedonia, which is to the west of Pella and Cyrrhus. Beyond these places, however, into Bottiaea and Pieria, they did not penetrate, but ravaged Mygdonia, Grestonia, and Anthemus. The Macedonians, on the other hand, did not even think of defending themselves with infantry, but calling upon their allies in the interior for additional cavalry, though few against many, they dashed in among the Thracian army wherever they chose. And wherever they charged no one could withstand them, for they were good horsemen and protected by cuirasses; but since they were constantly being hemmed in by superior numbers and found themselves

[1] 413–399 B.C. He was as famous for the splendour and success of his reign as for the crimes by which he obtained the throne.

πλασίῳ τῷ ὁμίλῳ ἐς κίνδυνον καθίστασαν· ὥστε
τέλος ἡσυχίαν ἦγον, οὐ νομίζοντες ἱκανοὶ εἶναι
πρὸς τὸ πλέον κινδυνεύειν.

CI. Ὁ δὲ Σιτάλκης πρός τε τὸν Περδίκκαν
λόγους ἐποιεῖτο ὧν ἕνεκα ἐστράτευσε, καὶ ἐπειδὴ
οἱ Ἀθηναῖοι οὐ παρῆσαν ταῖς ναυσὶν ἀπιστοῦντες
αὐτὸν μὴ ἥξειν (δῶρα δὲ καὶ πρέσβεις ἔπεμψαν
αὐτῷ), ἔς τε τοὺς Χαλκιδέας καὶ Βοττιαίους
μέρος τι τοῦ στρατοῦ πέμπει, καὶ τειχήρεις ποιή-
2 σας ἐδῄου τὴν γῆν. καθημένου δ' αὐτοῦ περὶ
τοὺς χώρους τούτους οἱ πρὸς νότον οἰκοῦντες
Θεσσαλοὶ καὶ Μάγνητες καὶ οἱ ἄλλοι ὑπήκοοι
Θεσσαλῶν καὶ οἱ μέχρι Θερμοπυλῶν Ἕλληνες
ἐφοβήθησαν μὴ καὶ ἐπὶ σφᾶς ὁ στρατὸς χωρήσῃ,
3 καὶ ἐν παρασκευῇ ἦσαν. ἐφοβήθησαν δὲ καὶ οἱ
πέραν Στρυμόνος πρὸς βορέαν Θρᾷκες ὅσοι πεδία
εἶχον, Παναῖοι καὶ Ὀδόμαντοι καὶ Δρῶοι καὶ
4 Δερσαῖοι· αὐτόνομοι δ' εἰσὶ πάντες. παρέσχε δὲ
λόγον καὶ ἐπὶ τοὺς τῶν Ἀθηναίων πολεμίους
Ἕλληνας μὴ ὑπ' αὐτῶν ἀγόμενοι κατὰ τὸ ξυμ-
5 μαχικὸν καὶ ἐπὶ σφᾶς χωρήσωσιν. ὁ δὲ τήν τε
Χαλκιδικὴν καὶ Βοττικὴν καὶ Μακεδονίαν ἅμα
ἐπέχων ἔφθειρε, καὶ ἐπειδὴ αὐτῷ οὐδὲν ἐπράσ-
σετο ὧν ἕνεκα ἐσέβαλε, καὶ ἡ στρατιὰ σῖτόν τε
οὐκ εἶχεν αὐτῷ καὶ ὑπὸ χειμῶνος ἐταλαιπώρει,
ἀναπείθεται ὑπὸ Σεύθου τοῦ Σπαραδόκου, ἀδελ-

imperilled by the horde that was many times their own number, they finally desisted, thinking that they were not strong enough to fight with the larger force.

CI. Sitalces now began to hold parleys with Perdiccas about the matters for which he had undertaken the expedition; and since the Athenians (who did not believe that Sitalces would come, though they sent gifts and envoys to him) had not arrived with their promised fleet, he despatched part of his army into the territory of the Chalcidians and Bottiaeans, and shutting them up within their walls ravaged their lands. But while he was staying in the neighbourhood of these places, the peoples which dwell to the south—the Thessalians, the Magnesians and other subjects of the Thessalians, and the Hellenes as far south as Thermopylae—became frightened lest the host should come against them also, and so were making preparations. The same alarm was felt also by the Thracians who inhabit the plain beyond the Strymon to the north, that is, the Panaeans, Odomantians, Droans, and Dersaeans, independent tribes. He gave occasion also to a rumour which spread even to the Hellenes hostile to Athens, that the Thracians might be led on by the Athenians in accordance with the terms of their alliance and come against them too. But meanwhile Sitalces kept on ravaging at one and the same time Chalcidice, Bottice, and Macedonia; and then, since none of the original objects of his invasion was being accomplished, and his army was without food and was suffering from the winter, he was persuaded by Seuthes son of Sparadocus, a

φιδοῦ ὄντος καὶ μέγιστον μεθ' ἑαυτὸν δυναμένου,
ὥστ' ἐν τάχει ἀπελθεῖν. τὸν δὲ Σεύθην κρύφα
Περδίκκας ὑποσχόμενος ἀδελφὴν ἑαυτοῦ δώσειν
6 καὶ χρήματα ἐπ' αὐτῇ προσποιεῖται. καὶ ὁ μὲν
πεισθεὶς καὶ μείνας τριάκοντα τὰς πάσας ἡμέρας,
τούτων δὲ ὀκτὼ ἐν Χαλκιδεῦσιν, ἀνεχώρησε τῷ
στρατῷ κατὰ τάχος ἐπ' οἴκου· Περδίκκας δὲ
ὕστερον Στρατονίκην τὴν ἑαυτοῦ ἀδελφὴν δίδωσι
Σεύθῃ, ὥσπερ ὑπέσχετο. τὰ μὲν οὖν κατὰ τὴν
Σιτάλκου στρατείαν οὕτως ἐγένετο.

CII. Οἱ δὲ ἐν Ναυπάκτῳ Ἀθηναῖοι τοῦ αὐτοῦ
χειμῶνος, ἐπειδὴ τὸ τῶν Πελοποννησίων ναυτικὸν διελύθη, Φορμίωνος ἡγουμένου ἐστράτευσαν,
παραπλεύσαντες ἐπ' Ἀστακοῦ καὶ ἀποβάντες
ἐς τὴν μεσόγειαν τῆς Ἀκαρνανίας τετρακοσίοις
μὲν ὁπλίταις Ἀθηναίων τῶν ἀπὸ τῶν νεῶν, τετρακοσίοις δὲ Μεσσηνίων, καὶ ἔκ τε Στράτου καὶ
Κορόντων καὶ ἄλλων χωρίων ἄνδρας οὐ δοκοῦντας
βεβαίους εἶναι ἐξήλασαν, καὶ Κύνητα τὸν Θεο-
λύτου ἐς Κόροντα καταγαγόντες ἀνεχώρησαν
2 πάλιν ἐπὶ τὰς ναῦς. ἐς γὰρ Οἰνιάδας αἰεί ποτε
πολεμίους ὄντας μόνους Ἀκαρνάνων οὐκ ἐδόκει
δυνατὸν εἶναι χειμῶνος ὄντος στρατεύειν· ὁ γὰρ
Ἀχελῷος ποταμὸς ῥέων ἐκ Πίνδου ὄρους διὰ
Δολοπίας καὶ Ἀγραίων καὶ Ἀμφιλόχων καὶ διὰ
τοῦ Ἀκαρνανικοῦ πεδίου, ἄνωθεν μὲν παρὰ Στράτον πόλιν, ἐς θάλασσαν δ' ἐξιεὶς παρ' Οἰνιάδας
καὶ τὴν πόλιν αὐτοῖς περιλιμνάζων, ἄπορον ποιεῖ

nephew and next to him in power,[1] to go back home at once. Now Seuthes had been secretly won over by Perdiccas, who had promised to give him his sister in marriage and a dowry with her. So Sitalces yielded, and after a stay of only thirty days in all, eight of which had been spent among the Chalcidians, returned home with his army with all speed. And Perdiccas afterwards gave his sister Stratonice to Seuthes as he had promised. Such, then, is the history of the expedition of Sitalces.

CII. During the same winter the Athenians in Naupactus, after the Peloponnesian fleet had been disbanded, made an expedition under the command of Phormio. They first skirted the coast in the direction of Astacus, and then, disembarking, invaded the interior of Acarnania with four hundred Athenian hoplites from the ships and four hundred Messenian. And after they had expelled from Stratus, Coronta, and other places such men as were regarded as disloyal, and had restored Cynes son of Theolytus to Coronta, they returned again to their ships. For it seemed impracticable in winter to make a campaign against Oeniadae, whose inhabitants alone of the Acarnanians were always hostile; for the river Achelous, which rises in Mount Pindus and flows through the country of the Dolopians, Agraeans, and Amphilochians and then through the Acarnanian plain, passes by the city of Stratus high up the stream, but by Oeniadae empties into the sea, where it surrounds the city with marshes, thus rendering military operations there impossible in

[1] Sadocus, Sitalces' own son, who had been received into Athenian citizenship (ch. xxix. 5; lxvii. 2), must have died before this time. The nephew Seuthes succeeded to the throne in 424 B.C. (IV. ci. 4).

3 ὑπὸ τοῦ ὕδατος ἐν χειμῶνι στρατεύειν. κεῖνται δὲ καὶ τῶν νήσων τῶν Ἐχινάδων αἱ πολλαὶ καταντικρὺ Οἰνιαδῶν τοῦ Ἀχελῴου τῶν ἐκβολῶν οὐδὲν ἀπέχουσαι, ὥστε μέγας ὢν ὁ ποταμὸς προσχοῖ αἰεὶ καὶ εἰσὶ τῶν νήσων αἳ ἠπείρωνται, ἐλπὶς δὲ καὶ πάσας οὐκ ἐν πολλῷ τινι ἂν χρόνῳ
4 τοῦτο παθεῖν· τό τε γὰρ ῥεῦμά ἐστι μέγα καὶ πολὺ καὶ θολερόν, αἵ τε νῆσοι πυκναί, καὶ ἀλλήλαις τῆς προσχώσεως τὸ μὴ σκεδάννυσθαι[1] ξύνδεσμοι γίγνονται, παραλλὰξ καὶ οὐ κατὰ στοῖχον κείμεναι, οὐδ' ἔχουσαι εὐθείας διόδους τοῦ ὕδατος
5 ἐς τὸ πέλαγος. ἐρῆμοι δ' εἰσὶ καὶ οὐ μεγάλαι. λέγεται δὲ καὶ Ἀλκμέωνι τῷ Ἀμφιάρεω, ὅτε δὴ ἀλᾶσθαι αὐτὸν μετὰ τὸν φόνον τῆς μητρός, τὸν Ἀπόλλω ταύτην τὴν γῆν χρῆσαι οἰκεῖν, ὑπειπόντα οὐκ εἶναι λύσιν τῶν δειμάτων πρὶν ἂν εὑρὼν ἐν ταύτῃ τῇ χώρᾳ κατοικίσηται ἥτις ὅτε ἔκτεινε τὴν μητέρα μήπω ὑπὸ ἡλίου ἑωρᾶτο μηδὲ
6 γῆ ἦν, ὡς τῆς γε ἄλλης αὐτῷ μεμιασμένης. ὁ δ' ἀπορῶν, ὥς φασι, μόλις κατενόησε τὴν πρόσχωσιν ταύτην τοῦ Ἀχελῴου, καὶ ἐδόκει αὐτῷ ἱκανὴ ἂν κεχῶσθαι δίαιτα τῷ σώματι ἀφ' οὗπερ κτείνας τὴν μητέρα οὐκ ὀλίγον χρόνον ἐπλανᾶτο. καὶ κατοικισθεὶς ἐς τοὺς περὶ Οἰνιάδας τόπους ἐδυνάστευσέ τε καὶ ἀπὸ Ἀκαρνᾶνος παιδὸς ἑαυτοῦ τῆς χώρας τὴν ἐπωνυμίαν ἐγκατέλιπεν. τὰ μὲν οὖν περὶ Ἀλκμέωνα τοιαῦτα λεγόμενα παρελάβομεν.

[1] Hude brackets τὸ μὴ σκεδάννυσθαι, following Stahl.

winter by reason of the water. Besides, most of the Echinades islands lie opposite to Oeniadae at no great distance from the mouths of the Achelous, so that the river, which is large, keeps making fresh deposits of silt, and some of the islands have already become part of the mainland, and probably this will happen to all of them in no great while. For the stream is wide and deep and turbid, and the islands are close together and serve to bind to one another the bars as they are formed, preventing them from being broken up, since the islands lie, not in line, but irregularly, and do not allow straight channels for the water into the open sea. These islands are uninhabited and not large. There is a story that when Alcmaeon son of Amphiaraus was a wanderer after the murder of his mother,[1] Apollo directed him by oracle to inhabit this land, intimating that he would have no release from his fears until he should find and settle in a country which at the time he killed his mother had not yet been seen by the sun, and was not even land then, for all the rest of the earth had been polluted by him. And he, in his perplexity, at last, as the story goes, observed this sand-bar formed by the Achelous, and he surmised that during the long time he had been wandering since he had slain his mother enough land would have been silted up to support life in. So he settled there in the region of Oeniadae, founded a principality, and left to the country its name Acarnania, after that of his son Acarnan. Such is the tradition which we have received concerning Alcmaeon.

[1] Eriphyle.

CIII. Οἱ δὲ Ἀθηναῖοι καὶ ὁ Φορμίων ἄραντες
ἐκ τῆς Ἀκαρνανίας καὶ ἀφικόμενοι ἐς τὴν Ναύπακτον ἅμα ἦρι κατέπλευσαν ἐς τὰς Ἀθήνας,
τούς τε ἐλευθέρους τῶν αἰχμαλώτων ἐκ τῶν
ναυμαχιῶν ἄγοντες, οἳ ἀνὴρ ἀντ' ἀνδρὸς ἐλύ-
2 θησαν, καὶ τὰς ναῦς ἃς εἷλον. καὶ ὁ χειμὼν
ἐτελεύτα οὗτος, καὶ τρίτον ἔτος τῷ πολέμῳ
ἐτελεύτα τῷδε ὃν Θουκυδίδης ξυνέγραψεν.

CIII. The Athenians and Phormio set out from Acarnania and arrived at Naupactus, and later, at the beginning of spring, sailed back to Athens, bringing with them the captured ships and also the prisoners of free birth whom they had taken in the sea-fights. These were exchanged man for man. And this winter ended, concluding the third year of this war of which Thucydides wrote the history.

Printed in Great Britain by
Richard Clay (The Chaucer Press), Ltd.,
Bungay, Suffolk

THE LOEB CLASSICAL LIBRARY

VOLUMES ALREADY PUBLISHED

Latin Authors

AMMIANUS MARECLLINUS. Translated by J. C. Rolfe. 3 Vols.

APULEIUS: THE GOLDEN ASS (METAMORPHOSES). W. Adlington (1566). Revised by S. Gaselee.

ST. AUGUSTINE: CITY OF GOD. 7 Vols. Vol. I. G. E. McCracken Vol. II. W. M. Green. Vol. III. D. Wiesen. Vol. IV. P. Levine. Vol. V. E. M. Sanford and W. M. Green. Vol. VI. W. C. Greene.

ST. AUGUSTINE, CONFESSIONS OF. W. Watts (1631). 2 Vols.

ST. AUGUSTINE, SELECT LETTERS. J. H. Baxter.

AUSONIUS. H. G. Evelyn White. 2 Vols.

BEDE. J. E. King. 2 Vols.

BOETHIUS: TRACTS and DE CONSOLATIONE PHILOSOPHIAE. Rev. H. F. Stewart and E. K. Rand.

CAESAR: ALEXANDRIAN, AFRICAN and SPANISH WARS. A. G. Way.

CAESAR: CIVIL WARS. A. G. Peskett.

CAESAR: GALLIC WAR. H. J. Edwards.

CATO: DE RE RUSTICA; VARRO: DE RE RUSTICA. H. B. Ash and W. D. Hooper.

CATULLUS. F. W. Cornish; TIBULLUS. J. B. Postgate; PERVIGILIUM VENERIS. J. W. Mackail.

CELSUS: DE MEDICINA. W. G. Spencer. 3 Vols.

CICERO: BRUTUS, and ORATOR. G. L. Hendrickson and H. M. Hubbell.

[CICERO]: AD HERENNIUM. H. Caplan.

CICERO: DE ORATORE, etc. 2 Vols. Vol. I. DE ORATORE, Books I. and II. E. W. Sutton and H. Rackham. Vol. II. DE ORATORE, Book III. De Fato; Paradoxa Stoicorum; De Partitione Oratoria. H. Rackham.

CICERO: DE FINIBUS. H. Rackham.

CICERO: DE INVENTIONE, etc. H. M. Hubbell.

CICERO: DE NATURA DEORUM and ACADEMICA. H. Rackham.

CICERO: DE OFFICIIS. Walter Miller.

CICERO: DE REPUBLICA and DE LEGIBUS; SOMNIUM SCIPIONIS. Clinton W. Keyes.

Cicero: De Senectute, De Amicitia, De Divinatione. W. A. Falconer.

Cicero: In Catilinam, Pro Flacco, Pro Murena, Pro Sulla. Louis E. Lord.

Cicero: Letters to Atticus. E. O. Winstedt. 3 Vols.

Cicero: Letters to His Friends. W. Glynn Williams. 3 Vols.

Cicero: Philippics. W. C. A. Ker.

Cicero: Pro Archia Post Reditum, De Domo, De Haruspicum Responsis, Pro Plancio. N. H. Watts.

Cicero: Pro Caecina, Pro Lege Manilia, Pro Cluentio, Pro Rabirio. H. Grose Hodge.

Cicero: Pro Caelio, De Provinciis Consularibus, Pro Balbo. R. Gardner.

Cicero: Pro Milone, In Pisonem, Pro Scauro, Pro Fonteio, Pro Rabirio Postumo, Pro Marcello, Pro Ligario, Pro Rege Deiotaro. N. H. Watts.

Cicero: Pro Quinctio, Pro Roscio Amerino, Pro Roscio Comoedo, Contra Rullum. J. H. Freese.

Cicero: Pro Sestio, In Vatinium. R. Gardner.

Cicero: Tusculan Disputations. J. E. King.

Cicero: Verrine Orations. L. H. G. Greenwood. 2 Vols.

Claudian. M. Platnauer. 2 Vols.

Columella: De Re Rustica. De Arboribus. H. B. Ash, E. S. Forster and E. Heffner. 3 Vols.

Curtius, Q.: History of Alexander. J. C. Rolfe. 2 Vols.

Florus. E. S. Forster; and Cornelius Nepos. J. C. Rolfe.

Frontinus: Stratagems and Aqueducts. C. E. Bennett and M. B. McElwain.

Fronto: Correspondence. C. R. Haines. 2 Vols.

Gellius, J. C. Rolfe. 3 Vols.

Horace: Odes and Epodes. C. E. Bennett.

Horace: Satires, Epistles, Ars Poetica. H. R. Fairclough.

Jerome: Selected Letters. F. A. Wright.

Juvenal and Persius. G. G. Ramsay.

Livy. B. O. Foster, F. G. Moore, Evan T. Sage, and A. C. Schlesinger and R. M. Geer (General Index). 14 Vols.

Lucan. J. D. Duff.

Lucretius. W. H. D. Rouse.

Martial. W. C. A. Ker. 2 Vols.

Minor Latin Poets: from Publilius Syrus to Rutilius Namatianus, including Grattius, Calpurnius Siculus, Nemesianus, Avianus, and others with "Aetna" and the "Phoenix." J. Wight Duff and Arnold M. Duff.

Ovid: The Art of Love and Other Poems. J. H. Mozley.

Ovid: Fasti. Sir James G. Frazer.

Ovid: Heroides and Amores. Grant Showerman.

Ovid: Metamorphoses. F. J. Miller. 2 Vols.

Ovid: Tristia and Ex Ponto. A. L. Wheeler.

Persius. Cf. Juvenal.

Petronius. M. Heseltine; Seneca; Apocolocyntosis. W. H. D. Rouse.

Phaedrus and Babrius (Greek). B. E. Perry.

Plautus. Paul Nixon. 5 Vols.

Pliny: Letters. Melmoth's Translation revised by W. M. L. Hutchinson. 2 Vols.

Pliny: Natural History.
10 Vols. Vols. I.–V. and IX. H. Rackham. Vols. VI.–VIII. W. H. S. Jones. Vol. X. D. E. Eichholz.

Propertius. H. E. Butler.

Prudentius. H. J. Thomson. 2 Vols.

Quintilian. H. E. Butler. 4 Vols.

Remains of Old Latin. E. H. Warmington. 4 Vols. Vol. I. (Ennius and Caecilius.) Vol. II. (Livius, Naevius, Pacuvius, Accius.) Vol. III. (Lucilius and Laws of XII Tables.) Vol. IV. (Archaic Inscriptions.)

Sallust. J. C. Rolfe.

Scriptores Historiae Augustae. D. Magie. 3 Vols.

Seneca: Apocolocyntosis. Cf. Petronius.

Seneca: Epistulae Morales. R. M. Gummere. 3 Vols.

Seneca: Moral Essays. J. W. Basore. 3 Vols.

Seneca: Tragedies. F. J. Miller. 2 Vols.

Sidonius: Poems and Letters. W. B. Anderson. 2 Vols.

Silius Italicus. J. D. Duff. 2 Vols.

Statius. J. H. Mozley. 2 Vols.

Suetonius. J. C. Rolfe. 2 Vols.

Tacitus: Dialogus. Sir Wm. Peterson. Agricola and Germania. Maurice Hutton.

Tacitus: Histories and Annals. C. H. Moore and J. Jackson. 4 Vols.

Terence. John Sargeaunt. 2 Vols.

Tertullian: Apologia and De Spectaculis. T. R. Glover. Minucius Felix. G. H. Rendall.

Valerius Flaccus. J. H. Mozley.

Varro: De Lingua Latina. R. G. Kent. 2 Vols.

Velleius Paterculus and Res Gestae Divi Augusti. F. W. Shipley.

Virgil. H. R. Fairclough. 2 Vols.

Vitruvius: De Architectura. F. Granger. 2 Vols.

Greek Authors

Achilles Tatius. S. Gaselee.

Aelian: On the Nature of Animals. A. F. Scholfield. 3 Vols.

Aeneas Tacticus, Asclepiodotus and Onasander. The Illinois Greek Club.

Aeschines. C. D. Adams.

Aeschylus. H. Weir Smyth. 2 Vols.

Alciphron, Aelian, Philostratus: Letters. A. R. Benner and F. H. Fobes.

Andocides, Antiphon, Cf. Minor Attic Orators.

Apollodorus. Sir James G. Frazer. 2 Vols.

Apollonius Rhodius. R. C. Seaton.

The Apostolic Fathers. Kirsopp Lake. 2 Vols.

Appian: Roman History. Horace White. 4 Vols.

Aratus. Cf. Callimachus.

Aristophanes. Benjamin Bickley Rogers. 3 Vols. Verse trans.

Aristotle: Art of Rhetoric. J. H. Freese.

Aristotle: Athenian Constitution, Eudemian Ethics, Vices and Virtues. H. Rackham.

Aristotle: Generation of Animals. A. L. Peck.

Aristotle: Historia Animalium. A. L. Peck. Vol. I.

Aristotle: Metaphysics. H. Tredennick. 2 Vols.

Aristotle: Meteorologica. H. D. P. Lee.

Aristotle: Minor Works. W. S. Hett. On Colours, On Things Heard, On Physiognomies, On Plants, On Marvellous Things Heard, Mechanical Problems, On Indivisible Lines, On Situations and Names of Winds, On Melissus, Xenophanes, and Gorgias.

Aristotle: Nicomachean Ethics. H. Rackham.

Aristotle: Oeconomica and Magna Moralia. G. C. Armstrong; (with Metaphysics, Vol. II.).

Aristotle: On the Heavens. W. K. C. Guthrie.

Aristotle: On the Soul. Parva Naturalia. On Breath. W. S. Hett.

Aristotle: Categories, On Interpretation, Prior Analytics. H. P. Cooke and H. Tredennick.

Aristotle: Posterior Analytics, Topics. H. Tredennick and E. S. Forster.

Aristotle: On Sophistical Refutations.

On Coming to be and Passing Away, On the Cosmos. E. S. Forster and D. J. Furley.

Aristotle: Parts of Animals. A. L. Peck; Motion and Progression of Animals. E. S. Forster.

Aristotle: Physics. Rev. P. Wicksteed and F. M. Cornford. 2 Vols.

Aristotle: Poetics and Longinus. W. Hamilton Fyfe; Demetrius on Style. W. Rhys Roberts.

Aristotle: Politics. H. Rackham.

Aristotle: Problems. W. S. Hett. 2 Vols.

Aristotle: Rhetorica Ad Alexandrum (with Problems. Vol. II.) H. Rackham.

Arrian: History of Alexander and Indica. Rev. E. Iliffe Robson. 2 Vols.

Athenaeus: Deipnosophistae. C. B. Gulick. 7 Vols.

Babrius and Phaedrus (Latin). B. E. Perry.

St. Basil: Letters. R. J. Deferrari. 4 Vols.

Callimachus: Fragments. C. A. Trypanis.

Callimachus, Hymns and Epigrams, and Lycophron. A. W. Mair; Aratus. G. R. Mair.

Clement of Alexandria. Rev. G. W. Butterworth.

Colluthus. Cf. Oppian.

Daphnis and Chloe. Thornley's Translation revised by J. M. Edmonds; and Parthenius. S. Gaselee.

Demosthenes I.: Olynthiacs, Philippics and Minor Orations. I.–XVII. and XX. J. H. Vince.

Demosthenes II.: De Corona and De Falsa Legatione. C. A. Vince and J. H. Vince.

Demosthenes III.: Meidias, Androtion, Aristocrates, Timocrates and Aristogeiton, I. and II. J. H. Vince.

Demosthenes IV.–VI.: Private Orations and In Neaeram. A. T. Murray.

Demosthenes VII.: Funeral Speech, Erotic Essay, Exordia and Letters. N. W. and N. J. DeWitt.

Dio Cassius: Roman History. E. Cary. 9 Vols.

Dio Chrysostom. J. W. Cohoon and H. Lamar Crosby. 5 Vols.

Diodorus Siculus. 12 Vols. Vols. I.–VI. C. H. Oldfather. Vol. VII. C. L. Sherman. Vol. VIII. C. B. Welles. Vols. IX. and X. R. M. Geer. Vol. XI. F. Walton. Vol. XII. F. Walton. General Index. R. M. Geer.

Diogenes Laertius. R. D. Hicks. 2 Vols.

Dionysius of Halicarnassus: Roman Antiquities. Spelman's translation revised by E. Cary. 7 Vols.

Epictetus. W. A. Oldfather. 2 Vols.

Euripides. A. S. Way. 4 Vols. Verse trans.

Eusebius: Ecclesiastical History. Kirsopp Lake and J. E. L. Oulton. 2 Vols.

Galen: On the Natural Faculties. A. J. Brock.

The Greek Anthology. W. R. Paton. 5 Vols.

GREEK ELEGY AND IAMBUS with the ANACREONTEA. J. M. Edmonds. 2 Vols.

THE GREEK BUCOLIC POETS (THEOCRITUS, BION, MOSCHUS). J. M. Edmonds.

GREEK MATHEMATICAL WORKS. Ivor Thomas. 2 Vols.

HERODES. Cf. THEOPHRASTUS: CHARACTERS.

HERODOTUS. A. D. Godley. 4 Vols.

HESIOD AND THE HOMERIC HYMNS. H. G. Evelyn White.

HIPPOCRATES and the FRAGMENTS OF HERACLEITUS. W. H. S. Jones and E. T. Withington. 4 Vols.

HOMER: ILIAD. A. T. Murray. 2 Vols.

HOMER: ODYSSEY. A. T. Murray. 2 Vols.

ISAEUS. E. W. Forster.

ISOCRATES. George Norlin and LaRue Van Hook. 3 Vols.

[ST. JOHN DAMASCENE]: BARLAAM AND IOASAPH. Rev. G. R. Woodward, Harold Mattingly and D. M. Lang.

JOSEPHUS. 9 Vols. Vols. I.–IV.; H. Thackeray. Vol. V.; H. Thackeray and R. Marcus. Vols. VI.–VII.; R. Marcus. Vol. VIII.; R. Marcus and Allen Wikgren. Vol. IX. L. H. Feldman.

JULIAN. Wilmer Cave Wright. 3 Vols.

LUCIAN. 8 Vols. Vols. I.–V. A. M. Harmon. Vol. VI. K. Kilburn. Vols. VII.–VIII. M. D. Macleod.

LYCOPHRON. Cf. CALLIMACHUS.

LYRA GRAECA. J. M. Edmonds. 3 Vols.

LYSIAS. W. R. M. Lamb.

MANETHO. W. G. Waddell: PTOLEMY: TETRABIBLOS. F. E. Robbins.

MARCUS AURELIUS. C. R. Haines.

MENANDER. F. G. Allinson.

MINOR ATTIC ORATORS (ANTIPHON, ANDOCIDES, LYCURGUS, DEMADES, DINARCHUS, HYPERIDES). K. J. Maidment and J. O. Burrt. 2 Vols.

NONNOS: DIONYSIACA. W. H. D. Rouse. 3 Vols.

OPPIAN, COLLUTHUS, TRYPHIODORUS. A. W. Mair.

PAPYRI. NON-LITERARY SELECTIONS. A. S. Hunt and C. C. Edgar. 2 Vols. LITERARY SELECTIONS (Poetry). D. L. Page.

PARTHENIUS. Cf. DAPHNIS and CHLOE.

PAUSANIAS: DESCRIPTION OF GREECE. W. H. S. Jones. 4 Vols. and Companion Vol. arranged by R. E. Wycherley.

PHILO. 10 Vols. Vols. I.–V.; F. H. Colson and Rev. G. H. Whitaker. Vols. VI.–IX.; F. H. Colson. Vol. X. F. H. Colson and the Rev. J. W. Earp.

PHILO: two supplementary Vols. (*Translation only.*) Ralph Marcus.

PHILOSTRATUS: THE LIFE OF APOLLONIUS OF TYANA. F. C. Conybeare. 2 Vols.

PHILOSTRATUS: IMAGINES; CALLISTRATUS: DESCRIPTIONS. A. Fairbanks.

PHILOSTRATUS and EUNAPIUS: LIVES OF THE SOPHISTS. Wilmer Cave Wright.

PINDAR. Sir J. E. Sandys.

PLATO: CHARMIDES, ALCIBIADES, HIPPARCHUS, THE LOVERS, THEAGES, MINOS and EPINOMIS. W. R. M. Lamb.

PLATO: CRATYLUS, PARMENIDES, GREATER HIPPIAS, LESSER HIPPIAS. H. N. Fowler.

PLATO: EUTHYPHRO, APOLOGY, CRITO, PHAEDO, PHAEDRUS. H. N. Fowler.

PLATO: LACHES, PROTAGORAS, MENO, EUTHYDEMUS. W. R. M. Lamb.

PLATO: LAWS. Rev. R. G. Bury. 2 Vols.

PLATO: LYSIS, SYMPOSIUM, GORGIAS. W. R. M. Lamb.

PLATO: REPUBLIC. Paul Shorey. 2 Vols.

PLATO: STATESMAN, PHILEBUS. H. N. Fowler; ION. W. R. M. Lamb.

PLATO: THEAETETUS and SOPHIST. H. N. Fowler.

PLATO: TIMAEUS, CRITIAS, CLITOPHO, MENEXENUS, EPISTULAE. Rev. R. G. Bury.

PLOTINUS: A. H. Armstrong. Vols. I.–III.

PLUTARCH: MORALIA. 15 Vols. Vols. I.–V. F. C. Babbitt. Vol. VI. W. C. Helmbold. Vols. VII. and XIV. P. H. De Lacy and B. Einarson. Vol. IX. E. L. Minar, Jr., F. H. Sandbach, W. C. Helmbold. Vol. X. H. N. Fowler. Vol. XI. L. Pearson and F. H. Sandbach. Vol. XII. H. Cherniss and W. C. Helmbold.

PLUTARCH: THE PARALLEL LIVES. B. Perrin. 11 Vols.

POLYBIUS. W. R. Paton. 6 Vols.

PROCOPIUS: HISTORY OF THE WARS. H. B. Dewing. 7 Vols.

PTOLEMY: TETRABIBLOS. Cf. MANETHO.

QUINTUS SMYRNAEUS. A. S. Way. Verse trans.

SEXTUS EMPIRICUS. Rev. R. G. Bury. 4 Vols.

SOPHOCLES. F. Storr. 2 Vols. Verse trans.

STRABO: GEOGRAPHY. Horace L. Jones. 8 Vols.

THEOPHRASTUS: CHARACTERS. J. M. Edmonds. HERODES, etc. A. D. Knox.

THEOPHRASTUS: ENQUIRY INTO PLANTS. Sir Arthur Hort, Bart. 2 Vols.

THUCYDIDES. C. F. Smith. 4 Vols.

TRYPHIODORUS. Cf. OPPIAN.

XENOPHON: CYROPAEDIA. Walter Miller. 2 Vols.

XENOPHON: HELLENICA. C. L. Brownson. 2 Vols.

XENOPHON: ANABASIS. C. L. Brownson.

XENOPHON: MEMORABILIA AND OECONOMICUS. E. C. Marchant. SYMPOSIUM AND APOLOGY. O. J. Todd.

XENOPHON: SCRIPTA MINORA. E. C. Marchant and G. W. Bowersock.

IN PREPARATION

Greek Authors

ARISTIDES: ORATIONS. C. A. Behr.

HERODIANUS. C. R. Whittaker.

LIBANIUS: SELECTED WORKS. A. F. Norman.

MUSAEUS: HERO AND LEANDER. T. Gelzer and C. H. WHITMAN.

THEOPHRASTUS: DE CAUSIS PLANTARUM. G. K. K. Link and B. Einarson.

Latin Authors

ASCONIUS: COMMENTARIES ON CICERO'S ORATIONS. G. W. Bowersock.

BENEDICT: THE RULE. P. Meyvaert.

JUSTIN–TROGUS. R. Moss.

MANILIUS. G. P. Goold.

PLINY: LETTERS. B. Radice.

DESCRIPTIVE PROSPECTUS ON APPLICATION

London — WILLIAM HEINEMANN LTD
Cambridge, Mass. — HARVARD UNIVERSITY PRESS